LEGAL AID PRACTICE
1996–97

AUSTRALIA
LBC Information Services
Brisbane ● Sydney ● Melbourne ● Perth

CANADA
Carswell
Ottawa ● Toronto ● Calgary ● Montreal ● Vancouver

Agents:
Steimatzky's Agency Ltd., Tel Aviv;
N.M. Tripathi (Private) Ltd., Bombay;
Eastern Law House (Private) Ltd., Calcutta;
M.P.P. House, Bangalore;
Universal Book Traders, Delhi;
Aditya Books, Delhi;
MacMillan Shuppan KK, Tokyo;
Pakistan Law House, Karachi, Lahore

LEGAL AID PRACTICE
1996–97

Peter Hurst
Lynn Graham and
Simon Morgans

LONDON   SWEET & MAXWELL   1996

Published in 1996 by
Sweet & Maxwell Limited of
100 Avenue Road
London NW3 3PF
Typeset by Wyvern Typesetting Ltd
Printed at The Bath Press, Bath, Somerset

No natural forests were destroyed to make this product;
only farmed timber was used and replanted

British Library Cataloguing in Publication Data

A CIP catalogue record for this book
is available from the British Library

ISBN 0-421 419 903

Preface

The purpose of the work is to complement the Annual Legal Aid Handbook which sets out all the current Legal Aid statutory provisions, as well as Notes for Guidance, but which does not provide any substantial commentary or background. The authors of the Legal Aid Practice have tried to put flesh on the bare bones of the legislation, in an attempt to provide a helpful practical guide through the increasingly complex legal aid maze.

Legal Aid continues to be the subject of intense scrutiny, not least because of the enormous cost of some high profile, but ultimately unsuccessful civil litigation, and the "apparently rich" recipients of Criminal Legal Aid. There is no doubt that the scrutiny and surrounding debate will continue, and that there will be further changes in the way in which legal aid is administered, and the way in which legal representatives are remunerated. As I write a White Paper is awaited and the Legal Aid Board is planning the introduction of a new Corporate Information System (CIS), which will increase the computerisation of its area offices and have a visible impact on its dealing with the profession, *e.g.* as to forms, wordings and the conduct of business by telephone.

Although the team of authors and the editorial staff at Sweet and Maxwell have both changed in the course of the writing of *Legal Aid Practice*, the authors have received great assistance from the editorial staff, and are very grateful to all those involved for their support and patience.

The law is stated as at December 1995.

Peter T. Hurst, LLB
Chief Master,
Supreme Court Taxing Office

March 25, 1996 Supreme Court Taxing Office London

Contents

Part D Criminal Legal Aid

Part E Supplementary

Table of Cases

TABLE OF STATUTES

TABLE OF STATUTORY INSTRUMENTS

PART A

THE ADMINISTRATION OF THE SCHEME

1. History and Development
2. The Present Scheme and it's Administration

Chapter 1

HISTORY AND DEVELOPMENT

It is instructive to look at the history and development of the availability of what is now generally referred to as legal aid. Much of the existing framework has its roots in the past, although the current system was only put in place in 1989.

EARLY HISTORY

In one form or another legal aid is as old as the practice of law itself. **01–01** Throughout history, lawyers have advised and represented the poor without charge. In 1495, the first English[1] statute was passed providing for legal aid. It was "An Act to admit such persons as are poor to sue *in forma pauperis*"[2] and it provided that:

    (a) the poor were not to be charged fees for the issue of writs;
    (b) the clerks, counsel and attorneys were to be assigned by the Chancellor to prepare such writs for them without payment; and
    (c) at the return of the writs, the Justices were to assign to the poor, counsel who should act without payment.[3]

The Act did not attempt to define "poor persons" and did nothing to remove their liability to pay their opponent's costs if unsuccessful. This was dealt with in the following reign by a statute which exempted an unsuccessful poor plaintiff from liability for costs, but subjected him to such "other punishment, as by the discretion of the Justices or Judge . . . shall be thought reasonable."[4] The effect of this provision is uncertain[5] but there is evidence that it could include corporal punishment.

Further defects in the Act of 1495, as it came to be interpreted, were that:

---

[1] Legislation had been enacted in Scotland 7 years earlier. See the Report of the Poor Representation (Scotland) Committee, Cmd. 5435 (1937), para. 1.
[2] Poor Persons Act 1495 (11 Hen. 7, c.12).
[3] Sergeants were in honour bound to advise paupers without charge, [1969] C.L.J. 205, 212.
[4] [1531] 23 Hen. 8, c.15.
[5] The note in [1917] 31 H.L.R. 485 suggested that the statute meant no more than that the court should have a discretion to punish a pauper who, having sued, did not prosecute an action, since such conduct would amount to contempt.

(a) in the common law courts[6] it was held to apply only to plaintiffs;

(b) the rule was adopted that no-one who was worth more than £5 could benefit by it;

(c) by George II's time poor persons had, at their own expense, to produce counsel's opinion as to the merits of their case; and

(d) despite the unambiguous wording of the Act, a poor person was not always exempt from paying court fees.

There were, however, two main reasons why the Act of 1495 was a failure. It made no provision for paying the poor person's legal advisers and it contained no machinery for distinguishing good cases from bad.

BETWEEN 1883 AND 1950

01–02 In 1883, the Acts of Henry VII and Henry VIII were repealed[7] and provision was made by rules of court litigation by the poor. The development of the procedure can be divided into the following four periods.

1883–1913

01–03 The rules first introduced were similar to the provisions of the repealed Acts, as interpreted by the court, and counsel's certificate on the merits was still needed. In addition, applicants or their solicitors were required to make an affidavit in support and the financial limits were raised from £5 to £25.[8]

In 1893, the Appeal (Forma Pauperis) Act provided that an applicant for leave to appeal to the House of Lords as a poor person must show proof of a *prima facie* case in addition to proof of lack of means.[9]

The conditions attaching to litigation by the poor were, however, so stringent as to make the procedure practically inoperative and an increasing public awareness of the consequent hardship led to demand for reform and ultimately to the amendment of the rules.[10]

---

[6] The Act was held not to apply in Chancery.

[7] By the Statute Law Revision and Civil Procedure Act 1883, subject, in the case of the 1495 Act, to the power to make rules of court, which was finally repealed with effect from October 2, 1950, when legal aid was made available in the Supreme Court. See the Legal Aid and Advice Act 1949, s. 17(3) (a) and the Legal Aid and Advice Act 1949 (Commencement) Order 1950. See the further repeals effected by the Statute Law (Repeals) Act 1973, s.1 (1) and Sched. 1, Pt. XII.

[8] R.S.C. 1883, Ord. XVI, rr. 22–31.

[9] The Appeal (Forma Pauperis) Act was repealed with effect from December 1, 1960 in consequence of legal aid being made available in the House of Lords. See the Legal Aid and Advice Act 1949, s. 17(3) (b) and the Legal Aid and Advice Act 1949 (Commencement No. 9) Order 1960. See the further repeals effected by the Statute Law (Repeals) Act 1973, s. 1(1), Sched 1, Pt. XII.

[10] A leading article in *The Times*, December 30, 1912, described the conditions as "prohibitive" and declared that: "No one can say a word in favour of retaining unchanged the

4

1914–1920

New rules[11] introduced the framework of the poor persons' procedure **01–04**
which continued until the Legal Aid and Advice Act 1949 came into force.
The financial limit was £50[12] but there was power to raise it to £100 in
special circumstances. The requirement of counsel's opinion and an
affidavit was abolished. Administration was put in the hands of "prescribed
officers", who constituted a Poor Persons Department.[13] An application for
admission as a poor person was made to one of these officers and was
referred by him to a number of solicitors and counsel acting without a fee
as "reporters" for investigation and to report whether, and on what terms,
the applicant ought to be admitted as a poor person. On receiving the
report, the court might admit the applicant as a poor person and assign
counsel and a solicitor to conduct his case from a list of practitioners willing
to act. The effect of admission as a poor person was to relieve the person
concerned of having to pay court fees or, in general, costs to any other
party but he still had to meet all out-of-pocket expenses.[14]

The procedure was again not effective and in 1919 the Lawrence
Committee was appointed to report on the working of the rules. The
committee found that very few non-matrimonial cases were being dealt
with and that a practice had grown up amongst the conducting solicitors of
demanding a sum of money from the poor person to cover out-of-pocket
expenses as a condition of acting.[15]

1921–1925

The main recommendations of the Lawrence Committee were implemented **01–05**
by amendments to the rules, which came into force on January 1, 1921
and which abolished the collection by court officials for "office expenses",
provided for payment to the Poor Persons Department by the poor person
himself of a deposit for out-of-pocket expenses at the time of making the

---

present system, which unites with curious infelicity opposite defects. It encourages litigants
who deserve no countenance, and it shuts out those who really need aid." See also the
recommendations of the Royal Commission on Divorce and Matrimonial Causes Cd. 6478
(1912), paras. 409–420.
[11] R.S.C. (Poor Persons) 1913, substituting new Ord. XVI, rr. 22–32. They came into force on
January 1, 1914 and were amended and replaced by R.S.C. (Poor Persons) 1914.
[12] Excluding clothes, household goods, trade tools and the subject-matter of the action; R.S.C.
(Poor Persons) 1914, r.22.
[13] These were, in the King's Bench and Chancery Division, masters in those Divisions, and in
the Probate Divorce and Admiralty Division, a registrar. In those district registries where a
prescribed officer was appointed, he was the district registrar; R.S.C. (Poor Persons) 1914,
r.31D.
[14] For further details, see the Report of the Committee on Legal Aid and Legal Advice in
England and Wales (Chairman: Lord Rushcliffe), Cmd. 6641 (1945).
[15] Report of the Committee to inquire into the Poor Persons' Rules, Cmd. 430 (1919).

application, and added an income test of £2 per week, or in special circumstances, £4 a week, to the existing capital test.[16] The Committee had also recommended that provision should be made for the trial of poor persons' divorce cases at Assizes and in 1922 provision was made for such cases to be heard at selected Assize towns.[17]

The system still continued to be ineffective and in 1923 a further committee was appointed, again under the chairmanship of P.O. Lawrence J. Its main recommendations were that there should be a large increase in the number of Assize towns where matrimonial cases could be heard, that administration should be transferred from the Poor Persons Department to the solicitors' profession, acting through committees appointed by the Law Society and by every provincial Law Society and approved by the Lord Chancellor, and that the system of the "reporting solicitor" should be abolished. It proposed that the local committee should, in each case, undertake all necessary inquiries and grant a certificate of admission as a poor person, that, in general, no money should be payable for profit costs or office expenses, and that a limit should be placed on out-of-pocket expenses by rules of court. In addition, it recommended that a grant should be paid by the Treasury towards the administrative expenses of the committees.[18]

1926–1950

01–06 The committee's recommendations were implemented by amendments made from time to time in the Rules of the Supreme Court.[19] The Law Society took over the offices and staff of the former Poor Persons Department and applications for legal aid were investigated and granted or refused by local committees.

During the Second World War the poor persons' procedure was in imminent danger of breakdown because of the shortage of solicitors and counsel owing to war service, the increase in applications for matrimonial proceedings and the fact that the pay of most members of the armed forces was above the financial limit. To overcome these difficulties, the Law Society created a Services Divorce Department to conduct any matrimonial

---

[16] R.S.C. (Poor Persons) 1920, Ord. XVI, rr. 22(2), 23, 31E.
[17] Matrimonial Causes at Assizes Order 1922; R.S.C. 1922, adding Ord. XXVIA, r.8.
[18] Report of the Poor Persons' Rules Committee Cmd. 2358 (1925).
[19] Rushcliffe, para. 20. The poor persons procedure did not apply generally in county courts and in *Cook v. Imperial Tobacco Co. Ltd* [1922] 2 K.B. 158 the Court of Appeal, not following *Chinn v. Bullen* (1849) 8 C.B. 447, held that proceedings could not be brought in those courts in *forma pauperis* because that procedure was purely statutory. The poor persons procedure was extended to actions remitted from the High Court to implement the Final Report of the Committee on Legal Aid for the poor, Cmd. 3016 (1928); R.S.C. (Poor Persons) 1928; adding R.S.C., Ord. XVI, r. 31DD.

cause in the High Court under the poor persons' procedure, somewhat modified, where any of the parties was in the services.[20]

The recommendations of the Rushcliffe Committee   01–07

By 1944 it had become apparent that the existing provisions for legal aid and advice were unsatisfactory and in that year the Lord Chancellor set up a committee under the chairmanship of the Lord Rushcliffe to consider the facilities then available for giving advice and assistance to the poor and to make recommendations for modifying and improving the existing system. The Committee reported in May 1945.

It was impressed by the evidence it had received that there was a need for a new approach to the whole question of legal assistance. It described the existing facilities for legal aid and advice as "a service which was at best somewhat patchy [and which] has become totally inadequate."[21] Its main recommendations were that:

(a) legal aid should be available in all courts;

(b) it should not be limited to those normally classed as poor, but should include a wider income group;

(c) those who could not afford to pay anything for legal aid should receive it free, and there should be a scale of contributions for those who could afford to pay something;

(d) the cost should be borne by the state, but the scheme should not be administered either as a department of state or by local authorities;

(e) administration should be carried out by the legal profession through the Law Society, which should act in co-operation with the Bar Council and should be answerable to the Lord Chancellor, who would be advised on matters of general policy by a central advisory committee;

(f) the means of an applicant for legal aid should be investigated by the National Assistance Board[22] and the merits of the case by committees of lawyers;

(g) barristers and solicitors should receive adequate remuneration for their services under the Scheme.[23]

The Rushcliffe Committee also made recommendations as to how legal aid and advice should be made available in accordance with its proposals.

---

[20] See the Rushcliffe Committee's Report, paras. 26–31 and 71–81 for creation and work of this Department and the other steps taken to meet the war-time difficulties. Through its conversion into the Law Society's Divorce Department, see the Society's First Report (1949–51), para. 18.

[21] See the Rushcliffe Committee's Report, para. 126.

[22] Now the Legal Aid Assessment Office of the Benefits Agency which carries out assessments of means on behalf of the Board; see below, para. 02–09.

[23] See the Rushcliffe Committee's Report, paras. 127, 156, 171.

The Government accepted the recommendations with slight variations[24] and invited the Law Society to prepare a detailed scheme.

In 1946, a comprehensive report was adopted by the Council of the Society for submission to the Lord Chancellor and subsequently for discussion with the legal profession.[25] It was on their proposals, amplifying the Rushcliffe Committee's recommendations, that the Bill which became the Legal Aid and Advice Act 1949 and the subordinate legislation made under it,[26] were based.

Provision was made for the Legal Aid and Advice Act 1949[27] to be brought into force by the Lord Chancellor and he was given power to appoint different days for different purposes.[28] The power was first exercised to bring into force, with effect from September 1, 1949, the purely administrative provisions of the Act relating to the functions of the Law Society in starting the new scheme and to the constitution of the Lord Chancellor's Advisory Committee (dissolved in 1994).[29]

At that time it was hoped that the whole of the remainder of Part I of the Act would be brought into force on July 1, 1950. However, in October 1949, the Government announced its decision, in view of the general economic situation of the country, to defer this indefinitely except for the provisions of the Act relating to legal aid and proceedings in the High Court or in the Court of Appeal, including proceedings remitted from the High Court to a county court or the Mayor's and City of London Court.

LEGAL ADVICE

01–08 The Rushcliffe Committee was required to consider, in addition to legal aid, the facilities in England and Wales for giving legal advice. There had never in the past been any provision for this other than from private charitable sources, including advice given gratuitously by practitioners.

The Rushcliffe Committee found the facilities available for giving legal advice to be more sporadic than those for legal aid and it also found that there was no organised provision for legal advice throughout the country, comparable either with the provision for legal aid in criminal matters or

---

[24] See the White Paper on the Legal Aid and Advice Bill 1948, Cmd. 7563 (1948).

[25] See L.S. Gaz., June 1970, 399.

[26] Principally the Legal Aid (General) Regulations 1950, the Legal Aid (Assessment of Resources) Regulations 1950 and the Legal Aid Scheme 1950.

[27] At that time, Pt. I dealt primarily with legal advice and with legal aid in civil proceedings, and Pt. II with legal aid in criminal proceedings. Pt. II was revoked and replaced by the Criminal Justice Act 1967, Pt. IV.

[28] Legal Aid and Advice Act 1949, s. 17(2). For the transitional provisions relating to the *in forma pauperis* and poor persons' procedures, see *ibid.* s. 17(3)–(6), and Legal Aid (General) Regulations 1950, reg. 20.

[29] See below, para. 02–04, for the duties of this committee.

with that provided by the poor persons procedure for legal aid in civil matters in the High Court and the Court of Appeal. The committee recommended the establishment of facilities for legal advice all over the country which were to be administered by The Law Society and paid for out of public funds. The Law Society made proposals for implementing this recommendation, under which advice centres would be established in 250 places, staffed by just under 100 solicitors employed full-time by the Society, reinforced in less populous areas by solicitors in private practice engaged part-time on the work.[30] For reasons of national economy, implementation of these proposals was deferred, although the necessary provisions were included in the Legal Aid and Advice Act 1949.

Between 1950 and the Present

From 1950, the Scheme was extended piecemeal, as economic circum- **01–09** stances permitted. County Court proceedings were included from January 1956. Cover for claims was added from March 1960[31] with most appeals to the House of Lords being added in December 1960 and proceedings in magistrates' courts and at quarter sessions from May 1961, January 1965 and August 1969 (depending on the type of case). Criminal legal aid was granted by the criminal courts.

There was mounting criticism that the scheme, was placing an undue emphasis on litigation rather than on the avoidance of it.[32] In order to meet the financial difficulties, and encouraged by practitioner's response to the legal aid scheme, The Law Society made proposals in 1958 for a more economical service, whereby legal advice would be given by practising solicitors in their own offices. These proposals were accepted and, on 2 March 1959, the new statutory scheme was introduced simultaneously with a voluntary scheme run by solicitors in private practice.

It soon became apparent that the arrangements for going beyond the provision of purely oral advice, and supplying assistance for claims under

---

[30] Pollock, "Legal Aid as a Social Service", (1970) L.S. Gaz. June 1970, 399. (This article gives the history of the statutory advice scheme.) And see Lund, (1948) 92 Sol. Jo. 716, at p. 728.

[31] Legal aid for "claims" was intended to bridge the gap between the legal advice scheme and legal aid for proceedings. The scope of the advice scheme at that time was very limited, its purpose being to provide a person with oral advice on legal questions in which he had an interest and to do no more than that. The solicitor was not permitted to write letters on the client's behalf or to obtain information or do anything in the way of asserting or protecting the client's rights. Legal aid for claims was designed to cover this situation by providing for legal aid in taking steps to assert or dispute a claim where the question of taking proceedings had not yet arisen. The scope of the modern legal advice scheme is very wide and covers all the work previously covered by legal aid for claims, see Part B.

[32] See generally, Dworkin, "The progress and future of legal aid in civil litigation" (1965) 28 M.L.R. 432, and Pollock in L.S. Gaz., February 1960, 98.

section 5 of the Legal Aid and Advice Act 1949, which was brought into force shortly afterwards, were cumbersome and that the financial limits prevented many people from receiving the assistance they needed at a sufficiently early stage. For these and other reasons, a number of the existing Poor Man's Lawyer centres, which had existed from about 1890, instead of being rendered unnecessary by introduction of the statutory scheme, remained in steady demand.

Criticisms

01–10 The growth of the legal aid scheme was spectacular. Its development was hampered by the economic position of the country but it was considered to be a success although aspects which were criticised included the fixed upper limit of eligibility in respect of an applicant's income, the obligation to pay the whole excess of disposable capital over £125 by way of a contribution, the low limits of eligibility and that legal aid was not available for any tribunal other than the Lands Tribunal. Criticisms which remain familiar today.

There were also criticisms of deficiencies in the statutory advice scheme and in the provision of legal aid for claims but in 1968 The Law Society made proposals for overcoming these. Under the scheme — which was usually referred to as "the £25 scheme" because that figure represented the amount of costs which a solicitor could incur under it on his own authority — the best elements of the existing arrangements for legal advice, claims and legal aid were to be combined into a single scheme. The proposals, although generally welcomed, were criticised as being inadequate to deal with the problems of the poor and disadvantaged, particularly those living in over-crowded urban areas. It was said that there were too few solicitors in practice in those areas, that much of the work would be uneconomical and therefore unattractive, that few solicitors had sufficient knowledge of the subjects on which advice and assistance were needed (*e.g.* as to welfare benefits), and that some sections of the public were reluctant to go into a solicitor's office, regarding it as unfamiliar and unsympathetic. With a view to overcoming these difficulties there was pressure for the setting up of legal centres which would be independent of the legal aid and advice scheme and be staffed by lawyers employed exclusively to look after the needs of the poor.

In many parts of the country, local law societies and independent groups of lawyers initiated a variety of experiments and charitable foundations, including The Nuffield Foundation, made grants to support them or fund research to gauge the extent of the so called "unmet need" for legal services. This led to the establishment of Law Centres[33] and the involvement of the "advice sector" in the provision of legal services.

---

[33] e.g. North Kensington Law Centre (L.S. Gaz., September 1970, 634); Citizens' Rights Office (New L.J., 30 April 1970, 414). Solicitors employed there full-time were permitted to act as panel members under the legal advice and legal aid schemes.

The Legal Advice and Assistance Act 1972, coming into force on 2 April **01–11**
1973, replaced and rationalised the former provisions for legal advice and
for claims by the introduction of the legal advice and assistance scheme
which became known as "the Green Form Scheme". The system today has
very many of the features of the old scheme in terms of scope, the
application of a means test, an extendable costs limit and the operation of
the solicitor's charge subject to a list of exemptions.

When the statutory Green Form Scheme was introduced, The Law
Society's voluntary scheme was brought to an end. The concept of "panel"
membership was abolished and the client could consult any solicitor
willing to undertake work under the Scheme. Information to assist in
identifying a solicitor was improved by The Law Society and failure to
advise as to the availability of legal aid, advice and assistance could render
a solicitor liable in negligence or lead to disciplinary action.

1974–1988

The Legal Aid Act 1974 was a consolidation Act which repealed and **01–12**
replaced the Legal Aid and Advice Acts 1949 to 1972, and Part IV of the
Criminal Justice Act 1967, without making any changes in the law. With a
few exceptions, the whole of the Legal Aid Act 1974 came into force on
May 8, 1974.

Use of both so called Green Form legal advice and legal aid grew over
the years and there was also a general upsurge of interest in the provision
of legal services in areas of particular need, including the setting up of
advice and law centres and the creation of voluntary duty solicitor and rota
schemes.

With effect from April 1, 1979, the Lord Chancellor restricted the scope
of legal aid in proceedings for divorce or judicial separation using the
power in section 7(2) of the Legal Aid Act 1974. This decision attracted
considerable criticism but legal aid was restricted in this way at the same
time as, by the Matrimonial Causes (Amendment No. 2) Rules 1976, the
special procedure was extended to all types of undefended divorce cases.

Various changes have been made to widen the scope of civil legal aid,
e.g. for proceedings before a Commons Commissioner and the Employment
Appeal Tribunal. Legal aid has not, however, been extended to all statutory
tribunals and extensions to the system tend to have reflected more general
changes in the legal system.

The Legal Aid Act 1982 gave applicants for criminal legal aid a right of
review to the Law Society's Legal Aid Area Committees following disparities
in grant/refusal rates of criminal legal aid as between different magistrates'
courts. At the same time, the Law Society was given other limited powers
in relation to criminal legal aid, *e.g.* to deal with prior authorities.

The growth of use of the legal aid system continued with changes in
financial eligibility, in an attempt to keep pace with inflation, and increases

in the rates of remuneration payable. With the passage of time, the percentage of the population financially eligible for assistance decreased and the legal profession became dissatisfied with the rates of remuneration.

1989 on

01–13   Following the inception of a Legal Aid Board for Scotland, the Legal Aid Act 1988 set up a new, non-departmental public body the Legal Aid Board for England and Wales, as well as providing a new framework for the provision of publicly funded advice, assistance or representation to those who might otherwise be unable to obtain it on account of their means. The Legal Aid Board (the Board) took over the administration of legal aid on April 1, 1989 from the Law Society. While the Legal Aid Act 1988 (the 1988 Act) allows the Board wide flexibility in the delivery of legal services, *e.g.* by grants and contracts, much of the current system is based on the historical development of legal aid.

After 1989 expenditure increased from £685 million in 1990-91 to a figure in excess of £1,300 million in 1994-95 — a doubling of expenditure in a very short time. Annual increases in the eligibility limit and remuneration rates no longer necessarily take place and, indeed, in 1993 the eligibility conditions were tightened and contributory Green Forms abolished. Both the cost of the current system and the desire to fund the provision of quality legal services more effectively at a controllable cost led the Lord Chancellor[34] to undertake a Fundamental Review of legal aid.

The Future

01–14   Under consideration is a cash limited system with set priorities and regional committees advising on local needs and the allocation of funds. Legally aided services would be provided by contracted quality assured suppliers on a block contract basis as to the type, volume and price of services to be provided. Pilot projects may be run by the Legal Aid Board but the Lord Chancellor sees the failures of the current scheme as not targeting need, not ensuring quality and channelling money to costly legal solutions.

The Lord Chancellor has also issued a consultation paper on the grant of legal aid to the apparently wealthy as well as to non-United Kingdom citizens. This explores options to prevent abuse and address what many see as the unfairness of the present scheme following a number of highly publicised expensive cases in relation to the grant of both criminal and civil legal aid and may lead to some changes, particularly in the area of means assessment (e.g. to limit the disregard allowed for the equity in property

---

[34] Green Paper — "Legal Aid — Targeting Need". Cm 2854.

which is the subject matter of the dispute, and to allow for assets to be frozen and then used towards legal costs after conviction). The Green Form scheme has also been publicised as being open to abuse by fraudulent solicitors and subject to costs generation by solicitors "touting" for work.

The Fundamental Review aside, (which is to lead to a White Paper in early 1996) the Legal Aid Board has introduced the concept of quality assured publicly funded legal services through its scheme of franchising. The Board is also exploring alternative methods of delivery of legal services, e.g. through non-solicitor advice agencies.

The introduction of standard fees and prescribed hourly rates has not controlled legal aid expenditure and cuts in financial eligibility have not sufficed to make the *status quo* an option.[35]

---

[35] The Lord Chancellor's address "The Future for Legal Aid" to the Social Market Foundation January 11, 1995 in which he said: "There must be change."

13

Chapter 2

THE PRESENT SCHEME AND ITS ADMINISTRATION

LEGAL AID ACT 1988

02–01 The basis for the present scheme is the Legal Aid Act 1988 (the 1988 Act) which received royal assent on July 29, 1988 and was substantially brought into force on April 1, 1989. The 1988 Act is, as were the previous Acts dealing with legal aid, essentially an enabling Act, and the details of the scheme are set out in the various Regulations made under the Act.

The principal change brought about by the 1988 Act was the transfer of responsibility for administration of the scheme from the Law Society to a new body called the Legal Aid Board (the Board). The Board is a body corporate but has no Crown immunity. It is a non-departmental public body (a 'quango').

The main purpose of the 1988 Act is stated to be "to establish a framework for the provision under Parts II, III, IV, V and VI of advice, assistance and representation which is publicly funded with a view to helping persons who might otherwise be unable to obtain advice, assistance or representation on account of their means".[1-2]

Advice and assistance are defined in terms similar to those used in the previous legislation[3] but the term "legal aid" which had been used in the previous legislation to cover the situation where the assisted person was being represented in proceedings (as distinct from merely receiving advice and assistance) has been replaced with the term "representation".[4]

Although in many respects the 1988 Act reproduces provisions similar to those contained in the previous legislation, the 1988 Act does provide for the Board to assume wider powers, including the power to enter into contracts (a system now known as "franchising").[5]

[1-2] Legal Aid Act 1988, s. 1.
[3] For definition of "advice" see para. 03–10 and for definition of "assistance" see para. 03–11.
[4] For definition of "representation" see para. 07–02.
[5] For the Board's powers generally see para. 02–03 and chap. 39.

LEGAL AID BOARD

Under the 1988 Act, the Board is given the general function of securing **02–02** that advice, assistance representation are available in accordance with the 1988 Act and of administering the 1988 Act.[6] The Board's functions do not, however, extend to the grant of representation under Part VI of the 1988 Act for the purpose of proceedings for contempt.[7] The 1988 Act also provides that certain other functions are not to be conferred on the Board unless the Lord Chancellor so directs by order and only to the extent specified in the order. These additional functions are:

(a) determination of the costs of representation under Part IV (civil legal aid);

(b) functions as respects representation under Part V (criminal legal aid) other than determination of the costs of representation for the purposes of proceedings in magistrates' courts; and

(c) determination of the financial resources of persons for the purposes of the 1988 Act.[8]

It is clear that the scheme envisages that the Board may ultimately take over responsibility for legal aid taxations (from the appropriate taxing officers), the grant of criminal legal aid (from the courts) and determination of the resources of people applying for legal aid (from the Legal Aid Assessment Office of the Benefits Agency in the case of civil legal aid and from the courts in the case of criminal legal aid). These provisions reflect the declared intention of the Lord Chancellor that the Board shall ultimately have overall responsibility for legal aid.

The 1988 Act provides that there must be at least 11, and not more than 17 members of the Board and that the members and the chairman shall be appointed by Lord Chancellor.[9] The 1988 Act requires that there should be at least two solicitors appointed to the Board after consultation with the Law Society[10] and that the Lord Chancellor shall consult with the General Council of the Bar with a view to the inclusion on the Board of at least two barristers.[11]

---

[6] Legal Aid Act 1988, s. 3(2).

[7] *ibid.* s. 3(3). See also Chap. 37.

[8] *ibid.* 3(4). The Legal Aid Act also specifically provides that the Board may, from time to time, prepare and submit to the Lord Chancellor proposals for the assumption by it of any functions in relation to the provision of advice, assistance or representation under the Legal Aid Act; see *ibid.* s. 4(8).

[9] *ibid.* 3(5); but any vacancy among the members of the Board or any defect in the appointment of any member does not affect the validity of any proceedings of the Board of any committee appointed by the Board; see *ibid.* Sched. 1, para. 11(5). Further, the Lord Chancellor is empowered to vary by order the minimum and maximum numbers for membership of the Board to such other number as he thinks appropriate; see *ibid.* s. 3(6).

[10] *ibid.* 1988, s. 3(7).

[11] *ibid.* s. 3(8).

15

The Lord Chancellor is required, in appointing members of the Board, to have regard to the desirability of securing that the Board includes members who have expertise in or knowledge of the provision of legal services, the work of the courts and social conditions and management.[12] Mediation is likely to be added having regard to proposals for divorce reform.

In Schedule 1 to the 1988 Act there are provisions dealing with tenure of members, members' interests and their remuneration.

Powers of the Board

02–03 Subject to express provisions in the 1988 Act, the Board is empowered to do anything which it considers necessary or desirable to provide or secure the provision of advice, assistance and representation under the 1988 Act or which is calculated to facilitate or is incidental or conducive to the discharge of its functions. The 1988 Act also enables advice, assistance and representation to be provided in different ways in different areas of England and Wales and in different ways in different fields of law.[13]

Without prejudice to the general function referred to above, the Board is also given specific power to:

(a) enter into any contract including a contract to acquire or dispose of land;[14]

(b) make grants (with or without conditions including conditions as to repayment);

(c) make loans;

(d) invest money;

(e) promote or assist in the promotion of publicity relating to the functions of the Board;

(f) undertake any inquiry or investigation which the Board considers necessary or expedient in relation to the discharge of its functions; and

(g) give the Lord Chancellor such advice as it may consider appropriate in relation to the provision of advice, assistance and representation under the 1988 Act.[15]

The 1988 Act also makes express provision for advice, assistance or representation to be made available by means of contracts with or grants or loans to, other persons or bodies but this power is only exercisable if the

---

[12] *ibid.* s. 3(9). The Board members are paid but work part-time only; this enables Board members to be appointed who also have other posts and can bring to bear their expertise from those other posts.

[13] *ibid.* s. 4(1); but the Board may not borrow money or acquire and hold shares in bodies corporate or take part in forming bodies corporate; see *ibid.* s. 4(3).

[14] Contracts to acquire or dispose of land may not be exercised without the approval in writing of the Lord Chancellor; see *ibid.* s. 4(7).

[15] *ibid.* s. 4(2).

Lord Chancellor so directs and to the extent specified in the direction and in accordance with any directions given by the Lord Chancellor.[16] In the case of contracts to secure the provision of representation under Part IV (civil legal aid), the power is only exercisable in the classes of case prescribed in Regulations.[17] These contracting powers are the powers which enable the Board to enter into contracts with one or more firms for the purpose of representation of assisted persons involved in multi-party actions[18] and they also form the basis for the system of franchising.[19] They can be used to contract for the funding of cases on a block, rather than individual case by case, basis.

Duties of the Board

From time to time the Board is required to publish information as to the **02–04** discharge of its functions in relation to advice, assistance and representation[20] and to furnish to the Lord Chancellor with such information as he may require relating to its property and to the discharge or proposed discharge of its functions.[21]

Each year, as soon as possible after March 31, the Board is required to produce an annual report to the Lord Chancellor on the discharge of its functions during the preceding 12 months[22], and the Lord Chancellor may direct from time to time the matters which are to be included in the report.[23] The Legal Aid Advisory Committee, which previously advised the Lord Chancellor on Legal aid issues, was dissolved in 1994.

The Board's annual report is a useful source of statistical and other information regarding the Board's activities, including details of Regulation changes and significant cases. The Board also makes available for purchase the Legal Aid Handbook and issues guidance on the Exercise of Devolved Powers to franchisees. The Handbook not only contains the Board's Notes for Guidance on its decision-making but also all the relevant statutory material and useful reference material ranging from performance standards (targets) to details of forms and area offices.

Although the Board is required to have regard in discharging its functions, to any guidance given by the Lord Chancellor,[24] the 1988 Act specifically

---

[16] *ibid.* s. 4(4).
[17] *ibid.* s. 4(5).
[18] See Chap. 40.
[19] See Chap. 39.
[20] *ibid.* s. 5(1).
[21] *ibid.* s. 5(2). The Board is also required to permit any person authorised by the Lord Chancellor to inspect and make copies of any accounts or documents of the Board and give such explanations of them as that person or the Lord Chancellor may require; see *ibid.* s. 5(7).
[22] *ibid.* s. 5(3).
[23] *ibid.* s. 5(4).
[24] *ibid.* s. 5(5).

provides that any such guidance must not relate to the consideration or disposal, in particular cases, of applications for advice, assistance or representation, or any supplementary or incidental applications or requests to the Board where advice, assistance or representation has been made available.[25] This is so as to ensure the Board's independence in dealing with individual cases.

The Legal Aid Board achieved corporate accreditation in late 1993 for the BS 5750 quality accrediation (now ISO 9000). It is committed to total quality and continuous improvement in its performance. It considers that it is particularly important in Legal Aid that discretionary decisions are justifiable. It has defined its masters, who may have conflicting interests as "stakeholders", each of whom has to be borne in mind when a decision is made. The stakeholders are the applicant (or assisted person), the legal adviser, the court and the Government (the taxpayer). What is the right decision for the applicant may not be the right decision for the court or the taxpayer if legal aid is granted when it should not be; what may be the right decision for the taxpayer may not be right for the applicant if legal aid is refused when it should be granted. The Board considers that its decision must be capable of justification to the stakeholders in any particular case. The standards on the consistency of decision-making which are included in the Legal Aid Handbook address justifiability.

LEGAL AID FUND

02–05 There are two separate funds which are made available to the Board to enable it to discharge its functions. The term "Legal Aid Fund" (the Fund) is generally used to mean the demand led fund which the Board is required under the 1988 Act to establish and maintain.[26] There is, however, an additional cash-limited fund which is made available to the Board to meet the administrative costs of running the scheme.

The greater part of the Fund is used for payment of the remuneration and expenses incurred by legal representatives in connection with the provision of advice, assistance or representation.[27] The Fund also has to meet any costs awarded to a successful unassisted party under section 13 (assistance by way of representation ABWOR) or section 18 (civil legal aid).[28] The Fund is also liable for any repayment of contribution to assisted persons under section 16(4) (civil legal aid) or section 23(7) (criminal legal aid).[29] Subject to those payments the only other payments which may be made out of the

---

[25] *ibid.* s. 5(6).
[26] *ibid.* s. 6(1).
[27] *ibid.* s. 6(2)(a).
[28] *ibid.* s. 6(2)(b).
[29] *ibid.* s. 6(2)(c).

Fund are such other payments for the purposes of the 1988 Act as the Lord Chancellor may, with the concurrence of the Treasury, determine.[30]

The money paid into the Fund consists of:

(a) any contribution payable to the Board under the Act;

(b) any *inter partes* costs award in favour of an assisted person;

(c) any sum payable out of property recovered or preserved for an assisted person;

(d) any costs paid to a successful unassisted party under section 13 or 18 which are ordered to be repaid to the Board;

(e) the sum paid by the Lord Chancellor which is required from the Treasury to meet the cost of running the legal aid scheme, subject to the receipts referred to above; and

(f) such other receipts of the Board as the Lord Chancellor, with the concurrence of the Treasury, determine.[31]

The Board is required to keep separate accounts in respect of the two funds (the legal aid fund and the administration costs) and to prepare a statement of accounts in respect of each financial year.[32] These accounts must be audited by persons appointed by the Lord Chancellor in accordance with a scheme of audit approved by him and the auditors are required to prepare a report to the Lord Chancellor on the accounts and statement which are furnished by the Board.[33] On completion of the audit the auditors must send to the Lord Chancellor a copy of their report together with the Board's statement of accounts. The Lord Chancellor in turn must send these to the Comptroller and Auditor General[34] who may inspect the accounts and any records relating to them.[35] These statements of accounts and auditors' reports must be laid by the Lord Chancellor before each House of Parliament.

The Board itself works through a number of committees. There is a separate operational Management Board chaired by the Chief Executive.

LEGAL AID HEAD OFFICE

The senior permanent member of staff appointed by the Board is the Chief **02–06** Executive.[36] His appointment, and the appointment of any other

---

[30] *ibid.* s. 6(2)(d).
[31] *ibid.* s. 6(3).
[32] *ibid.* s. 7(1). The term "financial year" means the period beginning with the day on which the Board was established (*i.e.* April 1, 1989) and ending with March 31, 1990 and each subsequent period of 12 months ending with March 31 in each year; see *ibid.* s. 7(8). These accounts are to be kept, and the statement of accounts prepared, in such form as the Lord Chancellor may, with the approval of the Treasury, direct; see *ibid.* s. 7(2).
[33] *ibid.* s. 7(3). The Legal Aid Act also sets out the qualifications for an appointed auditor; see *ibid.* s. 7(4).
[34] *ibid.* s. 7(5).
[35] *ibid.* s. 7(6).
[36] *ibid.* Sched. 1, para. 9(1). Currently Stephen Orchard.

employment specified (by direction of the Lord Chancellor) is subject to consultation with, and the approval of, the Lord Chancellor.[37]

Apart from the Chief Executive, the Legal Aid Head Office functions are divided into four discrete categories, each under the responsibility of a member of the Board's Management Board. The Management Board deals with policy and operational matters and is chaired by the Chief Executive.

Secretariat

The Secretariat is the focus of contact between the Board, the Lord Chancellor's Department, the legal profession and all other bodies. It services the Board's committees and works on policy, in collaboration with other parts of the organisation, for approval by the Board. The Secretariat is also responsible for the duty solicitor arrangements, publicity and public relations.

The Legal Department

The Legal Department provides legal advice to the organisation, handles any complex litigation in which the administration is involved and answers queries about the legal aid legislation from outside the organisation. It also deals with complaints about the administration of legal aid which have not been resolved at local level.

Finance and Personnel

The Accounts Department deals with payment of costs authorised by area offices and with contributions from legally aided persons as well as receipt of costs and damages which must, under the Regulations, be paid into the Fund. It includes the Board's Debt Recovery Unit which deals with the recovery of contributions, statutory charge liabilities and costs orders. It also includes an Investigation Section which is responsible for prevention and discovery of fraud against the Fund. In addition, the Accounts Department has various administrative functions.

The Personnel and Training Department's main responsibility is to develop the organisation's structure and human resources to meet the total quality objectives that have been defined by the Board. It is, in addition, responsible for policy, procedures and advice on all personnel and training issues. There is also a separate Quality Assurance Department (also known as SQA (Supplier Quality Assurance)) which deals with all quality issues, including franchising (also known as SQA). The Board is committed to the

---

[37] *ibid.* Sched. 1, para. 9(3).

management concept of total quality and holds the British Standards quality standard ISO 9000 (formerly BS 5750).

Information Systems Department

The Information Systems Department (ISD) is responsible for the development, implementation and support of all computer systems in legal aid. It is responsible for the running of, and data entry to, the central computer and is developing a new administration/computer system known as CIS (Corporate Information System) for implementation in 1996.

This system will replace all the Board's existing computer and administration systems at both local and central level. It will deal with case recording, document production, accounting and the collection of management information.

Its introduction will make the Board's administration less paper dependent and is likely to be allied with an increase in the conduct of business by telephone (rather than paper) as well as in customer care/awareness.

Prior to introduction all the Board's external forms will be re-designed and renumbered. Forms changes are always consulted upon outside the Board.

AREA OFFICES

For administrative purposes England and Wales is divided into 13 **02–07** geographical areas. These are, in turn, divided into five groups or regions (London/Brighton group, North East Group, North West Group, Midlands Group and Wales and the West Group). Each area office is run by a Group or Area Manager who is appointed by the Board to be the Area Director in accordance with the Regulations.[38] Group Managers are responsible for all the offices within that group and are members of the Management Board. The Area Directors are given wide powers under the Regulations[39] but, in practice, decisions are delegated by the Area Directors to members of the area office staff.

The functions of the area offices are:

(a) to grant or refuse applications for legal aid certificates[40];

---

[38] For the definition of Area Director see reg. 3 of the General Regulations. Reg. 4 further provides that Area Directors shall exercise functions delegated to them by the Board or conferred on them by the Civil Legal Aid (General) Regulations.
[39] See reg. 6 of the General Regulations.
[40] See Chaps 7 and 8.

(b) to deal with requests for amendments to certificates[41];

(c) to deal with requests for authority to incur expenditure in civil proceedings[42];

(d) to discharge or revoke certificates[43];

(e) to assess bills of costs for work done under legal aid certificates in certain circumstances[44];

(f) to decide whether the statutory charge applies under section 16(6) of the 1988 Act[45];

(g) to consider applications for extensions of the Green Form costs limit[46];

(h) to assess Green Form and ABWOR bills[47] and duty solicitor costs claims;

(i) to consider requests that the Green Form charge be waived[48];

(j) to grant approval of ABWOR[49];

(k) to deal with requests for authority to incur expenditure under an ABWOR approval[50];

(l) to withdraw approval of ABWOR[51];

(m) to consider criminal legal aid review applications requests for amendment of, and for authorities under criminal legal aid orders[52];

(n) to assess bills of costs for work done in Magistrates' Courts under criminal legal aid orders.[53]

(o) to assess bills of costs for work done under representation in contempt proceedings.[54]

Each regional group has a Group Duty Solicitor Manager who overseas the operation of the duty solicitor arrangements. Each area office also has a Franchise Manager supported by Liaison Managers and auditors who are responsible for the implementation of franchising including audits[55] of franchised firms (franchisees) and applicants for franchises.

As part of its commitment to quality the Board recognises the need to have a system for dealing with and learning from complaints.

---

[41] See Chap. 13.
[42] See Chap. 14.
[43] See Chap. 15.
[44] See Chaps. 16, 19 and 20.
[45] See Chap. 18.
[46] See Chap. 31.
[47] See Chap. 3.
[48] See Chap. 3.
[49] See Chap. 4.
[50] See Chap. 4.
[51] See Chap. 4.
[52] See Chap. 20.
[53] See Chap. 20.
[54] See Chap. 37.
[55] See Chap. 39.

Complaints by individuals or solicitors (*e.g.* regarding delay) should be addressed to the relevant area office. The name of the assisted person and the Board's reference should be clearly stated at the top of any written complaint which should be boldly marked "Complaint". As part of its customer care approach the Board has a leaflet to assist those who are dissatisfied. Complaints will be fully investigated and any appropriate action taken. The Board's published Customer Service Standards (see the Legal Aid Handbook and the Board's Annual Report) include a commitment to address complaints promptly and efficiently. If a complaint is made an explanation will be given and, if the Board is at fault, an apology and information also given on what has been done to put things right.

AREA COMMITTEES

Area committees are appointed by the Board for each of the legal aid areas   **02–08** covered by the area offices.[56] The members of the area committees consist of solicitors and barristers in private practice who meet in sub-committees of not fewer than three members and who deal with:

   (a) appeals against refusal to grant legal aid certificates and against discharge/revocation of legal aid certificates;
   (b) applications for review of assessments of costs claims and for certification of points of principle of general importance;
   (c) refusal of applications for approval of ABWOR;
   (d) refusal of requests for authority to incur expenditure under an ABWOR approval;
   (e) appeals against withdrawal of approval of ABWOR;
   (f) review of an application for a legal aid order;
   (g) renewal of an application for amendment of a legal aid order;
   (h) requests for authority to incur expenditure in criminal proceedings in a magistrates' court or in the Crown Court.

The arrangements for the appointment of area committee members by the Board are set out in the Legal Aid Board Area Committee Arrangements.[57]

LEGAL AID ASSESSMENT OFFICE

Assessment of the financial eligibility of those applying for legal aid under   **02–09** Part IV of the 1988 Act (civil legal aid) is undertaken on behalf of the Board

---

[56] See reg. 4 of the General Regulations. Area Committees are generally speaking autonomous but for the position re control by the courts, see Chap. 35. Area committees operate in accordance with the Legal Aid Board Area Committee Arrangements.
[57] See Legal Aid Handbook 1995, p. 497.

by the Legal Aid Assessment Office which forms part of the Benefits Agency (formerly the Department of Social Security).[58] The detailed Regulations relating to financial eligibility under Part IV are set out in the Civil Legal Aid (Assessment of Resources) Regulations 1989.

Individual assessments are undertaken by "assessment officers"[59] and there is no right of appeal from the assessment of an applicant's means. Applicants can, however, ask the appropriate area office to request the assessment officer to reconsider the assessment and/or to provide a breakdown of how the assessment was reached.[60]

The 1988 Act contemplates that the responsibility for the determination of the financial resources of applicants may be conferred on the Board.[61]

THE SCHEME IN OUTLINE

02–10 There are four types of legal aid provided by the 1988 Act:
  (a) advice and assistance including ABWOR;
  (b) civil legal aid;
  (c) criminal legal aid; and
  (d) advice and representation provided by duty solicitors at magistrates' courts and by duty and own solicitors at police stations.

Legal advice and assistance, which is usually known as the Green Form Scheme, covers the provision of advice and assistance on matters of English law on a non contributory basis for those who qualify financially. Legal advice and assistance also includes ABWOR which extends to representation as opposed to Green Form advice and assistance which does not cover representation.

Civil legal aid is representation for the purposes of such proceedings before courts or tribunals or at statutory inquiries in England and Wales as are specified by the 1988 Act. It is normally both means and merits tested, although there are special arrangements relating to certain proceedings in respect of children which allow for non means, non merits tested (free) or means tested only legal aid.

02–11 Criminal legal aid covers representation in criminal proceedings before magistrates' courts, the Crown Courts, the criminal division of the Court of

---

[58] The address of the Legal Aid Assessment Office is Albert Edward House, No. 3 The Pavilions, Ashton-in-Ribble, Preston, PR2 2PA. (DX 700419, telephone 01722 898061 or 898064).
[59] For the definition of assessment officer see reg. 3 of the General Regulations.
[60] See Chap. 6. For the position regarding control by the courts see Chap. 35.
[61] See s. 3(4) of the Legal Aid Act 1988.

Appeal or the Courts-Martial Appeal Court and the House of Lords exercising its appellate jurisdiction from the Crown Court or the criminal division of the Court of Appeal. Representation is means and merits tested and extends to any proceedings preliminary or incidental to the proceedings, including bail proceedings, whether before the court in question or another court.

Advice at police stations is provided by duty solicitors on a rota or panel basis in accordance with the Legal Aid Board Duty Solicitor Arrangements 1994 and the Legal Aid Board Legal Advice and Assistance at Police Stations Register Arrangements 1994. It also extends to the use of own solicitors. It is not means tested and covers advice and assistance to those who are arrested and held in custody or to volunteers. A volunteer is someone who, for the purpose of assisting with an investigation, attends voluntarily at a police station or other place where a constable is present or accompanies a constable to a police station or other place without being arrested. Duty solicitors at magistrates' courts also provide advice and representation in accordance with the Legal Aid Board Duty Solicitor Arrangements 1994. These Arrangements have replaced any voluntary arrangements which were previously in place.

The Board is responsible for the administration of advice and assistance, civil legal aid and the duty solicitor schemes. In relation to criminal legal aid, the Board assesses criminal legal aid costs claims for magistrates' court proceedings and also deals with reviews against the refusal of criminal legal aid as well as certain other applications relating to criminal legal aid. The grant of criminal legal aid is dealt with by the Criminal Courts rather than the Legal Aid Board. Bills for proceedings in Crown Courts are assessed by Crown Court determining officers. It is the Lord Chancellor's Department which is the responsible department in relation to the magistrates' courts, although they are administered locally, while the Crown Courts fall within the jurisdiction of the Court Service.

It should be noted that, according to section 31(1)(a) of the 1988 Act, except as expressly provided, the fact that the services of a legal representative are given under the Act does not affect the relationship between or rights of legal representative and client or any privilege arising out of such relationship.

The legal representative is not precluded from disclosing to any person authorised by the Legal Aid Board to request it, any information which relates to advice, assistance and representation provided to a client or former client of his where that client is or was a legally assisted person. The information must be requested for the purpose of enabling the Legal Aid Board to discharge its functions under the Legal Aid Act 1988.[62] See Chapter 36 for confidentiality.

---

[62] See Legal Aid (Disclosure of Information) Regulations 1991.

THE FUTURE

02–12 The Board is committed to the expansion of franchising and is undertaking research regarding the delivery of legal services. This includes a Non Solicitor Agencies Project which involves the delivery of legal advice and assistance by agencies in the advice sector who receive funding from the Board once it is satisfied as to certain quality standards. A qualified solicitor is not involved.

The Lord Chancellor is undertaking a Fundamental Review of legal aid and a Green Paper on the subject was published in Spring 1995. This may result in radical change to the legal aid system in England and Wales following concerns regarding the increasing costs of a demand led legal aid fund.

Prior to the publication of the Green Paper the idea of a cash limited-fund with fund-holders similar to those in the reform of the National Health Service was floated but options being considered are now based on a cash limited rather than demand led legal aid fund operated through block funding of certain work which would be undertaken by firms quality assured. This would involve the allocation of limited funds through the prioritisation of types of work — there could be national priorities but also identification of local needs by Regional Legal Services Committees. Criminal legal aid would not necessarily be cash limited but would form the subject of a separate fund. Possible changes in the legal aid arrangements for matrimonial proceedings would be in tandem with the reform of divorce law moving to an emphasis on mediation.[63]

---

[63] See also para. 01–13 and 01–14.

PART B

ADVICE AND ASSISTANCE

Chapter 3

GREEN FORM SCHEME

INTRODUCTION

For advice and assistance under the 1988 Act, a solicitor or the solicitor's **03–01** competent and responsible representative employed in his office or otherwise under his immediate supervision must assess whether client is eligible for advice and assistance.[1]

All such advice and assistance is provided under Part III of the 1988 Act (unless it is provided under a contract under Part II of the Act, in which case it may be provided under Part II or III, depending on the provisions of the contract); it is generally known as advice and assistance under the Green Form Scheme. This is simply because the forms used are presently green in colour. When the idea of expanding the Legal Aid and Advice Act 1949 to cover advice was first put forward (by the Law Society), it was referred to as the "£25 Scheme" because this was the value of the advice which it was proposed should be covered by the scheme.

Financial eligibility

Advice and assistance to which Part III of the 1988 Act applies is available **03–02** to any person whose financial resources are such as, under Regulations, make him eligible for advice or assistance.[2] The relevant regulations are the Legal Advice and Assistance Regulations 1989 and the Legal Advice and Assistance (Scope) Regulations 1989.

A person receiving advice and assistance (a client) cannot be required to pay any additional sums to his legal representatives for the work covered by the Green Form.[3]

The 1988 Act makes provision for clients to be liable to pay contributions towards the cost of the advice and assistance.[4] However, since April 1993,

---

[1] See the Legal Advice and Assistance Regulations 1989, reg. 20 for the solicitors power to entrust functions under the Regulations to others.

[2] Legal Aid Act 1988, s. 9(1).

[3] *ibid*, ss. 9(5) and 31(3).

[4] *ibid.* s. 9(6).

when financial eligibility for Green Form advice and assistance was reduced, the Legal Advice and Assistance Regulations 1989 have not made any provision for those eligible to have to pay contributions.

Regulations may be made which make advice and assistance available to persons without reference to financial circumstances[5] and in such circumstances, Regulations may prescribe that clients pay a fixed fee instead of a contribution.[6-7]

Eligibility is governed by the Legal Advice and Assistance Regulations 1989, regs. 11(1), 13, Sched. 2.

Although a client who is financially eligible for Green Form advice and assistance will not have to pay a contribution (to the solicitor), he may have to make payment for the advice and assistance via the charge in favour of the solicitor created by section 11 of the 1988 Act.

Assessment of financial eligibility — general

03–03 The solicitor is responsible for the assessment of the client's financial eligibility for Green Form advice and assistance (either the solicitor will himself have carried out the assessment or it will have been carried out by a representative of the solicitor). This involves determining disposable income and disposable capital.[8] The solicitor may entrust this function to a representative provided such representative is:

    (a) competent;

    (b) responsible;

    (c) (i) employed in the solicitor's office and so under the solicitor's immediate supervision; or

       (ii) employed elsewhere but nevertheless under the solicitor's immediate supervision.[9]

There are circumstances in which other persons' means may be treated as those of the client.[10]

When the client (or any other person whose means are to be assessed) is either directly or indirectly in receipt of either income support or family credit, the solicitor must take that person's disposable income as being below the current sum specified in the Legal Advice and Assistance Regulations 1989, reg. 11(1) (*i.e.* below the eligibility limit — so that the client is eligible for advice and assistance).

Any client who applies for advice and assistance must provide the solicitor with the information necessary for the solicitor to determine

---

[5] *ibid.* s. 9(2).
[6-7] *ibid.* s. 9(7).
[8] Legal Advice and Assistance Regulations, Sched. 11.
[9] *ibid.* reg. 20.
[10] *ibid.* reg. 13(1).

whether he is financially eligible.[11] Such information must be furnished in a form approved by the Board.[12] This is presently the Green Form GF1.[13]

The solicitor must not provide advice and assistance until he has determined that the client is financially eligible and the client has signed the Green Form.[14] The solicitor will have failed to comply with the Regulations if advice and assistance are provided before this is done.

The solicitor is assisted in completing the Green Form by a "key card". New key cards (including any amendments to financial eligibility provisions) are issued by the Board each April.

A client (or the person to receive advice and assistance on the client's behalf)[15] must sign the Green Form after the solicitor has assessed that he or she is eligible. The signature is to confirm the truth of the information provided.[16-17]

Assessment of financial eligibility — the assessment

The solicitor should first determine the client's disposable capital. "Capital" means the amount or value of every resource of a capital nature.[18] What is the client's disposable capital will usually depend on what he owns but occasionally (such as where advice and assistance is being given to a child it is just and equitable to do so[19]) the means of other persons will be relevant and spouses "and co-habitants" means are aggregated (see paragraph 03–04).[20]

Any question as to financial eligibility must be decided by the solicitor having regard to any guidance issued by the Board.[21] As yet, the Board has not issued guidance on this.

---

[11] *ibid.* reg. 9(4).

[12] *ibid.* reg. 9(6).

[13] It is understood that the Legal Aid Board is planning changes to its systems which may result in all forms being white and printable from computers.

[14] *ibid.* reg. 13(5).

[15] *ibid.* reg. 10 and p. 42.

[16] If such help has previously been given, the solicitor (if he or she did not provide it) must obtain authority from the Area Director to provide further advice and assistance. *ibid.* reg. 16. If the solicitor previously gave advice and assistance he or she should consider whether to apply for an extension of the financial limit on the existing green form, rather than accepting a fresh application. Whether the matter is the same or a new matter, is not always easy to determine. The Board has issued guidance on this. See p. 47. If more than six months has elapsed since the solicitor submitted his claim for payment from the Board, the application for advice and assistance should be treated as being in respect of a separate matter and a fresh application for advice and assistance must be made.

[17] The reference to prosecution is a reference to the Legal Aid Act 1988, s. 39.

[18] Legal Advice and Assistance Regulations 1989, Sched. 2, paras. 1 and 4.

[19] *ibid.* Sched. 2, para. 5.

[20] *ibid.* Sched. 2, refers at all times to the means of "the person concerned" who is defined in para. 1 as the person whose disposable capital and disposable income are to be assessed.

[21] *ibid.* Sched. 2, para. 3.

Spouses and cohabitants

03-04 Spouses and cohabitants means must be aggregated unless[22]

    (a) the spouse or cohabitant[23] has a contrary interest in the matter in respect of which the person concerned[24] (the client) is seeking advice and assistance; or

    (b) the person concerned (the client) and his spouse or cohabitant are living separate and apart; or

    (c) in all the circumstances of the case it would be inequitable or inpractical to do so.

However, the regulations do not require the resources of gay or lesbian couples to be aggregated as they are not spouses or "a man and a woman" (which are the terms used in the Regulations).

It may not always be easy to decide whether a couple are living "separate and apart". This is likely to be so if they live in separate households and are experiencing a breakdown in their relationship. But it is possible to be living together, *i.e.* not living separate and apart, even if the couple are living under separate roofs.

The words "living separate and apart" denote an attitude of mind in which the couple regard themselves as withdrawn from each other. Thus, *e.g.* where one spouse is confined to a mental hospital suffering from a serious illness from which they are unlikely to recover, but the other spouse visits them in hospital, they may not be "living separate and apart." On the other hand, if the visiting spouse ceases to visit, and becomes interested in another person receiving no communication from the hospital the parties may be said to be "separate and apart".

Similarly, it is possible to be living apart under the same roof. In *Hollens v. Hollens*[25] where, after a violent quarrel, the parties remained in the same house but did not speak to each other or eat together and the wife did nothing for husband, it was held that they lived apart. In *Fuller v. Fuller*[26] where one of the parties was taken into the household "in another capacity" (*e.g.* lodger or paid housekeeper) they were living apart. In *Mouncer v. Mouncer*[27] the test was whether they were sharing a common life together.

18   These issues must be decided by the solicitor "having regard to any guidance issued by the Board."

03-05   The Regulations also set out the rules for computing the capital of the

---

[22] *ibid.* Sched. 2, para. 7(2).
[23] *ibid.* Sched. 2, para 2.
[24] The "person concerned" is defined in para. 1 of Sched. 2 as "the person whose disposal income and disposable capital are to be assessed." In most cases this will be the client.
[25] (1971) 115 S.J. 327.
[26] [1973] 2 All E.R. 650.
[27] [1972] 1 All E.R. 289.

person concerned.[28] Although not specifically made exempt, the motor vehicle of the person concerned is regarded as a normal possession and is not, unless it is particularly valuable, taken into account. Whether a vehicle is particularly valuable — so that it is not rightly considered "a normal possession" is a matter for the solicitor to decide.

There have been cases where the meaning of "household furniture and effects" and similar phrases have been considered, e.g. *Northey v Paxton*[29] and *Re Masson*.[30] However, in *MacPhail v. Philips*[31], Barton J. said (at p. 160) "In a case of this kind, very little assistance is gained from the citing of authorities".

The Regulations[32] set out the deductions to be made for a spouse (or cohabitant) whose resources are required to be aggregated and whom the person concerned has living with him, and a dependent child (or dependent relative) wholly or substantially maintained by the person concerned, and whom the person concerned has living with him.

So far as spouses and cohabitants are concerned, it seems logical to treat "living separate and apart" as being the opposite state from "living with" so that, if means are aggregated, the allowance applies and, if means are not aggregated, there is no allowance. The relevant allowances appear on the Green Form key code issued by the Board.

Children

A "child"[33] is defined as a person under the age that is for the time being **03–06** the upper limit of compulsory school age by virtue of section 35 of Education Act 1944 together with an Order in Council made under that section. This is presently age 16.

There is no specific requirement that the child should be a child of the person concerned (or of his spouse or cohabitant if their means are aggregated), whether natural and legitimate, natural and illegitimate or adopted or a stepchild. It is sufficient that the child should be a dependent child wholly or substantially maintained. However, if a person concerned receives fostering or boarding out payments in respect of a child, it will be difficult for the solicitor to conclude that the child is "wholly or substantially" maintained by him.

Whether a child is "dependent" and "substantially maintained" is a question to be decided by the solicitor in comparing the child's assets to those of the persons concerned. Clearly, small part-time earnings are

---

[28] See Legal Advice and Assistance Regulations 1989, Sched. 2, para. 8.
[29] (1988) 60 L.T. 30.
[30] (1917) 86 L.J. Ch. 753.
[31] [1904] 1 I.R. 155.
[32] Legal Advice and Assistance Regulations 1989, Sched. 2, para. 8(c).
[33] Legal Advice and Assistance Regulations, reg. 3.

unlikely to affect the position as are small receipts of maintenance by the child.

If a child applies for advice and assistance, the resources of any person who, under section 26(3) and (4) of the Social Security Act 1986 is liable to maintain him or who usually contributes substantially to his or her maintenance, or who has care and control of him not being a person who has such care and control by reason of any contract or for some temporary purpose, may be treated as the child's resources, if, having regard to all the circumstances, including the child's age and resources and any conflict of interest it appears just and equitable to do so.[34]

A child who is at boarding school is still "living with" the person concerned if that is where the child has his home. Where a child spends time in more than one household, e.g. because his mother and father are living apart, it is a question of fact with whom he is living. Unless there are issues between the relevant adults, the payment of maintenance and the receipt of child benefit are indications as to with whom the child lives.

Other factors

03–07   Solicitors have two further factors to consider before they can finally determine the disposable capital of the person concerned. First, they must leave out of account the value of the subject-matter of any claim in respect of which advice and assistance is sought.[35] Thus, e.g. the client is seeking advice on defending a claim in respect of ownership of a caravan, the value of his interest in that property (which is subject-matter of the claim) must be left out of account in determining his capital.

Secondly, the solicitor must consider whether it appears to him that the person concerned has arranged his resources so as to make himself financially eligible. In which case the solicitor must look at the resources as if they had not been arranged.[36-38] Given the low threshold for financial eligibility on income, this is a situation which is likely only rarely to be confronted by a solicitor. It is largely a hangover from the time when Green Form financial eligibility was much more generous.

While the solicitor need not make particular and searching inquiries in this area, if he has any suspicion that such steps have been taken then, bearing in mind the nature of his relationship with the Board, he should make reasonable inquiry.

If the solicitor then applies paragraph 6 of Schedule 2 to the Legal Advice and Assistance Regulations 1989 and as a result the client declines to instruct him, the solicitor should advise the client that if he or she applies

---

[34] Legal Advice and Assistance Regulations 1989, Sched. 2, para. 5.
[35] *ibid.* Sched 2, para. 7(1).
[36-38] *ibid.* Sched. 2, para. 6.

to another solicitor for advice and assistance, he must still disclose the same information and that if the client does not he might be in breach of section 39 of the 1988 Act.

The provisions of the Regulations suggest that to determine financial eligibility, the solicitor should deduct from the client's disposable capital the allowances prescribed by paragraph 8(c) of Schedule 2 to the Legal Advice and Assistance Regulations 1989 and enter this sum on the Green Form. Underneath this on the form is space to enter the capital of any relevant spouse or cohabitant. These two figures should then be added together to give the disposable capital figure for the purpose of the Green Form Scheme. In fact, the key card indicates that the full amount of capital without any deduction for paragraph 8(c) allowances, should be entered on the Green Form and that the paragraph 8(c) allowances are notionally added on to the regulation 11(1)[39] prescribed capital limit to assess eligibility. The net result is the same.

After determining disposable capital, the solicitor must determine the disposable income of the person concerned. Income means a total income from all sources which the person concerned has received or may reasonably expect to receive in respect of the seven days up to and including the date of the application.[40]

The Legal Advice and Assistance Regulations 1989 provide detailed income computation provisions.[41] They also provide for certain bona fide payments of maintenance made or to be made in respect of the seven days up to and including the date of the application for advice and assistance to be a deduction from the disposable income calculation.[42]

Errors or mistakes

Finally, they also[43] make provision for where there has been an error or **03–08** mistake in the assessment of the disposable income, disposable capital or maximum contribution or the person concerned.[44]

The Legal Advice and Assistance Regulations 1989[45] appear to offer two options to the solicitor:
    (a) to reassess or "as the case may be";
    (b) to amend the assessment.
In the latter case, the amended assessment is substituted for the original

---

[39] Reg. 11(1) Legal Advice and Assistance Regulations 1989.
[40] Legal Advice and Assistance Regulations 1989, Sched. 2, para. 1.
[41] *ibid.* Sched. 2, para. 9.
[42] *ibid.* Sched. 2, para. 10.
[43] *ibid.* Sched. 2, para. 11.
[44] Civil Legal Aid (Assessment of Resources) Regulations 1989, reg. 14 is its equivalent for civil legal aid.
[45] Sched. 2, para. 11.

assessment. The solicitor should select whichever option is more favourable to the client. There is no requirement to reassess a client's means if his means change. If the client is eligible for advice and assistance at the date of application, the solicitor may continue to provide advice and assistance under the Green Form thereof to — even if the client were to come into a large sum of money.

AVAILABILITY

Introduction

03–09   Part III of the 1988 Act (sections 8–16) is entitled "Advice and Assistance". Section 8 is entitled "Scope of this Part". Section 2(2) defines advice and section 2(3) defines assistance. The Regulations which apply to advice and assistance are:
   (a) the Legal Advice and Assistance Regulations 1989;
   (b) the Legal Advice and Assistance (Scope) Regulations 1989; and
   (c) the Legal Aid in Criminal and Care Proceedings (Costs) Regulations 1989.[46]

The meaning of "advice"

03–10   "'Advice' means oral or written advice on the application of English Law to any particular circumstances that have arisen in relation to the person seeking the advice and as to the steps which that person might appropriately take having regard to the application of English law to those circumstances."[47]

The advice may, therefore, be provided orally or in writing (which term should be widely interpreted) or both orally and in writing.

Only advice on the application of English law is within the definition. However, the 1988 Act makes provision for the Lord Chancellor to extend this to other laws to enable the United Kingdom to comply with any international agreement.[48] The advice must be on the application of English law to any particular circumstances that have arisen in relation to the person seeking the advice. Therefore, e.g. advice on circumstances that have arisen in relation to the client's neighbour are not within the definition.

---

[46] The relevant Board Notes for Guidance are numbers 2–01 to 2–46 (*Legal Aid Handbook 1995*).
[47] Legal Aid Act 1988, s. 2(2).
[48] *ibid.* s. 2(8).

The advice may go on to deal with the steps which the person seeking the advice might appropriately take, having regard to the application of English law to the circumstances. Advice, therefore, does not include taking steps on the person's behalf or for him.

The meaning of assistance

> "'Assistance' means assistance in taking any of the steps which a **03–11** person might take, including steps with respect to proceedings, having regard to the application of English law to any particular circumstances that have arisen in relation to him, whether by taking such steps on his behalf (including assistance by way of representation) or by assisting him in taking them on his own behalf."[49]

Assistance therefore may be either in the form of helping the person to take steps himself or of taking the steps on his behalf. Taking steps on the person's behalf includes assistance by way of representation.[50-51]

Who may provide advice and assistance and to whom

Advice and assistance under Part III of the 1988 Act may be provided only **03–12** to a person. Section 2(10) of the 1988 Act provides:

> "In this Act 'person' does not include a body of persons corporate or uncorporate which is not concerned in a representative, fiduciary or official capacity so as to authorise advice, assistance or representation to be granted to such a body."

Section 9 of the 1988 Act deals with the availability of advice and assistance. It provides that advice and assistance are available to anyone who, under the Regulations, is financially eligible.

However, section 8(4) of the 1988 Act enables Regulations to be made restricting the availability of described categories of advice and assistance to described categories of persons.

It follows that, unless expressly excluded by Regulations, advice and assistance is available to any person who is financially eligible.

Advice and assistance under Part III of the 1988 Act must be provided by a "legal representative" but the solicitor legal representative may deleg-

---

[49] Legal Aid Act 1988, s. 2(3).
[50-51] Legal Advice and Assistance Regulations 1989, reg. 3(1) and Legal Advice and Assistance (Scope) Regulations 1989, reg. 2 provides "' ABWOR means 'assistance by way of representation' which amounts to representation under Part III of the Act and for which approval of the Board may be required in individual cases."

ate work to a partner or to a representative who is under their immediate supervision and who is competent and responsible.[52]

Advice and assistance — restrictions and exclusions

03–13 A solicitor must not accept an application for advice and assistance from a child unless the Area Director has granted him authority to do so. The Area Director will grant such authority only where he is satisfied that it is reasonable in the circumstances that the child should receive advice and assistance.

Section 2(5) the Act 1988 provides that regulations can specify what is, or is not, included in advice and assistance of any description.

Furthermore, section 8(3) provides that Regulations can exclude particular descriptions of advice and assistance from all or part of Part III of the 1988 Act.

The Legal Advice and Assistance (Scope) Regulations 1989 exclude certain conveyancing services and the making of wills (except for certain categories of client) from Part III of the 1988 Act.

Conveyancing

03–14 Conveyancing services are largely excluded. Advice and assistance for conveyancing is available only where it is provided in relation to a rental purchase agreement or a conditional sale agreement, or where it is provided to give effect to an order of the court or (in proceedings under the Matrimonial Causes Act 1973 or the Matrimonial and Family Proceedings Act 1984) the terms of an agreement.[53]

Wills

03–15 Advice and assistance in the making of wills is also largely excluded. The exceptions relate to the position of the client. Subject, of course to their financial eligibility advice and assistance can be given to:
   (a) those aged 70 or over;
   (b) those who are blind (or partially sighted), deaf (or hard of hearing), or dumb or who suffer from a mental disorder of any description, or who are substantially and permanently handicapped by illness, injury or congenital deformity;

---

[52] "Legal representative means an authorised advocate or authorised litigator, as defined by section 119(1) of the Courts and Legal Services Act 1990." At the time of writing, only solicitors and barristers fall within this definition.
[53] Legal Advice and Assistance (Scope) Regulations 1989, reg. 3.

(c) parents or guardians (within the meaning of section 87 of the Child Care Act 1980) of any person to whom any description in (b) applies, where they want to provide in their will for such person; or

(d) the mother or father of a minor child who is living with them and for whom they wish to appoint a guardian under section 4 of the Guardianship of Minors Act 1971, where the mother or father is not living with the minor's other parent.[54]

Receiving legal aid

Whenever a person is in receipt of civil or criminal legal aid in connection with any proceedings, he or she can not be given advice or assistance in connection with those proceedings under the Green Form Scheme. Section 8(5) of the 1988 Act achieves this by providing that Part III of that Act does not apply to any advice or assistance given in such circumstances. **03–16**

Unless ABWOR has been approved, no representation can be provided as representation is defined separately from advice and in the 1988 Act and (save for ABWOR) is not included within the definition of advice and assistance. From this, it follows that no court issue fees are claimable as disbursements. **03–17**

Work done in assessing a client's entitlement to welfare benefits or in verifying an assessment by the DSS or other benefit-granting body (such as a local authority) is taken by the Board as being advice or assistance under Part III of the 1988 Act.[55] **03–18**

The Board also views work done to enable a client to make a personal application for a grant of representation to an estate as being advice or assistance under Part III of the 1988 Act, although the court fees cannot be claimed as a disbursement.[56] **03–19**

Applying for a passport or driving licence and similar work is not viewed by the Board as work "having regard to the application of English law" so as to be within advice and assistance. **03–20**

Advice and assistance can be given about child maintenance and assessment/enforcement by the Child Support Agency. However, the Board will only pay for form-filling so far as it has a legal element and it is therefore reasonable for the solicitor (rather than the client) to do that work. The Board has also said that, in the case of free-standing assessments, it is expected that the solicitor will be able to carry out the work necessary to assist in obtaining an assessment within the Green Form initial costs limit. **03–21**

---

[54] *ibid.* reg. 4.
[55] See the Board's Notes for Guidance 2.26.
[56] See the Board's Notes for Guidance 2.27.

MCKENZIE ADVISERS

03-22   In *McKenzie v. McKenzie*[57] the Court of Appeal held that the county court judge had been wrong to prevent an unrepresented husband from having a lawyer sitting beside him during the case to help him by giving advice making suggestions from time to time and so on. The Court of Appeal held that the husband had been entitled to have such help and that the lawyer had been entitled to give it. Since then, people giving such help been known as "McKenzie Advisers".

Is there any reason why advice and assistance under the Green Form Scheme should not cover the services of a McKenzie Adviser? In particular, may the Green Form Scheme be used to fund McKenzie advisers at tribunals where neither assistance by way of representation nor legal aid is available?

Although the application for advice or assistance must be made in England or Wales there is no restriction in the 1988 Act or in the Regulations on *where* advice and assistance may be given.[58] The fact that it may be given in court or in a tribunal does not mean that it is not advice and assistance within the provisions of the 1988 Act and the Regulations.

However, a solicitor is unlikely to be able to provide significant help to his client as a McKenzie Adviser within the Green Form initial cost-limit. It will probably appear to him that the cost of giving advice and assistance is "likely to exceed" the initial cost-limit so he will be obliged to apply for an "extension".[59]

03-23   Is the legal aid area office likely to grant such an extension? The Area Director is bound to consider[60]:

(a) whether it is reasonable for the advice and assistance to be given; and

(b) whether the estimate of the costs to be incurred in giving advice and assistance is reasonable.

The Board's Notes for Guidance says that the area office will bear in mind that it will normally be unreasonable to grant an extension:

(a) where full legal aid is available for the proceedings and the client will be better served by being fully represented in such proceedings;

(b) unless the solicitor can satisfy the area office that, by reason of either the difficulty of the case or the importance to the client or the inability of the client to act on his or her own without legal

---

[57] [1970] 3 All E.R. 1034.
[58] Subject to specific examples, section 47(b) of the 1988 Act provides that it extends only to England and Wales.
[59] Legal Advice and Assistance Regulations 1989, reg. 21.
[60] Under the provisions of regulation 21(2).

help, it is necesary for the client to have the services of a solicitor acting as a McKenzie Adviser.

The Notes for Guidance make it clear that when a Green Form bill **03–24** including a claim for acting as a McKenzie Adviser is submitted to an area office, the office will call for the solicitor's file to ensure that there is no element of representation in the claim. This will not be paid for as it is outside the scope of advice and assistance (where ABWOR has not been granted).

Solicitors who act as McKenzie advisers have a difficult path to tread. Tribunal chairmen sometimes find the artificiality of the McKenzie Adviser procedure an irritation and encourage solicitors to represent their client.

THE APPLICATION FOR ADVICE AND ASSISTANCE

Introduction to the application

It is a principle of professional conduct that a solicitor is under a duty to **03–25** consider and advise his client on the availability of legal aid (which must include advice and assistance) where the client might be entitled to assistance under the 1988 Act.

Applications for such Green Form advice and assistance are made to the solicitor (in contrast to applications for civil legal aid which are made to the legal aid area office but which are almost invariably submitted by solicitors for the applicant). The solicitor is responsible for the proper management of the application in accordance with the provisions of the 1988 Act, the regulations and the Boards Notes for Guidance.

The solicitor must therefore decide whether (and what) advice and assistance may be given. The solicitor must consider whether what he is asked to do is covered by the scheme, whether the client is financially eligible and, in certain cases, must obtain area office approval before he can give advice and assistance. As the charge, or any property recovered or preserved, created by section of the 1988 Act 11, is in the solicitor's favour (not the Board's), it must be applied by him unless he wishes to waive it at his own (not the Board's) expense.

Solicitors are not obliged to provide advice and assistance but when they **03–26** do, they owe duties to the Board as well as to the client. Broadly, the scheme provides for advice and assistance on English law as it affects the client to be provided. The application for advice and assistance must be made in England and Wales (even if this means making an application from abroad to a solicitor in England and Wales by post)

The relevant legislation is:

(a) Part III Legal Aid Act 1988;

(b) Legal Advice and Assistance Regulations 1989;

41

(c) Legal Advice and Assistance (Scope) Regulations 1989;

(d) Legal Aid in Criminal and Care Proceedings (Costs) Regulations 1989.

Making an application — attendance by the client in person

03–27   Regulation 9(1) and (3) provides that the applications shall be made to the solicitor from whom the advice and assistance is sought and that (subject to regulation 10 (attendance on behalf of client) shall be made by the client in person.

Because of the provisions of regulation 20, the solicitor may entrust any function under the regulations to 'a partner of his or a competent and responsible representative of his who is employed in his office or otherwise under his immediate supervision'. So, the application may be made to such a person.

From this requirement, to make the application in person, it follows that if, e.g. a solicitor goes to visit a client at home and it is there that the client makes the application for advice and assistance, a solicitor will not be able to claim for the travel to the client under the Green form, scheme although he can claim for the return travel from the client's house.[61] Franchised solicitors with appropriate devolved powers may claim outward travel costs (but not time) to visit a client and may accept applications for advice and assistance by post or by telephone.[62]

There is no restriction, by nationality, domicile, residence or otherwise on who may apply for and be granted advice and assistance. However, special provisions apply to children, patients and to persons resident abroad.

Making an application — attendance on behalf of the client

03–28   Another person may attend on behalf of the client 'for good reason'.[63]

Although questions arising under assessment of resources must be decided by the solicitor having regard to any guidance issued by the Board[64], the interpretation of the provisions of the Regulations themselves is not placed within the solicitor's discretion. Therefore, if he has any doubt as to what might constitute 'good reason' he should contact the area office.

---

[61] Whether the return costs will be allowed on an assessment of the solicitor's claim will depend upon whether the area office considers it was reasonable to incur those costs. They are more likely to be allowed if the client is housebound and does not live a great distance from the solicitor' office.

[62] Regs. 9(3A) and 30(4).

[63] Reg. 10(1).

[64] Clients abroad can not take advantage of the provision as special provision for them is made by reg. 15.

The following are examples of what might constitute 'good reason:'

The client is confined to home, hospital or prison or with severe mobility problems caused by physical or psychological incapacity, *e.g.* severe arthritis or agoraphobia

However, the Board is understood to take a narrow view of this Regulation and expects "authorisation" normally to be given in person and/or in writing. The person authorised must have sufficient knowledge of the client and the problem and of the client's financial circumstances to make a proper application and to give proper instructions.

Making an application — attendance on behalf of the client: children and patients

A 'child' means a person under the age that is for the time being the upper **03–29** limit of compulsory school age by virtue of section 35 of the Education Act 1944 together with any Order in Council made under that section (i.e. a person under the age of 16).[65]

A 'patient' means a person who, by reason of mental disorder within the meaning of the Mental Health Act 1983, is incapable of managing and administering his property and affairs.[66]

Solicitors may accept applications on behalf of children and patients by specified persons in specified circumstances. In such cases, there is no requirement that the child be present.[67]

Where an application is made on behalf of another, the client remains the person on whose behalf the application is made. The "client" is the person seeking or receiving advice and assistance or on whose behalf advice and assistance is sought.[68]

Where the client is a child, an application may be accepted on the child's behalf from his or her parent, guardian or other person in whose care the child is, or from any person acting for the purposes of any proceedings as the child's next friend or guardian *ad litem*.

Where the client is a patient, an application may be accepted on the patient's behalf from a receiver appointed under Part VII of the Mental Health Act 1983, from the patient's nearest relative or guardian within the meaning of Part II of the Mental Health Act 1983, or from a person acting for the purposes of any proceedings as the patient's next friend or guardian *ad litem*.

With the Area Director's prior authority, an application on behalf of

---

[65] Reg. 3.
[66] *ibid.*
[67] reg. 14(3).
[68] reg. 3.

either a child or a patient may be accepted from any other person. The Area Director will give such authority if he considers that it is reasonable in the circumstances for advice and assistance to be given to such other person, *e.g.* if there is good reason why the parent or guardian can not make the application (*e.g.* conflict of interest) and there is sufficient connection between the child or patient and the other person to ensure that the other person is likely to accept responsibility in the interests of the child or patient and the other person has sufficient knowledge of the child or patient, the problem and the financial circumstances to give proper instructions to the solicitor. Applications for prior authority must be made on form GF5.

Making an application — attendance by client in person: children and patients

03–30　A solicitor must not (unless his firm has a legal aid franchise in the relevant category of work at the relevant office) accept an application for advice and assistance from a child unless the application is in relation to proceedings which the child is entitled to begin, prosecute or defend without a next friend or guardian *ad litem* or the solicitor has been authorised to do so by the Area Director. The Area Director must withhold such authority unless he is satisfied that it is reasonable in the circumstances that the child shall receive advice and assistance.[69]

There is no equivalent provision for patients. Therefore, a solicitor may accept an application from and provide advice and assistance to a patient without authority. Of course, if the solicitor doubts whether this is wise, he may be able to accept an application from and provide advice and assistance to a person on behalf of the patient.

Authority to advise a child direct will usually be given if there is good reason why the parent or guardian is not applying, *e.g.* conflict of interest as the child is in care and needs separate representation and the child is able to give instructions and to understand the nature of the advice and assistance. Applications for prior authority must be made using the Board's form GF5

Making an application — post

03–31　The regulations make provision for postal applications for advice and assistance from clients resident outside England and Wales. However (unless the solicitor's firm has a franchise in the relevant category of work

---

[69] reg. 14(1).

at the relevant office), the prior authority of the Area Director is required.[70]

The Boards Notes for Guidance specify the basis upon which the Area Director's authority will be given. They provide: "The rule is that where the client resides outside England and Wales, a solicitor can, with the prior authority of the area office, accept a postal application for advice and assistance . . . Such authority will be given where there is good reason why the client cannot attend personally but not where the client's residence is purely temporary and the solicitor can, without disadvantage to the client, postpone giving advice and assistance until the client returns to England and Wales. As mentioned above applications for prior authority must be made on form GF5."

Whether or not the client is resident in England and Walls, if the Solicitor's firm has a franchise in the relevant category of work at the relevant office, Green Forms may be sent by post to clients for signature.

Making an application — where the application must be made

The application for advice and assistance must be made to a solicitor in **03–32** England and Wales although, there is no express provision to this effect this seems to be the only reasonable interpretation of this position. Section 47(6) provides, generally, that "this Act extends to England and Wales only". A wider interpretation would allow solicitors anywhere in the world to provide advice and assistance, which is unlikely to be what Parliament intended.

Making an application — information to be provided

A client applying to a solicitor for advice and assistance must provide the **03–33** solicitor with the information necessary to enable the solicitor to determine:
  (a) the client's disposable capital;
  (b) where appropriate, whether the client is in receipt of income support, family credit or disability working allowance; and
  (c) where the client is not in receipt of income support, family credit or disability working allowance, his disposable income.[71]

The above information is required to enable the solicitor to decide whether the client is financially eligible to receive advice and assistance (and, if the client requires ABWOR — whether he should pay a contribution.

It is sometimes thought that receipt of one or more of the following pay- **03–34**

---

[70] reg. 15.
[71] reg. 9(4)

ments renders a client automatically eligible for Green Form advice and assistance:

(a) disability living allowance;

(b) attendance allowance paid under section 64 or Schedule 8 paragraphs 4 or 7(2);

(c) constant attendance allowance paid under section 104 as an increase to a disablement pension; or

(d) any payment made out of the social fund.

This is not the case. However, by paragraph 9A of Schedule 2 to the Legal Advice and Assistance Regulations 1989, receipt of some payments is to be disregarded in computing disposable income.

A client applying to a solicitor for advice and assistance relating to the making of a will must provide the solicitor with the information necessary to enable the solicitor to determine whether the advice and assistance would fall within regulation 4(2) of the Legal Advice and Assistance (Scope) Regulations 1989.[72]

The client must also give the solicitor sufficient information about the case to enable the solicitor to determine whether what is sought is:

(a) "advice" as defined in section 2(2) of the 1988 Act: "oral or written advice on the application of English law to any particular circumstances that have arisen in relation to the person seeking the advice and as to the steps which that person might appropriately take having regard to the application of English law to those circumstances"; and, or

(b) "assistance" as defined in section 2(3) of the 1988 Act: "assistance in taking any of the steps which a person might take, including steps with respect to proceedings, having regard to the application of English law to any particular circumstances that have arisen in relation to him, whether by taking such steps on his behalf (including assistance by way of representation) or by assisting him in taking them on his own behalf".

03–35 The key concepts are "English law", (e.g. advice cannot be given on Scottish law) and that the advice must relate to circumstances that have arisen in relation to the client (e.g. the circumstances must not have arisen in relation to a friend or relative).

The solicitor will also need to know whether the client has previously been given advice and assistance for the same matter by another solicitor. This is because "the client must not, (except where regulation 6, 7 or 8 applies[73]) be given advice and assistance for the same matter by more than one solicitor without the prior authority of the Area Director, and such authority may be given on such terms and conditions as the Area Director

---

[72] reg. 9(5)

[73] reg. 6, 7 and 8 apply to duty solicitors at police stations and magistrates' courts.

in his discretion may see fit to impose.[74-75] Form GF 5 should be used to apply for such prior authority. Solicitors with an appropriate legal aid franchise may grant their own authorities.

In practice "one solicitor" is treated as one firm of solicitors because legal aid pays firms rather than individuals. Thus, if a client changes solicitors within the same firm, no authority is needed. However, if the solicitor changes firms and wishes to take the client with him, the Board's view is that authority is needed.

Separate matters

It is not always easy to decide whether matters are separate. Regulation 17 **03–36** provides:

"where two or more separate matters are involved, each matter shall be the subject of a separate application for advice and assistance provided that matters connected with or arising from proceedings for divorce or judicial separation, whether actual or prospective between the client and his spouse, shall not be treated as separate matters for the purposes of advice and assistance."

It is the solicitor's decision which "sooner or later he will have to justify" as to which matters are separate.

Although advice and assistance on welfare law and entitlement to welfare benefits can be given and be the subject of an individual application for advice and assistance, the Board expects that welfare benefits advice, which is incidental to advice on another matter, e.g. incidental to advice and assistance on divorce or on a claim for personal injuries, should be given under the Green Form for the other matter. A separate Green Form for the welfare benefits advice would be appropriate only if more than associated advice were required or, for reasons particular to an individual case, an unusually large amount of work has to be done in respect of the welfare benefits advice and assistance. Similarly, where a client makes an application for Green Form advice and assistance for welfare benefits advice, the Board expects that only one Green Form will be signed even if several benefits are involved. In other words, separate benefits do not generally constitute separate matters.

The submission of a Green Form claim for payment does not terminate the relevant Green Form. Therefore, if further work has to be done after the Green Form has been submitted for payment, the solicitor must continue under the original Green Form, applying for an extension on form GF3 if necessary. As the solicitor will not have the original Green Form (it will have been submitted to the Board with the claim for payment), the Board

---

[74-75] reg. 16(1)

advises that the solicitor should complete the front of another Green Form to show the client's name and address and should clearly strike through the rest of the form, writing boldly in the space on the left hand side "Green form sent by us (firm name) for payment on (date) under lead name (name of first claim on consolidated claim for costs form GF2). Further work carried out".

As the non-termination of Green Forms can cause problems in practice, the Board has said that when six months has expired after the submission of a Green Form claim for costs, any further advice and assistance on the relevant matter should be treated as being a separate matter and a separate application for advice and assistance must be made.

Making an application — the Board's forms

03–37   Regulation 9(6) provides that the information required by regulation 9 shall be furnished in a form approved by the Board. These are the Green Form (form GFl) and the form for advice and assistance for wills (form GF4).

The Board's current key card should be used when completing the Green Form.

The Green Form GF1 (capital)

03–38   There is aggregation of the means of the client and his or her spouse or cohabitee. Allowances are made for dependants by adding on the allowances made for them in para 8(c) of Schedule 2 to the Legal Advice and Assistance Regulations 1989 to the capital eligibility limits prescribed by regulation 11(1) Legal Advice and Assistance Regulations 1989. This is not strictly in accordance with the provisions of the Legal Advice and Assistance Regulations 1989 which prescribed deductions) but the outcome is the same.

The Legal Advice and Assistance Regulations 1989 make no provisions for contribution from capital so the capital computation is simply to establish whether the client is eligible for advice and assistance.

The Green Form GF1 (income)

03–39   The eligibility figures are said already to have made allowance for notional expenditure such as rent, mortgage and community charge. If the client is in receipt of income support, family credit or disability working allowance the rest of this section may be ignored because (subject to being eligible on capital grounds —[76] the client will, by regulation 13(2) be eligible for advice and assistance without a contribution.

---

[76] Regulation 9(2) in fact concerns "any of the persons whose disposable incomes are to be assessed". Thus, if any person whose means are to be aggregated with those of the client

To be completed and signed by client

"I am over the compulsory school leaving age (or, if not, the solicitor **03–40**
is advising me under regulation 14(2A) Legal Advice and Assurance
Regulations 1989)".

An affirmative answer to this question means that the client is not a child.[77]
A negative answer means that unless an appropriate franchise is held, the
solicitor must obtain the Area Director's authority before accepting the
application for advice and assistance.

"I have/have not previously received help from a solicitor on this matter under the Green Form"

This statement relates to the provisions of regulation 16 of the Legal Advice **03–41**
and Assistance Regulations 1989 which provides that a person must not be
given advice and assistance for the same matter by more than one solicitor
without the prior authority of the Area Director. It follows that, if the
statement is made in the affirmative (*i.e.* "have not" is deleted), the solicitor
must, unless an appropriate franchise is held, obtain the Area Director's
authority before providing advice and assistance unless the matter is treated
as a separate matter by the Board.

What is or is not the same matter may not always be easy to decide. The
Board in recognising that there are some long running, though intermittent,
matters has said that for practical purposes it will treat certain matters as
being separate. The effect of the Board's guidance is that if a claim for costs
in the matter (whether covered by regulation 17 or not)[78] has been
submitted more than six months before the client seeks fresh advice and
assistance on it the matter should be treated as separate.[79]

If the client says that he or she has previously received advice and
assistance from a solicitor about the matter, the solicitor should either seek
authority from the area office to accept an application for advice and
assistance on the same matter or contact the former solicitors to find out

---

is in receipt of income support or family credit his or her income will be taken as not
exceeding the amount above which a contribution would be payable (see s. 9(6) of the
Legal Aid Act 1988, reg. 11 of the Legal Advice and Assistance Regulations 1989 and Sched.
3 of those Regulations). If that person's actual income is less than this amount, it is the
lesser amount which is relevant for the purposes of aggregation.

[77] "Child" is defined in reg. 3 as "a person under the age that is for the time being the upper
limit of compulsory school age by virtue of section 35 of the Education Act 1934 together
with any order in counsel made under that section."

[78] Reg. 17 ensures that more than one Green Form is not signed when the client visits the
solicitor for advice and assistance in connection with divorce and judicial separation.

[79] In theory, once a Green Form has been signed, it remains "open" for all time and the
advice and assistance does not terminate on submission on a claim for costs. The Board's
guidance standardised various area office time periods which had developed to match the
practical difficulties caused by never-closing green forms.

whether their bill was submitted more than six months previously. If so, the matter is treated by the Board as a separate matter and no authority is required. Franchised Solicitors can grant themselves authority if they have a franchise in the relevant category of work at the relevant office.

If authority is granted or the matter is treated as a separate matter the client must make a fresh application for advice and assistance to the new solicitor. If authority is refused and the matter is not treated as a separate matter, the Solicitor cannot provide advice and assistance to the client.

"I understand that I might have to pay my Solicitor's costs out of any money or property which is recovered or preserved for me"

03–42   This is a reference to the solicitor's statutory charge created by section 11(2) of the 1988 Act.[80]

"As far as I am aware, the information on this page is correct. I understand that if I give false information I could be prosecuted

03–43   This relates to section 39 of the Act 1988 and to regulation 36. Given the nature of the relationship between the solicitor and the Board if, while he is providing advice and assistance to the client or at any time thereafter, the solicitor considers that the client has provided incorrect or inadequate information which has resulted or will result in a loss to the Fund, the solicitor should report that fact to the Board.

Form GF4

Form GF4 simply reflects regulation 4 of the Legal Advice and Assistance (Scope) Regulations 1989. Either the client or the solicitor must sign form GF4 to confirm which of the qualifying provisions apply.

GREEN FORM IN PRACTICE

A personal injury claim

03–44   The client attends the solicitor's office where he is seen by either the solicitor or the solicitor's representative. In this case it is a representative of the solicitor. The client makes an application for Green Form advice and assistance. In practice, the client takes a rather passive part and it is the representative who, using the Green Form key card and information provided by the client, determines whether the client qualifies for Green

---

[80] See also regulations 32 and 33 and the schedule to the Regulations.

Form advice and assistance and whether the Area Director's authority is needed.

The executive knows that he can do work to the value of £X (equivalent to two hours work) without an extension, but that if it appears to him that the cost of giving advice and assistance is likely to exceed this amount, he must apply for an extension unless he has an appropriate franchise and can self-grant an extension.

The client signs a Green Form and the representative starts work, taking a statement and giving preliminary advice. He now advises the client about the charge under section 11, that it may be necessary to apply for legal aid and what this means.

If the firm has a franchise the representative takes care to comply with his firm's manual which will reflect the Franchise Specification and Transaction Criteria as to the administrative steps which must be taken, what information must be recorded and what must be confirmed with the client.

03–45 At the second appointment, some time later, the representative realises that an extension will be needed, partly to cover the cost of making an application for legal aid. He expects to have to do about an hour's further work including making the application for legal aid. He gives the client Form L17 statement of earnings by present employer which will be needed for the application for legal aid, and asks him to have the employer complete it and return it to the client. He also gives the client a Form CLA4A (financial application Form) to complete and bring to his next appointment.

The representative completes Form GF3 (application for Green Form extension) which they send to the area office. The extension is granted and Form GF3 is returned suitably endorsed. If the firm has a personal injury franchise the representative, in accordance with the procedures set out in his firm's manual (which will have been approved by the Board) and in accordance with the Board's Guidance on the Exercise of Devolved Powers, self-grant an appropriate extension.

The representative sees the client again. At this appointment Form CLA1 (application for legal aid non matrimonial) is completed by the executive (some parts could have been completed by the client) and signed by the client and the supervising solicitor.[81] The client hands the representative forms L17 and CLA4A who checks that the have been properly completed.

The representative sends the application to the legal aid area office knowing that, once an application has been submitted, the area office will be reluctant to grant a further Green Form extension for the case because it will shortly examine the merits in detail. If the situation is urgent the representative could apply for emergency legal aid. If the firm has a personal injury franchise emergency legal aid can be self-granted.

03–46 The application for legal aid is refused. The solicitor and the client each

---

[81] The solicitor signs to say he has explained the statutory charge to the client.

receive notice of refusal. The ground for refusal is under section 15(3)(A) of the 1988 Act it appears unreasonable to the Board that the applicant should be because granted civil legal aid. The reason for refusal is that "bearing in mind the probable cost and the likely award of damages, the proceedings are not justified".

The solicitor considers that a further Green Form extension is needed to explain the position to the client, to obtain a medical report and to appeal against the refusal. He knows that the area office will bear in mind when considering the application for an extension the relevant note for guidance which provides.

> "has legal aid (whether civil or criminal) or ABWOR been refused? If it has, the extension may still be granted. In particular a limited extension may be granted to prepare an appeal against refusal to an area committee in the case of civil legal aid provided the appeal is not in connection with repeated applications for legal aid."

03–47   The solicitor applies for a Green Form extension of £60 to cover a G.P.'s report and advising the client about the appeal. He knows that the Board will almost invariably pay only for the preparatory work in connection with the appeal and not for representation at the hearing itself.[82]

The appeal is successful and the offer of legal is sent to the client. Once the certificate is issued:

(a) the solicitor may do no further work under the Green Form, even if part of the extension remains unused, because of the provisions of section 8(5) of the 1988 Act.

(b) The cost of the Green Form work which the solicitor will claim from the Board form part of the statutory charge created by section 16(6) of the 1988 Act by virtue of the provisions of section 16(9)(b) of the 1988 Act.

Divorce proceedings

03–48   This application for advice and assistance proceeds in the same way as the application for advice and assistance for the personal injury claim with two main differences.

First, the initial costs limit, where advice on a petition is given, is the equivalent of three (not two) hours' work.

Secondly, if a civil legal aid certificate "to prosecute a suit for divorce" or "to defend a suit for divorce" is issued, it is very wide in its scope. It will cover the decree proceedings themselves. Usually such certificates will bear limitations stating that the certificate covers the decree proceedings only while the suit is defended. While a certificate covers the decree

---

[82] Notes for Guidance 6–13 *Legal Aid Handbook 1995.*

proceedings, no work at all can be done under the Green Form because the scope of the certificate covers, or is capable of being amended to cover, all matters in connection with the proceedings.

However, if as is more usual, the certificate is issued for specified ancillary proceedings, *e.g.* in relation to property or children, the decree proceedings are not covered by the certificate and work in connection with the decree proceedings themselves may continue to be carried out under the Green Form.

REMUNERATION OF LEGAL REPRESENTATIVES
LEGAL AID ADVICE AND ASSISTANCE — COSTS

How to apply

Legal advice and assistance (Green Form) costs are claimed on the **03–49** conclusion of the case by submitting form GFI — Green Form (with both the front and the costs claim on the back fully completed) or where the form has a relevant franchise, form GF7, plus form GF6, Green Form consolidated claim for fees to the appropriate area office. With the form should also be submitted:

(a) completed form GF4 where advice has been given regarding the making of a will;

(b) any authorities and extensions granted by the area office in relation to the Green Form;

(c) vouchers for disbursements claimed;

(d) any fee notes where counsel has been instructed. Note that, unlike Civil legal aid, counsel will not be paid direct.

It is useful to keep a copy of the Green Form including the costs claim on the back in case of queries and the possibility of further advice being sought. Further advice on the same matter must be provided under the same Green Form unless six months have elapsed since the claim for payment was submitted. There are no provisions enabling payments on account in Green Form cases. It is in the practitioners interest to submit the claim as soon as possible on the conclusion of the matter.

The Board pays the amount of the "assessed deficiency". Any charge **03–50** arising is in the solicitor's favour and not in favour of the Board. If there is a recovery or preservation, the solicitor takes his costs from that money or property and accounts for any balance to the client. Some property is exempt from the charge, by virtue of Schedule 4 to the Legal Advice and Assistance Regulations 1989 and there is provision, under Regulation 33 of the Legal Advice and Assistance Regulations 1989 for the solicitor to apply for authority to waive the charge.

Although it has not been tested in the courts, it is the Board's view that, in the event of the solicitor's charge operating so that there is no deficiency to assess, the solicitor is entitled, from the charged property, only to such costs and disbursements as would have been allowed on assessment by the Board in accordance with regulation 30 of the Legal Advice and Assistance Regulations 1989 (although no claim is made and no assessment takes place). This view is based on the combined effect of section 11(5) of the 1988 Act and regulations 29(4) and 30 of the Legal Advice and Assistance Regulations 1989.

Although the legislation appears to envisage an assessment by the Board, even where the solicitors charge operates, in practice when the solicitor can take his costs from, *e.g.* damages recovered, no claim is submitted. The solicitor should simply deduct the costs, charged at the appropriate rates, from the damages.

03–51   The exceptions to the solicitor's charge listed in Schedule 4 to the Legal Advice and Assistance Regulations 1989 are not exactly the same as the list of *exemptions* to the legal aid statutory charge which is contained in regulation 94 of the Civil Legal Aid (General) Regulations 1989. Some of the differences arise from the nature of Green Form advice (*i.e.* that representation is not covered except under ABWOR). However, in the matrimonial context, it is worth noting that, although the exception and exemption in respect of both periodical payments and the first £2,500 of stated orders and agreements in a domestic context are the same, there is a Green Form exception in paragraph (b) of Schedule 4 which excepts the client's main or only dwelling or any household furniture or tools of trade. There is no corresponding exemption in relation to civil legal aid. If there is a recovery or preservation which is not within the exceptions, the solicitor may apply to the area office or the charge to be waived under Regulation 33 of the Legal Advice and Assistance Regulations 1989. Waiver will be granted only if it would cause grave hardship or grave distress to enforce the charge or if it could be enforced only with unreasonable difficulty because of the nature of the property.[83]

03–52   In order to avoid either rejection of the claim or delay in payment when submitting a costs claim the solicitor should check that:

(a) the front and back of form GF1 have been fully completed with *all* questions answered, otherwise the claim will be rejected. No duplicate of the form needs to be submitted but it is useful to keep a copy for reference;

(b) all necessary documents are enclosed (any authority, extension and/or GF4);

(c) details of the operation of the solicitor's charge and any request

---

[83] Legal Aid and Advice Regulations 1989, reg. 33.

for authority not to enforce it are given. The latter should be done by way of a covering letter attached to the *back* of the papers;

(d) the solicitor's account number has been correctly inserted.

The amounts of costs

The costs claimed must be based on the rates set out in Schedule 6 to the **03–53** Legal Advice and Assistance Regulations 1989 at the time the work was undertaken. Higher rates are paid to franchised firms. Claims for costs in respect of Green Form advice are assessed in accordance with the Schedule 6 rates and the provisions of regulations 6 and 7 of the Legal Aid in Criminal and Care Proceedings (Costs) Regulations 1989 as if the work done was work done by a solicitor in criminal proceedings in a magistrates' court.[84]

This means that a reasonable amount must be allowed for work actually and reasonably done, based on the set rates. The fact that an authority or extension to the costs limit has been granted does *not* mean that the costs incurred will be paid. The Board is not estopped from disallowing or reducing costs claimed, e.g. because the Green Form was not properly completed, the work done was not advice on a matter of English law or the amount claimed was excessive. Note also that the solicitor's costs may be reduced if what was at stake in the matter did not justify incurring the amount of costs actually incurred. Enhanced (or reduced) rates are not payable.

Where the rates of payment are increased in the period when work is being done, the solicitor must apportion the work between the appropriate rates shown as "old rate" and "new rate". The Board will not necessarily recalculate or return a claim which does not take any increased rate into account.

The initial costs limit (the "prescribed limit" under section 10 of the 1988 **03–54** Act) is fixed by reference to a multiple of twice (or three times where a divorce or judicial separation petition — but not an amended or supplemental petition — is drafted) the "relevant sum" which is the criminal legal aid preparation rate prescribed by Schedule 6. The Board is of the view that, for the purpose of determining the initial costs limit, the applicable preparation rate is the rate which applied when the last act of advice/assistance was undertaken, although the preparation and submission of the costs claim is not part of the advice/assistance. It cannot be remunerated and does not suffice to trigger a new increased limit. The area office may call for the solicitor's file if it appears that the solicitor has sought to manipulate the limit.

---

[84] Legal Advice and Assistance Regulations 1989, reg. 30.

Assessment procedure

03–55   Assessments are carried out by the Area Director; that is to say by staff authorised to act on his behalf.[85] If the claim is allowed as sought, payment will be authorised and appear in the solicitor's next settlement. If the claim is reduced, it will be returned to the solicitor with the Notice of Assessment section at the back of the Green Form GF1 completed to show the amount assessed as allowed. The solicitor (and counsel) then have the option of accepting the assessment and resubmitting the claim or making representations to the appropriate area committe.[86]

Submitting written representations triggers a "review" of the assessment when the area committee can confirm, increase *or* decrease the assessment. This is widely referred to as an "appeal". There is no printed form of appeal but the representations (which will, therefore, be in the form of a letter) must be made within 21 days of receipt of notification of the assessment.

Although there is no right of audience on a review, the practitioner appellant will probably be permitted to address the area committee where this is requested on applying for the review. This will be at the practitioner's expense even if he is successful in getting the assessment increased.

03–56   A solicitor or counsel who is dissatisfied with the decision of an area committee on a review may, within 21 days of receipt of notification of the committee's decision, apply to that committee to certify a point of principle of general importance. It is important to note that the point must be one of *principle* (that is to say going to the 1988 Act and the Regulations and their application rather than merely to quantum) and also of *general importance* (that is to say that the circumstances of the case are such that it would not be right to describe the case as a "one off"). The solicitor/counsel should clearly and succinctly summarise the point or points in respect of which certification is sought, referring as appropriate to the 1988 Act and the Regulations and the circumstances of the case. If a point of principle is certified by the area committee, the solicitor/counsel will be informed of the exact wording of the point accepted by the area committee. Then it is for the solicitor/counsel to appeal in writing to the Costs Appeals Committee of the Board within 21 days receipt of notification of the certification.[87] This Committee consists of legally qualified Board members (usually two) and a Law Society representative and it may reverse, confirm or amend the decision of the area committee.[88] The amount allowed may be reduced or increased or continued.

It is important to note that the reference to the Costs Appeals Committee is not automatic even where a certification is granted and that there is no

---

[85] Legal Aid and Advice Regulations 1989, reg. 3(1).
[86] *ibid.* reg. 29(7).
[87] Notes for Guidance 13–05 *Legal Aid Handbook 1995.*
[88] reg. 29(10).

right of appeal from the area committee's decision save to the Costs Appeals Committee from which there is then no further appeal.

Appeals to the Costs Appeals Committee should not be sent to the area **03–57** office but to the Legal Aid Head Office marked "Costs Appeals Committee". There is no form for this. The solicitor should send a copy of the letter from the area office notifying him of the certification, the documents returned to him by the area office and any further written submissions which he wishes to make. The Legal Aid Head Office will obtain a report from the area office which will provide the correspondence between the solicitor and the area office so that any submissions previously made need not be repeated. The solicitor should consider submitting his full file even if it was not previously submitted. There is no right of audience and, although the area committee may be prepared to hear oral representations, on a review of an assessment, the Costs Appeals Committee will not do so. The decision of the Costs Appeals Committee is notified in writing and the area office actions the decisions which may include a recoupment if the amount allowed is reduced.

Chapter 4

ASSISTANCE BY WAY OF REPRESENTATION (ABWOR)[1]

INTRODUCTION

04–01 Although assistance by way of representation (ABWOR) covers representation, it is dealt with in Part III of the 1988 Act (covering advice and assistance which does not normally include representation). Section 8(2) specifically applies Part III to assistance by way of representation "if, and to the extent that, regulations so provide" and the relevant Regulations are regulations 6 to 9 of the Legal Advice and Assistance (Scope) Regulations 1989. These Regulations and the other relevant Regulations, the Legal Advice and Assistance Regulations 1989, both use the term ABWOR, defined as "assistance by way of representation". ABWOR may or may not:

(a) be means tested;

(b) require the prior approval of the Board or a magistrates' or county court;

(c) be subject to the usual Green Form advice and assistance financial limit on costs or no limit at all (subject to justification of costs on assessment).

04–02 There are four types of ABWOR:

(a) ABWOR for which the prior approval of the Board's Area Director is required, *i.e.* ABWOR under regulations 7(1)(a), 7(2) (unless the solicitor is the court duty solicitor) or 9 of the Legal Advice and Assistance (Scope) Regulations 1989. In such cases the client must be financially eligible for ABWOR. Note, however, that no means test is applied to proceedings before a Mental Health Review Tribunal.[2]

---

[1] For sources see Legal Aid Act 1988, Pt. III (ss. 8–13); Legal Advice and Assistance Regulations 1989 as amended; Legal Advice and Assistance (Scope) Regulations 1989; Legal Aid in Criminal and Care Proceedings (Costs) Regulations 1989; *Legal Aid Handbook 1995*, Notes for Guidance 3–01–3–28.

[2] The financial eligibility test for ABWOR for representation before Mental Health Tribunals was abolished by reg. 5A of the Legal Advice and Assistance Regulations 1989 as amended.

(b) ABWOR for which the approval of the magistrates' court or county court is required, *i.e.* ABWOR under regulation 7(1)(b) or 8 of the Legal Advice and Assistance (Scope) Regulations 1989 respectively. The client must be financially eligible for ABWOR.

(c) ABWOR in criminal proceedings in the magistrates' court for which no prior approval is required, *i.e.* by the court duty solicitor under regulations 7(2) or (4) of the Legal Advice and Assistance (Scope) Regulations 1989 — no means test is applied.[3]

(d) ABWOR in respect of warrants of further detention or extensions of such warrants, *i.e.* ABWOR under regulation 7(1)(c) of the Legal Advice and Assistance (Scope) Regulations 1989 and regulation 5 of the Legal Advice and Assistance Regulations 1989 — again, no means test is applied.

Financial eligibility

A means test of both income and capital must be satisfied in order to qualify where the approval of the Board or court is required, although a means test is no longer applied to representation before a Mental Health Review Tribunal. The same assessment criteria contained in Schedule 2 to the Legal Advice and Assistance Regulations 1989 are applied as to Green Form. The limits and contribution arrangements are not, however, the same as for the Green Form Scheme. While Green Form is no longer contributory, ABWOR remains so. There is no contribution if the relevant weekly disposable income is up to £64, but between £64 and the upper limit of £156 a weekly contribution of one-third of the excess income over £64 is payable to the solicitor. The contribution is payable from the date of approval of ABWOR to the conclusion of the proceedings or until ABWOR is withdrawn.[4] Note, however, that the contribution for court-granted ABWOR under regulation 7(1)(b) or 8 of the Legal Advice and Assistance (Scope) Regulations 1989 is limited to one week's contribution[5] and that in any proceedings where the total contribution is likely to exceed the cost of giving ABWOR, the solicitor should not require the client to pay more than would be expected to meet the solicitor's reasonable costs.[6] Where the costs are less than any contribution made by the client, the solicitor must refund the balance.[7] The limits are more generous than for Green Form and some clients who are not eligible for Green Form will qualify for ABWOR although a

04–03

---

[3] See Chapter 5.
[4] Legal Advice and Assistance Regulations 1989, reg. 12(3).
[5] *ibid.* reg. 12(4).
[6] Legal Advice and Assistance Regulations 1989, reg. 28(1A) substituted by the Legal Advice and Assistance (Amendment) Regulations 1993.
[7] *ibid.* reg. 28(2).

contribution[8] may be payable. If the ABWOR income or capital limit is exceeded the client will not be eligible.

04–04   The ABWOR disposable capital limit is £3,000 to which dependants' allowances for capital are added. Income support is a passport to ABWOR so that where the solicitor is satisfied that the applicant or anyone whose resources may be treated as those of the applicant in accordance with Schedule 2 to the Legal Advice and Assistance Regulations 1989 is in receipt of income support, then the solicitor is required to take that person's disposable capital as not exceeding the capital limit.[9] Receipt of family credit or disability working allowance is *not* a passport to ABWOR and a capital (but not income) assessment must be carried out.

Schedule 2 to the Legal Advice and Assistance Regulations 1989 governs the assessment of resources for both Green Form and ABWOR but note that, although paragraph 3 provides that "any question arising under the Schedule shall be decided by the solicitor" the solicitor must have regard to any guidance which may from time to time be given by the Board. Such guidance would be in the form of the Notes for Guidance issued by the Board but if a solicitor has a particular query he may consider it advisable to put the point to the Board's area office, bearing in mind that if the area office takes a different view this will otherwise only be discovered on his application for payment.

Availability

04–05   The Legal Advice and Assistance (Scope) Regulations 1989 set out the proceedings for which ABWOR is available. By the Schedule to the Regulations, ABWOR is available for the following magistrates' court proceedings:

(a) for or in relation to an affiliation order within the meaning of the Affiliation Proceedings Act 1957;

(b) for or in relation to an order under the Matrimonial Proceedings (Magistrates' Courts) Act 1960 or Part I of the Domestic Proceedings and Magistrates' Courts Act 1978;

(c) under the Guardianship of Minors Act 1971 and 1973;

(d) under section 43 of the National Assistance Act 1948 section 22, of the Maintenance Orders Act 1950 section 4 of the Maintenance, Orders Act 1958, section 18 of the Supplementary Benefits Act 1976 or section 24 of the Social Security Act 1986;

(e) in relation to an application for leave of the court to remove a child from a person's custody under sections 27 or 28 of the Adoption Act 1976 or proceedings in which the making of an order

---

[8] *ibid.* reg. 11(2), 12, 13.
[9] *ibid.* reg. 13(3).

under Part II or section 29 or 55 of the Adoption Act 1976 is opposed by any party to the proceedings;

(f) under Part I of the Maintenance Orders (Reciprocal Enforcement) Act 1972 relating to a maintenance order made by a court of a country outside the United Kingdom;

(g) under Part II of the Children Act 1975;

(h) under section 10A of the Fire Precautions Act 1971.

Paragraph 1 of the Schedule provides that the cover includes giving notice of appeal or applying for a case to be stated, within the ordinary time for so doing, and matters preliminary thereto.

The only proceedings for which ABWOR *only* is available are those under section 10A of the Fire Precautions Act 1971. Apart from that exception, civil legal aid is available as well as ABWOR.

The statutes referred to in (a), (c) and (g) have been repealed but by the operation of the saving provisions in the Interpretation Act 1978, ABWOR cover is available for Children Act 1989 proceedings where the Children Act replaces the repealed provisions. The Interpretation Act 1978 provisions also make civil legal aid available for proceedings under section 24 of the Social Security Act 1986 even though that is not specifically mentioned in the list of proceedings for which civil legal aid is available (compare the ABWOR provisions).

There is no provision corresponding to section 15(3)(b) of the 1988 Act to enable ABWOR applications to be refused on the basis that civil legal aid is more appropriate. The Board's Notes for Guidance confirm that ABWOR applications will not be refused on that basis.[10] The solicitor, therefore, has a free choice as to whether to apply for ABWOR or civil legal aid.

The advantages of ABWOR are: **04–06**

(a) means assessment by the solicitor;

(b) small (but continuing) contribution, if any, by a client who is financially eligible;

(c) speed of grant of approval.

(d) firms with an appropriate legal aid franchise can grant their own ABWOR;

But civil legal aid should be applied for:

(a) where the client is not financially eligible for ABWOR;

(b) if the proceedings are to be commenced other than in the magistrates' court or are likely to be transferred up (as ABWOR can never cover proceedings other than in the magistrates' court).

ABWOR is also available:

(a) where a magistrates' court requests a solicitor to provide ABWOR or approves a proposal from a solicitor that ABWOR be provided;

(b) in connection with an application for a warrant for further

---

[10] See *Legal Aid Handbook 1995*, Notes for Guidance 7–23.

detention or for an extension of such a warrant under section 43 or 44 of the Police and Criminal Evidence Act 1984;

(c) for representation in criminal proceedings in prescribed circumstances, *i.e.* by a duty solicitor in accordance with regulation 7 of the Legal Advice and Assistance Regulations 1989 and Regulation 7(2) and (4) of the Legal Advice and Assistance (Scope) Regulations 1989;

(d) where a country court requests a solicitor to provide ABWOR or approves a proposal from a solicitor that ABWOR be provided;

(e) for proceedings before a Mental Health Review Tribunal;

(f) for disciplinary proceedings before a prison governor controller of a "contracted out" prison;

(g) for a discretionary life prisoners whose case is referred to the Parole Board under sections 34(4) or (5) or 39(4) of the Criminal Justice Act 1991.[11]

The application for ABWOR

04–07 Where the authority of the Area Director is required for the provision of ABWOR (*i.e.* for the civil proceedings in the magistrates' court listed in the Schedule to the legal Advice and Assistance (Scope) Regulation 1989, for criminal proceedings in the magistrates' court within regulation 7(2) of the Legal Advice and Assistance (Scope) Regulations 1989 outside the duty solicitor scheme, and for proceedings before a Mental Health Review Tribunal or prison governor the application should be made to the solicitor's local area office. However in the case of Mental Health Review Tribunals and prison disciplinary proceedings the application may be sent to the legal aid area in which the hospital or prison is situated.

Any approval granted will *not* operate retrospectively and should, therefore, be applied for at the earliest opportunity as there is also no provision to deem costs pre-dating an approval as incurred under that approval—although Green Form costs are recoverable (where the client qualifies and the Green Form has been completed). It may be necessary for the solicitor to obtain a Green Form extension or extensions before applying for ABWOR.

The application must be made on a form approved by the Board and the solicitor is required to supply such information as may enable the Area Director to consider and determine it.[12] The form is currently form ABWOR 1. This includes details of the client, the solicitor, the nature of the proceedings for which representation is sought and, on the back, details about any opponent and a short statement of the case including, if

---

[11] *London Borough of Sutton v. Davis (costs) (No. 2)* [1994] 2 F.L.R. 569.
[12] Legal Advice and Assistance Regulations 1989, reg. 22(4).

appropriate, details of any opponent's financial circumstances and of any corroborative evidence. The front of the form may be signed *for* the conducting solicitor (*i.e.* the nominated solicitor who has responsibility for the case even if its actual conduct is delegated) and he is not required *personally* to sign a declaration included in the form that he holds a valid practising certificate. The statement must be signed by the client and includes the client's authority to enforce or write off any costs order which may be made in the client's favour in the proceedings. Any relevant supporting documents should also be submitted to the area office.

The solicitor should take care in completing Form ABWOR 1, to ensure **04–08** that the statement contains all the relevant facts, is legible and any relevant documents are enclosed.

A little extra time spent on preparation of the application may lead to a grant rather than a refusal on the basis of lack of information or that reasonable grounds for taking/defending the proceedings have not been made out. It should be remembered that the Board's area offices no longer raise queries but make decisions on the information sent to them.

If the situation is urgent an application may be made over the telephone in which case it is advisable to ensure that all the information to be contained in Form ABWOR 1 is available when telephoning the area office. The area office will, over the telephone, be seeking the information which would be submitted in a written Form ABWOR 1.

If time permits, it is advisable to make a written application followed by a telephone call to ascertain the outcome. The time which it takes for an ABWOR application to be dealt with will vary from time to time and area office to area office but an application is likely to take a period of days (rather than weeks) to determine (bearing in mind that there is no means assessment to be undertaken). The Board currently has no target for dealing with applications for ABWOR.

The Area Director *must* refuse an application *unless* it is shown that the **04–09** client has reasonable grounds for taking, defending or being a party to proceedings[13] although this requirement does not apply to Mental Health Review Tribunals, prison disciplinary and discretionary life panel proceedings.

The Area Director *may* refuse an application if it appears unreasonable that approval should be granted in the particular circumstances of the case.[14] An application will not be refused on the basis that civil legal aid should be applied for, although on the basis of section 15(3)(b) of the 1988 Act, civil legal aid applications may be refused if ABWOR is more appropriate.

The application for ABWOR may be granted in whole or in part and the **04–10**

[13] Legal Advice and Assistance Regulations 1989, reg. 22(5).
[14] *ibid.* reg. 22(6).

Area Director may impose such conditions as to the conduct of the proceedings as he thinks fit. It is a condition of every approval (except where a firm had an appropriate legal aid franchise) that the prior permission of the Area Director is required:

(a) to obtain a report or opinion of an expert; or

(b) to tender expert evidence; or

(c) to perform an act which is either unusual in its nature or involves unusually large expenditure;

unless such permission has been included in the grant of approval.

An approval of ABWOR includes an extension to what would otherwise be the appropriate advice and assistance costs limit and the Area Director may prescribe such higher costs limit as he thinks fit. This is not usually done so that the costs which may be incurred are unlimited, subject to the scope of the ABWOR and costs assessment.[15]

If the application is approved, the area office sends the solicitor a form of approval (ABWOR 2) together with claim form. The solicitor should carefully check the wording of the notification immediately on receipt, so that any error or omission in the wording of an approval may be corrected. Refusals are notified by letter to the solicitor.

Note that neither the approval nor refusal is copied direct to the client (unlike a civil legal aid certificate). Documents submitted in support will be returned.

Once an approval has been granted it will be a matter for the solicitor to start collecting any weekly contribution that is payable. This costs claim will be dealt with on the basis that the appropriate contribution has been collected (even if that is not the case).

Appeal to the area committee

04–11   Where the Area Director refuses an application for ABWOR, refuses prior authority under regulation 22(7) of the Legal Advice and Assistance Regulations 1989 or withdraws ABWOR under regulation 25 of the Legal Advice and Assistance Regulations 1989, there is a right of appeal to the Area Committee.[16] Although the Legal Advice and Assistance Regulations 1989 provide for an appeal to be made by giving notice on a form approved by the Board[17] there is currently no form of notice of appeal and, therefore, notice should be given by letter.

04–12   Notice of appeal must be given within 14 days of the date of the refusal decision (calculated up to the date of receipt at the appropriate area office). Pursuant to regulation 37(2) of the Legal Advice and Assistance Regulations

---

[15] Legal Advice and Assistance Regulations 1989, reg. 22(7), (8).
[16] Legal Advice and Assistance Regulations 1989, reg. 26(1).
[17] *ibid.* reg. 26(2).

1989, time may be extended, even after the time period has expired, if the Area Director thinks fit. If an appeal is made out of time, the letter of appeal should include grounds for an extension. There is no appeal against an Area Director's refusal to extend time.

On an appeal, the area committee is required to:

(a) dismiss the appeal; or

(b) in the case of an application for ABWOR or a prior authority, grant the application subject to such terms and conditions as it thinks fit; or

(c) in the case of a decision to withdraw approval, quash that decision.[18]

The area committee considers the matter afresh. Its decision is final and it is required to give notice in writing of its decision and the reason for it to both the client and the solicitor.[19]

Any decision of the area committee will not be retrospective and the time **04–13** which it takes for an appeal to be determined will depend on the appeals awaiting consideration by the committee in the area concerned. If the case is urgent, attention should be drawn to this in the letter of appeal. There is no right of audience before the area committee and attendances will not be permitted. It is important, therefore, that the letter of appeal makes the grounds of appeal clear and refers to any relevant documents. Additional or fresh documents or information not forwarded with the original application may be submitted in support of the appeal.

Firms without a legal aid franchise have devolved to them the Area **04–14** Director's power to grant and reform ABWOR. If a firm refuses ABWOR, the client has the same rights of appeal as if the Area Director had made the refusal. In practice, firms are more likely to advise clients whose applications would be refused, not to apply.

Amendment of ABWOR granted by the area office

The Regulations are silent as to the possible amendment of an ABWOR **04–15** approval. It is The Board's view that an ABWOR may be amended and it has a standard form (ABWOR 6) for that purpose.

An amendment could extend the ABWOR to other steps or proceedings (following an approval in part under Regulation 22(7) of the Legal Advice and Assistance Regulations 1989) and the most usual amendment would be to delete a limitation.

Where the refusal of an amendment would have the effect of refusing ABWOR or bringing it to an end, the Board will allow an appeal to be made to the area committee, although Regulation 26 of the Legal Advice

---

[18] *ibid.* reg. 27(1).
[19] *ibid.* reg. 27(2).

and Assistance Regulations 1989 does not directly provide for this. If appropriate, the ABWOR should be withdrawn to have the effect of providing a right of appeal and bringing the assisted person's liability for contributions to an end. If the assisted person wishes to change solicitor other than within the same firm, a fresh application for ABWOR must be made.

Particular Types of Proceedings

Civil proceedings in the magistrates' courts

04–16 The proceedings for which ABWOR is available are listed in the Schedule to the Legal Advice and Assistance (Scope) Regulations 1989. ABWOR may be granted for proceedings under the Children Act 1989 where that Act replaces a repealed provision.

Note for Guidance 3–12 the *Legal Aid Handbook 1995* gives examples of decisions in some of the most common types of ABWOR cases. Practitioners should consult this Note as to the likelihood of a grant/refusal as it will be followed by the area office/area committee.

If the client is outside the ABWOR capital limit but within the maximum civil legal aid limit, or is outside the ABWOR income limit but within the civil legal aid limit then an application for civil legal aid under Part IV of the 1988 Act, may be made in respect of the magistrates' court proceedings listed in paragraph 2 of Part 1 of Schedule 2 to the 1988 Act, as amended by Schedule 15 to the Children Act 1989, that is:

(a) proceedings under the Guardianship of Minors Acts 1971 and 1973;

(b) proceedings under section 43 of the National Assistance Act 1948, section 22 of the Maintenance Orders Act 1950, section 4 of the Maintenance Orders Act 1958, or section 18 of the Supplementary Benefits Act 1976;

(c) proceedings in relation to an application for leave of the court to remove a child from a person's custody under section 27 or section 28 of the Adoption Act 1976 or proceedings in which the making of an order under Part II or section 29 or section 55 of the Adoption Act 1976 is opposed by any party to the proceedings;

(d) proceedings under Part I of the Maintenance Orders (Reciprocal Enforcement) Act 1972 relating to a maintenance order made by a court of a country outside the United Kingdom;

(e) proceedings under Part II of the Children Act 1975;

(f) proceedings for or in relation to an order under Part I of the Domestic Proceedings and Magistrates' Courts Act 1978;

(g) proceedings under the Children Act 1989.

    (h) appeals under section 20, where they are to be made to a magistrates' court, and proceedings under section 27 of the Child Support Act 1991.

    (i) proceedings under section 30 of the Human Fertilisation and Embryology Act 1990.[20]

Only these proceedings can be covered and the particular requirements of summary jurisdiction civil legal aid (the old yellow legal aid) no longer exist. Applications are made to the usual area office and an assessment of means by the Legal Aid Assesment Office will be required except in relation to certain specified proceedings under the Children Act.

When the 1988 Act was drafted, civil legal aid for proceedings in the magistrates' court was intended only to cover those cases where the applicant did not qualify financially for ABWOR but fell within the civil legal aid financial limits. Section 15(3)(b) of the 1988 Act contains a statutory ground for refusing Part IV civil legal if, in the particular circumstances of the case, it appears to the Board more appropriate that the applicant should be given ABWOR. Following the implementation of the Children Act 1989 and the legal aid changes made as a consequence this section will be of little application. The reverse does not apply so the solicitor may elect to apply for ABWOR where civil legal aid is available. **04–17**

Cover for enforcement of an order under the Guardianship of Minors Acts 1971 and 1973 or the Children Act 1989 is not available in the magistrates' court as these are not proceedings *under* the Acts but rather proceedings in relation to an order which is made under the Acts — a distinction drawn by both Part I, Schedule 2, to the 1988 Act and the Schedule to the Legal Advice and Assistance (Scope) Regulations 1989. Enforcement may be covered by civil legal aid in the higher courts where there is no finite list of proceedings for which civil legal aid is available.

Civil legal aid under Part IV of the 1988 Act is also available for the domestic proceedings which are covered by ABWOR.[21] On the face of the Schedule dealing with civil legal aid it does not appear that proceedings for or in relation to an affiliation order within the meaning of the Affiliation Proceedings Act 1957 (*e.g* making or opposing applications to vary an affiliation order made before or since April 1, 1989) are covered—unlike ABWOR where those proceedings are specifically mentioned in paragraph 2(a) of the Schedule to the Legal Advice and Assistance (Scope) Regulations 1989. Civil legal aid is, in fact, available because of the saving provisions of paragraph 6 of Schedule 3 to the Family Law Reform Act 1987 which saves old legislation in relation to any affiliation order made under the Affiliation Proceedins Act 1957 and section 17(2) of the Interpretation Act **04–18**

---

[20] Inserted by the Legal Aid (Scope) Regulations 1994.
[21] Legal Aid Act 1988, Pt. 1, Sched. 2, para. 2.

1978 which preserves the availability of legal aid under the Legal Aid Act 1974 (despite its repeal) and under the 1988 Act.

04–19   ABWOR is available in relation to orders made under the Matrimonial Proceedings (Magistrates' Courts) Act 1960 and a civil legal aid certificate would also be available for variation or enforcement proceedings, although this does not appear to be the case from the face of paragraph 2, Part I, Schedule 2 to the 1988 Act. The Matrimonial Proceedings (Magistrates' Courts) Act 1960 was repealed by the Domestic Proceedings and Magistrates' Courts Act 1978. However, the saving provisions in the Domestic Proceedings and Magistrates' Courts Act 1978 (particularly paragraph 3 of Schedule 1) have the effect of making full legal aid but not ABWOR available for proceedings in a magistrates' court "for or in relation to an order made under the Matrimonial Proceedings (Magistrates' Courts) Act 1960."

04–20   ABWOR is available for proceedings under section 10A of the Fire Precautions Act 1971. This Act provides for an appeal to the magistrates' court and the Legal Advice and Assistance (Scope) Regulations 1989 as amended make ABWOR available for the prosecution of such appeals. Civil legal aid is *not* available and it is not clear whether it will be made available at some future date.

04–21   ABWOR is not available for proceedings in the magistrates' court under the Child Support Act 1991 or section 30 of the Human Fertilisation and Embryology Act 1990, although civil legal aid is available.

Mental Health Review Tribunals

04–22   ABWOR is available under regulation 9(a) of the Legal Advice and Assistance (Scope) Regulations 1989 to a person whose case or whose application is to be the subject of the proceedings before the Mental Health Review Tribunal. The Board accepts that ABWOR is available both to the patient *and* to a "nearest relative" if that person is making the application. No means test is applied regardless of which the client is. The application may be sent to the area office where the hospital involved is situated. The Board has stated that solicitors should prepare the case (*i.e.* obtain the hospital statment and interview the client) using the Green Form limit before applying for ABWOR (where the client qualifies for Green Form advice and assistance). Where the client does not qualify for Green form, an immediate ABWOR application which is not means tested can be made.

An approval of ABWOR will not automatically authorise the obtaining of an independent psychiatric report. The solicitor applying should, therefore, specify in the application for ABWOR any reports for which authority is sought although authority may be applied for subsequently using Form ABWOR 6. The Board expects solicitors to exercise their professional judgment in deciding whether a report is needed, but authority will usually be granted if the responsible medical officer's report contains recommendations which are not acceptable to the client.[22]

Authority for the instruction of counsel will normally be refused because it is expected that solicitors should be sufficiently experienced to deal with Mental Health Review Tribunal cases. Although clients are free to instruct any solicitor of their choice, the Law Society has set up a panel of solicitors with expertise in this work. Details can be obtained from the Panel Administrator, Specialisation Unit, The Law Society. Note that a special higher rate of payment applies.[23] See decision ABWOR 7 of the Board's Costs Appeals Committee regarding travel by Mental Health Return Tribunal Panel members.

Disciplinary proceedings before prison governors or controllers

ABWOR is available to a prisoner in proceedings before a prison governor only where the governor or controller has permitted the prisoner to be legally represented in those proceedings.[24] Representation is at the discretion of the governor or controller and not a right.[25] **04–23**

ABWOR may be refused only if it appears unreasonable that approval should be granted in the particular circumstances of the case (there is no need to show reasonable grounds for defending the proceedings).

Note that the normal ABWOR payment rates (rather than any enhanced rate) apply.

Discretionary lifer tribunals (Parole Board)

ABWOR is available to a discretionary life prisoner, as defined by section 34(1) of the Criminal Justice Act 1991, whose case is referred to the Parole Board under sections 34(4) or (5) or 39(4) of the Criminal Justice Act 1991.[26] ABWOR may be refused only if it appears unreasonable that approval should be granted in the particular circumstances of the case (there is no need to show reasonable grounds for taking the proceedings). **04–24**

Note that the higher Mental Health Review Tribunal rate of payment

---

[22] *Legal Aid Handbook 1995*, Note for Guidance 3–15.
[23] Legal Advice and Assistance Regulations 1989, Sched. 6 as amended by Legal Advice and Assistance (Amendment) (No. 2) Regulations 1992, reg. 2(2), (3).
[24] Legal Advice and Assistance (Scope) Regulations 1989, reg. 9(b) as substituted by Legal Advice and Assistance (Scope) (Amendment) Regulations 1992, reg. 3 (and amended by the Legal Aid (Scope) Regulations 1994 to add in controllers of privatised prisons).
[25] *R. v. Secretary of State for the Home Department, ex parte Tarrant; R. v. Board of Visitors of Albany Prison, ex parte Leyland; R. v. Board of Visitors of Wormwood Scrubs Prison, ex parte Tangnay, Clark, Anderson* [1984] 1 All E.R. 799. These decisions were made in relation to boards of visitors rather than prison governors.
[26] Legal Advice and Assistance (Scope) Regulations 1989, reg. 9(c).

applies.[27] Part of the documentation supplied by the prison authoritites will include a psychiatric report. Solicitors may seek prior authority under regulation 22(7) of the Legal Advice and Assistance Regulations 1989 to instruct a psychiatrist of their own. If authority is sought, a copy of the prison psychiatrist's report should be provided to the area office by the solicitor together with the solicitor's observations as to why the prison report is regarded as unsatisfactory and why a further report is necessary.

Discretionary lifers may instruct the solicitor of their choice and this may lead to large claims for payment for travel where a non-local solicitor is instructed subject to costs assessment. The basis of assessment of ABWOR claims is as if the work done was work done by a solicitor in criminal proceedings in magistrates' courts.[28]

There is no ABWOR regulation comparable to regulation 48(1) of the Civil Legal Aid (General) Regulations 1989, which gives the Board power to restrict costs allowable to a distant solicitor, but having regard to the general intention of the Regulations and by reference to the Boards Costs Appeals Committee and decision CRIMLA31, claims for travel will be approached carefully and consideration will be given as to whether local agents should have been instructed. See also decision ABWOR 7 regarding travel by Mental Health Review Tribunal panel members.

General

Effects of ABWOR approval and cover granted

04–25 The Regulations allow the Area Director to grant an application for approval in whole or in part and subject to such conditions as to the conduct of the proceedings as he thinks fit. The most common limitation is to the obtaining of blood tests in cases involving parentage (paternity). Requests for an amendment to an ABWOR approval including the deletion of a limitation should be made using Form ABWOR 6. The Board considers that an ABWOR may also be amended to cover different/additional proceedings for which ABWOR is available but not to show a change of solicitor. The approval of ABWOR contains an extension to the usual Green Form financial limit which would otherwise be applicable and although the Area Director may fix an increased limit as he thinks fit this is not generally done.

Where ABWOR is approved in respect of proceedings in a magistrates' court and the client is or becomes a party to proceedings, the solicitor shall (as soon as practicable) give notice of the approval to any other party to

---

[27] Legal Advice and Assistance Regulations 1989, Sched. 6 as amended by Legal Advice and Assistance (Amendment) (No. 2) Regulations 1992, reg. 2(2), (3).
[28] Legal Advice and Assistance Regulations 1989, reg. 30(1).

the proceedings and to the court. There is no prescribed form for this and notice may be given by letter or by the use of a solicitor's "in house" form in similar terms to a Notice of Issue of a civil legal aid certificate.

Costs

The Board expects the solicitor to advise an assisted party as to obtaining a **04–26** costs order in the same way as he would advise a fee-paying client of moderate means. Where order for costs is made, there is no procedure for the assessment of costs except by the area office. Therefore, the costs question must be adjourned to enable an assessment to be obtained and the assessed amount notified to the court. Wasted costs orders may be made.

An ABWOR approval protects the assisted person against costs in that the amount of his liability must not exceed the amount (if any) which is a reasonable one for him to pay having regard to all the circumstances, including the financial resources of all the parties and their conduct in connection with the dispute. The amount of his liability is required to be determined in accordance with Schedule 5 to the Legal Advice and Assistance Regulations 1989. Points to note are:

(a) if the ABWOR approval does not relate to the whole proceedings or has been withdrawn, the court is required to determine the client's liability for that part of the proceedings covered by the approval;

(b) the court may refer any relevant question of fact to the Clerk to the Justices for investigation and report back to the court;

(c) the assisted person's dwelling house, clothes, furniture and tools and implements of his trade are disregarded as for the assessment of disposable capital and may not be subject to execution to enforce the order for costs;

(d) a party (other than the assisted person) may file an affidavit of means and circumstances relevant to the determination of costs liability and the court may order an oral examination of the assisted person and any party who has filed such an affidavit;

(e) the court may direct payment by instalments or that payment be suspended until a fixed date or *sine dine*;

(f) a party in whose favour an order is made may apply for the order to be varied within six years of the date of the order on the grounds of material additional information or a change in the assisted party's circumstances,

(g) special provision is made for clients who are concerned solely in a representative, fiduciary or official capacity, children and patients.
An unassisted party who is successful in proceedings where the other party has ABWOR, may seek an order for costs against the Board and the court must allow the Area Director an opportunity

to make representations before making an order. The provisions are the same as those contained in section 18 of the 1988 Act regarding civil legal aid. Points to note are:

(a) Before an order is made, the court is required to consider what order for costs should be made against the assisted party and to determine his liability.

(b) An order may only be made if:
   (i) an order for costs would be made in the proceedings apart from the provisions of the 1988 Act;
   (ii) regarding costs incurred in a court of first instance, the proceedings were instituted by the assisted party and *the court is satisfied* that the unassisted party will suffer *severe financial hardship* unless the order is made; and
   (iii) the court is satisfied that it is just and equitable.

(c) Costs means as between party and party, and includes the costs of applying for an order payable by the Board.

(d) Proceedings are treated as finally decided in favour of an unassisted party if:
   (i) no appeal lies against the decision with leave and the time for applying for leave has expired; or
   (ii) leave to appeal is granted or is not required but no appeal is brought within the time-limit for appeal.

(e) No appeal lies against such an order or the refusal to make such an order, except on a point of law.

Cover

04–27 The cover for proceedings in the magistrates' court includes giving notice of appeal or applying for a case to be stated within the ordinary time as well as work preliminary to those steps.[29]

The ABWOR approval may be limited in scope or by reference to a financial limit and may contain conditions. The solicitor should check the terms of any approval on receipt, clearly marking his file with any limitations or conditions so that they are not overlooked at a later stage.

The approval will not include the instruction of counsel, the obtaining of expert reports, the tendering of expert evidence or performing an act which is either unusual in its nature or involves unusually large expenditure *unless* specific permission has been sought when applying for the approval of ABWOR and is then included in the approval. However, firms with an appropriate legal aid franchise are able to take these steps without authority from the area office.

The Costs Appeals Committee of the Board has decided that the scope of

---

[29] Legal Advice and Assistance (Scope) Regulations 1989, Sched. para. 1.

an ABWOR includes negotiations for settlement of the proceedings covered, provided that the negotiations reasonably relate to the scope of the particular ABWOR approval. The scope does not include implementation of any settlement save to obtain a final order within the scope of the ABWOR approval.[30] Negotiations as to a transfer of property could fall within an ABWOR covering maintenance proceedings but the preparation of any agreement or transfer could not be covered.

An ABWOR approval covering financial relief will not cover applying to the court for a first child maintenance order except in relation to a stepchild or children, *unless* additional cover is specifically stated. This is in view of the jurisdiction of the Child Support Agency. If cover for child maintenance is sought, the solicitor should make the basis of the court's, rather than the Child Support Agency's, jurisdiction clear in the application. In the light of the transitional provisions for the Agency's jurisdiction, the area office will generally assume that cover for variation of a child maintenance order is sought, that cover for a first child maintenance order (other than as to a stepchild or children) is not sought and it will make no assumption that the court has jurisdiction in first order cases.

Prior authority

Points to note regarding the prior authority of the Area Director for **04-28** expenditure are:

    (a) Except where the firm holds an appropriate legal aid franchise the requirement for authority is mandatory to:

        (i) obtain a report; or

        (ii) opinion of an expert; or

        (iii) tender expert evidence; or

        (iv) perform an act which is either unusual in its nature or involves unusually expenditure.

    This applies even if the court has ordered the work to be done (e.g. obtaining blood tests) and this has been confirmed by the Costs Appeals Committee of the Board in a point of principle decision.[31]

    (b) If authority is not applied for in the ABWOR application itself, the Board's Form ABWOR 6 must be used. A separate form must be completed for each application (although they may relate to a single ABWOR approval). Applications made by letter will be rejected. No queries will be raised.

    (c) Authority cannot be granted retrospectively.

    (d) In the absence of prior authority, payment cannot be made out of the fund. There is no statutory requirement for any authority

---

[30] See decision ABWOR 2.
[31] See decision ABWOR 1.

granted to stipulate the maximum amount (compare civil legal aid) but this is normally done.

(e) The Board's Note for Guidance 3–14 *in the Legal Aid Handbook 1995* deals with prior authorities in ABWOR cases, indicating that authority will be given if the expenditure is necessary and reasonable having regard to the nature of the proceedings and the likely benefit to the client but not if a fee paying client would be advised not to incur the expense or to use a cheaper alternative.

(f) Prior authority will not normally be required in respect of an enquiry agent's fees unless those fees involve "unusually large expenditure". The Board's Notes for Guidance suggest that £200 for enquiry agents' fees as interpreters' charges would constitute an unusually large expenditure. If authority is refused on the basis that an authority is not required then it would be reasonable to expect the fees to be met provided that they are justified on the assessment of costs. On the other hand, if authority is not sought and it is subsequently considered (on assessment) to have been required, then no payment can be made for the disbursement/costs incurred.

Blood tests

04–29 In cases involving parentage (paternity) an ABWOR approval may be issued limited to obtaining blood tests (which encompasses DNA tests). If an approval is issued which is not limited in this way but blood tests are required, then prior authority must be sought even if the court has ordered the tests.[32] Except where the other party is the Child Support Agency, a solicitor applying for prior authority should give some information of the other party's position including whether he is in receipt of ABWOR or legal aid as the Area Director will consider asking the solicitor to request an unassisted party to make a contribution towards the expenditure. This will only be done where there is positive evidence that any unassisted party can afford to share the expense without hardship. The assisted person must not be prejudiced and the prior authority will be granted to the full amount even if the unassisted party fails or refuses to contribute.

In cases involving the Child Support Agency, the Board would expect a successful assisted party to seek a costs order (including the costs of blood/DNA tests) against the Agency if it will not fund the costs of tests itself (the Agency's policy in this area is under review).

---

[32] See decision ABWOR 1.

Counsel

If the prior authority of the Area Director for the instruction of counsel is **04–30** not applied for or is refused costs will be assessed on the basis that the solicitor alone conducted the case, *unless* the Area Director considers (on the costs assessment) that the proper conduct of the proceedings required counsel.[33] Therefore, the instruction of counsel may be applied for in advance or justified on assessment. The solicitor will wish to consider applying for authority in appropriate cases so that his position is protected on assessment.

The Board has indicated that approval will be given if the cases pose unusually complex evidential problems or novel or difficult points of law, but not if the reason for instructing counsel is that:

(a) the case is contested, protracted or involves the cross-examination of witnesses or arguments on points of law;

(b) the personal circumstances or convenience of the solicitor;

(c) the other side is represented by counsel; or

(d) it would be more appropriate to instruct a solicitor agent.

Approval is unlikely to be granted in Mental Health Review Tribunal cases — see para. 04–22 above.

Change of solicitor

There are no provisions in the Legal Advice and Assistance Regulations **04–31** 1989 for the amendment of an ABWOR approval, although the Board does amend approvals to delete/amend limitations or conditions or to alter the proceedings covered. This is done by way of a standard letter in response to an application from the solicitor on mandatory Form ABWOR 6. However, should a client holding an ABWOR approval wish to change solicitor (*i.e.* another firm rather than within the same firm) a fresh ABWOR will need to be applied for. Authority from the Area office may need to be sought for the client.[34]

Approval in part

If an Area Director grants an approval only in part, the Board is of the view **04–32** that there is a right of appeal to the area committee as the refusal of cover constitutes a refusal of an application for approval which gives rise to a right of appeal.[35]

---

[33] Legal Advice and Assistance Regulations 1989, reg. 29(5).
[34] Legal Advice and Assistance Regulations 1989, reg. 9.
[35] *ibid.* reg. 26.

Withdrawal of ABWOR

04–33 The Area Director is required to withdraw ABWOR *from such date as he considers appropriate where, as a result of information which has come to his knowledge,* if he considers that:

    (a) in respect of proceedings in the magistrates' court specified in the Schedule to the Legal Advice and Assistance (Scope) Regulations 1989, the client no longer has reasonable grounds for taking, defending or being a party to the proceedings or for continuing to do so; or

    (b) the client has required the proceedings to be conducted unreasonably so as to incur an unjustifiable expense to the Fund; or

    (c) it is unreasonable in the particular circumstances that the client should continue to receive ABWOR.[36]

The Area Director may act on information from any source (this can include the opponent) and there is no equivalent of the civil legal aid "show cause" procedure so that theoretically ABWOR could be withdrawn without prior notification to the client or solicitor. In practice, the solicitor may well have reported the position to the area office, the area office will be likely to issue a show cause letter (copied to both the client and solicitor) and there is in any event a right of appeal to the area committee.[37] Note that if the ABWOR is withdrawn *only* the solicitor is informed. *He is under an obligation* to "forthwith";

    (a) inform his client of the withdrawal; and

    (b) in case of proceedings in the magistrates' court listed in the Schedule to the Legal Advice and Assistance (Scope) Regulations 1989, send a copy of the notice of withdrawal (which may be issued by the area office in the form of a letter) to the court and to any other party to the proceedings.[38] If the area committee decides to quash the Area Director's decision to withdraw an approval of ABWOR the solicitor is required, in respect of proceedings in a magistrates' court, to notify any other party and the court, if any, in which the proceedings are pending.[39]

Withdrawal does not affect or prejudice any subsequent application for representation or for approval of ABWOR in respect of the same proceedings.[40]

04–34 The withdrawal of ABWOR is dealt with in the Board's Notes for Guid-

---

[36] *ibid.* reg. 25(1).
[37] *ibid.* reg. 26(1)(c).
[38] *ibid.* reg. 25(2).
[39] *ibid.* reg. 27(3).
[40] *ibid.* reg. 25(3).

ance[41] where some of the circumstances in which ABWOR will be withdrawn are listed. ABWOR is withdrawn in a very small number of cases as, where the solicitor is without instructions or where there is no disagreement between him and the client, the solicitor may simply submit his costs claim for assessment without the ABWOR being withdrawn. However, since ABWOR contributions became payable until the conclusion of the proceedings or until ABWOR is withdrawn, increasing numbers of approvals have been withdrawn due to non payment of contribution.

There are no provisions for ABWOR to be discharged — the ABWOR continues until it is withdrawn or the work covered is concluded. It should be noted that there are no specific obligations to report to the area office (compare the civil legal aid position) but it is the view of the Board that there is an implied obligation to report the matters mentioned in regulation 25 of the Legal Advice and Assistance Regulations 1989 (*i.e.* loss of grounds, requiring proceedings to be conducted unreasonably or if it is unreasonable that the client should continue to receive ABWOR). In addition, the solicitor can suffer a costs penalty in that only such work as appears to have been actually and reasonably done will be allowed on assessment.[42] It will also be assumed that any contribution payable is actually paid so it will not be in the solicitor's interest to delay in reporting any failure to pay an assessed contribution.

ABWOR COSTS WHERE THE AREA DIRECTOR (OR FRANCHISED FIRM) HAS APPROVED THE ABWOR

ABWOR costs are claimed on the conclusion of the case by submitting the **04–35** ABWOR 3 — report on case form — to the area office which granted the approval. The form provides for payment at different rates according to the category of work undertaken and requires details of the fee earner's initials for time spent. The solicitor must, therefore, ensure that adequate time recording systems are in place to show the fee earner, the category of work undertaken as well as the actual time spent. With the form should also be submitted:

(a) any related Green Form costs claim and any authorities and extensions granted by the area office in relation to the Green Form itself;

(b) all authorities and amendments granted by the area office under the ABWOR;

(c) vouchers for disbursements claimed;

---

[41] *Legal Aid Handbook 1995*, Notes for Guidance 3–17.
[42] Legal Advice and Assistance Regulations 1989, reg. 30(1).

(d) all relevant fee notes where counsel has been instructed, whether authorised or not.

There is a three-month time-limit from the conclusion of the proceedings for submission of the costs claim[43] although this can be extended as the Area Director thinks fit.[44] A copy of the claim should be kept by the solicitor in case of queries and the possibility of further advice being sought where the existence of the claim is relevant.

04-36   There are specific provisions for payments on account of disbursements (but not profit costs).[45] Payments must be applied for using Form ABWOR 5 and the amount sought and the time likely to elapse before a final claim can be submitted will be the most important factor considered although no test is specified. No other payment on account will be made, *i.e.*, for profit costs or counsel's fees. Note that:

(a) a minimum of £30 inclusive of VAT must be claimed per case (but this could be made up of more than one item);

(b) no payment will be made where any requisite authority (under regulation 22(7) of the Legal Advice and Assistance Regulations 1989) has not been obtained;

(c) the disbursement must have been incurred *or be about to be* incurred — this is not defined;

(d) if there is no deficiency prompting the solicitor to make a claim for payment, he must submit a statement of costs on the conclusion of the case where a payment on account has been made. The payment (or in appropriate cases, part of it) must be repaid to the Fund where it exceeds the assessed deficiency, if any.[46]

04-37   The Board pays the amount of the "assessed deficiency" as in a Green Form case. In ABWOR (as in Green Form) cases any charge arising is in the solicitor's favour and not in favour of the Board. If there is a recovery or preservation, the solicitor recoups his costs and accounts for any balance to the client. It may be, therefore, that he makes *no claim* for costs to the Board as there is no deficiency. Although it has not been tested, it is the view of the Board that in the event of the solicitor's charge operating so that there is no deficiency to assess, the solicitor is entitled only to such costs and disbursements as would have been allowed on assessment by the Board in accordance with regulation 30 of the Legal Advice and Assistance Regulations 1989 (although no claim is made and no assessment takes place). This may be a source of difficulty, in particular where it is not clear whether counsel's fees would have been allowed on assessment (in the absence of authority) or whether prior authority was actually required under

---

[43] *ibid.* reg. 30 and Legal Aid in Criminal and Care Proceedings (Costs) Regulations 1989, reg. 5(1).
[44] Legal Advice and Assistance Regulations 1989, reg. 37(2).
[45] *ibid.* reg. 30A.
[46] *ibid.* reg. 30A(2), (3).

regulation 22(7) of the Legal Advice and Assistance Regulations 1989. A possibility might be to seek an informal assessment from the relevant area office which would be persuasive but not binding but capable of being reviewed by the Area Committee.

Exceptions to the solicitor's charge are listed in Schedule 4 to the Legal Advice and Assistance Regulations 1989. The list of exceptions is *not* exactly the same as the list of *exemptions* to the civil legal aid statutory charge which is contained in regulation 94 of the Civil Legal Aid (General) Regulations 1989. Some of the differences arise from the nature of Green Form advice (*i.e.* that representation is not covered except under ABWOR). However, in the matrimonial context it is worth noting that, although the exception and exemption in respect of both periodical payments and the first £2,500 of stated orders and agreements in a family context are the same, there is a Green Form/ABWOR exception in paragraph (b) of Schedule 4 which excepts the client's main or only dwelling or any household furniture or tools of trade. There is no corresponding exemption in relation to civil legal aid. **04–38**

In order to avoid either rejection of the claim or delay in payment when submitting a costs claim the solicitor should check that:

- (a) the front and back of Form ABWOR 3 have been fully completed with *all* questions answered, otherwise the claim will be rejected;
- (b) the full reference number, including the final letter, has been given (this final letter is a computer digit which is actually needed by the area office);
- (c) the solicitor's account number has been correctly inserted;
- (d) if counsel has been instructed and his legal aid account number has been correctly inserted, he will receive any payment direct;
- (e) all necessary documents are enclosed;
- (f) Form ABWOR 3 is signed *twice*; the declaration as to certification must be signed *personally* by the solicitor who has responsibility for the case even if its actual conduct is delegated by the solicitor. If the form is not correctly signed, the claim will be rejected.

The amount of costs

The costs claimed must be based on the rates applicable at the time the work was undertaken. The rates are set out in Schedule 6 to the Legal Advice and Assistance Regulations 1989. Enhanced rates are not payable[47]. **04–39**

Where counsel has been instructed and the Area Director considers that the proper conduct of the proceedings required counsel, or the instruction of counsel was previously approved under regulation 23 of the Legal Aid in Criminal and Care Proceedings (Costs) Regulations 1989, the Area Director

---

[47] Legal Advice and Assistance Regulations 1989, reg. 30(1), (c).

assesses the solicitor's claim excluding counsel's fees and pays the assessed deficiency (if any) to the solicitor. The Area Director also assesses counsel's fees and pays him the amount allowed less the amount, if any, by which the solicitor's charge arising under section 11 of the 1988 Act, together with the amount of any contribution payable by the clients exceeds the amount allowed to the solicitor.[48] The solicitor must then account to counsel for that excess amount. This can only arise where, despite the operation of the solicitor's charge, a claim has to be made against the Fund (*i.e.* where the costs incurred exceed the recovery or preservation) —, *e.g.* profit costs, including disbursement, allowed at £500, counsels fees assessed at £200 but the charge and contribution total £550. Counsel is paid £150 by the Board and £50 by the solicitor.

04-40 Where the claim relates to ABWOR in respect of which counsel has been instructed without prior approval under regulation 23 of the 1989 Regulations and the Area Director considers that the proper conduct of the proceedings did not require counsel, the Area Director is required to:

  (a) determine the assessed deficiency on the basis that counsel had not been instructed and the solicitor had conducted the case on his own;

  (b) allow the amount for counsel that would have been allowed had counsel been authorised or justified and pay counsel *to the extent* of the assessed deficiency; and

  (c) pay the balance of the net assessed deficiency, if any, to the solicitor.[49] This is known as "the maximum fee principle".

Counsel is paid direct in any event and the solicitor has to bear any shortfall if there are insufficient moneys to pay his costs in full after the payment of counsel.

The solicitor should be mindful of the wording of the ABWOR approval as work outside the scope of the approval will not be covered. The Costs Appeals Committee of the Board has decided that settlement negotiations reasonably related to the scope of the particular ABWOR approval are covered.[50]

Assessment procedure

04-41 Assessments are carried out by the Area Director, that is to say by staff authorised to act on his behalf.[51] If the claim is allowed as sought payment will be authorised and appear in the solicitor's next settlement. If the claim is reduced, payment of the reduced amount is authorised and the area office

---

[48] *ibid.* reg. 29(5).
[49] *ibid.* reg. 29(6).
[50] See ABWOR 2, point of principle decisions of the costs Appeals Committees of the Board.
[51] Legal Advice and Assistance Regulations 1989, reg. 3(1)—definition of "Area Director".

assessment is notified to the solicitor and, where appropriate, counsel who may within 21 days of *receipt* of notification of the assessment make written representations to the area committee. The representations should be by letter re-submitting relevant documents.

A claim may be assessed at nil or completely rejected. If the area office rejects the claim, *e.g.* where the client's means were incorrectly assessed as in scope, it can be argued there is no right of appeal (compare where the area office assesses the claim at nil and right of appeal is clear). The point has not been tested.

The area committee *reviews* the area office assessment and may confirm, increase or *decrease* the amount assessed. Although the correct terminology for the consideration of an assessment by the area committee is "review", the term "appeal" is widely used by both the area offices and practitioners.

There is no right of audience but the practitioner appellant will probably be permitted to address the area committee, at his own expense, if this is requested on applying for the review.

A solicitor or counsel who is dissatisfied with the decision of an area **04–42** committee on a review may, within 21 days of receipt of notification of the committee's decision, apply to that committee to certify a point of principle of general importance. It is important to note that the point must be one of *principle* (that is to say going to the 1988 Act and the Regulations and their application rather than merely to quantum) and also of *general importance* (that is to say that the circumstances of the case are such that it would not be right to describe the case as a "one off".[52] The solicitor/counsel should clearly and succinctly summarise the point or points in respect of which certification is sought, referring as appropriate to the 1988 Act and the Regulations and the circumstances of the case. If a point of principle is certified by the area committee, the solicitor/counsel will be informed of the exact wording of the point accepted by the area committee. Then it is for the solicitor/counsel to appeal in writing to the Costs Appeals Committee of the Board within 21 days of receipt of notification of the certification.[53] This Committee consists of legally qualified Board members and a Law Society representative and the Committee may reverse, affirm or amend the decision of the area committee.[54] The amount allowed may be reduced. It is important to note that the reference to the Costs Appeals Committee is not automatic and that there is no right of appeal from the area committee's decision save to the Costs Appeals Committee from which there is then no further appeal.

Appeals to the Costs Appeals Committee should not be sent to the area **04–43** office but to the Board's Legal Department at Legal Aid Head Office marked "Costs Appeals Committee". There is no form for this but the solicitor

---

[52] *ibid.* reg. 29(8).
[53] *ibid.* reg. 29(8), (9).
[54] *ibid.* reg. 29(10).

should send a copy of the letter from the area office notifying him of the certification, the documents returned to him by the area office and any further written submissions he wishes to make. Legal Aid Head Office will obtain a report from the area office which will provide the correspondence between the solicitor and the area office so that any submissions previously made need not be repeated. The solicitor should consider submitting his full file even if it was not previously submitted. There is no right of audience and, although the area committee may be prepared to hear oral representations on a review of an assessment, the Costs Appeals Committee will not do so. The decision of the Costs Appeals Committee is notified in writing and the area office actions the decision which may include a recoupment if the amount allowed is reduced. All decisions are publicised in the Board's focus newsletter and inserted in the next edition of the *Legal Aid Handbook*.

Costs orders

04–44 Where another party is ordered to pay costs to the assisted party the amount is required to be paid to the Clerk to the Justices who then passes it to the Board. Only the Clerk to the Justices is able to give a good discharge and the Board, if the solicitor has not already been paid by it, is required to pass to the solicitor the amount of his charge with any balance being paid to the client. The solicitor will, however, prefer to assign his charge to the Board and receive the amount of the costs order from the Board in addition to the costs payable out of the Fund. The report on case Form ABWOR 3 provides for this and the effect is that payment to the solicitor is not delayed while any costs ordered are collected. Any costs ordered would form part of the solicitor's charge and would normally be deducted by the Board before the assessed deficiency is paid. The assignment of the solicitor's charge to the Board enables him to receive full payment from the Board without delay. This applies only to costs and not to the solicitor's charge on property recovered or preserved under section 11(2)(b) of the 1988 Act.[55] There is no corresponding provision for other cases where ABWOR approval is required from the Area Director but the Clerk to the Justices is not involved. Given the nature of the other "proceedings" covered by ABWOR (*e.g.* Mental Health Review Tribunals, prison disciplinary proceedings and Discretionary lifer parels) costs orders will be rare but payment would have to be made to the solicitor.

Note that ABWOR costs must be assessed by the area office if a claim is to be made out of the Fund. There is no procedure for an area office assessment where the court makes a costs order for a stated amount. This

---

[55] *ibid.* reg. 31.

may be a cause of difficulty if the general costs indemnity principle is not to be breached.[56]

Costs of successful unassisted parties may be ordered to be paid out of the Fund pursuant to section 13 of the 1988 Act. Section 13 is in the same terms as section 18 of the 1988 Act which relates to civil legal aid and the court is required to give the Area Director who dealt with the ABWOR application an opportunity to make representations before any order is made.[57]   **04-45**

Where a client is or was in receipt of ABWOR and an order for costs has been made against him, the amount of his liability for costs, if any, is required to be determined in accordance with Schedule 5 to the Legal Advice and Assistance Regulations 1989. The unsuccessful assisted party's liability will be limited to the amount which it is reasonable for him to pay having regard to all the circumstances, including the means of all the parties and their conduct in connection with the dispute.[58] This limit on costs corresponds to the limit on costs against a person receiving civil legal aid.

APPROVAL OF ABWOR BY MAGISTRATES' COURTS AND COUNTY COURTS

A magistrates' court or county court may grant ABWOR to a party to proceedings. Although the provisions are contained in separate Regulations[59] they are identical (save that the opening phrase to the county court provision specifically refers to ABWOR "given by a solicitor"). They provide for the court to authorise ABWOR only if: **04-46**

   (a) the party is not receiving and has not been refused representation (*i.e.* ABWOR, civil or criminal legal aid) in the proceedings;
   (b) the court is satisfied that the hearing should proceed on the same day;
   (c) the court is satisfied that that party would not otherwise be represented; and
   (d) the court requests a solicitor who is within the precincts of the court for purposes *other than* providing court-approved ABWOR to provide ABWOR or approves a proposal from such a solicitor that he provide the party with ABWOR.

Where approval for the provision of ABWOR is given by the court rather than by the Board, the approval given does not include an extension to the Green Form legal advice and assistance financial limit. Therefore, it is

---

[56] *London Borough of Sutton v. Davis (costs) (No. 2) [1994]* 2.F.L.R. 569.
[57] Legal Advice and Assistance (Scope) Regulations 1989, reg. 35.
[58] Legal Advice and Assistance Regulations 1989, reg. 35.
[59] Legal Advice and Assistance (Scope) Regulations 1989, reg. 7(1)(b), (8).

subject to the usual costs limit which is twice the Green Form hourly rate.[60] The means test to be applied is the ABWOR means test.[61] The contribution payable is limited to one week's assessed contribution. It should be noted that the Board accepts that the usual Green Form costs limit applies irrespective of any previous costs incurred in giving advice or assistance relating to the same proceedings under a Green Form, that is to say the Board accepts that the representation constitutes a separate matter, even if the same solicitor is involved.

04–47   The Board will accept evidence of the grant of ABWOR by the court in the form of:

(a) an endorsement on the completed Form ABWOR 1;

(b) a county court order confirming that ABWOR was approved (subsequently submitted to the area office with Form ABWOR 1).

(c) a letter from the court confirming that ABWOR was approved (subsequently submitted to the area office with Form ABWOR 1).

The Board has suggested[62] that any endorsement on the ABWOR 1 should be in the following or similar terms:

I confirm that this court requested/approved a proposal that ABWOR be provided pursuant to regulation 7(1)(b)/8 of the Legal Advice and Assistance (Scope) Regulations 1989 in respect of a hearing on (insert date).
Signed —
Clerk to the justices/of the court
Dated —

The endorsement can most conveniently be put in the space for the statement of case as no statement of case is required. A completed Form ABWOR 1 must, however, be submitted with the costs claim in any event — to confirm the client's details and financial eligibility. The costs claim must be made using the ABWOR claim Form ABWOR 3. Claims made using the Green Form and consolidated claim Form GF2 will no longer be accepted.

The availability of ABWOR approved by magistrates' or county courts is intended to enable cases to proceed with representation where the court is satisfied that this is appropriate within the specific requirements of regulation 7(1)(b) and 8 of the Legal Advice and Assistance (Scope) Regulations 1989. If the solicitor is not a qualifying solicitor within the Regulations then any ABWOR granted will be *ultra vires*. It is a matter for the court to decide whether a solicitor qualifies but a solicitor who has been telephoned by the court in order to attend at court to provide ABWOR

---

[60] Legal Advice and Assistance Regulations 1989, reg. 4(1)(c).

[61] *ibid.* reg. 11(2), 9.

[62] Notice in L.S. Gaz., December 20, 1989 and see *Legal Aid Handbook 1995*, Note for Guidance 3–10.

would not come within the requirements of the Regulations. It is the Board's view albeit, untested by the courts, that court-granted ABWOR cannot be given to counsel direct nor can counsel be instructed by the solicitor in view of the specific references to "a solicitor" in the Legal Advice and Assistance (Scope) Regulations 1989.

In the magistrates' courts, ABWOR could be used for either civil or criminal cases and it is worthy of mention that this form of ABWOR can be used in the magistrates' courts to enable representation to be provided on council tax and Child Support Agency enforcement cases.

In the county court, this form of ABWOR could be used, e.g. to enable a respondent in injunction proceedings to be represented, or where legal aid is not normally granted, but the requirement that representation must not have been refused should not be overlooked. Note also that non-means tested representation is available under section 29 of the 1988 Act, for certain contempt proceedings usually amounting to contempt in the face of the court — This is not a form of ABWOR although representation is ordered by the court. Courts may purport to grant section 29 representation in cases involving contempt arising from breaches of orders (e.g. injunctions) — such grants are *ultra vires* and practitioners should be aware that payment will not be made out of the Fund.

ABWOR FOR WARRANTS OF FURTHER DETENTION OR EXTENSIONS TO WARRANTS OF FURTHER DETENTION

ABWOR is available in connection with applications for warrants of **04–48** further detention or for extension of such warrants under section 43 or 44 of the Police and Criminal Evidence Act 1984.[63] Note that this form of ABWOR is not means tested and no application form needs to be signed by the client.

The approval of the Board or the court is not required and assistance may be given by a duty solicitor or by an own solicitor but where the ABWOR is given by a duty solicitor in unsocial hours (as defined in regulation 2 of the Legal Advice and Assistance at Police Stations (Remuneration) Regulations 1989) the amount allowed is increased by one-third[64]. Unsocial hours are between 5.30 pm and 9.30 am on any weekday and any time on a day which is not a business day. A business day is any day other than a Saturday, Sunday, Christmas Day, Good Friday or a bank holiday under the Banking and Financial Dealings Act 1971[65]. If the ABWOR is provided by

---

[63] Legal Advice and Assistance Regulations 1989, reg. 5.
[64] *ibid.* reg. 30(2).
[65] Legal Advice and Assistance at Police Stations (Remuneration) Regulations 1989, reg. 2(1).

an own solicitor or by a duty solicitor other than in unsocial hours the claim must be assessed on the current standard hourly rates.

The claim for payment is made together with the relevant costs claim for advice at police stations using Advice at Police Stations Report DSPS. The usual Green Form costs limit of twice the hourly preparation rate applies as it is not excluded by regulation 4(2) of the Legal Advice and Assistance Regulations 1989. This cannot be retrospectively extended but the Board accepts that the full limit is available in that the ABWOR representation is separate from any other Green Form advice and assistance.

PART C

REPRESENTATION IN CIVIL PROCEEDINGS

Chapter 5

THE DUTY SOLICITOR SCHEMES

Introduction

The Board has appointed five group duty solicitor managers, one for each **05–01** of the groups into which the administration of legal aid has been split. The group duty solicitor manager will be able to provide information about local duty solicitor schemes, answer questions and supply application forms. They are located in the Board's Newcastle, Chester, Nottingham, London and Cardiff area offices.

The first court duty solicitor scheme was introduced in Bristol in 1972 on a voluntary basis following the introduction of a scheme in Scotland and a growing awareness of the disadvantage to defendants of not having assistance at court readily available. During the following decade, voluntary schemes were introduced in over 100 courts. The Law Society issued a guide to setting up schemes which laid down minimum conditions. Despite the spread of schemes it proved difficult to make progress at some courts due to opposition from solicitors with well established criminal practices who feared a loss of work and sometimes opposition from magistrates and justices' clerks. A combination of these difficulties, support from the Lord Chancellor's Legal Aid Advisory Committee and a recommendation from the Royal Commission on Legal Services[1] led to a power being included in the Legal Aid Act 1982[2] which provided for the introduction of a formal court duty solicitor scheme including remuneration arrangements. In addition, magistrates' courts were required to comply with directions from the Lord Chancellor to give effect to the court scheme.

Using the powers in the Legal Aid Act 1982, the Law Society — which **05–02** was at that time responsible for the administration of legal aid — set up the Legal Aid (Duty Solicitor) Scheme 1983 which set out the framework for the introduction of schemes in all courts throughout England and Wales. It established regional and local committees (the former with lay members —

---

[1] The Royal Commission on Legal Services: final report, Cmnd. 7648 (1979) p. 92.
[2] Legal Aid Act 1982, s. 1.

an innovation at the time), laid down criteria for selecting duty solicitors and specified the service which was to be provided by all duty solicitors. The Scheme allowed local committees some flexibility as to local arrangements but at the same time aimed to ensure that defendants would receive the same level of service irrespective of the court at which they appeared.

Research became available in the early 1970s indicating considerable difficulties in obtaining advice at police stations. The Judges' Rules — which were supposed to ensure that suspects could obtain advice — were not proving effective. It was not, however, until the *Confait* case[3] — where three juveniles whose conviction for murder was subsequently quashed — that the spur was provided for setting up the Royal Commission on Criminal Procedure. One of the Commission's recommendations was the establishment of the duty solicitor scheme to cover police stations.[4] The right to confidential advice and a power to establish a police station duty solicitor scheme were included in the Police and Criminal Evidence Act 1984. The court duty solicitor scheme provided the necessary framework to establish police station cover and a revised scheme came into effect on January 1, 1986 at the same time as the requirements of the Police and Criminal Evidence Act 1984 were introduced into police stations.

ADMINISTRATION

05–03 The duty solicitor schemes are run by a three-tier structure of committees in which the profession is well represented. Individual schemes are run by their local duty solicitor committee of which there are about 300 covering the whole of England and Wales. The local committees have a duty to help the Board provide a quality service to the public.[5] They must make appropriate arrangements for running the local scheme and are responsible for selecting duty solicitors. The members of the local committee must include at least three solicitors and a lay member and they may also include a justice of the peace, justices' clerk, representatives of the probation service, police and Crown Prosecution Service.[6] There must be a majority of solicitors.[7]

The next tier is the 24 regional committees whose role is to oversee the operation of the local schemes in their region, withdraw existing arrangements and substitute alternative ones, *e.g.* substitute a panel for a

---

[3] The *Confait* case, report by the Hon. Sir Henry Fisher (1977), HMSO.
[4] The Royal Commission on Criminal Procedure Report, Cmnd. 8092 (1981), para. 4.97.
[5] Duty Solicitor Arrangements 1994 24(1).
[6] ibid. 18.
[7] ibid. 20(1).

rota in the police station scheme which, if there is a low demand, will prove less costly[8] and to consider appeals from decisions of the local committees. The members of the regional committee must include a solicitor member of each local committee, a justice of the peace, a justices' clerk, two lay members and a police representative. Other members may include a member of the Legal aid area committee, a representative of the probation service and the Crown Prosecution Service and additional lay members.[9] Again, there must be a majority of solicitors on a regional committee.[10]

The final tier in the committee structure is the Board's national Duty Solicitor Committee which has a general overall responsibility for the operation of the duty solicitor schemes, revising the Duty Solicitor Arrangements as and when necessary, reviewing appeal decisions of the regional committees and setting performance targets for both the court and police station schemes. The targets for the latter include: the speed of passing cases to duty solicitors by the telephone referral service, the amount of telephone advice only given to suspects without an attendance at the police station and the cost of standby payments per suspect assisted.

SELECTION, RESELECTION AND DISCIPLINE

The selection criteria for court duty solicitors also applies to the selection **05–04** of police station duty solicitors except that the geographical proximity to court requirements do not apply to police station applicants. In addition, police station applicants will have to demonstrate experience of police station work. In practice, the majority of solicitors apply for membership of both schemes. The selection criteria for duty solicitors are set out in paragraphs 32 and 33 of the Board's Duty Solicitor Arrangements 1994.

The duty solicitor application form is available from the Board's group duty solicitor manager. The form covers both schemes and asks for details of the applicant's office and home and other professional details. Applicants for the court scheme must give details of the last 25 cases in court whilst police station scheme applicants must give similar information about such cases in the police station.

The primary control over the schemes to which application can be made is geographical proximity.[11] There are, however, other controls which may apply. There is a power to limit the number of court schemes to which an

---

[8] *ibid.* 14(5).
[9] *ibid.* 7.
[10] *ibid.* 9.
[11] See below para. 05–08.

individual duty solicitor can belong[12] and in London, for instance, a limitation of two court schemes is widely applied. There is no equivalent restriction for the police station scheme.

05–05   The general rule is that a solicitor does not have to be a member of both court and police station schemes. However, there is a power in the Board's Duty Solicitor Arrangements to require membership of the police station scheme as a condition of joining the court scheme.[13] This power was inserted in the Duty Solicitor Arrangements when the police station scheme was introduced at which time the idea of having to provide a 24-hour service was far less popular than it is now. There is no reverse equivalent of this power but the national Duty Solicitor Committee has a general power to make directions[14] and this is sometimes used to require membership of the court scheme as a condition of joining the police station scheme.

The suitability of solicitors to act as duty solicitors is of great importance as members of the public asking for the duty solicitor will not be offered a choice. Such clients will not generally have much experience of instructing a solicitor and will be heavily reliant on the effectiveness of the local duty solicitor committee to ensure that only properly experienced solicitors are deployed.

The key requirement for both court and police station applicants is to "have comprehensive experience of criminal defence work including advocacy in magistrates' courts throughout the previous 12 months".[15] There are some riders to this requirement. The period of 12 months can be halved if the applicant "was in recent full-time employment as a prosecuting solicitor or in another similar position".[16] An interval of up to 12 months due to sickness, pregnancy, etc., can be disregarded.[17] It should be stressed that experience need not have been gained in the local magistrates' court as a requirement for local experience could act as a restrictive practice.[18] If the applicant does not meet the experience requirement and the local committee considers the applicant *would* make a competent duty solicitor, the local committee may recommend to its regional committee in exceptional circumstances that the relevant requirement is waived.[18a]

05–06   The local committee assesses competence to become a duty solicitor by reference to the nature, frequency and quality of the applicant's advocacy including his ability to provide help to a number of defendants in a limited time, and to adequate knowledge of the procedure in magistrates' courts

---

[12] Duty Solicitor Arrangements 25(6).
[13] *ibid.* 15(1), 32(1)(g).
[14] *ibid.* 5(1)(b)
[15] *ibid.* 324(1)(f)(ii).
[16] *ibid.* 324(1)(f)(iii).
[17] *ibid.* 324(1)(f)(v).
[18] *ibid.* 324(1)(f)(iv).
[18a] *ibid.* 32(1)(f)(vi).

and of the law relating to the more common offences that come before the courts.[19] This provision allows the local committee to reject an applicant if it does not consider that he or she will be a suitable duty solicitor even if the applicant appears before a court regularly. In addition, applicants for the police station scheme must convince the local committee that they have adequate experience of providing advice to persons arrested and held in custody.

Unless the applicant claims to have "substantial experience", training must be undertaken before the local committee can select. The local committee is the judge of whether or not the applicant's "substantial experience" is sufficient to justify exemption from training. Attendance on separate training courses is required for the court and police station schemes.[20] Applicants who wish to join both schemes will have to attend both training courses. Suitable courses are run by a number of course providers and last one day. The Board's group duty solicitor manager has details of suitable courses if there is any difficulty in identifying them.

There are several additional requirements which apply to all applicants. **05–07** The applicant must have a current practising certificate or, in the discretion of the local committee, a conditional one.[21] The local committee may also reject an application if it considers that to do so would be in the interests of suspects or defendants where the applicant has been charged with or convicted of a criminal offence since the applicant's admission or has been subject to an adverse finding by the Adjudication Committee of the Solicitors Complaints Bureau or by the Solicitors Disciplinary Tribunal, or if there are hearings pending in either forum or for any other good reason.[22] An applicant cannot be a special constable as suspects and defendants might have doubts about such a solicitor's independence from the police.[23] The applicant must also have books and periodicals prescribed by the Duty Solicitor Committee.[24] The only items that have been prescribed for court duty solicitor applicants are Home Office Circulars 66/90, *Provision for Mentally Disordered Offender* and 12/95 *Mentally Disordered Offenders: Inter-Agency Working* , copies of which are supplied by the Board. Items required for police station duty solicitors are a copy of the Police and Criminal Evidence Act 1984, the Codes of Practice made under it, the current edition of the Law Society's *Advising the Suspect at the Police Station* and its training pack *Police Station Skills for Legal Advisers.*

The applicant must be willing to act personally as duty solicitor.[25] It would, therefore, be expected that the solicitor would undertake duties

---

[19] *ibid.* 33(2).
[20] *ibid.* 32(3), 33(3).
[21] *ibid.* 32(1)(d).
[22] *ibid.* 32(4).
[23] *ibid.* 32(1)(f)(i).
[24] *ibid.* 32(5).
[25] *ibid.* 32(1)(e).

personally and would not, for instance, regularly pass them to another duty solicitor in his firm.

05-08 The proximity of the court duty solicitor applicant's office to the relevant court depends on whether or not the local scheme is an attendance scheme, *i.e.* it requires the duty solicitor to be physically present at court at a specified time. The duty solicitor's personal attendance is required at all busy courts whilst, at all other courts, the duty solicitor will be called in if a defendant requires assistance. If an attendance scheme is in operation, the applicant will have to have an office which is within the area of the court or, if outside it, is reasonably accessible to the court for the convenience of any defendant who wishes to instruct the duty solicitor to continue to act for him or her.[26] The applicant should normally be in attendance at the office and the office should be open during the majority of normal business hours.[27] It is for the local committee to decide whether an office is reasonably accessible to a court. Accessibility relates to defendants, not the applicant, and some regard should probably be had to the availability of public transport. The office could be the applicant's home provided it complies with the requirements for an office.

If a call-in scheme is in operation, the office must still be reasonably accessible but there is a proviso that relevant local considerations should be taken into account.[28] This proviso provides more flexibility in the distance of the applicant's office from the relevant courts because courts with call-in schemes are likely to serve areas of small and scattered populations.

The geographical proximity requirement for the police station scheme is that the applicant's home or office must be within 45 minutes travel time from the relevant police station. The applicant does not, therefore, need to have an office provided that his or her home is within the 45 minutes travel time. Regional committees have the power to vary the 45 minute requirement and may, for instance, do so in rural areas where considerable distances have to be covered.[29] Regional committees also have the power to approve the substitution of "office only" for "home or office."[30] If the application is based on the proximity of an office then there is no requirement as there is for the court scheme that the office should normally be open and the applicant in attendance. In addition, the duty solicitor has to be willing to make arrangements to be reasonably accessible to the police station when on rota duty. In some instances this may mean staying in an hotel and the cost of such accommodation can be recovered. In

---

[26] *ibid.* 32(1)(a).
[27] *ibid.* 32(1)(b).
[28] *ibid.* 32(1)(c).
[29] *ibid.* 14(4)(a).
[30] *ibid.* 14(4)(b), 26(6).

addition, applicants can be required to satisfy the committee undertaking selection that he or she will be in a position to accept panel calls.[31]

An applicant must be interviewed by the local committee or by a **05–09** sub-committee. There is no possible exemption from interview because of "substantial experience" as there is for attending a training course. The only possibility of exemption is where the applicant has already been approved by another local committee; even if this is the case, the local committee to whom the application has been made has a discretion to interview.[32]

All members of a local committee may participate in the committee's deliberations prior to a decision being made. The decision itself can only be made by the solicitor and lay members.[33] At least one lay member must participate in selection. For this purpose, a lay member who is a member of court staff does not fulfill this requirement. If a lay member cannot attend, one who is entitled to attend must agree to the interview being conducted in his absence.[34] In addition, a member of the regional committee may be included on the selection.[35] Case studies for court and police station schemes are available to local committees to assist with interviewing and their use is encouraged with a view to achieving greater consistency in selection.

An application must be dealt with in 60 days by the local committee.[36] If the local committee decides not to select the applicant it must give reasons for its decision indicating which of the selection criteria have not been met.[37] Where an application has been rejected by a local committee[38] or where the local committee has not approved an application within the period of 60 days[39] there is an appeal to the regional committee. The appeal should be made within 28 days of the local committee's decision being notified to the applicant subject to the regional committee having the discretion to accept an appeal outside 28 days for good reason.[40]

All members of a regional committee may participate in a committee's deliberations prior to a decision being made. The decision itself can only be made by the solicitor or lay members.[41] A member of the local committee which made the decision resulting in the appeal must not participate.[42]

---

[31] *ibid.* 33(2).
[32] *ibid.* 34(1).
[33] *ibid.* 21.
[34] *ibid.* 34(2).
[35] *ibid.* 34(3).
[36] *ibid.* 35.
[37] *ibid.* 36.
[38] *ibid.* 37(1).
[39] *ibid.* 37(3).
[40] *ibid.* 37(1).
[41] *ibid.* 10(1).
[42] *ibid.* 10(2).

Each appeal to the regional committee is dealt with by way of a re-hearing.[43] The appellant must submit written representations when giving notice of appeal and must send a copy to the local committee.[44] The latter may submit written representations and send a copy to the appellant.[45] The appellant, but not the local committee, has the right to make oral representations to the regional committee[46] and must be given reasons for the appeal decision.[47] The regional committee has a power to refer back to the local committee where the latter has not followed the selection procedure.[48]

If the appellant is dissatisfied with the determination of the appeal by the regional committee a written request for a review by the national Duty Solicitor Committee can be submitted. This must be made within 28 days of the outcome of the appeal being notified to the appellant, although a request outside this period can be accepted for good reasons.[49] A statement of the reasons for which the review applicant claims the regional committee's decision was unreasonable must accompany the request.[50] The review is dealt with on a paper-only basis and the Duty Solicitor Committee must give reasons for its decision.[51]

05–10   Reselection of duty solicitors must take place every five years.[52] The Board's group duty solicitor manager is responsible for issuing the reselection form to relevant duty solicitors who must complete and return it if they wish to continue to be duty solicitors.[53] Applications for reselection are considered by the local committee who must be satisfied that the duty solicitor meets the reselection criteria. The reselection criteria for the court scheme include continued compliance with the original selection criteria, regularity of personal attendance at court as duty solicitor and compliance with the requirements in the Arrangements.[54] For police station reselection the criteria include continued compliance with the selection criteria, availability to receive telephone calls concerning requests for advice from suspects at the police station, willingness to accept calls when a panel duty solicitor, attending a police station in cases where the duty solicitor is normally required to attend and, where their use is permitted, the appropriate use of duty solicitor representatives.[55] In addition, a duty

---

[43] *ibid.* 15(7)(a).
[44] *ibid.* 15(7)(b).
[45] *ibid.* 15(7)(c).
[46] *ibid.* 15(7)(e).
[47] *ibid.* 15(7)(f).
[48] *ibid.* 15(7)(g).
[49] *ibid.* 16(3).
[50] *ibid.* 16(4).
[51] *ibid.* 15(1)(a).
[52] *ibid.* 38(1).
[53] *ibid.* 38(2).
[54] *ibid.* 39(1).
[55] *ibid.* 39(2).

solicitor must have undertaken a minimum of six hours' tuition during the past five years on a course or courses relevant to duty solicitor work.[56]

The local committee must either tell the duty solicitor that a solicitor has been reselected or, if not satisfied that the reselection criteria have been met, the duty solicitor must be invited to an interview. The solicitor must respond to this invitation within 21 days. If, after the interview, the local committee decides not to reselect it must give reasons for its decision.[57] The solicitor can then appeal to the regional committee[58] and, if the appeal is rejected, can request a review by the national Duty Solicitor Committee.[59]

The selection of duty solicitor representatives to provide advice at police stations is along similar lines to the selection of duty solicitors. However, it is important to note that only about half of the schemes allow the use of representatives. The Board's group duty solicitor manager will know whether a representative can be used on a particular scheme. It should be noted that the Law Society, with the full support of the Board, introduced an accreditation scheme for our solicitor representatives from February 1, 1995. From this date, the Board will only make payments from the Fund in respect of work undertaken by own solicitor representatives who are registered with the Board as accredited or probationary representatives. Duty solicitor representatives are being brought within the accreditation scheme, as will trainee solicitors, from February 1, 1997. The Board's group duty solicitor manager can provide up-to-date information on precisely what requirements are currently in force for representatives advising at police stations.

For the time being, only duty solicitor representatives selected by local committees will be able to deal with duty solicitor cases and then only when the regional committee has consented to the use of representatives.[60] The representative's application form must be obtained from the Board's group duty solicitor manager. The selection criteria for representatives include a requirement to be in the full or part-time employment of the duty solicitor or solicitors in the same firm and not in the employment of any other solicitor.[61] The applicant representative must have experience of providing advice at a police station having gained such experience by working in a solicitor's office. This latter requirement prevents an ex-police officer being able to become a duty solicitor representative immediately upon resignation from the police. The amount of experience depends on the type of representative. If the application is from a solicitor, *e.g.* a solicitor who does not have sufficient experience to be a duty solicitor in his or her right,

05–11

---

[56] *ibid.* 40.
[57] *ibid.* 38(3).
[58] *ibid.* 28(1).
[59] *ibid.* 16(1).
[60] *ibid.* 14(3).
[61] *ibid.* 45(1)(a).

four months, experience is required; three years experience is required for a solicitor's clerk or, if a trainee solicitor, six months, experience of which four must be of criminal cases. The applicant must be competent to act as a representative, have received appropriate training and have copies of the same publications as duty solicitor applicants. The local committee has a discretion to reject an application where it considers to do so would be in the interests of the suspect. A solicitor applicant may be refused where he only has a conditional practising certificate[62] or has been subject to an adverse finding by the Adjudication Committee of the Solicitors Complaints Bureau or by the Solicitors Disciplinary Tribunal.

Just as for duty solicitor applicants, representative applicants must be interviewed by the local committee except that the local committee has a discretion not to interview where the representative has already been selected by another local committee.[63] The same arrangements for local committee members to deliberate and decide upon selection apply to representatives.[64] If the local committee decides not to allow the application it must provide the applicant with a statement of the reasons for its decision.[65] There are appeal arrangements to the regional committee very similar to those which apply in respect of duty solicitor applications.[66]

Duty solicitor representatives are, like duty solicitors, subject to reselection every five years.[67] The local committee must be satisfied that the representative continues to meet the selection criteria.[68] If the local committee is not satisfied, it must invite the representative to an interview and, if it decides not to reselect, it must provide a statement of the reasons for its decision.[69] There is an appeal to the regional committee against non-reselection[70] but no provision for the Duty Solicitor Committee to review the appeal.

05–12   Both the local and regional committee have similar disciplinary powers over duty solicitors and representatives. Disciplinary steps are normally initiated by the local committee both because that committee is responsible for the activities of individual duty solicitors in connection with the local scheme and because the duty solicitor concerned will have a right of appeal to the regional committee. The local committee can either exclude or suspend a duty solicitor for a period of up to 12 months for failure to carry out duties, to meet any of the selection criteria, where he is in breach of any

---

[62] *ibid.* 45(1)(g).
[63] *ibid.* 46(1).
[64] *ibid.* 21, 46(2).
[65] *ibid.* 45(2).
[66] *ibid.* 47(1), (2).
[67] *ibid.* 48(1).
[68] *ibid.* 48(3).
[69] *ibid.* 48(4), (5).
[70] *ibid.* 47(3).

rule of the local scheme, where there is some other good cause[71] or where a police station duty solicitor fails to accept a reasonable number of calls whilst on panel duty.[72]

A court duty solicitor who forgets to attend court on his duty day may, for instance, be suspended for a couple of months whilst a police station duty solicitor who sends an unauthorised representative to deal with a duty solicitor case may be excluded.

The duty solicitor must be notified of the complaint and that he may make written representations or give notice of his intention to make oral representations within 21 days of the local committee having notified him of the complaint[73] and the committee must provide a written statement of the reasons for its decision if it decides to exclude or suspend.[74] There is also a provision that where a duty solicitor under investigation for or having been charged with a criminal offence or is subject to an investigation by the Solicitors Complaints Bureau, the duty solicitor can be suspended for a period of up to six weeks (which can be extended for a further six weeks).[75]

The effect of a decision to suspend or exclude takes effect immediately **05–13** subject to the local committee having a discretion to postpone the effect where the duty solicitor affected undertakes to submit notice of appeal within 28 days.[76] The regional committee has similar powers to discipline duty solicitors if, for instance, it is felt that a local committee should have taken action but had failed to do so.[77] The local and regional committees also have similar disciplinary powers over duty solicitor representatives.[78] Once excluded, an application cannot be made to a local committee to which the exclusion relates for twelve months.[79]

COURT DUTY SOLICITOR — SCOPE OF SERVICE

Once selected, the court duty solicitor should be supplied with the local **05–14** rules or instructions for the local scheme. These serve two purposes. First, they set out how the local scheme operates, *e.g.* whether it is an attendance or call-in scheme and, if the former, when the duty solicitor should arrive at court. They should also indicate how defendants will be informed of the duty solicitor cover. This may involve the jailer or court staff informing

---

[71] *ibid.* 27(3)(a).
[72] *ibid.* 27(3)(b).
[73] *ibid.* 27(3)(a).
[74] *ibid.* 27(3)(e).
[75] *ibid.* 27(3)(d).
[76] *ibid.* 27(3)(e).
[77] *ibid.* 15(5).
[78] *ibid.* 15(14), 27(10).
[79] *ibid.* 27(11).

the defendant or the duty solicitor doing so. Secondly, the local rules or instructions set out the "Scope of Service — Magistrates' Courts" from the Arrangements[80] which define the service which is to be provided by court duty solicitors to defendants. In most schemes duty solicitors can, as well as acting as duty solicitor, also act for clients who have previously instructed them. However, some of the busier schemes do not allow the duty solicitor to act for own clients.[81]

Court duty solicitors can provide advice to a defendant prior to appearing before the court and also representation. They are limited to providing representation in criminal proceedings.[82] For this reason the duty solicitor cannot provide representation in connection with council tax cases as failure to pay is not a criminal offence. However, in such cases the duty solicitor may be able to provide help under "assistance by way of representation"[83] provided the consent of the court is obtained.

05–15   The first task of the court duty solicitor is to tell the defendant that he is entitled to instruct any solicitor and to ask whether there is a solicitor whom he wishes to provide representation. If there is another solicitor then the duty solicitor must not act.[84] However, if the defendant wants to be represented by a named solicitor or firm who is not available, the duty solicitor may provide advice and representation on that occasion but must not thereafter act unless the defendant instructs the duty solicitor to do so in writing.[85]

Next, the duty solicitor is under a specific obligation to advise defendants in custody who wish to be assisted by the duty solicitor. The duty solicitor must also make a bail application for such defendants unless such assistance has been received on a previous occasion. Finally, for defendants in custody, the duty solicitor must provide representation on a guilty plea where the defendant wishes the case to be concluded at that appearance unless the duty solicitor considers that the case should be adjourned in the interests of justice or of the defendant or the defendant has previously received such assistance on the same charge.[86] However, the duty solicitor should not provide representation in committal proceedings or on a not guilty plea or, except in circumstances the duty solicitor considers exceptional, representation in connection with a non-imprisonable offence.[87]

05–16   So far as bailed defendants are concerned, the duty solicitor must provide advice and, if in the opinion of the duty solicitor the defendant requires it,

---

[80] *ibid.* 49–52.
[81] *ibid.* 25(7).
[82] Legal Adivce and Assistance (Scope) Regulations 1989, reg. 7(2).
[83] *ibid.* reg. 7(1).
[84] Duty Solicitor Arrangements 49(1).
[85] *ibid.* 49(2).
[86] *ibid.* 50(2)(a).
[87] *ibid.* 51 (1).

representation.[88] Again, for bailed defendants, the duty solicitor must not provide representation in committal proceedings or on a not guilty plea or, except in exceptional circumstances, representation in connection with a non-imprisonable offence.[89]

Whether or not a defendant is in custody, the duty solicitor must assist defendants who are before the court as a result of having failed to pay a fine or other sum or to obey an order of the court where they are at risk of imprisonment.[90] The duty solicitor must also help make an application for a legal aid order and must enquire whether the defendant wishes to instruct another solicitor and, if so, must insert the name of the other solicitor on the application form.[91]

The duty solicitor must neither represent a defendant who has been **05–17** represented by a court duty solicitor at an earlier hearing of the same case, except in connection with a failure to pay a fine,[92] or assist any defendant at a sitting where the duty solicitor or a member of his firm is representing the Crown Prosecution Service in the same courtroom.[93] Finally, the duty solicitor must remain at court until it is clear, preferably after consulting the clerk, that no further defendants require assistance.[94]

SERVICE PROVIDED BY POLICE STATION DUTY SOLICITOR

Where a suspect has been detained, the custody officer at the police station **05–18** must inform him of certain specified rights including "the right to consult privately with a solicitor . . . and the fact that independent legal advice is available free of charge".[95] The suspect must also be given a written notice setting out these rights in more detail.[96] The notice explains that the suspect can obtain advice from a named ("own") solicitor, the duty solicitor or a solicitor chosen from a list. The police may use the Law Society's *Solicitors' Regional Directory* for the latter purpose. Posters must also be prominently displayed in the charging area of every police station.[97] Suspects must also be reminded of their right to free legal advice at specified stages as the investigation progresses.[98]

---

[88] *ibid.* 50(2)(c).
[89] *ibid.* 51(1).
[90] *ibid.* 50(2)(b).
[91] *ibid.* 50(2)(d).
[92] *ibid.* 51(2).
[93] *ibid.* 51(3).
[94] *ibid.* 52.
[95] Code of Practice C, para. 3.1(ii) made under the Police and Criminal Evidence Act 1984, s.66.
[96] Code of Practice C, para. 3.2.
[97] *ibid.* para. 6.3.
[98] *ibid.* para. 6.5.

About one-third of suspects ask for a solicitor.[99] Of these, two-thirds ask for a named solicitor and one-third for the duty solicitor. Advice at police stations is not subject to any means testing[1] and no contribution is payable. This applies whether the suspect asks for an "own" solicitor or for the duty solicitor. If the suspect requests an "own" solicitor the police will try to contact that solicitor. It is the responsibility of the "own" solicitor as to how the advice is given, *i.e.* it may be given by the solicitor or by a clerk. The latter must be a "competent and responsible representative of his who is employed in his office or is otherwise under his immediate supervision and who may have to be registered under the accreditation scheme".[2]

Research for the Board found that training for advising at the police station was poor, haphazard and inadequate. Such work was downgraded to something that almost anyone in the office could be sent out on. Advice tended to be routinised rather than personal to the individual case and client and legal representatives were generally passive in their behaviour at the police station.[3] Discussions between the Board and the Law Society have resulted in the introduction of an accreditation scheme which is referred to above.

05–19   Where the suspect asks for the duty solicitor, the police are required to contact the Board's telephone referral service. The telephone referral service has in its computer details of each of the 380 or so police station schemes which cover England and Wales 24 hours a day, 365 days a year. There will either be a rota or panel in operation. Where a rota is in operation, a named duty solicitor will be on duty. The details of who is on the rota and at what time will have been supplied to the telephone referral service by the local scheme. When a panel is in operation, the telephone referral service goes through the list of duty solicitors on the panel which has been supplied by the local scheme, telephoning each one in turn until finding one willing to take the case. Arrangements are made to ensure a fair distribution of offers of cases to the panel duty solicitors.

Typically, rota schemes are used in connection with the busier schemes and panels for the less busy. However, this is not invariably the case as some very busy schemes use a panel during office hours as this avoids any duty solicitors having to hold themselves available when they may need to be in court. Many schemes operate a combination of both rota and panel, *e.g.* panel during office hours and rota at other times. Statistical information from the telephone referral service ensures that any scheme not providing an adequate service in terms of making a duty solicitor speedily available

---

[99] "Changing the Code: Police Detention under the Revised PACE Codes of Practice", Home Office Research Study 129 (1992) HMSO.
[1] Legal Advice and Assistance Regulations 1989, reg. 6(4).
[2] *ibid.* reg. 20.
[3] Research commissioned by the Legal Aid Board from Dr. Jacqueline Hodgson of Warwick University and see L.S. Gaz., September 2, 1992.

is identified and steps taken to resolve any problem. The Board may also influence the use of a rota as rota duty solicitors are entitled to a standby payment and a target is set for schemes with a view to ensuring that there is a balance between the cost of standby and the number of suspects assisted.

The Board's Duty Solicitor Arrangements set out detailed requirements **05–20** as to the responsibilities of police station duty solicitors. A duty solicitor on rota is obliged to accept a case referred by the telephone referral service unless already engaged with another suspect.[4] The rota duty solicitor or panel duty solicitor who has accepted a case must personaly provide initial advice by speaking directly to the suspect on the telephone unless the solicitor is at or near the police station in which case the advice can be given in person. Note that the initial telephone advice can only be given by the duty solicitor personally and that the advice must be given direct to the suspect. A conversation with the custody officer but not the suspect would not constitute compliance with this requirement. However, if the suspect is incapable — by reason of drunkeness or violent behaviour — of speaking to the duty solicitor, i.e. the police cannot bring him to the telephone, the initial advice can be postponed. In these circumstances, the duty solicitor must make arrangements to provide initial advice as soon as the suspect is capable of speaking to the solicitor.[5]

Next, the duty solicitor must tell the suspect, in specified circumstances, that he will attend the police station unless the solicitor is of the opinion that there are exceptional circumstances for not doing so in which case the solicitor must explain the circumstances to the suspect. The specified circumstances referred to are where the suspect has been arrested in connection with an arrestable offence[6] and the police intend to interview the suspect, where the police intend to hold an identity parade or where the suspect complains of serious maltreatment by the police.[7] If an interview is postponed until the solicitor is no longer on duty, he must make arrangements to ensure that the suspect's request is fulfilled either by continuing to act as a duty solicitor or by arranging for the suspect to receive advice from another duty solicitor.[8] In addition, where the suspect is to be charged with an arrestable offence, the duty solicitor must advise on the implications of the caution given when the suspect is charged.[9]

If the circumstances specified above do not apply, the duty solicitor exercises his discretion whether it is in the interests of the suspect to attend the police station. In assessing whether attendance is necessary in these circumstances the solicitor must have regard to whether advice can be

---

[4] Duty Solicitor Arrangements 53(1).
[5] ibid. 53(2).
[6] Police and Criminal Evidence Act 1984, s.24.
[7] ibid. 54(1).
[8] ibid. 54(3).
[9] Code of Practice C, para. 16.2 and Duty Solicitor (Amendment No. 2) Arrangements 1995.

provided over the telephone with sufficient confidentiality to deal adequately with the matter. Where the suspect is a juvenile or person at risk there is a presumption in favour of attendance.[10]

05–21   Although the duty solicitor is always obliged to give the initial advice to the suspect[11] any subsequent advice including attendances at the police may be delegated to a duty solicitor representative provided that the use of such a representative is allowed on the relevant scheme,[12] the representative has been selected by the local duty solicitor committee[13] and that the representative is employed by the duty solicitor's firm.[14] The local committee may decide only to select solicitors as representatives; typically solicitors who may not have sufficient experience to apply to become a duty solicitor.[15] Only half the police station schemes allow the use of representatives; in the other schemes all duty solicitor functions must be carried out by the duty solicitor personally and may not be delegated.

There are some provisos to be observed where the use of a representative is permitted. The representative must be able to attend the police station within 45 minutes and the suspect must be informed before the advice is given of the status of the representative.[16]

05–22   Special restrictions apply to services persons at a services establishment. In such cases, only a duty solicitor or a representative who is a solicitor[17] can provide assistance in connection with an investigation by the services police and where the suspect is suspected of offences contrary to the Services Discipline Acts where the investigation involves offences which cannot be dealt with summarily or the offence appears to the services police to be serious.[18] There must be a personal attendance on the suspect where the duty solicitor considers such attendance necessary for the protection of the suspect's interests.[19]

The duty solicitor may offer to continue to act for the suspect subject to telling the suspect that he is entitled to instruct any solicitor in similar terms to those required of court duty solicitors.[20]

---

[10] *ibid.* 55.
[11] *ibid.* 53(2).
[12] *ibid.* 26(4).
[13] *ibid.* 44 *et seq.*
[14] *ibid.* 45(1)(a), 57.
[15] *ibid.* 26(5).
[16] *ibid.* 57.
[17] *ibid.* 57.
[18] *ibid.* 56.
[19] *ibid.* 56.
[20] *ibid.* 58.

COURT DUTY SOLICITOR REMUNERATION

Court duty solicitors are paid for the time they spend at court irrespective **05–23** of the number of defendants they assist or, indeed, if they assist any at all. Only one form has to be completed and the names of any defendants assisted complete with brief details about them and the service provided is entered together with the period of time spent at court acting as as duty solicitor and, where claimable, travel time and expenses.

Duty solicitors required to be in attendance at court claim from the time they arrive at court to the time they depart except for any time spent acting for one of their own clients. They cannot normally claim for travel time and expenses as, by being required to be at court under an attendance scheme, their place of work is regarded as being at court. However, on a Saturday, Sunday or Bank Holiday an attendance duty solicitor can claim for the time[21] and expense[22] of travel from office or home to the court. In addition, the duty solicitor is entitled to enhance the normal rate of remuneration by 25 per cent on a day which is not a business day.[23] Duty solicitors on call-in schemes can always claim for travel time and expenses[24] in addition to claiming for being in attendance.

The normal rate of remuneration for court duty solicitors is the average of the rates for preparation and advocacy[25] whilst the rate for travel is the travel and waiting rate.[26] The rate is the rate applicable on the day when the solicitor acts as duty solicitor.[27]

All claims for remuneration must be submitted within three months[28] **05–24** which can be extended for good reason.[29] Claims are subject to assessment by the Board's "determining officers", *i.e* staff responsible for assessing claims. The assessment is in two parts. First, the determining officer allows such time as is considered reasonable in respect of the work done. Secondly, the work has to have been actually and reasonably done in accordance with the duty solicitor requirements.[30] An example of a claim being reduced in connection with the first might be where the duty solicitor has spent an unnecessary amount of time at court without assisting a single defendant. An example of the second might be where the duty solicitor has

---

[21] Legal Advice and Assistance (Duty Solicitor) (Remuneration) Regulations 1989, reg. 5(1).
[22] *ibid.* reg.. 6.
[23] *ibid.* reg. 5(3).
[24] *ibid.* reg. 5(1)(b), 6.
[25] *ibid.* reg. 5(2)(a) and Legal Aid in Criminal and Care Proceedings (Costs) Regulations 1989 Sched. 1, Pt.1, para. 1(1)(a).
[26] Legal Aid in Criminal and Care Proceedings (Costs) Regulations 1989, Sched. 1, Pt. 1, para. 1(1)(a).
[27] Legal Advice and Assistance (Duty Solicitor) (Remuneration) Regulations 1989, reg. 5(2).
[28] *ibid.* reg. 4(1).
[29] *ibid.* reg. 4(3).
[30] *ibid.* reg. 5(1)(a).

provided representation in connection with non-payment of the community charge which is not a criminal offence and is not, therefore, covered by the court scheme.

05–25   If costs are allowed or increased on review or appeal, these will be authorised for payment.[31] Where they are reduced, a "notice of assessment" is completed on the claim form and, if agreed by the solicitor, the assessed amount is paid. If the solicitor is dissatisfied with the assessment the solicitor can within 21 days of the "notice of assessment" apply to the area committee to review the decision.[32] The area committee can confirm, increase or decrease the costs.[33] If the solicitor is not satisfied with the decision, he may apply to the area committee within 21 days of the notification of the decision to certify a point of principle of general importance.[34] Where the area committee so certifies, the solicitor may within 21 days of receipt of notification appeal in writing to the Board's Costs Appeals Committee. The Committee may reverse, affirm or amend the decision of the area committee.[35]

POLICE STATION REMUNERATION

05–26   Unlike court duty solicitors, a separate "advice at police station report" costs claim form has to be completed in respect of each suspect assisted. Police station duty solicitors and own solicitors[36] use the same form. In addition, there is a separate form covering the standby payment and hotel expenses which can be claimed by duty solicitors who are on rota duty. Completed forms are submitted to the Board's area office in whose area the police station is situated.

As for the court duty solicitor scheme, the claim is assessed by a determining officer. The claim must be submitted within three months of the duty day for standby claims and the same period for advice and assistance claims.[37] The time-limit may be extended by the determining officer "for good reason".[38] The examples of good reasons given in the Board's Notes for Guidance[39] apply primarily to late submission of criminal bills, *e.g.* awaiting an account from counsel. For police station work it

---

[31] *ibid.* reg. 7(2)(a).
[32] *ibid.* reg. 8(1).
[33] *ibid.* reg. 8(2).
[34] reg. 9(1).
[35] reg. 9(3).
[36] Legal Advice and Assistance at Police Stations (Remuneration) Regulations 1989, reg. 2(1); "own solicitor" means a solicitor who gives advice and assistance . . . otherwise than as a "duty solicitor".
[37] *ibid.* reg. 4(1).
[38] *ibid.* reg. 4(3).
[39] *Legal Aid Handbook* 1995 17–23, p. 157.

should almost always be possible to submit a claim immediately the advice and assistance has been given. It is a question of fact for the determining officer to decide whether good reasons exist. If a good reason is held to exist then the claim is assessed in full.

There is clearly a real danger that the solicitor will fail to convince the determining officer that there is a good reason for late submission. In such cases the determining officer may still — the discretion remains with the determining officer — extend the time-limit but, at the same time, consider whether "it is reasonable in the circumstances to reduce the costs".[40] The solicitor must be given an opportunity to show why the costs should not be reduced. The amount of the reduction is likely to be related to how late the claim has been submitted.

Assuming the claim has been submitted in time, the determining officer **05–27** has to consider the claim and any accompanying information.[41] The latter may typically be a covering letter perhaps explaining why a lengthy attendance at the police station was necessary. The determining officer must then consider the claim and may allow for the following classes of work done:[42]

    (a) rota availability, *i.e.* a claim for the standby payment;
    (b) advice and assistance given to a suspect under arrest;
    (c) a volunteer[43];
    (d) travel and waiting;
    (e) advice and assistance over the telephone;
    (f) routine telephone calls.

Just as for the assessment of claims from court duty solicitors, the **05–28** assessement of police station claims is in two parts. First, the determining officer must allow such work as appears to have been actually and reasonably done classifying it under the classes set out above. Secondly, he allows such time in respect of each class of work as he considers reasonable.[44] For telephone calls, the first consideration only applies. If they were "actually and reasonably done" they are subject to a fixed payment and the second consideration does not, therefore, apply. In schemes where it is permissible for the duty solicitor to deploy a representative and the representative has been selected by the local committee, the work of the representative is claimed at the duty solicitor rate.[45] The costs allowed are set out in the Schedule to the Legal Advice and Assistance at Police Stations (Remuneration) Regulations 1989.[46] The claim can also include travel

---

[40] Legal Advice and Assistance at Police Stations (Remuneration) Regulations 1989, reg. 4(4).
[41] *ibid.* reg. 5(2).
[42] *ibid.* reg. 5(1).
[43] "'Volunteer' means a person who . . . attends voluntarily at a police station or any other place where constable is present . . . without having been arrested"; *ibid.* reg. 2(1).
[44] *ibid.* reg. 5(2).
[45] The definition of "duty solicitor" includes a representative; *ibid* reg. 2(1).
[46] *ibid.* Sched. 16(1).

expenses which will be subjected to an "actually and reasonably incurred" test provided that costs for travel time have been allowed[47] and also disbursements which are subject to the same test.[48] Disbursements may include, for instance, medical and interpreters' fees.

05–29   As advice and assistance at police stations is an offshoot of the Green Form Scheme there is a limit on the costs and expenses which can be incurred.[49] The limit — which has not been increased since the police station scheme was introduced in 1986 — is £90.[50] The limit does not include value added tax and does not apply to the standby payment which is, in any case, not claimed on the advice at police stations claim form. However, this limit can be retrospectively extended where the determining officer is satisfied that the assistance was required in the interests of justice to be given as a matter of urgency.[51] It is important that the solicitor completes the relevant section of the claim form to explain why it was considered necessary to exceed the £90 limit. Failure to do so may result in the claim being returned. Inevitably, as the £90 limit has not been increased, a large number of cases where there is an attendance at the police station will result in the limit being exceeded. This has, in practice, caused no real problems. The limit does not apply to franchisees[52]

If costs are increased these will be authorised for payment.[53] Where the determining officer considers the costs claimed should be reduced, a special form is completed to advise the solicitor of the revised figure. The revised amount is paid and any additional payment resulting from a review is paid at a later date.

05–30   A separate form has to be completed in respect of the standby claim and hotel expenses. The standby claim is only claimable by duty solicitors on rota. The form is completed with details of the period on duty which should not exceed 24 hours per standby claim form. The form has to be submitted with any advice at police stations claim forms which relate to the period of time covered by the rota duty. The reason for this is that the standby fee has to be reduced by the amount of fees paid in respect of police station advice and assistance given by the duty solicitor during the duty period up to a maximum of one half of the fees allowed for advice and assistance.[54] The reduction in the standby fee does not apply to franchisees.[55] In addition, if the solicitor has undertaken court duty solicitor work during the police station duty period, the court duty solicitor claim form also has to

---

[47] *ibid.* reg. 5(4)(b).
[48] *ibid.* reg. 5(4)(c).
[49] *ibid.* reg. 5(5)(1).
[50] Legal Aid and Assistance Regulations 1989, reg. 4(1)(a).
[51] *ibid.* reg. 5(6).
[52] *ibid.* reg. 5(7).
[53] *ibid.* reg. 6(2).
[54] *ibid.* Sched. 2.
[55] *ibid.* Sched. 2(2).

be submitted at the same time as the solicitor cannot claim costs for being a court duty solicitor and for being on standby at the same time. The same procedure which applies where the solicitor is dissatisfied with the assessment in court duty solicitor cases also applies in respect of police station claims.[56]

The standby claim form is also used by duty solicitors who have been on rota to claim hotel expenses. Such expenses may be incurred as the rota solicitor, to be selected, must be prepared to be reasonably accessible to the relevant police station whilst on duty.[57] This may sometimes result in a duty solicitor (particularly on a urban scheme where a duty solicitor's home may be at a considerable distance) having to use a hotel as a base from which to act as duty solicitor. Hotel expenses are linked to payment of the standby payment.[58]

---

[56] *ibid.* regs. 7, 8.
[57] Duty Solicitor Arrangements 33(2).
[58] Legal Advice at Police Stations (Remuneration) Regulations 1989, reg. 5(4)(a).

Chapter 6

FINANCIAL ELIGIBILITY, CONTRIBUTION AND ASSESSMENT AND REASSESSMENT OF RESOURCES

INTRODUCTION

06–01 Civil legal aid means "representation"[1] under Part IV of the 1988 Act. To receive civil legal aid a person must be financially eligible. The financial eligibility criteria are prescribed by Regulations. There is a maximum disposable income limit above which civil legal aid cannot be granted. There is an upper disposable capital limit above which civil legal aid will be refused if the Area Director considers that the person could afford to proceed without legal aid. The Regulations also make provision for contributions to the Fund out of disposable income and disposable capital above prescribed limits.

   When an Area Director receives an application for legal aid, regulation 18(1) of the Civil Legal Aid (General) Regulations 1989 requires him to refer so much of it as is relevant (in practice this generally means Form CLA4A setting out the applicant's means but other information may sometimes be relevant and there is a section of Form CLA4A for the provision of "extra information") to the Assessment Officer.[2]

   "Assessment Officer" is defined in regulation 3 of the Civil Legal Aid (General) Regulations 1989 and means a person authorised by the Secretary of State to assess disposable income and disposable capital and maximum contribution of the "person concerned". In practice, assessment of financial eligibility is carried out by the Benefits Agency Legal Aid Assessment Office at Preston.[3] Almost without exception, assessments are carried out entirely

---

[1] "Representation" is defined in the 1988 Act s. 2(4).
[2] This provision is subject to the Legal Aid Act 1988, s. 15(3B)-(30) — Children Act 1989 cases where civil legal aid must be granted whatever the applicant's means.
[3] The address of the DSS Assessment Office is: Benefits Agency, Legal Aid Assessment Office, Albert Edward House, No. 3 The Pavilions, Ashton-on-Ribble, Preston, PR2 2PA.

by post, the applicant completing appropriate forms supplying financial information.

The financial resources of an assisted person remain relevant throughout the life of a legal aid certificate — until it is discharged or revoked. Until the certificate is discharged or revoked, the assisted person's means may be reassessed and further contributions from disposable income or disposable capital may be called for.

Outside the "period of computation"

THE 1988 ACT

Civil legal aid is covered by Part IV of the 1988 Act (sections 14 to 18). **06–02** These sections cover the following areas:

Section 15(1) of the 1988 Act deals with financial eligibility for civil legal aid ("representation" under Part IV) and sections 15(6), 16(1)–(4) deal with the financial contribution which an assisted person may have to pay to the Board.[4] Section 15(1) provides:

"Subject to subsections (2) to (3D) below, representation under this Part for the purposes of proceedings to which this Part applies shall be available to any person whose financial resources are such as under regulations,[5] make him eligible for representation under this Part."

Section 15(6) provides:

"Except in so far as he is required under section 16 to make a contribution, a legally assisted person shall not be required to make any payment in respect of representation under this Part and it shall be for the Board to pay the solicitor for acting for him and to pay any fees of counsel for so acting."

Section 16(1) provides:

"A legally assisted person shall, if his financial resources are such as,

---

[4] Legal Aid Act 1988, s. 15(2) and (3) deal respectively with the first and second limbs of the merits test. The Legal Aid Act 1988 requires that, as well as being financially eligible, to be granted legal aid an applicant must have a case which is worth taking or defending. There are special provisions for Children Act 1989 proceedings. S. 15(4) provides that the Board may grant representation under Part IV with or without limitations and may amend, withdraw or revoke such representation. S. 5(3A)-(3E) make special provision for applications for legal aid for proceedings under the Children Act 1989.

[5] The Regulations dealing with financial eligibility under Part IV of the 1988 Act are the Civil Legal Aid (Assessment of Resources) Regulations 1989. These Regulations deal with financial eligibility and with the financial contributions which must be made by legally assisted persons.

under regulations,[6] make him liable to make such a contribution, pay to the Board a contribution in respect of the costs of his being represented under this part."

Section 16(2) provides:

"The contribution to be required of him by the Board shall be determined by the Board in accordance with the regulations and may take the form of periodical payments or one or more capital sums or both."

Section 16(3) provides:

"The contribution required of a person may, in the case of periodical payments, be made payable by reference to the period during which he is represented under this Part or any shorter period and, in the case of a capital sum, be made payable by instalments."[7]

Section 16(4) provides:

"If the total contribution made by a person in respect of any proceedings exceeds the net liability of the Board on his account, the excess shall be repaid to him."

THE CIVIL LEGAL AID (ASSESSMENT OF RESOURCES) REGULATIONS 1989

Introduction

06–03 These Regulations follow from sections 15(1) and 16(1)–(4) of the 1988 Act. They provide for the assessment of means and, if appropriate, the assessment of contribution of the "person concerned".

---

[6] Under the Legal Aid Act 1974, the financial eligibility limits and scale of contributions were prescribed in the Act. These were uprated annually by amending the Act. In practice, the contributions from capital were paid in one instalment and contributions from income were paid in 12 instalments over the 12 months following the Area Director's notification by the Legal Aid Accounts Department of receipt of the signed "offer" of legal aid with the first instalment (signifying acceptance of the "offer"). There was no reference to the possibility of contributions being "payable by reference to the period during which he is represented". It is likely that this option was introduced partly because of the rising cost of the Fund, partly because it might encourage the legally assisted persons to press their solicitors to attempt to conclude proceedings more quickly and partly because it would mean that a legally assisted person would be even more like a private litigant, while still having to pay no more than he could afford.

[7] In fact, because of the provisions of ss. 15(4) and 15(9), the contribution may not be only "in respect of the costs of his being represented under this Act". If the Board has paid the legally assisted person's solicitor for associated work carried out under a Green Form, then, on the issue of the legal aid certificate, the legally assisted person's account is immediately in deficit by the amount paid because of the provision of 15(9). The provision of 15(4) means that it is the surplus of contribution over the net liability as defined by 15(9) which

Regulation 3 provides:
"'person concerned'" means the person:
  (a) whose disposable income and disposable capital are to be assessed or reassessed; or
  (b) whose resources are to be treated as the resources of any person under these Regulations."
Although the "person concerned" will, in most cases, be the applicant for legal aid, this will not always be so. For example, regulation 7 provides that (unless he or she has a contrary interest) the resources of the applicant's spouse or cohabitant shall be treated as his or her resources.[8]

Computation of (disposable) capital, (disposable) income and maximum contribution — introduction

Regulation 4 requires the "Assessment Officer"[9] (of the Benefits Agency) to take into account the financial resources of the person concerned and to compute his income and capital in accordance with Schedules 2 and 3 to the Regulations. **06–04**

The term "disposable" means the amount of income and/or capital, as the case may be, which is available for the making of a contribution after the person concerned's income and capital have been computed in accordance with Schedules 2 and 3.[10]

In short "disposable" means the totality of income or capital after computation in accordance with the Regulations.

Regulation 4(4) specifies the amounts of disposable capital and disposable income above which contribution from the excess must be made

---

can be returned to the legally assisted person — not the surplus over the legal aid certificate (work under the legal aid certificate is properly "representation" under Part IV or "civil legal aid"). This means that the legal aid contribution will sometimes have to be used to pay for work carried out under a Green Form, despite the fact that s. 16(1) provides for the contribution to be made "in respect of the costs of his being *represented* under *this Part*'".

[8] Before amendment by the Civil Legal Aid (Assessment of Resources) (Amendment) Regulations 1990 (S.I. 1990 No. 484) which removed reg. 8. Reg. 8 provided that, subject to exceptions, where an application for legal aid:

  "is made by or on behalf of a child who is under the upper limit of compulsory school age, the resources of any person —
    (a) who is responsible in law for maintaining the child; and
    (b) "with whom the child is living or would normally live shall be assessed as taken into account in addition to the child's resources."

[9] "Assessment Officer" means a person authorised by the Secretary of State to assess the disposable income, disposable capital and maximum contribution of the person concerned; Civil Legal Aid (General) Regulations 1989, reg. 3

[10] If the Assessment Officer assesses these as "nil", this means that the financial resources of the person concerned are below those prescribed (above which a contribution is payable) by *ibid.* reg. 4(4) and are, therefore, below the eligibility limits fixed by *ibid.* reg. 4(2) and (3).

by a person who would like to receive legal aid. Although amounts of income and/or capital below such amounts are "available for the making of a contribution", regulation 4(4) provides that a contribution is payable only when the person who would like to receive legal aid has income and/or capital which exceed these amounts. As at April 1, 1995 these are:

    (a) the upper disposable income limit (above which legal aid must be refused) is £7,187 (£7,920 where the application includes a claim in respect of personal injuries);

    (b) the upper disposable capital limit (above which legal aid may be refused if it appears to the Area Director that the applicant could afford to proceed without legal aid) is £6,750 (£8,560 where the application includes a claim in respect of personal injuries); and

    (c) Contributions are payable as follows — where the applicant's disposable income in the period of computation exceeds £2,425, a monthly contribution in respect of disposable income payable throughout the period while the certificate is in force of one thirty-sixth of the excess and where the applicant's disposable capital exceeds £3,000 a contribution in respect of disposable capital not greater than the excess.

Computation of income — Schedule 2 — introduction

06–05   Paragraph 1 of Schedule 2 provides:

"The income of the person concerned from any source shall be taken to be the income which that person may reasonably expect to receive (in cash or in kind) during the period of computation and, in the absence of other means of ascertaining it, shall be taken to the income received during the preceeding year."

Regulation 3 provides:

"period of computation means the period of 12 months next ensuing from the date of application for a certificate or such other period of 12 months as in the particular circumstances of any case the Assessment Officer may consider to be appropriate."[11–13]

It can therefore be seen that the income assessment is intended to be

---

[11–13] In practice the Benefits Agency is understood to use the date of the applicants' signature on Form CLA4A (statement of, financial resources) rather than the date when the application was received and then forwards form CLA4A to the DSS Assessment Office. With Form CLA4A there should also be submitted to the legal aid area office either form L17 (statement of wages) or the social security reference number with confirmation that the applicant for legal aid is in receipt social security, or, if the applicant for legal aid is self-employed, the audited accounts for the previous year.

forward looking for a period of 12 months but that the Assessment Officer "in the absence of other means of ascertaining it" shall take this as the income received during the preceeding year. When the person concerned is self-employed, the Assessment Officer will usually compute income from the accounts for the last accounting period. Where the person concerned is a Schedule E taxpayer, in employment, the Assessment Officer will compute income from Form L17 wages statement which should be completed by the person concerned's employer.

Schedule 2 goes on to provide detailed directions to Assessment Officers on income which must be disregarded and on deductions which must be made in computing the income of the person concerned. Paragraph 14 is the final paragraph of the Schedule. It gives the Assessment Officer a "sweeping up" discretion. It provides:

"In computing the income from any source, there shall be disregarded such amount, if any, as the Assessment Officer considers to be reasonable having regard to the nature of the income or to any other circumstances of the case."

Computation of capital — Schedule 3 — introduction

Paragraph 1(1) of Schedule 3 provides: **06–06**

"subject to paragraph (2) and to the provisions of these Regulations, in computing the capital of the person concerned, there shall be included the amount or value of every resource of a capital nature belonging to him on the date the legal aid application is made."

It can therefore be seen that the capital assessment is not intended to be forward looking (unlike the income assessment) but to assess the position when the application for legal aid is made. This is subject to paragraph (2) which provides:

"(2) where it comes to the attention of the Assessment Officer that, between the date the legal aid application is made and the assessment, there has been a substantial fluctuation in the value of a resource or there has been a substantial variation in the nature of the resource affecting the basis of computation of its value, or any resource has ceased to exist or a new resource has come into the possession of the person concerned, the officer shall compute the capital resources of that person in the light of such facts and the resources as so computed shall be taken into account in the assessment."

Schedule 3 goes on to provide detailed directions to Assessment Officers on the valuation of assets and what must be disregarded and on the

115

treatment of debts of the person concerned. Paragraph 15 is the final paragraph of the Schedule. It gives the Assessment Officer a "sweeping up" discretion. It provides:

> "In computing the capital of the period concerned, there may also be disregarded such an amount of capital (if any) as the Assessment Officer may, in his discretion, decide having regard to all circumstances of the case."

Review of the Civil Legal Aid (Assessment of Resources) Regulations 1989

Regulation 1 — citation and commencement

06–07   This regulation says how the Regulations should be cited and that they come into force on April 1, 1989.

Regulation 2 — revocations

06–08   This regulation revokes all previous Regulations concerned with the assessment of resources for civil legal aid otherwise in force.

Regulation 3 — interpretation

06–09   Parts of this interpretation regulation require comment.

(a) Many of the "definitions" are taken from the Civil Legal Aid (General) Regulations 1989;

(b) "Area Committee", "Area Director" and "Assessment Officer" have the meanings assigned to them by regulation 3 of the Civil Legal Aid (General) Regulations 1989. This provides:

> "'Area Committee' means an Area Committee appointed by the Board in accordance with regulation 4.
>
> 'Area Director' means an Area Director appointed by the Board in accordance with regulation 4 and includes any person duly authorised to act on his behalf.
>
> 'Assessment officer' means a person authorised by the Secretary of State to assess the disposable *income, disposable capital and maximum contribution* of the person concerned."

By section 4 of the 1988 Act, the Board has wide powers to enable it to discharge its functions under the 1988 Act including the general function, prescribed by section 3(2) of securing that advice, assistance and representation are available in accordance with the 1988 Act and of administering the 1988 Act. Paragraph 11(2) of Schedule 1 to the 1988 Act provides:

"The Board may make such arrangements as it considers appropriate for the discharge of its functions, including the delegation of specified functions and shall make such arrangements for the delegation of functions to committees and persons as may be prescribed."

This enables the Board in practice to discharge many of its functions to "Area Committees" or to "Area Directors".

(c) A "child" is defined as a person under 16 years old (i.e. "under the age that is for the time being the upper limit of compulsory school age within the meaning of the Education Act 1944") or, being over that age, either "receiving full-time instruction at an education establishment or undergoing training for a trade, profession or vocation. The meaning of "full-time" of what is meant by "training" is not set out in the Regulations.[14]

(d) "Income", as well as including benefits and privileges also includes "any sum payable (whether voluntarily or under a court order, the terms of any instrument or otherwise) for the purpose of the maintenance of a child."

(e) "Period of computation" is the period used for the calculation of income and is the period of 12-months next-ensuring from the date of application for a certificate or such other period of 12 months as in the particular circumstances of any case the Assessment Officer may consider to be appropriate.

(f) "Person concerned" see Introduction

Regulation 4 — computation of disposable income, disposable capital and contribution

Regulation 4(1) requires the Assessment Officer to take into account the financial resources and compute the income and capital of the person concerned.   **06–10**

---

[14] The significance of the meaning of "child" diminished with the introduction of the Civil Legal Aid (Assessment of Resources) (Amendment) Regulations 1990 which omitted reg. 8. Reg. 8 provided broadly for the means of parents or guardians to be taken into account when assessing a child's means. The financial resources of children are now assessed like those of any other applicant for legal aid. Minors and children do not, however, have to complete their own forms of application. Reg. 16 of the Civil Legal Aid (General) Regulations 1989 provides for applications to be made on their behalf (though any certificate issued will be in the minor's or child's name). If any minor or child fails to provide the necessary information to the Assessment Officer, this, too, can be provided on the minor's or child's behalf and will be acceptable to the DSS Assessment Officer.

117

Regulation 4(2) provides:

"Subject to paragraph (3) below, legal aid shall be available to a person whose disposable income does not exceed £7,187 a year but a person may be refused legal aid where:
(a) his disposable capital exceeds £6,750; and
(b) it appears to the Area Director that he could afford to proceed without legal aid."

Regulation 4(3) provides:

"Where the subject-matter of the dispute in respect of which the legal aid application has been made includes a claim in respect of personal injuries.[15] Legal aid shall be available to a person whose disposable income does not exceed £7,920 a year but a person may be refused legal aid where:
(a) his disposable capital exceeds £8,560; and
(b) it appears to the Area Director that he could afford to proceed without legal aid."

Regulation 4(4) provides:

"A person who desires to receive legal aid shall be liable to make the following contributions —
(a) where his disposable income in the period of computation exceeds £2,425, a monthly contribution in respect of disposable income payable throughout the period while the certificate is in force of one thirty-sixth of the excess;
(b) where his disposable capital exceeds £3,000, a contribution in respect of disposable capital not greater than the excess.

Regulation 5 — subject matter of dispute

06–11 Regulation 5 concerns the "subject-matter of the dispute" in respect of which the legal aid application has been made and provides that the value

---

[15] "Personal injuries", by reg. 4(5), "includes any death and any disease or other impairment of a person's physical or mental condition". The higher limits apply provided the claim *includes* such a claim. It need not be the main element of the claim. Thus, claims for damages for assault/trespass and an injunction, where what is really sought is the protection of an injunction, may nevertheless be included. No definitive list has been prepared of what does and does not come within the term "personal injury" and borderline cases may be referred to the Area Director. A very high proportion of legally aided personal injury actions are succesful. They result in damages and/or costs being recovered. In such cases, the Board will usually recover all money expended on the assisted person's account (the solicitors/ barristers charges or fees) through the operation of the statutory charge or under the order for costs. Having higher financial eligibility limits in respect of personal injury actions has therefore, only a limited impact on the overall legal aid budget.

of it must be excluded in computing the income or capital of the person concerned. For example, if two parties are in dispute over the ownership of a plot of land or of money credited to an account, and either of them applies for legal aid, the value of the asset in dispute must be excluded by the Assessment Officer when he computes disposable capital. There is a link between the "subject-matter of the dispute" and the property which is subject to the charge under section 16(6) of the 1988 Act. If, at the outset, the applicant indicates that certain property is the subject-matter of the dispute, it is very likely, when the proceedings are concluded, to be determined to have been "in issue in the proceedings" and so potentially subject to the statutory charge if it is recovered or preserved.

Regulation 6 — application in representative, fiduciary or official capacity

Regulation 6 concerns applications made by a person who is concerned in the proceedings *only*, in a representative fiduciary or official capacity.[16] Persons within these categories will include, *e.g.* trustees or personal representatives of a deceased, who would come within the meaning of the terms "fiduciary" and "representative". "Official" might cover such persons as the Official Receiver. **06–12**

Regulation 6(a) requires the Assessment Officer in computing the income and capital of such a person and the amount of any contribution to be made to:

"Where so requested by the Area Director, assess the value of any property or estate or the amount of any fund out of which that person is entitled to be indemnified and the disposable income, disposable capital and maximum contribution of any persons (including that person if appropriate), who might benefit from the outcome of the proceedings;".

The Area Director is required by regulation 33 of the Civil Legal Aid (General) Regulations 1989 to take into account such resources and, in practice, the Assessment Officer will assess the personal resources of the applicant if he stands to benefit from the outcome of the proceedings as would, *e.g.* a personal representative who is also a beneficiary under the deceased's will. Regulation 6(b) provides that, otherwise, the personal resources of such a person must be disregarded.

---

[16] Reg. 33 is corresponding regulation in the Civil Legal Aid (General) Regulations 1989 relating to such applications.

Regulation 7 — resources of spouses etc

06–13 Regulation 7 provides for the aggregation of resources — both of spouses' resources and of the resources of "a man and a woman who are living with each other in the same household as husband and wife."[17] There is no aggregation, however, if the spouses or cohabitants have a "contrary interest" in the dispute in respect of which the legal aid application is made. One question on Form CLA4A is "is your partner your opponent in the case you are applying for legal aid for", and, in practice it is from the answer to this question that, in the absence of other information, the Assessment Officer will decide whether there is a contrary interest. An example might be a wife taking proceedings against her husband for damages for injuries sustained in a road traffic accident where the husband was the driver and the wife a passenger. It is not inconceivable that there could be other situations (*i.e.* where the partner is not the opponent in the proceedings) where there are genuine contrary interests. If so, they should be specifically drawn to the Area Director's attention.

Regulation 8 — resources of an applicant who is a child

06–14 Regulation 8, which deals with the assessment of resources of a child applicant was omitted by the Civil Legal Aid (Assessment of Resources) (Amendment) Regulations 1990.

Regulation 9 — deprivation or conversion of resources

06–15 The purpose of regulation 9 is to prevent abuses. It is the intent of the person concerned which is important. The regulation really needs little explanation. The words "whether for the purposes for making himself eligible for legal aid, reducing his liability to pay a contribution towards legal aid *or otherwise*' ' were added by the Civil Legal Aid (Assessment of Resources) (Amendment) Regulations 1990. The regulation prevents applicants from benefiting by using disposable capital to reduce their mortgage debt.[18]

Regulation 10 — notification of the assessment officer's decision

06–16 Regulation 10 deals with notification of the assessment officer's decision. In practice, the Assessment Officer sends Form L2 to the area office. It will

---

[17] Gay or lesbian couples do not come within this form of words as they are not respectively "a man and a woman".

[18] The conversion of an existing overdraft into a personal loan repayable within 12 months would not usually fall foul of regulation 9 (repayments of a loan over 12 months are off set

show the disposable capital, disposable income and maximum contribution. Where the financial resources of the person concerned are such that if income or capital are below the amount set out in regulation 4(4) — above which a contribution is required — the form will simply say "below". Where the applicant is in receipt of income support, this will be stated and, in either case, the maximum contribution will be shown as nil.[19]

The fact that the information is communicated in this limited way does not mean that more detailed information is not retained by the Assessment Officer. If an applicant wishes to question the assessment he or his solicitor may ask the Area Director for a breakdown of it, which the Area Director will, in turn, request from the Assessment Officer.

Regulation 11 — duty of the person concerned to report change in financial circumstances

Regulation 11 is primarily concerned with reassessment and should be looked at in conjunction with regulations 66, 67 and 68 of the Civil Legal Aid (General) Regulations 1989. Regulation 11 obliges the "person concerned" to inform the Area Director. The assisted person (who in most, but not all, cases will be the "person concerned") is under a similar obligation by virtue of regulation 66 of the General Regulations to inform his solicitor. When a solicitor is given information about a change in his client's financial circumstances, unless he knows that it will not affect the client's contribution or the continuation of the certificate he should forthwith inform the Area Director who will then decide whether to inform the Assessment Officer.[20]

06–17

Regulation 12 — further assessments (and "old" regulations 12 and 13 reassessments and further assessments)

Regulation 12 provides for further assessments of means while a legal aid certificate is in force. At any time while a certificate is in force, where it

06–18

---

against income — an overdraft is not off set against capital). However, the transfer of assets from an account is credit to one in deficit is unlikely to be effective as a means of reducing disposable capital in the account is credit.

[19] Sched. 3, para. 7 (computation of capital) provides:

"Where the person concerned or his spouse is in receipt of income support paid under the Social Security Act 1986, the person concerned shall, for the period during which income support is received, be deemed to have disposal capital not exceeding the figure for the time being specified in Regulation 4(4)(b)."

[20] If disposable income or disposable capital have changed by at least the amounts set out in reg. 12 of the Civil Legal Aid (Assessment of Resources) Regulations 1989 there is likely to be a reassessment of means leading to an increased or decreased contribution.

appears that the person concerned's means may have altered by his disposable income having increased by more than £750 or decreased by more than £300, or his disposable capital having increased by more than £750 or if the Area Director considers that his financial circumstances are such that he could afford to proceed without legal aid, the assessment officer will make a further assessment of the disposable capital, income or maximum contribution, as the case may be.

For the purposes of the further assessment, the period of computation (*i.e.* the period used to calculate income) is the 12 months following the date it was requested (or such other period of 12 months as the assessment officer may consider to be appropriate); the amount and value of every resource of a capital nature acquired since the date of the legal aid application is calculated as at the date it was received.

However, where the original period of computation began before April 12, 1993 and/or the certificate was granted before April 12, 1993, the position is governed by "old" regulations 12 and 13. The combined effect of these "old" regulations is as follows:

(a) Within the original computation period, in respect of income, means may be reassessed with a view to increasing or decreasing the contribution and/or to discharging the certificate; in respect of capital, means may be reassessed with a view to increasing the contribution and/or to discharging the certificate.

(b) Outside the original period of computation, in respect of income, means may be further assessed only with a view to discharging the certificate; in respect of capital, means may be further assessed or reassessed with a view to increasing the contribution and/or to discharging the certificate.

06–19   Old regulation 12 provides for reassessment of means on a change of financial circumstances, whether the change of circumstances is within or outside the period of computation. It obliges the Assessment Officer to carry out a reassessment unless it appears to him unlikely that any significant change in the liability of the person concerned to make a contribution would result from such a reassessment. Whereas on an application for legal aid, paragraph 1 of Schedule 3 to the Regulations provides that it is the capital held on the date the legal aid application is made which is relevant, regulation 12(2) provides that on a reassessment it is the value of capital received since the legal aid application on the date of its receipt which is relevant.

An "old" regulation 12 reassessment may lead to no action or, during the period of computation, in respect of income, to an increase or decrease in the contribution and/or to discharge of the certificate and, in respect of capital, to an increase (never to a decrease) in contribution or to the discharge of the certificate. There can be no decrease in the capital contribution because it is capital at the date of the legal aid application or the date of subsequent receipt of capital which is relevant. Outside the original periods of computation a reassessment may lead to no action or, in respect of income, to the discharge of the certificate and, in the case of capital, to an increased contribution and/or the discharge of the certificate.

"Old" regulation 13 makes specific provision for a further assessment **06–20** outside the original period of computation where the Area Director considers that the circumstances of the person concerned are such that he could afford to proceed without legal aid. A further assessment under regulation 13 is prospective. An income reassessment under "old" regulation 12, in contrast, is concerned with income during the original period of computation. As such, an "old" regulation 12 reassessment is a reworking of the original assessment. Such a reassessment may lead to a greater or lesser contribution being computed than that already determined or if the disposable income is sufficiently high, to the discharge of the certificate. A further assessment under "old" regulation 13 is a fresh assessment and the period of computation for such an assessment is, by "old" regulation 13(2)(a), the period of 12 months following the date of the Area Director's request. It follows that in respect of income such an assessment is concerned with income during that further period and can lead to "no change" or to the discharge of the certificate but cannot lead to an increased contribution from income.

"Old" regulations 12 and 13 (relating to pre April 12, 1993 cases) have **06–21** to be read with regulations 52 and 76 of the Civil Legal Aid (General) Regulations 1989. Regulation 52 concerns the Area Director's power to alter the contribution and to amend the certificate accordingly. Regulation 76 concerns the Area Director's power to discharge a certificate on financial grounds. Regulation 52(1) of the Civil Legal Aid (General) Regulations 1989 gives the Area Director the power to request the Assessment Officer to reassess. (This would result in an "old" regulation 12 reassessment.)

Regulation 52(3) requires the Area Director to amend a certificate where he redetermines the amount payable either pursuant to regulation 52 or *otherwise*. He may, therefore, be obliged to amend the certificate to show a higher contribution following either a reassessment under "old" regulation 12 or a further assessment under "old" regulation 13. However, where the reassessment is under "old" regulation 13 and in respect of income outside the original period of computation, this cannot lead to an increased contribution.

Under the "new" regulation 12 (post April 12, 1993 cases) the position **06–22** is clearer as further assessments of eligibility and/or contribution can be made from capital and/or income at any time.

The Regulations were changed in 1993 to introduce contributions throughout the life of legal aid certificates. Before this change, assisted persons had to pay contributions from income only during the first year of their legal aid but had to pay a year's worth of such contributions even if their certificate was discharged within a year. The change also enables reassessments of, and higher contributions from, income outside the original period of contribution.

06–23   Regulation 76(1) Civil Legal Aid (General) Regulations 1989 concerns income and provides:

> "The Area Director shall discharge a certificate (other than an emergency certificate) from such date as he considers appropriate where the Assessment Officer assesses that the person to whom it was issued has disposable income of an amount which makes him ineligible for legal aid."

Under this regulation, the Area Director has a discretion as to the date of discharge of a certificate but has no discretion not to discharge a certificate. Before contributions became payable throughout the life of a legal aid certificate, this regulation applied only to income during the original period of computation. It's application was limited to the original period of computation because the determining factor is "disposable income of an amount which makes him ineligible for legal aid" and "disposable income" (by regulation 4 of the assessment of resources regulation) means the amount of income "available for the making of a contribution". Income outside the original period or computation, before contributions became payable throughout the life of a certificate, was not so available for the making of a contribution.

06–24   Regulation 76(2) Civil Legal Aid (General) Regulation 1989 concerns capital and provides:

> "The Area Director shall discharge a certificate (other than an emergency certificate) from such date as he considers appropriate where the assessment officer assesses that the person to whom it was issued, having disposable income of an amount which makes him eligible for legal aid, has disposable capital of an amount which renders him liable to be refused legal aid, and it appears to the Area Director that, without legal aid, the probable cost to him of continuing the proceedings in respect of which the certificte was issued would not exceed the contribution which would be payable."

Under this regulation, the Area Director has a discretion as to the date of discharge of a certificate. However, if the assisted person has disposable capital of an amount which renders him liable to be refused legal aid, and it appears to the Area Director that the probable cost to the assisted person of continuing the proceedings (in respect of which the certificate was issued would not exceed the contribution which would be payable, the area Director must discharge the certificate under this regulation.

06–25   Regulation 76(3) Civil Legal Aid (General) Regulation 1989 refers to "current financial circumstances". It provides:

> "Subject to section 15(3B) to (3D) of the Act, where the Area Director

considers that the current financial circumstances of the assisted person are such that he could afford to proceed without legal aid, he may, with a view to discharging the certificate, require the assessment officer to assess the assisted person's current financial resources in accordance with the Civil Legal Aid (Assessment of Resources) Regulation 1989 and may discharge the certificate from such date as he considers appropriate."

This links with Regulation 12(1)(b) requiring the Assessment Officer to make a further assessment if the Area Director considers that the current financial resources of the person concerned are such that he could afford to proceed without legal aid.

Regulation 14 — amendment of assessment due to error or receipt of new conformation

Regulation 14 requires the Assessment Officer to make an amended **06–26** assessment where there has been an error or mistake and it would be just and equitable to do so or where new information which is relevant to the assessment has come to light. A regulation 14 amended assesment is, for all purposes, substituted for the original assessment.

A regulation 14 amended assessment may lead to an increased or decreased contribution being called for. It may also lead to the discharge of a legal aid certificate if the amended assessment shows a computation of disposable income or disposable capital above the limits prescribed by regulation 4.

There is no power in the Civil Legal Aid (General) Regulations 1989 to revoke a certificate as a result of a regulation 14 amended assessment (although *e.g.* a certificate can be revoked under regulation 78 or 79 if the assisted person failed or supply relevant information). However, the power to discharge a certificate on financial grounds, which is found in regulation 76 of the Civil Legal Aid (General) Regulations 1989, enables the Area Director to discharge a certificate from "such date as he considers appropriate". In theory a regulation 14 amended assessment showing that, on financial grounds, the assisted person should not have been granted legal aid, could lead to the certificate being discharged from the date it was issued. However, the Area Directors should act reasonably and their decisions may be challenged by judiciary review. Such a discharge could prejudice the assisted person's solicitors, who would be unable to recover costs from the Board.

Regulation 15 — Power of Assessment Officer to estimate the resources of the person concerned

06–27   Regulation 15 enables the Assessment Officer, in urgent cases, to estimate the disposable income, disposable capital and contribution of the person concerned. This regulation is likely to be relevant where the Area Director is unsure whether the applicant is likely to "fulfil the conditions under which legal aid may be granted under the Act" and the Regulations[21] and so is unwilling to issue an emergency certificate. The Area Director may then use the information in the estimated assessment either to issue or refuse a substantive certificate (or an offer of such a certificate) or an emergency certificate.

When the Assessment Officer receives the additional information he requires to make a (non-estimated) assessment, that assessment is substituted for all purposes for the estimate. This could lead to an increased or decreased contribution or to the discharge of the legal aid certificate.

How the Contribution Forms Part of an Assisted Person's Account

06–28   When a legal aid certificate is issued, an applicant becomes a legally assisted person and the Board opens an account for him, in his name.

Payments into the Legal Aid Fund, *e.g.* monthly contributions from disposable income or "one-off" contributions from disposable capital, are credited to the assisted person's account. Payments out, *e.g.* payments on account of disbursements or profit costs or payment of taxed or assessed costs, are debited to the account.

Only payments of contribution actually made are credited to the account. Assessed contributions which are not paid are not credited. Also credited are any receipts of costs or of damages.

If advice or assistance under the Green Form Scheme has been given in connection with the proceedings to which the certificate relates, the account may open with an actual or potential debit balance. This is because section 16(9)(b) of the 1988 Act draws in any sums "paid or payable for any advice or assistance under Part III in connection with those proceedings or any matter to which these proceedings relate" as part of the net liability of the Fund in an assisted person's account.

Section 16(4) of the 1988 Act provides:

"If the total contribution made by a person in respect of any

---

[21] Civil Legal Aid (General) Regulations 1989, Reg. 19(2)(a).

proceedings exceeds the net liability of the Board as his account, the excess shall be repaid to him."

When the "net liability" and the "excess" are calculated any amounts paid out in respect of Green Form advice are included in the calculation. In this way, an assisted person's legal aid contribution may sometimes go towards payment for Green Form advice and assistance.

If there is a deficiency on an assisted person's account with the Board and property is recovered as preserved for him in the proceedings for which he was legally aided, section 16(6) of the 1988 Act provides that the Board has a charge on such property to the extent of such deficiency.

Chapter 7

AVAILABILITY

INTRODUCTION

07–01 Part IV of the 1988 Act (sections 14–18) is entitled "Civil Legal Aid". Schedule 2 to the 1988 Act is entitled "Civil Proceedings; Scope of Part IV Representation", which is what is provided under Part IV of the 1988 Act. The Regulations which apply to civil legal aid are:

(a) Civil Legal Aid (General) Regulations 1989;
(b) Civil Legal Aid (Assessment of Resources) Regulations 1989;
(c) Legal Aid in Family Proceedings (Remuneration) Regulations 1991;
(d) Legal Aid (Disclosure of Information) Regulations 1991;
(e) Legal Aid in Contempt Proceedings (Remuneration) Regulations 1995;
(f) Legal Aid in Civil Proceedings (Remuneration) Regulations 1994.

THE MEANING OF "REPRESENTATION" (CIVIL LEGAL AID)

07–02 Section 2(4) of the 1988 Act defines "representation":

"'Representation' means representation for the purposes of proceedings and it includes —
(a) all such assistance as is usually given by a legal representative in the steps preliminary or incidental to any proceedings;
(b) all such assistance as is usually so given in civil proceedings in arriving at or giving effect to a compromise to avoid or bring to an end any proceedings; and
(c) in the case of criminal proceedings, advice and assistance as to any appeal;

and related expressions have corresponding meanings."

Referring to "assistance", the definition of "representation" in section 2(4) of the 1988 Act also pulls in "assistance" which is defined in section 2(3) of the 1988 Act as:

"'Assistance' means assistance in taking any of the steps which a

128

person might take, including steps with respect to proceedings, having regard to the application of English law to any particular circumstances that have arisen in relation to him, whether by taking such steps on his behalf (including assistance by way of representation) or by assisting him in taking them on his own behalf."

The key point is that "representation" is representation for the purposes **07–03** of proceedings. However, this includes, "assistance" of the kind usually given by a legal representative in the steps preliminary or incidental to any proceedings and "assistance" of the kind usually given (by a legal representative for the purpose of proceedings) in arriving at or giving effect to a compromise either to avoid or to bring to an end any (prospective) proceedings.

It follows that "representation" includes work usually carried out by solicitors before proceedings are commenced and includes work involved in reaching a compromise so that proceedings are never, in fact, commenced. However, proceedings must be in prospect. Representation is "for the purposes of proceedings" and if a case is at such an early stage that it is not clear whether there will be proceedings, representation is not appropriate. Advice and assistance under the Green Form Scheme may be given.

Except for special categories of case under the Regulations and some Children Act 1989 cases specified in Section 16 of the 1988 Act, civil legal aid will not be granted unless an applicant can satisfy the "merits tests" set out in the 1988 Act and or Regulations. These include the requirement that the applicant must show that he has reasonable grounds for taking, defending or being a party to proceedings and representation will not be granted to a "potential" defendant unless proceedings have actually been commenced against him.

The term "proceedings" is not defined in the 1988 Act. Its meaning has, however, been considered by the courts in cases involving the statutory charge and cases concerning claims for costs against the Fund under section 18 of the Act (formerly section 13 of the Legal Aid Act 1974).

These cases make it clear that "proceedings" does not necessarily mean the whole action, cause or matter. It follows that an application for legal aid may be made for representation in respect of part only of an action. An application for legal aid for representation for the whole action may, similarly, be granted for only one aspect of it.

THE PROCEEDINGS FOR WHICH "REPRESENTATION" (CIVIL LEGAL AID) IS AVAILABLE BEFORE SPECIFIED COURTS OR TRIBUNALS

Civil legal aid consists of representation under Part IV of the 1988 Act. By **07–04** section 14(1) of the 1988 Act, Part IV applies as follows:

"This Part applies to such proceedings before courts or tribunals or at statutory inquiries in England and Wales as —

(a) are proceedings of a description for the time being specified in Part I of Schedule 2 to this Act, except proceedings for the time being specified in Part II of that Schedule; and

(b) are not proceedings for which representation may be granted under Part V,

and representation under this Part shall be available to any person subject to and in accordance with sections 15 and 16."

Thus, representation under Part IV is limited to proceedings before "courts", "tribunals" or "statutory inquiries". The term "courts" is not defined in the 1988 Act. The terms "tribunals" and "statutory inquiry" are defined in section 43 of the 1988 Act.

"Statutory inquiry" has the meaning assigned to it by section 19(1) of the Tribunals and Inquiries Act 1971, which provides:

"'Statutory inquiry' means —

(a) an inquiry or hearing held or to be held in pursuance of a duty imposed by any statutory provision; or

(b) an inquiry or hearing, or an inquiry or hearing of a class, designated for the purposes of this section by an order under subsection (2) of this section;".

Subsection (2) provides:

"The Lord Chancellor and the Secretary of State may by order designate for the purposes of this section any inquiry or hearing held or to be held in pursuance of a power conferred by any statutory provision specified or described in the order, or any class of such inquiries or hearings."

By section 43 of the 1988 Act "Tribunal" includes an arbitrator or umpire, however appointed, and whether the arbitration takes place under a reference by consent or otherwise.

The term "tribunal" is, therefore, not narrowly defined. Section 43 of the 1988 Act says what is included in the term but does not draw a boundary round it. An inference which may be drawn, however, is that the tribunal must be one which performs an adjudicatory role, like an arbitrator or umpire.

It is also clear that statutory tribunals fall within the definition. Indeed, civil legal aid is specifically available for proceedings before some statutory tribunals.

Section 14(1)(a) of the 1988 Act applies Part IV only to proceedings specified in Part I of Schedule 2 to the 1988 Act except for proceedings for the time being specified in Part II of that Schedule.

Description of proceedings — Part I of Schedule 2 to the 1988 Act

1. Proceedings in, or before any person to whom a case is re- **07–05** ferred in whole or in part, by any of the following courts, namely:
   (a) the House of Lords in exercise of its jurisdiction in relation to appeals from courts in England and Wales;
   (b) the Court of Appeal;
   (c) the High Court;
   (d) any county court.
2. The following proceedings in a magistrates' court, namely:
   (a) proceedings under the Guardianship of Minors Act 1971 and 1973;
   (b) proceedings under section 43 of the National Assistance Act 1948, section 22 of the Maintenance Orders Act 1950, section 4 of the Maintenance Orders Act 1958, or section 18 of the Supplementary Benefits Act 1979;
   (c) proceedings in relation to an application for leave of the court to remove a child from a person's custody under section 27 or 28 of the Adoption Act 1976 or proceedings in which the making of an order under Part II or section 29 or 55 of the Adoption Act 1976 is opposed to any Part to the proceedings;
   (d) proceedings under Part I of the Maintenance Orders (Reciprocal Enforcement) Act 1972 relating to a maintenance order made by a court of a country outside the United Kingdom;
   (e) proceedings under Part II of the Children Act 1975;
   (f) proceedings for or in relation to an order under Part I of the Domestic Proceedings and Magistrates' Courts Act 1978.
   (g) proceedings under the Children Act 1989;
   (h) appeals under section 20, where they are to be made to a magistrates' court and proceedings under section 27 of the Child Support Act 1991.
   (i) proceedings under section 30 of the Human Fertilisation and Embryology Act 1990.
3. Proceedings in the Employment Appeal Tribunal.
4. Proceedings in the Lands Tribunal.
5. Proceedings before a Commons Commissioner appointed under section 17(1) of the Commons Registration Act 1965.
6. Proceedings in the Restrictive Practices Court under Part III of the Fair Trading Act 1973, and any proceedings in that court in

consequence of an order made, or undertaking given to the court, under that Part of that Act.

Paragraph 1 of Part I of Schedule 2 differs from the other paragraphs. Paragraph 1 provides that the scope of Part IV representation is not for "proceedings in any of the following courts" but for: "proceedings in, *or before any person to whom a case is referred in whole or in part by,* any of the following courts."

It follows that if one of those courts refers a case or part of a case to any person and that person has before him "proceedings" then representation continues to be available for those "proceedings". However, the position is qualified by section 14(1) of the Act.

The position, therefore, is that if one of the paragraph 1 courts refers a case or part of a case to a "court", "tribunal" or "statutory inquiry" (as defined in section 43) in England and Wales and that "court", "tribunal" or "statutory inquiry" has before it "proceedings", then "representation" is available. There must, however, be a formal "reference" (not merely an order by consent) as otherwise, *e.g.* to transfer a case as part of a case. The Board's view is that such a reference can be made only where it is specifically provided for by Regulations or Rules of Court.

07–06   Examples of referrals where legal aid continues to be available are:

(a) In a county court, where the court refers proceedings to (small claims) arbitration (in practice, legal aid is rarely granted for small claims arbitration proceedings because the applicant is unlikely to be able to satisfy the legal aid merits test — having regard to the size of the claim and the costs involved).

(b) In any of the paragraphs, where the court makes a reference to the European Court of Justice, representation under 1988 Act continues to be available for proceedings before the European Court. In *R v. Marlborough Street Stipendiary Magistrate, ex.p Bouchereau*,[1] it was held that a criminal legal aid order issued under the Legal Aid Act 1974 covered proceedings in the European Court following a reference of an issue by the magistrates' court to that court. The basis of this decision was that proceedings in the European Court of Justice were part of the proceedings before the magistrates' court and that the costs of the European Court of Justice proceedings were recoverable in, and a matter for, the national court. In the civil proceedings outlined above, (unlike in criminal proceedings) there is specific provision for a "reference" of a case or part of a case to be made. On a practical point, it should be noted that proceedings in the European Court of Justice

---

[1] [1977] 3 All E.R 365.

at Luxembourg, following such a reference, are commonly dealt with by written representations only.

Finally, in paragraph 1 of Part 1 of Schedule 2 it is worth emphasising **07–07** that legal aid for proceedings in the House of Lords (for which a separate application for legal aid must be made except where proceedings are under the Children Act 1989 — see regulations 46(2) and 18(2) (a) of the Civil Legal Aid (General) Regulations 1989) is available only for appeals from courts in England and Wales. Thus, it is available only for proceedings where civil legal aid would, under paragraph 1, have been available in the court below. It is not available to cover appeals from Scottish or Northern Irish courts nor to cover the House of Lords Privy Council jurisdiction.

The proceedings in the magistrates' court for which legal aid is available are listed in paragragh 2. These are proceedings of a domestic or family nature or which concern children. ABWOR is also available for most, but not all, such proceedings.

The remaining paragraphs 3, 4, 5 and 6 of Part 1 speak for themselves. Apart from the Employment Appeal Tribunal very few legally aided cases are undertaken in these courts or tribunals.

THE PROCEEDINGS FOR WHICH "REPRESENTATION" (CIVIL LEGAL AID) IS EXPRESSLY NOT AVAILABLE

Excepted proceedings — Part II of Schedule 2 to the 1988 Act

"1. Proceedings wholly or partly in respect of defamation, but so that **07–08** the making of the counterclaim for defamation in proceedings for which representation may be granted shall not of itself affect any right of the defendant to the counterclaim to representation for the purposes of the proceedings and so that representation may be granted to enable him to defend the counterclaim.

2. Relator actions.

3. Proceedings far the recovery of a penalty where the proceedings may be taken by any person and the whole or part of the penalty is payable to the person taking the proceedings.

4. Election petitions under the Representation of the People Act 1983.

5. In a county court, proceedings for or consequent on the issue of a judgment summons and, in the case of a defendant, proceedings where the only question to be brought before the court is as to the time and mode of payment by him of a debt (including liquidated damages) and costs.

5A. Proceedings for a decree of divorce or judicial separation unless the cause is defended, or the petition is directed to be heard in open court, or it is not practicable by reason of physical or mental

133

incapacity for the applicant to proceed without representation; except that representation shall be available for the purpose of making or opposing an application:

a for an injunction;

b for ancillary relief excluding representation for the purpose only of inserting a prayer for ancillary relief in the petition;

c for an order relating to the custody of (or access to) a child, or the education or care or supervision of a child, excluding representation for the purpose only of making application where there is no reason to believe that the application will be opposed;

d for an order declaring that the court is satisfied as to the arrangements for the welfare of the children of the family, excluding representation for the purpose only of making such an application there is no reason to believe that the application will be opposed; or

e for the purpose of making or opposing any other application, or satisfying the court on any other matter which raises a substantial question for determination by the court.

6. Proceedings incidental to any proceedings excepted by this Part of this Schedule."

The first exception is broadly defamation. However, if civil legal aid were unavailable for proceedings wholly or partly in respect of defamation without exception, (as was the position under the Legal Aid Act 1949), it would be open to any defendant to counterclaim for defamation to deprive the plaintiff of legal aid. Paragraph 1 of Part II therefore provides that the making of a counterclaim for defamation shall not of itself deprive the defendant to the counterclaim of legal aid.

07–09   There is some difficulty with the term "defamation", which is not defined in the 1988 Act. The standard definition of "defamatory" is that of Parke B. in the case of *Parmiter v. Coupland*[2] where he said: "a publication ... which is calculated to injure the reputation of another by exposing him to hatred, contempt or ridicule."

However, in *Tournier v. National Provincial and Union Bank of England*[3] the court of Appeal considered that such a definition was too narrow and that words which are "injurious to a man's character in business" would amount to defamation

Defamation, therefore, requires the reputation of the person concerned to have been touched. Slander and libel are, therefore, clearly within the meaning of "defamation" but there are three other forms of action which are similar to libel and slander yet are not within the meaning of

---

[2] (1840) 6 M.W. 105 at 108.
[3] [1924] 1 K.B. 461.

"defamation", although they are generally regarded as being part of the law of defamation — so the distinction is a fine one.

The three similar forms of action are actions for injurious falsehoods in which, subject to statutory exceptions, damage must be proved. They are:

(a) slander of title (casting doubt on the plaintiff's entitlement to property);
(b) slander of goods (disparaging the plaintiff's goods); and
(c) malicious or injurious falsehood (statements which are false but not defamatory and which are not slander of title or slander of goods).

Although the matter has not been tested in the courts, legal aid can (subject to the usual conditions) be expected to be granted for such proceedings provided there is no element whatsoever of a claim for defamation. This is perhaps most clearly evidenced by the claim for damages which is made.

Slander of title

This has four elements: 07–10

(a) A statement (written or spoken) to a third party in relation to the plaintiff's title to property (real or personal) must be made;
(b) The statement must be false;
(c) The statement must have been made maliciously (*i.e.* with a dishonest or other improper motive);
(d) The plaintiff must prove special damage (unless exempted by the provisions of section 3 of the Defamation Act 1952) and in practice proof of actual monetary damage is usually required.

Slander of goods

This has four elements: 07–11

(a) a statement (written or spoken) to a third party in relation to the plaintiff's goods must be made;
(b) the statement must be false;
(c) the statement must have been made maliciously (*i.e.* with a dishonest or otherwise improper motive);
(d) the plaintiff must prove special damage (unless exempted from proving special damage by the provisions of section 3 of the Defamation Act 1952).

Malicious falsehood

This has four elements: 07–12

(a) a statement (written or spoken) to a third party in relation to the plaintiff (but not in relation to his title to property or to his goods) must be made;

(b) the statement must be false;

(c) the statement must have been made maliciously (*i.e.* with a dishonest or otherwise improper motive);

(d) the plaintiff must prove special damage (unless exempted from proving special damage by the provision of section 3 of the Defamation Act 1952).

The practical distinctions between an action for defamation and an action for malicious falsehood can be summarised as follows:

(a) in an action for defamation it is necessary to prove that the words are defamatory — in an action for malicious falsehood there is no such requirement;

(b) in an action for defamation the falsity of any defamatory words is presumed and the burden of proving that they were true lies on the defendant — in an action for malicious falsehood the plaintiff has to plead and prove as part of the cause of action that the words were false;

(c) in an action for defamation it is not necessary for the plaintiff, in order to establish a prima facie case, to prove that the defendant was actuated by malice — in an action for malicious falsehood the plaintiff has to prove malice as part of the cause of action;

(d) in an action for libel it is not necessary for the plaintiff to prove that he has suffered damage; damage is presumed — in an action for malicious falsehood the plaintiff has to plead and prove as part of the cause of action that the publication has caused him special damage or that he is exempted from so doing by the provisions of section 3 of the Defamation Act 1952.

(e) a cause of action for defamation does not pass to the personal representatives of a deceased plaintiff nor does it survive against the estate of a deceased defendant — an action for malicious falsehood survives the death of either party.

(f) in an action for defamation the damages can, and almost certainly will, include damages for injury to the plaintiff's feelings — in an action for malicious falsehood the damages are restricted to actual or probable pecuniary loss.

07–13   It is evident that the distinction between "defamation" and similar proceedings can be a fine one. Legal aid area offices will need to be convinced that an application for legal aid for similar proceedings is not, in reality, one for defamation proceedings. One key factor will be the damages claimed. If there is any claim for damage to reputation or any claim for damage other than pecuniary loss, the legal aid application is unlikely to be granted.

An example of an application which might be granted is where, e.g. an employee is given a bad reference by his employer which he says is false.

Proceedings in such circumstances may often include no claim for defamation.

Finally, and most importantly, the wording of paragraph 1 of Part of **07–14** Schedule 2 excludes proceedings "wholly or partly" in respect of defamation. If, after legal aid has been granted, defamation is pleaded, the area office should be informed immediately and the certificate will be discharged (unless the assisted person is the plantiff and defamation is pleaded in the defendants counter claim) If the office is not informed, the certificate is almost certainly void or voidable from the date of the inclusion of the claim in respect of defamation.

Relator actions are, by paragraph II of Part II of Schedule "excepted pro- **07–15** ceedings". A relator action is one in which a person or body claiming to be entitled:

    (a) to restrain interference with the public right;

    (b) to abate a public nuisance; or

    (c) to compel the performance of a public duty;

must bring the action in the name of the Attorney-General. The practice is to describe the plaintiff as "the Attorney-General at the relation of (a) (b) relator".

The relator must bring the action in the name of the Attorney-General because he is the only person recognised by public law as entitled to represent the public in court proceedings and can take proceedings *ex officio or ex relatione* for a declaration as to public rights. Only the Attorney-General can sue on behalf of the public for the purpose of preventing public wrongs (though local authorities do have specific powers under the Local Government Act 1972). A private individual cannot sue on behalf of the public though he might be able to do so if he were to sustain injury as a result of a public wrong.

The Attorney-General decides in what cases it is proper for him to sue on behalf of relators and this discretion is absolute. The court has no power to review his decision.

A relator action may be brought by the Attorney-General alone, or by a relator in the name of the Attorney-General on his authority, but the relator is not the plaintiff. He may, however, be joined as a plaintiff if he has a cause of action himself arising out of the same facts and there are exceptional circumstances such that the Attorney-General considers that the relator should be joined as a plaintiff.

As all relator actions are "excepted proceedings" even when an individual has an action in his own right and is a co-plaintiff he cannot be granted legal aid for the action, and neither can a defendant to a relator action, e.g. a defendant to a relator action for the abatement of a public nuisance.

Proceedings for the recovery of a "penalty" where the proceedings may **07–16** be taken by any person and the whole or part of the penalty is payable to the person taking the proceedings are, by paragraph 3 of Part II of Schedule

2, excepted proceedings. "Penalty" is not defined in the 1988 Act but the requirement that the recovery proceedings must be proceedings which may be taken "by any person" effectively excludes from the exception actions for penalties imposed as compensation to a plaintiff or proceedings to enforce contract "penalty" clauses. The exception seems confined to proceedings to recover a penalty provided by the law of some part of the United Kingdom.

07–17 Election petitions under the Representation of the People Act 1983 are, by paragraph 4 of paragraph 2 of Schedule 2 excepted proceedings.

Section 121 of the Representation of the People Act 1983 provides for the presentation of parliamentary election petitions. A parliamentary election petition, complaining of an undue election or undue return, is the only means of questioning a parliamentary election or a return to Parliament.

07–18 Section 128 of the Representation of the People Act 1983 provides for the presentation of election petitions to question elections under the Local Government Act 1972.

07–19 In a county court, proceedings for or consequent upon the issue of a judgment summons are, by paragraph 5 of Part II of Schedule 2 "excepted proceedings". By section 147 of the County Court Act 1984, a "judgment summons" means a summons issued on the application of a person entitled to enforce a judgment or order under section 5 of the Debtors Act 1869 requiring a person, or where two or more persons are liable under the judgment or order, requiring any one or more of them, to appear and be examined on oath as to his or their means.

07–20 Section 5 of the Debtors Act 1869 provides for the committal to prison for a term not exceeding six weeks, or until payment of the sum due, of any person who may default in payment of any debt or instalment of any debt due from him in pursuance of any order or judgment.

However, by virtue of section 11 of the Administration of Justice Act 1970 the jurisdiction of a county court under section 5 of the Debtors Act 1869 to commit a person to prison for default in payment of a debt is exercisable only in respect of:

(a) arrears under a High Court or county court maintenance order (rule 87 of the Matrimonial Causes Rules 1977);

(b) arrears of income tax or any other tax or liability recoverable under section 65, 66 or 68 of the Taxes of the Management Act 1970;

(c) arrears of state pension provisions under Part III of the Social Security Pensions Act 1975; or

(d) arrears of Class I, II and IV contributions under Part I of the Social Security Act 1975.

07–21 In a county court, proceedings by defendants where the only question to be brought before the court is as to the time and mode of payment by him of a debt (including liquidated damages) and costs are, by paragraph 5 of Part II of Schedule 2 "excepted proceedings".

A legal aid certificate issued to cover taking or defending proceedings does not, without amendment, cover enforcement proceedings. Therefore, a solicitor acting for a defendant in a debt case where judgment is entered will require an amendment to cover the defence of enforcement proceedings. If there is no defence, not only is legal aid unlikely to be granted having regard to the merits test provided by section 15 of the 1988 Act and by regulations 28 to 30 of the Civil Legal Aid (General) Regulations 1989, but any application for aid should be refused on the ground that representation is not available.

Paragraph 5A of Part II of Schedule 2 makes undefended divorce or judicial separation decree proceedings "excepted proceedings" unless the petition is directed to be heard in open court or it is not practicable by reason of physical or mental incapacity for the applicant to proceed without representation. **07–22**

Paragraph 5A provides:

> "proceedings for a decree of divorce or judicial separation unless the cause is defended, or the petition is directed to be heard in open court, or is not practicable by reason of physical or mental incapacity for the applicant to proceed without representation; except that representation shall be available for the purpose of making or opposing an application —
> (a) for an injunction;
> (b) for ancillary relief, excluding representation for the purpose only of inserting a prayer for ancillary relief in the petition;
> (c) for an order relating to the custody of (or access to) a child, or the education or care or supervision of a child, excluding representation for the purpose only of making an application where there is no reason to believe that the application will be opposed;
> (d) for an order declaring that the court is satisfied as to arrangements for the welfare of the children of the family, excluding representation for the purpose only of making such an application where there is no reason to believe that the application will be opposed; or
> (e) for the purpose of making or opposing any other application, or satisfying the court on any other matter which raises a substantial question for determination by the court."

It may seem strange that divorce or judicial separation proceedings are generally "excepted proceedings" under the 1988 Act. This restriction on the availability of legal aid was introduced by the Legal Aid (Matrimonial Proceedings) Regulations 1977 and it was intended to act as a control on cost.

Where an applicant applies for legal aid to prosecute or defend a suit for divorce or judicial separation and shows that the matrimonial cause is likely to be defended or a certificate is granted to cover the decree proceedings on other grounds, the scope of the certificate is likely to be: **07–23**

(a) "to prosecute a suit for divorce (or judicial separation)"; or

(b) "to defend a suit for divorce (or judicial separation)"; or (more rarely)

(c) "to defend a suit for divorce (or judicial separation)" and "to cross pray" (for divorce);

the certificates will invariably bear the following endorsement and limitation:

"This certificate covers the decree proceedings so long as the cause remains defended. While it is so defended the certificate is limited to:

(i) all steps up to and including recovery of documents and, thereafter,

(ii) the obtaining of counsel's opinion on the merits of the cause continuing as a tested cause.'

When the decree proceedings cease to be defended, they are no longer covered by the certificate (but may be covered by a Green Form). However, the certificate remains in the terms quoted to prosecute defend a suit for divorce/judicial separation.

07–24 While the interpretation of the wording of the legal aid certificate, with particular regard to its scope, is a matter for decision by the taxing officer concerned in the light of any representations made by the solicitor with the normal remedies by way of objection and review in the event of dissatisfaction, the Senior Registrar of the Family Division agreed with the Law Society (which was then reponsible for legal and administration on the scope of certificates. This has since been updated and is set out below:

A. Certificates to prosecute or defend a suit for divorce *(1) Principles*

(a) Subject to any limitation, restriction or condition expressed therein, [such as the standard indorsement, referred to above] a certificate covers all the steps which are normally necessary for the purpose of prosecuting or defending a suit.

(b) Unless extended by amendment the certificate does not cover any step after the final decree other than applications for ancillary relief or custody or access made promptly after the final decree.

(c) The certificate will not cover any further steps in the decree proceedings if the cause at any time becomes undefended.

(2) Matters regarded as within the scope of the usual form of certificate

(a) certificate covering the prosecution or defence of proceedings for a decree of divorce is regarded as covering:-

(i) filing supplemental pleadings;

(ii) raising or opposing an issue as to domicile;

(iii) making or opposing an application for maintenance pending suit;

(iv) satisfying the judge as to the arrangements to be made for a child of the family;

(v) an application to remove a child of the family from the jurisdiction of the court, provided it is made before the final decree;

(vi) an application for an injunction of one of the following types, provided it is made any time up to the final decree:
(a) to prevent molestation of one spouse by the other,
(b) to require a spouse to leave the matrimonial home,

(vii) an application for an order under Section 8 of the Children Act 1989 provided it is made before or promptly after the final decree

(viii) an issue as to the status of a child provided it is raised at any time up to the making of an order for ancillary relief in respect of that child which is made before, on or promptly after the final decree;

(ix) an application for an injunction to restrain the other spouse from dealing with property to defeat an order for ancillary relief, provided it is made at any time up to the making of an order for ancillary relief, in respect of a party or a child of the family, which is made before, on or promptly after the final decree;

(x) an application for rescission of a decree nisi consequent upon the reconciliation of the parties;

(xi) making or opposing an application to expedite the making absolute of a decree nisi;

(xii) making or opposing an application before or promptly after the final decree, for: —
(a) a periodical payments order,
(b) a secured periodical payments order,
(c) a lump sum order,
(d) a transfer of property order,
(e) a settlement of property order,
(f) a variation of settlement order,
in respect of a party or a child of the family, but only so far as the court and not the Child Support Agency has jurisdiction;

(xiii) an application made before the final decree for a variation order;

(xiv) making or opposing an application for a periodical payments order or a lump sum order in respect of a party or a child of the family when the applicant has been unsuccessful in the main suit but only so far as the court and not the Child Support Agency has jurisdiction;

(xv) the registration in a magistrates' court of an order for ancillary relief provided that the application is made not later than six

141

months from the date of the order or the date of the final decree, whichever shall be the later;

(xvi) steps by a petitioner in connection with an application by the respondent under Section 10(2) of the Matrimonial Causes Act 1973;

(xvii) attendance before a Registrar on a summons for directions or pre-trial review.

(3) Matters regarded as outside the scope of the usual form of certificate

A certificate to prosecute or (as a respondent spouse) to defend a suit for divorce will not cover the initiation or opposing, as appropriate, of the following steps in such proceeding:

(i) On the part of the petitioner:
   (a) filing an answer to a separate cross-petition by the respondent;
   (b) filing a second petition;

(ii) on part of the respondent spouse: —
   (a) making cross-charges in an answer, followed by a prayer for divorce or some alternative matrimonial relief,
   (b) filing a separate cross-petition;
   (the cover afforded by such a certificate will be taken to extend to proceedings under a second petition or separate cross-petition which have taken place after an order for consolidation with the previous proceedings, but not otherwise)

(iii) an application for a variation order after the final decree;

(iv) the enforcement of an order for ancillary relief or costs;

(v) an application under section 7 of the Matrimonial Causes Act 1973;

(vi) an application for alteration of a maintenance agreement;

(vii) an application for provision to be made out of the estate of a deceased former spouse;

(viii) an application for an avoidance of disposition order;

(ix) protracted negotiations subsequent to, and to give effect to, an order for contact with a child;

(x) an application by the unsuccessful party for the decree nisi to be made absolute;

(xi) proceedings under section 17 of the Married Women's Property Act 1882;

(xii) opposing an intervention by the Queen's Proctor to show cause against the decree nisi being made absolute;

(xiii) resisting the respondent's application under section 10(1) of the Matrimonial Causes Act 1973 for rescission of the decree;

(xiv) an application for committal for breach of an injunction.
(It is emphasised that the above list is not exhaustive)

142

(4) Limitations and conditions

Where a legal aid certificate has been granted to continue to prosecute or to defend a defended suit for divorce, it will provide that the certificate covers the decree proceedings so long as the cause remains defended.

The certificate will also contain the following limitations.

"As to the defended suit itself, limited to: —

all steps up to and including discovery and, any summons for directions/pre-trial review and thereafter to obtaining counsel's opinion on the merits of the matter continuing as a contested cause. As to Children/ancillary matters, cover is in accordance with the notes for Guidance in the current Legal Aid Handbook."

Certificates for ancillary relief, custody, residence, or access (contact) will **07–25** bear the standard limitation "this certificate is limited to obtaining one substantive order only".

Paragraph 6 of Part II of Schedule 2 to the 1988 Act provides that "proceedings incidental to any proceedings accepted by this Part of this Schedule" are "exccepted proceedings".

Proceedings which are an incidence of such proceedings include enforcement proceedings and interlocutory proceedings, so that a legal aid certificate cannot be granted even for a specific step in any of the accepted proceedings or to enforce judgment obtained in such proceedings.

To Which Applicants May Civil Legal Aid Be Granted

As well as civil legal aid being available only for specified proceedings there are restrictions on the applicants to whom it can be granted. First, section 15 of the 1988 Act restricts availability to "any person".

Secondly section 15 goes on to restrict availability to financially eligible persons.

Thirdly, section 15(3A) expressly provides that civil legal aid is not available:

  (a) to any local authority; or
  (b) to any other body which falls within a prescribed description; or
  (c) to a guardian ad litem

for the purposes of proceedings under the Children Act 1989.

Section 2(10) provides in this Act "person" does not include a body of persons corporate or unincorporate which is not concerned in a representative, fiduciary or official capacity so as to authorise advice, assistance or representations to be granted to such a body. Because local authorities and some other bodies may be concerned in Children Act 1989

143

proceedings in a representative, fiduciary or official capacity the specific restriction in section 15(3A) ensures that they may not be granted legal aid for such proceedings. Clearly, however, civil legal aid is available to an individual — even if they are in a partnership. Finally, although section 47(6) provides that the 1988 Act extends to England and Wales only, a person's residence is not a criterion for eligibility. It is the locus of the proceedings, *i.e.* England or Wales which is the relevant factor.

Chapter 8

THE APPLICATION FOR A LEGAL AID CERTIFICATE

How to Apply For Legal Aid

An application for legal aid must be made in writing on a form approved **08–01** by the Board or in such other written form as the Area Director, to whom it is submitted, is willing to accept. In practice, Area Directors are not willing to accept applications for legal aid which are not submitted on an approved form.

The application must be lodged with an Area Director. The term Area Director is defined in regulation 3 of the Civil Legal Aid (General) Regulations 1989 as meaning an Area Director appointed by the Board in accordance with regulation 4 of those Regulations, including any person duly authorised to act on the Area Director's behalf. Paragraph 4 of the Legal Aid Board Area Committee Arrangements (as amended) provides that the persons who have been appointed by the Board to be Area Directors are the Group Managers and Area Managers for each office.

The application must contain sufficient information, and be supported by any necessary documents, to enable the Area Director to decide whether the applicant has reasonable grounds for taking defending or being a party to proceedings and also that it is reasonable for legal aid to be granted. An additional form (CLA4A, CLA4B or CLA4F) with the required additional documents — such as Form L 17 where the applicant is in employment must also be submitted containing all relevant information about the applicant's financial resources so that the DSS can determine his or her disposable income and capital and the maximum contribution.

The Right to Apply

Any person who wishes to receive legal aid in respect of proceedings may **08–02** apply:

(a) if resident in the United Kingdom, to any Area Director; or

(b) if resident elsewhere, to the Area Director of one of the legal aid areas nominated by the Board for this purpose. (The Board has now decided that application for legal aid from persons resident outside the United Kingdom may also be submitted to any area office.)

An application for legal aid for a minor or a patient (defined in regulation 3 of the Civil Legal Aid (General) Regulations 1989 as a person who, by reason of mental disorder within the meaning of the Mental Health Act 1983, is incapable of managing and administering his property and affairs) must be made on his or her behalf by a person of full age and capacity and, where the application relates to proceedings which are required by Rules of Court to be brought or defended by a next friend or guardian *ad litem* the next friend or guardian, or the person intending to act as such, must make the application.

08–03 Where the application relates to proceedings which have not actually begun, the person who, subject to any order of the court, intends to act in either of those capacities when the proceedings begin, must make the application. Furthermore, except where an application is made by the official solicitor, the Area Director may not issue a certificate applied for by a person on behalf of a minor or patient unless the person applying has signed an undertaking to pay to the Board (if required to do so) any sums which, by virtue of any provision of the 1988 Act or the Civil Legal Aid (General) Regulations 1989, the Area Director may require an assisted person of full age and capacity to pay from the issue or during the currency of a certificate or upon the discharge or revocation of a certificate.

08–04 Although an application on behalf of a minor or patient must be made by a person of full age and capacity, any certificate is issued in the name of the minor or patient but states the name of the person who has applied for it on his or her behalf. It is further provided in regulation 16 of the Civil Legal Aid (General) Regulations 1989 that the person named in the certificate as next friend or guardian *ad litem* of the minor or patient is to be treated for all purposes, including the receipt of notices, as the agent of the minor or patient in any matter relating to the issue, amendment, revocation or discharge of the certificate.

08–05 Finally, there is an overriding power vested in the Area Director to waive any of the requirements of regulation 16 where the circumstances appear to make it desirable. The help of a solicitor in completing an application for legal aid is available under the Green Form Scheme.

WHICH OFFICE TO APPLY TO

If a person resides in the United Kingdom he or she can apply to any area **08–06** office in the country for legal aid. Nothing in the Regulations requires an application to be submitted to the committee in the district in which the applicant lives or where the applicant's solicitor practices. However, as a general rule it is cheaper and more convenient to apply to the committee whose offices are nearest to where the applicant lives or works, or to where the applicant's solicitor practises. This is particularly likely to be the case if the application is refused and the applicant wishes to appeal to the appropriate area committee. It may be advantageous for the applicant to appear or to be represented at the appeal and, if this is heard by an area committee other than the nearest, the applicant may incur unnecessary expense.

Although there is no restriction on the committee to which the application may be made, the Civil Legal Aid (General) Regulations 1989 provide[1] that the papers relating to an application should be transferred to another area office if it appears to the Area Director who receives them that the application could, without prejudice to the applicant, be more conveniently or appropriately dealt with in another office. Such transfer will not be made without the applicant being given an explanation and, in exceptional circumstances, an opportunity to make representations about it (although the Regulations give the applicant no right to insist on this).

Examples of cases where an application may be transferred are:

(a) where it is made by a person who is not resident in the district and whose solicitor does not practice there;

(b) where the applicant is applying for legal aid to sue a local solicitor or a member of the area committee;

(c) where the Board has directed that all applications for legal aid arising out of a particular set of circumstances against a particular defendant should, for administrative convenience, be dealt with in one area office; or

(d) where the application is for judicial review of a decision of the area committee in the area to which the application has been submitted.

---

[1] Civil Legal Aid (General) Regulations 1989, reg. 17.

THE APPLICATION FORM

08–07 Every application must be made in writing on the form approved by the Board or in such other written form as the Area Director may accept.[2] As mentioned above, Area Directors will not accept applications otherwise than on approved forms (except in the case of an application for an emergency certificate which may be made in the first instance by telephone provided that the appropriate form is subsequently submitted).

The Board has approved a number of forms, of which the following are the most recently used:

These forms can be obtained from any area office or from a Citizens Advice Bureau or from a solicitor who deals with legal aid work and pamphlets explaining the working of the legal aid scheme and the financial conditions can be obtained from the same sources.

An application form should always be signed and dated and, when it has been completed, it must be lodged with an Area Director. The forms contain a warning of the penalties provided by section 39(1) of the 1988 Act for failing to provide information or furnishing false information.

08–08 A certificate may not, with certain exceptions relate to more than one action, cause or matter and a separate application must, therefore, be submitted in respect of each of these for which legal aid is sought[3]. This does not prevent a single application form relating to more than one set of proceedings provided that they can all be joined in a single action, cause or matter. Where, however, there are two or more sets of proceedings in respect of which consolidation will ultimately be sought, separate applications must be submitted in respect of each set of proceedings unless an order for consolidation has already been made at the time the application is submitted.

A separate application form should be lodged for each applicant, even when the application is made by persons who will be joint parties to proceedings or whose means will be aggregated for the purpose of contributing to the fund.

08–09 Where a solicitor is representing more than one child in proceedings under the Children Act, wardship or adoption, a separate Form CLA 5 must be filled out for each child applicant. To reduce form-filling and copying of documents for practitioners the Board will only require one set of accompanying documents although a separate means form is still required for each child. The Board suggests applications be completed and submitted in the following way:

    (a) Fill in *one* Form CLA5A leaving blank the applicant's name, signature and any other information which differs amongst the

---

[2] Civil Legal Aid (General) Regulations 1989, reg. 11(a).
[3] Civil Legal Aid (General) Regulations 1989, reg. 46.

applicants, *e.g.* date of birth. The form should not be signed at this stage.

(b) Write in print "ORIGINAL APPLICATION" in the top right-hand corner of Page 1.

(c) Photocopy the form the required number of times so that the words "ORIGINAL APPLICATION" appear on each copy. One of the applications should be submitted on the original Form CLA5.

(d) Write in the information particular to each child (name, date of birth, etc. The solicitor should then sign each application. It is important that any signatures are originals even if the form is a photocopy and the nominated solicitor must sign personally where he is instructed by a child/minor direct.

(e) Send the applications together to the area office. The photocopied applications must be firmly attached *behind* the original. Only one set of supporting enclosures is needed.

The area office will process the applications together as at present ensuring that they are cross-referenced and that original documents are returned once the legal decision has been made. If this procedure is not followed, applications must be made using original forms for each client.

This procedure may also be followed when submitting applications from spouses and co habitees who are applying to be represented in the same proceedings where no conflict of interest exists.

WHAT AN APPLICATION MUST CONTAIN AND WHAT MUST ACCOMPANY IT

Every application must contain such information and be accompanied by **08–10** such supporting documents (including any welfare report) as may be necessary to enable:

(a) the Area Director to determine the nature of the proceedings in respect of which legal aid is sought and whether it is reasonable that representation should be granted; and

(b) the Assessment Officer at the DSS to assess the disposable income, disposable capital and maximim contribution of the applicant.

The application must also state the name of the solicitor selected by the applicant to act under the certificate. The nominated solicitor is entitled to be paid for acting under a legal aid certificate only if he holds a valid current practising certificate at all times when work is done under the certificate. The solicitor or counsel acting for an assisted person is not permitted to entrust the conduct of any part of the case to any other person except another solicitor or counsel selected under section 32(1) of the 1988 Act[4] but regulation 65(2) of the Civil Legal Aid (General) Regulations 1989 provides that nothing in regulation 65(1) shall prevent a solicitor from entrusting the conduct of any part of the case to a partner or to a competent and responsible representative employed in the solicitor's office or otherwise under the solicitor's immediate supervision.

The application form indicates the information which is principally required and contains a number of questions which have to be answered. The applicant must also, if required to do so for the purpose of providing additional material, supply such further information or documents as may be required or attend an interview (in practice any interview will be with the Benefits Agency rather than with the area office). Failure to comply with this requirement is likely to prevent the applicant receiving legal aid since the Area Director will lack the information which must be available before the application can be granted.[5]

08–11   In *Kyle v. Mason*[6] the Court of Appeal considered that there were no grounds at all for the appeal which had been brought and could not understand why the appellants had been granted legal aid. It was informed that the committee had issued the certificate relying on a letter from the appellant's solicitor in support of the application. The solicitor appreciated that the letter was misleading although at the time it had been written under an honest, albeit mistaken, view as to the effect of the evidence. He submitted to an order for costs against him personally, the court saying that the case "underlined the care which must be taken when supplying information to legal aid committees". All relevant opinions from counsel must be submitted.

08–07   In general, Area Directors require an applicant to provide a statement giving all the relevant facts, and any relevant evidence in support. Reports by expert witnesses are not normally required unless they are already in existence. In certain cases, however, principally applications relating to proposed proceedings for personal injuries, some independent information will be needed. For example, confirmation of an injury suffered by the applicant may be required unless the result of the accident is self-evident, such as the loss of a limb. In the first instance this can take the form of a note from the applicant's doctor or a medical certificate rather than a full report.

08–12   A solicitor helping the person to complete an application for legal aid should, consider what evidence he would require to see before he would be prepared to advise that proceedings should be taken or defended. If

---

4 Civil Legal Aid (General) Regulations 1989, reg. 65(1).
5 *ibid.* reg. 78, which applies where a certificate has already been issued, and also the Legal Aid Act 1988, s. 39 with regard to proceedings for misrepresentation against an applicant or assisted person.
6 *The Times*, July 3, 1963.

counsel's opinion has already been obtained it should always be forwarded with the application, whether it is favourable or not.

It is not possible to give any exhaustive list of the relevant information which an Area Director will require in support of any particular application as each case must be decided on its own merits. Solicitors will know from their own experience and from previous dealings with the area office the sort of information which must be submitted. They should bear in mind that Area Directors wish to receive sufficient, but not excessive, information in support of an application and that it is not the Area Director's function to try the case. If the Area Director is satisfied that a legal aid certificate can properly be granted but that he should review the case at a later stage, a limitation will be imposed which may subsequently be removed on application for an amendment. Solicitors should also bear in mind that it is not the Area Director's function to sort through a miscellaneous bundle of documents and they should ensure that applications are submitted in a concise form.

FINANCIAL STATEMENT OF THE APPLICANT'S ITEMS

For all proceedings except "special Children Act proceedings", either: **08–13**
  (a) Form CLA4A (*i.e.* civil legal aid 4A statement of applicant's circumstances) shown below; or
  (b) Form CLA4B (*i.e.* civil legal aid 4B statement of applicant in receipt of income support) shown below; or
  (c) Form CLA4C (*i.e.* civil legal aid 4C statement of financial circumstances of an applicant for legal aid resident outside England and Wales shown below; or
  (d) Form CLA4F (*i.e.* civil legal aid 4F statement of financial circumstances of a child applicant under 16) shown below;
must also be completed and sent to the legal aid area office to provide it and the DSS assessment office with details of the applicant's means.

Except in the case of "special Children Act proceedings", where the applicant and his or her spouse or cohabitant is in employment, Form L17 wages statement completed by the employer is also required.

For "special Children Act proceedings" no means statement form and no L17 wages statement is required (such cases are not means tested) and Form CLA5A includes a certification by the solicitor that the client qualifies for non-means non-merits tested legal aid.

How an application is made by a resident outside the United Kingdom

08–14 Where a person is resident outside the United Kingdom and is not able to be present here in England or Wales while his application is considered, the application shall be:

    (a) written in English or in French; and

    (b) except where the applicant is a member of Her Majesty's Armed Forces, sworn:

        (i) if the applicant resides within the Commonwealth or the Republic of Ireland, before any justice of the peace or magistrate or any person for the time being authorised by law in the place where the applicant resides to administer an oath for a judicial or other legal purpose; or

        (ii) if the applicant resides elsewhere, before a British Counsular Officer or any other person for the time being authorised to exercise the functions of such an Officer or having authority to administer an oath in that place; and

    (c) accompanied by a statement in writing, signed by some responsible person who has knowledge of the facts, certifying that part of the application which relates to the applicant's disposable income and disposable capital.

The above requirements may be waived by the Area Director where compliance with them would cause serious difficulty, inconvenience or delay and the application otherwise satisfies the requirements contained in regulations 11 and 12 of the Civil Legal Aid (General) Regulations 1989.

Urgent applications

08–15 In cases when the need for a legal aid certificate is urgent this should be prominently marked on the application form and on any covering letter. Efforts should be made by the applicant or the solicitor to obtain an extension of time where this is possible and where it would enable the application to be dealt with without the need for an emergency certificate to be issued.

    The Civil Legal Aid (General) regulations 1989 provide two methods of dealing with urgent applications.

Emergency certificates

The Area Director may issue an emergency certificate without reference to **08–16** the Benefits Agency where he is satisfied that the applicant is likely to fulfil the conditions under which legal aid may be granted and it is in the interests of justice that applicant should, as a matter of urgency, be granted legal aid.

Estimated determinations

Where an applicant requires a certificate urgently and the Assessment **08–17** Officer at the Department of Social Security considers that the applicant's financial resources cannot be determined in time, the Assessment Officer may estimate the applicant's disposable income, disponsable capital and maximum contribution. The estimate is then treated as if it were an assessment, until the making of a full assessment, and section 17(1) of the 1988 Act (assisted person's partial protection against an order for *inter partes* costs) applies.

Where an emergency legal aid certificate is required, Form CLA3 (*i.e.* civil legal aid 3 application for emergency legal aid) must also be completed. However, for "special Children Act proceedings", on completing the certification on Form CLA5A the solicitor may begin work straight away because (providing Form CLA5A is received in the appropriate legal aid area office within three working days of receipt of instructions to act) costs from the time of receipt of instructions to act in the proceedings will be deemed to be within the certificate. In such cases, there should, therefore, be no need to apply for emergency certificates.

Where legal aid is needed very urgently (*i.e.* there is insufficient time to make a postal application for emergency legal aid) for proceedings other than "special Children Act proceedings", the solicitor may telephone the legal aid area office to apply for emergency legal aid. Thereafter, however, the appropriate, properly completed, forms must be sent to the office. When they are received, if legal aid was granted by telephone, the certificate will be issued bearing the date of the telephone grant.

Where legal aid is needed very urgently (*i.e.* there is insufficient time to make a postal application for emergency legal aid) for proceedings other than "special Children Act proceedings", but the legal aid area office is closed so that it is not possible to make an application by telephone, the deeming provision in regulation 103 (6) of the Civil Legal Aid (General) Regulations 1989 may apply. This provides that, in such circumstances, work done immediately prior to the issue of an emergency certificate shall be deemed to be work done while such a certificate is in force if the solicitor applies for an emergency certificate at the first available opportunity and the application is granted.

Of course, firms with an appropriate legal aid franchise may grant emergency legal aid themselves.

CONSIDERATION OF EMERGENCY APPLICATIONS

08–18   When an area office receives an application for an emergency legal aid certificate it will be granted if it is considered to be in the interests of justice that legal aid be granted as a matter of urgency and it appears likely that the applicant will fulfil the conditions under which legal aid may be granted under the 1988 Act and the the Civil Legal Aid (General) Regulations 1989, *i.e.* the means and merits tests.[7]

There is no right of appeal against this decision. However, if at the same time, the substantive application is refused, there is a right of appeal against this decision.

A franchised firm which has granted emergency legal aid must submit the application forms to the area office within seven days of the grant. The office will then issue an emergency certificate bearing the date of grant by the franchised firm. The office may, however, place a limitation on the certificate if it is considered appropriate. There is no right of appeal against the limitation on the emergency certificate though there is a right of appeal against the office's decision in relation to the substantive application.

CONSIDERATION OF APPLICATIONS

08–19   If an application is refused on the basis that the applicant is not financially eligible for legal aid, there is no right of appeal. However, a breakdown of the assessment of means may be requested and representations may be made if this appears to be wrong, though there is no formal procedure for this and no provision for this is made by the Civil Legal Aid (General) Regulations 1989.

If an application is refused on the basis that (although the applicant is financially eligible on income grounds) the applicant has disposable capital of an amount which renders him liable to be refused legal aid and it appears to the Area Director that the probable costs to the applicant in the proceedings would not exceed his assessed contribution, the applicant may appeal against the refusal. The basis of the appeal will not be to challenge

---

[7] Civil Legal Aid (General) Regulations 1989, reg. 19.

the assessment of means itself[8] but to challenge the Area Director's view of the probable costs.

If an application is refused or is not granted in the required terms, there is a right of appeal against this decision.

THE LEGAL MERITS CRITERION AND THE REASONABLENESS CRITERIA

15.—(1) The Primary Merits Criterion and Reasonableness Criteria are set out in Sections 15(2), 15(3) and 15(4A) of the 1988 Act, which are set out below:

(2) A person shall not be granted representation for the purposes of any **08–20** proceedings unless he satisfies the Board that he has reasonable grounds for taking, defending or being a party to the proceedings.

(3) A person may be refused representation for the purposes of any proceedings if, in the particular circumstances of the case it appears to the Board—

(a) unreasonable that he should be granted representation under this Part, or

(b) more appropriate that he should be given assistance by way of representation under Part III;

and regulations may prescribe the criteria for determining any questions arising under paragraph (b) above.

(4A) A person may not be refused representation for the purposes of any **08–21** proceedings on the ground (however expressed) that it would be more appropriate for him and a legal representative of his to enter into a conditional fee agreement (as defined by section 58 of the Courts and Legal Services Act 1990).[9]

Further criteria are specified by regulations.[10] The relevant regulations are set out below.

28.—(1) Without prejudice to the generality of sections 15(2) to (3C) and **08–22** (3E)[11] of the Act and subject to paragraph (2), an application for a certificate shall only be approved after the Area Director has considered all the questions of fact or law arising in the action, cause or matter to which the application relates and the circumstances in which the application was made.

(2) Where the application relates to proceedings to which section

---

[8] *ibid.* reg. 27(2).
[9] Less stringent criteria apply to proceedings under the Children Act 1989.
[10] Civil Legal Aid (General) Regulations 1989, regs. 28 to 33.
[11] S.3(C) relates to specified non means/non merits tested Children Act cases and s.3(3E) relates to specified non-means tested Children Act cases.

15(3B),[12] (3C) or (3E) of the Act apply, provided that the Area Director is satisfied that it does so relate and subject to regulation 27[13] (where applicable) he shall grant the application and Parts IV and V of these Regulations shall apply with any necessary modifications.

29. Without prejudice to regulations 28 and 32, an application may be refused where it appears to the Area Director that—

(a) only a trivial advantage would be gained by the applicant from the proceedings to which the application relates; or

(b) on account of the nature of the proceedings a solicitor would not ordinarily be employed.

30.—(1) Without prejudice to regulation 28, an application may be refused where it appears to the Area Director that—

(a) the applicant has available to him rights or facilities which make it unnecessary for him to obtain legal aid; or

(b) the applicant has a reasonable expectation of obtaining financial or other help from a body of which he is a member,

and that he has failed to take all reasonable steps to enforce or obtain such rights, facilities or help (including permitting the Area Director to take those steps on his behalf).

(2) Where it appears that the applicant has a right to be indemnified against expenses incurred in connection with any proceedings, it shall not, for the purposes of paragraph (1), be deemed to be a failure to take reasonable steps if he has not taken proceedings to enforce that right, whether for a declaration as to that right or otherwise.

31.—(1) The Area Director shall, when determining an application, also determine the sums for the time being payable on account of the applicant's contribution.

32.—(1) When determining an application, the Area Director shall consider whether it is reasonable and proper for persons concerned jointly with or having the same interest as the applicant to defray so much of the costs as would be payable from the fund in respect of the proceedings if a certificate were issued.

(2) In determining an application made by, or on behalf of, a person in connection with an action, cause or matter in which—

(a) numerous persons have the same interest; and

(b) in accordance with rules of court, one or more persons may sue or be sued, or may be authorised by a court to defend any such action, cause or matter on behalf of or for the benefit of all persons so interested,

the Area Director shall consider whether the rights of the applicant would be substantially prejudiced by the refusal of his application.

---

[12] Non means non merit tested proceedings under the Children Act 1989, s. 25.
[13] Reg. 27 relates to financial eligibility

(3) Where an application has been approved and the Area Director considers that it is reasonable that persons concerned jointly with or having the same interest as the applicant should contribute to the cost of the proceedings, he shall add the amount which would be payable by such persons to the sums (if any) payable by the applicant under regulation 31 and shall so notify him under regulation 43(2).

(4) The Area Director may subsequently redetermine the amount of any additional sums payable under paragraph (3) where he is satisfied that the applicant has, without success, taken all reasonable steps (including permitting the Area Director to take those steps on his behalf) to obtain such payment.

Application in representative, fiduciary or official capacity

33. Where an application is made in a representative, fiduciary or official capacity, the Area Director—
  (a) shall take into account the value of any property or estate or the amount of any fund out of which the applicant is entitled to be indemnified and the financial resources of any persons (including the applicant if appropriate) who might benefit from the proceedings; and
  (b) may (without prejudice to regulation 28) either—
      (i) approve the application, subject to the payment from the property or resources specified in sub-paragraph (a) of any sums which he may in his discretion determine, or
      (ii) refuse the application, if he concludes that to do so would not cause hardship.

The Legal Merits Criterion

The area office must be satisfied that, on the facts put forward and the law **08–23** which relates to them, there is a case or defence which should be put before a court for a decision. The availability and strength of evidence to support the facts alleged will be taken into account.

However, the area office sees only one side of the case and it is for the court to adjudicate on the issues. If the ultimate prospects of success are unclear, a limited grant may be appropriate, although the area office must, in every case, be satisfied that the applicant has reasonable grounds for taking, defending or being a party to the proceedings. The likelihood of success is a factor which the area office must bear in mind but it is of the essence of litigation that there are two opposing points of view on which the court is required to adjudicate. Litigation is also notoriously uncertain so that any attempt to restrict legal aid to certainties or near certainties would not only be doomed to failure (if the aim was 100 per cent. success rate) but would also be a denial to many applicants of an opportunity to obtain justice.

The aim therefore must be not to be over-cautious but not to grant legal aid for cases where there is little or no hope of success. If legal aid is granted in hopeless cases it raises the expectations of assisted persons too high, forces opponents to defend their rights and wastes public money, perhaps doubly if costs are awarded against the fund.

Therefore there are reasonable grounds to proceed if:

(a) there is an issue of fact or law which should be submitted to the court for a decision;

(b) the solicitor would advise the applicant to take or defend proceedings privately, *i.e.* if he had means which were adequate to meet the likely costs of the case or would make payment of the likely costs possible although something of a sacrifice; and

(c) the applicant shows that, as a matter of law, he has reasonable grounds for taking or defending proceedings, *i.e.* that there is a case or defence which has reasonable prospects of success, assuming the facts are proved.

Even if the application satisfies the legal merits criterion, it may still be refused under the reasonableness test.

The Reasonableness Criteria

08–24 A person may be refused legal aid if in the particular circumstances of the case it appears to the Board (*i.e.* the Area Director/area committee) unreasonable that it should be granted or more appropriate that ABWOR should be granted. This criterion is in addition to and not an alternative to the legal merits test. The discretion is wide on the face of it but there are well recognised circumstances in which the decision has to be made, and the most common cases are set out below. The criterion does not apply to certain applicants in specified proceedings under the Children Act 1989. In most cases the reasonableness test will be satisfied if, in all the circumstances, a fee-paying client of sufficient but not superabundant means would be advised to take proceedings.

Legal aid is likely to be refused as unreasonable if:

08–25 (a) the application reveals some illegal motive or the conduct of the applicant is such as to be unacceptable to the court (but moral character on its own should not be a bar to grant);

08–26 (b) the proceedings are not likely to be cost effective, *i.e.* the benefit to be achieved does not justify the costs.

The cost effectiveness factor may be outweighed by other matters—the importance of the case to the applicant (*e. g.* in relation to a negative equity situation), the possibility in divorce proceedings that the allegations in the petition are so serious that they could, if uncontested, affect matters of residence and finance, or the possibility in rent arrears cases that the client may be able to persuade the court not to make any order at all if it is unreasonable or would cause hardship. It is for the solicitor, on behalf of the applicant, to satisfy the area office that such factors exist and outweigh the lack of cost effectiveness.

Examples of cases which are not likely to be cost effective are:

(i) the amount of the claim is small;

(ii) the estimated costs of the proceedings are likely to exceed the benefit to the client—this will be relevant in probate actions where costs are likely to reduce the amount available in the estate in issue or give rise to the operation of the statutory charge;

(iii) the only matter at stake is loss of stature, dignity or reputation;

(iv) a substantive defence of a divorce petition where the marriage has broken down irretrievably and the only question in issue is whether or not the allegations in the petition are true;

(v) where rent or mortgage arrears are not in dispute and it is unlikely that an immediate order for possession would be made, and the only issue appears to be the terms on which a suspended order would be made.

(vi) where the proceedings are such that costs are unlikely to be recovered in the event of success, and the operation of the statutory charge would deprive the applicant of any significant benefit.

(vii) neighbour disputes—which can be dealt with by way of undertakings or where the property in issue is unlikely to justify the costs involved.

(c) the applicant has other rights and facilities making it unnecessary for **08–27** him/her to obtain legal aid or has a reasonable expectation of obtaining financial or other help from a body of which he is a member, *e.g.*: Trade Union; Commission for Racial Equality; Equal Opportunities Commission; AA/RAC, etc.; Estate (probate action); Firm where applicant is a member of a firm; or Cover under a policy of insurance which deals with legal costs. (The terms, conditions and adequacy of alternative funding may be a crucial factor when considering this test.)

(d) the applicant is a victim of a crime of violence who could obtain **08–28** compensation from the Criminal Injuries Compensation Board (CICB) and the circumstances are such that a reasonable fee-paying client of sufficient but not superabundant means would not take civil proceedings as well as, or instead of, applying to the CICB. Even if there is likely to be a sufficiently large difference between the damages likely to be obtained in court proceedings and CICB compensation to justify the proceedings, the area office will consider the likelihood of recovering from the opponent and if this is uncertain the application will be refused.

159

08–29 (e) a solicitor would not normally be employed in such proceedings, *e.g.* mortgage arrears or application to suspend warrant of possession or execution; application for extra time to meet High Court judgment; application to register county court or High Court maintenance order in magistrates' court (see also regulation 29(b)).

(f) the proceedings should be taken in a court other than the one specified in the application, *i.e.* where costs are lower but the proceedings still meet the needs of the applicant. This can apply to:

> maintenance,
> residence,
> adoption,
> protection.

08–30 (g) ABWOR is available for the proceedings and is more appropriate. This can only arise where both ABWOR and civil legal aid are available for the proceedings, which will give the applicant the same remedies, and the applicant is financially eligible under both schemes. ABWOR will be the choice because it is simpler and less expensive. The most common choice is between remedies relating to exclusion and protection orders in the Family Proceedings Court as opposed to injunctions and exclusion orders in the High Court and the county court. If the Family Proceedings Court can give the applicant the protection he/she needs then it may be unreasonable to grant legal aid for High Court or county court proceedings, but reasonable to direct the applicant towards ABWOR.

08–31 (h) the defendant has no means to satisfy any judgment against him/her or, in the case of injunction proceedings, any order obtained would be unenforceable in view of the respondent's/defendant's mental incapacity or minority/lack of assets (see *Wookey v. Wookey, Re S (A Minor)* [1991] 3 W.L.R. 135; [1991] 3 All E.R. 365).

08–32 (i) the applicant would get no personal benefit out of the proceedings.

08–33 (j) on an application for bail to the High Court it would seem more appropriate to rely on the Official Solicitor procedure under R.S.C., Ord. 70, *i.e.* where the application is simple without the need for a significant degree of preparation or legal argument. A civil legal aid application for bail to the judge in chambers should include information on the following:

> (i) whether the defendant is in the custody of the magistrates' court or Crown Court;
>
> (ii) the length of time the defendant would otherwise be likely to remain in custody pending trial;
>
> (iii) whether the defendant has already applied for bail to the magistrates' court and/or Crown Court (bail is often granted on a subsequent appearance when difficulties relating to sureties have been sorted out);
>
> (iv) whether the defendant has been represented on previous applications for bail;
>
> (v) why bail was refused and whether it is suggested that the reasons

given by the court for refusing bail were unreasonable or the grounds for refusing bail have altered;

(vi) any special social or other reasons for making an application for bail in the particular case.

(k) the application relates to an appeal from a decision of the Pensions **08–34** Appeal Tribunal where the Tribunal will meet the applicant's costs.

(l) the application is made in circumstances which themselves make a grant **08–35** unreasonable, for example where a company has assigned its cause of action to a director so that he may apply for legal aid.

(m) the applicant's previous legal aid history is such that a grant would be **08–36** unreasonable (*e.g.* in the light of previous failure to co-operate in means assessment or the revocation of an earlier certificate).

Criteria in the Regulations—Other Persons with an interest

In addition to the legal merits and reasonableness tests, the area office must, **08–37** pursuant to regulation 32, consider whether there are other persons concerned jointly with, or having the "**same**" interest as, the applicant in the outcome of the proceedings. If there are, it is a question of whether, in the circumstances, the applicant needs legal aid at all, and, if he does, whether the other persons involved should pay a contribution towards the costs.

However, if other persons are already joined as parties to the proceedings by the time the application is submitted, these additional questions will not normally need to be considered. This is because the area office will rely on the normal rules of taxation whereby costs between the non-legally aided parties and the assisted person will automatically be apportioned, so that only those items solely attributable to the assisted person, together with the appropriate proportion of the costs common to all the parties, will be allowed against the assisted person's certificate.

The solicitor and any counsel should be mindful of the fact that where the assisted person has no conflict of interest with another party sufficient to justify the additional costs of separate representation (by separate solicitors and/or counsel), it may be appropriate for one of the solicitors to represent the assisted persons and/or for there to be a joint instruction of counsel.

Failure to consider this at any appropriate point(s) may lead to costs being disallowed on taxation/assessment (in the event of work being unnecessarily duplicated). Should the assisted person decline to accept advice in that regard the show cause procedure may be invoked under regulation 77 of the Civil Legal Aid (General) Regulations 1989 (unjustifiable expense to the Fund).

Other persons have the "same" interest as the applicant if each person **08–38** (including the applicant) is seeking an identical outcome to the proceed-

161

ings, *e.g.* an order, injunction or declaration which would benefit all equally without the need for them to issue separate proceedings.

Other persons do not have the "same" interest as the applicant if each person has a special interest which might result in different orders for each, such as a claim for damages which must be individual to each person, even if the claims arise from a single event. In such a case, the other persons would have only similar interests not the "same" within the meaning of the regulation.

08–39 However, there may be cases where the persons concerned have both the "same" interest within the meaning of an application, and similar interests. This could happen where there is an application to the court for an order that the common parts of a block of flats be repaired (the "same" interest) and, in the same proceedings, a claim for damages for each person (a similar interest). In such a case whether or not regulation 32 would have to be invoked would depend on which was the main purpose of the proceedings.

Where there are other persons having the same interest, the application will be:

   (a) *Granted* if the applicant would be substantially prejudiced by not being able to take his own proceedings;
   (b) *Refused* if the other persons would proceed without the applicant, and the applicant would get what he wanted as a result of those proceedings.

08–40 If the decision is to grant, the other persons having the same interest will be asked to contribute towards the costs of the proceedings if the area office considers it reasonable, bearing in mind the respective benefits to be obtained from the proceedings by the applicant and the others having the same interest. The additional contribution is based, if possible, on an assessment of means but otherwise on a proportional division of the estimated costs of the proceedings. If a contribution from others is sought, payment of the total contribution will be requested in, and be a condition of, the offer of legal aid to the applicant. If the applicant takes all reasonable steps to collect the additional contribution but is unable to do so, the contribution may be varied.

An example would be where six home-owners will benefit from proceedings involving a liability to maintain a road. The area office is satisfied as to the legal merits but only two of the home-owners are parties to proceedings and only one of those has applied for legal aid. There are therefore four home-owners who would benefit from the issue of a legal aid certificate to the applicant while a share of the costs will be attributable to the other named party in accordance with the normal rules of taxation. The area office will estimate the likely costs of a fully contested trial allowable against any legal aid certificate (say £10,000). It will disregard the costs payable by the other named party. This estimate is then divided between those who would benefit from the issue of a legal aid certificate (the applicant for legal aid and the four other home-owners) producing a notional share of costs £2,000 for each home-owner. If means assessments are available, contributions will be requested in accordance with them (up to £2,000). If no assessment is available, then £2,000 will be sought from each of the four, although it is for the applicant to seek to recover this and arrange its payment.

THE BOARDS STANDARDS ON CONSISTENCY

The Board has published standards on consistency of decision-making in **08–41** connection with consideration of civil legal aid applications. These are set out below.

General preliminary procedures to be followed before consideration of the legal merits or reasonableness of a legal aid application

Principle

Unless consideration of the statutory criteria of legal merits and reasonableness is accompanied by consideration of the basic requirements of whether legal aid is available for the proceedings and whether the applicant is a person to whom legal aid could be granted, as well as being a person who is financially eligible for legal aid, the final decision may not be justifiable to any of the legal aid stakeholders. If legal aid is not available for the proceedings or the applicant is not eligible financially or is not a person to whom legal aid can be granted, it does not matter how strong the merits of the case are or how reasonable in principle it may be for legal aid to be granted. Any decision to grant, in those circumstances, would not be justifiable to:

(a) the applicant who may have to face the consequences of being granted an invalid certificate;
(b) the solicitor who may be acting under an invalid certificate and may risk non-payment of costs;
(c) the court who may be misled into thinking that the proceedings are properly legally aided;
(d) the taxpayer who may have to pay out of the legal aid fund for any mistake made.

Standard

A caseworker considering a legal aid application should not proceed to **08–42** consideration of its legal merits or reasonableness without first being satisfied that legal aid is available for the proceedings and that the applicant is a person to whom legal aid can be granted.

163

Is Legal Aid available for the proceedings?

General

08–43

1. Are the proceedings for which legal aid is sought to be heard by a court? (Other than a Coroner's Court, the Court of Protection or the Restrictive Practices Court.)

1. If YES go to question 5.
   If NO go to next question.

2. Are the proceedings for which legal aid is sought before:
   (a) a Coroner's Court or
   (b) the Court of Protection?

2. If YES legal aid is not available and the standard is NOT satisfied.
   If NO go to next question.

3. Are the proceedings for which legal aid is sought to be heard by:
   (a) the Employment Appeal Tribunal?
   (b) the Lands Tribunal?
   (c) a Commons Commissioner?

3. If YES go to question 21.
   If NO go to next question.

4. Are the proceedings for which legal aid is sought in the Restrictive Practices Court under Part III of the Fair Trading Act 1973? (Legal Aid Act 1988, Pt. I, para. 6, Sched. 2)

4. If YES go to question 21.
   If NO legal aid is not available and the standard is NOT satisfied.

Court Proceedings—Type of Court

5. Is the court one of the following courts or has the case been referred to any person by the following:
   (a) House of Lords?
   (b) Court of Appeal?
   (c) High Court?
   (d) County Court?
   (e) Magistrates' Court?
   (Legal Aid Act 1988, Pt. I, paras. 1 and 2, Sched. 2)

5. If YES go to next question.
   If NO legal aid is not available and the standard is NOT satisfied.

Court Proceedings—Type of Case

6. Are the proceedings for which legal aid is sought in relation to defamation?

6. If YES go to question 13.
   If NO go to next question.

7. Are the proceedings for which legal aid is sought in relation to undefended divorce?

7. If YES got to question 19.
If NO go to next question.

8. Are the proceedings for which legal aid is sought in respect of or incidental to:
(a) a relator action?
(b) the recovery of penalties?
(c) an election petition?

8. If YES legal aid is not available and the standard is not satisfied. (Legal Aid Act 1988, Pt. II, paras. 2–4, Sched. 2).
If NO go to next question.

9. Are the proceedings in a county court?

9. If YES go to next question.
If NO go to question 11.

10. If the proceedings are in a county court does the application relate to:
(a) taking or defending judgment summons proceedings?
(b) in the case of a defendant in a county court, a matter where only the time and mode of payment is in issue?

10. If YES legal aid is not available and the standard is not satisfied (Legal Aid Act 1988, Pt. II, para. 5, Sched. 2).
If NO go to question 21.

11. Are the proceedings in a magistrates' court?

11. If YES go to next question.
If NO go to question 21.

12. If the proceedings are in a magistrates' court do they come within any of the following categories:
(a) Guardianship of Minors Acts 1971 & 1973—now repealed,
(b) Social Security Administration Act 1992, s. 106 (or earlier legislation),
(c) ss. 27, 28, 29 or 55 of the Adoption Act 1976,
(d) Maintenance Orders (Reciprocal Enforcement) Act 1972 to enforce in England and Wales a maintenance order made by a Court outside the United Kingdom,
(e) Part II of the Children Act 1975—now repealed,
(f) Part I of the Domestic Proceedings and Magistrates' Courts Act 1978,
(g) Children Act 1989,

12. If YES go to question 21.
If NO legal aid is NOT available and the standard is NOT satisfied (Legal Aid Act 1988, Pt. I, para. 2, Sched. 2).

(h) Appeals under s. 20 (where they are to be made to a magistrates' court) and proceedings under s. 27 of the Child Support Act 1991,

(i) proceedings under s. 30 Human Fertilisation and Embryology Act 1990.

Defamation (Legal Aid Act 1988, Pt. II, para. 1, Sched. 2)

13. Does the applicant wish to take proceedings for defamation?

13. If YES legal aid not available and the standard is NOT satisfied.
If NO go to next question.

14. Does the claim for defamation first appear in a counterclaim by the defendant?

14. If YES go to next question.
If NO legal aid is not available and the standard is NOT satisfied.

15. Are the proceedings such that legal aid is available apart from the defamation issue?

15. If YES go to next question.
If NO legal aid is not available and the standard is NOT satisfied.

16. Is the application for legal aid by the plaintiff in the proceedings?

16. If YES go to question 21.
If NO legal aid is not available and the standard is not satisfied.

Undefended Divorce and Judicial Separation (Legal Aid Act 1988, Pt. II, para. 5A, Sched. 2)

17. Is the application by a petitioner to take divorce or judicial separation proceedings?

17. If YES go to next question.
If NO the standard does not apply.

18. Is the cause defended?

18. If YES legal aid is available and the application may be considered on its merits.
If NO go to the next question.

19. Has the petition been directed to be heard in open court?

19. If YES legal aid is available and the application may be considered on its merits.
If NO go to the next question.

20. Is it impracticable by reason of physical or mental incapacity for the applicant to proceed without representation?

20. If YES legal aid is available and the application may be considered on its merits.
If NO legal aid is not available and the standard is NOT satisfied but consideration may be given to representation on ancillary matters or for an injunction.

Is the applicant a person to whom legal aid can be granted? (Legal Aid Act 1988, ss.2(10) and 15(3A)

21. Is the applicant applying for legal aid as an individual on his or her own behalf?

   21. If YES this part of the standard is satisfied.
   If NO go to next question.

22. Is the applicant applying for legal aid as a partner or member of a firm on his or her own behalf?

   22. If YES this part of the standard is satisfied.
   If NO go to next question.

23. Is the applicant applying for legal aid as a company or other body corporate or unincorporate for the purpose of that company or body or is the applicant a local authority, prescribed body, guardian *ad litem* applying for legal aid in Children Act proceedings?

   23. If YES this part of the standard is NOT satisfied.
   If NO go to next question.

24. Is the applicant applying for legal aid in a representative fiduciary or official capacity, whether as a company or other body corporate or unincorporate or as an individual?

   24. If YES this part of the standard is satisfied.
   If NO this part of the standard is NOT satisfied and legal aid cannot be granted.

Fruitless litigation

Principle

If the application is to take proceedings for a purely monetary claim against a defendant who is uninsured or otherwise without means to satisfy any judgment, a grant of legal aid will not be justifiable: **08–44**

  (a) to the taxpayer, because costs will be paid out for nothing.

  (b) to the applicant, because a grant of legal aid would raise hopes which would not be satisfied. An applicant might indeed end up worse off financially if there is a contribution which is non-returnable.

Standard

Legal aid should only be granted for purely monetary claims where there is reason to believe that the defendant has sufficient means to meet the claim by insurance or otherwise.   **08–45**

Questions to be asked

1. Is the claim one for which there is compulsory insurance in respect of the accident with protection if the defendant is not insured? (*e.g.* motor accidents involving personal injury, damage and Motor Insurers Bureau)

1. If YES, the standard is satisfied. If NO go to next question.

2. Is the claim one in respect of which there is compulsory insurance but no protection if the defendant is not insured? (*e.g.* employees' insurance)

2. If YES, go to question 4. If NO go to next question.

3. Is the defendant privately insured or covered by the policy of a Third Party? (*e.g.* motor accident involving vehicle damage)

3. If YES, the standard is satisfied. If NO go to next question.

4. Has the defendant means to satisfy any judgment and pay costs?

4. If YES go to next question. If NO go to question 6.

5. How does the solicitor know the defendant has means? (*e.g.* is there a status report)

5. If there is satisfactory evidence that the solicitor has some basis for the answer YES to question 4, the standard is satisfied. If NO go to next question.

6. Is the conclusion that:
(a) The defendant by insurance or private means can satisfy any judgment?
(b) The defendant is not insured and has no means to meet the claim?
(c) There is no information about the defendant's means?

6. If YES to:
(a) The standard is satisfied and the application can be granted on this aspect.
(b) The standard is NOT satisfied and this factor should be considered as one of the grounds of refusal.
(c) The standard is NOT satisfied and this factor should be considered as one of the grounds of refusal. Alternatively, if the case has sufficient legal merits *and* the quantum of damages is substantial (*i.e.* over £1,000), consideration may be given to granting a certificate limited to obtaining evidence of means, including a status report subject to a maximum cost.

Cost benefit

Principle

If the application is to take proceedings in which the estimated costs to the **08–46**
applicant are likely to exceed the value of any benefit gained by the
applicant, a grant of legal aid will not be justifiable:
- (a) to the applicant if it raises expectations which cannot be satisfied
  because any award will be absorbed by payment of a contribution
  and/or the statutory charge;
- (b) to the courts if time and resources are used up by cases which
  would not be pursued in the absence of legal aid because the
  applicant, were he/she a person of moderate means, would not
  have paid privately for the proceedings;
- (c) to the taxpayer if money is spent for nothing, *i.e.* if the award in
  the proceedings is not sufficient to cover the statutory charge.

Standard

Legal aid should only be granted to pursue a case in which costs are likely **08–47**
to exceed the value of any benefit gained thereby where:
- (a) there is a high prospect of success and the opponent is likely to
  indemnify the applicant for the legal costs; or
- (b) what is at stake is of such overwhelming importance to the
  applicant that it overrides the question of costs.

Questions to be asked

1. Has the claim a monetary value?

1. If YES go to question 2.
   If NO go to question 7.

2. What is the approximate amount of the claim?

2. £ . . . .
   Go to question 3.

3. Is the amount of the claim less than £1,000?

3. If YES the standard is NOT satisfied and the application should be refused.
   If NO, go to question 4.

4. What is the estimated amount of costs?

4. £ . . . .

5. If 2 exceeds 4:
   (a) Is it by a margin of £1,000 or under?
   or
   (b) Is it by a margin of over £1,000?

5. (a) If YES, go to question 6(a).
   If NO, go to question 5(b).

   (b) If YES the standard is satisfied and the remaining questions may be ignored.

169

6. If 4 exceeds 2:
   (a) Is there a high prospect of success?

   (b) Is the opponent likely to indemnify the applicant for legal costs?

6. (a) If YES, go to question 6(b).
   If NO, the standard is NOT satisfied and the application should be refused.
   (b) If YES, the standard is satisfied and the remaining questions may be ignored.
   If NO, the standard is NOT satisfied and the application should be refused.

7. If the claim is NOT monetary is there a benefit which the applicant will gain from the proceedings?

8. Can the benefit be quantified in financial terms?

7. If YES, go to question 8.
   If NO, the standard is NOT satisfied and the application should be refused.

8. If YES, return to questions 2–6 and answer as if for monetary claims.
   If NO, the standard is NOT satisfied and the application should be refused UNLESS the benefit to the applicant is of such importance that it would justify the costs of the proceedings.

Persons other than the applicant having an interest in the proceedings

Principle

08–48   A decision to grant legal aid where persons other than the applicant are concerned jointly in the proceedings or have the same interest as the applicant, without either considering whether legal aid is necessary at all or calling for the appropriate contribution from such other person, would not be justifiable to the taxpayer because persons other than the applicant might benefit from the proceedings without contributing to the public purse.

Standard

08–49   Legal aid should only be granted where persons other than the applicant are concerned jointly in the proceedings or have the same interest as the applicant where:

   (a) the applicant would be substantially prejudiced by refusal of legal aid; and

170

(b) persons other than the applicant are called upon to make, if appropriate, a contribution towards the cost of the proceedings.

Questions to be asked

1. Are there persons other than the applicant with an interest in the proceedings?

   1. If YES go to question 2.
   If NO this standard does NOT arise and all remaining questions may be ignored.

2. Do the other persons have merely a "similar" interest to the applicant in the proceedings? (see NFG for definition).

   2. If YES this standard does NOT arise and all remaining questions may be ignored.
   If NO go to question 3.

3. Do the other persons have either a joint interest with or the same interest as the applicant in the proceedings? (see NFG for definition).

   3. If YES go to question 4.
   If NO this standard does NOT arise and all remaining questions may be ignored.

4. Can the other person proceed without the applicant, so that the applicant will get what he/she wants from the proceedings even if not a party?

   4. If YES the standard is NOT satisfied and the application should be refused.
   If NO, the standard is satisfied subject to question 5 below.

5. Is it reasonable on a grant to ask the other persons to contribute towards the costs of the proceedings, bearing in mind the respective benefits to be gained by them from the proceedings.

   5. If YES the standard is satisfied and the contribution should be calculated, called for and the appropriate offer is issued.
   If NO the standard is satisfied and the offer/certificate should be sent to the applicant in the usual way.

Other rights and facilities making it unnecessary for legal aid to be granted

Principle

If the applicant has the ability to pursue the proceedings other than through **08–50** legal aid, a decision to grant legal aid would not be justifiable to the taxpayer because of the use of public money where private money was available.

Standard

08–51 Legal aid should only be granted to a person who has other rights or facilities which make it unnecessary for him/her to obtain legal aid or who has a reasonable expectation of obtaining financial help from a body of which he/she is a member where:

  (a) the applicant has been unsuccessful in taking all reasonable steps to enforce or obtain such rights, facilities or help; or

  (b) restrictions on the rights, facilities or help make them disadvantageous compared with legal aid.

Questions to be asked

1. Has the applicant:
   (a) Other rights or facilities enabling him or her to take the proceedings, or
   (b) The expectation of obtaining financial help from a body of which he or she is a member?

1. If YES to either, go to question 2. If NO the standard does not arise and subsequent questions may be ignored.

2. Has the applicant been unsuccessful in taking all reasonable steps to enforce or obtain such rights, facilities or help?

2. If YES the standard is satisfied and subsequent questions may be ignored.
If NO go to question 3.

3. Are the other rights, facilities or help disadvantageous compared with legal aid? (e.g. are there restrictions on costs or the type of proceedings or, in the case of a restriction on choice of solicitor, does the applicant have valid reasons for not wishing that solicitor to act?)

3. If YES the standard is satisfied and the application may be granted subject to a limitation if appropriate. Note that the applicant's selection of a solicitor who is not approved by his trade union, which is then unwilling to provide assistance, will normally satisfy the standard.
If NO, the standard is not satisfied and legal aid is not available.

Reasonableness of granting legal aid where merits are below average but possible damages are large

Principle

08–52 Where the legal merits of a case are poor, a decision to grant legal aid merely because the amount at stake was large would not be justifiable:

172

(a) to the applicant in raising hopes which would probably not be fulfilled,

(b) to the taxpayer in expenditure of large sums on unmeritorious proceedings, or

(c) to the courts who would have to devote time and trouble to an unmeritorious case.

Standard

Where the prospects of success are below average it would be **08–53** unreasonable to grant legal aid merely because the amount at stake is large or the consequences to the applicant are great.

Questions to be asked

1. Is the amount of the claim £50,000 or over?

   1. If YES go to question 2. If NO the standard does not arise and all subsequent questions may be ignored.

2. Are the legal prospects of success:
   (a) Good?
   (b) Average?
   (c) Below average?

   2. (a) If YES the standard does not arise and all subsequent questions may be ignored.
   (b) If YES the standard may be satisfied but only if the costs are likely to be reasonably low compared with the amount of the claim.
   (c) If YES the standard is NOT satisfied and the application should be refused.

REFUSAL AND (PART REFUSAL) OF APPLICATIONS

When an application is refused, the area office will notify the solicitor and **08–54** the applicant of (a) the ground for refusal and (b) the reasons for refusal. The ground for refusal will be one of the statutory grounds in the 1988 Act. The reasons will be the reasons giving rise to the refusal under the stated statutory ground.

When an application is granted only in part, the applicant will be sent an offer of legal aid. He may either accept this and (if necessary) apply later for an amendment to cover the balance of what he applied for; or he may appeal against the decision to grant only in part. If an application is granted in full but the certificate is limited, *e.g.* limited to counsel's opinion, an offer will not be sent (unless the applicant has a contribution to pay — in such cases offers are always sent because applicants have to decide whether they are willing to pay the contributions and accept legal aid). Instead, a certificate will be issued on the basis that legal aid has been granted for the specified proceedings.[14] A later application can then be made for the removal of the limitation.

APPEALS

08–55 Appeals are determined by subcommittees of the relevant area committee. Notice of appeal, which should be given on the form sent by the Board with the refusal notice, should be given within 14 days' notice of the decision to be appealed.[15] In practice, this time-limit is not strictly applied by Area Directors and notices of appeal are frequently accepted out of time.[16]

Every appeal is by way of reconsideration of the application[17] and the appellant may submit further statements (orally or in writing) in support of his application. In practice, area committees will consider any further documentation submitted in support of the appeal.[18]

The appellant may conduct the appeal himself (with or without the assistance of any other person he may appoint for the purpose) or may be represented by counsel, a solicitor or a legal executive.[19]

The area committee must determine the appeal in such manner as seems to it to be just. In particular, it may:

    (a) dismiss the appeal;

    (b) direct the Area Director to offer a certificate subject to such terms and conditions as it thinks fit;

---

[14] It is common for certificates to bear limitations and many bear standard limitations requiring the solicitor to report to the area office at a certain point in proceedings. Most certificates will bear conditions requiring the solicitor to report when costs of the specified amount have been incurred.

[15] Civil Legal Aid (General) Regulations 1989, reg. 36.

[16] *ibid.* reg. 7(2).

[17] *ibid.* reg. 37.

[18] *ibid.* reg. 38(1).

[19] *ibid.* reg. 38. The Green Form Scheme cannot be used to enable "representation" to be provided (as it covers only advice and assistance) and an extension to the Green Form to enable a MacKenzie adviser will only be granted in exceptional cases because the procedure is essentially informal and the committee will be willing to help the appellant to put his case. (In a very small number of appeals involving multi-party actions the Board has been willing to finance legal representation by way of grant. However, such cases are very rare and no such provision is made by Regulations. The grants are made under the Board's general powers under the Legal Aid Act 1988.)

(c) direct the Area Director to settle terms and conditions on which a certificate may be offered;

(d) refer the matter, or any part of it, back to the Area Director for his determination or report.[20]

The area committee's decision on any appeal is final and it must give notice of its decision and the reasons for it to the appellant and to any solicitor acting for him.[21]

REPEATED REFUSAL OF CERTIFICATES

A person whose appeal is dismissed may, nevertheless, apply again for legal aid.[22] However, if a person has applied for and been refused a certificate on three separate occasions and the Area Director considers that his conduct amounts to an abuse of the 1988 Act, the Area Director may report the matter to the area committee.[23]

08–56

If the Area Director makes such a report, the area committee may inquire whether any other area office has received any application from the person and call for a report as to the circumstances of any such application. It may, if it considers that the person has abused the facilities provided by the 1988 Act, report to the Board making such recommendations as seem to it to be just.[24]

When the Board receives such a report, it must give the person named in it the opportunity to make representations in writing. These may be made by him or by someone on his behalf. It must also make such other inquiries as seem to it to be necessary. If the Board then considers that his conduct has amounted to an abuse of the facilities provided by the 1988 Act, it may make a "prohibitory direction".[25]

A prohibitory direction may provide that no consideration shall, for a period not exceeding five years, be given by any Area Director either (a) to any pending or future application by that person for a certificate with regard to any particular matter; or (b) in exceptional circumstances, to any pending or future application by him whatsoever.[26] The Board may, in its discretion, include within the terms of any prohibitory direction, any receiver, next friend or guardian *ad litem* who applies for a certificate on behalf of the person referred to in the prohibitory direction.[27]

08–57

---

[20] Civil Legal Aid (General) Regulations 1989, reg. 39.
[21] *ibid.* reg. 39(2).
[22] There will be little point in doing this unless there is further information available.
[23] Civil Legal Aid (General) Regulations 1989, reg. 40.
[24] *ibid.* reg. 40(2).
[25] *ibid.* reg. 41(1).
[26] *ibid.* reg. 41(1).
[27] *ibid.* reg. 41(2).

Chapter 9

THE ORDINARY CERTIFICATE — SCOPE AND LIMITATIONS/ CONDITIONS

LAYOUT

The form of certificate has a unique reference number which is shown at **09–01** the top together with the solicitor's account number and a case code which is used by the Board for statistical purposes. The first two numbers can be used to identify the area office which issued it, the next two indicate the type of legal aid (01 for civil legal aid, 37 for ABWOR), the next two the year of receipt of the application with the final numbers and letter being allocated in sequence from January each year. The final letter which should be quoted is an identifier required for computer purposes. The certificate is addressed to the assisted person and indicates whether it is financially connected with any other certificate. The description of legal aid is contained in paragraph 1 of the certificate with any conditions and limitations being contained in paragraph 2 and details of any contribution at paragraph 3. The name of the nominated individual solicitor is shown at paragraph 4 together with his reference. The solicitor's address appears at the bottom of the form together with the signature and address of the area office and the date of the certificate.

It is important to check the wording of any certificate issued and make a note of any restrictions. A certificate may be restricted by:

    (a) covering only part of the proceedings, *e.g.* covering only ancillary relief in divorce;

    (b) stipulating that the proceedings may only be taken in a particular court (*i.e.* the county court rather than the High Court);

    (c) imposing a special condition or conditions, *e.g.* as to the amount of costs to be incurred without further reference to the area office;

    (d) limiting the steps which may be taken.

The first two of these options are dealt with in paragraph 1 of the

177

certificate (in the description of legal aid, although a condition may be used to stipulate the forum in which proceedings must be commenced, *e.g.* in private law Children Act proceedings) and the second two in paragraph 2 of the certificate. The last option is commonly referred to as a "limited certificate".

09–02   Steps which are taken outside the scope or limitation of the certificate will not be remunerated but a certificate may be amended to remove or amend any restriction, stipulation, condition or limitation. Where an Area Director refuses an application for a certificate or an applicant is dissatisfied with the terms upon which the Area Director would be prepared to issue it, the applicant has a right of appeal to the area committee (save as to the means assessment or the Area Director's decision as to the amount and method of payment of the applicant's contribution). Note, however, that there is a right of a real against a decision as to sums payable where others have an interest or the application is made in a representative, fiduciary or official capacity.[1] In Children Act cases a certificate may be issued, rather than an offer or letter indicating the extent of the grant being dispatched — this is to avoid delay if the applicant is prepared to accept the certificate as granted. If he is not, then the certificate can be amended in the event of a successful appeal.

Paragraph 1 of the certificate — description of legal aid

09–03   The description of legal aid may cover only part of the proceedings, *e.g.*, it may permit the defending of an action but it will not cover a counterclaim unless this is specifically stated. It may only cover certain aspects of proceedings — this is most common in the matrimonial context — and it will only cover the normal steps in the proceedings which are specifically stated.

The description of legal aid must specify the parties to the proceedings unless it relates to family proceedings (as defined by regulation 3(1) of the Civil Legal Aid (General) Regulations 1989 and including proceedings under the Domestic Violence and Matrimonial Proceedings Act 1976).[2]

A certificate is not permitted to relate "more than one action, cause or matter" except in the case of:

(a) family proceedings; or

(b) an application for a grant of representation to enable the action which is the subject matter of the certificate to be brought; or

(c) an application for pre-action disclosure under section 33 of the Supreme Court Act 1981 or section 52 of the County Courts Act 1984 and subsequent court proceedings; or

---

[1] Civil Legal Aid (General) Regulations 1989, reg. 35.
[2] *ibid.* reg. 47.

(d) proceedings which, under the 1988 Act, may be taken to enforce or give effect to any order or agreement made in the proceedings to which the certificate relates. This includes proceedings in bankruptcy or to wind up a company but note that this covers only *taking* proceedings and that it is not permissible for defending bankruptcy proceedings to be included in a certificate covering other proceedings[3]

If the proceedings in question could be taken in different courts and the forum is not specified in the description of legal aid, then there is no restriction as to where the proceedings may be taken but if, *e.g.*, the solicitor decides to take the proceedings in the High Court this will have to be justified on taxation. If the certificate specifies that proceedings must be taken in a particular court, usually the county court, then it will only cover proceedings in that level of court and proceedings issued outside that level will be outside the scope of the certificate. Note, however, that no amendment is required to cover work done following the transfer of a case covered by a High Court certificate to a county court. Note also that in private law Children Act proceedings between individuals a condition may require the proceedings to be *commenced* at a particular level of court. **09–04**

Paragraph 2 of the certificate — conditions and limitations (if any)

Paragraph 2 of the certificate may contain special conditions as to the issue and continued existence of the certificate or as to the conduct of the proceedings including the costs to be incurred. The condition (other than a condition as to costs) could be a requirement to be satisfied either at the outset or subsequently. If a condition was not satisfied then any certificate issued could be withdrawn, but only by way of discharge (rather than revocation), following the show cause procedure. If, however, work is done and costs incurred in breach of a condition, *e.g.*, only to commence proceedings once certain requirements (*e.g.* as to the defendants, status) are met, then the costs would be unlikely to be allowed. The practitioner should, therefore, apply for the amendment or deletion of the condition, as appropriate. **09–05**

In private law Children Act proceedings between individuals a condition may be inserted requiring the proceedings to be commenced in the magistrates' (or county) court. This does not prevent a vertical transfer of the proceedings in accordance with the Children (Allocation of Proceedings) Order 1991 and no authority or amendment is required to apply for the transfer or continue to prosecute the proceedings if transferred.

---

[3] *ibid.* reg. 46(3).

The insertion of such a condition may be appealed to the area committee but the solicitor may prefer to commence the proceedings and seek a transfer. Public law Children Act cases can be transferred in accordance with the Children (Allocation of Proceedings) Order 1991 in any event.

The following are common forms of condition together with the meaning normally attached to them and comments on any likely points of difficulty. The identification codes used below are those used internally within the Board's area offices.

Civil legal aid conditions

L040

09–06 It is a condition of this certificate that if it covers ancillary relief it is restricted to the obtaining of one substantive order and if it covers contact residence order.

This condition has been in use for a period of some years. It prevents more than one order being obtained in respect of ancillary relief or contact. Its use means that once a final order has been obtained the solicitor must seek an amendment to the certificate to apply for a further order or variation or even to become involved in further negotiations. The aim is that the solicitor's application for an amendment will enable the area office to consider the merits of the aspect in respect of which further legal aid cover is sought.

L043

It is a condition of this offer than no certificate will be issued until the concurrent offers of legal aid sent to — have all been accepted and the first instalments of contribution payable have been paid.

This condition merely makes clear that related offers are being made and that they will only be processed together. This is to avoid those who do not accept an offer and make the first contribution from benefitting from a certificate issued to another applicant.

There is a similar condition (reference L064) which indicates that no costs are to be incurred until legal aid certificate(s) have been issued to certain named persons.

L044

It is a condition of this certificate that the solicitor shall not be entitled to payment in respect of any additional costs or disbursements incurred by reason of the fact that he/she does not carry on his/her practice at or near the place where his/her services are required in acting under this certificate.

This is the condition which is used to restrict costs pursuant to regulation 48 of the Civil Legal Aid (General) Regulations 1989.

L048

It is a condition of this certificate that the assisted person and/or his solicitor shall report forthwith if — ceases to be legally aided or to instruct solicitors privately.

This condition may be included in a certificate to ensure that the area office is able to consider the position if those who would benefit from the certificate cease to take action on their own behalf.

L049

It is a condition of the issue and continuation of this certificate that the assisted person shall pay an additional contribution of £ — to reflect the interest in the proceedings of others who are not legally aided, pursuant to regulation 32(3) of the Civil Legal Aid (General) Regulations 1989.

This is the condition which is included in offers which include a contribution element and is attributable to those who will benefit from the existence of the assisted person's certificate because they have an involvement in and the same interest as the applicant in the outcome of the proceedings. Where such a contribution is included it will be based either on an actual means assessment or on such other information which is made available to the area office. The contribution may be from capital or income (and payable accordingly). Note that such a contribution may be appealed to the area committee in accordance with regulation 35(2)(b) of the Civil Legal Aid (General) Regulations 1989 (either as to the amount or the method of payment). Note also that the amount of such a contribution may be redetermined where the area office is satisfied that the applicant has, without success, taken all reasonable steps to obtain such payment, including permitting the area office to take those steps (regulation 32(4) of the Civil Legal Aid (General) Regulations 1989). With ongoing contributions from income the condition is likely to be a source of difficulty — if the applicant is not able to successfully appeal the condition he will have a redetermination or be at risk of the certificate being discharged if income instalments are not kept up to date.

L057

Work done in the proceedings covered by this certificate but prior to its issue is deemed to be done while the certificate is in force (see regulation 12A(3) of the Civil Legal Aid (General) Regulations 1989) and costs may be claimed accordingly.

This is the wording which is used in the second paragraph of the certificate to make it clear that costs from instruction are deemed to be within the scope of the certificate in special Children Act cases.

L058

It is a condition of this certificate that any proceedings be commenced in the magistrates' court although they may be transferred in accordance with the Children (Allocation of Proceedings) Order 1991.

This is the wording which is used to require proceedings to be commenced in the magistrates' court (family proceedings court). L059 is the corresponding county court condition.

Costs conditions

L066

09–07 It is a condition that the solicitor shall report to the area office on form CLA30 if profit costs, disbursements and counsel's fees exceed £ —. If an extension is not obtained, subsequent profit costs may be deferred.

There are also related conditions (references L073 and L074) which include costs figures of £2,500 and £7,500 respectively. These conditions are part of the Board's system of case control. They are widely used in that they are included in all non-matrimonial, non-family certificates issued after September 1992. They mean that the Board will not routinely require reports from solicitors under regulation 70(2) of the Civil Legal Aid (General) Regulations 1989. The condition is effectively a request for a report pursuant to regulation 70(1) of the Civil Legal Aid (General) Regulations 1989.

They may also be used as an alternative to a solicitor's undertaking as to costs where an ongoing contribution is waived.

The sanction for a failure to report is that action may be taken by th Board under regulation 102 of the Civil Legal Aid (General) Regulations 1989 to defer the solicitor's profit costs and/or refer the solicitor's conduct to the Solicitors' Disciplinary Tribunal. The condition places the legally aided client in the same position as a fee-paying client, in that if the stated costs limit is exceeded and not subsequently extended, then the solicitor may not obtain payment. This is akin to the situation where a fee-paying client authorises a solicitor to incur costs only to a stated amount.

The solicitor's profit costs (excluding disbursements and counsel's fees) may only be deferred where the limit has been exceeded and not extended and it is considered that, had there been a report to the area office, the limit would not have been increased and the certificate would have been discharged. In the event of a deferments the disbursements and counsel's fees will be paid but the solicitor will only receive his profit costs for the balance of the specified limit.

If there is a late report (*i.e.* where the limit has been exceeded) rather than no report, then the solicitor is at risk of a regulation 102 of this 1989 Regulations deferment if the limit is not increased. Costs incurred in excess of the limit can still be paid either as a result of the limit being extended or there being no deferment.

The condition has no relevance on taxation but on receiving claims for payment the area offices will check the condition and consider whether a regulation 102 of this 1989 Regulations deferment would be appropriate.

Any decision to defer may be made by authorised area office staff but their decision can, on the solicitor's request, be reviewed by the area committee on whose behalf the delegated decision to defer has been made.

Solicitors will need to check certificates on receipt for any costs condition and to apply for an amendment to the costs figure when the amount in any condition is being approached (although that limit can be increased even though it has been exceeded).

Limitations will continue to be used as appropriate. However, in high cost cases (that is where costs and disbursements are expected to be over £2,500) it will be usual for certificates to be limited to obtaining further evidence and counsel's opinion thereafter. If proceedings have already been commenced, certificates will normally require counsel's opinion to be obtained before trial.

Although costs may only be deferred in very limited circumstances the prudent solicitor will monitor the costs which are being incurred and will ensure that an application for an amendment to the figure contained in the condition is sought in sufficient time for the stated amount not to be exceeded. Note that in each case the figure is the profit costs, disbursements and counsel's fees exclusive of VAT but that only the solicitor's profit costs may be deferred.

L076

To ensure that the appropriate proportion of costs is attributed to this certificate it is a condition of this certificate that on taxation the nominated solicitor makes the taxing officer aware of any period during which he was instructed on a private client basis by a party to the proceedings.

This condition will be used to ensure that where the solicitor is representing other parties to proceedings and he is also acting under a legal aid certificate, this is specifically drawn to the attention of the taxing officer who will then ensure that the costs are correctly apportioned as between the legally assisted person and any fee-paying clients.

Multi-party action conditions

L901

09–08 The certificate is issued subject to the condition that no work whatsoever shall be undertaken under this certificate without further authorisation by the area office. It should be noted that generic work is being undertaken under another certificate and the area committee has decided that no work shall be done under this certificate pending further review by the area office.

This condition has the effect of giving an applicant legal aid but preventing any work from being undertaken without the authority of the area office. The authority of the area office is normally given in the form of a letter and will depend on the need for work to be undertaken to protect the assisted person's position. Arrangements will be likely to be made to ensure that the generic costs are ultimately shared between the parties, if necessary, by a costs sharing order.

L903

This certificate is limited to all steps up to and including discovery and inspection of documents and obtaining counsel's opinion at that stage. It is a condition of this certificate that no generic work be carried out without the prior authority of the area office.

This limitation and condition enables the case to be taken to discovery and inspection of documents, followed by counsel's opinion being obtained but no generic work can be carried out without the prior authority of the area office. This condition will be used where generic work is being dealt with by a steering committee or where the area office wishes to retain an overview in relation to generic work. There are similar conditions (L094 and L095) which respectively cover the obtaining of counsel's opinion but not the issue of proceedings and which simply provide that no generic work should be carried out.

Any limitation on the steps which may be taken will be contained in paragraph 2 of the certificate. The limitation may actually not permit proceedings to be commenced or may enable proceedings to be taken up to a certain stage. The inclusion of limitations enables the Area Director to be satisfied that further steps should be taken in that if the cover is to be extended the solicitor must apply for the amendment of the limitation (to cover further steps) or for its removal. This gives the Area Director an opportunity to consider the case at that point.

The restrictions contained in paragraph 1 of the certificate will be made known in any notice of issue/amendment required to be served on other parties.[4] Conditions and limitations contained in paragraph 2 of the

---

[4] Civil Legal Aid (General) Regulations 1989, regs. 50(1), 54(2).

certificate need not be referred to in such a notice unless the certificate relates to an appeal.[5]

Regulation 46(1) of the Legal Aid (General) Regulations 1989 provides that a certificate may cover the whole or part of proceedings and may be extended to cover appellate proceedings other than those in the House of Lords or on appeal from a magistrates' court (except in special Children Act proceedings).

The power to issue a limited certificate has been accepted by the Court **09–09** of Appeal[6] and section 15(4) of the 1988 Act specifically refers to the fact that civil legal aid may be granted with or without limitations.

A fresh legal aid application must be made for House of Lords appeals or appeals against magistrates' court orders, except where non-means, non-merits tested legal aid is available (i.e. for special Children Act proceedings), in which case an existing certificate can be amended. Even if a further certificate is needed the Area Director is not required to obtain a reassessment of means.[7]

A certificate, including an emergency certificate may be amended to remove or vary existing limitations or impose new limitations.[8] An amendment may also widen or narrow the scope of the certificate and remove or vary any special conditions.

There is specific provision for a certificate to state that where a nominated **09–10** solicitor carries on his practice so far away from where his services will be required in acting that this will result in significantly greater expense to the Fund than would have been the case if another solicitor had been selected, he is not entitled to payment of any additional costs or disbursements incurred by reason of the fact that he does not carry on his practice at or near the place where his services are required. If such a provision is inserted in a certificate it will appear as a condition in paragraph 2 and the consequence will be that payment of the additional costs or disbursements will not be allowed on determination of costs.[9] Even where such a condition is not included in the certificate the distant solicitor will have to justify his costs and disbursements in the usual way and he will therefore, need to consider to what extent it would be appropriate for him to instruct a local solicitor agent.

The effect of limited certificates

Within its limitation, a limited certificate confers the same benefits on the **09–11** holder as does an unlimited certificate. Any limitation is subject to the

---

[5] *Scarth v. Jacobs-Paton, The Times*, November 1; 1978.
[6] *Dugon v. Williamson* [1963] 3 All E.R. 25.
[7] *ibid.* reg. 18(2).
[8] Civil Legal Aid (General) Regulations 1989, reg. 51.
[9] *ibid.* reg. 48.

185

ordinary rules of construction but it should be borne in mind that the case should be conducted reasonably and that it will not be appropriate to undertake all the work *permitted* in *every* case. The solicitor must exercise his judgement and not unreasonably continue the case. If the assisted person requires the solicitor to unreasonably continue the case, then the solicitor is under a duty to report to the Area Director[10] and if the solicitor or counsel is uncertain whether it would be reasonable for him to continue acting this must be reported to the Area Director.[11]

Forms of limitation

09–12 If a limited certificate is issued the area office will not draw particular attention to the limitation nor explain its meaning. It will be subject to the ordinary rules of construction but if a solicitor is in doubt as to whether certain steps are within the scope of the certificate (including any limitation), then he should seek clarification from the area office or apply for an amendment to the limitation.

The following comments deal with any likely points of difficulty:

(a) The interpretation of the wording of a legal aid certificate is always a matter for decision by the taxing officer in the light of any representations made by the solicitor whose remedy is to carry in objections. The area office's views can be sought as to the meaning of any particular wording but the area office will only be able to express a view for consideration by the taxing officer.

(b) Any limitations which include the obtaining of counsel's opinion may specify whether the opinion is to be on merits, on quantum or on merits and quantum. The area office may alternatively indicate that the opinion must cover a particular point or points. Where the area to be covered by the opinion is specified this is because the area office sees that subject area as being a source of difficulty and it will limit the certificate so as to enable that source of difficulty to be addressed at least possible cost. By way of an example, the area office will require an opinion on merits where it has no concern on quantum and does not wish the expense of establishing quantum to be incurred *until* it is satisfied that the merits are sufficiently strong to justify the continued existence of the certificate. The Board will expect any guidance on the contents of opinions in legal aid matters' issued by the Bar Council to be followed.

(c) Any certificate which covers obtaining counsel's opinion includes the gathering of evidence/information sufficient to enable counsel

---

[10] *ibid.* reg. 67(1).
[11] *ibid.* reg. 67(2).

186

to advise effectively. It is accepted that incomplete instructions should not be put to counsel but obviously the solicitor must justify the costs and disbursements incurred in preparing the matter for counsel on either assessment or taxation of the costs claim. If the solicitor wishes to be sure that payment will be received, then specific authority should be sought as appropriate, although the solicitor will only wish to seek authority where he feels at risk either as to the principle of a particular disbursement/act or as to the amount involved.

(d) If a certificate covers obtaining counsel's opinion, the area office will normally wish to see the written opinion. If, however, the solicitor is of the view that an opinion is not required at all, *e.g.* because he considers that he will be able to satisfy the area office as to the position by the preparation of a detailed report or, on the other hand because, *e.g.* negative medical or other evidence has been obtained and the expense of instructing counsel would not be justified, then he should contact the area office either seeking an amendment to the limitation or providing a written report as to the position.

(e) Any certificate which covers obtaining counsel's opinion will only cover the obtaining of one opinion. If, *e.g.* counsel advises that a further item of evidence should be gathered and placed before him for further advice, then an amendment to the limitation must be sought. Otherwise the work done after the obtaining of the opinion (beyond considering its contents and notifying the client) will be disallowed. This is so that the area office has the opportunity consider whether the expense of obtaining counsel's further opinion is actually justified. Note that although only one written opinion is covered an enquiry to counsel for clarification of genuine ambiguity may be allowed. The solicitor may however wish to clarify the position with the area office in any event. It is the view of the Board that a certificate covering counsel's opinion does extend to a conference. If a certificate specially indicates that counsel's opinion is to obtained only after a conference attended by the assisted person, then this indicates that the area office specifically wishes counsel to meet the client and discuss the case/ evidence with him/her. If it is intended in particular cases to restrict further preparatory work or the particular steps to be taken, this will be spelt out clearly in the terms of any limitation imposed. If that is not so, then it will be for the solicitor to justify a conference, unless he seeks an amendment to the certificate to ensure that the costs of a conference will be allowed. Such a request would effectively be for the insertion of a condition to be accepted on taxation. It is the view of the Board that there is no right of appeal against a refusal as a conference is within the scope of the certificate, although this would normally be subject to justification on taxation/assessment

(f) Emergency certificates will normally be limited in scope as they will only cover the urgent work which needs to be undertaken pending assessment of the assisted person's means. Ordinary certificates will often be limited — this is a method of ensuring that the solicitor must report to the area office (in seeking an amendment) and is, therefore, an element of case control. As part of its case control system the Board designates new non-matrimonial, non-family cases as low (up to £2,500), high (£2,500 to £7,500) and very high cost (above £7,500) — all inclusive of disbursements but exclusive of VAT. The designation will based on information given by the solicitor in the ordinary application Form CLA1, although the solicitor's estimate of costs (and prospects of success) will not necessarily be accepted by the area office. Very high cost cases will be dealt with by more senior staff in the area offices and both high and very high cost cases will generally be limited. Where proceedings have not been commenced the limitation will generally provide for further evidence and counsel's opinion to be obtained and after proceedings have been commenced the limitation will generally provide for counsel's opinion to be obtained before the matter proceeds to trial.

The following are common forms of limitation together with the meaning normally attached to them and comments on any likely points of difficulty.

Steps up to proceedings

L001

09–13 Limited to obtaining further evidence and thereafter counsel's opinion as to merits and quantum, to include the settling of proceedings or a defence (and counterclaim) if counsel so advises.

L067 and 068 which provide for counsel's opinion as to merits and as to quantum respectively, are otherwise the same as limitation L001. Note that this limitation specifically provides for the obtaining of further evidence as well as the settling of proceedings — including a counterclaim — if counsel so advises. The Board accepts that if there is a positive advice it is sensible for counsel to settle the necessary documents.

L002

Limited to obtaining a medical report.

There a number of similar wordings which enable particular specified types of reports to be obtained. They cover instructing the appropriate expert, considering the report and reporting to both the client and the area office. Generally, the limitation will not specify a maximum amount for obtaining the report and if the solicitor considers it would be prudent to do so, then he should apply for a specific authority to ensure that the full disbursement is recovered on taxation/assessment.

L006

Limited to obtaining further evidence and a solicitor's report.

This wording specifically enables further evidence to be obtained and then for the solicitor to report to the area office. In reporting the solicitor may seek an amendment to the effect that proceedings may be taken or may wish to obtain counsel's opinion. Costs incurred under this limitation must be justified in the usual way but there is another limitation (L008 — Limited to all steps up to but excluding commencement of proceedings; a solicitor's report is included but seeking counsel's opinion is not) which the Board considers to be somewhat wider in scope as the solicitor can gather all the evidence and take all the steps considered to be justified, short of commencing proceedings.

Medical negligence

L061

Limited to obtaining the appropriate medical reports (including if necessary **09–14** an application for pre-action discovery), obtaining independent medical report(s) (one per specialism) and thereafter to the preparation of papers for counsel and obtaining counsel's opinion, to include the settling of proceedings if counsel so advises.

This limitation includes an application for pre-action discovery. It enables more than one medical report to be obtained but only one per specialism. Note that it potentially includes the settling of proceedings and that an amendment/authority may be sought to increase the number of reports or specify the fees. The Board's Costs Appeals Committee has decided that it is not reasonable for a solicitor to examine original records as a matter of course but that where a solicitor has reason to believe that the copy records supplied are incomplete or inaccurate, this would be reasonable. It has also indicated that a certificate limited to obtaining or perusing medical records will cover inspection of original medical records.[12] The Committee has also decided that it is reasonable for the solicitor to consider in detail copies of the medical records relevant to the issues in the case.[13]

---

[12] See decision CLA4.
[13] See decision CLA7.

L077

Limited to all steps up to and including settling down, to include mutual exchange of factual witness statements under R.S.C., Ord. 38, r. 2A and mutual exchange of expert evidence under R.S.C., Ord. 38, r. 37 and to the preparation of papers for counsel and obtaining counsel's then opinion on merits, quantum and evidence.

Note that this limitation includes setting down as well as the mutual exchange of factual witness statements and expert evidence.

Steps after the issue of proceedings

L015

09–15 Limited to the issue of proceedings.

This limitation covers only the issue of proceedings and would be used to prevent a claim becoming statute barred (although query whether the reason(s) for delay would make the issue of an emergency certificate unlikely). The wording does not enable the proceedings to be served. It does not specify that the proceedings may be settled by counsel nor does it make any requirement as to forum which would need to be justified on taxation/assessment. There is a wider limitation L016 which also covers the service of proceedings as well as another limitation (L017) which covers the issue of proceedings and thereafter obtaining counsel's opinion.

L062

Limited to all steps up to but excluding trial but including obtaining counsel's opinion on merits, quantum and evidence.

This limitation includes setting down (as against limitation L063 which excludes setting down). There is also a more restrictive limitation L070 which includes setting down and thereafter mutual exchange of experts' reports. The solicitor should ensure that when any of these limitations are used counsel's opinion is obtained at the earliest opportunity and forwarded to the area office without delay. Otherwise there is a risk that the area office will seek to discharge the certificate shortly before trial with the possibility that if the certificate is discharged at a late stage the client cannot appeal to the Area Committee before the trial. The area offices cannot ensure that matters are put to the Area Committee before any particular hearing date.

There is a similar wording L026 which provides for a solicitor's report rather than counsel's opinion. Note also that there are two wordings L027 and L028 which cover all steps up to but excluding trial, and up to but excluding setting down respectively, but which do not require counsel's opinion to be obtained at that stage. Instead they cover the obtaining of counsel's opinion "if the solicitor considers it necessary". These wordings enable the solicitor to submit a report to the area office on merits, quantum and evidence himself if he considers that this will be sufficient to persuade the area office to lift the limitation and allow the matter to proceed.

L018

Limited to preparation and filing or delivery of a defence.

This limitation does not cover a counterclaim but only the defence. It is for the solicitor to justify the instruction of counsel under regulation 59(1) of the Civil Legal Aid (General) Regulations 1989 (*i.e* that the proper conduct of the proceedings requires the instruction of counsel).

L030

Limited to an application for the settling aside of a judgment/order and, if the solicitor considers it necessary, to the preparation of papers for counsel and obtaining counsel's opinion.

Where this limitation is used, paragraph 1 of the certificate will make it clear that the certificate covers applying to set aside the judgment/order and if successful for the assisted person to be represented in the proceedings but the scope of the certificate is then narrowed by this limitation. The wording does not specifically refer to applying for a stay of execution but this will be covered. There is a more restrictive wording — L031 which covers only applying for a stay of execution.

Matrimonial and children

L032

As to the defended suit itself, limited to all steps up to and including **09–16** discovery and any summons for directions/pre-trial review and thereafter to obtaining counsel's opinion on the merits of the matter continuing as a contested cause. As to children/ancillary matters, cover is in accordance with the Notes for Guidance in the current Legal Aid Handbook.

This limitation is inserted in all certificates covering defended matrimonial proceedings. The Board's Notes for Guidance make it clear that "legally aided cases must not be defended without good reason". Before lifting the limitation the area office will need to be satisfied that the case cannot be disposed of as an undefended suit "without detriment to the proper interest of the parties or either of them". When applying for the limitation to be lifted the solicitor should in particular indicate the position in relation to any negotiations.

The Notes for Guidance in the *Legal Aid Handbook* are currently at Note for Guidance 8–09 *Legal Aid Handbook 1994*. They have been agreed with the Senior District Judge of the Family Division and indicate in detail the matters which are regarded as within the scope of the certificate as well as the matters which are regarded as outside the scope of the certificate. The

191

principles are that, subject to any limitation, restriction or condition particular to the certificate, it will cover all the steps which are normally necessary to prosecute or defend a suit. The certificate will not, however, cover any step after the final decree other than applications for ancillary relief or orders under section 8 of the Children Act 1989 made promptly after the final decree.

It should be noted that the certificate will not cover any further steps in the decree proceedings if the cause at any time becomes undefended. Should the cause become undefended the solicitor should report to the area office so that the wording of the certificate may be amended to cover the specific steps which are necessary in relation to children/ancillary matters.

While the suit remains defended the solicitor should check in the Notes for Guidance whether a particular step is covered or not. In general terms the cover is wide and includes supplemental pleadings, maintenance pending suit, leave to remove a child from the jurisdiction (before final decree), non-molestation and ouster injunctions, section 8 Children Act applications (made before or promptly after the final decree), an application for an injunction to restrain the other spouse from dealing with property, ancillary relief (excluding child maintenance where the Child Support Agency has jurisdiction) and attendance on a summons for directions or pre-trial review.

It does not cover second or cross-petitions (unless consolidated with the previous proceedings), enforcement of ancillary relief/costs orders, avoidance of disposition orders, protracted negotiations subsequent to and to give effect to an order for contact or an application for committal for breach of an injunction.

If the solicitor has any doubt as to the extent of the cover he should apply for an amendment to the certificate when the area office will, if appropriate, confirm that the step envisaged is already covered and refuse the application.

Note that all ancillary relief certificates will exclude child maintenance where the Child Support Agency has jurisdiction — see L075 and L078 below.

L056

Limited to all steps up to and including obtaining and consideration of court directed blood tests.

Note that this wording extends to DNA tests. If negative tests are obtained a putative father may still be permitted to be represented under a legal aid certificate if representation on quantum is justified.

Judicial review

L037

Limited to an application for leave and if successful the filing and service **09–17** of notice of motion. To include, if necessary, applying for an injunction or stay.

This wording will generally be used in emergency certificates. It covers either a paper or oral application for leave in the Divisional Court although the costs must be justified in the usual way. It does not cover renewing the application for leave in the Court of Appeal. There is a more restrictive wording (L072) which allows the obtaining of counsel's opinion and, if so advised, applying for leave and an injunction or stay (in accordance with wording L037. Limitation L072 does not specify that counsel's written opinion must be obtained and submitted to the area office. If a written opinion is not obtained the solicitors should ensure that notes of any conference are available. Both wordings require amendment for the matter to proceed beyond service of the Notice of Motion. If the solicitor wishes to apply for bail he should indicate this in the application so that it may be specified.

L038

Limited to all steps up to and including service of the respondent's evidence and thereafter obtaining counsel's opinion on merits and evidence.

This wording is used in ordinary certificates. It includes applying for an injunction or stay but does not include renewing the application for leave in the Court of Appeal. If the respondent does not serve any evidence, then the solicitor should consider reporting on the merits to the area office which will not necessarily require counsel's opinion to be obtained. If the solicitor wishes to apply for bail he should indicate this in the application so that it may be specified.

L075

If this certificate relates to child maintenance, it only covers maintenance in respect of a stepchild(ren) of an absent parent, unless additional cover is expressly stated.

This limitation is routinely used with any certificate wording which potentially covers child maintenance, any certificate which covers ancillary relief. The purpose of the limitation is to restrict the cover regarding child maintenance to maintenance in respect of step-child or children, *unless* additional cover for child maintenance is expressly stated. This enables the area office to consider whether the court, rather than the Agency has jurisdication for the proposed application and whether it would, in any event, satisfy the civil legal aid merits test. The area office would consider the merits either if such a proposed application was included in the original legal aid application or if an amendment to extend the limitation was sought. If further cover is given in respect of child maintenance, then the certificate would include additional wording reading "To include representation on application for child maintenance" in the first paragraph of the certificate.

L078

In so far as this certificate relates to child maintenance, it covers maintenance in respect of a stepchild(ren) of an absent parent only.

This wording has the same aim as wording but it is used only to restrict certificate wordings which include variation of periodical payments where the Child Support Agency, rather than the court, has jurisdiction. This wording reflects the transitional arrangements for the take on of business by the Child Support Agency and may be replaced by a restrictive wording which will be increasingly used as the Agency takes on further cases.

Variation and removal of limitations

09–18   Limitations may be varied or removed in accordance with regulation 51 of the Civil Legal Aid (General) Regulations 1989 which deals with amendments to the certificate. Normally amendments are on the application of the nominated solicitor or assisted person although the Area Director may amend a certificate of his own volition (this would only be likely to be done to correct an administrative, rather than a legal, mistake[14] or possibly to restrict further work under the certificate).

On receiving an application to remove a limitation the Area Director may:

(a) remove the limitation altogether, by amending the certificate to that effect;

(b) impose a fresh limitation which will normally be less restrictive;

(c) issue a notice (which will be in the form of a letter) to the assisted person that the application for an amendment may be refused and his certificate discharged and inviting him to show cause why the application should be granted. Note that an Area Director can refuse to delete a limitation in an emergency certificate without having to institute the so-called show cause procedure.[15]

Scope of civil legal aid certificates

09–19   (a) A certificate may cover the whole or part of proceeding.[16] A

---

[14] Civil Legal Aid (General) Regulations 1989, reg. 51(a).
[15] *ibid.* reg. 55.
[16] *ibid.* reg. 46(1).

certificate may cover only part of the proceedings in the sense that it is limited either by way of a limitation or in that it specifies being represented in relation to a particular aspect of proceedings *e.g.* a certificate may cover only ancillary relief in matrimonial proceedings which are defended or may cover only defending proceedings but not counterclaiming).

(b) Civil legal aid certificates cover only those proceedings which are specified. This means that if a certificate is expressed to cover an action based in negligence it will not extend to nuisance. A certificate will also only cover the specific proceedings which are mentioned by court reference number and/or by the naming of the parties. The solicitor should check on receipt that any court reference and names contained in the certificate are correct. The certificate can be amended to correct an administrative mistake pursuant to regulation 51(a) of the Civil Legal Aid (General) Regulations 1989. Note, however, that certificates relating to family proceedings do not have to specify the parties.

(c) Subject to any limitation or condition contained in the certificate, it will cover all usual steps in the proceedings. It will not cover steps outside the usual conduct of proceedings and it will not cover work after the proceedings have been concluded (save as specified). It will, however, cover steps preliminary or incidental to the proceedings where they would usually be undertaken by a legal representative — if the solicitor is in any doubt as to the extent of a certificate he should seek clarification from the area office. Certificates do not cover applying to be joined, setting aside orders, prosecuting or defending appeals (save that defending an appeal against an interlocutory order is covered) nor enforcing an order which has been obtained in the proceedings. A certificate may be specifically amended to take additional steps such as these, although there are restrictions on amending certificates to appeal to the House of Lords or from the magistrates' court and a single certificate can only cover one action, cause or matter except in the case of:

   (i) family proceedings (for this purpose this includes adoption proceedings); or

   (ii) an application for a grant of representation necessary to enable the proceedings covered by the certificate to be brought; or

   (iii) an application for pre-action discovery under section 33 of the Supreme Court Act 1981 or section 52 of the County Courts Act 1984 and subsequent court proceedings; or

   (iv) proceedings which may be taken to enforce or give effect to any order or agreement in the proceedings covered. This

195

specifically extends bankruptcy or winding up proceedings.[17] Note, however, that unless the wording of the certificate specifically covers more than one set of proceedings an application for an amendment would need to be made. Pre-action discovery applications are normally included in medical negligence certificates and applying for a grant of representation will be included in the certificate where the need for that is made clear to the area office in the original legal aid application.

(d) A certificate which indicates that the assisted person is "To be represented . . ." cover either taking or defending proceedings and this wording is generally used rather than "To take . . ." or "To defend . . .", although the latter terms may be used where a certificate is issued part way through an existing court action to cover continuing to prosecute or defendit. Note that certificates do not cover a counterclaim or the defence of a counterclaim without a specific amendment.

(5) A certificate may specify the level of court in which the proceedings are to be conducted. If the certificate is silent then the proceedings may be conducted at any level, subject only to the fact that civil legal aid must be available *e.g.* to cover the particular proceedings in the magistrates' court. The solicitor must then justify the forum on taxation/assessment of costs.

(e) Where the certificate specifies that the proceedings are to be conducted in a particular level of court, in the county court, then an amendment is not required if the proceedings are transferred to another court at the same level. An amendment is, however, required if the proceedings are transferred to a court of a different level although if a certificate specifies that proceedings in the High Court are covered, then no specific amendment is needed in the event of a transfer from the High Court to a county court. Certificates covering private law Children Act proceedings may include a condition as to the commencement of proceedings.

(f) It should be noted that a certificate covers only the solicitor who is nominated under it. That solicitor may, however, delegate the conduct of any part of the case to a partner or to a competent and responsible representative employed in his office or otherwise under his immediate supervision.[18] In practice this means that the certificate will cover work done within a particular firm so long as the nominated solicitor remains with that firm. If there is a change of firm (even if the same solicitor continues to deal with the case) then an amendment to the certificate must be sought for costs to

---

[17] *ibid.* reg. 46(3).
[18] Civil Legal Aid (General) Regulations 1989, reg. 65(2).

be recovered under the certificate although it may be possible for a retrospective, corrective amendment to be issued.[19] It is the view of the Board that should the nominated solicitor cease to be with the firm (or organisation), then there can be no delegation and costs cannot be recovered. Law Centres and other such agencies should take particular care to ensure that there is a solicitor who is able to be nominated and delegate work as appropriate.

(8) The *Legal Aid Handbook* contains detailed Notes for Guidance as to the scope of matrimonial certificates which list the matters which are regarded as within and as outside the scope of the usual form of certificate covering defended proceedings. If the solicitor wishes to represent the assisted person in relation to an aspect of the case which is not mentioned in either list, then clarification of the position should be sought from the area office. If an amendment is sought in any particular case where the area office considers that the step is already covered, it may either refuse the amendment indicating its view or it may nonetheless amend the certificate for the avoidance of any doubt. Should defended matrimonial proceedings become undefended, the solicitor should report the position to the area office by seeking a specific amendment to cover those aspects of the proceedings in respect of which cover is required.

(g) In any matrimonial matter, defended or not, the solicitor should note that the certificate will only cover child maintenance in respect of stepchildren of the absent parent unless wider cover is specifically stated) and that only one substantive order in respect of ancillary relief or contact may be obtained. In relation to Children Act matters the certificate will normally only cover those section 8 applications which are specified, however, note that a specific amendment is not need to oppose the making of any section 8 order in care or supervision proceedings and that any certificate covering family proceedings within section 8(3) of the Children Act 1989 does cover the proceedings being concluded by a different type of section 8 order (so as to allow for the making of orders on the court's own motion).

(h) Cover for enforcement proceedings will normally specify the method of enforcement to be adopted. If it does not, it will be regarded as covering one application for enforcement only and it should be borne in mind that:

(i) legal aid is not available for proceedings for or consequent upon the issue of a judgement summons in the county court;

(ii) maintenance orders providing for payment direct to a child

---

[19] *R. v. Legal Aid Board ex parte Nicolson, The Times,* June 24, 1994.

can only be enforced by that child acting by a next friend or guardian *ad litem*.[20] A separate application by the child is not, however, required to register such an order in the family proceedings court;

(iii) legal aid certificates, other than those to prosecute or defend a suit for divorce, do not cover registration in a family proceedings court, unless this is specifically mentioned.

(i) The Board considers that asking for a penal notice to be endorsed on an order is within the scope of a certificate but an amendment is required to apply for committal (but not for a warrant of committal where a suspended committal order has been made).

(j) It is accepted that the costs of conveyancing work and the work unecessary to implement an order are usually covered whether the order is made by consent or not.[21] This does not, however, extend to matters which would not normally be dealt with by a solicitor. For example, it does not extend to actually making any payment for which the client is liable or which enable the object of the order to be fulfilled. If the solicitor is in doubt as to the position, he should seek clarification from the area office.

(k) Any cover in respect of an appeal will be specified in the first paragraph of the certificate and the solicitor should take care to ensure that the work done remains within the limitation as work outside the limitation will not be remunerated. It should be noted that certificates covering an appeal are often expressed (in the first paragraph of the certificate) to be in respect of obtaining counsel's opinion (or petitioning the House of Lords for leave to appeal), although they may then be amended to indicate that thereafter the prosecution of the appeal is covered.

---

[20] *Shelley v. Shelley* [1952] P. 107.
[21] *Copeland v. Houlton* [1955] 1 W.L.R. 1072 and *S v. S* (LAT) [1991] Fam. Law 271.

Chapter 10

EMERGENCY CERTIFICATES

MAKING AN EMERGENCY APPLICATION

There is provision for "any person who desires legal aid as a matter of **10–01** urgency" to apply to any Area Director for an emergency certificate on a form approved by the Board or in such other manner as the Area Director may accept as sufficient in the circumstances of the case.[1]

Although it would be theoretically possible to submit an emergency application to any Area Director the application should be made to the solicitor's usual area office unless the solicitor has established in advance that for some particular reason, *e.g.* the application relates to judicial review proceedings against that area or to a multi-party action for which there is a nominated area, the application should be sent elsewhere. If an application is sent to an inappropriate area office it will be transferred to another area office where it can be more conveniently or appropriately dealt with. This should only be done where the applicant would not be prejudiced[2] but the reality is that this could be done in any event because an emergency application can be made over the telephone and an application could be considered in that way while the papers were on the way from one area office to another. If the solicitor is in doubt as to which office would be the appropriate area office, *e.g.* because the applicant already has an existing certificate in another area, the case involves a local solicitor as a party or relates to a particular claim in respect of which the Board may have nominated one area office (*e.g.* all claims relating to a particular drug), then he should draw attention to the position in a covering letter or make inquiries with his local area office before submitting the application at all.

Written emergency applications are made on Form CLA3 which must be submitted with the appropriate non-emergency application Form (CLA1, 2 or 5), the appropriate statement of means (*i.e.* applicable to the particular applicants circumstances) and any supporting documents (including

---

[1] Civil Legal Aid (General) Regulations 1989, reg. 19(1).
[2] *ibid.* reg. 17.

confirmation of means) unless the ordinary application has already been submitted. In the latter case the ordinary application reference number (taken from the area office acknowledgemt letter) should be clearly stated so that the forms can be connected in the area office. Form CLA3 must make clear the proceedings involved and the urgent step(s) to be covered by any emergency certificate issued.

The form also contains important notes for the applicant who should read and understand them. It is particularly important that the applicant appreciates that if a certificate is issued he must co-operate in the assessment of his means even if, *so far he is aware, no work* is undertaken by the solicitor and the proceedings do not go ahead. A failure to co-operate in the means assessment could result in a revocation of the emergency certificate in which case the assisted person will be liable for the solicitor's costs as paid out of the Legal Aid Fund as well as such additional costs as would have been payable if he had been a private, rather than a legally aided, client.

The contents of the emergency application form together with the ordinary application form must be sufficient to enable the Area Director to determine:

(a) the nature of the proceedings;

(b) the circumstances in which emergency legal aid is sought;

(c) whether the applicant is likely to fulfil the conditions under which legal aid may be granted; and

(d) whether it is in the interests of justice that the applicant should, as a matter of urgency, be granted legal aid.[3]

10–02 The Area Director is empowered to issue an emergency certificate subject to conditions as to the furnishing of additional information if the applicant cannot reasonably furnish the information normally required.[4] If an application is made over the telephone then an emergency certificate may be granted subject to receipt of a written application (and supporting documents) within the time period stipulated on the telephone. If the written application is not forthcoming or is submitted outside the stipulated time period, no certificate will be issued or the certificate will only date from the processing of the written application and the solicitor will not be able to recover the costs incurred previously. It is important that, if an emergency certificate is obtained over the telephone, the specific requirements as to the submission of a written application are not overlooked and it is helpful to have the completed application prepared when a telephone application is made so that this can be sent to the area office straight away with no possibility that the submission of the written application is overlooked. Telephone applications should only be made in

---

[3] Civil Legal Aid (General) Regulations 1989, reg. 19(2).
[4] *ibid.* reg. 19(3).

cases of real emergency. Note that the solicitor is at risk if he has not obtained the client's signature to the necessary forms (fully completed) and is subsequently unable to do so (*e.g.* because the client disappears and the solicitor finds himself without instructions).

REFUSAL OF AN EMERGENCY APPLICATION

An application for an emergency certificate may be refused on one of the **10–03** same grounds as an application for an ordinary certificate, that is to say:
  (a) where legal aid is not available for the particular proceedings; or
  (b) on financial ineligibility; or
  (c) where the applicant has not shown he has reasonable grounds for taking, defending or being a party to the proceedings; or
  (d) where it appears unreasonable that the applicant should receive legal aid in particular circumstances of the case; or
  (e) additionally because —:
    (i) the applicant is unlikely to fulfil the conditions under which legal aid may be granted; or
    (ii) on the grounds that it is not in the interests of justice that legal aid be granted as a matter of urgency[5] — an area office may decline to deal with a telephone application on this basis although the Board is committed to accepting telephone applications in public law Children Act cases which are subject only to the means test.
  The ground that the applicant is unlikely to fulfil the conditions under which legal aid may be granted could be employed in circumstances where the Board was of the view that, even if financially eligible, the applicant would not pay the assessed contribution. This has not been tested but is understood to have been intended by the draftsman to cover the non-payment of a contribution. It should be noted that although there is no specific requirement in the (General) Regulations Civil Legal Aid that a reason applying the particular ground for refusal to the application in question be given, it is the practice of the Board to give such a reason.
  It is the current practice in area offices for the substantive (ordinary) **10–04** application to be considered at the same time as any written emergency application. If an emergency application is refused on the legal merits (rather than pending an assessment of means or because it is considered that it is not in the interests of justice that legal aid be granted as a matter of urgency), then the refusal of the ordinary application will follow closely on the emergency refusal. If this is not the case it may be indicated by the

---

[5] *ibid.* reg. 20.

area office, when the emergency application is refused, that the substantive application has been approved subject to a means assessment. The speed with which a decision on the substantive application can be obtained is important because there is no provision for an appeal to the area committee against the refusal of an emergency application.[6] However, if an emergency certificate is refused, the application may be renewed by letter (marked "urgent") or by telephone, although it will only be likely to be granted if fresh information is provided or the circumstances have changed since it was previously considered. On an appeal against a refusal of a substantive application, the area committee may allow the appeal whereupon the refusal of the emergency application will be reconsidered and an emergency certificate may be issued although this would be a matter for the Area Director.[7] Any certificate granted on appeal would not be backdated.

10–05 If an emergency application is refused over the telephone the solicitor should consider whether to submit a written application. He will normally wish to do this unless the emergency has passed. If a written application is submitted and the area office does not fax or telephone the outcome, then the solicitor may wish to contact the area office by telephone to find out whether a decision has been reached. The application reference should be ascertained from the area office. When "chasing" emergency applications — it is usually better to telephone later, rather than earlier, in the day to enable the application to have been received, entered in the area office computer and considered by a caseworker.

The Legal Aid Board's customer service standards (targets) include for 1995–96 a commitment to give emergency applications a high priority. The Board expects to provide a decision within 24 hours of receipt but indicates that in exceptional circumstances it may take up to 48 hours to reach a decision.[8] Note that some area offices will fax out the result of the application.

10–06 The layout of the form of emergency certificate is very similar to the ordinary certificate layout. The description of legal aid and conditions and limitations paragraphs are not, however, numbered (1) and (2) although they serve the same purpose. On receiving any emergency certificate the solicitor should check the wording and date of the certificate to confirm that it accords with any telephone grant, that it contains no errors (or omissions) and in order to note the cover granted. Emergency certificates will only be issued to cover the steps which are urgent. It is particularly important that the solicitor checks the scope of the certificate and ensures that amendments to the certificate are requested as they become necessary.

---

[6] Civil Legal Aid (General) Regulations 1989, reg. 35(1)(c) inserted for clarification by the Civil Legal Aid (General) (Amendment) (No. 2) Regulations 1994.

[7] *ibid.* regs. 35(1), 39(1).

[8] Legal Aid Board Customer Service Standards, Legal Aid Handbook 1994, p. 495.

Amendment applications can, if necessary, be made by telephone but where there is sufficient time to apply for an amendment in writing this should be done using mandatory Form CLA30, as the area office may decline to deal with an application for an amendment over the telephone or may refuse it if it considers that there is time for a written application to be made.

Where the Board is satisfied that an emergency certificate should be **10–07** issued but supporting documents regarding information as to means are not submitted, the area office may issue an emergency certificate but allow the assisted person a stated period of time, usually 21 days, to submit those documents. If they are not forthcoming within the time stipulated (or as extended by the area office) the emergency certificate will be revoked or discharged. A "show cause" letter is sent to the assisted person with the certificate and the original rejected means form. The show cause letter is copied to the solicitor who may wish to remind his client of the importance of resubmitting the means form and supporting documentation.

Where the area office is not satisfied that an emergency certificate should be granted and the means information is defective, it will notify the solicitor only of the refusal of the emergency application and return the rejected means assessment form for completion and return within a stated period, usually 21 days. If the necessary means information/documents are not submitted the substantive (ordinary) application will be abandoned and the file closed. The solicitor should bear in mind that only he is notified of the refusal and that he will need to get the client to resubmit the means form and documents in the stated time if the file is not to be treated as abandoned and closed. If a file is closed a new application will need to be submitted.

GRANT OF EMERGENCY APPLICATIONS

Specific examples of decisions in emergency cases are contained in the **10–08** *Legal Aid Handbook 1995* at Note for Guidance 5–03 but generally practitioners should bear in mind that:
   (a) civil legal aid must be available;
   (b) the civil legal aid merits and reasonableness tests must be satisfied;
   (c) the client must be financially eligible and likely to pay any assessed contribution; and
   (d) it must be in the interests of justice that emergency legal aid is granted.
The area office should not refuse emergency legal aid merely because the applicant has sufficient disposable capital over the £3,000 contribution limit to fund the current steps, but will be likely to refuse an emergency application where:
   (a) financial eligibility is in doubt; or

(b) there is a history of non co-operation in previous means assessments or of failure to pay legal aid contributions; or

(c) there has been delay on the part of the applicant or solicitor which has helped to create the emergency[9] (see Legal Aid Handbook 1995 Note for Guidance 5–01); or

(d) an adjournment or more time can be obtained.

Legal Aid Handbook 1995, Note for Guidance 5–01 suggests that it will almost always be in the interests of justice for an emergency certificate to be granted where:

(a) the applicant's liberty is threatened; or

(b) any delay would cause the risk of miscarriage of justice, or unreasonable hardship to the applicant, or exceptional problems in handling the case.

ISSUE AND EFFECT OF AN EMERGENCY CERTIFICATE

10–09 An emergency certificate is issued where no means assessment has yet been requested by the Area Director or where it has been requested and has not been completed. There is provision for the Assessment Officer to make an estimate of the disposable income and capital of the relevant person and of his contribution where the Area Director informs the Assessment Officer that a certificate is required as a matter of urgency and the Assessment Officer cannot complete the assessment in the time available. The estimate is treated as an assessment for the purposes of calculating the applicant's contribution, although the Assessment Officer does proceed to make a final assessment which then replaces the estimate.[10] The use of this provision hinges upon the Area Director's contacting the Assessment Officer and, given the possibility of an emergency certificate being issued or an urgent assessment being obtained, it is very rarely used.

When an emergency certificate is issued the Area Director must send the original and a copy to the nominated solicitor and a further copy to the applicant.[11] Emergency certificates are no longer a different colour from ordinary, full certificates following increased computerisation in the area offices.[12]

If the solicitor has given the applicant's correspondence address as "c/o himself", then any copy certificate will be sent to the solicitor. The area office (and assessment office) will use the correspondence address for all

---

[9] See *Legal Aid Handbook 1995*, Notes for Guidance 5–01.

[10] Civil Legal Aid (Assessment of Resources) Regulations 1989, reg. 15.

[11] Civil Legal Aid (General) Regulations 1989, reg. 21(3).

[12] Before this change all emergency legal aid certificates were pink and all substantive certificates were blue.

purposes until notified otherwise and the solicitor should consider carefully whether this is appropriate in the circumstances of any particular case.

An emergency certificate has the same effect as a substantive, ordinary certificate and the holder of an emergency certificate is deemed to be an assisted person while it is in force.[13] This means that the holder has the benefit of section 17 of the 1988 Act which limits the liability of a legally assisted party for costs.

The provisions as to the notification of issue of certificates apply equally to emergency certificates as to ordinary certificates so that when an emergency certificate is issued the solicitor is required to serve the usual notice.[14]

The solicitor can undertake work under the certificate as soon as it has been issued — the solicitor does not have to wait to physically receive the certificate if it has been granted following a telephone application or if he has been informed by the area office that the application has been granted (with effect from a particular date). It is important for a solicitor submitting the written application following a telephone grant to refer to the telephone grant, its date and give the name or reference of the caseworker who dealt with the application. Likewise, if the solicitor telephones the area office and is informed that an application has been granted it is important that he should obtain the reference of the caseworker informing him of this, as well as *exact* details of the cover (including any limitations and/or conditions) provided by the certificate. Where proceedings are being taken the court will accept the filing of the certificate once it has been received by the solicitor and if the certificate reference number is known notice of issue can be served on the other parties without the solicitor having actually received the certificate.

Once an emergency certificate has been issued the solicitor can apply for payments on account of disbursements incurred or about to be incurred[15] and may also, if appropriate, apply for specific authority under regulation 59 (to instruct counsel, leading counsel or more than one counsel) or regulation 61 (to incur costs) of the Civil Legal Aid (General) Regulations 1989, unless any necessary authorities were sought and obtained when the certificate was issued.

EMERGENCY WORK BEFORE THE ISSUE OF A CERTIFICATE

An emergency certificate, in common with all other legal aid cover (with **10–10** the exception of special Children Act proceedings), will not be back-dated

---

[13] *ibid.* reg. 21(4).
[14] *ibid.* reg. 3(1), 50.
[15] *ibid.* reg. 101(1).

and will only operate from its issue.[16] It is therefore important that emergency legal aid is applied for at the earliest opportunity where an emergency certificate is needed. However, a "deeming provision" does enable work done by a solicitor immediately before the issue of an emergency certificate to be deemed to be work done under an emergency certificate but:

(a) the work must be done at a time when an emergency certificate could not be applied for because the appropriate area office was closed (although strictly speaking there is no appropriate area office this implies that the solicitor need not approach an office other than his usual area office if that office is closed for some particular local reason, *e.g.* disruption due to adverse transport or weather conditions); *and*

(b) the solicitor applies for an emergency certificate at the first available opportunity (the solicitor should telephone the area office as soon as it opens and if he cannot do this himself he should delegate the task in order to ensure that he keeps his case within the confines of the provision); *and*

(c) the application is granted.[17]

It should be noted that:

(a) the provision is limited to work done by a solicitor. This would not cover work done by counsel although it would include work delegated under regulation 65(2) of the Civil Legal Aid (General) Regulations 1989, *i.e.* to a partner or to a competent and responsible representative who is the solicitor's employee or otherwise under his immediate supervision;

(b) the application for an emergency certificate has to be granted and if it is not the work cannot be paid for. The prudent solicitor will ensure that the Green Form is used as far as possible (although this will only be up to the financial limit including any extension previously obtained) and will wish to consider whether to ask the client to put him in funds in case the emergency application is not granted.

DURATION OF EMERGENCY CERTIFICATES

10–11 An emergency certificate remains in force until it:

(a) is discharged or revoked;

(b) is merged in a substantive, ordinary certificate; or

---

[16] *ibid.* reg. 103(1).
[17] *ibid.* reg. 103(6).

(c) expires by effluxion of time (including any extension of the duration of the certificate).[18]

There is a specific requirement that the Area Director shall revoke an emergency certificate where the assisted person is assessed as out of scope on income.[19] There is also a specific requirement that an emergency certificate be revoked where the assisted person is assessed as having disposable capital of an amount which renders him liable to be refused legal aid and it appears to the Area Director that, without legal aid, the probable costs of the proceedings would not exceed the contribution payable.[20]

The Area Director may either revoke or discharge an emergency certificate where the assisted person has failed to attend for an interview or provide information or documents when required to do so, or has failed to accept an offer of a substantive certificate.[21] It is important that those applying for and holding emergency certificates do understand the importance of co-operating in the assessment of means as well as that the failure to accept an offer of legal aid will, in all probability, result in the revocation of the emergency certificate. It should be noted that no emergency certificate can be revoked on this ground until both the assisted person and the solicitor have been given notice that the certificate may be revoked and that the assisted person may show cause why it should not be, and the assisted person has been given an opportunity to show cause.[22] The period of notice which is normally given is 10 days from the date of the letter showing cause and on receiving his copy of the letter the solicitor should check that the letter has been correctly addressed (contacting the area office immediately if it has not). He should also consider stressing the seriousness of the assisted person's position to him.

Once a show cause notice has been served in relation to the possible *revocation* of an emergency certificate no further work may be done or steps taken under the certificate except as authorised by the Area Director.[23] The area office practice is to issue a show cause letter even if the more likely outcome is that the certificate will be discharged rather than revoked. If there are urgent steps which need to be taken in order that the assisted person's position is not prejudiced, the solicitor should contact the area office (by telephone or letter depending on the degree of urgency) and seek authority to undertake that limited work. The area office will need to be persuaded that the work must be undertaken and the solicitor will need to be ready to justify the assisted person's failure to co-operate in the means

---

[18] *ibid.* reg. 22.
[19] *ibid.* reg. 75(1).
[20] *ibid.* reg. 75(2).
[21] *ibid.* reg. 75(3).
[22] Civil Legal Aid (General) Regulations 1989, reg. 75(5).
[23] *ibid.* reg. 75(6).

assessment. If the assisted person has failed to accept an offer of a substantive certificate it is most unlikely that the area office will be prepared to authorise further steps under the emergency certificate as the solution is for the assisted person to accept the offer, although special arrangements would have to be made for this to be done out of time (rather than a new application being submitted in the usual way).

MERGER IN SUBSTANTIVE CERTIFICATE

10–12 Where a substantive certificate is issued, the emergency certificate merges in the substantive certificate which then takes effect from the date of issue of the emergency certificate (but only to the extent of the emergency certificate).[24]

There is a specific requirement that, where an emergency certificate is merged into a substantive certificate, the substantive certificate must state the date of issue of the emergency certificate and that the emergency certificate has been continuously in force from then until the issue of the substantive certificate.[25] This should not be stated if the emergency certificate expires and is not extended until after the expiry in which case there will be a period of time during which the certificate is not in force (but see below regarding expiry). Although it has not been tested, it is unlikely that the solicitor could charge privately during any such gap in the emergency legal aid cover — he should diarise the date of expiry of the certificate and apply for its extension.[26]

EXPIRY AND EXTENSION OF EMERGENCY CERTIFICATES

10–13 An emergency certificate may be limited in time as well as in scope although the current usual area office practice is for emergency certificates not to state a time-limitation. The solicitor should check this on receipt of the certificate and make an appropriate diary note if the certificate is indeed limited in time as, so, and the certificate is not extended, then any work done after expiry will not be covered. An Area Director (whose decision is final) may extend the duration of an emergency certificate where:

    (a) the applicant has been made an offer of legal aid and has failed to accept it or appealed against its terms; or

    (b) the application for a substantive, ordinary certificate has been

---

[24] *ibid.* reg. 23(1).
[25] *ibid.* reg. 23(2).
[26] *ibid.* reg. 24.

refused and either notice of appeal has been given within the time-limit (14 days from the date of notice of refusal) or the time-limit has not expired; or

(c) there are exceptional circumstances.

Where an emergency certificate is extended under (a) or (b) above, then no further work may be done or steps taken under the certificate.[27] In those circumstances the extension of time is just that — it does not enable further work to be undertaken but suspends the expiry of the certificate so that an offer of legal aid may be accepted or an amended offer may be made or an appeal against the refusal of an ordinary certificate may be allowed. The emergency certificate can then merge into the substantive certificate even though no work can be undertaken in the period of the extension. Although this has not been tested this probably means that neither legal aid nor private client funding is available although it is not entirely clear that Green Form advice is excluded.[28]

Where an Area Director extends the duration of an emergency certificate under (c) above, i.e. because there are exceptional circumstances, then further work may be undertaken although this work would be likely to be limited. An example of exceptional circumstances would be where, through no fault of the assisted person, a means assessment had not been completed in the time allowed for the duration of the certificate and the emergency was continuing.

Where an emergency certificate is extended the Area Director must issue a notice of the extension to the solicitor (with an additional copy) and to the assisted person.[29] The extension does not actually constitute an amendment within Part VII of the Civil Legal Aid (General) Regulations 1989 so as to give rise to a right of appeal.

If an emergency certificate is extended the solicitor must:

(a) notify any counsel instructed forthwith[30]; and

(b) if proceedings have been commenced or on their commencement:

(i) send a copy of the notice of extension by post to the court; and

(ii) serve notice of the extension (but not the extension itself) on the other parties to the proceedings (as well as to any others who become parties).[31]

A notice of issue/amendment form can be amended for this purpose. It is unclear what should happen when notice of the extension is served on the

---

[27] Civil Legal Aid (General) Regulations 1989, reg. 24(2).
[28] Legal Aid Act 1988, s. 8(5).
[29] Civil Legal Aid (General) Regulations 1989, reg. 25(1).
[30] ibid. reg. 25(2).
[31] ibid. reg. 25(3).

other parties. They will have been unaware of any limitations contained in the original emergency certificate and of the specific duration of the emergency certificate and will not know the basis of the extension and the extent to which, if any, further steps may be undertaken.

Chapter 11

FILING OF DOCUMENTS AND SERVICE OF NOTICES

INTRODUCTION

If a litigant is legally aided both the court and his opponent will be affected. **11–01**
Specific provision is therefore made for the certificate and any other
documents defining the scope of the cover granted to be filed in court and
for the assisted person's opponent(s) to receive notice, although not copies
of the documents themselves. The principle is that the court is entitled to
full information as to the assisted person's position, including information
on his contribution (if any), but that the opponent is entitled only to be
informed of the nature of the proceedings and, in the case of appeals, of
the scope of the certificate having regard to the appeal. Note, however, that
defending an interlocutory appeal is regarded as being included within the
scope of the original certificate and no amendment is required.

FILING DOCUMENTS IN COURT

What must be filed

A solicitor is required to file the following by post (but see below) to the **11–02**
appropriate court office or registry:
  (a) a certificate (including an emergency certificate)[1];
  (b) notice of revocation or discharge of a certificate, including an
      emergency certificate[2];
  (c) an amendment to a certificate including an emergency certificate[3];
      and
  (d) a notice that an emergency certificate has been extended.[4]

---

[1] Civil Legal Aid (General) Regulations 1989, regs. 3(1), 50(4).
[2] *ibid.* reg. 82(2)(b).
[3] *ibid.* reg. 54(2)(a).
[4] *ibid.* reg. 25(3)(a).

The requirements as to the filing of documents do not apply to certificates covering authorised summary proceedings where the requirement is that the solicitor files the document with the Clerk to the Justices before or at the first hearing after its issue. Any document sent to a court office or registry or filed or exhibited may be made available, on request, for the use of the court at any stage of the proceedings.[5]

There is no requirement to file authorities although obviously these should be produced on taxation or assessment. Although there is no specific provision requiring it, notice of rescission of a discharge or a revocation should be given. The area office will not issue a formal notice as such and the court should, where the original notice of discharge or revocation has already been filed, be provided with a copy of the area office's letter indicating the rescission of the discharge or revocation and with a notice of issue/amendment appropriately amended.

Time for filing

11–03 There is no time-limit prescribed in the relation to the issue of a certificate (including an emergency certificate) where a copy (taken to be the top copy) is required to be sent (if proceedings have begun, or otherwise upon their commencement).[6] Amendments are required to be sent "forthwith" if proceedings have begun or otherwise upon their commencement.[7] No time-limit is prescribed in relation to the extension of an emergency certificate. Notice of discharge or revocation is required to be sent either forthwith or forthwith upon receipt of notice of dismissal of an appeal to the area committee and there is provision for the notice to be in a form approved by the Board.[8] There are no specific requirements at all in relation to notice of rescission of a discharge or revocation.

Note that if a notice of discharge or revocation is filed with the court immediately on receipt in the belief that there will be no appeal and there is a successful appeal or the revocation is rescinded due to a mistake of fact, then the letter informing the solicitor of the successful outcome of the appeal or the rescission of the revocation should be filed with the court. Where there is a discharge or revocation of a certificate and proceedings have been commenced the solicitor's retainer does not determine until he has served any requisite notice.[9] This applies only where proceedings have been commenced; where proceedings have not been commenced the

---

[5] *ibid.* reg. 9.
[6] *ibid.* reg. 50(4).
[7] *ibid.* reg. 54(2)(a).
[8] *ibid.* reg. 82(2).
[9] *ibid.* reg. 83(2).

retainer determines immediately on receipt of notice of discharge or revocation or on receipt of notice of dismissal of an appeal.[10]

The delay in the determination of the solicitor's retainer where proceedings have been commenced presents a possible difficulty in that notice cannot be given until any appeal has been dismissed. If there are any hearings in that period the solicitor should notify the court of the position and ask the area office to expedite the appeal. Technically it would be possible for the court to insist upon the solicitor's attendance but it is more likely that the case would be adjourned pending clarification of the legal aid position, or that the solicitor would be excused from attendance. The solicitor could not be privately funded in this period although as his retainer has not been determined he still has an obligation to protect his client's interest, *e.g.* by forwarding any notices received from the court.

SERVICE OF NOTICES ON OTHER PARTIES

Whenever an assisted person becomes a party to proceedings, or a party to proceedings becomes legally aided, his solicitor must serve all other parties, even those who subsequently become parties, with notice of issue of the certificate.[11] This applies equally to emergency certificate.[12-13] **11–04**

There is no prescribed notice but law stationers will provide forms of notice for this purpose. It is the solicitor's responsibility to effect service but where he commences proceedings in a country court or in accordance with Order 112, rules 3 or 4 of the Rules of the Supreme Court 1965 or rule 101 or 103 of the Matrimonial Causes Rules 1977, and at the same time files a copy of the notice it will be annexed to the originating process for service.[14]

The solicitor must also in the same way serve notice of the fact of extension of an emergency certificate[15] (except an amendment altering the assisted person's contribution)[16] and of the discharge or revocation of a certificate,[17] There is no specific requirement to serve notice of the rescission of a discharge or revocation but this should be done in the same way where notice of the discharge or revocation itself has been given.

Failure or delay in serving the requisite notice can result in an order for

---

[10] *ibid.* reg. 83(1).
[11] *ibid.* reg. 50(1).
[12-13] *ibid.* reg. 3(1).
[14] Civil Legal Aid (General) Regulations 1989, reg. 50(3).
[15] *ibid.* reg. 25(3).
[16] *ibid.* reg. 54(2)(b).
[17] *ibid.* reg. 82(2)(a).

costs against the solicitor personally.[18] It may also form the basis of a complaint to the Solicitors' Complaints Bureau. The service of notices is important in that the specific provisions are intended to enable parties who are litigating with others who are legally aided to know their position in relation to costs. It is important not to overlook service of the appropriate notices and while there is no prescribed form of notice (although there is provision for this in relation to notice of discharge (revocation) it is important that whatever form of notice is given it is correct in all material aspects in particular it must distinguish between discharge and revocation). Although notice could be served by letter it is important that the letter should not mislead if it is to constitute valid notice so as not to put the solicitor at risk of an order for costs and, in the case of notice of discharge or revocation, to constitute notice sufficient to determine the retainer and have the effect of taking the solicitor off the record.

WHAT SHOULD BE INCLUDED IN THE NOTICE?

11–05 The notice of issue of a legal aid certificate (including an emergency certificate) should not contain or refer to any condition or limitation imposed on the certificate. Conditions and limitations are potentially a weakness which the assisted person is not required to disclose to opposing parties. Following a Court of Appeal decision[19] (which related clearly to appeals) limitations on the work which may be done in connection with an appeal must be disclosed. This is so that any opposing party does not take unnecessary steps in connection with the appeal.

What then is the position when a limitation or condition which has not previously been disclosed is deleted by way of an amendment? In relation to amendments the requirement is to serve only of the *fact* of an amendment.[20] Although it has not been tested it is the view of the Board that amendments which amend the description of proceedings contained in paragraph 1 of the certificate must be served and that the opposing party is entitled to know the extent of the legal aid cover. Normally, however, limitations and conditions will be in paragraph 2 of the certificate and not fully disclosable, except in the case of appeals. This means that where a limitation or condition not previously disclosed is deleted, or indeed amended, by an amendment, the opposing party will be alerted to the fact but not the content of that limitation or condition. Should that party then request further details he would not be entitled to receive them as of right.

---

[18] *Sinclair-Jones v. Kay* [1989] 1 W.L.R. 114.
[19] *Scarth v. Jacobs-Paton* [1978] *The Times*, November 2, 1978.
[20] Civil Legal Aid (General) Regulations 1989, reg. 54(2)(b).

214

SANCTION FOR FAILURE/DELAY

The sanction for failure/delay in serving a requisite notice could be an order **11–06** for costs made against the solicitor personally or a referral to the Solicitors' Complaints Bureau at the instigation of an opposing party or the Board.

HOW CAN NOTICE BE SERVED?

Under the Civil Legal Aid (General) Regulations 1989 notice can be served: **11–07**
- (a) on someone acting in person by:
    - (i) personal delivery or
    - (ii) delivery/sending by post to his address for service or if he has no such address by:
        - — delivery to his residence or sending by post to his last known residence; or
        - — in the case of a proprietor of a business, by delivery or sending by post to his last known place of business;
- (b) on someone acting by a solicitor by:
    - (i) delivery/sending by post to the solicitor's address for service; or
    - (ii) by document exchange.[21]

Service by document exchange is deemed to have been effected on the second day after the day of delivery to the document exchange (where the box is held or which transmits daily to that document exchange).[22]

The provisions as to service do not appear to apply to the filing of documents with the court office but arguably do so; otherwise documents could only validly be sent to the court by post. The provisions also make no reference to transmission by facsimile or the giving of notice by telephone.

Where the area office is dealing with a minor or patient the next friend or guardian *ad litem* (or where there is none the solicitor of the minor or patient) is treated as the agent of the minor or patient, including as to the receipt of notices,[23] although this requirement can be waived by the Area Director where the circumstances appear to make it desirable.

Note also that where a correspondence address is given for an applicant/assisted person the area office will use that address for all communication with the applicant/assisted person until informed otherwise. This is of relevance where the solicitor's address is given because of, *e.g.*

---

[21] *ibid.* reg. 8(1).
[22] *ibid.* reg. 8(2).
[23] *ibid.* reg. 16(4).

accomodation difficulties and the solicitor then receives the applicant's/ assisted person's copy of all communications which will then need to be forwarded or otherwise notified to the applicant/assited person without delay.

Chapter 12

THE CONDUCT OF AN ASSISTED PERSON'S CASE

INTRODUCTION

The fact that a litigant is being financially supported by the Fund makes **12–01** little difference to the way in which the case is conducted, since it is a general principle of the legal aid system that an assisted person's advisers should, as far as possible, have the same freedom in the conduct of the case as they would if the assisted person were meeting all the expenses personally.

Even where a full legal aid certificate has been issued for the taking or defending or being a party to proceedings, solicitors should keep under constant review the reasonableness of the proceedings continuing at public expense. If a solicitor wastes costs by failure to conduct the proceedings with reasonable competence and expedition, the taxing officer has power to reduce the costs or even disallow them completely.[1]

Family Division guidelines

In an application for ancillary relief — in which the wife sought ancillary **12–02** relief for herself and the two children of the marriage — various properties were to be considered, and the husband owned his own company. It was agreed that the wife should have the matrimonial home but all valuations of the property involved were bitterly contested. Further, the parties' costs totalled £60,000 and were out of all proportion to the assets. In the light of this, Booth J., with the concurrence of the President of the Family Division, set out guidelines to be followed designed to limit costs in the preparation of a substantial ancillary relief case:

    (a) Affidavits should be confined to relevant facts and should not be prolix or diffuse. Normally each party should file only one substantive affidavit.

---

[1] Civil Legal Aid (General) Regulations 1989, reg. 109.

(b) Inquiries under rule 77 of the Matrimonial Causes Rules 1977 should be contained in one comprehensive questionnaire.

(c) Property valuation should be obtained from a valuer jointly instructed by both parties; if separate valuers are instructed then their reports should be exchanged and the valuers should meet and attempt to resolve the differences between them.

(d) Expensive exercises should not be undertaken for the purpose of attempting to arrive at a precise valuation of shares in a private family company that will not be sold.[2]

(e) All professional witnesses should be careful to avoid a partisan approach and should maintain proper professional standards.

(f) Non-expert evidence should be carefully selected and witnesses as to facts should avoid emotive issues. Further deponents of affidavits should be available for cross-examination on notice from either side.

(g) Solicitors should co-operate to prepare agreed bundles of documents for the hearing; duplication of documents should always be avoided.

(h) A chronology of material facts should also be agreed and made available to the judge.

(i) In a substantial case, it may be desirable to have a pre-trial review to define the issues, to explore the possibility of settlement and to ensure readiness for hearing if a settlement cannot be reached.

12–03   Dealing specifically with the matter of costs, the learned judge stated that solicitors and counsel should keep their clients informed of the costs at all stages of the proceedings and, where appropriate, should ensure they understand the implications of the statutory charge. The court will require an estimate of the costs on each side before it can make a lump-sum award.[3] The desirability of reaching a settlement should be borne in mind throughout the proceedings. While it was necessary for legal advisers to have sufficient knowledge of the financial situation of both parties before advising a client on a proposed settlement, the necessity to make further inquiries of an opponent about financial matters had to be balanced by a consideration of what those inquiries might be likely to achieve and the increased costs which would be incurred.[4]

No legal representative acting for an assisted person may entrust the conduct of any part of the case to any other person, except another legal representative selected from among those willing to provide advice and assistance or representation under the 1988 Act.[5] There is nothing to prevent a solicitor entrusting the conduct of any part of the case to a partner

---

[2] See also *P.v.P.* [1989] 2 F.L.R 241.
[3] See *Practice Direction* [1982] 2 All E.R. 800.
[4] *Evans v. Evans* [1990] 1 W.L.R. 575; [1990] 2 All E.R.147.
[5] Civil Legal Aid (General) Regulations 1989, reg. 65(1); Legal Aid Act 1988, s. 32(1).

or a competent and responsible representative employed in his office or otherwise under his immediate supervision.[6]

As the public interest is involved, certain safeguards have had to be provided of which the most important is the reservation to the Area Director of an overriding right to bring legal aid to an end should it be decided that it is no longer reasonable for the assisted person to continue with the case under the certificate.[7]

Provision is made in the Civil Legal Aid (General) Regulations 1989 for reports about an assisted person's case to be given, where necessary, to the Area Director.[8] This has two consequences: first, it keeps the Area Director informed and enables the Director to discharge the certificate should it be considered that the circumstances require it; secondly, it enables a litigant, solicitor and counsel to be spared what can be the invidious and difficult responsibility of deciding whether their client's case, the chances of success having become doubtful, should be continued at the expense of the Fund and to the possible prejudice of the opposing party who may, even though successful, find it impossible to recover the costs. **12–04**

Notwithstanding the relationship between or rights of a legal representative and a client or any privilege arising out of such a relationship, the legal representative is not precluded from disclosing to any person authorised by the Board any information relating to the cases of clients or former clients who are or were legally aided.[9] It is exceptional for a court to order that the cost of proceedings be paid by some person other than a party to the proceedings. It is even more exceptional for such an order to be made against a non-party where the applicant had a cause of action against him and could have joined him in the proceedings. The courts are well aware of the financial difficulties faced by parties opposed by legally aided litigants at first instance, where the opportunity to claim against the Board is very limited. Nevertheless, the Regulations lay down conditions designed to ensure that there is no abuse of legal aid by a legally assisted person and those are designed to protect the other party to the litigation as well as the Fund.[10]

The Area Director is given the power by the Regulations to revoke or discharge certificates for abuse of legal aid, for failure to attend for interview or to provide information or documents and, in certain other circumstances, when appropriate.[11–12]

Another safeguard created by the Regulations is a requirement that before certain steps, which are likely to be particularly expensive, are taken on

---

[6] *ibid.* reg. 65(2).
[7] *ibid.* reg. 77.
[8] *ibid.* regs. 66–73.
[9] Legal Aid (Disclosure of Information) Regulations 1991, reg. 2.
[10] *Symphony Group plc v. Hodgson* [1993] 4 All E.R. 143.
[11–12] Civil Legal Aid (General) Regulations 1989, regs. 78,79,80.

behalf of an assisted person, the specific authority of the Area Director must be obtained. As these are of special importance they are dealt with separately where the method of obtaining authority before incurring any unusual expenditure is also described. Failure to obtain any such authority may mean that the costs incurred will not be allowed on taxation and it is important, therefore, for a practitioner always to consider, before taking any step in proceedings, whether authority is essential or desirable.

THE GENERAL PRINCIPLE

12–05   An assisted person's solicitor and counsel are entitled to the same freedom in conducting their client's case as they would possess were the assisted person meeting all the costs personally, save where specific exceptions are made by the legislation. The basis of the legal aid scheme is to put the assisted person on the same footing as an unassisted person who has reasonable means to pursue the action or the defence. Except where otherwise provided by the Civil Legal Aid (General) Regulations 1989, the normal rules of procedure apply in proceedings in any court to which an assisted person is a party.

The basis on which the court decides whether or not proceedings have been conducted reasonably is described as follows:

"The correct viewpoint to be adopted by a taxing officer is that of a sensible solicitor sitting in his chair and considering what in the light of his then knowledge is reasonable in the interests of his lay client (who) . . . should be deemed a man of means adequate to bear the expense of the litigation out of his own pocket, and by 'adequate' I mean neither 'barely adequate' nor 'super abundant'".[13]

Accordingly, when considering any problem as to whether expenses should be incurred to attain justice in an assisted case, the legally aided litigant's solicitor and counsel should approach it in the same way as they would were their client a person whose private means enabled him to fight that particular case in a reasonable way. Any taxation is on the standard basis, that is a reasonable amount in respect of all costs reasonably incurred and any doubts which the taxing officer may have as to whether the costs were reasonably incurred or were reasonable in amount will be resolved in favour of the paying party.[14]

---

[13] *Francis v. Francis and Dickerson* [1956] P. 95; [1955] 3 W.L.R. 973, *per* Sachs J.
[14] R.S.C., Ord. 62, r. 12(1).

DECIDED CASES AND INHERENT JURISDICTION

In considering the conduct of an assisted person's case, the court may **12–06** exercise its penal powers under R.S.C., Ord. 62, rr. 10, 11 or C.C.R., Ord. 38, r. 1(3) or under the Civil Legal Aid (General) Regulations 1989, regs. 102, 109. All those provisions are supplementary to the wasted costs jurisdiction and the inherent jurisdiction of the court.

The Court of Appeal has stated that it would bear in mind the difficulties inherent in conducting litigation and, on occasions, in keeping within relevant time-limits. The existence of unreasonable delay was the principal criticism made of the conduct of litigation today and it was up to all concerned to do what they could to eliminate it.[15]

THE POSITION BEFORE THE CERTIFICATE IS ISSUED

Where a solicitor acts on behalf of an applicant for legal aid, the costs for **12–07** any work done before the certificate is issued are irrecoverable from the Fund (unless recoverable under the Green Form Scheme). Pre-certificate costs may be recovered *inter partes* or from the client on a solicitor and own client basis. It may, however, be essential for certain steps to be taken without delay, if the client's position is not to be prejudiced. If the cost involved is not great, the applicant may be prepared to pay personally but, if not, the right course for the solicitor to adopt is to advise immediate application for an emergency certificate.

STEPS BEFORE PROCEEDINGS ARE STARTED

Before advising an assisted person to take proceedings, the solicitor should **12–08** make the same inquiries and investigations as would normally be carried out for a private client, provided they are within the scope of the certificate and are designed to achieve the purposes which are contemplated by it.[16]

When deciding the grounds on which proceedings are to be instituted the assisted person's solicitor should take care not to incur unnecessary costs. If unnecessary costs are incurred, they will not be allowed on the legal aid taxation.

---

[15] *Sinclair-Jones v. Kay* [1989] 1 W.L.R. 114.
[16] *Francis v. Francis and Dickerson* [1956] P. 87; [1955] 3 W.L.R. 973.

Instructing Counsel

When counsel should be instructed

12–09 It is for the assisted person's solicitor to decide whether counsel's services are required but the client has the right to select his legal representative.[17] In two cases the Regulations provide for the Area Director's authority to be sought before counsel can be instructed:

(a) in authorised summary proceedings; and

(b) When a Queen's Counsel or more than one counsel is to be instructed.

These are dealt with elsewhere. Otherwise, as in a privately funded case, the solicitor may, subject to any instructions from his client, instruct counsel whenever the circumstances require it but this is subject to the risk that the taxing officer may take a different view on the legal aid taxation; leaving counsel with no right to any fees and the solicitor in the same position so far as the costs incurred in instructing counsel are concerned. No fee is marked on any brief to counsel which is simply endorsed "legal aid" with the reference number of the certificate. The instructions must include a copy of the certificate and any amendments to it and any authority to incur costs. In the case of authorised summary proceedings, instructions must show the authority for counsel to be instructed.[18]

Certificates limited to counsel's opinion

12–10 Where a civil legal aid certificate is granted, limited to obtaining counsel's opinion, that limitation is interpreted to allow solicitors to obtain fresh evidence when seeking counsel's opinion, to enable counsel to advise effectively. In addition, the Board has indicated that it will allow a conference to be attended and paid for, even though it is not specifically mentioned in the limitation. There is no need for specific authority for a conference but it will still have to be justified and usually the area office specifically refers to a conference if it deems one to be necessary. Solicitors may request specific reference to a conference. As a general premise, certificates limited to obtaining counsel's opinion will continue to cover obtaining only one written opinion. Thus, obtaining further opinions or preparatory work to this end is outside the scope of the limitation. However, an inquiry to counsel for clarification of a genuine ambiguity in the opinion itself may be allowed. Any further preparatory work, whether suggested by

---

[17] Legal Aid Act 1988, s. 32(1).
[18] Civil Legal Aid (General) Regulations, reg. 59(2).

counsel or not, will not be within the scope of the limitation unless a further amendment is authorised by the area office.[19]

THE CHOICE OF COURT

When granting an application for legal aid, the area committee will **12–11** normally decide the court in which proceedings should be brought. If this is to be the High Court it is unusual for it to be specified in the certificate. Where, however, the committee considers that proceedings should only be brought in a county court it will usually restrict the certificate accordingly. If the scope of a certificate is restricted in this way to proceedings in a particular court it will have to be amended if it is to cover proceedings after they have been transferred to another court. No amendment is needed if the certificate does not specify a particular court.

In a borderline case the committee will leave it to the assisted person, acting on the advice of his solicitor and counsel, to decide in which court the proceedings should be brought. The assisted person's advisers will have to bear in mind that if the proceedings are started in the High Court, the assisted person could suffer financially if the amount recovered is such that only costs on the county court scale are allowed.[20] The costs payable out of the Fund to the solicitor and counsel will be taxed on the High Court scale and the difference will have to be borne by the assisted person out of the contribution or, if this is insufficient, will be recoverable by way of the statutory charge on any damages recovered.

STARTING PROCEEDINGS

Certificates are frequently granted which authorise the taking of "all **12–12** necessary steps up to but not including", e.g. the issue of a writ or setting down for trial, but unless there is a limitation of this sort on the certificate it is unnecessary for the Area Director to be consulted before proceedings are commenced and the assisted person's solicitor may issue a writ as soon as it is considered appropriate to do so. The solicitor should ensure that the certificate covers the proceedings which are contemplated and extends to any parties it may be intended to sue.

The solicitor is responsible, in the first instance, for paying the court fees and all the other disbursements in connection with the proceedings (save

---

[19] Legal Aid Board Guidance to Legal Aid Practitioners, December 1990.
[20] County Courts Act 1984, ss. 19, 20, 29.

for counsel's fees) and is entitled to recover them in due course from the Fund.

Because time may be needed in which to make an application to the Area Director, it is particularly important in a legally aided case for the solicitor to keep in mind the provisions of the Limitation Acts and other time-limits, such as the need to serve a writ within four months of its issue. If no steps are taken until near the end of the relevant period it may not be possible to obtain any necessary authority in time; and even where the court has a discretion to extend the limit it may not be prepared, when exercising it, to take into account any delay that has resulted from obtaining a certificate or having one amended.

EXPERT AND OTHER WITNESSES

12–13 A solicitor who instructs an expert may be rendered liable, as a matter of professional etiquette, and by contract, to pay a higher fee than that allowed on taxation, unless specific steps are taken to limit the liability for the witness's fee when first giving the instructions. A legal aid taxation determines only the amount which is to be paid to the solicitor out of the Fund, whilst the amount payable by the solicitor to the expert is regulated by the contract between them. In a legal aid case where the balance cannot be obtained from the client, a solicitor is well advised to make it a term of the instructions to the expert that the latter's fees will not exceed the sum allowed on taxation. The practice of engaging an expert on terms that remuneration will be restricted to the amount allowed on taxation is desirable in the interests of litigants and such an expert should receive fair treatment on taxation.

A solicitor ought to use his best endeavours to secure the allowance on taxation of a proper fee for such an expert.

A solicitor can properly apply for authority to carry in objections or to apply to the court for review on the grounds that he is dissatisfied with the decision of a taxing officer in so far as it relates to the fees of an expert.[21] It may be possible to obtain prior authority to employ a particular expert and in those circumstances a maximum fee will be prescribed by the Area Director.[22]

SETTLEMENTS AND PAYMENT INTO COURT

12–14 An assisted person has the same right as any other litigant to settle an action or to enter into a compromise to avoid proceedings or to bring them to an

---

[21] *Per* Phillips J. in *Cementation Construction Ltd. v. Keaveny* (July 8, 1988; unreported).
[22] Civil Legal Aid (General) Regulations 1989, reg. 61.

end.[23] It is unnecessary for the Area Director to approve the arrangements or even to be consulted. It may be wise, in a doubtful case, to consult the Area Director as to whether the statutory charge will attach to any damages or other property to be recovered or preserved in the compromise. In certain circumstances the assisted person may be under a duty to offer to submit to judgment, so as to avoid further costs being unjustly incurred. If the legally assisted person insists on the case being unreasonably continued the solicitor and counsel are under a duty to report the fact to the Area Director.[24]

In litigation concerning the drug Opren, a legally aided plaintiff refused a global settlement and the legal aid certificate was discharged on the premise that a certain sum had been refused. On judical review, it was found that the sum was a provisional figure based on incomplete material and the discharge was quashed. The court also considered the extent to which litigation costs should be contrasted with the amount which would be recovered if the action was successful, as a factor to be taken into account in determining whether the certificate should be discharged.[25]

A legally aided litigant is also in the same position as an unassisted person in respect of the rules governing payment into court. If the payment in is declined and the assisted person does not then recover more than the amount paid in, the costs will normally be awarded against the assisted person as from the date of payment in. The assisted person's liability for costs is limited by section 17(1) of the 1988 Act which provides that it is not to exceed the amount, if any, which is a reasonable one for him to pay having regard to all the circumstances including the financial resources of all the parties and their conduct in connection with the dispute.

If a defendant considers that the legally aided plaintiff is unreasonably refusing to accept a payment in, the facts may be reported to the Area Director.[26]

The statutory charge extends to an assisted person's rights under any **12–15** compromise which is arrived at to avoid proceedings or to bring them to an end, and also to any sum which is taken out of court. This is so whether or not the assisted person is liable to make a contribution to the Fund. When advising a legally aided client whether to accept a proposed settlement or to take money out of court, it is important that a warning is given of the effect that the statutory charge will have on the amount which the client will receive. The matter can be serious for an assisted person as, in some cases, the whole of the sum awarded by way of damages may be absorbed, particularly where the assisted person is rendered liable to pay part of his opponent's costs through having obtained less than the amount paid into court.

---

[23] *Re Trusts affecting 26 Clarendon Villas* [1955] 3 ALL E.R. 178.
[24] Civil Legal Aid (General) Regulations 1989, reg. 67.
[25] *R. v. Legal Aid Area Committee No. 10 (East Midlands), ex p. McKenna* [1990] C.O.D. 358, D.C.
[26] Civil Legal Aid (General) Regulations 1989, reg. 70.

REPORTS TO COMMITTEES

12–16 In certain circumstances which are dealt with below, an assisted person's solicitor or counsel has the right or duty, in spite of the normal rules of professional privilege, to make a report about the client's case to the Area Director. Costs incurred by reason of any report made by an assisted person's solicitor under these provisions will be taxed on the standard basis.[27]

The assisted person must forthwith inform his solicitor of any change in his circumstances or of any changes in the circumstances of his case which he has reason to believe might affect the terms or the continuance of his certificate.[28]

Duty to report abuse of legal aid

12–17 Where, during the course of an assisted person's case, the solicitor or counsel has reason to believe that the assisted person has required the case to be conducted unreasonably, so as to incur an unjustifiable expense to the Fund, or has unreasonably required that the case be continued, the solicitor or counsel are under a duty forthwith to report the fact to the Area Director. Similarly, if there is reason to believe that the assisted person has intentionally failed to comply with any provision of the Civil Legal Aid (General) Regulations 1989 concerning information to be furnished, or has knowingly made a false statement or representation in furnishing such information, there is again a duty to report the fact to the Area Director.[29] If the solicitor or counsel is uncertain whether or not it would be reasonable to continue acting for the assisted person, the circumstances must be reported to the Area Director.[30] Where the circumstances described above arise, any solicitor or counsel for the assisted person may give up the case if so minded, and that right is without prejudice to any other right which the solicitor or counsel may have to give up the case.[31]

Duty to report on refusing or giving up a case

12–18 Where a solicitor refuses to act for an assisted person, or gives up a case having been selected, the solicitor is under a duty to inform the Area Director of the reasons behind the decision.[32] Where counsel, having been

---

[27] Civil Legal Aid (General) Regulations 1989, reg. 111.
[28] *ibid.* reg. 66.
[29] *ibid.* reg. 67(1).
[30] *ibid.* reg. 67(2).
[31] *ibid.* reg. 69(3).
[32] *ibid.* reg. 69(1).

selected to act for an assisted person, refuses to accept instructions or decides to give up the case, counsel is under a duty to inform the Area Director of the reasons for the decision. Where counsel entrusts the case to another member of the Bar, he must inform the Area Director of his reasons for so doing if required to do so.[33]

Where a solicitor or counsel gives up an assisted person's case because of the assisted person's abuse of legal aid, the solicitor is under a duty to report the circumstances in which the right was exercised to the Area Director.[34] It is open to the Area Director to discharge or revoke the assisted person's certificate having received such a report, but if this is not done, the Area Director must require the assisted person to select another solicitor to act for him.[35]

Duty to report progress of proceedings

The assisted person's solicitor is under a duty to make a report to the Area Director where the assisted person declines to accept a reasonable offer of settlement, or of a sum which is paid into court. The solicitor is also under a duty to notify the Area Director where a legal aid certificate is issued to another party to the proceedings.[36] This last requirement, although sensible on the face of it, is likely to lead to difficulties since it is an unfortunate failing of many solicitors not to give the appropriate notice of the issue of a legal aid certificate and accordingly the original assisted person's solicitor might simply not know of the issue of a legal aid certificate to any other party to the proceedings. It is apparently not possible at the moment for the area committee's computer system to provide the necessary information.

12–19

If the Area Director requires information from time to time regarding the progress and disposal of the proceedings from the assisted person's solicitor and counsel, they are under a duty to provide the appropriate information.[37]

The Board may require the assisted person's solicitor to certify, in a report to the Area Director, that it is reasonable for the assisted person to continue to receive legal aid in respect of the proceedings. Such a report and certificate must be on an approved form.[38] Where a request is made by the Board for a certificate of reasonableness, the assisted person's solicitor must make the report within 21 days, failing which, the Area Director will give notice to the solicitor and to the assisted person that the legal aid certificate may be discharged and will invite the assisted person to show cause why the certificate should not be discharged. In that regard, the Civil Legal Aid

---

[33] *ibid.* reg. 69(2).
[34] *ibid.* regs. 67, 69(4).
[35] *ibid.* reg. 69(5).
[36] *ibid.* reg. 70(1).
[37] *ibid.* reg. 70(1).
[38] *ibid.* reg. 70(2).

(General) Regulations 1989 applying to discharge of certificates will apply with any necessary modifications.[39]

Duty to report death or bankruptcy of an assisted person

12–20 Where the assisted person dies or has a bankruptcy order made against him, the solicitor is under a duty, upon becoming aware of the situation, to report the fact to the Area Director.[40]

Duty to report completion of a case

12–21 Where the assisted person's solicitor has completed the case, or has completed the work authorised by the solicitor, or is for any reason unable to complete the work, he must report forthwith to the Area Director.[41] Thus, where a limited certificate has been issued and a stage in the proceedings has been reached in which the limitation becomes effective, it is necessary to report to the Area Director for consideration as to whether the limitation should be removed or enlarged or the certificate discharged.

Duty to report not affected by professional privilege

12–22 An assisted person is entitled to the benefit of professional privilege and neither the solicitor nor counsel may, in general, disclose any information about the assisted person's affairs which they have obtained as a result of acting for that person. However, neither solicitor nor counsel is precluded by reason or any privilege arising out of the relationship between counsel, solicitor and client from disclosing to an Area Director or an area committee any information or from giving any opinion which that person is required to disclose under the 1988 Act or the Regulations or which may enable them to perform their functions.[42]

For the purpose of providing information under the 1988 Act or the Regulations, to enable an Area Director or area committee to perform its functions, any party may disclose communications in relation to the proceedings concerned, sent to or by the assisted person's solicitor whether or not they are expressed to be "without prejudice".[43] The Regulations require an Area Director to discharge a certificate if it is considered that it is no longer reasonable for it to remain in force.[44]

---

[39] *ibid.* regs. 70(3), (4), 86.
[40] *ibid.* reg. 71.
[41] *ibid.* reg. 72.
[42] *ibid.* reg. 73(1).
[43] *ibid.* reg. 73(2).
[44] *ibid.* reg. 77.

No question can arise of breach of privilege in any of the cases referred to above because in each of them the assisted person's solicitor or counsel is under a duty, imposed by the Regulations, to make the appropriate report.

Power of the court to refer abuse to the Area Director

At any time during the hearing of any proceedings to which the assisted **12–23** person is a party, if the court considers that the assisted person has:
  (a) in relation to any application for a certificate, made an untrue statement as to his financial resources or has failed to disclose any material fact concerning them when the statement was made, or the failure occurred before or after the issue of the certificate and notwithstanding that it was made or occured in relation to an application to another area office in connection with the same proceedings; or
  (b) intentionally failed to comply with the Regulations by not furnishing his solicitor or the Area Director with any material or information concerning anything other than his financial resources; or
  (c) knowingly made an untrue statement in furnishing such information;
the court may, on its own motion or on the application of the Board, make an order referring to the Area Director the question whether the assisted person's certificate should continue.[45] If the assisted person satisfies the court that he has used due care and diligence to avoid misstatement or failure, no order need be made, but the assisted person's solicitor must nevertheless report the circumstances to the Area Director.[46]

UNJUSTIFIABLE AND FRUITLESS LITIGATION

When litigation may cease to be reasonable

A litigant's advisers must continue to keep in mind the financial risks **12–24** involved in going on with a case. Where their client is bearing the cost himself, it is for him to decide whether to continue incurring the risk, and the duty of the solicitor and counsel is discharged if they give him the best advice they can. Where the cost is underwritten by the Fund with little or only limited liability attaching to the assisted person, his advisers may be

[45] *ibid.* reg. 68(1).
[46] *ibid.* reg. 68(2).

in an invidious position because, while they have a duty to their client, they are also bound to ensure that he does not misuse the legal aid scheme by continuing with an unmeritorious case which may result in a waste of public money or in hardship to an opponent. There are three main areas in which they may find themselves in this dilemma:

No cause of action

12–25 It may happen that after a certificate has been granted, an assisted person's solicitor or counsel finds that the client has no case or no defence. Supporting evidence may be unobtainable, adverse evidence may be produced or for some other reason it may be apparent that the assisted person cannot be advised to go on. The proposed action may be found not to be maintainable in law. The grant of a certificate is not a warranty that the holder has a good cause of action and means no more than that, on the facts before them, the committee considered that he had reasonable grounds for taking, defending or being a party to proceedings.[47]

Change in the prospects of success

12–26 Although an action may have been properly begun or legitimately defended, it may become apparent at any time that the assisted person's chances of success have altered. This is particularly likely to occur if the opponent pays money into court, or offers to settle, which poses the assisted person with the same, often difficult, choice as any other litigant. If the solicitor and counsel take the view that there is no reasonable likelihood that the assisted person will be awarded any greater sum than the amount already paid into court, or the settlement which has been offered is as advantageous as can fairly be hoped for, they will have to consider their own position if the assisted person refuses to accept their advice.[48]

Fruitless litigation

12–27 Although an assisted person may have a good cause of action, it may emerge at any stage, either before proceedings have begun or while they are in progress, that any judgment which is obtained is likely to be fruitless. This may be because inquiries show that the defendant will be unable to meet the judgment or because the costs incurred will, through the operation of the statutory charge, absorb the greater part or even the whole value of the property. When considering whether it is reasonable for a client to continue with proceedings in such circumstances, it is relevant for the assisted person's solicitor or counsel to bear in mind that one of the grounds on which the certificate may be refused is where it appears to the Area

---

[47] Legal Aid Act 1988, s. 15(2).
[48] Civil Legal Aid (General) Regulations 1989, reg. 67.

Director that only a trivial advantage would be gained by the applicant from the proceedings.[49]

The decision which must be taken in such a case may not be easy, particularly where, even though the defendant may seem unlikely to be in a position immediately to meet any judgment that is obtained, the assisted person is anxious to proceed. It may be argued that the defendant's financial position may improve in the meanwhile, although nothing more tangible can be produced on which to base this hope than the possibility of the defendant's income increasing as a result of advancement in employment. The hope that the defendant might win the football pools would not be sufficient. A further factor which may have to be taken into account is the assisted person's own financial position since an order for quite a small sum, even if paid by instalments, might be of considerable benefit to the assisted person if that person was, *e.g.* an old-age pensioner or permanently incapacitated for work.

Clearly, the prospects for recovery are greatly improved if the defendant is insured and solicitors should take steps to discover this in the same way as if acting for a privately funded client.

The duty of solicitors and counsel

Where the legal adviser is confident that the case ought not to proceed

The solicitor or counsel may reach a definite decision that there are no **12–28** reasonable grounds for going on with the client's case. This may be because they are satisfied that any judgment which might be obtained would inevitably be fruitless or for any of the other reasons already referred to. In such circumstances, the adviser is fully entitled to give up the case. A solicitor has a right to give up an action properly begun where he finds that it could not be successfully continued.[50] Before giving up the case, the solicitor should advise the client that, in his view, it is no longer reasonable to continue. If the assisted person accepts this advice, no difficulty will arise and the solicitor will merely have to apply to have the certificate discharged[51] and thereafter take the remaining steps to enable the matter to be disposed of. If the client refuses to accept the advice, he should be warned that the Regulations give the solicitor or counsel the right to give up a case where they have reason to believe that the assisted person has required the case to be conducted unreasonably, so as to incur an unjustifiable expense to the Fund, or has

---

[49] *ibid.* reg. 29.
[50] *Lawrence v. Potts* [1834] 6 Conv. 428.
[51] Civil Legal Aid (General) Regulations 1989, reg. 77.

required unreasonably that the case be continued.[52] If, notwithstanding this warning, the client persists in his attitude, the solicitor or counsel may then withdraw from the case.[53] In such circumstances, the solicitor must make a report to the Area Director.[54]

Although a practitioner is fully entitled to give up the case in the above circumstances and in practice would almost always do so, the Regulations do not impose an obligation to withdraw. Whether or not he withdraws, the solicitor or counsel must forthwith report the facts to the Area Director.[55] The solicitor who unreasonably starts or continues a case will be regarded as behaving improperly and may render himself personally liable to an order to pay the costs,[56] but "it is not for solicitors or counsel to impose a screen through which a litigant has to pass before he can put his case before the court."[57] In other words, solicitor and counsel merely have to be satisfied that the assisted person's case is properly arguable (and will not ultimately be fruitless).

Where the legal adviser is uncertain whether the case will proceed

12–29 The solicitor or counsel acting for a legally aided person is under a duty to report to the Area Director if in any doubt as to whether it is reasonable to continue acting.[58] The legal adviser need not give up the case but may leave it to the Area Director to decide whether the certificate should be discharged or amended.

Where the assisted person runs up unnecessary costs

12–30 A solicitor may be presented with a problem rather similar to that of unjustifiable litigation when he is faced with an importunate client who, not being personally liable for the expense, increases costs unnecessarily by continually writing, calling or telephoning. This may put the solicitor in a difficult position because he must maintain his client's confidence and yet avoid unnecessary expense to the Fund. Any such inflated costs may be disallowed on taxation and, if a combination of firmness and tact proves unsuccessful, the solicitor should warn his client that he may have to consider making a report to the Area Director to enable the Director to consider serving notice on the client to show cause why the certificate

---

[52] *ibid.* reg. 67(1) (a).
[53] *ibid.* reg. 69(3).
[54] *ibid.* reg. 69(4).
[55] *ibid.* reg. 67(1) (b).
[56] *ibid.* reg. 109.
[57] *Orchard v. South Eastern Electricity Board* [1987] Q.B. 565.
[58] Civil Legal Aid (General) Regulations 1989, reg. 67(2).

should not be discharged.[59] In extreme circumstances, the solicitor may have to give up the case altogether on the grounds that the assisted person is requiring it to be conducted unreasonably so as to incur unjustifiable expense to the Fund.[60]

The right of other parties to report

Any party may give information to the Area Director with a view to persuading the Director to discharge, amend or revoke an assisted person's certificate.[61] The Civil Legal Aid (General) Regulations 1989 require the Area Director to discharge the certificate if, as a result of information which has come to his knowledge, he considers it is unreasonable in the particular circumstances that the assisted person should continue to receive legal aid[62] and this information may come from any source, including the assisted person's opponent or the latter's solicitors. Such a party may disclose to the Area Director communications relating to the proceedings and to or by the assisted person's solicitor whether marked "without prejudice" or not.[63] If information which might lead the Area Director to amend an assisted person's certificate, or to discharge it, should come to the knowledge of the opponent's solicitor, it should be forwarded by that solicitor to the Area Director for consideration, so that the solicitor's own client does not remain at risk in respect of costs any longer than is necessary. Failure to do this may, in certain circumstances, amount to professional negligence.

12–31

The powers of the court

The court has two main powers in dealing with litigation which appears to be unjustifiable or is likely to be fruitless, namely the right to adjourn proceedings and to make orders for costs. If at any time it appears to the court that it may no longer be reasonable, due to any of the considerations already referred to, for an assisted person to continue with the proceedings, it may adjourn the case to give the Area Director the opportunity of discharging the certificate.[64] The court also has wide powers, if it is satisfied that it is unreasonable for proceedings to have been brought or defended or the assisted person should not have continued with them beyond a

12–32

---

[59] *ibid.* reg. 81.
[60] *ibid.* reg. 67.
[61] *ibid.* reg. 73(2).
[62] *ibid.* reg. 77(c).
[63] *ibid.* reg. 73(2).
[64] *ibid.* reg. 68.

certain stage, to make orders for costs against the assisted person or the solicitor.[65] Ancillary to these is the court's power to refer a case to a taxing officer for inquiry and report.[66]

The duty of the Area Director

When a certificate may or must be discharged

12–33 At any time during the conduct of an assisted person's case, the Area Director may have to decide whether it is reasonable for that person to continue receiving legal aid. The circumstances in which this question may arise are first, where a report is made to the Director by the assisted person's solicitor or counsel on giving up the case[67] and secondly, where the Director receives information from any source in other circumstances.[68] In each case, the Director must consider whether:

(a) the assisted person no longer has reasonable grounds for taking, defending or being a party to the proceedings or for continuing to do so; or

(b) the assisted person has required the proceedings to be conducted unreasonably so as to incur an unjustifiable expense to the Fund; or

(c) it is unreasonable in the circumstances that the assisted person should continue to receive legal aid.[69]

If any of those questions are answered in the affirmative, the Director must discharge the certificate.[70] Before doing so, however, the Director must serve notice on the assisted person that the certificate may be discharged (or revoked) and that the assisted person may show cause why this should not be done.[71] The test to be applied when considering whether or not to discharge a certificate is similar to that to be applied when considering an application for legal aid. That is, it must be decided what advice would properly have been given to the applicant if that person were of adequate, but not overabundant means, and were paying for the litigation personally.[72]

The division of responsibility between the Area Director and the legal advisers

12–34 There may sometimes be a risk of confusion between the duty of the Area Director to ensure that legal aid is not abused and the right of the assisted

---

[65] *ibid.* reg. 124.
[66] R.S.C., Ord. 62, rr. 10, 11.
[67] Civil Legal Aid (General) Regulations 1989, reg. 69(4).
[68] *ibid.* reg. 77.
[69] *ibid.* reg. 77.
[70] *ibid.* reg. 77.
[71] *ibid.* reg. 81(1)(a).
[72] *Francis v. Francis and Dickerson* [1956] P. 87; [1955] 3 W.L.R. 973.

person's legal advisers to be free to decide how the action should be conducted. It has been held that:

(a) It is not the function of the Area Director to intervene in the way in which a case is conducted except in respect of the overriding duty to deprive an assisted person of legal aid if he requires the case to be handled unreasonably so as to waste public money.

(b) It is for the Area Director to see that the merits of the case have been fully considered but the responsibility for the way in which it is conducted thereafter is that of the legal advisers.

(c) It is an essential part of the Area Director's duty to exercise his own independent judgment of the facts and where there is the possibility of a proper and agreed solution to make sure that it is explored by the assisted person's advisers. To do this is not to interfere with the actual conduct of the case.

(d) Throughout the proceedings, the Area Director is under a duty to discharge the certificate if it appears that the assisted person no longer has any reasonable grounds for continuing with the case or that, for some other cause, it would be unreasonable for him to continue to receive legal aid.[73]

APPEALS

The need to apply for legal aid

It is necessary to make a fresh application for a new certificate to make or **12–35** defend an appeal to the House of Lords or an appeal from the magistrates' court.[74]

In the case of any other appeals, where the proceedings in the court below have been legally aided, the certificate may be amended to include making or defending an appeal or making an interlocutory appeal. Applications for an amendment should be made to the Area Director as soon as possible. Defence of an interlocutory appeal is regarded as being included within the scope of the original certificate. Clearly, if there is no existing certificate covering the proceedings in the court below, a full application for legal aid must be made in respect of the appellate proceedings.

In a case in which the plaintiff was brain damaged, allegedly as a result of whooping cough vaccine, judgment was given at first instance for the defendants. Counsel gave an advice in favour of appeal and further advised that the judgment should not itself be treated as a ground for refusing legal

---

[73] *Iverson v. Iverson* [1967] P. 134; [1966] 2 W.L.R. 1168.
[74] Civil Legal Aid (General) Regulations 1989, reg. 46(2).

aid. On judicial review of the Legal Aid Appeal Committee's refusal of legal aid, the court held that the Committee had failed to have regard to all the material considerations and that in such circumstances a committee might be required to give extended reasons for its decision to refuse to grant legal aid or to discharge a certificate.[75]

12–36　It may not always be possible to obtain legal aid before the time for appealing elapses. Consequently, many appeals are out of time. To avoid difficulty, prompt notification should be given to the opposite side of the intention to appeal against the order and of the fact that application is being made for a legal aid certificate. The notice of appeal itself should contain an application to extend the time for appeal. In such circumstances, the Divisional Court of the Family Division may be expected to give leave without any prior application for the necessary extension of time of the hearing of the appeal. The Master of the Rolls has criticised the disparity of treatment between assisted and non-assisted parties in requiring compliance with rules for setting down an appeal resulting from delays in the grant of legal aid and stated that the situation could be remedied by the introduction of changes to the Legal Aid Regulations and the Rules of the Supreme Court.[76]

Where the appellant is in receipt of assistance by way of representation for proceedings in a magistrates' court, this will cover giving notice of appeal and applying for a case to be stated within the ordinary time for so doing.

12–37　The legal aid certificate to appeal or an amendment of an existing certificate (initially limited to bespeaking relevant parts of the transcript) can be granted by the Area Director very quickly. However, thereafter there may be some unavoidable delays and, for this reason, application for legal aid or amendment of an existing certificate should be made as soon as possible after the conclusion of the original hearing. Prompt notification should be given to the opposite side of the intention to appeal and of the fact that application for legal aid is being made immediately. It is understood that the Court of Appeal takes the view that where such a notification is given, the opposing parties would normally be expected to consent to an extension of time, corresponding to the time allowed in High Court appeals and, if failure to consent to such an extension thus necessitates an application to the court, the court may well order the other party to pay the costs of the application.

Where the liberty of the subject is at stake and a solicitor considers that his legally aided client has grounds for an appeal, he should not delay lodging the notice of appeal while awaiting further legal aid.[77]

---

[75] *R. v. Legal Aid Area No. 8 (Northern) Appeal Committee, ex p. Parkinson, The Times,* March 13, 1990.

[76] *Norwich and Peterborough Building Society v. Steed* [1991] 1 W.L.R. 449.

[77] *Jordan v. Jordan* [1992] 2 F.L.R. 701; *The Times,* June 22, 1992.

The conduct of an appeal

In general, the same principles apply to the conduct of a legally aided **12–38**
appeal as to a trial. In particular, a solicitor and counsel acting for an
assisted person have the same rights and are subject to the same obligations
in respect of the conduct of proceedings which may be likely to be fruitless
or unjustifiable as have already been described.

Abandonment of proceedings

An assisted person has the same right to abandon or withdraw or **12–39**
discontinue the whole or part of an action, defence or counterclaim as an
unassisted litigant.[78] This is subject to the normal liability to pay the
opponent's costs, *e.g.* when the plaintiff discontinues an action without
leave,[79] but the liability is limited by section 17(1) of the 1988 Act which
restricts the extent to which the order for costs can be made against an
assisted person to an amount which is a reasonable one for him to pay
having a regard to all the circumstances.

Where an assisted person abandons any proceedings for which a
certificate has been issued, an immediate application should be made to
the Area Director to have the certificate either discharged or amended to
cover any outstanding matter. It could amount to an abuse of legal aid for
an assisted person to appear as such when the object for which the
certificate was issued has been abandoned.

DUTIES OF ASSISTED PERSON

A legal aid application must contain the information necessary to determine **12–40**
the nature of the proceedings and whether it is reasonable that
representation should be granted and to assess the disposable income,
disposable capital and (maximum) contribution of the applicant (but see
Chapter 20 regarding special Children Act proceedings).[80] An applicant is
required to supply such further information or documents as may be
required or attend for an interview.[81] This is backed by the Area Director's
power to revoke or discharge a certificate where the assisted person fails to

---

[78] R.S.C., Ord. 21.
[79] R.S.C., Ord. 62, r. 5(3).
[80] Civil Legal Aid (General) Regulations 1989, reg. 12(1).
[81] *ibid.* reg. 12(3).

attend for an interview or to provide information or documents when required to do so.[82] Means assessments are now conducted by post with the appropriate means form and supporting documents being submitted with the application itself. Interviews are extremely rare. This does not, however, reduce the applicant's obligation to complete the application form, including the statement of means, honestly and fully.

12–41   Where an applicant is liable to pay a contribution, he is notified of the amount of his contribution and of the terms upon which a certificate will be issued to him (*i.e.* as to the payment of that contribution). This is done in a form of offer which is specifically required to draw attention to the applicant's liability for payment of his contribution, the operation of the statutory charge and the limit of his liability under an order for costs. Therefore, where there is a contribution there is an obligation to pay it and that is confirmed by the applicant in his acceptance of the offer of legal aid. If no contribution is payable (and no offer is issued) the certificate issued to the assisted person draws attention to the statutory charge and the limit on the assisted person's liability under an order for costs.[83] If the assisted person fails to keep instalments of his contribution up to date and any payment is more than 21 days in arrears, his certificate may be discharged from such date as the Area Director considers appropriate.[84] The Board has increased the controls in this area and revocation or discharge will speedily follow any contribution falling into arrears.

12–42   An applicant may also be required to sign an undertaking to pay to the Board any sum which he receives from an organisation or body which might reasonably be expected to give him financial help towards the costs of the proceedings (without there being a right of indemnity in the applicant's favour, *e.g.* from a trade union).[85] This is rarely employed and once a legal aid certificate has been issued there is a restriction on "topping up" contained in regulation 64 of the Civil Legal Aid (General) Regulations 1989 which means that neither the assisted person's solicitor nor counsel could be involved in the direct use of such funds in connection with the litigation. Furthermore, the assisted person is obliged to report changes in his financial circumstances even where there is no such undertaking.

An applicant or assisted person is required to comply with the Regulations as to the information to be provided by him and intentional failure to disclose, or knowingly making any false statement or false representation in furnishing any information required by the Regulations, renders the applicant or assisted person liable to criminal prosecution.[86]

---

[82] *ibid.* reg. 79.
[83] *ibid.* reg. 42, 43.
[84] *ibid.* reg. 80(b).
[85] *ibid.* reg. 44.
[86] Legal Aid Act 1988, s. 39(1).

The availability of such a prosecution is reinforced by a specific provision which enables the Board to recover its loss in a county court where an applicant or assisted person fails to comply with the Regulations as to the information to be furnished by him (*i.e.* fails to disclose information) or makes a false statement or false representation in furnishing information for the purposes of the 1988 Act.[87]

The availability of criminal prosecution and recovery of the Board's loss **12–43** in a county court (even where the county court limit is exceeded) are backed by an obligation on the assisted person's solicitor or counsel to report where he has reason to believe that the assisted person has intentionally failed to furnish information or has knowingly made a false statement or false representation.[88] Additionally, a court has power during the hearing of any proceedings to which an assisted person is a party, on the application of the Board or of its own motion, to make an order referring to the Area Director the question whether the certificate should remain in force, where the court considers that the assisted person has, in relation to any application for a certificate, made an untrue statement as to his financial resources, or failed to disclose any material facts concerning them. Statements and failures before or after the issue of a certificate are covered, as are statements or failures in connection with an application to another area office in connection with the same proceedings.

The court may also make such an order where it considers that the **12–44** assisted person has intentionally failed to furnish his solicitor or the Area Director with any material information concerning anything *other than* his financial resources or knowingly made an untrue statement in furnishing such information.[89]

No order may be made in relation to mis-statements or failures to disclose details relating to financial resources if the court is satisfied by the assisted person that he used due care or diligence to avoid such mis-statement or failure, but the assisted person is then obliged to report the circumstances to the Area Director.[90]

The obligation to make full and accurate disclosure of information regarding financial resources and any other material information is further backed by the Area Director's power to revoke or discharge a certificate where, as a result of information which has come to his knowledge, by a reference from the court or otherwise, it appears that the assisted person has:

(a) made an untrue statement as to his financial resources or failed to disclose any material fact concerning them, either before or after the issue of a certificate and even if it was in relation to an

---

[87] *ibid.* s. 39(4).
[88] Civil Legal Aid (General) Regulations 1989, reg. 67(1)(b).
[89] *ibid.* reg. 68(1).
[90] *ibid.* reg. 68(2).

application to another area office in connection with the same proceedings; or

(b) *intentionally* failed to comply with the Regulations by not furnishing to the Area Director *or* the solicitor any material information concerning any matter other than his financial resources; or

(c) knowingly made an untrue statement in furnishing such information.[91]

A certificate cannot be revoked or discharged due to mis-statement or non-disclosure regarding financial resources if the Area Director is satisfied by the assisted person that he used due care or diligence to avoid the mis-statement or failure.[92] This proviso does not apply to non-financial mis-statements or failures to disclose.

12–45   The assisted person is under a specific obligation to inform his solicitor of any change in his circumstances or in the circumstances of his case which he has reason to believe might affect the terms of continuation of his certificate.[93] The provision is widely drafted and requires immediate notification of changes in the assisted person's circumstances, financial or otherwise, and of changes in the circumstances of the case which *might* affect the assisted person's contribution position or the continued existence of the certificate. Note that this is backed by an obligation on the solicitor (and counsel) to give the Area Director information regarding the progress and disposal of the case as the Area Director may from time to time require and, without request from the area office, to report unaccepted but reasonable offers of payments into court and to notify the Area Director of the issue of a legal aid certificate to another party to the proceedings.[94] There is no direct obligation on the assisted person to provide the area office with information regarding his circumstances on request (*i.e.* to carry out a check on continuing financial eligibility) but if an assisted person does not respond to such a request (which can be issued under section 4(1)(a) of the 1988 Act, the area office will institute a means assessment (under regulation 52(1) or 76(3)) with which the assisted person must co-operate, failing which his certificate will be revoked or discharged for failure to co-operate.[95] The assisted person's obligation is to inform the solicitor but it is limited to those changes which the *assisted person* has reason to believe might affect the position. This will extend to marrying (and co-habiting) and, *e.g.* to the disappearance of witnesses or evidence and changes in the

---

[91] *ibid.* reg. 78(1).
[92] *ibid.* reg. 78(2)
[93] *ibid.* reg. 66.
[94] *ibid.* reg. 70(1).
[95] *ibid.* reg. 79.

known circumstances of the defendant which could affect his ability to meet any judgment obtained.

This is backed by a specific requirement that the person whose means **12–46** are assessed or reassessed or whose resources are treated as the resources of any other person (*e.g.* spouses or cohabitees) must inform the Area Director of any change in financial circumstances since the original assessment *and* which he has reason to believe might affect the terms on which the certificate was granted or its continuation.[96] This obligation is clarified in the legal aid application form and legal aid certificate where the amounts which trigger a reassessment of means are specifically referred to.[97] It follows that the assisted person is under an obligation to inform both the solicitor and the Area Director of changes in his financial circumstances although the solicitor is not specifically required to report these changes to the Area Director. Additionally, there is an indirect obligation to deal with the area office's inquiries as to current means, failing which the assisted person's certificate can be revoked or discharged on non-co-operation in a formal means assessment triggered by the assisted person's failure to provide information to the area office.

To summarise, the applicant or assisted person must: **12–47**
  (a) co-operate in the assessment and reassessment of means;
  (b) supply information fully and accurately both before and after the issue of the certificate;
  (c) pay any contribution called for on the terms accepted in the acceptance of his offer;
  (d) pass to the Board any sum received towards the costs of proceedings where an undertaking to that effect has been given;
  (e) report changes in his circumstances or in the circumstances of the case which may affect his contribution or the continuation of the certificate;
  (f) report to the Area Director changes in his financial circumstances since the original assessment and those which might affect the contribution or the continuation of the certificate.

Additionally, there are some implied obligations backed by discharge and/ or revocation. Therefore the assisted person must not:
  (a) require the proceedings to be conducted unreasonably so as to incur an unjustifiable expense to the Fund; or
  (b) require unreasonably that the case be continued (including refusing to accept a reasonable offer of settlement or a sum which is paid into court); or
  (c) act in such a way that it becomes unreasonable in the particular circumstances that he should continue to receive legal aid.

---

[96] Civil Legal Aid (Assessment of Resources) Regulations 1989, reg. 11.
[97] *ibid.* reg. 12(1).

The assisted person must also co-operate with the Board's inquiries as to his current means which may lead to further means assessment.

Chapter 13

AMENDMENT OF LEGAL AID CERTIFICATES

PERMISSIBLE AMENDMENTS

Section 15(4) of the 1988 Act makes it clear that Part IV, civil, legal aid **13–01** may be amended. Under regulation 51 of the Civil Legal Aid (General) Regulations 1989 the Area Director may amend a certificate to:

(a) Correct some (administrative) mistake in the certificate, *e.g.* if one of the parties is incorrectly named — such an amendment can operate retrospectively[1]; or

(b) Extend the certificate to:

   (i) proceedings (*i.e.* where only steps up to (but excluding) proceedings were previously covered); or

   (ii) other steps (*i.e.* where additional steps short of proceedings are to be covered); or

   (iii) other proceedings (this is subject to regulation 46(3) so that a certificate may only be extended to other proceedings which it is permissible to cover in a single certificate, *e.g.* proceedings following an application for pre-action disclosure under section 33 of the Supreme Court Act 1981 or section 52 of the County Courts Act 1984); or

   (iv) proceedings which may be taken to enforce or give effect to any order or agreement made in the proceedings in respect of which the certificate was issued (regulation 46(3)(f) of the Civil Legal Aid (General) Regulations 1989 specifically includes taking proceedings in bankruptcy or to wind up a company); or

   (v) the bringing of an interlocutory appeal. R.S.C. Ord. 59, r. 1A deals with the distinction between final and interlocutory

---

[1] This is not normally so: *Wallace v. Freeman Heating* [1955] 1 W.L.R. 172; [1955] 1 All E.R. 418. On the correction of errors see *R. v. The Law Society, ex parte Gates, The Times,* March 31, 1988, *Thew v. Reeves,* [1981] 3 W.L.R. 190; [1981] 2 All E.R. 964, C.A. and *R. v. Legal Aid Board, ex parte Nicolson, The Times* June 24, 1994.

appeals and final and interlocutory orders. The residual general test is that an order is not final unless it would have finally determined the whole case whichever way the court had decided the application.[2] Note, however, that an ancillary relief order (including in the Family Division) is no longer interlocutory. Therefore, a specific amendment is always required to either prosecute or defend an appeal against such an order. Previously, an amendment was only necessary to prosecute such appeals. For the position regarding bringing or defending a final appeal see para. 13–04; or

(vi) proceedings in the Court of Justice of the European Communities (Luxembourg) on a reference for a preliminary ruling (although it is not specifically stated in the 1988 Act, it is the view of the Board that a certificate could be issued to cover such proceedings. It is, however, unlikely that such a certificate would be applied for as a certificate capable of amendment would probably be in existence, given the nature of a reference); or

(vii) representation by an EC (EEC) lawyer; this has the same meaning as in the European Communities (Services of Lawyers) Order 1978 (that is a person entitled to pursue his professional activities under the designation, in Belgium of an advocat — advocaat; in Denmark of an advokat; in Germany of a Rechtsanwalt; in France of an avocat; in the Hellenic Republic of a dikegoros; in the Republic of Ireland of a barrister or solicitor; in Italy of an avvocato; in Luxembourg of an avocat — avoue; and in the Netherlands of an advocaat).

(c) Add or substitute parties to the proceedings.

13–02   Regulation 47 of the Civil Legal Aid (General) Regulations 1989 requires that a certificate, other than one relating to family proceedings (for the definition of family proceedings, see regulation 3 of the Civil Legal Aid (General) Regulations 1989), shall specify the parties to the proceedings in respect of which it was issued. Care must be taken to ensure that a client's certificate covers all appropriate defendants. If, during the course of the proceedings, it becomes apparent that additional defendants should be joined or substituted in place of existing defendants, a request must be made to the area office for an appropriate amendment (using Form CLA30). Solicitors should not assume that an amendment will be automatically forthcoming. For example, it may be that the proceedings against the original proposed

---

[2] See *White v. Brunton* [1984] Q.B. 570; [1984] 2 All E.R. 606, C.A. — now enacted in R.S.C. r.1 A(3).

defendant would have been likely to prove fruitful, whereas proceedings against an alternative defendant might not be justified having regard to the inability of the new proposed defendant to satisfy any judgment.

Care should also be taken to ensure that a proposed defendant is correctly described in a certificate. A slight mistake in the spelling of a defendant's name would not generally invalidate the certificate but where, *e.g.* the incorrect initial of the first name of the defendant was set out in the certificate, the court treated the assisted person as not being legally aided vis-à-vis the opponent.[3] It should be borne in mind, however, that in the particular case there was a person with the surname and initials set out in the certificate (the named defendant was in fact the father of the correct defendant). It is submitted that had there been no person connected with the parties to the proceedings who bore the incorrect initials set out in the certificate, a corrective amendment with retrospective effect would have been permitted. Although the court held that the certificate was invalid as against the opponent, it did, nonetheless, hold that the certificate was valid as against the Fund and that the solicitors who had acted for the assisted person were entitled to be paid for the work done under the certificate. It might seem surprising that a certificate could be deemed to be valid for one purpose and not for another. However, that principle is to be found in another context in regulation 74 of the Civil Legal Aid (General) Regulations 1989 whereby a revoked certificate is deemed never to have existed in so far as the assisted person is concerned but it is deemed to exist for the purposes of an application by a successful unassisted party for costs out of the Fund pursuant to section 18 of the 1988 Act. **13–03**

(d) Extend the certificate to any steps having the same effect as a cross-action, a reply to a cross-action or a cross-appeal. **13–04**

A certificate to defend proceedings does not include bringing a counterclaim unless this is specifically stated.[4] It should also be borne in mind that a certificate issued to a plaintiff for the purpose of taking proceedings does not cover defending a counterclaim. It may be, *e.g.* that a plaintiff's own claim against the defendant has sufficient merit to justify the grant or continuation of legal aid after a defence has been filed but that the plaintiff has no defence to a counterclaim in the proceedings. In those circumstances, it would be open to the Area Director to grant legal aid for prosecuting the

---

[3] See above, para. 13–01 and *R. v. The Law Society, ex parte Gates* (1988), *The Times*, March 31, 1988.
[4] *Thew v. Reeves* [1981] 3 W.L.R. 190; [1981] 2 All E.R. 964, C.A.

plaintiff's own claim but not to include defending the counterclaim.

An amendment is always required for the purpose of a cross-appeal. If the order which is being appealed against is a final order, both appellant and respondent, if legally aided in the court below, will require amendments to their certificates whether it be for bringing the appeal, defending it or cross-appealing. Where, however, the appeal is against an interlocutory order, the appellant requires an amendment to his or her certificate[5] but the defendant does not require any amendment unless it is proposed to cross-appeal.

It should be noted that a certificate cannot be amended to cover an appeal to the House of Lords or for an appeal from the magistrates' court (except in the latter case where non-means, non-merits tested legal aid for Children Act proceedings applies)[6].

13–05   (e) Reduce the scope of the certificate so that it no longer extends to certain of the proceedings.

It is open to an Area Director to withdraw legal aid wholly or in part.[7] This may happen, e.g. where a certificate was issued in broad terms but counsel subsequently advises that part of the claim cannot be sustained. Although the Civil Legal Aid (General) Regulations 1989 are silent on the point, in practice, an Area Director will allow an assisted person a right of appeal to the area committee where a certificate is amended by withdrawing part of the cover originally provided by the certificate. For the procedure on appeal against refusal of an amendment see para. 13–18.

The view of the Board is that this power can also be used to restrict the work which can be undertaken where a voluntary embargo on work, or certain work, under a certificate is not accepted by an assisted person. This could arise where the Board has given notice to an assisted person to show cause why his ordinary (as opposed to emergency) certificate should not be discharged or revoked or where the Board is not in a position to issue a show cause letter (e.g. because a further assessment of means is taking place but has not been concluded) and the assisted person will not accept the embargo. If the Board is in a position to issue a show cause letter but it would be appropriate for the certificate to be speedily discharged, it will generally shorten the time given for the assisted person to respond to the show cause

---

[5] See above, para 13–01.

[6] Civil Legal Aid (General) Regulations 1989, reg. 46(2).

[7] For complete withdrawal of legal aid see Chap. 15 on revocation and discharge of certificates. Note, however, that section 15(4) permits civil legal aid to be withdrawn. If this is separate and distinct from the power to discharge it is not normally exercised.

letter rather than to rely on this provision. Note that if the scope of a certificate is limited in this way, there is a right of appeal to the area committee if the limitation is not deleted following a request to do so (as this would constitute a refusal of an amendment).

(f) Authorise a change of solicitor — see para. 13–08 below.[8]

APPLYING FOR AN AMENDMENT

Part II of the Civil Legal Aid (General) Regulations 1989 applies to **13–06** applications for the amendment of certificates as it applies to an application for a certificate albeit with any necessary modifications. This has the effect of requiring the application to contain the information and documents necessary to enable the Area Director to determine it and also imposes on the assisted person an obligation to provide such further information or documents as may be required. Note, however, that the area offices will deal with amendment applications on the basis of the information submitted and will not raise any queries.

Applications for amendments must be made using the Board's mandatory form (currently Form CLA30) which can be sent following a telephone grant. Applications made by letter will be rejected. The use of a mandatory form is intended to enable the Board to easily identify amendment applications and to elicit the necessary information.

The information which is required will depend upon the precise amendment sought. If, *e.g.* a certificate was limited in the first instance to obtaining counsel's opinion, clearly a copy of the opinion will have to be submitted in support of an application for an amendment to remove that limitation. Solicitors should bear in mind that area offices do not keep copies of all the documents which were originally submitted in support of an application for legal aid and any of these which are relevant to an application for an amendment to the certificate should be re-submitted to the area office when the amendment is requested. Points to be borne in mind are:

(a) no queries will be raised. It is therefore important to complete the application form fully to avoid refusal of the application (although a refusal can be appealed or a further application made);

(b) two applications in respect of the same certificate can be made on one form. If more than two applications are being made, two forms will need to be completed and fastened together;

(c) any documents submitted should be put *behind* the form so that

---

[8] Civil Legal Aid (General) Regulations 1989, reg.51.

the form can be easily identified in the area office. No covering letter is needed;

(d) if a costs condition is to be increased an appropriate amendment application must be made, i.e. amending the scope of the certificate does not automatically increase the costs figure contained in any costs condition.

POWER TO ALTER CONTRIBUTION AND AMEND CERTIFICATE

13–07 The Area Director may, if he considers it to be desirable, ask the Assessment Officer to re–assess the assisted person's financial resources and contribution.[9] The Area Director must then amend the certificate from such date as he considers appropriate to show the assisted person's re-determined contribution.[10]

The Area Director must also amend the certificate where he waives or revives contribution payments because he considers the costs incurred or likely to be incurred under the certificate will not be more than the contribution already paid.[11]

CHANGE OF SOLICITOR

13–08 Section 32 of the 1988 Act permits those entitled to legal aid to select the solicitor and, if necessary, counsel they wish to act for them. However, where a legal aid certificate has already been issued, the assisted person is not automatically entitled to have the certificate transferred into the name of another nominated solicitor. A request must be made to the area office which issued the certificate seeking an amendment.

The area office will need to know the reasons why the client wishes to change solicitor so that it can decide whether a change, with the resulting increase in costs, is justified and reasonable in all the circumstances. The application form will contain sufficient detail for the area office to consider the position generally, having regard to the stage reached and the costs involved in the case.[12] A change at a late stage when significant work has been done and costs incurred or at a point when only limited steps are (or remain) to be taken may be hard to justify.

Generally, an amendment will be approved where the client has lost

---

[9] *ibid.* reg. 52(1).
[10] *ibid.* reg. 52(3)(a).
[11] *ibid.* reg. 52(2), (3)(b).
[12] See below para.13–10.

confidence in his or her solicitor, unless there is some other reason to discharge the certificate or it is apparent that the reason for the loss of confidence is that the solicitor is giving reasonable advice which the assisted person is not prepared to accept. If that is so, then the assisted person will be asked to show cause why the amendment should not be refused and the certificate discharged. A second or subsequent change of solicitor request will be increasingly difficult to justify.

Assisted persons must bear in mind that a change of solicitor almost always increases the costs incurred on their behalf. Although these costs are likely to be recoverable from the Fund, they are unlikely to be recoverable *inter partes*. If the assisted person recovers money or property in the proceedings, he or she may end up paying these additional costs by virtue of the statutory charge.[13]

When a legal aid certificate is amended to enable new solicitors to   **13–09** conduct the assisted person's case, the normal practice is for the original solicitors to hand the papers over to the new solicitors on an undertaking that, at the end of the case, the new solicitors will either have a consolidated bill taxed or make the papers available to the original solicitors so that they may prepare a bill for taxation of their costs. The Law Society endorses this – see Commentary 5 to Principle 12.18 in *The Guide to the Professional Conduct of Solicitors* 1993.

Solicitors should bear in mind that, once a legal aid certificate has been issued, the assisted person's solicitor has the statutory right to be paid out of the Fund and cannot take payment from elsewhere.[14] It follows, therefore, that no lien arises in respect of costs and disbursements payable under a legal aid certificate and, unless solicitors have a lien in respect of pre-certificate costs and disbursements, they are not, in the Board's new, entitled to refuse to hand over the papers to the new solicitors. Papers relating to pre-certificate costs and disbursements (other than those covered by a Green Form) will be subject to a solicitor's lien but this lien is protected by regulation 103 of the Civil Legal Aid (General) Regulations[15]. Solicitors who have undertaken pre-certificate work in relation to the matter in question should not, therefore, refuse to hand over the papers to new solicitors unless they can show that their entitlement to costs cannot adequately be protected.

An application for an amendment to show a change of nominated soli-   **13–10** citor may be made by the assisted person or by the new solicitor. It is the Board's view that an amendment is not needed when there is a change of solicitor within a firm — this is treated as a delegation of the case.[16] However, if the nominated solicitor leaves the firm, an amendment will be

---

[13] See Chap. 18.
[14] Legal Aid Act 1988, s.15 and Civil Legal Aid (General) Regulations 1989, reg. 64.
[15] See below para.13–13.
[16] See *Legal Aid Handbook 1995*, Note for Guidance 9–03.

required as he will not be able to have the ultimate responsibility for the case and its conduct under the certificate.[17-18]

If the area office is approached by the assisted person, seeking a change of solicitor amendment, it will ask for the name and address of the new solicitor to be nominated if that information is not given. The confirmation of that solicitor that he is prepared to act will not necessarily be sought although the reason(s) for the proposed change must be given. If the proposed new solicitor makes the application, the mandatory application form must be used.

If there is some particular urgency this should be indicated as the area office may contact the currently nominated solicitor for his views (to check that the assisted person has not received unpalatable advice) before sanctioning the change. Although there are no stated criteria for such an amendment, the area office will need to be satisfied that it would be reasonable for the change to be authorised in all the circumstances of the case. Relevant factors, apart from the continued satisfaction of the civil legal aid merits test sufficient to justify the continuation of legal aid, will include:

    (a) the reason(s) for the change;

    (b) the stage the proceedings have reached (if the bulk of the work has been undertaken an amendment is less likely to be granted than would otherwise be the case, bearing in mind the increased costs arising from the transfer of the conduct of the case) and the work remaining to be undertaken (if a certificate was limited only to obtaining counsel's opinion or obtaining a specified report then a change would be unlikely to be authorised);

    (c) the number of changes of solicitor previously authorised (the area office will be less likely to grant a subsequent change of solicitor than a first change of solicitor).

13–11   Any amendment (except appropriately worded corrective amendments under regulation 51(a) of the Civil Legal Aid (General) Regulations 1989) will not be retrospective and if a matter is particularly urgent then the solicitor will wish to consider making an application for an amendment over the telephone. If such an application were granted this would be subject to receipt by the area office of a written application within a stipulated time period but this does enable the solicitor to start work straightaway on the basis of the amendment. Regulation 64 of the Civil Legal Aid (General) Regulations 1989 which prohibits private funding is untested but it may arguably apply to any solicitor or counsel so that *no* work by the proposed solicitor will be remunerated privately or otherwise pending a change of

---

[17-18] See *Thew v. Reeves* [1981] 3 W.L.R. 190; [1981] 2 All E.R. 964, C.A. and *R. v. Legal Aid Board, ex parte Nicolson, The Times,* June 24, 1994. To avoid difficulties the solicitor could stress the urgent need for an amendment or, in appropriate cases, obtain the client's consent to discharge.

solicitor, unless the nominated solicitor instructs the proposed solicitor as his agent.

It should be noted that the Board's customer service standards (targets) for 1995–96 include a target to decide 80% of amendment applications in two weeks and 95% in four weeks.[19]

ISSUE OF AMENDMENT

Where a certificate is amended the Area Director is required to send two copies of the amendment to the solicitor and one to the assisted person.[20] In the case of an amendment to show a change of solicitor a copy of the amendment is also sent to the former solicitor. Explanatory notes include guidance to the former solicitor. This requires him to forward to the new solicitor as soon as possible the papers relating to the case, together with the details of his costs, disbursements and counsel's fees (if any) incurred prior to the date of the amendment so that they may be included in the new solicitor's bill for taxation or assessment at the conclusion of the case, and, where appropriate, be recovered from the other side. Attention is also drawn to the fact that a payment on account may be made if the solicitor considers it unlikely that there will be a taxation within six months. If the solicitor wishes to make such an application he should notify any counsel instructed and make the application on behalf of himself and counsel using Form CLA28 (application for payment on account of profit costs, disbursements and/or counsel's fees) enclosing a breakdown of the profit costs, disbursements and counsel's fees together with either: **13–12**

    (a) counsel's fee note(s); or

    (b) confirmation that counsel has been informed and *does not* wish to make application for a payment on account of his fees.

The normal practice on a change of solicitor is for the former solicitor to pass his papers to the new solicitor on the new solicitor's undertaking that he will either have a consolidated bill taxed or make the papers available to the original solicitor so that he may prepare a bill for taxation of his costs.[21] The original solicitor has no lien over the papers *except* in respect of costs for which the client has undertaken *personal* liability (*i.e.* private client costs). This lien is protected by a specific provision.[22] The solicitor has no lien in respect of costs and disbursements incurred under the Green **13–13**

---

[19] Legal Aid Board Customer Service Standards, Legal Aid Handbook 1995, p. 521.
[20] Civil Legal Aid (General) Regulations 1989, reg.54(1).
[21] See above, para. 13–09.
[22] Reg. 103(2).

Form or a civil legal aid certificate as he is entitled to payment out of the Fund.[23]

In short, where there is no lien in respect of pre-certificate costs and disbursements and an undertaking is given by the new solicitor in relation to the eventual taxation of the original solicitor's costs (or the making available of the papers) the former solicitor has no reason to withhold the papers.

It should be noted that the Board does not consider that it has ownership of the papers in a legally aided case. The normal rules apply so that after a solicitor has been paid the assisted person would be entitled to not only the return of any papers belonging to him but also to receive any papers which do not belong to the solicitor. If the solicitor has not yet been paid, he will not wish to release the papers other than on the basis of an undertaking, in case his costs are not included in a consolidated bill or the papers are not returned to him to enable him to support his own claim. If an assisted person seeks the release of the papers himself, rather than their transfer to another solicitor, the solicitor should explain his position to the assisted person and urge him to consult a new solicitor so that the papers can be transferred to that new solicitor following the grant of an amendment to the certificate.

SERVICE OF NOTICE OF AMENDMENT

13–14 Where proceedings have begun or when they are begun, the solicitor receiving an amendment must forthwith:
   (a) send a copy of it to the court; *and*
   (b) serve notice of the fact of the amendment (but not a copy of it) on all other parties to the proceedings and on those who become parties.

Solicitors should note there is no requirement to serve notice of an amendment under regulation 52 of the Civil Legal Aid (General) Regulations 1989 (an amendment relating to an assisted person's financial contribution)[24] nor is it necessary to disclose details of any limitation to the certificate which is either imposed or varied by amendment (although the *fact* of the amendment must be disclosed).[25] The notice is required to be in a form approved by the Board but currently the Board has not made any specific requirements clear (and the forms produced by law stationers will be acceptable).[26]

---

[23] Legal Aid Act 1988, s.9(5) (Green Form) and Legal Aid Act 1988, S.15 and Civil Legal Aid (General) Regulations 1989, reg. 64, (Civil Legal Aid).
[24] Civil Legal Aid (General) Regulations 1989, reg.54(2).
[25] See Chap. 11.
[26] *ibid.* reg. 54(2)(b) as amended.

If no proceedings have been commenced the nominated solicitor is not required to take any action with regard to the amendment but he should bear in mind that the steps referred to above must be taken as soon as proceedings are issued. Failure to serve notice without delay may lead to a wasted costs order being made in respect of the costs of another party thrown away as a result of that party's ignorance of the amendment.

The above provisions do not apply to authorised summary proceedings[27] **13–15** and, where an assisted person is party to such proceedings, his or her solicitor must, before the first hearing which takes place after the amendment has been issued or at that hearing, file the amendment with the Clerk to the Justices.[28]

The copy of any amendment sent to the appropriate court office or registry forms part of the papers for the court in the proceedings.[29]

RIGHT TO SHOW CAUSE ON APPLICATION TO REMOVE LIMITATION

An Area Director must not refuse an application to amend a certificate, **13–16** except an emergency certificate, by removing a limitation until:
   (a) notice has been served on the assisted person that the application may be refused and his certificate discharged and that he may show cause why the application should be granted; and
   (b) the assisted person has been given an opportunity to show cause why the application should be granted.[30]

In these circumstances, the area office will send a show cause letter to the assisted person with a copy to the solicitor which will give a stated period within which a written response is to be received at the area office — this is usually 10 days but the time period which is not laid down by Regulations may be reduced in urgent cases. It is important that the time period is not overlooked and the solicitor will wish to consider whether he should obtain the assisted person's instructions to respond to the show cause letter on his behalf. Once a response to the show cause letter has been received, or after the stated time period has elapsed if no response is received by then, the area office will consider whether to remove the limitation or refuse the amendment and discharge the certificate. The amendment will be refused and the certificate discharged if no response is received.

---

[27] *Sinclair-Jones Kay* [1988] 2 All E.R. 611, C.A.
[28] Civil Legal Aid (General) Regulations 1989, reg. 54(4).
[29] *ibid.* reg 54(3).
[30] *ibid.* reg. 55.

253

REFUSAL OF AMENDMENT

13–17 Where an amendment is refused, the Area Director is required to notify the assisted person's solicitor in writing (but not the assisted person) giving his reasons for the refusal.[31] There are no stated criteria for dealing with applications for amendment but the Area Director will consider whether the amendment is reasonable in terms of the prospects of success and whether it is justified in all the circumstances of the case. This will include considering whether a fee-paying client of moderate means would take the steps envisaged. Effectively, the area office will apply the legal merits and reasonableness tests.

Notification of refusal is by way of a standard letter which gives details of the right of appeal.

RIGHT OF APPEAL AGAINST REFUSAL OF AN AMENDMENT AND DETERMINATION OF SUCH AN APPEAL

13–18 There is a right of appeal against a refusal of an amendment. Notice of appeal is required to be given "on a form approved by the Board" within 14 days of the Area Director's decision to refuse the application.[32] There is currently no form of appeal nationally approved by the Board and notice of appeal should therefore be given by letter (or by any form in local use) which should be sent to the appropriate area office clearly stating:

    (a) the certificate reference number;

    (b) the grounds of the appeal, enclosing any further information or documents which will be of assistance to the area committee and *resubmitting* any documents returned by the area office with the notification of refusal;

    (c) any particular urgency — any hearing date should be given in the heading and the letter marked "urgent" at the top;

    (d) any reason why the appeal is out of time (*e.g.* the notification of refusal may have been delayed in the post).

On an appeal against the refusal of an amendment, the area committee is required to reconsider the application and determine the appeal in such a manner "as seems to it to be just", although there is specific provision for the committee to dismiss the appeal or direct the Area Director to amend the certificate as the area committee thinks fit.[33]

The area committee's decision is final and it is required to give notice of

---

[31] *ibid.* reg. 56.
[32] *ibid.* reg. 57(1).
[33] *ibid.* reg. 58(1).

its decision, and the reasons for it, to the assisted person and to his solicitor in a form approved by the Board.[34] Currently notification is by letter.

Where there is no *right* of audience there is provision for the area **13–19** committee to consider whether it is necessary for the assisted person to be permitted to conduct his appeal or be represented on it.[35] In those circumstances, the decision as to whether the appellant may attend or be represented on an appeal need not actually be made by the area committee. The decision can be made by the Area Director including "any person duly authorised to act on his behalf"[36] and will be in response to a *request* for permission to attend/be represented.

However, if the refusal of the amendment has also resulted in the discharge of a certificate, then there is a right of audience in any event.[37] There is also specific provision that the appellant may conduct his own appeal, with or without assistance, or be represented by counsel or a solicitor or legal executive if the committee's decision "finally determines" the applicant's right to receive legal aid.[38] This is expressed to be subject to the consideration by the area committee of whether to allow an assisted person to conduct his own appeal or be represented.

If the area office does not indicate that the assisted person may attend or be represented at an area committee hearing, then the solicitor and assisted person will wish to consider whether to ask the area office for this to be allowed. The area office can make this decision in advance of the committee meeting although the costs of any representation would not be met out of the Legal Aid Fund.

---

[34] *ibid.* reg. 58(2).
[35] *ibid.* reg. 58(3).
[36] *ibid.* reg. 6(1),3(1).
[37] *ibid.* reg. 38(1).
[38] *ibid.* reg. 38(2).

Chapter 14

ACTS FOR WHICH AUTHORITY MUST OR MAY BE OBTAINED

INTRODUCTION

14–01 The Regulations provide that before certain acts are done in the conduct of an assisted person's case the authority of the Area Director must be obtained, if the certificate does not already authorise them. The costs relating to them may otherwise be irrecoverable from the Fund.

The Area Director's authority may also be sought before other specified acts are done, if these are not authorised by the certificate, but this is not mandatory. In addition, there is a general right to seek the Area Director's authority where the assisted person's solicitor considers it is necessary to do an act, which is either of an unusual nature, or will involve unusually large expenditure. In these cases, if authority is given, the propriety of the act cannot be challenged when the solicitor seeks payment of the legal aid costs. If it is not given, either because it has not been sought or because of refusal, it will be for the discretion of the taxing officer on the legal aid taxation or the Area Director, if the costs are to be assessed, to decide whether to allow the amount claimed.

14–02 It is important to distinguish between acts for which authority is required and acts for which an amendment to the certificate is required. An amendment is required where the certificate is limited in such a way as to prohibit the conduct of that part of the proceedings which the assisted person wishes to pursue. An authority is required if the scope of the certificate permits the conduct of that part of the proceedings but the assisted person's solicitor wishes to ensure that costs and disbursements are not disallowed on the legal aid taxation.

The assisted person's solicitor or counsel may not receive or be a party to the making of any payment for work done in any proceedings in connection with which a certificate has been issued (whether within the scope of the certificate or otherwise), except such payments as may be made out of the Fund.[1] Where a certificate is limited or relates to part only

---

[1] Civil Legal Aid (General) Regulations 1989, reg. 64.

of the proceedings, it may be possible for solicitors to recover their costs direct from the client.[2]

THE BASIS ON WHICH AN APPLICATION SHOULD BE CONSIDERED

There is no difference, in principle, between the considerations which **14–03** govern an application for authority to do a particular act and those which relate to an ordinary application for legal aid, the same test should therefore apply to both. The Area Director will consider what advice would reasonably be given to a private client in similar circumstances, where the client was of adequate means to meet the likely cost.[3]

ACTS FOR WHICH AUTHORITY IS MANDATORY

Civil legal aid is expressed to be by solicitor and, so far as necessary, **14–04** counsel but there is provision for regulations to prescribe the circumstances in which representation is to be by counsel only or by solicitor only and to regulate representation by more than one counsel.[4] The Regulations made for civil legal aid are contained in Part VIII of the Civil Legal Aid (General) Regulations 1989.

Under the Civil Legal Aid (General) Regulations 1989 the solicitor may instruct counsel where it appears to him that the proper conduct of the proceedings requires this, but authority is required either:

    (a) in the certificate; or

    (b) from the Area Director (on specific application);

for:

    (a) the instruction of counsel in authorised summary proceedings; and

    (b) the instruction of Queen's Counsel; or

    (c) more than one counsel.[5]

The so called "Two Counsel" rule was abrogated following a resolution by the Bar Council on the May 31, 1977. *Inter alia* the Bar's Rules are now that Queen's Counsel may accept instructions to appear as an advocate without a junior. Queen's Counsel is entitled to assume that a junior is also to be instructed at the hearing unless the contrary is stated when instructions are first delivered. Queen's Counsel should decline to appear as an advocate without a junior if he would be unable properly to conduct the

---

[2] *Littaur v. Steggles Palmer* [1986] 1 W.L.R. 287.
[3] *Francis v. Francis and Dickerson* [1956] P. 87; [1955] 3 W.L.R. 973.
[4] Legal Aid Act 1988, s. 2(7).
[5] Civil Legal Aid (General) Regulations 1989, reg. 59(1).

case or other cases or to fulfil his professional or semi-professional commitments unless a junior were also instructed in the case in question.

14–05   Where counsel, instructed as junior counsel, takes silk during the course of the case, the Area Director will take into consideration the fact that Queen's Counsel is permitted, and should normally be willing to settle pleadings and other documents, to appear at the trial or any hearing and do any other ordinary work of a junior in regard to which he was instructed before his appointment, at any time before the first anniversary of his appointment. It is open to leading counsel in such circumstances to continue to act as a junior. Once the first anniversary of the appointment has passed, leading counsel should refuse to act as junior unless such a refusal would cause harm to the client. Leading counsel may then, at his discretion, continue to act for any purpose in regard to the matter or proceeding until the second anniversary of his appointment. If a newly appointed leading counsel withdraws from the case it is of course open to the solicitor to instruct fresh junior counsel.

14–06   An authority may be included in the certificate if sought in the original application for legal aid but sometimes it is only after a certificate has been issued that the solicitor establishes that this is necessary and that an application would be justified. If such an authority is sought and granted in a certificate it will be included in paragraph 2 of the certificate (conditions and limitations). Factors taken into account by the area office in considering applications for authority for counsel will include:

(a) that a difficult point of law is involved;

(b) that the sum at stake is large or the question at issue is of particular importance to the assisted person; or

(c) that the unusual nature of the case requires counsel experienced in some special field.

The fact that:

(a) the opposing side has instructed leading counsel;

(b) junior counsel who has been instructed is not sufficiently experienced to conduct it by himself;

(c) the hearing is likely to be protracted or that documents are voluminous; or

(d) junior counsel who has settled the proceedings has since taken silk;

will not normally of themselves be considered sufficient to obtain the appropriate authority.

It is, of course, open to the Area Director to authorise the instruction of two junior counsel where, for instance, the case is likely to be protracted rather than difficult, or where there are voluminous documents.

In relation to any instructions delivered to counsel, there must be included a copy of the certificate and any amendments, and any authority to incur costs granted under the Civil Legal Aid (General) Regulations 1989. The instructions must be endorsed with the legal aid reference number and,

258

in the case of authorised summary proceedings, show the authority for counsel to be instructed. No fees are to be marked on any of the papers delivered to counsel.[6]

Notwithstanding authority to employ leading counsel having been obtained from the Area Director, it is still necessary to obtain the specific instructions of the client, after explaining the probable cost and the effect upon the client's assets and those in dispute (because of the operation of the statutory charge) before leading counsel is instructed.[7]

Joint plaintiffs or defendants jointly represented

Difficulty sometimes occurs where only one of two joint plaintiffs is assisted **14–07** and the other is unwilling to share the expense of instructing leading counsel, since separate representation will not normally be allowed on this ground alone. It may be possible to overcome the problem by agreement with the unassisted plaintiff to share the extra cost. If no agreement is made, the normal practice on taxation is for counsel's fees to be apportioned equally between the joint plaintiffs. If, however, the Area Director authorises the assisted person to accept responsibility for the whole of the fee payable to leading counsel and the amount, if any, by which junior counsel's fee may be increased in consequence, no apportionment will be made and the whole amount should be allowed on the legal aid taxation. It is incumbent upon a solicitor applying for authority to make full disclosure of the facts and the solicitor and counsel should ensure that the form of authority sufficiently covers what is required. Joint defendants always have the right to separate representation and it is only when they choose to be represented by the same counsel that a problem may arise; the same considerations then apply.

ACTS FOR WHICH AUTHORITY IS OPTIONAL

General authority by the Board

The Board may give general authority to solicitors acting for assisted **14–08** persons in a particular class of case to incur costs by:
   (a) obtaining a report or opinion from one or more experts or tendering expert evidence;
   (b) employing a person to provide a report or opinion (other than as an expert); or

---

[6] *ibid.* reg. 59(2).
[7] *Re A Solicitor, (Taxation of Costs)* [1982] 1 W.L.R. 745; [1982] 2 ALL E.R. 683.

(c) requesting transcripts of shorthand notes or tape recordings of any proceedings.

Where such an authority is given, the Board must specify the maximum fee payable for any such report, opinion, expert evidence or transcript.[8] No such general authorities have so far been given by the Board.

Authority given by the Area Director

14–09 There are five instances in which an assisted person's solicitor may apply to the Area Director for prior authority to take certain steps which appear to be necessary for the proper conduct of the proceedings.[9]

Obtaining expert evidence

14–10 A solicitor may, if this has not been authorised by the certificate, apply to the Area Director for authority to obtain a report or opinion from an expert, or to tender expert evidence, in a case of a class not included in any general authority given by the Board.[10] The Area Director will need to know not only the cost of obtaining the report or opinion, but also the costs that will be incurred if it becomes necessary at a later stage for the expert to give evidence at the hearing. It is therefore normal to provide this information at the outset so that the total commitment is known.

Obtaining reports from witnesses who are not experts

14–11 Authority may be obtained to pay any person who is not an expert to prepare a report and, if required, give evidence provided that general authority has been given.[11-12] Although the regulation refers to "a person" a company or other organisation could be instructed to prepare such a report and the Board would still consider it had jurisidiction.

The solicitor must decide whether it would be appropriate to be protected on taxation. The most common expense which may fall within this category is probably the fees of an inquiry agent. It is important to note that authority may only be given for the preparation of a report and the giving of evidence; there is no jurisdiction under this head to authorise inquiry agent's fees which do not lead logically to the preparation of a report. For example, service of documents as opposed to, say, a status report on a defendant.

Exceeding the general authority of the Board

14–12 No general authorities have so far been given by the Board but the 1989 Regulations provide that if the solicitor is conducting a case of a class which

---

[8] Civil Legal Aid (General) Regulations 1989, reg. 60.
[9] *ibid.* reg. 61(1).
[10] *ibid.* reg. 61(2)(a).
[11-12] *ibid.* reg. 61(2)(b).

is included in a general authority, authority may be obtained from the Area Director to pay a higher fee than that specified by the Board or to obtain more reports or opinions, or to tender more evidence (expert or otherwise) than has been specified in the Board's general authority.[13]

Unusual steps or unusually large expense

A solicitor acting for an assisted person is sometimes in the difficult position **14–13** of having to make a judgment as to whether to take a certain step which is unusual or which will be particularly expensive, and which is not authorised by the certificate, in the knowledge that by the time the case reaches taxation, it may be difficult for the taxing officer to appreciate how matters appeared at the time the decision was made. The 1989 Regulations make provision to meet the difficulty that the client cannot give instructions in such a case, which will be effective for the purpose of legal aid taxation. They provide a general residuary power to deal with special cases where the solicitor wishes to do some particular act, such as bringing a witness from abroad, that it is either of an unusual nature or is likely to involve unusually large expense. The solicitor is entitled to seek the authority of the Area Director to perform such an act.[14] Examples may be:

(a) employing legal advisers abroad;
(b) arranging for a country solicitor to be present at a consultation in London or at a trial there;
(c) obtaining an order for exhumation of a corpse;
(d) making a journey abroad on behalf of the assisted person;
(e) bringing a witness or the assisted person from another country to give evidence

It is important to note that the act must be not just unusual but unusual *in its nature* and that this involves the performing of an act by the solicitor himself. What is "unusual in its nature" will depend on what are considered to be the current norms — over a period of years something which falls into this category could become more usual and no longer qualify. It will not, however, cover such expenses as inquiry agents' or interpreters' fees.

In addition, the act must involve costs being *incurred* by the solicitor in performing an act which involves unusually large *expenditure*. This will not necessarily be the actual performance of the act by the solicitor himself. It is not a static concept in that inflation has a bearing, but is interpreted by the Board to mean an unusually large global figure rather than merely something charged in excess of a rate known to have been allowed previously on taxation or assessment. An expenditure would certainly have to be over £100 for the Board to consider that it had jurisdiction to deal with an application for authority but the Area Director should, in cases

---

[13] *ibid.* reg. 61(2)(c).
[14] *ibid.* reg. 61(2)(d).

falling under this head and no other, make a decision which may be that there is no jurisdiction (as opposed to simply advising the solicitor to justify the expenditure on taxation).

In very exceptional circumstances, the authority may extend to authorising the assisted person's travelling expenses to see an expert, where the report is essential and the assisted person cannot afford the expenses involved in travelling to see the expert. This apart, an assisted person's travelling expenses will not be authorised and are unlikely to be allowed on taxation assessment following the normal principles of taxation.

Obtaining a transcript

14–14   An assisted person's solicitor may apply to the Area Director for authority to obtain any transcripts of shorthand notes or tape recordings of any proceedings, if authority has not been given in the certificate to obtain it.[15]

When considering such a request, the Area Director will normally adopt the test of reasonableness. The Area Director may not agree to a transcript of proceedings being obtained but may limit the authority to so much as is needed for the purpose of the case. For an appeal, part only of the transcript of the evidence given in the court below may be sufficient, or possibly the judgment alone. An assisted person's solicitor will have to keep this in mind if it is decided to obtain a transcript without authority because of the need to satisfy the taxing officer of the reasonableness of the expenditure on taxation.

The work in respect of which authority is sought cannot be undertaken "in house" but must involve the instruction of an external individual or agency. The rate allowed will depend on market forces, that is the availability and charges in the particular geographical area at the relevant time.

14–15   The Board has indicated that if the solicitor or his partner or employee is involved in the provision of non-legal services then authority to use those services will be refused unless the area office is satisfied that:

(a) the business providing the service (*e.g.* photograph or transcript services) has been legitimately set up and does exist as a separate entry;

(b) those involved appear to have the necessary expertise to undertake the work involved;

(c) it appears unlikely that those involved would have to give evidence, other than formal evidence;

(d) the expenditure is justified in terms of the work to be undertaken and the amount involved, at least one other estimate being available;

(e) the client has been informed of the position and agrees that the

---

[15] *ibid.* reg. 61(2)(e).

disbursement should be incurred using the business connected with the solicitor.[16]

This is to ensure that the client's interests are protected, having particular regard to any contribution payable by the client and the possible operation of the solicitor's statutory charge.

Where prior authority for any of the above steps is given, it will specify **14–15A** the number of reports or opinions that may be obtained or the number of persons who may be authorised to give expert evidence, and the maximum fee to be paid in each case.[16a]

How to Apply for Authority

To be included in the certificate

Authority for any particular act can be sought when applying for legal aid **14–16** and, if it is granted, the authority will be included in the certificate. It is desirable to adopt this course whenever it is known at the time of applying for a certificate that the act in question is necessary and can be justified, particularly if time is short as in an appellate matter, in authorised summary proceedings or in any other urgent case.

From the Area Director

In any case where the assisted person's solicitor seeks authority, this must **14–17** be obtained before the intended act is done, or the expense incurred, because there is no power for authority to be given retrospectively. Although the Area Director may amend the certificate where it appears that there has been some mistake in it, this does not entitle the Director to authorise *ex post facto* an act which has already been done unless the authority to do the act had in fact been given before the certificate was issued.[17] The meaning of a certificate or authority will be strictly construed on its own wording.[18]

Applications must be made using the Board's mandatory form 31. **14–18** Applications made by letter will be rejected. Points to note are:

(a) a single form can be used to make up to two applications under one certificate;

(b) three or more applications under a single certificate can be made

---

[16] See also principle 11–05 of the *Guide to the professional conduct of solicitors.*
[16a] Civil Legal Aid (General) Regulations 1989 Reg 61(3).
[17] *Wallace v. Freeman Heating Company Ltd* [1955] 1 W.L.R. 172.
[18] *Taj Din v. Wandsworth London Borough Council* [1982] 1 W.L.R. 418.

by filling in two or more forms and fastening them together securely;

(c) the application should be marked "urgent" only if it is objectively urgent;

(d) no covering letter should be submitted and additional information or documents should be *behind* the form, so that the form can easily be seen for identification purposes in the area office;

(e) queries will not be raised and the application should be completed fully, submitting any relevant documents, otherwise it is at risk of refusal when there is no right of appeal although a further application can be made;

(f) for Children Act cases where the leave of the court is required, that leave should be obtained before applying for any authority (as the authority will be refused without it);

(g) where applicable, the maximum authority sought must be indicated as well as hourly rates for preparation and travel, travel expenses if relevant and the daily court attendance rate if the expert is to give evidence (some indication of fees, even if not a formal quote, will therefore have to be obtained);

(h) although form 31 inquires about alternative quotes do not have to be obtained, if they have been, and the solicitor wishes to use the more expensive quote, he must justify this (otherwise the lower amount will be authorised);

(i) the area office may grant authority for an unnamed expert at an amount/rate lower than applied for (this enables the solicitor to seek an expert prepared to do the work at that price).

Solicitor and counsel should satisfy themselves that whatever authority has been given is in specific terms and covers exactly what is wanted. Copies of all relevant authorities and of the certificate should be included in counsel's instructions.[19]

14–19 When applying for authority for counsel it is important to make clear *exactly* what is sought. "Briefing counsel" only covers the brief itself and any necessary consultation on the brief after its delivery. Consultations or other work prior to the preparation and delivery of the brief are not covered.[20] An authority for "instructing counsel" is wider than one for "briefing counsel". It covers the involvement of counsel generally in the further conduct of the proceedings *including* being briefed to appear, subject only to assessment/taxation. An authority for "instructing leading counsel alone" permits him to settle pleadings or draft such other documents as are normally drafted by junior counsel where he has agreed to appear as an advocate without a junior. The solicitor should make it

---

[19] Civil Legal Aid (General) Regulations 1989, reg. 59(2).
[20] *Din v. Wandsworth London Borough Council (No.3)* [1983] 1 W.L.R. 1171.

clear whether he is seeking authority to *instruct* counsel or *brief* counsel and also whether he is seeking authority for Queen's Counsel alone, Queen's Counsel and junior counsel or more than one junior counsel. The solicitor should check the authority on receipt and seek clarification from the area office if he has any doubt as to its meaning.

The following should be noted in relation to appeals to the House of Lords. Leading counsel may not settle an application for leave to appeal to the House of Lords, although authority may be granted for him to advise on the merits of such an appeal but only where he conducted the appeal hearing in the Court of Appeal.

In House of Lords cases the following authority wordings will normally **14–20** be used:

    (a) authority is included to instruct leading and junior counsel but only after leave to appeal has been obtained;

    (b) authority is included to instruct leading counsel alone but only after leave to appeal has been obtained.

The authority wordings reflect the House of Lords' Practice Directions regarding the use of leading counsel and the fact that a conference (or consultation with leading counsel) before leave is obtained would only exceptionally be considered to be justified on taxation. If specific authority for such a conference is sought from the area office it would be likely to be refused.

In addition to the authority of the Area Director, the prior approval of the client must also be sought to instruct Queen's Counsel and take unusual or unusually expensive steps. Even if the solicitor has obtained the Area Director's authority if he does not also have the client's authority then such expenses may be disallowed on taxation. The client must be informed of the additional cost involved and its effect in relation to the operation of the statutory charge.[21] The area office will make no inquiries regarding authority from the client.

The solicitor's relationship with any expert or other potential witnesses is **14–21** not a matter for the Board. When instructing experts, the solicitor should seek to limit their fees to whatever is allowed on taxation unless prior authority is sought in which case the maximum fee (and rates) authorised should be agreed with the expert. If no clear agreement is reached, the solicitor may find himself in dispute with the expert. If no agreed fee has been fixed or the fee is not limited to the amount allowed on taxation, the solicitor may be liable to pay any balance to the expert.

Although the fact that a case is legally aided does not affect the solicitor's contractual relationship with an expert or in respect of any other disbursement, particularly in relation to the solicitor's obligation to pay the

---

[21] *Re A Solicitor (Taxation of Costs)* [1982] 1 W.L.R. 745; [1982] 2All E.R. 683.

disbursement,[22] the solicitor should consider the possibility of making an application for a payment on account under regulation 101(1)(a) of the Civil Legal Aid (General) Regulations 1989 (which extends to disbursements both incurred or about to be incurred). Applying for payment on account using form CLA28 enables the disbursement to be paid without delay and reduces the likelihood of a dispute between the solicitor and expert instructed. If an expert or other person instructed does not receive prompt payment of his fee he may report the solicitor to the Solicitors' Complaints Bureau.

If authority is given, the authority will specify the number of reports or opinions that may be obtained or the number of persons who may be authorised to give expert evidence and the maximum fee to be paid to each. In other cases, a limit will normally be placed on the costs which may be incurred so that it is desirable to give an estimate of the probable expense involved.

The effect of the authority

14–22 If prior authority has been obtained for any of the acts which have been referred to, it will be unnecessary to satisfy the taxing officer on the legal aid taxation, or the Area Director on assessment of fees, that it was reasonable to do the act in question, since no question as to the propriety of any step or act in relation to which prior authority has been obtained may be raised on any taxation of costs.[23]

Failure to obtain authority has different results depending on whether the act is one for which authority must be obtained or is one where it is optional. Where it is mandatory the costs *will be disallowed* on the legal aid taxation. But where costs are incurred in instructing Queen's Counsel or more than one counsel without authority to do so having been given, no payment in respect of the costs may be allowed on any taxation, *unless it is also allowed* on an *inter partes* taxation under an order for costs made in the assisted person's favour, since the 1989 Regulations provide unambiguously that, save in such circumstances, no payment in respect of those costs shall be allowed on any taxation.[24]

In a case where it is optional, and authority has not been obtained, the matter is discretionary so that, where costs are incurred in instructing counsel, or in taking any step, or in doing any act for which authority could have been obtained, without that authority having been obtained, payment in respect of the costs may still be allowed on taxation if the step taken was reasonable.[25]

---

[22] Legal Aid Act 1988, s. 15(8).
[23] Civil Legal Aid (General) Regulations 1989, reg. 63(1).
[24] *ibid.* reg. 63(3). See also *Hunt v. East Dorset Health Authority* [1992] 2 All E.R. 539.
[25] *ibid.* reg. 63(4).

Where costs are incurred in accordance with, and subject to, the limit imposed by a prior authority, no question may be raised on any taxation as to the amount of the payment to be allowed for that particular step, or act, unless the solicitor or the assisted person knew, or ought reasonably to have known, that the purpose for which the authority was given had failed or become irrelevant or unnecessary, before the costs were incurred.[26] Hindsight must not be used, the correct approach being that of the reasonable solicitor doing the best for his client in the light of his then knowledge.[27] If prior authority has been obtained but the limit imposed by that authority has been exceeded, an amount in excess of the specified limit may be allowed if the expense actually incurred is considered reasonable on taxation or assessment.

Where authority is refused

If the Area Director refuses an application for authority, written reasons for **14–23** the decision must be supplied. There is no right of appeal against a refusal by an Area Director to give an authority, and there is nothing in the 1989 Regulations to prevent a second or subsequent application being made, though it is obviously desirable for it to be supported by further information or fresh argument and the written reasons provided by the Area Director would no doubt highlight the shortcomings of the previous application.[28]

---

[26] *ibid.* reg. 63(2).
[27] *Francis and Francis v. Dickerson* [1956] P. 87; 3 W.L.R. 973.
[28] Civil Legal Aid (General) Regulations 1989, reg. 62.

Chapter 15

DISCHARGE AND REVOCATION

<small>MEANING AND CONSEQUENCES</small>

Discharge

15–01 A person whose certificate is discharged ceases, from the date of the discharge, to be an assisted person in the proceedings to which the certificate related,[1] *but* he retains all the benefits of being legally aided in the life of the certificate so that the effects of discharge are as follows:

(a) cover ceases at the date of discharge;

(b) if no proceedings have been started, the retainer of the solicitor and counsel ends on receipt of notice of discharge or, where there is an appeal against the discharge, on receipt of notice of the appeal being dismissed[2];

(c) if proceedings have been started the retainer of the solicitor does not determine until he has served any notice required[3];

(d) notice of discharge must be given[4];

(e) the costs of the proceedings must be submitted for taxation or assessment as soon as practicable after the determination of the retainer[5];

(f) the Fund remains liable for payment of the costs as taxed or assessed[6];

(g) the protection to the assisted person against an order for costs applies in respect of costs incurred up to the date of discharge[7];

(h) other parties retain the right to an order for costs out of the Fund in respect of costs incurred when the certificate was in force[8];

---

[1] Civil Legal Aid (General) Regulations 1989, reg. 74(2).
[2] *ibid.* reg. 83(1).
[3] *ibid.* reg. 83(2).
[4] *ibid.* reg. 82. and see Chap. 11.
[5] *ibid.* reg. 84(a).
[6] *ibid.* reg. 84(b).
[7] *ibid.* reg. 86(2).
[8] *ibid.* reg. 74(2).

(i) the statutory charge may operate in the usual way and where the discharge is based on death or bankruptcy will include recovery or preservation for the former assisted person's personal representatives, trustee in bankruptcy or the Official Receiver[9];

(j) the former assisted person remains liable for his contribution as determined or redetermined up to the amount of costs as taxed or assessed — the contribution may be redetermined immediately prior to discharge[10];

(k) payment of the assisted person's own costs up to the discharge are dealt with in the usual way (as against his contribution, costs recovered, the statutory charge and the Fund.[11]

Effects of revocation

The effect of revocation is that the former assisted person is required to be **15–02** deemed never to have been an assisted person in relation to the proceedings except for the purposes of section 18 costs orders again of the Legal Aid Fund. The final two points which apply to discharge ((j) and (k) above) do not apply to revocation although the others, with the exception of protection against cost orders ((g) above), are common to both discharge and revocation. The points which apply to revocation only are:

(a) the former assisted person is liable to the Fund for all costs paid out less any contribution paid at the time of the revocation[12];

(b) the solicitor has the right to recover from the former assisted person the difference between the legal aid costs and the full amount of his solicitor and own client costs[13];

(c) the former assisted person is deemed never to have been an assisted person so that his protection against an order for costs is lost entirely. The other parties to the proceedings still have a right to an order for costs against the Fund in respect of the period when the certificate was in force.[14]

GROUNDS FOR DISCHARGE AND REVOCATION[15]

Obligatory discharge

A full certificate must be discharged by the Area Director from such date **15–03** as he considers appropriate where:

---

[9] *ibid.* reg. 85(1), (2).
[10] *ibid.* reg. 86(2).
[11] *ibid.* reg. 74(2).
[12] *ibid.* reg. 86(1).
[13] *ibid.* reg. 86(1).
[14] *ibid.* reg. 74(2).
[15] For emergency certificates, see Chap. 10.

(a) an assisted person is assessed as financially ineligible (*i.e* his disposable income exceeds the current income limit)[16];

(b) the assisted person, although eligible on income, has disposable capital in excess of the current capital limit and it appears to the Area Director that, without legal aid, the probable cost of the proceedings would be less than the contribution payable[17];

(c) where, as a result of information which has come to the Area Director's knowledge, he considers that the assisted person no longer has reasonable grounds for taking, defending or being a party to the proceedings or for continuing to do so[18];

(d) where, as a result of information which has come to his knowledge, the Area Director considers that the assisted person required the proceedings to be conducted unreasonably so as to incur an unjustifiable expense to the Fund[19]; or

(e) where it is unreasonable, in the particular circumstances, that the assisted person should continue to receive legal aid[20].

Discretionary discharge

15–04 The Area Director may discharge a certificate from such date as he considers appropriate:

(a) where the assisted person consents; or

(b) where the assisted person is more than 21 days in arrears with the payment of his contribution; or

(c) on being satisfied, following a report from the solicitor or otherwise that:

    (i) the assisted person has died;

    (ii) the assisted person has had a bankruptcy order made against him;

    (iii) the proceedings to which the certificate relates have been disposed of; or

    (iv) the work authorised has been completed[21].

The Area Director may also discharge a certificate from such date as he considers appropriate where the current financial circumstances of the assisted person are such that the Area Director considers that he could afford to proceed without legal aid and the assisted person's current

---

[16] Civil Legal Aid (General) Regulations 1989, reg. 76(1).
[17] *ibid.* reg. 76(2).
[18] *ibid.* reg. 77(1)(a).
[19] *ibid.* reg. 77(1)(b).
[20] *ibid.* reg. 77(1)(c).
[21] *ibid.* reg. 80.

financial resources are reassessed with a view to discharging the certificate.[22] In deciding whether an assisted person could afford to proceed, the Area Director will take into account the assisted person's financial circumstances as against the stage the proceedings have reached and therefore the costs which are likely to be incurred in bringing the proceedings to a conclusion. Such an assessment will only be requested outside the original period of computation in old cases where the certificate was granted before April 12, 1993 (as otherwise the assisted person's means could be reassessed or further assessed on a change of circumstances in any event).[23] If the Area Director decides not to discharge the certificate, a contribution or increased contribution from income or capital may be requested. The assisted person then has the option of paying the contribution, in which case the certificate will continue, or declining to do so, although in the case of capital contributions the contribution will still remain payable even if the certificate is discharged.

No indication is given as to when it would be appropriate to discharge other than from the date of the decision to do so. On the face of it there is nothing to preclude either a date in the past or in the future being fixed. An example might be where an assisted person delayed reporting an improvement of his financial circumstances which was then found to make him financially ineligible. In those circumstances the discharge could be effective from the date when he should have reported the change. Normally the date of the decision is used.

Discretionary discharge or revocation

The Area Director may revoke or discharge a certificate: **15–05**

    (a) where the assisted person has made an untrue statement about or failed to disclose any material fact concerning his financial circumstances, either before or after the issue of the certificate and even if this related to an application to another area office in connection with the same proceedings. The assisted person will avoid discharge/revocation if he can satisfy the Area Director that he used due care or diligence to avoid the mis-statement or failure to disclose[24];

    (b) the assisted person has intentionally failed to supply the Area Director or solicitor with any material information *not* relating to his financial circumstances[25];

---

[22] *ibid.* reg. 76(3).
[23] Civil Legal Aid (Assessment of Resources) Regulations 1989, regs, 12, 13 and 14.
[24] Civil Legal Aid (General) Regulations 1989, reg. 78(1)(a).
[25] *ibid.* reg. 78(1)(b).

    (c) where the assisted person has knowingly made a false statement in supplying material (but non-financial) information[26];

    (d) where the Area Director is satisfied that the assisted person has failed to attend for an interview or to provide information or documents when required to do so.[27] This is used as the basis for discharge or revocation following a failure to co-operate with the Legal Aid Assessment Office.

The requirement to show cause

15–06 A certificate cannot be revoked or discharged *except*:

    (a) on financial grounds;

    (b) with the assisted person's consent;

    (c) where the assisted person is more than 21 days in arrears of his contribution;

    (d) where the assisted person has died;

    (e) where the proceedings have been disposed of; or

    (f) the work authorised by the certificate has been completed; *unless* the assisted person has been served with notice that the Area Director may revoke or discharge his certificate and that he may show cause why it should not be revoked or discharged and he has been given an opportunity to show such cause.[28]

This means that the so-called "show cause procedure" must be instituted where discharge or revocation is being considered:

    (a) on the merits

    (b) on the basis of an untrue statement or failure to disclose financial or non-financial information;

    (c) for failure to attend for an interview or to provide information or documents when required;

    (d) on the basis that an assisted person has had a bankruptcy order made against him.

Note that the court has no power to discharge or revoke a certificate although it can, on the Board's application or its own motion, refer to the Area Director (*i.e.* area office) the question of whether the assisted person's certificate should continue where the court considers there has been a false statement or non-disclosure.[29] The Board would not normally apply to the court but would consider the possible false statement or non-disclosure itself in the usual way.

---

[26] *ibid.* reg. 78(1)(c).
[27] *ibid.* reg. 79.
[28] *ibid.* reg. 81(1).
[29] *ibid.* reg. 68 and see Chap. 36.

Procedure

Where there is no requirement to give the assisted person an opportunity **15–07** to show cause why his certificate should not be discharged, the area office will simply issue a standard notice of discharge showing the basis upon which the certificate has been discharged. Two copies of the form are sent to the solicitor and a further copy is sent direct to the client (unless the client's address is shown as care of the solicitor's office in which case the copy for the client will be sent to the solicitor and must be forwarded by the solicitor). Where a certificate is being discharged on the payment of a bill (*i.e.* the costs have already been determined) no notice is required but it may take the form of a letter to the solicitor — this is referred to as an informal discharge although only the absence of the formal notice (and the need to serve it) differs from the usual procedure.

Where the assisted person is required to be given an opportunity to show **15–08** cause why his certificate should not be discharged, a standard letter will be sent to the assisted person indicating the specific reason(s) why consideration is being given to the discharge or revocation of the certificate and giving the assisted person time to respond. The time given is normally 10 days but this can be reduced in urgent cases to as little as 24 hours although this would be unusual. No time limit is specified by Regulations.

In addition to the show cause letter itself, the solicitor is sent a letter instructing him to take no further action under the certificate and asking him to contact the area office for guidance if urgent work is needed. There is no specific regulatory basis for the imposition of an embargo on work under a certificate by way of a show cause letter/notice or other letter/ notice except in the case of emergency certificates.[30] Generally, solicitors respond positively to an instruction from an area office that they should not undertake further work. If limited urgent work is necessary, the area office will, depending on the circumstances, be prepared to agree to that work being undertaken — this could cover applying for a hearing to be adjourned.

Occasionally it will not be possible to reach an agreement as either the solicitor and/or the client is not prepared to accept a voluntary embargo. In those circumstances it is the Board's view that it can rely on its general powers to impose an embargo and amendment to the certificate can be used to prevent all further work or some specific steps being taken under the certificate.[31] This should be regarded as exceptional and if such an amendment is imposed and a request to delete it is then refused this

---

[30] Civil Legal Aid (General) Regulations 1989 reg. 75(6). Although see the Board's general powers in section 4 of the Legal Aid Act 1988 and Re A Solicitor (Wasted Costs Order) [1993] 2 F.L.R. No. 6.

[31] *ibid.* reg. 51(e).

constitutes the refusal of an amendment giving rise to a right of appeal to the area committee.[32]

The Board may also use an amendment to limit or prevent further work being undertaken where it would not be appropriate to invoke the show cause procedure, *e.g.* where allegations in particular as to financial eligibility/disclosure are currently being considered and/or a further assessment of means is pending and it is considered appropriate that any inquiries or further assessment be concluded. If there is no appeal made against an amendment made of the Board's own volition, then an application to amend the certificate (by reversing the previous amendment) could be made which would give rise to an appeal if refused.[33]

The Board has a power to withdraw civil legal aid under section 15(4) Legal Aid Act 1988. This is not supported by regulations but (unless it is the power to discharge) could be used in appropriate cases, *i.e.* where the withdrawal was justified. The consequences of withdrawal (as opposed to discharge) are unclear.

15–09 If a show cause letter is received, the solicitor should check that it has been sent to the assisted person's correct address. It would also be prudent to contact the assisted person by letter explaining that the certificate will be discharged or revoked in the absence of a reply direct to the area office (or the client may instruct the solicitor to reply on his behalf).

Any reply should clearly state:

    (a) the certificate reference number;

    (b) the assisted person's name;

    (c) any particular degree of urgency;

    (d) the reason(s) why the certificate should not be discharged or revoked having regard to the specific reason(s) given in the show cause letter and enclosing copies of any relevant documents (it must be recalled that the area offices do not retain copy documents on their files and that these need to be resubmitted when the case is considered);

    (e) if applicable, any reason why the response will be received at the area office outside the stipulated time limit, *e.g.* where the letter was apparently delayed in the post or the assisted person has been away from home.

15–10 If no response is received following the sending of a show cause letter the certificate will be discharged or revoked and notice of discharge or notice of revocation sent to both the solicitor and the assisted person. The notice indicates the ground for the discharge or revocation and two copies are sent to the solicitor and a further copy direct to the client (unless the

---

[32] *ibid.* reg. 57(1).
[33] *ibid.* reg. 57.

274

client's correspondence address for the Board is care of the solicitor who must in those circumstances forward the notice to the client).

If representations are received they will be considered and a decision made on behalf of the Area Director resulting in either a discharge or revocation of the certificate with the appropriate notice being given or confirmation that the certificate is not going to be discharged or revoked, although the area office may wish to insert some new limitation or condition in the certificate depending on the circumstances of the case. If the certificate is to remain in force, a letter will be sent to the solicitor with a copy direct to the assisted person and with or without any amendment to the certificate.

Where a certificate is discharged or revoked (or not) following "representations" (*i.e.* information supplied) by any person the Area Director may, if he thinks fit, inform that person whether or not the certificate has been discharged or revoked.[34]

Appeal against discharge or revocation

Where a certificate is discharged or revoked in cases where the assisted **15–11** person must be given an opportunity to show cause, then (and only then) there is a right of appeal to the area committee against the discharge or revocation. Where there is a right of appeal the provisions as to the conduct and determination of appeals against the refusal of legal aid apply.[35] They are that:

(a) notice must be given within 14 days of the date of notice of discharge/revocation (*not* of its receipt);

(b) the appeal is by way of reconsideration;

(c) the appellant may submit further information, orally or in writing;

(d) the appellant may conduct the appeal himself, with or without assistance, or be represented;

(e) the area committee may dismiss the appeal or direct the Area Director to reinstate the certificate subject to such terms and conditions as the area committee thinks fit (the area committee may therefore impose a new limitation or condition), or direct the Area Director to reinstate the certificate and settle its terms and conditions or refer the matter back to the Area Director for his determination or report.[36]

The area committee's decision on an appeal is final (subject to judicial review) and the committee is required to give notice of its decision and the

---

[34] *ibid.* reg. 82(5).
[35] *ibid.* reg. 81(2).
[36] *ibid.* regs. 36–39, 81(2).

reasons for it to both the appellant and to his solicitor.[37] This is done by a standard letter and, if appropriate, the issue of a form of amendment to the certificate.

If an appeal is successful and the discharge or revocation is rescinded it is not beyond doubt to what extent the rescission has retrospective effect.

It is possible for a revocation to be rescinded where the revocation was based on a mistake of fact and in those circumstances the rescission has retrospective effect so that the certificate is treated as being continuously in force.[38] If the rescission of a revocation is sought then full details should be given to the area office as soon as possible and, if possible, the original notice of revocation should be returned to the area office. This will not be possible where the notice has been filed and served.

Notice of any rescission of the revocation should be given to "reverse" any notice of revocation. The revocation will be rescinded by letter and the most convenient way for the solicitor to give notice of any rescission is for him to amend a standard form of notice of issue/amendment of certificate.

The Board considers that a discharge can, in certain circumstances, be rescinded and the show cause procedure instituted, e.g. where a false statement or failure to disclose is not known at the time of the discharge. Proceedings for misrepresentation/non-disclosure can be taken in appropriate circumstances.[39]

---

[37] *ibid.* reg. 81(3).
[38] *Langford v. Gibb*, The Times, January 26, 1984.
[39] Legal Aid Act 1988, s. 39 and see Chap. 36.

Chapter 16

THE RIGHT OF AN ASSISTED PERSON TO COSTS

INTRODUCTION

A legally aided litigant, if successful, is in no different position from any **16–01** other so far as the right to costs is concerned, and this is so despite the fact that the costs must be paid into the Fund. This may, in certain circumstances, lead to the Fund making a profit.

If an assisted person succeeds in his action, the court will make an order for costs upon precisely the same principles as would apply if legal aid were not involved. The assisted person has no beneficial entitlement to the costs,[1] and the party liable can obtain a discharge for them if they are paid to the assisted person's solicitor and he is required to pay them into the Fund.

It is the duty of an assisted person to claim costs if in the same circumstances a paying client would do so in his own interests. Section 31(1) of the Legal Aid Act 1988 provides that the rights conferred on a person under the Act will not affect the rights or liabilities of other parties, or the principles on which the courts' discretion is normally exercised.[1a]

THE GENERAL PRINCIPLE

If an assisted person is successful in proceedings, that person is entitled to **16–02** the usual order for costs, whether making a contribution towards the costs or not. This follows from section 31(1)(b) of the 1988 Act under which the rights conferred by the 1988 Act on a person receiving advice, assistance or representation are not to affect the rights or liabilities of other parties to

---

[1] *A Debtor v. Law Society (No. 5883 of 1979) The Times,* February 20, 1981, C.A.
[1a] *Knight v. Lambeth L.B.C.* (CCRTI 94/0330/E) November 28, 1994 C.A. and see *Scherer v. Counting Instruments* (1986) 1 W.L.R. 615.

the proceedings or the principles on which the discretion of any court or tribunal is normally exercised.

The provisions of the 1988 Act are such as to give the assisted person the same right to an order for costs as any other successful party. For the purposes of determining the costs of the legally assisted person in pursuance of an order for costs or an agreement for costs, the services of the solicitor and counsel are treated as having been provided otherwise than under the 1988 Act, and the solicitor is treated as having paid counsel's fees.[2] This is so even though costs are normally awarded only in the nature of an indemnity[3] and the assisted person may not be under any personal liability. In respect of the proceedings for which a certificate was granted on or after February 25, 1994, solicitors are paid fixed fees for certain items of work and prescribed hourly rates for preparation, advocacy, travelling and waiting and attending on counsel. The prescribed fees and hourly rates apply to High Court and county court proceedings as well as in family proceedings.[4] The Civil Legal Aid (General) Regulations 1989 enable the assisted person's solicitor to recover *inter partes* costs over and above those determined at the prescribed rates from the party against whom an order for *inter partes* costs has been made.[5] The unassisted party is liable to pay the *inter partes* costs even though these may amount to more than the amount paid out of the Fund to the assisted person's solicitor and counsel. This can arise since legal aid costs are taxed or assessed on the standard basis,[6] but it may be appropriate to obtain an order for costs on the indemnity basis which could result in the unassisted paying party being ordered to pay money into the Fund which is not subsequently paid out to the assisted party's legal advisers.

A precedent for this situation is that an unassisted paying party has always had to pay the full amount found due on taxation, but until recently a 10 per cent deduction was made from that amount before payment was made to the assisted person's lawyers. Since the 1988 Act specifically provides that the services of solicitor and counsel are to be treated as having been provided otherwise than under the 1988 Act it is clear that the discretion in relation to costs must be exercised on ordinary principles.[7]

---

[2] Legal Aid Act 1988, s. 31(2).
[3] *Gundry v. Sainsbury* [1910] 1 K.B. 645, C.A.
[4] Legal Aid in Civil Proceedings (Remuneration) Regulations 1994 (S.I. 1994 No. 228); Civil Legal Aid (General) (Amendment) Regulations 1994 (S.I. 1994 No. 229); Legal Aid in Family Proceedings (Remuneration) (Amendment) Regulations 1994 (S.I. 1994 No. 230).
[5] Civil Legal Aid (General) Regulations 1989, reg. 107B.
[6] *ibid.* regs. 105, 107.
[7] Legal Aid Act 1988, s. 31(2).

SECURITY FOR COSTS

An assisted person has the same rights as any other litigant to apply for an **16–03** order that his opponent shall give security for costs, since the object of such an order is to give the defendant security against such costs as are likely to be awarded to him if successful at the trial. Where an assisted plaintiff is ordinarily resident abroad an order for security may be made in an appropriate case.[8]

WHAT COSTS ARE PAYABLE?

How ascertained

Where costs are awarded to an assisted person they are taxed or agreed in **16–04** the ordinary way.[9–10] This is subject to certain provisions which take account of the special position of an assisted person and which are dealt with later.

Costs on the standard basis subject to the Civil Legal Aid (General) Regulations 1989

Where the opponent is liable to pay costs, the costs will be taxed on the **16–05** standard basis subject to the 1989 Regulations.[11] The legal aid element of the costs will be taxed in accordance with the prescribed rates but as against the paying party the taxation will take place on the standard basis at rates which are not restricted to those prescribed. The assisted person's legal representatives are not prevented from recovering from the paying party, sums in respect of costs by any rule of law which limits the costs recoverable by a party to proceedings to the amount which he is liable to pay his legal representatives.[12] On taxation there will be allowed a reasonable amount in respect of all costs reasonably incurred; any doubts which the taxing officer may have as to whether the costs were reasonably incurred or reasonable in amount will be resolved in favour of the paying party.[13] Costs incurred by reason of any application for authority to incur costs and of any report made by an assisted person's solicitor in respect of

---

[8] *Jackson v. John Dickinson & Co (Bolton) Ltd* [1952] 1 All E.R. 104, C.A.; *Freidman v. Austay (London) Ltd* [1954] 1 W.L.R. 466; *Williams v. Williams* [1953] 1 W.L.R. 905.

[9–10] Civil Legal Aid (General) Regulations 1989, Pt. XII.

[11] *i.e.* Legal Aid in Civil Proceedings (Remuneration) Regulations 1994 and the Legal Aid in Family Proceedings (Remuneration) Regulations 1991 as amended.

[12] Civil Legal Aid (General) Regulations 1994, reg. 107B(3)(a).

[13] R.S.C., Ord. 62, r. 12(1).

the conduct of proceedings, will be taxed on the standard basis under regulation 107A(2) of the 1989 Regulations but will not necessarily be allowed against the paying party.

Costs incurred in:

    (a) notification of extension of an emergency certificate;

    (b) notification of issue of a new certificate;

    (c) notification of an amendment to a certificate;

    (d) notification of revocation or discharge of a certificate; or

    (e) in relation to an assisted person's liability for costs

are costs in the cause.[14]

Costs on the indemnity basis

16–06   In an appropriate case, a court may properly award costs to an assisted person on the indemnity basis,[15] notwithstanding the fact that the legally assisted person's solicitor or counsel may only recover costs at the prescribed rate out of the Fund.[16] However, it is now possible to recover *inter partes* costs from a paying party in excess of the prescribed legal aid costs.[17] On the taxation on the indemnity basis all costs will be allowed except in so far as they are of an unreasonable amount or have been unreasonably incurred and any doubts which the taxing officer may have as to whether the costs were reasonably incurred or were reasonable in amount will be resolved in favour of the receiving party.[18]

Interest on Damages

16–07   Where the Board receives damages paid in favour of an assisted person, it must pay to that person a sum representing gross interest and while the damages were being held by the Board.[19] The Board is required to maintain a general account at a bank or building society in which to deposit damages. The rate of interest payable to the assisted person is half a per cent per annum less than the rate payable on damages deposited in the general account.[20] No interest is payable where damages received do not exceed £500 or where the period during which they are held by the Board is less than twenty eight days. Interest is payable for the period beginning on the third business day after the date on which the Board receives the damages down to and including the date on which the Board determines

---

[14] Civil Legal Aid (General) Regulations 1989, regs. 111, 25, 50, 54, 82, 124.
[15] Legal Aid Act 1988, s. 31(1)(b).
[16] Civil Legal Aid (General) Regulations 1989, Pt. XII.
[17] *ibid.* reg. 107B (3)(a).
[18] R.S.C., Ord. 62, r. 12(2).
[19] Civil Legal Aid (General) Regulations 1989 Regulation 92A (1).
[20] *ibid.*, Regulation 92A (2) and (3).

the amount to be retained under the Statutory Charge Provisions in accordance with Regulation 92(2) of the 1989 General Regulations.[21]

Interest on Costs

Following the decision of the House of Lords in *Hunt v. R.M. Douglas* **16–08** *(Roofing) Ltd,*[22] it is now clear that interest on costs runs from the date of judgment at eight per cent.[23] Normally one would expect the client to be entitled to that interest. The 1988 Act provides that the fact that the services of counsel or a solicitor are given under the 1988 Act will not affect the relationship between or rights of counsel, solicitor and client or any privilege arising out of such relationships,[24] but since the client has not stood out of any money (except the contribution) it would seem logical for the Board to stand in the shoes of the client in relation to the interest. Subject to reimbursement of the Board in respect of costs which it has paid out in accordance with the 1989 Regulations[25] and any interest thereon, any costs recovered from the paying party (and presumably any interest thereon) belong to the solicitor.[26]

It is the duty of an assisted person's solicitor to safeguard the interests of the Fund on any *inter partes* taxation pursuant to an order for costs made in favour of the assisted person even where the assisted person may have no interest in the result of the taxation.[27]

All costs are payable to the Board

Any sums recovered by virtue of an order or agreement for costs made in **16–09** favour of a legally assisted person with respect to the proceedings must be paid to the Board.[28] This is part of the general rule that all sums due to an assisted person, with limited exceptions, must be paid for the credit of the assisted person's account with the Board and is dealt with in Chapter 18.

---

[21] *ibid.,* Regulation 92A (4) (5).
[22] [1983] 3 W.L.R. 975.
[23] Judgment Debts (Rate of Interest) Order 1993 (S.I. 1993 No. 564).
[24] Legal Aid Act 1988, s. 31(1)(a).
[25] Civil Legal Aid (General) Regulations 1989, reg. 92(1)(b).
[26] *ibid.,* reg. 107B(4).
[27] *ibid.,* reg. 110.
[28] Legal Aid Act 1988, s. 16(5).

Chapter 17

THE LIABILITY OF AN ASSISTED PERSON FOR AN OPPONENT'S COSTS

INTRODUCTION

17–01   If a litigant loses the case, the existence of legal aid does not affect the need for the court to decide, in accordance with the normal principles, whether any order for costs should be made against the legally assisted person, and the court is under a duty to restrict the amount of any order it may make to the amount, if any, which is a reasonable one for the assisted person to pay having regard to all the circumstances, including the financial resources of all the parties and their conduct in connection with the dispute.[1] There is no need for the assisted person to apply for the benefit of the statutory protection, for the court must give effect to it whenever it makes an order for costs against a legally assisted party.

Sections 16, 17 and 18 of the 1988 Act are capable of producing the result that, whilst a legally aided unsuccessful plaintiff would not be at risk of losing her own home to the enforcement of costs, a legally aided successful defendant who had acted reasonably could be. The court expressed the view that urgent reconsideration should be given to the legislation.[2] In a dispute in which both parties were legally aided the court held that litigants should request an order for costs in their favour with the determination of the assisted person's liability postponed. Section 17(3) of the 1988 Act protects an assisted person's home from execution. A charging order is execution for these purposes.[3]

17–02   The determination of the amount which the assisted person is to pay must be made at the end of the trial of the action, but the court has the power to adjourn it or to refer any question of fact, including the party's means, to a taxing master, district judge or the Clerk of the Parliaments, to the chief

---

[1] Legal Aid Act 1988, s. 17(1).
[2] *Almond v. Miles, The Times,* February 4, 1992.
[3] *Parr v. Smith 1994* NPC 5 C.A.

clerk of a Crown Court or to a clerk to the justices, for inquiry and report. The determination of the amount payable must be made by the court which tried or heard the proceedings. An assisted person is given a further degree of protection in that the dwelling house, clothes, household furniture and the tools and implements of the trade, are left out of account in the same way that they are left out of account in the determination of disposable income and capital. The assisted person has no right to apply for variation of an order for costs made against him, but the party in whose favour it is made can apply at any time within six years on the ground that further information about the assisted person's means has become available or that there has been an improvement in his financial position.

THE GENERAL PRINCIPLE

The fact that a party to proceedings is legally aided does not prevent the **17–03** court in a proper case from making an order that that party should pay the opponent's costs. This follows from section 31(1)(b) of the 1988 Act which provides that the rights conferred by the 1988 Act on a person receiving advice, assistance or representation, are not to affect the rights or liabilities of other parties to the proceedings or the principles on which the discretion of the court or any tribunal is normally exercised.[4] The effect of the subsection is to impose a duty upon the court to consider the question: "Who is to pay the costs of the proceedings?" in accordance with normal principles.[5] Thus, where there has been no impropriety by a party in conducting a successful defence held to be unfounded in law that party is entitled to its costs.[6]

SECURITY FOR COSTS

Where an assisted person is required to give security for costs, that person **17–04** must find the security personally, there being no provision enabling it to be paid out of the Fund. However, the amount of any security must not exceed the amount which could be ordered to be paid by the assisted person under section 17(1) of the 1988 Act, *i.e.* an amount, if any, which is a reasonable one to be paid having regard to all the circumstances, including the financial resources of all the parties and their conduct, in connection with

---

[4] Legal Aid Act 1988, s. 31(1)(b).
[5] *Cope v. United Dairies (London) Ltd* [1963] 2 Q.B. 33.
[6] *Richardson v. West Lindsey District Council* [1990] 1 W.L.R. 522 and *Hornby v. Cripps* (LTA94/5749/C) January 13 1995 C.A.

the dispute.[7] Security has been ordered where the assisted plaintiff was ordinarily resident abroad.[8-9]

THE STATUTORY PROTECTION GIVEN TO AN ASSISTED PERSON

The nature of the protection

17–05 Although the court can make an order for costs against an assisted person, section 17(1) of the 1988 Act limits the amount which can be ordered to be paid. It provides that:

> "The liability of a legally assisted party under an order for costs made against him with respect to any proceedings shall not exceed the amount (if any) which is a reasonable one for him to pay having regard to all the circumstances including the financial resources of the parties and their conduct in connection with the dispute."

There is thus a distinction to be drawn between an order for costs on the one hand, and the amount to be paid on the other. The financial circumstances of many assisted persons are such that they are in no position to pay their own costs, let alone those of their opponents, with the result that the court often has no option when applying section 17(1) but to exempt them from liability altogether. This can cause hardship to a successful unassisted party and the position with regard to such parties is dealt with later. The statutory protection is personal to the assisted party and does not extend to costs which are payable not directly by that person but out of property in which he has an interest.

The court's duty to apply section 17(1) of the 1988 Act

17–06 Once the court has decided to make an order for costs against an assisted person, section 17(1) imposes a duty upon it to decide what limit is to be imposed on those costs and it is unnecessary for the assisted person to apply for the benefit of the subsection.[10] The effect of the 1988 Act is to make it necessary for the court to deal with costs in two stages.

> "Where there is a determination of liability for costs in an action to which an assisted person is a party, that determination involves two phases though they sometimes take place at the same time. The first phase is the determination by the court in its discretion, whether or

---

[7] Civil Legal Aid (General) Regulations 1989, reg. 123.
[8-9] *Caldwell v. Sumpters* [1972] Ch. 478.
[10] *Cope v. United Dairies (London) Ltd* [1963] 2 Q.B. 33 at 43.

not it is proper that an order for costs should be made against the assisted person. This phase, by reason of . . . the Act, is carried out without reference to any consideration as to the party being, or having ever been, an assisted person. The second phase, which arises in relation to a person who is or has been assisted is a separate determination as to the amount, if any, of the liability for costs which the assisted person should be ordered to pay. Frequently, in fact, these two phases fall to be dealt with at different stages. Thus where costs are awarded against an assisted person on an interlocutory application the amount must not be assessed at that stage."[11]

The stage at which the determination must be made

At the trial or hearing

The determination of an assisted person's liability under section 17(1) of the 1988 Act must be made when the proceedings have concluded. Thus, no costs attributable to the period during which the assisted person's certificate was in force are recoverable from him until the court has determined the amount of the liability in accordance with section 17(1). Where the assisted person's certificate does not relate to or has been amended so that it no longer relates to the whole of the proceedings, the court must nevertheless make a determination in respect of that part of the proceedings to which the certificate does relate. The determination must be made by the court which tried or heard the proceedings.[12] The court need not exercise its powers immediately because the Civil Legal Aid Regulations (General) 1989 confer the following discretions. **17–07**

Power to postpone or adjourn the determination The court, if it thinks fit, may postpone or adjourn the determination for such time and to such place, including chambers, as it may decide.[13] **17–08**

Power to refer any question of fact for investigation If it thinks fit, the court may refer to a master, district judge or the Clerk of the Parliaments any question of fact relevant to the determination, for investigation in chambers or elsewhere and require the master, etc, to report the findings on that question to the court. The power extends, in the case of an appeal from a decision of the Crown Court or a court of summary jurisdiction, to the chief clerk or the clerk to the justices of the court from which the appeal was brought.[14] **17–09**

---

[11] *ibid.* at p. 41.
[12] Civil Legal Aid (General) Regulations 1989, regs. 124(1), (2) and (3).
[13] *ibid.* reg. 124(a).
[14] *ibid.* reg. 127(b).

Interlocutory proceedings

17–10 The requirement that the assisted person's liability is to be determined where proceedings have been concluded,[15] means that it cannot take place during any interlocutory application. In such a case, therefore, the matter must be raised at the trial or final hearing of the case so that a determination can then be made and incorporated in the final order. Similarly, when the costs of interlocutory proceedings are reserved, not only should they be dealt with at the hearing of the main suit and included in the final order, but a determination should also be made under section 17(1) of the 1988 Act.

The Basis on which the Determination should be made

17–11 The assisted person's liability is not to exceed "the amount (if any) which is a reasonable one for him to pay having regard to all the circumstances including the financial resources of all the parties and their conduct in connection with the dispute."[16]

The amount (if any) which is a reasonable one for him to pay

17–12 When a party is legally aided, the court has a wide discretion in deciding what costs he should be ordered to pay, but it must exercise this reasonably. Whatever one might think of the conduct of an assisted party, it would not be right to make an order for costs against him which would be unreasonable having regard to his means.[17-18] Under section 17(1) the courts can, and frequently do, relieve an assisted person from paying any costs at all.

Having regard to all the circumstances

17–13 The principal factor which the court takes into account is the means of the parties; any other circumstances are not often regarded as relevant. Such circumstances might include, *e.g.* that the assisted person's case was lost on a technicality although the assisted person was morally entitled to succeed.

Including the financial resources of all the parties

17–14 This is the most important single factor. The court may make the necessary inquiries itself before deciding what order to make or may ask a master or district judge to do so under the procedure already described.

In determining the amount of an assisted person's liability, any document

---

[15] *ibid.* reg. 124(1).
[16] Legal Aid Act 1988. s. 17(1).
[17-18] Willmer L.J. in *Crystall v Crystall* [1963] 1 W.L.R. 574.

286

which may have been sent to the court office or registry, or filed or exhibited under the Civil Legal Aid (General) Regulations 1989, is evidence of the facts stated in it,[19] and the court may, if it thinks fit, order the assisted person or anybody who has filed an affidavit, to attend for oral examination as to his means and as to any other facts which may be relevant.[20] It may also allow any party to give evidence and to call witnesses; not only for the resources of the parties to be considered, but also their outgoings and their present and future liabilities.

The assisted person's means The financial position of the legally aided   **17–15**
party is likely to be the decisive consideration in determining what order should be made against him.

In determining the assisted person's liability, his house, clothes, household furniture and the tools and implements of his trade are left out of account to the same extent as they are left out of account in the determination of disposable income and disposable capital.[21–22]

The fact that the assisted person has recovered damages in the action will affect his means and is a factor which the court may take into account. The court will have to bear in mind, however, that the damages will be subject to the statutory charge in favour of the Fund and in some cases may absorb the whole of them, leaving nothing available with which to pay the opponent's costs.

The means of other parties An assisted person's opponent has the right to   **17–16**
file an affidavit (other than in authorised summary proceedings) exhibiting a statement setting out the rate of his own income and amount of his own capital and any other facts relevant to the determination of his means in accordance with section 17(1) of the 1988 Act. If such an affidavit is filed, a copy of it must be served together with the exhibit on the assisted person's solicitor who must immediately serve that person with a copy of the certificate and send a copy of the affidavit to the Area Director.[23]

Oral examination Where the court has made an order referring a question   **17–17**
of fact to the master, district judge, etc., the person conducting the investigation may order the assisted person and any party who has filed an affidavit as to means to attend for oral examination as to his means and as to any other facts which may be relevant to the determination of the amount of the assisted person's liability for costs. A party ordered to attend for oral examination may be permitted to give evidence and to call witnesses.[24]

---

[19] Civil Legal Aid (General) Regulations 1989, reg. 126 (b).
[20] *ibid.* reg. 128(1).
[21–22] *ibid.* reg. 126(a).
[23] Civil Legal Aid (General) Regulations, reg. 125(1), (2).
[24] *ibid.* regs. 128(2), (1).

Their conduct in connection with the dispute

17–18 Conduct which may be considered relevant includes:
   (a) failure by an unassisted party until a late stage in proceedings to disclose documents which, had they been produced earlier, might have led to his legally aided opponents dropping their action;
   (b) acting reasonably and honourably throughout;
   (c) being guilty of behaviour contributing to the dispute;
   (d) bringing a divorce petition, but not proceeding with the allegation in it or persisting with the petition where there are no grounds for doing so.[25]

Agreeing costs inter partes and setting off costs

17–19 An assisted person may sometimes wish, *e.g.* in order to achieve a settlement, to agree to pay costs to the opposing party without asking for the statutory limitation on liability and there is nothing to prevent such an agreement being made, even if the court has made an order under section 17(1) of the 1988 Act.[26]

In practice, the courts do not normally consider it necessary to quantify an assisted person's liability under section 17(1) of the 1988 Act in a case where that person's liability to pay costs is ordered to be set off against costs which he is entitled to receive from his opponent, unless there is a risk that there will be a shortfall.

Persons acting in a representative fiduciary or official capacity

17–20 Where no order for costs is made against an assisted person who is concerned in the proceedings in a representative, fiduciary or official capacity, section 17(1) of the 1988 Act applies, but, unless there is reason to the contrary, personal resources are not to be taken into account. Instead, regard is to be had to the value of the property or estate or the amount of the Fund out of which the assisted person is entitled to be indemnified.[27]

Minors and Patients

17–21 When an order for costs is made against a minor who is an assisted person, section 17(1) of the 1988 Act applies. In deciding the amount of costs to

---

[25] *Crystall v. Crystall* [1963] 1 W.L.R. 574; *Re Spurlings Will Trusts* [1966] 1 W.L.R. 920; *Singlehurst v. Singlehurst* [1963] 107 S. J. 236; *Gooday v. Gooday* [1969] 1, C.A.; *Armstrong v. Armstrong* [1970] S.L.T. 247; *McDonnell v. McDonnell* [1977] 1 W.L.R. 34; *Bezzi v. Bezzi* [1956] 1 W.L.R. 116;
[26] *Salsbury v. Woodland* [1970] 1 Q.B. 324; [1969] 3 All E.R. 863 at 881.
[27] Civil Legal Aid (General) Regulations 1989, reg. 131.

be awarded, the minor's means would be taken as including the means of any person whose resources have been taken into account by the Assessment Officer in assessing the disposable income and capital of the minor.[28]

In a case where an order for costs is made against a next friend or guardian *ad litem* of an assisted person who is a minor or a patient, that person will have the benefit of section 17(1) of the 1988 Act as it applies to an assisted person and that person's means will be taken to be those of the minor (to the extent described in the previous paragraph) or of the patient.[29]

Where a person is legally aided for part only of the proceedings

The protection conferred by section 17(1) of the 1988 Act is limited to the period during which a person is in receipt of legal aid and if the certificate is not granted until after the opponent has incurred some costs, the assisted person will have no protection against those costs.[30] Where a person is issued with a certificate limited to part only of proceedings, he will be protected in respect only of costs incurred in connection with that part.[31] **17–22**

Where an assisted person's certificate is revoked, that person is deemed never to have been an assisted person in relation to the proceedings to which the certificate related,[32] and there is no question, therefore, of his being protected against liability for his opponent's costs. Where, however, a certificate is discharged, the provisions of section 17(1) of the 1988 Act apply in so far as the costs were incurred while the holder of the certificate was an assisted person.[33]

Where more than one of the parties is legally aided

Opposing parties

The fact that both parties to proceedings are legally aided does not prevent the court from making an order for costs against the loser in the normal way.[34] The amount which the unsuccessful party will be ordered to pay will be limited by section 17(1) of the 1988 Act in the same way as if his opponent were not legally aided. **17–23**

General principles There is no general principle that the incidence of **17–24**

---

[28] *ibid.* reg. 132.
[29] *ibid.* reg. 133.
[30] *Re Spurlings Will Trust* [1966] 1 W.L.R. 920.
[31] *Littaur v. Steggles Palmer* [1985] 1 W.L.R. 287.
[32] Civil Legal Aid (General) Regulations 1989, reg. 74(2).
[33] *ibid.* reg. 74(2).
[34] Legal Aid Act 1988, s. 31(1)(b).

legal aid should be made to fall on other parties and, unless there is good reason for doing so, the court will not depart from the normal principle that costs follow the event.[35]

Joint parties

17–25 Where two or more joint parties are entitled to costs against the legally aided person or persons, the court has power to make different determinations for the costs to be paid to each of them.[36]

Where an order for costs is made against joint parties who are not all legally aided, the limitation under section 17(1) of the 1988 Act of the liability of any party who is legally aided will not affect that of any unassisted party to pay the whole of the costs since they are jointly and severally liable for them. It follows that that person's rights to claim a contribution from the assisted party will be limited to the amount of the latter's liability as determined by the court.

The orders which the court may make

Generally

17–26 Where the court makes an order for costs against an assisted person it may order that payment shall be limited to such amount as the court thinks reasonable having regard to all the circumstances and that amount may be paid in instalments or otherwise and may include an amount to be determined on taxation.[37]

Where the court thinks it reasonable that no payment should be made immediately or that the assisted person should have no liability for payment, it may direct that payment under the order for costs be suspended either until a date determined by the court or indefinitely.[38] These provisions complement the provisions of section 17(1) of the 1988 Act.

Where a plaintiff is legally aided, a court has jurisdiction in interlocutory proceedings to make an order for costs in favour of the defendant directing that those costs be set off against any damages and/or costs to which the legally aided plaintiff may become entitled in the action.[39]

By whom the liability is to be determined

17–27 The amount of an assisted person's liability for costs must be determined by the court which tried or heard the proceedings.[40] This provision is

---

[35] *Johnson v. Ribbins* [1977] 1 W.L.R. 1458, C.A.
[36] *Re Spurlings Will Trust* [1966] 1 W.L.R. 920 at 941.
[37] Civil Legal Aid (General) Regulations 1989, reg. 129(a).
[38] *ibid.* reg. 129(b).
[39] *Lockley v. National Blood Transfusion Service* [1992] 1 W.L.R. 492, C.A.; and see *Cook v. Swinfen* [1967] 1 W.L.R. 457, C.A; *Brookes v. Harris, The Times* April 22, 1995 Ferris J.
[40] Civil Legal Aid (General) Regulations 1989, reg. 124(3).

mandatory and there does not appear to be any machinery for delegation, although it is clearly open to the court to require a master or district judge to undertake an inquiry and report upon which the court may then make the necessary order.

Determining the amount

17–28 The practice of the court relying solely on the assisted person's assessed contribution has been judicially criticised.[41] It is for the assisted person's solicitor to provide the court with whatever information is required to make the appropriate order.

Possible orders

17–29 The following are the most common orders which may be made under section 17(1) of the 1988 Act.

17–30 **No order for costs** The court may decide that an assisted person's means are such that he is unable to pay anything towards his opponent's costs and will make no order for costs against him; in such a case the correct order is that there be judgment for the opponent with costs, but that the assisted person should have no present liability for such costs. This is because the court has to deal with the matter in two stages: first, deciding that the assisted person is liable for his opponent's costs and secondly, determining that it is not reasonable for him to pay anything in respect of them. This leaves it open to the successful party to apply for a variation of the order should the assisted person's financial position later improve from that level.[42] The Court of Appeal has questioned the practice of making "football pools" orders against unsuccessful assisted parties as leave to enforce cannot be given unless there is additional information or change of circumstances. Where there are prospects for enforcement, successful litigants may prefer an order for costs with the determination of the party's liability postponed.[43]

17–31 **Payment of a fixed sum** Where an order is made for a specific amount it is unnecessary for the costs to be taxed.

17–32 **Payment of taxed costs subject to a limit** Such an order has the effect of making the assisted person liable to pay his opponent's costs as taxed or the sum specified in the order, whichever is the less.

17–33 **Payment of taxed costs or a fraction of them** Such an order will have the same effect as that referred to in the previous paragraph save that no limit is imposed by the court.

---

[41] *Gooday v. Gooday* [1969] P. 1 at 10.
[42] Civil Legal Aid (General) Regulations 1989, reg. 130.
[43] *i.e.* under *ibid.* reg. 127(A); *Parr v. Smith*; (January 26, 1994, C.A.; unreported).

17–34 **Postponement of payment** The court has power to order payment by instalments (the first instalment is normally to be paid one month after the assisted person's final instalment of contribution) and may also suspend the order for payment either to a given date or indefinitely.[44]

"Bullock" and "Sanderson" Orders

17–35 Where the court considers that it was reasonable for a plaintiff to sue two defendants claiming against them in the alternative, it has a discretion as to whom to order the unsuccessful defendant to pay the costs of the successful one. Thus, it may order the plaintiff to pay the successful defendant's costs and allow him to include these in the costs payable to him by the unsuccessful defendant (a "Bullock" Order),[45] or by ordering payment of the costs direct to the successful defendant by the unsuccessful defendant (a "Sanderson" Order).[46] It has been held that where the plaintiff in such a case is legally aided and a Sanderson Order is made, no inquiry into the plaintiff's means need be made and no question arises of a limited order for costs being made under section 17(1) of the 1988 Act, because the order is not made against him but against the unsuccessful defendant.[47]

There does not appear to have been a decision of the court where a Bullock Order has been made. It would seem that section 17(1) of the 1988 Act would apply to the order for costs against the assisted plaintiff, and that the most satisfactory order would normally be that he should pay a fixed amount, determined in the usual way, plus any sum received from the unsuccessful defendant up to the full amount of the successful defendant's costs. It may be that such an order could not properly be made, since it would not quantify the assisted person's liability as required by section 17(1) of the 1988 Act. It might be possible for the difficulty to be overcome by the successful defendant applying for the order to be varied as soon as the unsuccessful defendant makes payment to the assisted person.[48]

Enforcement of Orders

17–36 If an order for costs is made against an assisted person, he is liable to have it enforced against him by execution in the normal way, except that his house and household furniture and the tools of his trade are protected from execution in all parts of the United Kingdom to the same extent as they are left out of account by the court when determining his liability under section 17(1) of the 1988 Act. The protection is only in respect of liability for costs

---

[44] *ibid.* reg. 129.
[45] *Bullock v. London General Omnibus Company* [1907] 1 K.B. 264, C.A.
[46] *Sanderson v. Blyth Theatre Company* [1903] 2 K.B. 533, C.A.
[47] *Dailey v. Diggers Ltd* [1951] 1 K.B. 661.
[48] Civil Legal Aid (General) Regulations 1989, reg. 130(b).

and does not extend to execution to enforce an award of damages made against the assisted person. Furthermore, the assisted person is protected only against costs incurred by his opponent during the currency of the certificate.[49]

Variation of orders

The party in whose favour an order for costs is made may, within six years **17–37** from the date on which it was made, apply to court for the order to be varied on the ground that:

(a) material information as to the assisted person's means, being information which could not have been obtained by that party with reasonable diligence at the time the order was made, is available; or

(b) there has been a change in the assisted person's circumstances since the days of the order.

The court may vary the order as it thinks fit on any such application but, apart from this discretion to vary, the determination of the court is final.[50]

---

[49] *ibid.* reg. 124.
[50] *ibid.* reg. 130.

Chapter 18

AN ASSISTED PERSON'S ACCOUNT WITH THE BOARD — THE STATUTORY CHARGE

Introduction

18–01 The Board has the right to recover, from the following sources, the costs and expenses which are paid out of the Fund to an assisted person's legal adviser:

(a) first, from any costs recovered by an assisted person;

(b) then, from any contributions paid by the assisted person into the Fund; and

(c) finally, from any damages or other property or sums recovered or preserved for the assisted person.

To this end, any money due to an assisted person must be paid direct to the solicitor named in the legal aid certificate or any amendment to the certificate,[1] who must account for it to the Board, and the Board is empowered to enforce any order or agreement made in the assisted person's favour. In addition, the Board has a statutory first charge, which it has no power to waive,[2] over any property recovered or preserved in the proceedings to which the assisted person's certificate related and may enforce this to the extent necessary to balance the assisted person's account with the Fund.[3]

---

[1] As to the position where an assisted person wishes to nominate a new solicitor to act under the certificate see para. 13–08.

[2] The Board has, however, power to postpone enforcement of the statutory charge; see para. 18–86 *et seq.*

[3] Including a person who was formerly assisted; Civil Legal Aid (General) Regulations 1989, reg. 85(1) provides that the charge applies to any property recovered or preserved by a person whose certificate has been revoked or discharged and for that purpose the reference to a person whose certificate has been discharged includes his personal representatives, his trustee in bankruptcy or the Official Receiver, as the case may be, where the certificate has been discharged by reason of the assisted person's death or bankruptcy — Civil Legal Aid (General) Regulation 1989, reg. 86.

Certain payments (protected payments or exemptions) are exempt from the statutory charge and need not be paid to the assisted person's solicitor or into the Fund. Examples are periodical payments of maintenance and the first £2,500 of any money recovered or preserved in matrimonial/family proceedings.

When a legally aided case has been concluded, the Board balances the assisted person's account and retains any sums recovered in respect of costs from the assisted person's opponent.[4]

If the costs recovered are less than the sums paid out, a sufficient amount to meet the deficit (which is referred to in the 1988 Act as "the net liability" of the Board on the assisted person's account) is retained out of any contributions which the assisted person may have made.[5] Should there still be a deficiency, the statutory charge will be enforced to the necessary extent. If, when all amounts due to the Board have been recovered, there is a credit balance, this will be paid to the assisted person. The effect of these provisions is to make the assisted person liable to pay for the cost of the case from any contribution or from the proceeds of the litigation. To that extent, civil legal aid operates as a loan rather than a gift.[6]

Should there continue to be a deficiency, despite the above payments, this will be borne by the Fund, and ultimately by the taxpayer. The assisted person's liability is limited to the contribution payable under the certificate.[7]

COSTS PAYABLE TO AN ASSISTED PERSON

The position should always be clarified with the area office where the **18–02** solicitor wishes to retain monies but also see Chapter 16 regarding *inter partes* costs.

The Board may take proceedings in its own name to enforce any order or agreement for costs made in favour of the assisted person.[8]

THE RIGHT OF THE FUND TO CONTRIBUTIONS

If any costs recovered from the other side are insufficient to cover in full **18–03** the costs and expenses paid by the Board to the assisted person's solicitor and counsel, the Board looks to the assisted person's contribution[9] to meet

---

[4] Legal Aid Act 1988, s. 16(5).
[5] *ibid*, s. 16(6) and s. 43.
[6] See comments of the Master of the Rolls in *Davies v. Eli & Lilly & Co.* [1987] 3 All E.R. 94 at 97–98 and *Watkinson v. Law Society* [1991] 2 All E.R. 953.
[7] See Chap. 6.
[8] Civil Legal Aid (General) Regulations 1989, reg. 91(1).
[9] As to the position regarding contributions generally, see Chap. 6.

the shortfall.[10] Should the assisted person be unsuccessful in the proceedings and be ordered to pay costs, damages or any other sums to the opponent, the assisted person's liability to pay any contribution to the Board will remain unaffected.[11]

Whatever the outcome of the proceedings, an assisted person should continue to pay the instalments of the contribution as they become due even if an order for payment of damages and costs is obtained against the assisted person's opponent. This is necessary because the assisted person's liability for his contribution continues, notwithstanding any order made against the opponent, until payment is actually received from the opponent into the Fund or until the certificate is discharged.[12]

Where a certificate is discharged, the assisted person remains liable to pay any outstanding contribution up to the date of discharge but the liability for any further payments ceases. Where a certificate is revoked, the Board is entitled to recover from the assisted person the full amount paid out of the Fund on that person's behalf, less any contributions which have already been paid.[13] In addition, the solicitor who has acted under the certificate has the right to recover from the assisted person the difference between the amount paid or payable out of the Fund and the full amount of any solicitor and own client costs if these exceed the costs payable under the certificate.

PROPERTY RECOVERED OR PRESERVED FOR AN ASSISTED PERSON

All payments to be made to the assisted person's solicitor

18-04 If there is still a deficiency on an assisted person's account with the Board after credit has been given for any costs recovered from the opponent, and for contributions paid by the assisted person, the Board will look to the proceeds of the litigation.[14]

In order to give effect to this, regulation 87 of the Civil Legal Aid (General) Regulations 1989 provides that, with certain exceptions, all sums which are payable to an assisted person as a result of the proceedings for which a certificate was issued must be paid to the nominated solicitor or, if the assisted person is no longer represented, to the Board, and only the

---

[10] Legal Aid Act 1988, s. 16(9).
[11] Unless the assisted person's resources are redetermined by the Legal Aid Assessment Office, as they may be if there is a change in his financial position as a result of the outcome of the proceedings.
[12] Civil Legal Aid (General) Regulations 1989, reg. 86(2).
[13] *ibid.* reg. 86(1).
[14] Legal Aid Act 1988, s. 16(1).

solicitor or the Board can give a good discharge for such sums.[15] This will be the case even though the certificate has been discharged or revoked as, for the purpose of regulation 87, an assisted person includes someone in respect of whom a certificate has been but is no longer in force.[16] An assisted person's solicitor who has reason to believe that an attempt may be made to circumvent the provisions of regulation 87 has a duty to inform the Board accordingly.[17]

The sums which must be paid to the Board are all moneys payable to an assisted person in connection with the proceedings to which the certificate relates:

(a) by virtue of any agreement or order made in the action, cause or matter to which the certificate relates, whether such agreement was made before or after the proceedings were taken; or

(b) moneys payable in respect of the action, cause or matter to which the certificate relates upon the distribution of property of a person who has been adjudicated bankrupt or has entered into a deed of arrangement, or of a company in liquidation; or

(c) moneys which were paid into court by or on behalf of the assisted person in any proceedings to which the certificate relates which have been ordered to be repaid to the assisted person; or

(d) moneys standing in court to the credit of any proceedings to which the certificate relates.[18]

Regulation 87 is subject to regulations 89 and 94 of the Civil Legal Aid (General)[18] Regulations 1989. Payment of any sum under an order for costs in favour of an assisted person in authorised summary proceedings must be made to the Clerk to the Justices, who is required to pay it to the Board or as the Board directs, and only the Clerk to the Justices is able to give a good discharge for it.[19]

Where any moneys recovered or preserved for an assisted person in proceedings are ordered to be paid into or remain in court and invested for the benefit of the assisted person, the statutory charge attaches only to such part of those moneys as, in the opinion of the Area Director, will be

---

[15] Civil Legal Aid (General) Regulations, 1989, reg 87. Prior to the transfer of administration of the Legal Aid Scheme to the Board, the Law Society expressed the view that it is the duty of an assisted person's solicitor to bring to the notice of a party from whom costs are recoverable that only the solicitor or [the Board] (formerly the Law Society) can give a good discharge for such costs. The standard form notice of discharge draws attention to this point. In authorised summary proceedings any sum payable under an order for costs in favour of an assisted person must be paid to the Clerk to the Justices who must pay it to the Board; only the Clerk can give a good discharge; Civil Legal Aid (General) Regulations 1989, reg. 89(a).

[16] *ibid.* reg. 3-definition of "assisted person".

[17] *ibid.* reg. 87(2).

[18] *ibid.* reg. 87(1).

[19] *ibid.* reg. 89(a).

sufficient to safeguard the rights of the Board.[20] Any balance is not subject to regulation 87 and may be paid to the assisted person. The exemptions[21] are also not subject to regulation 87 and may be paid direct to the assisted person although the prudent solicitor may wish to protect himself and the fund by payment through his hands and to the Board, particularly where there could be any doubt as to the application of the exemption provisions.

How payment is to be made

18–05   A solicitor who receives sums due to an assisted client is permitted, in the course of normal accounting transactions, to retain these in payment or part payment of costs or disbursements due to the solicitor.[22] Subject to this, the duty to pay the Board any money received on behalf of an assisted person is mandatory.[23]

Should a solicitor acting for an assisted person, in breach of this duty, pay to the client money which should have been paid into the Fund and, as a result of the default or omission the Fund incurs a loss, the appropriate area committee may defer payment of all or part of the solicitor's profit costs[24] in connection with the proceedings to which the certificate relates until the solicitor has complied with the Regulations.[25] The effect of this provision is to deny the solicitor payment of any profit costs unless and until he is able to recover the money in question and pay it into the Fund. This may require the solicitor to take steps to recoup the money from the assisted person who may by that stage have disposed of the money, or be reluctant to return it to the solicitor.

The Board may also refer to the Solicitors' Complaint's Bureau the conduct of any solicitor who has failed to comply with the Regulations and, if the solicitor is disciplined, the Board may retain any sum, payment of which has previously been deferred, in accordance with a finding of the Solicitors' Disciplinary Tribunal.[26]

In cases where both damages and costs are due to an assisted person, the damages are usually recovered before the costs can be taxed, either

---

[20] *ibid.* reg. 93. Where this provision applies, the Area Director is required to notify the court in writing of the amount required to safeguard the rights of the Board.

[21] *ibid.* reg. 89(b) and 94.

[22] The solicitor should only take advantage of this provision where he is immediately and without doubt entitled to payment of a certain sum. This will only apply where costs have already been taxed by the court or assessed by the area office or agreed with the assisted person's opponent under Civil Legal Aid (General) Regulations 1989. The position should be confirmed without delay with the area office.

[23] Civil Legal Aid (General) Regulations 1989, reg. 87, unless the Board has made a direction under the proviso referred to above, or the payment is an exemption.

[24] *ibid.* reg. 102(a).

[25] The Regulation specifically refers to profit costs and there is, therefore, no power to defer payment in respect of disbursements or counsel's fees.

[26] Civil Legal Aid (General) Regulations 1989, reg. 102(b).

inter partes or under an order for legal aid taxation.[27] In such cases, it is the normal practice of the Board's area offices to authorise payment of part of the damages to the assisted person against an undertaking signed by the nominated solicitor that the (total) liability of the Fund for costs, disbursements and counsel's fees will not exceed a specified sum. The amount, if any, in respect of which the solicitor gives an undertaking will vary with the circumstances. If, e.g. the client's opponent is an insurance company or some other organisation where it is extremely unlikely that an order for *inter partes* costs will not be satisfied, it may be sufficient for the undertaking to cover the difference between any *inter partes* costs and any additional costs allowed on the legal aid taxation. In giving an undertaking solicitors should, however, bear in mind the possibility of costs which are being claimed *inter partes* being taxed off but allowed on the legal aid taxation, thereby increasing the shortfall for which the assisted person will be liable. If the financial standing of the opponent is uncertain or the amount of the *inter partes* costs payable is unknown, the solicitor should always bear in mind the possibility that *inter partes* costs may in practice not be recovered and in those circumstances the Board is entitled to look to any damages or costs which are subject to the statutory charge.

THE STATUTORY CHARGE

The nature of the charge

Section 16(6) of the 1988 Act provides that: **18–06**

"Except so far as regulations otherwise provide[28]
(a) any sums remaining unpaid on account of a person's contribution[29] in respect of the sums payable by the Board in respect of any proceedings; and
(b) a sum equal to any deficiency by reason of his total contribution being less than the net liability of the Board on his account, shall be a first charge for the benefit of the Board on any property which is recovered or preserved for him in the proceedings."

For the purpose of section 16(6) the net liability of the Board on an assisted person's account in relation to any proceedings means the aggregate of the sums paid or payable by the Board on the assisted person's

---

[27] For legal aid taxation generally see Chap. 20.
[28] Civil Legal Aid (General) Regulations 1989, reg. 94.
[29] A charge will be created even though the assisted person has a nil contribution: *R.v. Judge Fraser Harrison ex parte* Law Society [1955] 1 Q.B. 287, D.C.

account in respect of those proceedings to any legal representative[30] and any sums paid or payable for any advice or assistance (under the Green Form Scheme) in connection with those proceedings or any matter to which those proceedings relate, less any amount recovered by the Board by virtue of an order or agreement for costs made in the assisted person's favour with respect to those proceedings or by virtue of any right of his to be indemnified against expenses incurred by him in connection with those proceedings.[31]

The wording of section 16(6) of the 1988 Act is based on that relating to a solicitor's right to seek a charging order under section 73 of the Solicitors' Act 1974, and the authorities under that section are relevant in considering the interpretation of section 16(6).[32] There are, however, two important distinctions. One is that under the Solicitors' Act 1974 no charge comes into existence until the court makes an order, though it may then relate back to the recovery and preservation of the property[33]; the other is that the charge under the 1988 Act is restricted to property recovered or preserved for the assisted person in the proceedings to which the certificate related, whereas section 73 of the Solicitors' Act 1974 is wider and refers to any property which is recovered or preserved through the solicitor's instrumentality.[34]

18–07   A charge of this type has been a feature of the modern legal aid system since it was established by the Legal Aid Act 1949. The underlying principle of the charge is to put the assisted person as far as possible in the same position in relation to proceedings as an unassisted person, who is responsible at the end of the proceedings to pay whatever legal costs are not being paid by the other side. The statutory charge, therefore, generally applies where a solicitor would have a lien or charge over property recovered or preserved for a private client.

Thus, when an assisted person is wholly or partly successful in the proceedings covered by the certificate, the statutory charge converts legal aid from a gift into a loan.[35] Not only does the charge prevent the assisted person from making a profit at the expense of the Fund, and thereby the

---

[30] "Legal representative" means an authorised advocate or authorised litigator, as defined by the Courts and Legal Services Act 1990, s. 119(1); Legal Aid Act 1988, s. 43.

[31] Legal Aid Act 1988, s. 16(9). As to rights of indemnity see *ibid.* s. 40.

[32] See *Till v. Till* [1974] Q.B. 558, C.A. at 567 where Denning, M.R. said he had no doubt that the words "recovered or preserved" in the Legal Aid Act 1974, s. 9(6) which have been repeated with minor changes in the Legal Aid Act 1988, s. 16(6) had the same meaning as in the Solicitors' Act 1974.

[33] See *Cordery on Solicitors* (8th ed. 1988).

[34] An order may be made under the Solicitors Act 1974, s. 73 although the client has no interest in the property; *Bailey v. Birchall* (1965), II Hemm. & M. 371. This cannot be so under the Legal Aid Act 1988, s. 16(6) but for the position where an attempt is made to defeat the charge by diverting the proceeds of litigation to a third party; see para 18–35.

[35] See comments by Denning M.R. in *Davies v. Eli Lilly & Co* [1987] 3 All E.R. 94 at 97–98 and in *Watkinson v. The Legal Aid Board* [1991] 2 All E.R. 953.

taxpayer, but it is also a deterrent against running up costs unreasonably in so far as they are not borne out of any contribution payable by the assisted person.

Broadly, the charge ensures that the costs of an assisted person are borne as follows:

Costs paid by other side	equal to or greater than	costs paid or payable out of fund	no charge
Costs paid by other side	less than	costs paid or payable out of fund	calculate assisted person's contribution
Costs paid by other side plus assisted person's contribution	equal to or greater than	costs paid or payable out of fund	no charge
Costs paid by other side plus assisted person's contribution	less than	costs paid or payable out of fund	possible charge in respect of balance
No costs paid by the other side	nil contribution and exemption from charge *or* nil contribution and no recovery or preservation	legal aid fund bears all the assisted person's costs	

The charge which arises under the 1988 Act is expressed to be a first charge, the only exception being a bona fide purchaser for value without notice who takes a conveyance of the property.[36] In practice, where there is an existing charge, the Board treats the statutory charge as applying to the equity of redemption only. If, however, the chargee had benefited from the litigation the Board would doubtless seek to recoup any deficiency on the assisted person's account in priority to that benefit.[37]

---

[36] Legal Aid Act 1988, s. 16(6). Civil Legal Aid (General) Regulations 1989, reg. 95(4) provides: "Without prejudice to the provisions of the Land Registration Act 1925 and the Land Charges Act 1972, all conveyances and acts done to defeat, or operating to defeat, any such charge shall, except in the case of a bona fide purchaser for value without notice, be void as against the Board."

[37] See *Scholey v. Peck* [1893] 1 Ch. 709, and the notes in the *Supreme Court Practice* on solicitors' liens and charging orders under the subtitle "priorities".

What property is subject to the charge?

18–08 The terms of section 16(6) of the 1988 Act are very wide and refer to any property which is recovered or preserved for the assisted person in the proceedings. All forms of real and personal property, damages and other sums recovered or preserved would be included.[38] It is immaterial what the nature of the property is and where it is situated and property within the charge includes the rights of a person under any compromise or settlement arrived at to avoid the proceedings or to bring them to an end.[39]

It also includes any sums recovered by virtue of an order for costs made in the assisted person's favour in the proceedings which are not already payable[40] to the Board.[41] These may, *e.g.* include costs awarded in the Court of Appeal to a litigant who is assisted there but who was unassisted and unsuccessful in the court below; the order carrying the costs of the court of first instance as well as those in the Court of Appeal.

The fact that a payment made to an assisted person is expressed to be made *ex gratia* or without admission of liability will not of itself prevent it from being subject to the charge. Since the reference in section 16(7) of the 1988 Act to property recovered or preserved for an assisted person includes that person's rights under any compromise arrived at to avoid proceedings or bring them to an end, a payment which is made as part of a settlement, albeit with a denial of liability and on condition that the assisted person discontinues the action and submits to judgment, will be subject to the charge. But if a defendant were to insist that an assisted person should discontinue or submit unconditionally to judgment and then later offered the assisted person money or other property *ex gratia*, the charge would not apply.[42]

The test is whether the property is recovered or preserved as part of the compromise but the Board will, in all cases, need to be satisfied that the payment was not made as a result of an agreement between the parties to evade the operation of the statutory charge.[43]

---

[38] Property includes money; *The Law Society v. Rushman* [1955] 1 W.L.R. 681, C.A.

[39] Legal Aid Act 1988, s. 16(7).

[40] By virtue of *ibid.* s. 16(5).

[41] *ibid.* s. 16(7).

[42] Nor would the provisions of the Civil Legal Aid (General) Regulations 1989, reg. 87 as to payment to the assisted person's solicitor. The Area Director should, however, be informed as it might be necessary to redetermine the assisted person's means. The Board will also wish to be satisfied that any arrangement made between the parties is not, in effect, a compromise of the proceedings, as it would be if the agreement were made before the proceedings were concluded, or indeed an attempt by the assisted person to evade the charge.

[43] As to evasion of the charge generally, see paras. 18–35 and 18–63.

Property excluded from the charge

The Civil Legal Aid (General) Regulations 1989 exclude four classes of **18–09**
property from the charge[44]:
    (a) The exemptions (protected payments)—these are discussed later.[45]
    (b) Certain money in court—where an order is made that any sums which have been recovered or preserved for an assisted person in any proceedings are to be paid into or remain in court and are to be invested for the assisted person's benefit, the charge will attach only to that part of those moneys as, in the Area Director's opinion and communicated in writing to the court, will be sufficient to safeguard the rights of the Board.[46]
    (c) The costs of a legal aid taxation and costs in connection with challenging certain taxations. Where an assisted person has a financial interest in the taxation that person is not required to make any contribution to the Fund on account of the costs of the taxation proceedings, and the charge created by section 16(6) of the 1988 Act does not apply in relation to any resulting increase in the net liability of the Fund arising out of the cost of the taxation proceedings. The costs of taxation should, therefore, be shown separately in the solicitor's bill and liability for those costs, save where they are recovered *inter partes*, is borne by the Fund.[47] A similar protection against liability by way of contribution or under the statutory charge is provided to an assisted person in respect of the costs of carrying in objections under regulation 113 of the Civil Legal Aid (General) Regulations 1989 or applying to a judge to review a taxation under regulation 114 of those Regulations.[48]
    (d) Pre-certificate costs—the operation of the charge may have to be modified when a solicitor has acted for an assisted person before legal aid is granted or where the solicitor has a lien over documents needed for the proceedings.[49]

When does the charge apply?

The basic requirements for the charge to apply are as follows: **18–10**
    (a) there must be arrears of contribution or a net deficiency on the account of the assisted person with the Board;

---

[44] Legal Aid Act 1988, s. 16(6) creates a charge except in so far as Regulations provide otherwise.
[45] See Chap. 3.
[46] Civil Legal Aid (General) Regulation 1989, reg. 93.
[47] *ibid.* reg. 119(2).
[48] *ibid.* reg. 118 — where the assisted person has no interest in the outcome of the taxation, or would, but for the provisions of that regulation have an adverse interest to that of the nominated solicitor.
[49] See Chap. 20.

(b) property must have been recovered or preserved for the assisted person in the proceedings; and

(c) there must be nothing in the Civil Legal Aid (General) Regulations 1989 exempting the charge.

If any of the three criteria above do not apply, the charge does not arise.

The general approach which should be adopted in considering whether the charge arises should be to look at the reality of the situation, not the legal labels which the parties seek to apply to a given set of facts.[50]

Is there a net deficiency?

18–11 The way the amount of the charge is calculated is covered in detail below.[51] In deciding whether the charge applies, it is simply necessary to determine whether there is some deficiency on the assisted person's account with the Board, however small. It is necessary to calculate:

(a) the total debit on the assisted person's account—this is the total of the costs payable out of the Fund (less the cost of any taxation proceedings),[52] together with any Green Form or ABWOR costs in connection with the proceedings to which the certificate relates[53];

(b) the total credit on the account—this is the total contribution actually paid by the assisted person under the certificate plus the total costs *actually* recovered for the Fund from the assisted person's opponent.[54]

If the total credit equals or exceeds the total debit, the charge does not arise, and the Board will refund any excess contribution to the assisted person.[55] It is important to bear in mind:

(a) that it is impossible to calculate the exact net deficiency until the total costs under the client's certificate have been finalised, either by taxation by the court, assessment by the area office or an undertaking from the assisted person's solicitor—no decision can be made about this aspect of the charge if a further bill may be submitted by the solicitor under the certificate;

(b) although in the vast majority of cases it is only necessary for the Board to calculate the net deficiency on one certificate, there are some circumstances, particularly matrimonial proceedings and multi-party actions, where more than one certificate must be taken

---

[50] For examples of this approach, see *Manley v. The Law Society* [1981] 1 W.L.R. 325; *Stewart v. The Law Society* [1987] 1 F.L.R. 222; and *Watkinson v. Legal Aid Board* [1991] 1 W.L.R. 419.

[51] See para. 18–36.

[52] Civil Legal Aid (General) Regulations, 1989, reg. 119 (2).

[53] Legal Aid Act 1988, s. 16(9).

[54] *ibid.* s. 16(9).

[55] *ibid.* s. 16(4).

into account—this is because in such cases the assisted person's account with the Board is not represented by a single certificate.[56]

(c) the charge applies to the lesser of (i) the deficiency on the assisted person's account and (ii) the amount recovered or preserved (after taking into account any £2,500 exemption).

Meaning of "recovered or preserved"

Property is "recovered" if the assisted person successfully obtains property that is at the end of the proceedings there is a gain for the assisted person.[57]   **18–12**

Property is "preserved" if the assisted person successfully fends off a claim by someone else to his or her property, that is at the end of the proceedings the assisted person keeps all or part of what that person regards as his or her own.[58]

The charge may arise even if the assisted person is only partially successful. Where, e.g. an assisted person who seeks an outright transfer of property recovers only a part of or a beneficial interest in that property, or a share in the proceeds of sale of that property, the charge applies to whatever is recovered. Similarly, an assisted person who is granted legal aid to defend a claim against his or her property may lose part of it but manage to hold on to part of what was being claimed. Even though the assisted person ends off in a worse position than before the proceedings began, the charge applies to that part of the property preserved from the opponents's attack.[59]

Even where there is no issue as to title there may be a preservation where someone else's claim to possession is defeated or where the assisted person avoids an order for sale of the property.

It may be difficult to determine in certain cases whether property has been recovered or preserved where there are several items of property in issue and a party has both gains and losses. This situation is dealt with in more detail below.[60]

Judicial guidance on recovery and preservation

The most authoritative guidance on many aspects of the law relating to the statutory charge is that contained in the judgments of the House of Lords in the case of *Hanlon v. The Law Society*.[61] At page 214 Lord Scarman said: **18–13**
"... it is not difficult to construe 'property recovered' as property

---

[56] See para. 18–60.
[57] See *Hanlon v. The Law Society* [1980] 2 All E.R. 199 at 214–215 and dicta from *Curling v. The Law Society* [1985] 1 W.L.R. 470.
[58] See *Hanlon op. cit.* at 215.
[59] This follows from *Till v. Till* [1974] Q.B. 558 and earlier authorities on the Solicitors' Acts.
[60] See paras. 18–35 and 18–63.
[61] [1980] 2 All E.R. 199.

obtained." Authorities under the Solicitors' Acts 1934–1974 on the meaning of recovery and preservation are also useful but not necessarily directly applicable to the statutory charge. Note that at page 209 of *Hanlon*, Lord Simon suggested that the generous construction by the courts of the solicitor's charge in favour of the solicitor may not apply to a charge for a social service.

The clearest judicial statement of the meaning of recovery or preservation was set out in the case of *Foxon v. Gascoigne*[62] which was approved in *Till v. Till*[63] and *Hanlon*:

> ". . . where the Plaintiff claims property, and establishes a right to the ownership of the property in some shape or other, there the property has been recovered . . . Where a Defendant's right to the ownership of property is disputed and that right has been vindicated by the proceedings, there the property has been preserved."

However, the title of a party in proceedings is not important. In some cases a plaintiff or petitioner may preserve property; in others a defendant or respondent may recover property.

Property must be "in issue"

18–14 The charge cannot arise if the property recovered or preserved was never in issue in the proceedings. The property must be the subject-matter of the proceedings for which legal aid was granted.

In *Hanlon*, Lord Simon said at page 206:

> "In other words, property has been recovered or preserved if it has been in issue in the proceedings: recovered by the claimant if it has been subject to the successful claim, preserved by the respondent if the claim fails. In either case it is a question of fact, not of theoretical 'risk'. In property adjustment proceedings, in my view, it is only property the ownership or transfer of which has been in issue which has been 'recovered or preserved' so as to be the subject of a legal aid charge. What has been in issue is to be collected as a matter of fact from pleadings, evidence, judgment and/or order. I can see no reason for extending the words to items of property the ownership or possession of which has never been questioned."

Further, Lord Scarman said at page 214: "A person recovers or preserves in legal proceedings only what is in issue between the parties; and one discovers what is in issue by looking at the pleadings and the evidence."

18–15 To decide what property is in issue it is necessary to look carefully at the

---

[62] [1874] 9 Ch. App. 654 at 657.
[63] [1974] Q.B. 558.

papers. The starting point is to look at what has been recovered or preserved for the assisted person at the end of the case and then to see whether that property was ever disputed by the other side. The most important documents to consider are usually:

(a) the pleadings including in matrimonial cases, the petition and respondent's answer;

(b) affidavits as to ancillary relief, which often explain more clearly the pleadings and what each side is hoping to obtain from the litigation;

(c) correspondence setting out rival claims, in particular the first letters between the parties which often show the initial stance of the parties, and any open "without prejudice" offers.

Property can be put in issue at any time and, in deciding whether an assisted person has preserved property within the meaning of section 16(6) of the 1988 Act, it is necessary to look at what the worst result would have been for the assisted person had he or she conceded all that the opponent was claiming and then see if that situation has been improved upon. For example, if an opponent during proceedings claims to be entitled to certain property which was not previously in issue but subsequently abandons the claim, the property will have been preserved and the statutory charge will apply.

If one party claims certain property and the other party is silent as to that claim, it will usually be right to conclude that the property was in issue in the proceedings and the statutory charge applies, unless the facts show that the opponent has at all times conceded the assisted person's right to that property.

Similarly, the mere fact that an assisted person's opponent offers a certain **18–16** item of property to the assisted person does not necessarily imply that that property is not in issue. A party may claim the whole of certain property but be prepared to offer, openly or without prejudice, that the property be divided. The whole property remains in issue unless there is a concession, as a matter of prior entitlement, that the other party is entitled to a particular share of it.[64]

Conversely, the fact that a party's assets are at risk as a result of litigation does not of itself mean that they are in issue. If a legally assisted defendant successfully defends a damages claim, the statutory charge will not apply to the assets which the assisted person had available to meet that claim, even if the plaintiff only brought the claim because he knew the assisted person had certain assets.[65] However, if an assisted person's assets are specifically claimed in an action, where, e.g. the plaintiff claims to be

---

[64] See Lord Scarman in *Hanlon op. cit.* at p. 214.
[65] This would arise in respect of assets out of which an assisted person is not required to make any capital contribution, e.g. the value of his or her dwelling house and the first £3,000 of disposable capital.

307

entitled to a specific fund of money such as the contents of a building society account, the charge would apply if the legally assisted defendant successfully opposed the claim.[66]

A party may put property in issue regardless of the strength of his or her claim to that property. For example, a husband might, for tactical or bargaining reasons, claim entitlement to the entire matrimonial home, even if, on the facts, the best the husband could possibly hope for would be a half share; in such a case any interest in the home retained by the wife would be subject to the charge. Practitioners who are acting for an opponent of an assisted person should always, therefore, bear in mind when advising their client that the making of an unrealistic claim may make an action difficult to settle without an agreement to pay full costs to the assisted person so as to avoid any liability imposed by virtue of the statutory charge.

Property recovered under a compromise or settlement

18–17 Property within the charge includes the rights of a person under any compromise or settlement arrived at to avoid the proceedings or bring them to an end.[67] It follows that property recovered or preserved as a result of such a compromise or settlement can still be subject to the charge whether or not it was in issue in the proceedings.[68] Further, the charge will also apply if there is a compromise or settlement after a certificate has been issued but before proceedings are commenced.[69] Section 16(7) of the Legal Aid Act 1988 and the *Van Hoorn* case are intended to ensure that the charge cannot be avoided where, under a compromise, the assisted person receives something in substitution for the property in issue.

When proceedings are settled, the full terms of the settlement do not always appear in the final order and may be set out in a separate agreement or correspondence which will have to be considered before a decision can be made as to whether the charge applies.

It also sometimes happens that parties agree terms and then subsequently, expressly or informally, agree to an alternative course of action. For example, a court order may require a house to be sold and the proceeds divided between the parties; thereafter one party may instead agree to buy out the other. Practitioners should take care to ensure that any departure from the terms of an order are not such as to constitute an attempt to evade the operation of the statutory charge. If the appropriate area office considers that the circumstances are suspicious, the assisted person's solicitor may be asked to explain how and why the new agreement came to be reached and

---

[66] For property affected by interlocutory orders, see para. 18–23.
[67] Legal Aid Act 1988, s. 16(7).
[68] *Van Hoorn v. The Law Society* [1985] Q.B. 106.
[69] *ibid.* at 109.

the area office may insist that the parties return to court for a new order. Provided that there has not been any attempt to evade[70] the charge, it is the actual final agreement between the parties which determines the existence and scope of the charge and not any earlier superseded agreement.

Where possession of property is in issue

The statutory charge can apply to property, the possession of which was in **18–18** issue, even if ownership of the property was never in dispute. In the case of *Curling v. The Law Society*[71] there was no dispute as to the legally assisted wife's entitlement to a half share in the matrimonial home. The wife sought an order for immediate sale, but the husband sought a *Mesher*[72] Order to the effect that the property should not be sold and he should be allowed to remain in it for a certain period of time. Eventually the parties agreed that the husband would buy out the wife's half share in the property at market value. The wife accordingly succeeded in recovering her half share without delay as she had sought. The Court of Appeal held that recovery of possession of the wife's half share at that time amounted to "property recovered" and the charge applied. Neil J. stated[73]:

> "... the fact that a party to legal proceedings recovers in the proceedings that to which he or she in law is already entitled cannot by itself prevent the attachment of the statutory charge ... in my opinion the recovery of possession of property may constitute the recovery of property within section 9(6),[74] just as the defeat of a claim by another party to a possessory interest in property may constitute the preservation of property."

Oliver J.[75] explained the principle further:

> "Where, even though the title may not be in issue, the proceedings are necessary in order to reduce it into or restore it to the possession of the owner, it seems that, quite literally, the property has been 'recovered'. For instance a landlord seeking to forefeit a lease or a landowner seeking to evict a squatter who claims no title but merely refuses to move is pursuing property the title to which is not in issue. But I find it unarguable that the property reduced to possession by the judgment has not been 'recovered' by the proceedings. Equally, if a trustee for sale wrongly refuses to concur in selling so that proceedings

---

[70] See paras. 18–35 and 18–63.
[71] [1985] 1 All E.R. 705; [1985] 1 W.L.R. 470.
[72] *Mesher* [1985] 1 All E.R. 705.
[73] [1985] 1 All E.R. 705 at 711; [1985] 1 W.L.R. 470.
[74] Of the Legal Aid Act 1974, now s. 16(6) of the Legal Aid Act 1988.
[75] [1985] 1 All E.R. 705 at 715.

are necessary under section 30 of the Law of Property Act 1925 to compel a sale and the distribution of the proceeds, I would have thought it quite clear that, as a result of the proceedings, the beneficiary had 'recovered' his share. It seems to be entirely inappropriate and irrelevant in such a case to seek to assess the increment to the plaintiff of the value of his interest. He has, quite literally recovered (*i.e.* got into his hands) property which he would not have in his hands had it not been for the proceedings."

The following points arise from the Court of Appeal's decision in the *Curling* case:

(a) Where possession is recovered, the charge nevertheless applies to the whole value of the property recovered, not just to the value to the assisted person of obtaining possession at an earlier date.[76]

(b) Where possession is recovered or preserved, the charge cannot in practice apply unless the person gaining or keeping possession also owns the asset. In the example given above, had the squatter managed to avoid a possession order, he or she would have preserved possession but would have no chargeable property.

Preservation of possession

18–19 It used to be thought that the principles of *Curling* did not apply in reverse, *eg.* where an assisted person is seeking to avoid a sale of his or her property and succeeds in obtaining an order avoiding or delaying such sale. The case of *Parkes v. Legal Aid Board*[77] has established that the charge applies in all cases where possession is either recovered or preserved, although, at the time of writing, an appeal to the Court of Appeal was pending. The facts were that Miss Parkes and Mr Bradbury had a relationship and child before Mr Bradbury left and issued an application under section 30 of the Law of Property Act 1925 seeking an order for sale of the property in which Miss Parkes and the child still lived. Miss Parkes wished to remain in the property and so contested the application and ultimately there was a consent order under which a *Mesher* Order was made so that the property would be sold when the child reached seventeen, ceased full time education, died, or Miss Parkes remarried or cohabited. On the sale, proceeds would be divided equally. The court found that there was no dispute as to each party's beneficial interest. The finding of fact about whether the first £3,800 of the proceeds was in issue should not be regarded as a precedent for any other cases.

The court held that the principles of *Curling* apply equally to recovery or

---

[76] See comments of Oliver J., above.
[77] *Parkes v. Legal Aid Board, The Times,* 4 May 1994.

preservation of possession and the charge attached to Miss Parkes' share in the property. She had preserved her share by avoiding an order for sale. Note, however, that the effect of applying the charge in section 30 cases is not as harsh as it used to be as the power to postpone enforcement of the charge has been made available.

The effects of *Curling* and *Parkes* apply to many other categories of case:

(a) Mortgage possession actions. The charge will apply where an assisted person avoids an order for immediate possession.

(b) Landlord and tenant cases. A tenant who avoids loss of possession may be subject to the charge if he has any interest which is chargeable. A personal statutory right to remain in property is not chargeable but a formal contractual tenancy may be and the appropriate method of protecting the charge could be by surrender of any leasehold documents.

(c) Enforcement proceedings may give rise to the preservation of possession of property. For example, if a legally aided debtor is opposing a charging order or garnishee proceedings against his or her bank account, the charge will apply if a settlement is reached under which the charging order or garnishee order is not enforced.

Nature of property recovered

The charge applies regardless of the nature of the property recovered or preserved or where it is situated.[78] It applies to anything of value, including: **18–20**

(a) money, whether a lump sum or damages, liquidated or unliquidated;

(b) objects such as jewellery, paintings or livestock;

(c) intangible and financial assets such as stocks and shares, cheques and bills of exchange, insurance policies and debts owed;

(d) land or interests in land, including legal leases; or

(e) foreign land or other property abroad.[79]

Contingent recovery and Mesher Orders

In matrimonial proceedings it is sometimes ordered that a party will receive property at some time in the future or on the happening of a future event, *e.g.*, a *Mesher* Order where the court allows one party to remain in the matrimonial home until the children reach a certain age or cease full-time education, whereupon the property is to be sold and the proceeds divided. In such cases: **18–21**

---

[78] s. 16(7) Legal Aid Act 1988,

[79] The difficulty with unusual or foreign property is not whether the charge arises but how the Board can register enforce its charge; see para. 18–97.

(a) the statutory charge arises at once (and is valued at the date of the order) in respect of an assisted person who is allowed to remain in the former matrimonial home, where that person has recovered or preserved possession of the home[80];

(b) an assisted person who is prevented by the court order from living in the home has not recovered or preserved anything for the purpose of the statutory charge at the time of the order and the charge will only apply and be valued when the property comes to be sold.[81]

Charge on money in court

18–22 If money is paid into court during a case and that money is subsequently paid out to the paying party's legally aided opponent, either by an acceptance of an offer or under a court order, the assisted person who receives payment has recovered property and the charge applies.

If, however, an assisted person pays money into court, either as an offer of settlement or under a court order, and the assisted person is then allowed to take the money back out of court at the end of the case, the charge will not generally apply to that money. This follows from authorities confirming the solicitor's lien[82] which established that the payment of money into court does not put that money in issue, even though it does put the money at risk.

The position would, however, be different if money which an assisted person had paid into court had been ordered to be paid from an identified source which was already in issue in the proceedings; in that case on payment out to the assisted person the sum would have been preserved and the charge would apply.

Where property which has already been recovered or preserved is ordered to be paid into or remain in court[83] the appropriate area office must notify the court of the amount of money sufficient to safeguard the rights of the Board[84] and the charge will then only apply to the amount specified. This will be an estimate of the maximum amount of the charge.[85] Note that

---

[80] *Parkes v. Legal Aid Board, The Times,* 4 May 1994 although at the time of writing an appeal to the Court of Appeal was pending.

[81] The Board will, however, wish to protect the potential charge by registration under reg. 95 of the Civil Legal Aid (General) Regulations 1989. For the position regarding enforcement of the charge and the payment of interest in such cases see para. 18–75 *et seq.*

[82] See in particular *Wadsworth Rhodes v. Sugden* [1886] 29 C.L.D. 517. For a discussion of the operation of the statutory charge on money in court see *Keith Ian McKay v. Legal Aid Board,* Gage J., June 16, 1995, unreported. In the particular case, decided on its facts, the statutory charge applied.

[83] This is common where the assisted person is a child or a patient.

[84] This will be an estimate of the maximum amount of the statutory charge.

[85] Civil Legal Aid (General) Regulations 1989, reg. 93.

payment out should only be made to the assisted person's solicitor or, if he is no longer represented, to the Board, *i.e.* so as to obtain a good discharge.

Interlocutory orders and Mareva injunctions

Sometimes assets which are not directly in issue in proceedings are nevertheless affected by injunctions and other orders made by the court during the proceedings.

18–23

If a Mareva[86] injunction, freezing and preventing dealing in the assets of a debtor or potential debtor, is made before the debtor applies for legal aid, the assets frozen by the order would not be taken into account in the assessment of the debtor's means for legal aid purposes. Those assets would be regarded as not being available to the assisted person and not, therefore, "disposable". The question then arises as to whether the statutory charge applies if such assets are unfrozen part way through the proceedings and the assisted person thereby gains access to them.[87]

The general position is that a Mareva or similar injunction does not put property in issue for the purposes of the charge. None of the judgments in *Hanlon* suggest that interlocutory orders determine what is in issue.[88] Subject to what is said below, where assets are unfrozen during proceedings, the proper course is for the assisted person's solicitor to advise the appropriate area office so that the assisted person's means can be reassessed.[89] This may well lead to a recoupment from the assisted person of the costs paid out by the Board (*i.e.* by way of (increased) contribution) and the discharge of his or her certificate.

However, there may be cases where the statutory charge will arise on the lifting of an interlocutory order. Examples are where:

(a) the asset which was subject to the interlocutory order was itself in issue in the proceedings. In those circumstances it would not be possible to ascertain finally whether the charge applied until the proceedings were concluded, because only at that stage would it be known if the assisted person had preserved both possession and ownership.[90]

(b) There may be cases where the interlocutory issues are a major source of dispute between the parties and at the end of the case one party manages to retain an asset which might have been lost to him or her during the proceedings. In such a case, applying the

---

[86] *Mareva Compania Naviera SA v. International Bulk Carries SA "The Mareva"* [1980] 1 All E.R. 213.
[87] For the assessment of an applicant's means generally, see Chap. 6.
[88] [1980] 2 All E.R. 199 at 209 and 214.
[89] Civil Legal Aid (General) Regulations 1989, reg. 52.
[90] See para. 18–32.

approach in *Curling*, the statutory charge would arise on the basis that the assisted person had kept hold of and preserved his or her property.

Charge over orders for costs

18–24   Where an order for costs is made in favour of an assisted person, those costs must be paid into the Fund[91] and no question of the statutory charge arises. This is because those costs belong to the Board and are not recovered for the assisted person.[92] Where sums are recovered under an order for costs, which relates to a period before legal aid is granted or after the certificate is discharged or revoked so that the costs would benefit the assisted person rather than the Board, those costs are subject to the statutory charge.[93] In such cases the costs may need to be apportioned between the Board and the solicitors.[94]

The charge will also apply to an order for costs out of the fund under section 18 of the 1988 Act in favour of a successful unassisted party who was in receipt of legal aid at some stage. If A is assisted throughout the proceedings but B initially defends the proceedings privately and subsequently becomes an assisted person, B, if successful, may be entitled to an order that his or her pre-certificate costs be paid out of the Fund under section 18. The statutory charge would, however, apply to those costs[95] and this might mean that B would benefit very little from the order.[96]

Recovery outside the certificate

18–25   The charge cannot apply to property already recovered or preserved before the certificate was issued. If, however, there was an order or agreement providing for recovery or preservation and legal aid is granted to enforce or give effect to that order or agreement, the charge would apply.

If property is recovered or preserved while a certificate is in force in relation to the proceedings, but the recovery or preservation takes place in an aspect of the proceedings not covered by the certificate, the property will still be subject to the charge. This is because the recovery takes place in the proceedings to which the certificate related.[97]

---

[91] Legal Aid Act 1988, s. 16(5).
[92] See *Debtor v. The Law Society, The Times,* February 21, 1981.
[93] Legal Aid Act 1989, s. 16(7). This is so after discharge or revocation of a certificate: Civil Legal Aid (General) Regulations 1989, reg. 85.
[94] Civil Legal Aid (General) Regulations 1989, reg. 103.
[95] By virtue of Legal Aid Act 1988, s. 16(7).
[96] See *Re H* [1992] 3 All E.R. 380; Refer to *O'Sullivan v. Herdmans Ltd. (No. 2) [1988] 1 W.L.R. 1973, H.L.*
[97] See *Hanlon v. Law Society* [1980], 2 All E.R. 199 where the House of Lords made it clear that proceedings a matrimonial cases means the whole proceedings i.e. action, cause or matter.

Where a certificate has been revoked or discharged, the charge applies to any property recovered or preserved as a result of the former assisted persons continuing to take, defend or be a party to the proceedings to which the certificate related.[98] This is so even if that person obtains a second certificate in the same proceedings.[99]

Where a certificate has been discharged owing to death or bankruptcy of the assisted person, the charge applies to property recovered or preserved by his personal representatives, his trustee in bankruptcy or the Official Receiver.[1]

Where property is recovered or preserved after discharge or revocation, but in the part of the proceedings which would not have been covered by the certificate had it remained in force, the charge will still apply. Regulation 85 of the Civil Legal Aid (General) Regulations 1989 extends the charge to "any property recovered or preserved as a result of the person whose certificate has been revoked or discharged continuing to take, defend or be a party to the proceedings to which the certificate related." The Board construes the words "the proceedings to which the certificate related" as covering the entirety of the proceedings and not just the part covered by the certificate.

Relationship between the statutory charge and the subject matter of the dispute

When income and capital are assessed for legal aid purposes, the value of the "subject matter of the dispute in respect of which the legal aid application has been made" is disregarded.[2]   **18–26**

It follows that if a person who applies for legal aid is defending a claim to an asset in his possession, the value of that asset is not taken into account in determining that person's financial eligibility. However, should that person be given legal aid and successfully defend the opponent's claim to that asset, the statutory charge will apply to the value of the asset as property preserved. For all practical purposes the term "subject matter of the dispute" means the same as being in issue in the proceedings for the purpose of the charge.[3]

Furthermore, if an assisted person acquires an asset at the end of the proceedings but contends that the charge does not apply because the asset was never in issue in the proceedings, the Board will wish to consider the way in which the asset was treated when the assisted person's financial resources were assessed. If at the time of the assessment the assisted person

---

[98] Civil Legal Aid (General) Regulations 1983, reg. 85(1).
[99] See also Chap. 40 regarding multi-party actions.
[1] Civil Legal Aid (General) Regulation 1989, reg. 85(2).
[2] Civil Legal Aid (Assessment of Resources) Regulations 1989, reg. 5 and see Chap. 6.
[3] This approach was supported by Lord Simon in *Hanlon v. The Law Society* [1980] 2 All E.R. 199 at 209. See also *Till v. Till* [1974] 1 1974 Q.B. 558 All E.R. 1096 at 1102.

argued that the asset should be disregarded in the assessment as being the subject matter of the dispute it will be difficult for the assisted person later to say that the statutory charge does not apply to that asset. Alternatively, if, on the facts of the case, the asset never was in issue and was wrongly regarded as being the subject matter of the dispute, the charge would not apply but a further reassessment of the assisted person's means might well be appropriate.[4]

Recovery must be for the assisted person

18–27 Section 16(6) of the 1988 Act provides:

"Except so far as regulations otherwise provide—

(a) any sums remaining unpaid on account of a person's contribution in respect of the sums payable by the Board in respect of any proceedings; and

(b) a sum equal to any deficiency by reason of his total contribution being less than the net liability of the Board on his account,

shall be a first charge for the benefit of the Board on any property which is recovered or preserved for him in the proceedings."

It follows that the charge can only apply to a person who benefits from the proceedings. In the vast majority of cases the final order or agreement in the action will provide for any property or damages which are recovered to be paid to the assisted person. In those circumstances no difficulties arise. If, however, the order or agreement on its face provides for someone other than the assisted person to benefit, the charge may still apply depending on the circumstances.

Where property is recovered or preserved by both the assisted person and a third party and the amount recovered by the assisted person is sufficient to cover the deficiency, this will generally be accepted by the Board and the property recovered or preserved by the third party will be ignored, unless there are problems concerning enforcement of the charge against the assisted person.[5]

If, however, the assisted person recovers little or nothing under the order or agreement and all the property or money is to go to a third party, the Board will wish to investigate the full circumstances leading up to the making of the order or agreement. The general approach which the Board adopts is to look at the reality of what has happened and to see whether the assisted person has benefitted even though the order is nominally in favour of another person. Property recovered for the assisted person's

---

[4] See Chap. 6.
[5] See para. 18–33.

benefit is recovered "for him" within the meaning of those words in section 16(6) of the 1988 Act.[6]

Set out below are some of the circumstances in which the Board will regard the recovery or preservation as being for the assisted person so as to give rise to operation of the statutory charge.

Payment to trustees and representatives

Where legal aid is applied for in a representative, fiduciary or official **18–28** capacity, the applicant is only nominally bringing the proceedings. An example is where a trustee of a fund defends a claim to that fund on behalf of the beneficiaries. The means of the trustee personally will not be assessed; instead the means of the beneficiaries will be assessed and the value of any property or estate or the amount of any fund out of which the applicant is entitled to be indemnified will be taken into account.[7] In such cases the beneficiaries could be said to be the true assisted persons as they are the persons in respect of whom a contribution has been assessed within the meaning of section 16(6) of the 1988 Act and the charge will apply to any property ordered to be paid or reclaimed by the trustee.

Claims brought or defended by minors or patients do not require a certificate in the name of the trustee or representative. An application for legal aid for a minor or patient is made by a person of full age and capacity who will normally be the next friend or guardian *ad litem* of the minor or patient.[8] In such cases the certificate will be in the name of the minor or patient and the charge will apply to property recovered or preserved for the minor or patient, even if there are restrictions on how the property may be used.[9]

Payment to creditors or friends of the assisted person

It sometimes happens, particularly in matrimonial proceedings, that orders **18–29** are made which provide for a variety of payments to be made to third parties out of property recovered or preserved or the proceeds of sale of a former matrimonial home. The purpose is often to ensure that existing debts of the marriage are paid off and the parties can make a fresh start. The general rule which the Board adopts is that property ordered to be paid direct to a creditor of an assisted person is, nevertheless, property recovered

---

[6] See *Manley v. The Law Society* [1981] 1 W.L.R. 335; *Stewart v. The Law Society* [1987] 1 F.L.R. 223; *Watkinson v. Legal Aid Board* [1991] 2 All E.R. 953. See also paras. 18–35 and 18–63 regarding evasion of the statutory charge.

[7] Civil Legal Aid (General) Regulations 1989, reg. 33; Civil Legal aid (Assessment of Resources) Regulations 1989, reg. 6.

[8] Civil Legal Aid (General) Regulations 1989, reg. 16.

[9] See para. 18–84 for structured settlements. See also para. 18–30 for the position where money is ordered to be paid to a child who is not the assisted person.

for the assisted person.[10] The charge would clearly apply if the order provided for the money to go to the assisted person who would then use the money to pay the creditor; the charge cannot be avoided by framing the order so as to by-pass the assisted person who in reality will benefit financially. Similarly, if payment is made to a friend or member of the assisted person's family at the request of the assisted person, the recovery is in reality for the assisted person. Furthermore, such arrangements may be treated by the Board as evasion of the charge.[11]

Sometimes it is unclear from the order or agreement who the third parties are and why the order provides for payment to them. Practitioners should bear in mind that the Board will require solicitors to provide full details of how and why any order or agreement reached was made so as to provide for payment to third parties. The Board will wish to know the connection between the recipient and the parties to the proceedings, *e.g.* whether the recipient is a creditor of either party or both and, if so, the nature and amount of the debt.

Payment of joint debts accrued during a marriage, such as credit card bills, are commonly ordered to be paid out of property otherwise recovered or preserved. An example would be where an order provides for the matrimonial home to be sold with the net proceeds to be used first to discharge outstanding bills and the balance to be split between the parties. In general, the Board takes the view that the full net proceeds payable to a party, before payment of an appropriate share of any outstanding bills, should be treated as property recovered for that party. The Board does, however, make an exception where the debt is an existing mortgage or is closely linked to the property, when the assisted person cannot fairly be treated as having recovered the full net proceeds. An example would be repayment of a loan which was used to carry out repairs or improvements to the property. The Board would raise no objections to such a loan being paid before the charge is applied. The Board will also permit arrears of mortgage, gas and electricity bills relating to the property to be paid from the proceeds of sale before the charge applies.

Payment to a child of the assisted person

18–30 Where an order is made providing for payment to a child of the assisted person, the Board will wish to look at the circumstances and reasons why such an order was made. Maintenance orders in favour of children cause no problem since these are exempt from the charge in any event.[12] Arranging for a lump sum or property adjustment order to be made in favour

---

[10] See *Manley v. The Law Society* [1981] 1 All E.R. 401 at 410.
[11] See para. 18–35 for evasion of the statutory charge generally.
[12] Civil Legal Aid (General) Regulations 1989, reg. 94 and para. 18–32.

of a child or children, rather than an assisted person, may, however, lead to a challenge by the Board.

In *Draskovich v. Draskovich*[13] the court refused to make a consent order transferring the husband's share in the matrimonial home to his children where this had the effect of defeating the statutory charge. Balcombe J. stated that: ". . . in the absence of special circumstances, one does not settle property on the children."[14]

In *Griffiths v. Griffiths*[15] an order was made providing for lump sums representing a proportion of the proceeds of sale of the former matrimonial home to be set aside for the children. The Court of Appeal upheld the order, notwithstanding its effect on the statutory charge, because the husband had not met his obligations towards the children since leaving the home and had spent his share of the sale proceeds on durables for himself.

Where practitioners consider that an order for payment to a child in matrimonial proceedings is justified they should be prepared to justify their view to the Board. In particular, the Board will generally wish to consider:

(a) the purpose for which any money paid to a child is to be used and whether it is intended to meet expenses which would otherwise be paid for by the assisted person;

(b) whether the making of the order was primarily to reduce the impact of the charge, *e.g.* where the assisted person has brought about the payment with the help of legal aid and has subsequently required it to be made to the child when there was no other compelling legal or financial reason to do so;

(c) whether payment to the child is indirectly for the benefit of the assisted person, for example, to ensure that the assisted person remains entitled to state benefits.

If, however, payment to the child is for some other good reason connected with the welfare of the child, the Board will not treat the charge as applying. This is more likely to be the case where the final order was contested or where the court did more than simply approve a consent order drawn up by the parties.

Recovery must be in the proceedings for the charge to apply

The charge can only apply to property recovered or preserved "in the **18–31** proceedings"[16] for which legal aid has been granted, or in a settlement to

---

[13] [1981] Fam. Law 87.
[14] See also *Chamberlain v. Chamberlain* [1973] 1 W.L.R. 1557.
[15] [1984] Fam. 70.
[16] Legal Aid Act 1988, s. 16(6).

avoid the proceedings or bring them to an end.[17] It is not necessary for proceedings actually to have been commenced.[18]

The word "proceedings" is not defined in the 1988 Act but in general everything being dealt with through the court under a particular action, cause or matter number should be treated as one set of proceedings. In matrimonial cases the costs of all aspects of the proceedings are a charge on property recovered or preserved in one aspect of those proceedings.[19]

Sometimes a court may assign a new action number to proceedings for its own convenience, e.g. where a case is transferred from one court to another or where enforcement proceedings follow on from the main action. In such cases, where the proceedings and substance remain the same, the charge will be applied as if there had been no change.

Where an assisted person is involved in two separate sets of proceedings, the costs of one set are not a charge against the property recovered or preserved in the other set. There is, therefore, no roll-over of the charge from one set of proceedings to another although there may be cases where a settlement of one set of proceedings expressly or impliedly brings other proceedings to an end, in which case the Board may apply the charge to both sets of proceedings.

The general rule is that only one set of proceedings can be included in any one certificate, except where the Regulations provide to the contrary.[20] Even where two sets of proceedings are properly joined on one certificate in accordance with the Regulations the charge cannot be rolled-over; costs must be calculated separately for each set of proceedings and charged only against any recovery or preservation in those particular proceedings.

Exemptions from the statutory charge

18-32   Property recovered or preserved in certain situations or proceedings may be wholly or partially exempt (i.e. protected) from the charge.[21] The following are exempt:

(a) *Interim payments.* The High Court and County Court Rules allow for a plaintiff to apply for an interim payment from the defendant

---

[17] *ibid.* s. 16(7).
[18] *Van Hoorn v. Law Society* [1984] 3 All E.R. 136 at 139.
[19] See *Hanlon v. Law Society* [1980] 2 All E.R. 199 and para. 18–64.
[20] For exemptions see reg. 46(3) of the Civil Legal Aid (General) Regulations 1989 and para. 18–66. See also *Richards v. Richards* [1984] A.C. 174 where the House of Lords held that an application for an ouster injunction should not be made in existing matrimonial proceedings but in separate proceedings under s. 1 of the Matrimonial Homes Act 1967 or the Domestic Violence and Proceedings Act 1976 and, further, that an application for a non-molestation injunction should also be brought in separate proceedings unless it arose out of or in connection with existing matrimonial proceedings (*e.g.* where the petitioner in divorce proceedings alleges violence).
[21] Civil Legal (General) Regulations 1989, reg. 94.

pending the final disposal of an action where it is almost certain that the plaintiff would recover substantial damages at the end of the case. Such payments are often ordered where the plaintiff would suffer hardship if he or she were to have to await the final outcome of the case before receiving any money. In making these payments exempt from the statutory charge Parliament has ensured they can be released to the plaintiff, rather than being paid into the Legal Aid Fund which would defeat the purpose of the order.

An interim payment is, however, exempt only so long as the payment remains interim. Once a final award of damages is made, the interim damages are included in the calculation for the purpose of the statutory charge. If at that time damages and costs recovered are insufficient to meet the charge, the assisted person may be liable to reimburse the balance to the Board out of what was originally an interim payment. Practitioners should bear this in mind when seeking an interim payment for an assisted person and should also bear in mind that the charge cannot be avoided by securing an interim payment and then discontinuing the proceedings.

(b) *Payments under section 5 of the Inheritance (Provision for Family and Dependants) Act 1975.*

(c) *Periodical payments of maintenance.* This means sums paid towards the support of a spouse, former spouse, child or any other person for whose support the payer has previously been responsible or has made payments. The purpose of this exemption is to avoid the necessity for periodical payments to be made to the Board until any charge liability has been extinguished, thus preventing the assisted person from obtaining the benefit of the maintenance. However, only genuine maintenance payments are exempt. A payment of what is in reality a lump sum but is described as maintenance or a payment in lieu of maintenance is subject to the charge. Where genuine arrears of maintenance are paid in a lump sum such a payment is exempt from the charge but lump sums recovered by back-dating increases in maintenance or capitalising future maintenance payments will attract the charge.[22]

(d) *The £2,500 matrimonial exemption.* There is an exemption from **18–33** the charge in respect of the first £2,500 of any money, or the value of any property, recovered or preserved by virtue of:

(i) an order made, or deemed to be made, under the provisions of section 23(1)(c) or (f), 23(2), 24, 27(6)(c) or (f), or 35 of the Matrimonial Causes Act 1973; or

---

[22] See *Stewart v. The Law Society* [1987] 1 F.L.R. 223 and *Watkinson v. Legal Aid Board* [1991] 2 All E.R. 953.

      (ii) an order made or deemed to be made, under the provisions of section 2 or 6 of the Inheritance (Provision for Family and Dependants) Act 1975 or any provision repealed by that Act; or

     (iii) an order made, or deemed to be made, after September 30, 1977, under section 17 of the Married Women's Property Act 1882; or

     (iv) an order for the payment of a lump sum made, or deemed to be made, under the provisions of section 60 of the Magistrates' Courts Act 1980; or

     (v) an order made, or deemed to be made, under the provisions of section 2(1)(b) or (d), 6(1) or (5) or 20(2) of the Domestic Proceedings and Magistrates' Courts Act 1978; or

     (vi) an order made, or deemed to be made, under the provisions of Schedule 1 to the Children Act 1989; or

    (vii) an agreement made after March 1, 1981 which has the same effect as an order made, or deemed to be made, under any of the provisions specified in sub-paragraph (d)(i) to (vi).[23]

See also para. 18–73 below regarding the £2500 exemption.

(e) *Old matrimonial orders.* Where the legal aid certificate was issued before May 3, 1976, any money or property, of whatever amount or value, recovered or preserved by virtue of an order made, or deemed to be made, under any of the provisions specified in sub-paragraph (d)(i) or (ii) before August 1, 1976 or which, if made on or after that date, gives effect to a settlement entered into before that date.[24]

(f) *Employment Appeal Tribunal payments.* Any payment made in accordance with an order made by the Employment Appeal Tribunal, or in accordance with a settlement entered into after November 1, 1983 which has the same effect as such an order.[25] This provision enables successful assisted persons to benefit from orders made in their favour notwithstanding the fact that costs are not usually recovered in the Employment Appeal Tribunal.

18–34 (g) *Statutory prohibitions.* Any sum, payment or benefit which, by virtue of any provision of, or made under, an Act of Parliament cannot be assigned or charged is exempt from the statutory charge.[26] This exemption applies to certain specific sums, particularly in the field of state benefits, forces pay/pensions, civil service pensions and some local authority pensions, where there is a statutory provision that the sum cannot be charged or assigned.

---

[23] Civil Legal Aid (General) Regulations 1989, reg. 94.
[24] *ibid.* reg. 94(e). There will be no certificates which are still covered by this exemption.
[25] *ibid.* reg. 94(f).
[26] *ibid.* reg. 94(g).

Examples include pensions protected by section 203 of the Army Act 1955[27] or the Air Force Act 1955 or section 5 of the Superannuation Act 1972.

The most important application of this last exemption is in the field of state benefits. Section 187 of the Social Security Administration Act 1992 declares void any charge on:

(a) any benefit as defined by section 122 of the Social Security Contributions and Benefits Act 1992 (including unemployment benefit, sickness and invalidity benefit, attendance allowance, non-contributory invalidity pension, invalid care allowance, guardian's allowance, retirement pension and age additions, injury and disablement benefits and mobility allowance);

(b) any income-related benefit (including income support, family credit and housing benefit);

(c) child benefit.

If any of the payments or benefits referred to above are recovered or preserved by an assisted person the charge will not apply to those payments or benefits. The fact that they are protected against assignment could also have the wider consequence of making it unreasonable to grant legal aid to a person to attack, *e.g.* another person's pension since, nothing could be gained from the proceedings (as any order purporting to assign it would be invalid).[28]

Evasion of the charge

The courts have stated on numerous occasions that they will look to the reality of a transaction rather than the labels which the parties attach to it. The parties "cannot assert that black is white and expect the courts to believe it."[29] **18–35**

If, in reality, property which by its nature is not exempt from the charge is recovered or preserved for an assisted person, the Board will treat the charge as arising even if the wording of the order or settlement suggests that it does not. Examples include:

(a) arranging for a scheme whereby payments are made via a trust to creditors of the assisted person rather than to the assisted person directly,[30]

---

[27] For the effect of s. 203 of the Army Act 1955 on court orders see *Roberts v. Roberts* [1986] 1 W.L.R. 437 and *Happe v. Happe* [1990] 1 W.L.R. 1282. Note that the Naval and Marine Pay and Pensions Act 1865 does not contain such an absolute bar. See *Cotgrave v. Cotgrave* [1992] Fam. 33.

[28] As to the test to be applied by the Board in deciding whether it is reasonable for legal aid to be granted see Chap. 8.

[29] *Per* Denning L.J. in *Customs and Excise Commissioners v. Pools Finance (1937) Ltd.* [1952] 1 All E.R. 77.

[30] See *Manley v. The Law Society* [1981] 1 W.L.R. 335.

    (b) seeking an order that property recovered is to be used first for other purposes in priority to the charge[31]; and

    (c) recovering a lump sum and calling it maintenance.[32]

The clearest guidance on the question of evasion of the charge is contained in the case of *Manley v. The Law Society*.[33] In considering the £40,000 which had been placed on trust to pay the assisted person's creditors Lord Denning M.R. said:

> "The court should always look for the truth of the transaction. It should not let itself be deceived by the stratagems of lawyers, or accountants. It should not allow them to pull the wool over its eyes, it should not allow them to dress up a transaction in clothes that do not belong to it . . . To my mind, once we pull aside the curtain of words and the supposed rights, the truth is that this £40,000 was to be used to pay off David Manley's debts at his request. It is, therefore, the subject of the statutory charge in favour of the legal aid fund."

Legal advisers should, therefore, in general treat assisted persons for the purpose of the statutory charge in the same way as they would treat private clients having regard to their lien for costs.[34] This approach must, however, be subject to consideration of the exemptions of the statutory charge which are provided for in the Regulations.[35] There is nothing to prevent an assisted person from agreeing to an order for the payment of a lump sum of exactly £2,500, (which will be exempt from the charge)[36] and high maintenance payments, rather than a larger lump sum, where the excess over £2,500 would be subject to the charge, and lower maintenance payments.

    Taking steps to utilise the exemptions from the statutory charge so as to minimise its impact is regarded by the Board as perfectly acceptable. The test of whether any arrangement amounts to avoidance of the charge (which is acceptable) or evasion (which is not acceptable) is not dependent on the honesty or bona fides of the assisted person or his or her legal advisers, but rather on the question of whether the proposed arrangement is an artificial one designed with the intention to defeat the charge.

---

[31] *Clark v. Clark (No. 1)* [1989] 1 F.L.R. 174.

[32] See *Stewart v. The Law Society* [1987] 1 F.L.R. 223 and *Watkinson v. Legal Aid Board* [1991] 2 All E.R. 953.

[33] [1981] 1 W.L.R. 335.

[34] For solicitor's lien see para. 13–08. For the duties of legal advisers in such circumstances see para. 13–13. Regarding the nature of the charge see the comments of the Master of the Rolls in *Davies v. Eli Lilly + Co* [1987] 3 All E.R. 94 at 97–98 and *Watkinson v. Law Society* [1991] 2 All E.R. 953.

[35] Civil Legal Aid (General) Regulations 1989, reg. 94.

[36] *ibid.* reg. 94(d).

WHAT DOES THE CHARGE COVER?

General approach

The statutory charge will only arise where an assisted person (or former **18–36** assisted person[37] has recovered or preserved property in the legally aided proceedings and there is a net liability of the Board on that person's account with the Fund. An assisted person's account on conclusion of the case will almost always contain at least one debit item, being the nominated solicitor's claim for costs and disbursements and any counsel's fees.[38]

For practical purposes, the amount of statutory charge will be the value of the property recovered or preserved or the amount of the net liability, whichever is the smaller.[39] There may be more than one bill submitted by the nominated solicitor and, additionally, any costs incurred in enforcing orders in favour of an assisted person (whether for recovery or preservation of property or for payment of costs to the assisted person) will also be included as a debit on the assisted person's account even where the Board takes those proceedings in its own name. Any Green Form costs paid or payable in connection with the legally assisted proceedings, or any matter to which those proceedings related, will also form a debit on that person's account.[40] The total of all the costs (excluding the costs of taxation proceedings) incurred under the certificate and any enforcement costs or related Green Form costs form the total debit on an assisted person's account.

The first credit on an assisted person's account will be his or her contribution, if any, under the legal aid certificate.[41] Any *inter partes* costs which are actually recouped by the Board are also credited to the account and a balance is then taken to see if there is a net liability of the Board on the account.

Costs recovered *inter partes* are no longer restricted to prescribed rates and, where the amount recovered exceeds the amount determined under prescribed rates, the Board pays the excess to the solicitor. This means that in prescribed rate cases the legal aid only costs will form a debit on the assisted person's account which cannot be recouped.

If the account is in credit the excess will be repaid to the assisted person

---

[37] Civil Legal Aid (General) Regulation, 1989, reg. 85(1).
[38] Unless, for any special reason, all the costs incurred under the certificate have been disallowed as might happen if the certificate did not cover the proceedings.
[39] Civil Legal Aid (General) Regulations 1989, reg. 92(2)(c).
[40] Legal Aid Act 1989, s. 16(9); also, for the purposes of the assisted person's contribution, under *ibid.* s. 16(4).
[41] For contributions generally, see Chap. 6.

up to the total amount paid by him or her by way of contribution.[42] If, however, the total amount paid out of the Fund exceeds the total amount received the statutory charge will come into play where the assisted person has recovered or preserved property.

18–37 It should be borne in mind that the charge cannot exceed the lesser of the amount recovered or preserved (after taking into account any exemption such as the first £2,500 in matrimonial proceedings[43]) and the net liability of the Board on the assisted person's account. If the net liability is greater than the chargeable amount recovered or preserved the Fund pays the balance. If, on the other hand, the amount recovered or preserved is greater than the net liability the charge applies only to the extent of the net liability and any balance goes to the benefit of the assisted person.

It is also important to bear in mind that, whilst in many respects the statutory charge mirrors the solicitor's lien for costs where property is recovered or preserved on behalf of a private paying client, the two charges are fundamentally different in one important respect. The private client is liable to pay his or her own solicitor's bill in any event and the solicitor's lien is simply a means of protecting the solicitor's entitlement to payment. On the other hand, the assisted person's liability to pay costs incurred under his or her legal aid certificate, otherwise than by way of a contribution under the certificate, arises solely by virtue of there having been property recovered or preserved on the assisted person's behalf under the certificate.

Cost of Green Form legal advice and assistance

18–38 In calculating the net liability of the Board on an assisted person's account there must be included any sums paid or payable for advice or assistance given to the assisted person in connection with proceedings covered by the certificate or any matter to which those proceedings related. Only to the extent that the amounts payable for advice or assistance were paid out by the Board (rather than recovered from the client by way of contribution or charge for the benefit of the legal representative[44]) will any net liability be increased.[45] All Green Forms are now non-contributory[46] but it is still possible, in principle, for any related Green Form costs to have been recouped by the solicitor under the solicitor's Green Form charge.

Where the Green Form costs are incurred in giving advice in connection with the proposed proceedings, but prior to the issue of a legal aid certificate, no problem will generally arise in deciding that those costs form part of the net liability of the Board on the assisted person's account.

---

[42] *ibid.* s. 16(4).
[43] Civil Legal Aid (General) Regulation, 1989, reg. 94(d).
[44] Legal Aid Act 1988, s. 11.
[45] See Chap. 3.
[46] See Chap. 3.

Section 16(9) of the 1988 Act does, however, also include in the net liability any Green Form costs paid for advice or assistance on "any matter to which those proceedings relate". For example, any advice or assistance given to matrimonial client in connection with welfare benefits or other advice[47] on the financial liabilities of the parties with regard to mortgage arrears and the like following the breakdown of a marriage would be subject to the statutory charge where a legal aid certificate was issued in relation to those matrimonial proceedings. Similarly, costs incurred in connection with assistance by way of representation (ABWOR) in matrimonial proceedings in a magistrates' court would form part of the charge liability under a certificate in respect of subsequent divorce or judicial separation proceedings. If practitioners are unsure as to whether previously incurred costs in respect of advice and assistance will be included in calculating the assisted person's net liability the advisable course is to seek clarification from the appropriate legal aid area office.

By contrast, costs incurred in related proceedings for which a legal aid certificate has been issued are not aggregated for the purpose of calculating the amount of the statutory charge.[48]

Costs of taxation proceedings

An assisted person who has a financial interest in the taxation of his or her **18–39** solicitor's legal aid bill is not required to pay any contribution to the Fund in respect of the costs of the taxation proceedings, nor are those costs taken into account in calculating the net liability of the Board on the assisted person's account for the purpose of the statutory charge.[49] Where the charge arises, therefore, the nominated solicitor's bill must be split as between those items which relate to the costs of taxation[50] and all other items.

The purpose of this provision in the Regulations is to ensure that an assisted person cannot be personally liable for the additional costs which are necessitated as a result of there having to be a legal aid taxation of the solicitor's bill where a certificate is in force, as compared with the preparation of a solicitor and own client bill — the costs of which cannot be charged to the client.

This exemption from the charge in respect of taxation proceedings extends to costs incurred in carrying objections to the taxation, applying to a judge to review the taxation[51] or appealing from a review of the taxation.[52]

---

[47] For the position where there is more than one Green Form see Chap. 3.
[48] See para. 18–31.
[49] Civil Legal Aid (General) Regulations 1989, reg. 119(2).
[50] See Chap. 20.
[51] Civil Legal Aid (General) Regulations 1989, reg. 114.
[52] *ibid.* reg, 115.

The procedure for challenging legal aid taxations is dealt with elsewhere[53] but for the purposes of the statutory charge it is important to bear in mind that the exemption from the statutory charge (and any contribution liability) extends not solely to the costs incurred in mounting that challenge but also to any costs incurred in consequence of any order made as a result of the challenge. This means that the assisted person's statutory charge liability will not increase where additional legal aid costs are allowed following objections, a review or an appeal from the taxation. The assisted person would, however, benefit from any reduction of the costs allowed following a challenge to the taxation as it would then be the costs finally allowed which were debited to the assisted person's account with the Board.

WHEN IS THE CHARGE VALUED?

18–40 Where money is recovered or preserved, whether in the form of damages or a lump sum, the value of the charge is the amount actually received or held on to by the assisted person, after taking into account any legitimate set-off.[54]

Where other types of property are recovered or preserved a value must be placed on every item in order to quantify the charge. The charge operates on property which is actually recovered or preserved, not on the basis of property which is ordered to be transferred but which is never received. Therefore, the general rule is that property should be valued at the time it is recovered or preserved, which will not necessarily be the date of the order or agreement under which the recovery takes place. It all depends on precisely what the assisted person is getting in the proceedings. Guidance on particular types of property are given in the next paragraphs but the following example illustrates the approach.

Suppose the matrimonial home which is thought at the conclusion of the proceedings to have an equity of £40,000 is ordered to be sold with the wife receiving £30,000 out of the net proceeds of sale. It has always been accepted that the wife is entitled to half of the property, but the other half has been in issue. After sale, the net proceeds in fact amount to only £33,431.10. Half of this sum, £16,715.55 belongs to the wife absolutely because of her original undisputed ownership of a half-share of the property.

The wife will, in fact, receive £30,000, so the value of the property that she has recovered for the purpose of the charge is £13,284.45. When one takes into account the £2,500 exemption, the chargeable recovery is

---

[53] See Chap. 20.
[54] For set-offs see Legal Aid Act 1988, s. 16(8).

£10,784.45. These were the precise figures and approach approved by the House of Lords in *Simpson v. Law Society.*[55]

Land and interests in land

Where the order or agreement provides for land to be transferred to the **18–41** assisted person or declares that the assisted person has a certain interest in land, the value of the charge is the value of the assisted person's interest in the equity recovered or preserved. Where a house worth £100,000 is transferred to the assisted person subject to a pre-existing mortgage of £95,000, in truth the assisted person cannot have recovered more than £5,000. That is the most that could be obtained if there were any attempt to enforce the statutory charge. It follows that if the house has a negative equity when it is recovered or preserved, the value of the statutory charge is nil.

Where property is transferred to the assisted person, typically where a house in joint names of husband and wife is transferred to the sole name of the wife, there will be some delay between the date of the order and the date that the legal transfer of title is effected. Unless some problem arises about the transfer, the transfer of legal title is a nominal transfer and it is the order or agreement which establishes that the assisted person is entitled to the equity in the property. This approach is supported by *Re Flint (A bankrupt)*[56] where, for bankruptcy purposes, the court treated a matrimonial order as transferring the husband's interest immediately, even if legal title was not passed. This is because the rules of equity treat as done that which ought to be done.

Therefore, the general rule is that when an assisted person recovers or preserves land or an interest in land, and there is nothing in the order or agreement which delays the recovery, the charge should be valued as at the date of the order or agreement. The relevant values should be specified by the solicitor on Form CLA36.

If the assisted person chooses to sell the land immediately after recovery **18–42** to allow the charge to be paid off, the Board should be prepared to accept a value for the charge based on the actual net proceeds of sale. Otherwise where the assisted person chooses to sell at a later date, the value of the charge should be taken as the value of the equity at the date of the order. In such a case, the costs of sale of the property should not be deducted from the value of the charge, because the sale is the result of a voluntary act by the assisted person, who would have been entitled to retain the full equity of the property had it not been sold. However, where the sale price of the property differs greatly from the valuation given at the time of the

---

[55] [1987] 2 All E.R. at 481, 482.
[56] [1993] 2 W.L.R. 537 at 543.

order, that may be an indication that the original valuation was not correct. The Board should therefore be prepared to take into account the actual sale price of the property in deciding what was the true value of the property at the date of the order.

Where an order or agreement provides for the property to be sold and the assisted person to have a certain share of the proceeds of sale, the value of the charge is the value of the money actually received, not the notional share of the equity at the date of the order.[57]

Proceeds of sale

18–43 Where an order provides that a property is to be sold and the net proceeds of sale are to be divided between the parties to the proceedings, the question arises as to what deductions can be made from the sale price of the property for the purpose of calculating any statutory charge liability. The following items of expenditure are, in the Board's view, allowable deductions:

(a) all legal fees and expenses and all estate agents' fees relating to the sale;

(b) any outstanding mortgage and arrears of mortgage provided that the mortgage was entered into prior to the grant of legal aid and not with the intention of evading the statutory charge[58];

(c) any other debts secured on the property or directly referable to it and which the order expressly provides may be deducted. Examples would be outstanding gas and electricity bills, if the order expressly so provides,[59] and any amount owing on a loan taken out to effect repairs or improvements to the property.

It follows from (b) above that if there is a negative equity when the property is recovered or preserved, the value of the statutory charge is nil.

18–44 The following would not be allowed as deductions:

(a) any charges or other expenditure incurred in relation to the property where the purpose of incurring that expenditure was specifically with a view to evading the charge[60];

(b) any charge which does not rank in priority to the statutory charge[61];

(c) repayment of any debts owing by the assisted person other than

---

[57] *Simpson v. Law Society* [1987] 2 All E.R. 481.

[58] As to priority between the statutory charge and other charges see para. 18–56. As to evasion of the charge, see para. 18–35.

[59] Note, however, that if it were apparent that an applicant for legal aid, or an assisted person, had made a firm decision not to pay household bills this might affect the assessment of the applicant's means as the Legal Aid Assessment Office might not give credit for such payments.

[60] As to evasion generally, see para. 18–35.

[61] As to priority generally, see para. 18–56.

debts secured on or specifically referable to the property.[62] This includes payments, specified in the order to other creditors, family or friends of the assisted person which are treated as property recovered for the assisted person and count towards the charge.

Landlord and tenant actions

The statutory charge arises where a landlord with legal aid successfully evicts a tenant, licensee or squatter from his property, whether or not the person removed was claiming ownership or any legal right to remain in the property. This follows from *Curling v. The Law Society*.[63] It is also apparent from the *Curling* principle that if the possession of the entirety of the landlord's property was in issue, the full value of the landlord's property is subject to the statutory charge, just as if the title of the property had been in issue. **18–45**

Where the legally-aided landlord is resident on the property, or is otherwise claiming possession only of part of his property, the charge still arises but its value will be very small. If the tenant only had possession of one room with shared use of some facilities, the value of the charge is strictly the value of only that part of the property, or perhaps more correctly, the enhanced value to the landlord of the property without the tenant. Where there is a resident landlord, a tenant has very little security and does not enjoy full Rent Act protection, recovery of possession is unlikely to affect the value of the property greatly.

Note that where a legally-aided tenant successfully defends possession proceedings and manages to remain in the property, he may have no chargeable interest. It is only where the tenant has preserved a formal and marketable lease of the property that there can be a chargeable gain, with the value of the charge being the market value of the lease.

Stocks and shares

Generally speaking, no difficulty arises where the chargeable assets are stocks or shares in a publicly quoted company. The value, for the purposes of the statutory charge, will be taken to be the market value at the time of the order providing for recovery and preservation, unless the assisted person decides to satisfy the charge by selling the stocks and shares, rather than raising the money from elsewhere, in which case the value will be treated as the value which the stocks and shares actually realise, after taking into account any commission payable on sale. **18–46**

---

[62] See *Manley v. Law Society* [1981] 1 All E.R. 401.
[63] [1985] 1 All E.R. 705 at 715.

Difficulties can arise, however, where the chargeable assets are stocks or shares in a private company which is owned partly by the assisted person and/or that person's opponent. In those circumstances there may be restrictions on the sale of stocks and shares. If agreement cannot be reached between the Board and the assisted person as to the appropriate valuation[64] the Board is entitled to require that the stocks and shares be lodged with it in satisfaction of the charge.

Objects and life policies

18–47 In matrimonial proceedings, the final order may well provide for the division of the contents of the matrimonial home. Strictly the contents of the home may be subject to the charge and there is no relevant exemption except for the usual £2,500 figure. However, in the majority of cases the contents of the home will never really have been in issue in the proceedings and the charge will not arise at all except in relation to specific items which have been fought over.

Where an object or item of personal property is recovered or preserved in proceedings it is likely that there will be some evidence available as to its value as at the date of recovery or preservation (generally the date of the order).

As part of the Board's case control system (*i.e.* to ensure the grant and continuation of legal aid is justified), the assisted person's solicitors will have been asked to indicate the value of any claim at the outset and it will be difficult for an assisted person subsequently to say that the item was worth less than the amount originally quoted. If, however, the assisted person chooses to satisfy the charge by selling the chargeable asset shortly after its recovery, rather than by raising the money from elsewhere, the Board will accept a valuation of the charge by reference to the actual proceeds of sale, subject to any reduction in the value of a chargeable asset by any act or omission on the part of the assisted person.[65]

If agreement cannot be reached between the assisted person and the Board regarding the value of the chargeable asset and the assisted person is not willing to take steps to sell the asset to pay off the charge, the Board may enforce the charge in any manner which would be available to a chargee in respect of a charge given *inter partes*.[66] This would include taking possession of the chargeable asset and the Board making its own arrangements for sale. The costs incurred in connection with the sale, whether by auction or otherwise, would first be deducted from the proceeds of sale and the balance would be used to meet the net liability on the

---

[64] As to the cost of paying for a valuation see para. 18–49.
[65] See para. 18–50.
[66] Civil Legal Aid (General) Regulation, 1989, reg. 95(2).

assisted person's account. If the account was still in debit, the Legal Aid Fund would then meet the difference, but if the net proceeds of sale were more than the net liability, the balance would be refunded to the assisted person.

Where the benefit of a life policy is transferred to the assisted person, the value for the purposes of the charge is the surrender value, not the amount of any future payment which might be made under the policy.

Who pays for valuation?

Where a chargeable asset is recovered or preserved all relevant information **18–48** must be looked at in determining its value (unless the chargeable asset is sold when its value will generally be taken to be the net proceeds of sale).[67] The Board requires solicitors acting for assisted persons to give an indication (in the original legal aid application and any applications for amendments of the value or the amount of any dispute between the parties and the likely costs. The purpose of this is to ensure that public funds are not wasted on pursuing claims which are not cost-effective and which would be unlikely to be pursued by a private client.[68]

A value will also be specified by the solicitor when reporting the outcome of the case (in form CLA 36). In addition, the pleadings, affidavits, correspondence and any orders or agreements made in the proceedings may contain useful information as to the value of the chargeable asset. On the basis of all that information the Board will form a view as to the amount of the charge. The assisted person and his as her solicitor will always, of course, have the right to put forward their own additional views as to the value of the chargeable asset.

If agreement cannot be reached, the appropriate area office will generally advise the assisted person's solicitors of the value which the area office considers is appropriate having regard to all the information available. The Board will assume that the property in issue in the proceedings justified the costs of the action so that, if the action is wholly successful, the level of costs should be a guide to the general level of the value of the property. This may be of particular relevance in boundary disputes — see para. 18–68, below.

If the assisted person then wishes to dispute the area office valuation it **18–49** will be necessary for the assisted person to produce some evidence to the contrary. If this includes the cost of obtaining an independent valuation the Board will expect the assisted person to pay for this himself or herself. The Board cannot oblige an assisted person to obtain a valuation, nor is the Board obliged to obtain a valuation on its own behalf.

---

[67] See para. 18–51.
[68] For the private or fee-paying client test, see Chap. 8.

It is open to an assisted person who disputes the amount of the charge (or that the charge arises at all) to take proceedings against the Board for judicial review or a declaration.[69] Before doing so the solicitor should ensure that the case is referred to Legal Aid Head Office for consideration either by himself or by the relevant area office. This is to avoid any unnecessary costs.

A separate legal aid certificate would, in principle, be available for such proceedings. The costs incurred under the separate proceedings would not then be aggregated with the costs of the original proceedings for the purpose of calculating the charge liability under the original certificate. The costs incurred under the later certificate would, however, be subject to the charge in so far as the assisted person was successful in the declaration proceedings, unless the assisted person were to recover costs from the Board in those proceedings.[70]

Changes in value after order

18–50   The value of property recovered or preserved is generally taken as the value of the property at the date of the order, but if the order provides for the property to be sold or the assisted person chooses to sell the property immediately after the recovery in order to pay off the charge, then the actual proceeds of sale fix the amount of the charge. In such cases the full sale proceeds are subject to the charge, regardless of whether these are more than the value of the property at the date of the order or less. This approach applies even if, as may well be the case where the assisted person is trying to sell a house, there is a considerable delay before the sale finally takes place.

If the assisted person acquires property subject to the statutory charge and is neither obliged to sell it pursuant to the order nor chooses to sell it immediately after recovery in order to pay off the charge, the charge is valued as at the date of the order.

Subsequently, if the assisted person chooses to sell the property, the proceeds of sale may be greater than the chargeable value, in which case the assisted person keeps the balance, or they may be less than the value of the charge, in which case the assisted person will be indebted to the Board for the balance. Sometimes the difference in value will be due to a fluctuation in market values between the date of order and the date of the sale, but it may well be that the actual price which is fetched on sale indicates that the property was not correctly valued as at the date of the

---

[69] See Chap. 35.

[70] An assisted person who is successful in proceedings against the Board would normally recover full costs unless that person's behaviour in connection with the proceedings against the Board were such that the court considered it inappropriate for the costs to be borne by the Board. A letter before action should be sent before commencing proceedings.

order. The actual sale price realised may be the best evidence of the value at the time of the order.

Where the value of the charge depends on the proceeds of sale, **18–51** sometimes the value of the property will change significantly between the time of recovery and the time of sale. Whether this alters the valuation for the purposes of the charge depends on the circumstances.

In general, a change brought about as a result of some act or omission on the part of the assisted person will not affect the original valuation. If the assisted person takes some step which reduces the value of the asset before it is sold, he should be treated as liable under the statutory charge on the basis of the original value. An example would be where he recovered a house and then let it to a protected tenant so that its value was reduced by an inability to give vacant possession on completion. The statutory charge value should be the value with vacant possession.

On the other hand, if the property has reduced in value as a result of circumstances beyond the assisted person's control, the lower value should be accepted. If, *e.g.* the assisted person recovers a racehorse but before the horse can be sold to satisfy the statutory charge it is stolen or dies, the Board should accept that the statutory charge liability has been extinguished. A similar approach should be adopted if the horse died before the assisted person was able to pay off the charge, assuming there had been no undue delay.

Where enforcement of the charge cannot be postponed, the assisted person must either surrender the property to the Board, sell it to redeem the charge or pay off the charge from other funds. The assisted person should not be allowed to benefit from any delay in doing so. For example, if a painting is recovered and the assisted person wishes to pay off the charge and keep the painting, the value of the painting may increase while there is delay in making payment. It would be legitimate in such a case to require payment according to the value of the painting at the time the charge is redeemed. The Board would be entitled in such a case to enforce the charge by selling the painting at the enhanced value.

It may be necessary to revise a valuation where new information comes to light after the date of the order. If, before the charge is redeemed, a painting is found to be an old master and had been wrongly attributed to a lesser painter, it should be valued as an old master for the purpose of the charge.

Recovery superseded by later events

Sometimes an order providing for recovery or preservation is never **18–52** implemented, either because the parties subsequently agree formally or informally to deal with the property in some different way, or because some supervening event prevents the order being implemented or unscrambles what has previously been transferred.

335

The Board is entitled in the first instance to look at the order to see what has been recovered or preserved. If it is alleged that there has been some superseding agreement or event so that property is not recovered or preserved, the Board will consider whether there has been an attempt to evade the charge. If an arrangement has been made with the intention of evading the statutory charge, it will be disregarded and the statutory charge applied according to the original order.

Subject to this, where an order has been superseded by an agreement between the parties, the Board should be provided with details of the subsequent agreement and give effect to the charge as if that were the final order. In the absence of attempts to evade the charge, what matters is the reality of what is recovered or preserved, not what property is theoretically recovered or preserved under an order which has been overtaken by events. A typical example is where the order provides for the matrimonial home to be sold with the parties receiving certain percentages of the proceeds. Assume the wife's half-share in the property had never been in dispute. Subsequently it may be agreed that the wife will remain in the property but buy out the husband's interest for an agreed lump sum. The value of the property subject to the charge is half the equity in the property at the date of the agreement to buy out the husband, less the lump sum.

18–53 Sometimes recovery or preservation is frustrated by events beyond the control of the assisted person. Examples include:

(a) Insolvency of one party to the proceedings. Where a husband becomes bankrupt shortly after an order that he transfer property to his wife in divorce, earlier dispositions may be set aside.[71]

(b) Death of one party. Where one party dies before implementing an order there may be difficulties in enforcing the order as against the estate and further proceedings may be necessary.

If the assisted person, through no fault of his or her own, has been denied or deprived of recovering or preserving property, the statutory charge should not be applied.

If the assisted person eventually recovers or preserves the property, or some other property, as a result of separate proceedings or negotiations with a trustee in bankruptcy or the executors of the estate, questions can arise as to whether the costs in the earlier proceedings should count towards the statutory charge. If the later negotiations were primarily concerned with enforcing the original order, then the recovery should be taken as "in" the earlier proceedings and the costs of those proceedings would form part of the charge. If there were entirely separate proceedings to obtain property which were not merely enforcing the original order, the earlier costs would not form part of the statutory charge.

---

[71] See Insolvency Act 1988, s. 339 and related provisions.

Setting off gains and losses

Generally speaking, the statutory charge will apply to the net gain by an **18–54** assisted person from the legally aided proceedings. If, therefore, an assisted person who originally owned half of the former matrimonial home recovers his or her former spouse's half share in legally aided matrimonial proceedings, the charge will only apply if the opponent's half share is recovered for no consideration or at an undervalue. If the terms of the order are that one party should buy out the other party at market value there will be no net recovery such as to give rise to the charge.

There are, however, circumstances where the Board would not allow a set off to be taken as reducing the amount of the statutory charge. This can best be understood by considering two hypothetical cases. In the first example, A is granted legal aid to take proceedings against B for damages for breach of contract. In those proceedings B counterclaims damages against A, also for breach of contract. The value of B's counterclaim is estimated by the assisted person to be £5,000 and the assisted person has £5,000 savings from which any order against him could be paid. In considering the assisted person's financial eligibility for legal aid the potential counterclaim of £5,000 will not be regarded as the subject matter of the dispute as it is not a claim that the opponent is entitled, as of right, to a specific fund of money.[72] The £5,000 would, therefore, be taken into account in the assessment of A's means.[73]

If the proceedings are then disposed of by order or agreement which provides for payment of £10,000 to A on his claim and £5,000 to B on his counterclaim, in practice B will seek to set off the £5,000 against the amount due from him to A and will pay to A's solicitors[74] only the sum of £5,000. The Board will then accept that the amount recovered by the applicant in the proceedings is £5,000 only and no property has been preserved as the opponent's claim was not a claim to an entitlement, as of right, to a specific fund.

In the second example, A is granted legal aid to take proceedings for damages for breach of contract against B and in those proceedings B counterclaims for the return of a painting valued at £5,000. In this case, in the assessment of A's means for legal aid purposes, the value of the painting would be disregarded as being the subject matter of the dispute.[75] If the order or agreement which disposed of the proceedings provided for B to pay A £10,000 damages and for A to return the painting worth £5,000 to

---

[72] See para. 18–26.
[73] Disposable capital of £5,000 would produce a capital of contribution of £2,000. For the position regarding contributions generally see Chap. 6.
[74] But not to the assisted person personally; see Civil Legal Aid (General) Regulations 1989, reg. 87.
[75] Civil Legal Aid (Assessment of Resources) Regulations 1989, reg. 5.

B, the assisted person would be regarded as having recovered £10,000 and not the difference between the amount of the damages awarded and the value of the successful counterclaim. If, on the other hand, A were to recover £10,000 damages and to resist B's claim to the return of the painting, the £10,000 damages would be property recovered for the purpose of the statutory charge and the £5,000 value of the painting would be property preserved for the purpose of the charge. The total value of the chargeable assets available to meet the net liability on the assisted person's account would, therefore, be £15,000.

The general rule to bear in mind when considering the amount which an assisted person has recovered where there is a set off is that the Board will only seek to apply the charge to money or property which the assisted person actually has recovered or preserved and not to a hypothetical gain which does not reflect the true position.

Several properties in issue

18-55 The principle referred to above also applies where there is more than one property in issue in the proceedings. The general approach should be to apply the statutory change asset by asset, rather than globally, to see whether overall the assisted person has gained or lost.

Suppose A is granted legal aid to take proceedings against B to establish A's right to a property (Whiteacre) which is in B's name and B in turn makes a similar claim against A with regard to another property (Blackacre) which is in A's name. The value of Blackacre will be disregarded in the assessment of A's means for legal aid purposes as it would be treated as the subject matter of the dispute between the parties.[76] There are various ways in which the proceedings may be concluded.

(a) If A recovers Whiteacre and defeats B's claim to Blackacre the charge will apply in so far as A is concerned to both properties, Whiteacre having been recovered and Blackacre having been preserved.[77]

(b) If A recovers Whiteacre but loses Blackacre the charge will apply to Whiteacre as property recovered. A will not, however, be entitled to set off against the value of Whiteacre, for the purposes of calculating the statutory charge, the value of Blackacre.

(c) If A is unsuccessful in his claim to Whiteacre and also loses

---

[76] *ibid* reg. 5. If the property were the assisted person's main or only dwelling in which he or she resided the asset would be disregarded in the assessment of means in any event; para. 10 of Sched. 3 to the Civil Legal Aid (Assessment of Resources) Regulations 1989.

[77] In these circumstances it is likely that A will obtain an order for costs against B but *inter partes* costs only reduce the incidence of the statutory charge to the extent that they are actually recovered.

Blackacre there will, of course, be no statutory charge as no property will have been recovered or preserved.

Priority of charge

Section 16(6) of the 1988 Act provides that any deficiency on an assisted **18–56** person's account by reason of that person's total contribution under the certificate being less than the net liability of the Board on his or her account "shall be a *first* charge for the benefit of the Board on any property which is recovered or preserved for him in the proceedings."

In principle, therefore, the Board's charge ranks in priority over all other charges. In practice, however, the Board accepts that, where legal aid is granted to enable a person to pursue a claim relating to a property on which there is an existing mortgage, it is only the equity in that property which can actually be recovered or preserved for the purpose of the charge. In reality, therefore, the situation where there is an existing charge is not that it is given priority over the statutory charge but that the statutory charge only arises on the net value of the property recovered or preserved.

When, however, money is borrowed on the security of the property after legal aid has been granted, the Board will not generally permit the subsequent charge to have priority over the statutory charge. An exception would be, *e.g.* where a further advance was required to enable urgent repairs (as opposed to improvements) to be made to the property.

If subsequent charges were permitted to rank in priority to the statutory charge an assisted person could effectively evade the charge by taking out further advances on the property and disposing of the money so advanced, leaving the property with a nil equity.[78] Furthermore, the Regulations specifically provide that, without prejudice to the provisions of the Land Registration Act 1925 and the Land Charges Act 1972, all conveyances and acts done to defeat, or operating to defeat, the statutory charge are void as against the Board except in so far as a bona fide purchaser for value without notice is concerned.[79]

Set off of costs

The Court has a discretion to order a set off of an opponent's costs against **18–57** the costs payable by the opponent to an assisted person even if the Fund will lose as a result.

The following principles should be borne in mind:

---

[78] An example would be where an assisted person purported after the certificate had been issued to create a charge in favour of a relation in return for a loan. For evasion of the charge generally, see paras. 18–35 and 18–63.

[79] Civil Legal Aid (General) Regulations, 1989, reg. 95(4).

(a) section 16(8) of the 1988 Act only permits a set off where there is a court order to that effect;

(b) interlocutory costs ordered against an assisted person will normally be set off against costs awarded in his favour at the end of the case[80];

(c) in practice the court will usually try to make an order which does not penalise an unassisted party[81];

(d) there are certain cases where the court clearly intends the costs liability to lie with the unassisted party and it would be unfair to the Fund to order to order a set off[82];

(e) the 1988 Act also limits the circumstances in which a set off is permissible to cases where a legal representative's lien for costs would not prevent it.[83]

Recovery in part of the proceedings

18–58 Where legal aid is granted for matrimonial proceedings the amount for which the statutory charge attaches is not limited to the costs incurred in the financial issue or issues under which the recovery or preservation takes place, but it also covers all other costs incurred in those proceedings.[84] The Board considers that the principles of the *Hanlon* case still apply after the implementation of the Children Act 1989.

In non matrimonial proceedings there are less likely to be discrete aspects of the proceedings but, if there are, the *Hanlon* principle should be applied and all the certificate costs should count towards the charge. For example, if a party is unsuccessful at first instance but recovers property following an appeal to the Court of Appeal, the first instance costs still form part of the charge. Similarly, the costs of unsuccessful interlocutory proceedings must count towards the charge.

Costs of enforcement proceedings

18–59 The *Hanlon* principle should not be applied where property is preserved only in enforcement proceedings. Suppose a defendant with legal aid is unsuccessful in a damages claim and has judgment entered against him. No specific property was at issue in the action. If the plaintiff then tries to

---

[80] See *Lockley v. Blood Transfusion Service* [1992] 1 W.L.R. 492.

[81] See, *e.g. Cook v. S* [1967] 1 All E.R. 299.

[82] See *Currie & Co. v. The Law Society* [1977] Q.B. 990 where the court declined to order a set off as between costs ordered to be paid by the solicitors for the unassisted party and costs ordered against the assisted party, the court's intention in making the order against the solicitors being to punish them for negligence in that case.

[83] See *Cordery on Solicitor* (8th ed., 1988).

[84] *Hanlon v. Law Society* [1980] 2 All E.R. 199.

enforce the judgment by a charging order against the defendant's house or garnishee proceedings against his bank account, the charge will arise if the defendant manages to fend off these attacks on his property. In such a case it would be surprising if all the costs of the main and unsuccessful action counted towards the charge.

The correct approach is to draw a line after the main action and treat the enforcement proceedings as separate proceedings. Therefore only the costs of opposing the enforcement proceedings should count towards the charge on the defendant's property.

On the other hand, from the plaintiff's point of view, enforcement action is simply an additional step in obtaining the ultimate recovery of damages. The plaintiff's costs of both the main action and the enforcement proceedings count towards the charge on any property recovered for him.

More than one certificate in one action

Problems sometimes arise as to the scope of the statutory charge in cases **18–60** where more than one certificate is issued to an assisted person in relation to a set of proceedings. The most common situation arises in matrimonial cases where parties frequently return to court many times to deal with different aspects of a divorce over a long period. Broadly there are two basic situations which give rise to problems:

(a) An assisted person recovers property in divorce proceedings covered by a certificate which is subsequently dicharged. He or she then obtains a new certificate to make an application in the same proceedings, perhaps relating to a different aspect of the dispute such as maintenance or residence/contact. Clearly the costs under the first certificate are a charge on the original property recovered but do the costs under the second certificate also form part of the charge?

(b) An assisted person obtains a certificate but recovers no chargeable property before that certificate is discharged. Subsequently the assisted person obtains a new certificate and applies within the same proceedings and recovers a lump sum. The charge clearly applies to the costs under the second certificate, but does it extend to the first?

There is no clear authority on these points, although there are a number of **18–61** judicial comments and Regulations which bear upon the issue. There are two opposing points of view which derive respectively from the decision in *Hanlon v. The Law Society*[85] and *Watkinson v. Legal Aid Board.*[86]

The *Hanlon* decision suggests that it is the proceedings which determine

---

[85] [1980] 2 All E.R. 199.
[86] [1991] 2 All E.R. 953.

the scope of the charge and the number and scope of any legal aid certificates is irrelevant. On this interpretation the charge always applies to different certificates which relate to the same proceedings. The starting point is section 16(6) of the 1988 Act which refers to property recovered or preserved for the assisted person "in the proceedings" and the word "proceedings" in this context is given a wide interpretation in the case of *Hanlon*. Although there was only one relevant certificate in *Hanlon*, that certificate covered custody, access and an injunction application within the divorce as well as proceedings under sections 23 and 24 of the Matrimonial Causes Act 1973, under which property was recovered. Their Lordships rejected the argument that the charge arose only in respect of the costs of that part of the proceedings in which the recovery took place: the charge applied to all the costs incurred under the certificate. Although the head note to the law report on *Hanlon* talks of the charge covering "the totality of the proceedings covered by the legal aid certificate" it is doubtful whether their Lordships intended to restrict the charge to one certificate. Lord Scarman[87] referred to "the totality of the legally-aided proceedings."

Lord Lowry discussed the possibility of there being more than one certificate and stated[88]: "For my own part, I doubt whether the number of certificates issued is the real test. So to hold could leave an assisted person at the mercy of an administrative decision."

There are, however, indications to the contrary in Lord Scarman's judgment and, in particular, he stated[89]: "In most cases a reference to the legal aid certificate will determine the extent of the charge" and went on to say: "Accordingly, I agree that the charge, if it arises, constitutes a security for the costs of the divorce proceedings included in the certificate."

When considering the case of *Hanlon* it is important to bear in mind that their Lordships were considering whether the charge should apply to all or only part of the costs incurred under one certificate and the above remarks of Lord Scarman are not, therefore, necessarily inconsistent with the observations of Lord Lowry.

The *Watkinson* decision suggests that it is the certificate which always determines the scope of the charge and each certificate must, on that approach, be looked at in isolation. The actual decision in *Watkinson* is not controversial. The case concerned an assisted person who had secured an upward variation in periodical payments and under an amendment to her existing certificate was applying for a further variation. At the hearing the parties reached an agreement that the husband would pay a lump sum of £10,000 in return for which the assisted person's right to periodical payments would cease. Because periodical payments are exempt from the

---

[87] [1980] 2 All E.R. 199 at 213.
[88] *ibid.* at 224.
[89] *ibid.* at 213.

statutory charge[90] it was argued that the lump sum paid in lieu was also exempt. The Court of Appeal rejected this argument and held that the £10,000 was subject to the charge. The result was that the Board could recoup the costs paid out under the certificate in both its original and amended forms.

However, in his judgment in *Watkinson*, the Master of the Rolls went on to state, *obiter*, that the result would have been different if the final application for variation had been made under a new certificate, rather than under an amendment to the old certificate. The Master of the Rolls recommended to solicitors that they should never apply to have a certificate amended when they could instead apply for a fresh certificate and that once the purpose of the certificate had been fulfilled they should make every effort to have it discharged. In the light of those remarks, it has even been suggested that solicitors who continue to work under amended certificates when they could have obtained new certificates are guilty of negligence.

A factor to be taken into account when considering the relative merits of **18–62** the *Hanlon* and *Watkinson* approaches is regulation 85 of the General Civil Legal Aid (Regulations) 1989 which states:

> "Where a certificate has been revoked or discharged, section 16(6) of the Act (which provides for a charge upon property recovered or preserved for an assisted person) shall apply to any property recovered or preserved as a result of the person whose certificate has been revoked or discharged continuing to take, defend or be a party to the proceedings to which the certificate related."

This regulation makes it clear that the charge cannot be avoided by having a certificate discharged and going on to take the proceedings privately. It would seem illogical that the charge should apply if proceedings were continued privately after a certificate had been discharged but could be avoided by obtaining a new certificate to cover the proceedings as was suggested in the case of *Watkinson*. Furthermore, regulation 85 is not specifically worded so as to restrict its application to cases where the proceedings are continued privately after a certificate has been discharged. The regulation is wide enough to cover the case of a person continuing to take, defend or be a party to the proceedings under a fresh certificate.

Applying regulation 85, the Board takes the view that if costs are incurred under a certificate which is then discharged and a subsequent certificate is later issued relating to the same proceedings, the costs under both certificates are a charge on the property recovered or preserved under the second certificate. The charge applies to the costs incurred under the second certificate under normal principles and to the costs incurred under

---

[90] Civil Legal Aid (General) Regulations 1989, reg. 94(c).

the first certificate through the operation of regulation 85. Applying the *Hanlon* principle to regulation 85 the words "the proceedings to which the certificate related" would cover all aspects of the proceedings so that the charge would apply to the costs incurred under both certificates where, *e.g.* the first certificate related solely to an injunction application whilst the second certificate covered ancillary relief.

18–63   Regulation 85 does not, however, deal with the case where property is recovered under the first certificate and then further costs are incurred under a subsequent certificate. In these cases it is sometimes difficult or impossible for the Board to apply the charge on *Hanlon* principles, particularly where the original property recovered or preserved has been released to the assisted person and may have subsequently been disposed of.

The view taken by the Board is that neither the extreme *Hanlon* approach nor the extreme *Watkinson* approach is correct; prima facie the certificate establishes the scope of the charge but the charge extends beyond the certificate where:

    (a) property is recovered or preserved after the certificate is discharged or revoked;

    (b) a single certificate does not represent the true account of the assisted person with the Board, which may be the case where two simultaneous certificates exist in relation to the same proceedings; or

    (c) there is an attempt to evade the charge.

Applying these principles the Board has issued guidance to its area offices to the effect that:

    (a) costs incurred under a particular certificate are a charge not only on the property recovered or preserved under that certificate but also on property recovered or preserved in the same proceedings after the certificate has been discharged or revoked (whether or not a second certificate has been issued)[91];

    (b) where property has been recovered or preserved under a certificate which is then discharged, the costs incurred under a subsequent certificate do not constitute a charge on the property originally recovered where the second certificate is issued some time, say one year, after the first certificate was discharged and the facts of the case do not suggest a deliberate attempt to evade the charge.[92]

As to the second point, the Board will look at the question of whether, at the time the original certificate was discharged, there were still ancillary issues to be determined upon which no final order had been made and the purpose in having the original certificate discharged and waiting some time

---

[91] Civil Legal Aid (General) Regulations 1989, reg. 85.
[92] For evasion generally, see paras. 18–35 and 18–63.

before proceeding with the other issues was to ensure that the cost of the subsequent issues would not be a charge on the property recovered or preserved. Where, however, all the ancillary issues have been disposed of by means of a final order and, sometime later, further issues arise in relation to, say, the children, the Board will not treat those subsequent costs as being a charge on property which was recovered or preserved some time earlier.

Two proceedings in one certificate

A certificate rarely includes more than one action, cause or matter.[93] Where **18–64** it does, however, the charge will only apply to the costs which relate to the proceedings in which the recovery or preservation took place. The legal aid costs incurred in the different proceedings, and any *inter partes* costs recovered, will have to be apportioned accordingly. Any contribution paid by the assisted person will, however, be divided equally between the different sets of proceedings for the purpose of determining the deficiency on the assisted person's account in respect of those proceedings.

It is sometimes difficult to decide what amounts to separate "proceedings" for the purposes of the charge. There is no definition of "proceedings" in the 1988 Act or the Regulations. Every case in the county court has a particular case number and every case in the High Court has a particular action number, and everything under a particular court reference can generally be regarded as one set of proceedings. Sometimes the court reference will not remain constant because of transfer of proceedings from one court to another or owing to appeals. Allocation of a new number in such cases does not give rise to separate proceedings for the purpose of the charge and all the costs should be included. Similarly, enforcement procedures are sometimes given a new court reference number but, subject to the points made in para. 18–59 above, enforcement proceedings should be treated as part of the main action.

Disputes are more likely to arise where no formal proceedings have been issued and where, *e.g.* the solicitor is pursuing a number of possible avenues to achieve a result for his client. The approach in such cases should be that as the solicitor has chosen to carry out all the work under a single certificate, there should only be one set of proceedings at issue, and all the costs should count towards the charge. If, *e.g.* the solicitor is negotiating for compensation under some form of insurance or compensation scheme with a view to avoiding court proceedings, there will clearly be a limit as to how much such work can properly be undertaken under the certificate. However, assuming the work is covered by the certificate, consideration may be given to apportioning costs incurred under the certificate between

---

[93] See Civil Legal Aid (General) Regulations 1989, reg. 46(3) for the exceptions.

those which relate to potential court proceedings and those which relate to some other avenue entirely.

Several defendants in one set of proceedings

18–65 Certificates often entitle proceedings to be taken against more than one defendant and all parties or potential parties to the proceedings must be specified in the certificate. A single action brought against two defendants counts as a single set of proceedings so if, *e.g.* damages are recovered from one defendant but the claim fails against the other, all the costs under the certificate form a charge on the damages recovered, not just the costs attributable to the unsuccessful defendants. This is another application of the *Hanlon* principle that one must look at the whole costs of the proceedings, not just the part of the proceedings in which the recovery took place.

There are three areas of difficulty:

(a) Where separate actions are brought against the separate defendants, a fresh certificate must be issued so that each action is covered by its own certificate. The costs incurred under the original certificate up to the time that separate proceedings were commenced would form part of the charge against damages recovered from either defendant; thereafter costs incurred under one certificate would not usually be charged on property recovered under the other certificate.

(b) Sometimes damages will be recovered from one defendant but the action will proceed against the other. Consideration may be given at this point to whether the certificate should be discharged if the additional benefit of proceeding against the other defendant would not justify the additional costs. Where one defendant settles, all the costs incurred to that date would be charged on the damages recovered from him, but thereafter a line must be drawn at some point and subsequent costs incurred as against the continuing defendant should not retrospectively be charged back to the recovery from the defendant who settled.

(c) When considering separate proceedings against separate defendants it sometimes happens that a settlement of one action will effectively bring about the end of the other action. If a settlement to action A is arrived at to avoid or bring to an end proceedings in action B, the costs in both sets of proceedings would be charged against the recovery.

Children Act 1989

18–66 As the Children Act 1989 changed the basis upon which courts make orders in relation to children, issues sometimes arise as to whether cases concerning children should be treated as free-standing Children Act proceedings for the purposes of the statutory charge, or whether they are simply part of wider matrimonial proceedings. The problem arises because in family proceedings a single certificate can relate to more than one action, cause or matter.

Hanlon established that in divorce proceedings all aspects of the divorce, including disputes relating to children, were part of the proceedings and contributed to the statutory charge. The view taken by the Board is that the Children Act 1989 did not alter this general position so in a normal matrimonial certificate the costs relating to the children should not be apportioned separately.

Outside the context of divorce/judicial separation there may be cases of genuine free-standing Children Act proceedings where the costs should be apportioned separately and not count towards the charge on any property recovered in other proceedings.

Normal means and merits tested Children Act proceedings, covering **18–67** issues such as contact and residence, should not be combined on the same certificate as proceedings which are subject to the special non-means/non-merits tested or means tested only Children Act arrangements.[94] The special arrangements apply to certain public law issues affecting children, and it is unlikely that property will be recovered or preserved under a certificate covering public law aspects. If this does happen, consideration should be given to treating the private law proceedings leading to the recovery or preservation as separate proceedings from the public law Children Act proceedings, with costs being apportioned accordingly. Where, as should be the case, the public and private law aspects are dealt with under separate certificates, they should always be treated as separate proceedings for the purposes of the charge.

Note that property recovered or preserved under Schedule 1 to the Children Act 1989 is subject to the £2,500 exemption[95] and enforcement of the charge may be postponed subject to the usual restrictions.[96]

Boundary disputes

Boundary disputes often result in costs being incurred which are far in **18–68** excess of the real benefit to be obtained and generally will not satisfy the civil legal aid merits test.

Where legal aid is, however, granted to an assisted person for the purpose of taking or defending proceedings relating to a boundary dispute, problems may arise at the end of the proceedings in quantifying the value of any

---

[94] *Legal Aid Handbook 1995*, Note for Guidance 7–07 and 7–08.
[95] Civil Legal Aid (General) Regulations 1989, reg. 94(d)(viii)
[96] *ibid.* reg. 96(1)(d).

property recovered or preserved for the purpose of the statutory charge. The Board requires solicitors acting for applicants and assisted persons to given an indication as to the amount in issue (in the application form and when applying for any subsequent amendment)[97] and there may also be other information available from the pleadings, any affidavits or correspondence and from the final order or agreement which gives some indication of the amount in issue.

Generally speaking, however, the value will be taken to the value to the assisted person from successfully taking or defending the proceedings and not merely the value of the strip or piece of land in dispute taken in isolation. Where the parties dispute, e.g. the correct position for a boundary fence between their respective properties, the strip of land which lies between the two proposed positions for the boundary fence would almost certainly have little or no value if sold on the open market. That strip of land might, however, substantially affect the value of the party's respective properties. It might, e.g. provide a right of way or in some other way affect the enjoyment of one property or the other. In those circumstances the amount recovered or preserved by an assisted person who is successful in such proceedings will be taken to be the enhanced value of the property. This is the prospective value which solicitors will be expected to disclose to the Board in the legal aid application. Unless the assisted person can produce evidence to the contrary, the Board will assume that the enhancement in the value of the property to the assisted person justified and at least equalled the costs incurred under the assisted person's certificate.

Legal advisors should bear in mind when advising a client who seeks legal aid for the purpose of a boundary dispute that it will be difficult to maintain at the end of the case that the amount in issue was worth little or nothing and, at the same time, to justify having fought the proceedings at public expense under a legal aid certificate.

Representation by contract and multi-party actions

18–69   Section 16(10) of the 1988 Act provides:

> "Where a legally assisted person has been represented in any proceedings in pursuance of a contract made with the Board on terms which do not differentiate between the remuneration for his and other cases, the reference in sub-section (9)(a) above to the sums paid or payable by the Board on his account in respect of the proceedings shall be construed as a reference to such part of the remuneration payable under the contract as may be specified in writing by the Board."

---

[97] See Chap. 7 which deals with the civil legal aid merits test.

Contracts are used for the provision of advice, assistance and representation to multi-party actions which are defined as any action or actions in which 10 or more assisted persons have causes of action which involve common issues of fact or law arising out of the same cause or event.[98]

Section 16(10) of the 1988 Act enables the Board to apportion certain costs incurred under a contract between the various assisted persons so as to prevent all those costs being borne on the certificates of assisted persons who are chosen to prosecute lead actions. These cost-sharing arrangements relate solely to generic costs.[99] The approach towards the use of this power is set out in paragraphs 53 to 56 of the Board's Multi-Party Action Arrangements 1992.

18–70 Where a multi-party action is being pursued under a contract between the Board and the nominated solicitors the costs which specifically relate to any individual are debited to that individual's account with the Fund and are not the subject of any costs-sharing arrangement. Those specific costs will form part of the deficiency on that person's account for the purpose of the statutory charge together with an appropriate proportion of the generic costs.

Note for Guidance 16–07 in the *Lepal Aid Handbook 1995* deals with the circumstances in which the costs for an early leaver (from the action) may be specified.

The Board's contracting powers could also be used for the finding of cases on a block, rather than case by case basis. In those circumstances the amount of the charge could be fixed other than by reference to the actual costs of the particular case.

Interest on damages

18–71 Although damages recovered for an assisted person are subject to the statutory charge, the damages still belong to the assisted person. Therefore any interest accruing on such damages must also belong to the assisted person. Generally, interest on damages is not subject to the statutory charge because the interest is not in issue in the proceedings.

Where the Board retains damages on behalf of an assisted person, the Board's obligation to pay interest has now been put on a statutory footing. Regulation 92A Civil Legal Aid (General) Regulations 1989 obliges the Board to pay interest, subject to certain limitations, by reference to the interest paid by the bank on the Board's general deposit account. Any surplus interest on money held may simply be retained by the Board like interest on any other Board assets.

---

[98] Civil Legal Aid (General) Regulations 1989, reg. 152. For Multi-Party Action Arrangements generally, see Chap. 40.
[99] See Chap. 40.

Regulation 92A was inserted to regularise the tax position of interest payments because now that the payment is a statutory obligation on the Board, there is no requirement under the Taxes Acts to deduct income tax at source. The regulation does not suggest that interest payments may be subject to deduction through the statutory charge and this provides further confirmation that the charge does not apply to such interest. The regulation does not directly apply to interest on damages while in the hands of solicitors, but logically such interest should be treated no differently.

One situation where interest on damages will be subject to the statutory charge is where the interest accrues on the damages before it is recovered by the assisted person. Where a defendant is late in paying damages, he may have to pay interest on those damages under the Judgments Acts. The amount actually paid in satisfaction of the judgment debt may, therefore, include an element of interest but this should be treated like other property recovered or preserved and will be subject to the statutory charge.

Interest on costs

18–72   Where costs are awarded in favour of an assisted person, those costs belong to the Board and not to the assisted person.[1] Interest on costs also belongs to the Board. Neither an assisted person nor his or her solicitors can profit from interest on costs but an assisted person may indirectly benefit from the interest where the statutory charge arises.

If, after taking into account the amount of *inter partes* costs recovered from the assisted person's opponent there is still a deficiency on the assisted person's account,[2] the interest on costs will then be applied to reduce further the deficiency.

To the extent that interest on costs results in there being a credit balance on the assisted person's account, that balance remains in the Legal Aid Fund and does not go to either the assisted person or his or her legal representatives.[3] Note, however, that in prescribed rates cases, any interest

---

[1]   *The Debtor v. The Law Society (No. 5883 of 1970), The Times,* February 21, 1981, C.A.
[2]   Legal Aid Act 1988, s. 16(9).
[3]   The argument that interest on costs belongs to the Board follows from the case of *The Debtor v. The Law Society op. cit.* which established that the principal sum in respect of *inter partes* costs belongs to the Board. The fairness of this has been criticised on the basis that the Board can sometimes make a profit by virtue of interest on costs. It could be argued that, to the extent that an assisted person has, for the time being, financed the proceedings by virtue of having a contribution (contributions do not earn interest for the benefit of assisted persons, the benefit of interest on costs ought fairly to go to the assisted person. Equally, to the extent that the burden of costs has been borne by the solicitors acting under the legal aid certificate after taking into account any payments on account of costs or disbursements, the benefit of interests on costs ought fairly to go to the solicitors. Finally, to the extent that the Board has financed the proceedings by way of payments on account of costs or disbursements, the benefit of interest on costs ought fairly to go to the Fund.

recovered in excess of the interest due on prescribed rate costs must be paid back out to the solicitor.[4]

Applying the £2,500 exemption

The first £2,500 of any money, or of the value of any property, recovered **18–73** or preserved in certain proceedings is exempt. Note that the exemption applies to the money or property recovered or preserved and not to the first £2,500 of the costs incurred under the certificate. If the value of the property recovered is more than £2,500 greater than the amount of the chargeable costs, the exemption has no effect on the value of the charge. However, it may still assist the assisted person. Suppose chargeable costs are £5,000 but the assisted person recovers a lump sum of £2,500 and a matrimonial home worth £100,000. The amount of the charge will be £5,000 and the exemption makes no difference to this. However, the exemption will allow the £2,500 lump sum to be released freely to the assisted person and will mean that the full impact of the charge will apply to the matrimonial home.

The exemption applies to the "first" £2,500 recovered or preserved, so if, unusually, there are several orders providing for otherwise chargeable recovery, the exemption must apply to the recovery/preservation under the first order. It is more usual for one final order to cover several different recoveries, *e.g.* where a wife receives the matrimonial home, together with a lump sum of money and other personal property and insurance policies. If so, the assisted person is entitled to choose which of the simultaneous recoveries the £2,500 is to apply to.

In practice it is likely that the exemption will be applied in the following order:

    (a) first, to any assets which the assisted person does not wish to sell and over which enforcement of the charge is not postponeable, *e.g.* insurance policies or personal property;

    (b) next to any money payable under the order which can be released to the assisted person free of the charge;

    (c) finally, to the matrimonial home over which enforcement of the charge is likely to be postponed so that the assisted person would gain no immediate benefit from the exemption.[5]

The exemption should always be applied at the time the property is **18–74** recovered or preserved and the chargeable property is valued. Therefore when a house is transferred to the assisted person, the exemption should apply to the equity in the house at the date of the order. Where the assisted

---

[4] Civil Legal Aid (General) Regulations 1989, reg. 92(1)(d).

[5] *Simpson v. Law Society* [1987] 2 All E.R. 481.

person recovers proceeds of sale the exemption should apply to the chargeable proceeds actually received.

The £2,500 exemption can only ever be applied once in any set of proceedings. "Proceedings" is given the widest possible meaning for this purpose. The total value of property exempt under this head cannot exceed £2,500 regardless of how, when and to whom it is paid. If both sides are assisted in matrimonial proceedings each, of course, has a £2,500 exemption, but any lump-sum payment to a child of the marriage even if otherwise valid would not attract any additional exemption.

Where a sum of money is recovered to enable the assisted person to purchase a home and postponement of enforcement of the charge is possible, the assisted person is nevertheless entitled to be paid £2,500 before consideration is given to postponing the charge over the balance. The exemption is taken as overriding the normal obligation to pay money recovered into the Fund.[6]

Note also that the £2,500 exemption operates in addition to any other exemptions so, for example, any exempt periodical payments would not count towards the £2,500 exemption.

ENFORCEMENT OF THE CHARGE

Generally

18–75　The charge on property recovered or preserved for an assisted person which arises under section 16(6) of the 1988 Act or which is created by virtue of the Civil Legal Aid (General) Regulations 1989[7] vests in the Board.[8] The Board is given power in the Regulations to enforce its charge in any manner which would be available to a chargee in respect of a charge given *inter partes* but the Board is prohibited from agreeing to the release or postponement of enforcement of its charge except where the Regulations[9] apply and then only in accordance with the provisions of those Regulations.[10]

Except where an order or agreement provides that money or property is to be used for the purpose of purchasing a home for the assisted person or

---

[6] Civil Legal Aid (General) Regulations 1989, regs. 87, 90. Note that the decision of the Court of Appeal in *Simmons v. Simmons* [1984] 1 All E.R. 83 on this point should no longer be regarded as good authority following the views of the House of Lords in *Simpson v. Law Society op. cit.*

[7] Civil Legal Aid (General) Regulations 1989, regs. 96, 97 and 98.

[8] *ibid.* reg. 95(1).

[9] *i.e. ibid.* regs. 96, 97 or 98.

[10] *ibid.* reg. 95(2).

his or her dependants[11] or where substitution of the charged property is permitted[12] the Board is bound to enforce its charge forthwith.

Where it is necessary to take proceedings against the opponent of an assisted person to enforce or give effect to an order or agreement for the recovery or preservation of property for the benefit of the assisted person and to which the charge will apply, the Board may take those proceedings in its own name.[13]

Where the Board takes proceedings in its own name it may authorise any person to swear an affidavit, file a proof, receive a dividend or take any other step in the proceedings in its name and any costs incurred by the Board in any such enforcement proceedings constitute a first charge on any property or money which is recovered in those enforcement proceedings,[14] that is to say they form part of the charge amount.

Where it is necessary to take proceedings to give effect to an order or agreement[15] made in connection with the proceedings to which the assisted person's certificate relates for the payment of money to the assisted person, those enforcement proceedings may be taken by the assisted person with the appropriate Area Director's consent, provided that they are proceedings for which representation may be granted under the 1988 Act.[16]

Money

Subject to limited exceptions, all money payable to an assisted person must **18–76** be paid to his or her solicitor or, if the assisted person is no longer represented by a solicitor, to the Board and only the solicitor (or the Board) is capable of giving a good discharge for moneys so payable.[17]

This means that if the money was paid directly to the assisted person or elsewhere the paying party would still be treated as owing the money and the Board would be entitled to take proceedings to recover the money again.

The exceptions to this are:

(a) Magistrates' court proceedings where costs must be paid to the Clerk to the Justices who then pays it on to the Board.[18]

(b) Money ordered to be paid into and remain in court and invested for the benefit of the assisted person. This will often be the case

---

[11] See paras. 18–94 and 18–95.
[12] See para. 18–09.
[13] Civil Legal Aid (General) Regulations 1989, reg. 91(1).
[14] ibid., reg. 91(3).
[15] Including an agreement made before the proceedings were taken.
[16] Civil Legal Aid (General) Regulations 1989, reg. 91(2). The Area Director could not, e.g. give consent to proceedings being taken in courts outside England and Wales.
[17] ibid. reg. 87(1); subject to ibid. regs. 89 and 94 (exemptions from the charge, see para. 18–32).
[18] ibid. reg. 89(a).

where the assisted person is a child or is under a disability. In such cases the Board should notify the court in writing of the amount necessary to safeguard the interests of the Fund, after obtaining an undertaking or estimate from the solicitors if necessary. This will then be the amount which is subject to the charge, and the court will be free to release the balance to the assisted person.[19]

(c) Property which is exempt from the charge can be released directly to the assisted person.[20] However, solicitors would be well advised to check with the area office0before doing so. If it later appeared that the property was not exempt the solicitors would be in breach of the Regulations and likely to have their costs deferred.

Note that the Regulations require all monies to be paid to the solicitor or to the Board, not just those which are subject to the charge. This ensures that the money is safeguarded pending determination of the amount due under the charge.

18–77 In addition to money due directly under an order or agreement, there are three other situations where the money must come to the solicitor or the Board. They are examples of the general rule:

(a) Where the paying party has become bankrupt, has entered into a deed of arrangement, or is a company in liquidation, and money is due to the assisted person in respect of the proceedings. Where this happens, the solicitor or the Board must notify the trustee in bankruptcy, trustee or assignee of the deed of arrangement, or liquidator of the company, that a certificate has been issued to the assisted person. This should then ensure that any monies due to the assisted person on the distribution of the assets of the paying party will be paid to the solicitor or to the Board.[21]

(b) Where money has been paid into court by the assisted person and the court has ordered this to be repaid to him.[22] Note that although money paid out of court in this way cannot be released directly to the assisted person, it will not necessarily be subject to the statutory charge.

(c) Where money is standing in court to the credit of the legally aided proceedings, having been paid in by the other side, and is payable to the assisted person. Here such money will almost certainly have been "recovered" for the purposes of the statutory charge.[23]

A solicitor acting for an assisted person who has reason to believe that his or her client may try to circumvent the requirement for money to be

---

[19] *ibid.* reg. 87 is expressly subject to the exemptions in reg. 94. See also *Simpson v. Law Society* [1987] 2 All E.R. 481.
[20] *ibid.*
[21] *ibid.* reg. 87(1)(b), 88.
[22] *ibid.* reg. 87(1)(c).
[23] *ibid.* reg. 92.

paid to the solicitor is obliged by the Regulations to inform the Board, which means in practice the appropriate area office.[24]

When money is recovered or preserved for the assisted person, the solicitor must forthwith inform the appropriate Area Director[25] and send to the Area Director a copy of the order or agreement by virtue of which the money was recovered.[26]   **18–78**

The solicitor is then obliged to pay that money to the Board unless[27]:

(a) the solicitor is able to give an undertaking as to costs[28] as a result of which the Area Director is satisfied that the rights of the Fund will be safeguarded by payment to the Board of a sum less than the full amount recovered; or

(b) the money is to be used for the purpose of purchasing a home for the assisted person or his or her dependants.[29]

The Board will then enforce its charge on the money recovered by the assisted person by retaining the money in the Fund to meet any deficiency on the assisted person's account.

If failure to notify promptly means that the Board is unable to recover the charge, any loss to the Fund is likely to be recovered from the solicitors costs claim under Regulation 102 of the Civil Legal Aid (General) Regulations 1989, *i.e.* by deferment of profit costs.

Undertaking as to Costs

The discretion under Regulation 90(2) of the Civil Legal Aid (General) Regulations 1989 to allow a solicitor to release money to the assisted person can only be exercised where the Area Director is satisfied that the Fund will be safeguarded. The Fund can only be safeguarded by determining the maximum amount which may be due to the Fund and requesting that this be paid in. As the charge cannot be quantified until costs have been taxed or assessed, it is necessary to obtain a formal undertaking from the solicitors that total costs will not exceed a given amount.   **18–79**

An undertaking as to costs must cover everything which might count towards the charge, so the figure given by the solicitor must include counsel's fees, disbursements, VAT, earlier Green Form costs, costs incurred

---

[24] *ibid.* reg. 87(2).

[25] The term "Area Director" means an Area Director appointed by the Board in accordance with reg. 4 of the Civil Legal Aid (General) Regulations 1989 and includes any person duly authorised to act on his behalf; *ibid.* reg. 3. In practice the Area Director, who will be the Group or Area Manager for the relevant area office, will have delegated this responsibility to members of his or her staff.

[26] Civil Legal Aid (General) Regulations 1989, reg. 90(1)(a). There is a form (currently Form CLA36) to be used for this purpose.

[27] *ibid.* reg. 90(1)(b).

[28] See para. 18–79.

[29] Civil Legal Aid (General) Regulations 1989, reg. 96 and paras. 18–94 and 18–95.

by previous solicitors acting under the certificate, and costs under any other certificate issued to the assisted person in the same proceedings. The undertaking may be given by completing a standard form.

An alternative to requiring money to be paid into the Fund is for the area office to allow the solicitors to retain the money, subject to their undertaking not to release it to any other party. This would be sensible if the money needed to be held for a short while pending recovery of costs from the other side. The area office will only agree to such a proposal if it is satisfied that in all the circumstances the Fund will be safeguarded.

Once solicitors have given an undertaking, they will not be allowed costs in excess of it. Solicitors should obviously proceed cautiously when giving such undertakings.

Objects

18–80   Where an item of personal property is recovered or preserved for an assisted person, the assisted person's solicitor is obliged to notify the appropriate Area Director immediately and send to the Area Director a copy of the order or agreement by virtue of which the property was recovered or preserved.[30]

Sometimes the assisted person is able to satisfy his or her statutory charge liability arising out of recovery or preservation of an item of real property by payment of a sum of money to the Board sufficient to meet the deficiency on his or her account with the Legal Aid Fund. If, however, the assisted person cannot raise sufficient money to meet the charge liability the Board will look to the item of property to meet the deficiency. The Board has no power to postpone enforcement of the charge in the case of recovery or preservation of items of personal property.[31]

18–81   The Board may enforce its charge in any manner which would be available to a chargee in respect of a charge given *inter partes*. In practice, the Board will call for the item in question to be lodged at the appropriate area office or, if this is not practicable[32] to take steps to hand over control of the item to the Board.

The Board will then make arrangements for the valuation[33] and sale of the item and the net proceeds of sale will be credited to the assisted person's account with the Board. If there is a credit balance on the assisted

---

[30]   *ibid.* reg. 90(1)(a).

[31]   But the exemption in respect of the first £2,500 may apply; see Civil Legal Aid (General) Regulations 1989, reg. 94(d) and para. 18–32.

[32]   *e.g.* where an item is recovered or preserved which could not reasonably be lodged at the appropriate area office, such as a horse.

[33]   As to valuation of assets see paras. 18–34 and 18–49.

person's account,[34] the excess will be paid to the assisted person. If, however, there is still a deficiency on the account, the Fund will be liable for the balance.[35]

Insurance policies

Where the item which has been recovered or preserved is an insurance **18–82** policy the charge will apply to the value of that policy.[36]

The same principles apply as apply to personal property[37] but the assisted person will be asked by the appropriate area office if he or she is able to satisfy the charge by payment of a sum of money into the Fund.

If this is not possible the Board will call for the insurance policy to be lodged with it with a view to arranging a sale where this is possible. The net proceeds of sale will then be credited to the assisted person's account in the same way as for personal property.[38]

Mobile homes

Where the property which is recovered or preserved by an assisted person **18–83** is a mobile home the power to postpone enforcement of the charge does not arise, even if the mobile home is to be used as a home for the assisted person or his or her dependants.[39]

It is a condition of postponement that the assisted person should agree that interest shall accrue on the amount of the charge from the date on which it is first registered[40] and registration of the charge in accordance with the Regulations[41] is not possible in the case of a mobile home.

The Board has, therefore, no power or discretion to postpone enforcement and legal advisers should bear this in mind when advising assisted persons.

In practice, if the charge arises where a mobile home has been recovered or preserved the Board will ask the assisted person if he or she is able to raise a sum of money to meet the charge, failing which the Board has no

---

[34] After taking into account costs, disbursement and counsel's fees, any sums paid or payable for advice and assistance in connection with the proceedings or in any matter to which the proceedings related and after giving credit for any contribution actually paid by the assisted person and costs actually recovered from the assisted person's opponent.

[35] Unless arrears of contribution or *inter partes* costs are recovered.

[36] As to valuation, see paras. 18–47 and 18–48.

[37] See above, under objects.

[38] *ibid.*

[39] Civil Legal Aid (General) Regulations 1989, reg. 96. Nor where money to purchase a mobile home is recovered or preserved:

[40] *ibid.* see reg. 97(4) (in the case of property which is recovered or preserved) and reg. 96(3)(b) (in the case of money which is recovered or preserved).

[41] *ibid.* reg. 95(3).

alternative but to make arrangements for valuation and sale of the mobile home.[42]

Structured settlements

18–84 Where damages are awarded to an assisted person in the form of a structured settlement, the payments made under the structured settlement are not exempt from the charge. They are not periodical payments of maintenance which are exempt from the charge[43] and the Board has no power to postpone enforcement.

In practice, structured settlements will seldom create a problem in so far as the charge is concerned as full costs will normally be recovered from the paying party. If, however, there is a shortfall between the costs payable under the legal aid certificate and the costs recovered *inter partes* the charge will apply to that shortfall.

Legal advisers should bear this in mind when seeking an order or agreement for a structured settlement. If, *e.g.* there is likely to be costs shortfall of, say, £5,000 it may be preferable to reach an agreement whereby a lump sum of £5,000 is initially paid to the assisted person to satisfy the charge. Otherwise, all the initial payments which are intended for day to day provision for the assisted person will have to be paid to the Board until a sufficient sum has been paid into the Fund to meet the deficiency on the assisted person's account.

Enforcement of the statutory charge over land

18–85 Where a statutory charge over land cannot be postponed, the assisted person must be requested to pay in sufficient funds to redeem the charge. If the charge is not paid off and the conditions for postponement are not met, it may be necessary for the Board's Debt Recovery Unit to take proceedings against the assisted person to obtain an order from the court that the property be sold. In cases where the assisted person is refusing to sign the necessary interest agreement to enable postponement a warning of court action usually leads either to the agreement being duly signed or to the charge being paid off.

Note that the court always has a discretion when dealing with possession of a person's home, and will only order property to be sold if, in all the circumstances, it is considered reasonable. The court has wide powers to adjourn the application, stay or postpone enforcement on terms.[44]

---

[42] See above, under objects, paras. 18–80 and 18–81.
[43] Civil Legal Aid (General) Regulations 1989, reg. 94(c).
[44] See views of Lord Denning M.R. in *Quennel v. Maltley* [1979] 1 All E.R. 568; Administration of Justice Act 1970, s. 36 and Administration of Justice Act 1973, s. 8.

In cases where postponement of enforcement is possible but cannot take place only because the assisted person refuses to sign the interest agreement, it is likely that possession or sale would be suspended to give a final chance for the assisted person to sign the agreement.

POSTPONEMENT

The position on or before December 1, 1988

Prior to December 1, 1988 the position was that the Law Society (which at **18–86** that time administered civil legal aid) had power to postpone enforcement of the charge on property recovered or preserved but no similar power where money was recovered or preserved.[45]

This anomaly created difficulties because it sometimes frustrated the purpose of a court order providing that a former matrimonial home be sold and the proceeds divided in such a way as to enable the parent having custody of the children to purchase another property for occupation by them as a home. Unless full costs were recovered from an assisted person's opponent, the assisted person was first obliged to meet any statutory charge liability which sometimes resulted in there being insufficient funds available to purchase a new property.

On December 1, 1988 new Regulations[46] were introduced which permitted postponement of enforcement of the charge both in the case of property recovered or preserved and in the case of money recovered or preserved. These provisions were subject to certain restrictions, which are referred to below, and they applied to all statutory charges on property recovered or preserved under orders or agreements made after December 1, 1988. Until August 1994 postponement of enforcement of a charge over a home was only possible within certain proceedings. That restriction also no longer applies.[47]

Postponed enforcement over land

When the statutory charge applies to land enforcement of the statutory **18–87** charge can be postponed provided all the requirements of the Regulations are satisfied. Postponement of a charge over a home is now possible

---

[45] See *Simpson v. The Law Society* [1987] AC 861.
[46] Civil Legal Aid (General) (Amendment) (No. 2) Regulations 1988.
[47] Civil Legal Aid (General) Regulations 1989, reg. 97 as amended by the Civil Legal Aid (General) (Amendment) (No. 2) Regulations 1994.

regardless of the nature of proceedings in which the recovery took place.[48] Previously postponement was only possible where an order or agreement was made in proceedings under:

(a) the Married Women's Property Act 1882;
(b) the Matrimonial Causes Act 1973;
(c) the Inheritance (Provision for Family and Dependants) Act 1975; or
(d) Schedule 1 to the Children Act 1989.

In all other cases including, e.g. proceedings under the law of Property Act 1925 the Board had no power to postpone enforcement of its charge.

18–88   There are five conditions required for postponement:

(a) under the terms of a court order or agreement, the property is to be used as a home for the assisted person or his or her dependants[49];
(b) the assisted person wishes to use the property as a home for himself or herself and dependants[50];
(c) the assisted person agrees in writing that the charge will bear interest[51];
(d) the charge is or can be registered on the property[52];
(e) the Area Director is satisfied that the property will provide adequate security for the charge.[53]

Even when all these conditions are met, there is a discretion whether to allow postponement, but where all the conditions are satisfied, postponement should only be refused in very exceptional circumstances. Examples might be where the assisted person had just won a fortune on the lottery and so should be expected to pay the charge off without delay, or where the assisted person had not been honest in dealings with the Board. Note that in any case where the certificate has been revoked, no question of postponement arises and the full legal aid costs must be recovered without delay.[54]

The information necessary to determine whether all the conditions are satisfied and to exercise any discretion should be clear from the Board's compulsory forms — currently Forms CLA 36 (notification of property recovered or preserved) and CLA 37 (request to defer enforcement of the statutory charge).

The Regulations on postponement of the charge suggest a sequence of events which is not always easy to reconcile with reality. For example, Regulation 97 requires the Area Director to "direct" that that regulation applies. This should not be taken to mean that there must always be a

---

[48] Civil Legal Aid (General) Regulations 1989, reg. 97 as amended by Civil Legal Aid (General) Amendment (No. 2) Regulations 1992.
[49] Civil Legal Aid (General) Regulations 1989, reg. 97(1).
[50] *ibid.* reg. 97(3).
[51] *ibid.* reg. 97(3),(4).
[52] *ibid.* regs. 95(3), 97(4).
[53] *ibid.* reg. 97(3).
[54] *ibid.* reg. 86.

separate specific direction in every case; any notification from the area office agreeing to delay enforcement of the charge will suffice. In any event, the Board does not have to follow slavishly regulations of a procedural nature which are designed solely for its own protection.[55]

Further guidance on each of the conditions necessary for postponement is given below.

Postponed enforcement over money

In the case of money to buy a home there is a specific exemption to the general rule under regulation 90 Civil Legal Aid (General) Regualations 1980 that all money received by a solicitor on behalf of an assisted person must be paid into the Fund. However, postponement is only possible where all the requirements of the Regulations are met.[56]   **18–89**

The conditions are very similar to those for postponed enforcement over land; save that the postponement is only possible in certain proceedings. The conditions are:

(a) a sum of money has been recovered or preserved which, under the terms of a court order or agreement is to be used to purchase a home for the assisted person or his or her dependants[57];

(b) the recovery has taken place in specified proceedings; Regulation changes have expanded the list of proceedings[58];

(c) the assisted person wishes to use the property as a home for himself or herself and dependants[59];

(d) the assisted person agrees in writing that the charge will bear interest[60];

(e) the charge can be duly registered on the property[61];

(f) the Area Director is satisfied that the property will provide adequate security for the charge.[62]

Note that any money recovered or preserved must either go into the home and satisfy the other conditions, or it must be paid into the Fund. There is no power to allow money which is subject to the statutory charge to be used for other purposes such as paying off other debts or buying other assets. To do so would contravene regulations 90(4) and 95(3) of the Civil Legal Aid (General) Regulations 1989. This contrasts with the wider

---

[55] *See Re H* [1992] 3 All. E.R. 380.
[56] Civil Legal Aid (General) Regulations 1989, regs. 90(3), (4) and 95(3).
[57] *ibid.* reg. 96(1).
[58] *ibid.*
[59] *ibid.* reg. 96(2).
[60] *ibid.* reg. 96(2), (3).
[61] *ibid.* reg. 96(3).
[62] *ibid.* reg. 96(2).

discretion which the Board has over total proceeds of sale when a house which is already subject to the statutory charge is sold.

18–90   Money subject to postponement may either be a specific lump sum, or may be some share of the proceeds of sale of another property. Although all money subject to the charge must be used "for the purpose of purchasing a home" for the assisted person or his dependants, these words are given a wide meaning. Subject always to being satisfied that the Board will be adequately secured, the money may be used, not just towards the basic purchase price of the new property, but also towards:

(a) costs of purchase, including conveyancing and removal fees;

(b) reasonable repair work to the structure of the property;

(c) reasonable costs of furnishing the property.

These all come within the notion of buying a "home" including the costs of making the property habitable for the assisted person and dependants. Carrying out improvements to the property would not be covered, unless this is necessary to meet the particular needs of the assisted person or his or her dependants *e.g.* due to disability.

18–91   When the Board has agreed to postpone enforcement, the money subject to the charge can be released towards completion of the purchase of the new property.[63] It is vital that the conveyancing on this purchase is done either by the solicitor who acted under the certificate, or by a conveyancer who will ensure that the money goes into the new property and who co-operates in getting the Board's charge executed and registered on the property. The solicitor must give the area office sufficient information to allow the charge to be registered.[64] Regulation 96(5) of the Civil Legal Aid (General) Regulations 1989 as amended allows a solicitor to release money where an agreement to defer enforcement has been made, but only to a conveyancer who has given the Board a suitable undertaking.

Note that the property to be purchased was not itself recovered in legally aided proceedings so it is not subject to the statutory charge under section 16(6) of the 1988 Act. The view taken by the Board is that the statutory charge on the money can be traced through to the property although a contractual charge is requested to be executed by the assisted person. The form of charge needed is attached to the Board's Form CLA37.

18–92   There will often be a delay between money being recovered and completion of the new purchase. Solicitors should be permitted to retain the money pending completion. Sometimes the assisted person may not even have found a new property when the money comes through, or a proposed purchase will fall through. If the money has not been used to purchase a home one year after the order or agreement under which it was recovered, it must be paid into the Fund.[65] However, as with any time-limit,

---

[63] *ibid.* reg. 96(4).
[64] *ibid.* reg. 96(6).
[65] *ibid.* reg. 96(7).

the area office has a discretion under regulation 7 of the Civil Legal Aid (General) Regulations 1989 to allow more than a year and more time will normally be given if the assisted person still genuinely intends to purchase a home and the delay is not their responsibility.

Note that in addition to the money subject to the charge the assisted person is entitled to use other money or loans towards the purchase price. There is also nothing in the Regulations obliging the assisted person to purchase the property in his or her sole name, although if this is not done it may be difficult to show that the property provides adequate security.

Sale shortly after recovery

Where a property has been recovered or preserved and all the conditions **18–93** for postponement have been met, the assisted person may prefer to sell the property and purchase a new home. Before the statutory charge is registered, the assisted person may ask for the charge to be placed on the new property instead. Provided the assisted person agrees to the charge bearing interest and the new property provides adequate security, the Board may agree to postpone the charge.[66]

As in the case of money recovered to buy a property, the assisted person should execute a contractual charge in favour of the Board over the new property.

Property to be used as a home

Postponement is only allowed where the order of a court or the terms of **18–94** the agreement reached recite that property is to be used as a home for the assisted person or his or her dependants, or the money is to be used for the purpose of purchasing such a home.[67] A copy of the order or agreement should be submitted to the area office. No particular form of words is necessary in the order or agreement, and it is not necessary to refer to the Regulations expressly (although see below).

If no such words appear, the solicitor will be informed that there is no power to postpone enforcement. It may well be that omission of the words was an oversight and postponement of enforcement is still requested. If so, the solicitors may seek to put matters right by applying to court for any order to be amended or expanded under the "Slip Rule"[68] or by obtaining a statement signed on behalf of both sides that the property is to be used as a home. The view taken by the Board is that the words "any agreement reached" in regulations 96 and 97 of the Civil Legal Aid (General)

---

[66] *ibid.* reg. 97(5), (6).
[67] *ibid.* reg. 96(1), 97(1).
[68] See C.C.R., Ord. 15, r. 5.

Regulations 1989 can mean not just the agreement under which the property was recovered or preserved, but a subsequent agreement between the parties following the original order or agreement.

On August 19, 1991 the Senior District Judge of the Family Division issued a Practice Direction giving a form of words which should always be acceptable for the purposes of regulations 96 and 97 of the Civil Legal Aid (General) Regulations 1989. This reads as follows:

> "And it is certified for the purpose of the Civil Legal Aid (General) Regulations 1989 [that the lump sum of £X has been ordered to be paid to enable the Petitioner/Respondent to purchase a home for himself/herself (or his/her dependants) [that the property (*address*) has been preserved/recovered for the Petitioner/Respondent for use as a home for himself/herself (or his/her dependants)]".[69]

18–95 When the Regulations were amended on August 1, 1994 to allow the charge to be postponed in a wider category of cases, transitional provisions were introduced which allowed postponement to take place even if the order or agreement did not provide for the property to be used as a home.[70] The exemption applies where the order or agreement was made *before* August 1, 1994 and where under the unamended regulations postponement was not possible. For example, if a property was recovered in section 30 Law of Property Act proceedings under an order dated July 1994, it is unlikely that the order would cover use as a home. After August 1, 1994 the Board can agree to postponement without requiring the order to be amended, but it will only do so if it is satisfied that the property will indeed be used as a home.

It does not suffice for the order or agreement to say that the property is to be used as a home; the assisted person must actually intend to use the property as a home in accordance with the order or agreement.[71] This intention will be communicated by the assisted person in completing the Board's form CLA37 requesting postponement.

The property must be a home for the assisted person "or his dependants". Postponement is therefore possible even if the property will not be a home for the assisted person and will only be a home for his dependants.

There is no definition in the Regulations of who is and who is not a "dependant", but it is assumed that the phrase is intended to have a wide meaning and should cover all those who would be entitled to make applications under the Inheritance (Provision for Family and Dependants) Act 1975. Dependants will, therefore, be taken as including a spouse or former spouse of the assisted person, a child of the assisted person, any person who during any marriage was treated by the assisted person as a

[69] Practice Direction 1991, 3 All E.R. 896.
[70] See Civil Legal Aid (General) Amendment (No. 2) Regulations 1994, regs. 3(5) and (6).
[71] Civil Legal Aid (General) Regulations 1989, regs. 96(2), 97(3).

child of the family and any other person who is maintained by the assisted person, *i.e.* the assisted person is making a substantial contribution in money or money's worth towards the reasonable needs of that person.[72]

Proceedings under which postponement is possible

Where a home has been recovered or preserved, the Board's power to **18–96** postpone does not depend on the proceedings in which the land was recovered or preserved.[73]

Where money is recovered or preserved to buy a home postponement can only take place under one of the six statutes listed in Regulation 96(1) Civil Legal Aid (General) Regulations 1989. Postponement can take place even if proceedings were never issued, provided the proceedings could have been covered by the certificate. The statutes now covered are[74]:

 (a) the Married Women's Property Act 1882;
 (b) the Matrimonial Causes Act 1973;
 (c) the Inheritance (Provision for Family and -Dependants) Act 1975;
 (d) Schedule 1 to the Children Act 1989 — this Schedule contains all the provisions in the Act for making financial orders in favour of children;
 (e) section 30 of the Law of Property Act 1925;
 (f) Part III of the Matrimonial and Family Proceedings Act 1984 — financial orders made in the jurisdiction but following a foreign divorce.

Omissions to note which may cause difficulties are:

 (a) landlord and tenant actions concerning possession of a home;
 (b) mortgage possession actions;
 (c) Guardianship of Minors Acts 1971 and 1973 although such cases should have been concluded following the Acts' repeal by the Children Act 1989.

Can the charge be duly registered?

The charge can only be postponed if it is *duly* registered. This requirement **18–97** is made express in the case of charges over money (regulation 96(3)(a) of the Civil Legal Aid (General) Regulations 1989 and substitutions (regulation 98(3)(a)), and is implicit in the case of postponement over land.

---

[72] Inheritance Provision for Family and Dependants Act 1975, s. 1.
[73] Civil Legal Aid (General) Regulations 1989, reg. 97(1) as amended by Civil Legal Aid (Amendment)(No. 2) Regulations 1994.
[74] Paras. (e) and (f) below were inserted by Civil Legal Aid (General) (Amendment) (No. 2) Regulations 1994.

The only permissible types of registration are as follows:

(a) in the case of unregistered land, there must be a Class B land charge within the meaning of section 2 of the Land Charges Act 1972, or a caution against first registration under section 53(1) of the Land Registration Act 1925,

(b) in the case of registered land, there must be either a registrable substantive charge or a caution against dealings under section 54(1) of the Land Registration Act 1925;

(c) in the case of land in Scotland, by recording a standard security within the meaning of Part II of the Conveyancing and Feudal Reform (Scotland) Act 1970.[75]

18–98 Apart from in respect of land in Scotland, registration can only take place under the Land Registration Act 1925 or the Land Charges Act 1972, and as these Acts extend only to England and Wales, the charge cannot be postponed or substituted to land in Northern Ireland or abroad (even if registration abroad would appear to provide adequate security).

Postponement is also not possible for mobile homes. Even if arrangements could be devised so that the Board were satisfied a mobile home provided adequate security for the charge, postponement is not permissible. The charge cannot be registered as required by the Regulations.

Adequate Security

18–99 The property over which the charge is registered must provide adequate security for the charge.[76] The Board will look for sufficient equity to cover the likely amount of the charge. In cases where the bill has not been paid and the charge cannot yet be quantified, it will consider the solicitor's estimate of costs in the notification of property recovered or preserved (currently Form CLA36).

Since the amount of the statutory charge cannot be greater than the value of the equity in property recovered or preserved, it will be unusual for land which has been recovered or preserved not to provide adequate security. Property prices may fall after registration of the charge, but the Board should be prepared to agree to postponement if there is adequate security in the property at the time it is being considered, unless there is some compelling factor to show that the value of the property will fall significantly in the near future.

In the case of a charge over money to buy a home, the Board will particularly wish to be satisfied that there will be sufficient equity in the property to cover the charge, bearing in mind that some of the money may

---

[75] Civil Legal Aid (General) Regulations 1989, reg. 95(3A).
[76] *ibid.* regs. 96(2), 97(3), 98(2)(c), 98(4)(c).

not go towards the purchase of the property but towards other aspects of the home.

It is legitimate for the Board to take into account the extent of protection which will be afforded by registration. A full charge, or in the case of unregistered land a Class B land charge, provides the best security, but a far lower degree of protection is afforded if all that can be obtained is a caution *e.g.* where the assisted person is not the sole owner). This is because an interest protected only by a caution can be over-reached by any disposition by all the owners, *e.g.* taking out a second mortgage could account for all the remaining equity in the property.

If it is felt that a caution provides inadequate security, the Board may decline to agree to postponement of the charge unless the assisted person and any other owner(s) of the property agree to execute a contractual charge in favour of the Board.

Where the assisted person is requesting postponement in relation to a property which has not yet been bought, the Board will require the property to be bought in the sole name of the assisted person, or require all those buying the property to execute the charge in favour of the Board.

THE PAYMENT OF INTEREST

Interest agreement

The requirement that the assisted person agrees in writing that the charge **18–100** will carry interest is central to postponement.[77] The interest agreement is incorporated in the form requesting deferment of enforcement (currently Form CLA37). Completion of the form cannot guarantee postponement as the Board must still be satisfied of the other conditions.

The interest agreement contains other terms apart from the obligation to pay interest. In particular there is a term requiring the assisted person not to do anything to reduce the value of the property on which the charge is registered. The Board is entitled to insist on such additional terms such as this as part of its general discretion and within its general powers under section 4 of the 1988 Act.

The obligation to pay interest is a contractual one between the assisted person and the Board, whereas the assisted person's obligations under the statutory charge itself arise automatically by law. In order to ensure that the Board's entitlement to interest takes priority over subsequent entries with the Land Registry the interest agreement will if available, be submitted to the Land Registry on initial registration of the charge.

---

[77] *ibid.* regs. 97(3),(4) and 96(2), (3).

The signing of the interest agreement is often misunderstood by assisted persons as being a choice to pay interest or not. The choice, imposed by the Regulations, is either to agree to a charge bearing interest or to face enforcement proceedings. The solicitor should make the position clear to his or her client who may need specific advice in addition to being supplied with the Board's leaflet "Paying Back the Legal Aid Board". An assisted person may delay signing the interest agreement pending quantification of the charge and deciding whether to pay it off or seek postponement.

The interest agreement will normally be signed personally by the assisted person, but can be signed on his or her behalf by someone who is duly authorised to do so.

WHEN DOES INTEREST RUN?

18–101 On August 1, 1994 the Regulations regarding interest were changed. The amended Regulations apply where the assisted person signed the interest agreement on or after August 1, 1994. Where the assisted person has already signed the interest agreement before that date, interest is calculated as if the new Regulations had not been made, whether or not the charge is subsequently substituted onto a new property.[78]

When does interest start to run? — Interest agreement before August 1, 1994

18–102 Interest runs from the date the charge is first registered.[79] This is the date the charge is entered on the register and will be clear from any formal notification from the Registry. Where the charge is over money to buy a new property, interest only begins to run when the charge is registered on that new property, even if a long time has elapsed since the original order. If the order provided for an existing property to be sold and the proceeds to go into the new property, it may be that a charge was registered on the old property, but that does not give rise to the running of interest.[80]

When does interest start to run? Interest agreement on or after August 1, 1994

18–103 The new Regulations preserve the notion that interest runs from the date of registration, but the way this operates is affected by a new requirement that the amount the interest is calculated upon cannot be greater than the costs

---

[78] Civil Legal Aid (General) (Amendment) (No. 2) Regulations 1994, reg. 3.
[79] Civil Legal Aid (General) Regulations 1989, regs. 96(3)(b), 97(4).
[80] Civil Legal Aid (General) (Amendment) (No. 2) Regulations 1994, reg. 3(4).

paid on taxation or assessment. Therefore in a case where the charge is registered on July 1, but no bill is paid until August 1, no interest is in fact claimed between July and August because the amount interest is charged on is zero. For practical purposes, one can say that interest runs from the date of registration or the date the bill is paid, whichever is the later.

For cases which were not postponable prior to August 1, 1994 but which became postponeable as a result of the amended Regulations interest cannot be claimed for any period before August 1, 1994. This exemption ensures that by signing the interest agreement an assisted person will not become liable for back-dated interest where the charge was registered and bill paid between 1988 and 1994, but no enforcement action has been taken pending the Regulation changes which allow for postponement.

When does interest stop running?

Once interest is running it continues to run until the charge is paid off.[81] **18–104** Interest does not cease to run on the death of the assisted person or sale of the property.

What sum is interest calculated on? — Interest agreement before August 1, 1994

The unamended Regulations provided that interest ran on the amount **18–105** which the Board would have retained but for postponement of the charge.[82] This meant that interest was payable for periods before the bill was actually paid and before the charge was quantified. This gave rise to complaints of unfairness.

What sum is interest calculated on? — Interest agreement after August 1, 1994

The amended Regulations provide that interest is calculated on the amount **18–106** outstanding on the charge at any given time.[83] This is defined to mean the amount paid out by the Board on taxation or assessment (*i.e.* interest only runs on final bills, not on payments on account) and cannot be more than the value of the property at the time it was recovered or preserved.[84]

---

[81] Civil Legal Aid (General) Regulations 1989, reg. 99(1).
[82] *ibid.* regs. 92(b), 96(3)(b), 97(4).
[83] *ibid.* regs. 99(4) — (6) as amended.
[84] *ibid.* reg. 99(6).

What effect do payments towards the charge have on interest?

18–107 An assisted person can make payments towards the charge at any time but any sums paid must first be set off against accumulated interest, before they reduce the capital outstanding.[85]

Interest continues to accrue at a constant rate unless sufficient is paid in to start reducing the capital. This means that an assisted person has little incentive to make early payments unless they reduce the capital.

Once a charge is accruing interest, it may be that costs are recovered from the other side which reduce the deficit on the account. Again, any such sum will be used first to reduce the accumulated interest, then to reduce the capital.

Interest rates

18–108 Interest on the charge is simple rather than compound and tends to be a little higher than other compound interest rates.

The system of interest being payable on the charge came into force on registrations on or after December 1, 1988. The rates applicable since then have been as follows:

December 1, 1988 to	December 31, 1991	12%[86]
January 1, 1992 to	August 31, 1993	10.5%[87]
September 1, 1993 onwards		8%[88]

Note that it was intended to reduce the interest rate from 12 per cent from 11 per cent in October 1991, but this change was expressed to apply in respect of proceedings begun on or after October 14, 1991.[89] Since the rate was changed to 10.5 per cent for all registrations from January 1, 1992, it is very unlikely that any cases were concluded in time for this rate to be applicable.

Substitutions

18–109 Where an interest bearing charge has been registered on a property the Board has a discretion to release that charge and allow a replacement

---

[85] *ibid.* reg. 99(3).
[86] Legal Aid (General) (Amendment) (No. 2) Regulations 1988 Preserved by the Civil Legal Aid (General) Regulations 1989 as from April 1, 1989.
[87] Civil Legal Aid (General) (Amendment) (No. 3) Regulations 1991.
[88] Civil Legal Aid (General) (Amendment) (No. 2) Regulations 1993.
[89] Civil Legal Aid (General) (Amendment) (No. 2) Regulations 1991.

charge to be substituted on a new property.[90] A charge can be substituted more than once.[91]

Any charge registered before December 1, 1988 will not be interest-bearing and substitution would take place under the old rules, not under the Civil Legal Aid (General) Regulations 1989.[92] No substitution should take place unless the new property will provide adequate security for the charge and the charge can be duly registered on the new property. Otherwise such substitutions will be looked at in the same way as substitutions under the current regime although the Board may require the charge to be paid off rather than substituted if this can be done without hardship to the assisted person.

For substitutions, the following requirements are mandatory[93]:   **18–110**

    (a) there must be a registered interest-bearing charge on the existing property;

    (b) the assisted person must wish to purchase a new property in substitution for the existing one;

    (c) the assisted person must agree in writing that a charge will be registered on the new property and will bear interest;

    (d) the Board must be satisfied that the new property will provide adequate security for the charge. Substitution cannot take place if there is insufficient equity to cover the charge.

The application to substitute is made by letter and will be dealt with by the Land Charge Section of the Board's Debt Recovery Unit at Legal Aid Head Office. The assisted person will be sent a questionnaire giving details and confirming that interest will continue to be payable if the substitution takes place. If substitution is agreed to, the assisted person will execute a contractual charge in favour of the Board.

When an interest-bearing charge is substituted to a new property, interest simply continues to accrue just as if the substitution had not taken place.

If all the essential conditions for substitution are satisfied, all the **18–111** circumstances of the case must be taken into account in deciding as a matter of discretion whether to allow substitution to proceed. The following guidelines may be applied:

    (a) Is it reasonable to expect the assisted person to pay off the charge rather than have the charge transferred to the new property, bearing in mind the financial circumstances of the assisted person and all other facts?

    (b) Substitution will usually be agreed if otherwise the assisted person or his or her dependants would suffer hardship.

---

[90] Civil Legal Aid (General) Regulations 1989, reg. 98(1).
[91] *ibid.* reg. 98(4).
[92] See *Hanlon v. Law Society* [1980] 2 All E.R. 199 at 210–211 and 224–226.
[93] Civil Legal Aid (General) Regulations 1989, regs. 98(1) and (2).

(c) The reason for the assisted person wishing to move house is important. Substitution should generally not be agreed to if the assisted person simply wishes to trade up to a bigger house.

(d) The assisted person may be allowed to buy the new property jointly with somebody else but if so, they must both execute the contractual charge in favour of the Board. The resources of the other person should be taken into account in deciding whether it is reasonable for the charge to be paid off, especially if they are living together as a family.

(e) Every case must be considered on its own merits, and any specific compassionate grounds or mitigating circumstances should be taken into account.

(f) Sometimes the assisted person wishes to trade down and buy a smaller property, using the difference in value to pay off all existing debts. The Board would expect the statutory charge to be paid off at the same time as the other debts, unless the assisted person would be unable to afford the new property or would otherwise suffer hardship.

DEALINGS WITH REGISTERED CHARGES

18–112 Once the Board has a registered substantive charge the property cannot be disposed of without the Board's consent or without paying off the charge. Where the charge is protected only by a caution against dealings, the Board has the right be notified of the proposed dealings with the land.[94] The Board, as a proprietor of a charge or caution, must be asked for any appropriate consent.

In deciding whether to consent its concern is to ensure that the security of the statutory charge is not prejudiced. It would not be acceptable for an assisted person to transfer the property from sole names into joint names if that would result in a full charge being replaced with a caution. In such a case the assisted person and other joint purchaser should execute a contractual charge in favour of the Board. On the other hand a transfer from joint names into the sole name of the assisted person may well benefit the Board and be agreed to, although if the assisted person is buying out another party, it is first reasonable to see whether the assisted person has sufficient funds to pay off the statutory charge at the same time.

The most common application for the Board's consent is made where the assisted person wishes to borrow money on the security of the property and requests that the borrowing is added to the first mortgage or otherwise takes

---

[94] Land Registration Act 1925, s. 55(1).

priority over the statutory charge. The Board has a discretion to defer the statutory charge to a further advance, but this discretion is exercised sparingly.

Like all dealings with the charge after registration, these requests are dealt with by the Land Charge Section of the Board's Debt Recovery Unit at Legal Aid Head Office.

REDEMPTION OF THE CHARGE

Once enforcement of the charge has been postponed, there is nothing in **18–113** the Regulations saying how long the postponement may last. Ultimately, it is the registration of the charge which governs when it must be paid, so that a charge must be paid off:

   (a) when the property is sold, unless there is an agreement to substitute;

   (b) on the death or bankruptcy of the assisted person;

   (c) upon the assisted person exercising any of the powers of an owner under section 18 or section 21 of the Land Registration Act 1925, unless the Board agrees to the transaction. The Board's standard form contractual charges provide for repayment of the charge in those circumstances if the Board requires it.

Redemptions are generally dealt with by the Board's Debt Recovery Unit at Legal Aid Head Office which should be contacted quoted the civil legal aid reference number as well as the full name (including any changes since the charge was registered) and address of the assisted person as well as the title number or land charge reference number. The *minimum* information required is the assisted person's full name at the time of registration and the title number or land charge reference.

Chapter 19

THE REMUNERATION OF SOLICITORS, COUNSEL AND LEGAL REPRESENTATIVES

INTRODUCTION

19–01 Legal representatives acting for assisted persons have a statutory right to costs. These are payable to them out of the Fund and they may not look for payment to their clients or to any other source. The amounts due are normally ascertained by legal aid taxation carried out by a taxing officer on the standard basis subject to the Regulations,[1-2] but in certain cases they are assessed by the Area Director without taxation. Counsel's fees are fixed by taxation or assessment and are not agreed in advance with the instructing solicitor.

This chapter contains the general provisions relating to the costs payable to solicitors and counsel: the detailed procedure and the principles to be applied on taxation are dealt with in chapter 20.

In respect of any legal aid certificate granted on or after February 25, 1994, the Legal Aid in Civil Proceedings (Remuneration) Regulations 1994 and the Legal Aid in Family Proceedings (Remuneration) Regulations 1991 as amended, will apply.[3] Where a certificate was granted before February 25, 1994 to an assisted person whose solicitor represents any other assisted person in the same proceedings under a certificate granted on or after February 25, 1994 the provisions do not apply as regards the costs payable under the later certificate.[4]

Proceedings in respect of which a certificate was granted before February

---

[1-2] Legal Aid in Civil Proceedings (Remuneration) Regulations 1944; Legal Aid in Family Proceedings (Remuneration) Regulations 1991 as amended.

[3] Legal Aid in Civil Proceedings (Remuneration) Regulations 1994, reg. 1(1); Legal Aid in Family Proceedings (Remuneration) (Amendment) Regulations 1994, reg. 1(1).

[4] Legal Aid in Civil Proceedings (Remuneration) Regulations 1994, reg. 1(4); Legal Aid in Family Proceedings (Remuneration) (Amendment) Regulations 1994, reg. 2(2).

25, 1994 are treated as if the Remuneration Regulations had not been made, notwithstanding any amendment issued under Part VII of the Civil Legal Aid (General) Regulations 1989 on or after that date.[5]

The Legal Aid in Civil Proceedings (Remuneration) Regulations 1994 apply to proceedings to which Part IV of the 1988 Act apply except proceedings in the House of Lords; proceedings in the Court of Appeal; proceedings in the magistrates' courts; proceedings to which regulation 3(2)(a) (care proceedings) or regulation 3(2)(b) (prescribed family proceedings or, in a magistrates' court, any family proceedings other than care proceedings) of the Legal Aid in Family Proceedings (Remuneration) Regulations 1991 apply; proceedings for contempt under section 29 of the 1988 Act; or proceedings relating to particular courts and tribunals to which Part XV of the Civil Legal Aid (General) Regulations 1989 applies.[6-8]

In legally aided cases authority must, unless it is contained in the **19–02** certificate, be obtained from the Area Director before certain acts are done or steps are taken, such as instructing leading counsel or more than one counsel, or adding parties to the proceedings. Failure to obtain authority may result in the costs being disallowed on the legal aid taxation; where authority is obtained no question may be raised on taxation as to the amount of the payment to be allowed. Costs which are disallowed on taxation cannot be recovered from the assisted person. Prior authority may be obtained for certain other acts, such as engaging an expert witness, lodging an interlocutory appeal or bespeaking a transcript. If such authority is not obtained, payment will depend on whether the costs are allowed on the legal aid taxation or assessment. Where authority is obtained, no question as to the propriety of any step or act in relation to which prior authority has been obtained under the Civil Legal Aid (General) Regulations 1989 may be raised on any taxation of costs.[9]

The Board has given guidance as to the general circumstances in which costs and counsel's fees will normally be allowed in relation to such matters as instructing leading counsel, experts' and witnesses' fees and unusual expenditure.[10]

---

[5] Legal Aid in Civil Proceedings (Remuneration) Regulations 1994, reg. 1(4); Legal Aid in Family Proceedings (Remuneration) (Amendment) Regulations 1994, reg. 2(3).
[6-8] Legal Aid in Civil Proceedings (Remuneration) Regulations 1994, reg. 3.
[9] Legal Aid (General) Regulations 1989, reg. 63(1).
[10] Notes for Guidance, paras. 38 et seq.

THE RIGHT TO COSTS

The statutory right

19–03 Section 31(3) of the 1988 Act provides that:

> "A person who provides advice, assistance or representation under this Act shall not take any payment in respect of the advice, assistance or representation, except such payment as is made by the Board or authorised by, or by regulations under this Act."

Effect is given to the statutory right in one of the following ways:

(a) by a legal aid taxation conducted on the standard basis under regulation 107A(2) of the Civil Legal Aid (General); Regulations 1989 and in accordance with R.S.C., Ord. 62, r. 12[11];

(b) by assessment and taxation where agreed costs have been paid[12];

(c) by their being assessed by the Area Director; or

(d) by the solicitor or counsel electing, as they are entitled to do in certain (matrimonial) proceedings, to have their costs fixed instead of taxed.

Basis of Taxation

19–04 On any assessment, review or taxation of the costs of an assisted person in proceedings where the costs are or may be paid out of the Fund, the costs will be determined on the standard basis, subject to the relevant remuneration Regulations. The current Regulations are the Legal Aid in Civil Proceedings (Remuneration) Regulations 1994 and the Legal Aid in Family Proceedings (Remuneration) Regulations 1991.[13] Subject to that, any assessment, review or taxation will be carried out in accordance with Part XII (Costs of assisted persons) of the Civil Legal Aid (General) Regulations 1989. The assessment review or taxation must be conducted, together with any determination of the costs of the proceedings required, in accordance with any direction or order given or made in the proceedings.[14]

Costs that can be paid only out of the Fund

19–05 Except in so far as he is required to make a contribution towards the costs of being represented, a legally assisted person may not be required to make any payment in respect of the costs due to his legal representative for work

---

[11] Civil Legal Aid (General) Regulations 1989, reg. 107.
[12] *ibid.* reg. 106A.
[13] *ibid.* reg. 107A(1), (2).
[14] *ibid.* reg. 107A(3).

done on his behalf under the certificate and it is for the Board to pay the legal representative:[15] "The Fund alone is in law responsible for the solicitor's bill; and the lay client's contribution, if any, goes into the Fund and not direct to the solicitor."[16]

Where an order for costs is made in favour of an assisted party, the assisted person's legal representatives are not prevented from recovering from the paying party the sums in respect of costs to which they are entitled, either by any rule of law which limits the costs recoverable by a party to proceedings to the amount which he is liable to pay his legal representatives, or by regulation 64 of the Civil Legal Aid (General) Regulations 1989.[17] This means that the legal representatives may recover from a paying party amounts in excess of the rates prescribed by the Regulations and once the Board has been reimbursed its outlay, any costs recovered from the paying party belongs to the solicitor.[18]

Different considerations apply where a legally assisted person's certificate **19–06** is revoked. That person is then deemed never to have been an assisted person in relation to those proceedings and can be called upon to pay the full amount of the costs to the Board.[19] The legal representatives are, however, still paid out of the Fund.

Save as outlined above, neither solicitor nor counsel may receive or be a party to the making of any payment for work done in any proceedings during the currency of the legally assisted person's certificate *whether within the scope of the certificate or otherwise* except payments made out of the Fund.[20] This is an absolute rule which prevents a client from being charged for work done even if it is outside the scope of the certificate. There is, however, a distinction to be drawn: the matter was considered by the Court of Appeal[21] where it is was held that on its true construction the word "proceedings" (in regulation 65 of the Legal Aid (General) Regulations 1980 which is identical to regulation 64 of the Civil Legal Aid (General) Regulations 1989) has a narrow meaning which reflects the fact that legal aid may be, and often is, granted to deal with one issue arising out of an action as a whole and therefore refers only to the specific proceedings for which legal aid was granted, even though those proceedings might only be incidental to the whole action. Accordingly, where a legal aid certificate has been granted to a defendant to purge his contempt of court in civil proceedings brought against him, the solicitor who represents him in the contempt of court proceedings will not be precluded from receiving payments from the defendant for representing him in the main civil

---

[15] Legal Aid Act 1988, s. 15(6).
[16] *Rolph v. Marston Valley Brick Company Ltd* [1956] 2 Q.B. 18 at 23, *per* Devlin J.
[17] Civil Legal Aid (General) Regulations 1989, reg. 107B(3).
[18] *ibid.* reg. 107B(4).
[19] Civil Legal Aid (General) Regulations 1989, reg. 74.
[20] *ibid.* reg. 64.
[21] *Littaur v. Steggles Palmer* [1986] 1 W.L.R. 287.

proceedings brought against him by the plaintiff, nor will the solicitor be precluded from claiming a lien on the papers appertaining to those civil proceedings. Apart from that exposition of the law, it is not possible to require a client to top up fees under a legal aid certificate.

Care should be taken by counsel and solicitors in family proceedings not to dissipate assets available to the parties by costs of the legal actions pursued. The Fund and therefore the taxpayer looks for protection to the good sense of the practitioner and his client which imposes upon them high standards of trust and care.[22]

Directions to tax

19–07   The Regulations provide for legal aid costs to be taxed. They direct that, where in any proceedings to which an assisted person is a party:

    (a) judgment is signed in default, the judgment must include a direction that the costs of any assisted person shall be taxed under regulation 107A(2) of the Civil Legal Aid (General) Regulations 1989;

    (b) the court gives judgment or makes a final decree or order in the proceedings, this must include a direction (in addition to any other direction as to taxation) that the costs of any assisted person are to be taxed under regulation 107A(2) of the Civil Legal Aid (General) Regulations 1989; and

    (c) the plaintiff accepts money paid into court, the costs of any assisted person are to be paid under regulation 107A(2) of the Civil Legal Aid (General) Regulations 1989.[23]

Before making an order for costs, a judge must be satisfied of two things: first, that the proceedings are proceedings to which an assisted person is a party and secondly, that judgment is being given or a final order made in those proceedings.[24] In order to ensure that these two criteria are met, the Regulations provide that any certificate or notice of revocation or discharge must be made available on taxation and that the costs of proceedings to which an assisted person is a party, must be taxed in accordance with any direction or order given irrespective of the interest, if any, of the assisted person in the taxation. An order for the taxation of the costs of a review of taxation or of the costs of an appeal from the decision of a judge on such a review is deemed to be a final order.[25]

---

[22] *Clark v. Clark, The Times*, March 31, 1988.
[23] Civil Legal Aid (General) Regulations 1989, reg. 107(3).
[24] *Rolph v. Marston Valley Brick Company Ltd* [1956] 2 Q.B. 18 at 28, *per* Devlin J.
[25] Civil Legal Aid (General) Regulations 1989, regs. 107(1), (2).

Dismissal of appeal by consent

Where an appellant to the Court of Appeal does not wish to continue with   **19–08**
his appeal, it can be dismissed by consent on paper without a hearing. A
form of consent must be signed and sent to the Registrar of Civil Appeals.
Where any party is legally aided, the dismissal by consent form should
request legal aid taxation of his costs. There is no need for a separate
attendance at court.[26]

Taxation on discharge or revocation of a certificate

It may sometimes happen that no direction is made for there to be a legal   **19–09**
aid taxation, either through inadvertence or because of the way in which
the proceedings come to an end. To cover this contingency, the Regulations
provide that, where in any proceedings to which an assisted person or
former assisted person is a party:

(a) the proceedings are or have been brought to an end without a
direction having been given; or

(b) a judgment or order in favour of an opposing party which includes
a direction that the assisted person's costs be taxed on the standard
basis has not been drawn up or entered by him; or

(c) a retainer is determined under regulation 83[27] in such
circumstances as to require a taxation;

the costs of the assisted person will be taxed under regulation 107A(2) of
the Civil Legal Aid (General) Regulations 1989 on production of a copy of
the notice of discharge or revocation of the certificate at the appropriate
taxing office.[28] In the Supreme Court taxing office, references will be given
on notices of discharge or revocation which need not previously have been
filed in court.

The power of the court to deprive a solicitor of his costs

Upon an assessment or taxation, the relevant authority may allow costs in   **19–10**
respect of any item or class of work at less than the rates prescribed by the
Remuneration Regulations where it appears reasonable to do so having
regard for the competence or despatch of which the item or class of work
was done. This power is without prejudice to the powers under regulation
109 of the Civil Legal Aid (General) Regulations 1989.[29]

---

[26] *Re K (A Minor), The Times,* January 3, 1990; R.S.C., Ord. 59, r. 1.
[27] Civil Legal Aid (General) Regulations 1989, reg. 83.
[28] *ibid.* reg. 107(4).
[29] Legal Aid in Civil Proceedings (Remuneration) Regulations 1994, reg. 6(1) and (2).

The requirement that the court must make a direction for taxation under the 1988 Act, does not affect its power to deprive a solicitor of his costs. Where it appears to the court[30] or to a taxing master or district judge[31] that costs have been wasted in the taxation proceedings or in the proceedings which gave rise to the taxation proceedings, he may exercise the powers conferred on the court by section 51(6) of the Supreme Court Act 1981.[32]

Where the court decides to make an order under section 51(6) of the Supreme Court Act 1981, disallowing wasted costs, or ordering a legal representative to meet such costs or part of them, it must (having given the legal representative concerned a reasonable opportunity to appear and show cause why such an order should not be made[33]) specify in the order the costs which are to be so disallowed or met, and may make such other order as it thinks fit.[34] Before making such an order the court may direct a taxing master or district judge to inquire into the matter and report back to them.[35] When conducting such an inquiry the taxing master or district judge has all the powers and duties of the court under R.S.C., Ord. 62, r. 11(6) and (8).[36] The court may, instead of proceeding as set out above, refer the matter to a taxing master or district judge to deal with the matter under R.S.C., Ord. 62, r. 28(2) and (3).[37] Slow action by the legal aid authorities, and delay in obtaining counsel's written opinion that contributed to the tardy prosecution of a case entitled solicitors to have set aside an order that they were personally liable for wasted costs.[38]

Where a party entitled to costs:

(a) fails without good reason to commence or conduct proceedings for a taxation of those costs in accordance with Order 62 or any direction or;

(b) delays lodging the bill for taxation, a taxing master or district judge may:

(i) disallow all or part of the costs of taxation that he would otherwise have awarded that party; and

(ii) after taking into account all the circumstances (including any prejudice suffered by any other party as a result of such failure or delay as the case may be, and any additional interest payable under section 17 of the Judgments Act 1838, because of the failure or delay) allow the parties so entitled less than

---

[30] Under R.S.C., Ord. 62, r. 11(3).
[31] *ibid.* r. 28(2).
[32] R.S.C., Ord. 62, r. 28(2).
[33] *ibid.* r. 11(4).
[34] R.S.C., Ord. 62, r. 11(1)(a).
[35] *ibid.* r. 11(1)(b).
[36] *ibid.* r. 11(2).
[37] *ibid.* r. 11(3).
[38] *Trill v. Sacher (No. 2), The Times,* November 14, 1992.

the amount he would otherwise have allowed on taxation of the bill or wholly disallow the costs.[39]

19–11 The Civil Division of the Court of Appeal, the High Court and any county court have a complete discretion as to the costs of, and incidental to, all proceedings before the particular court, and the court has full power to determine by whom and to what extent the costs are to be paid. This power does not include orders that the costs of solicitors' successful appeals against wasted costs orders be paid out of central funds.[40]

In any such proceedings the court may disallow, or order the legal or other representative concerned to meet the whole or any part of any wasted costs. "Wasted costs" means any costs incurred by a party:

(a) as a result of any improper, unreasonable or negligent act or omission on the part of any legal or other representative or any employee of such a representative; or

(b) which in the light of any such act or omission occurring after they were incurred, the court considers it is unreasonable to expect that party to pay.[41]

Where a person has commenced proceedings in the High Court but those proceedings should, in the opinion of the court, have been commenced in a county court, the person responsible for determining the amount which is to be awarded to that person by way of costs, must have regard to those circumstances. Where that person reduces the amount which would otherwise be awarded to the person in question, the amount of the reduction must not exceed 25 per cent and on any taxation of the costs payable by that person to his legal representative regard must be had to the amount of the reduction.[42]

19–12 The above provisions apply in relation to any civil proceedings in the Crown Court as they apply in relation to any proceedings before the other courts mentioned above.[43]

In any civil proceedings in the magistrates' court the court may disallow or order the legal or other representative concerned to meet the whole or any part of any wasted costs. "Wasted costs" has the same meaning as detailed above (in para. 19–09). Rules may make provision as to the destination of any payment required to be made including provision for the reimbursement of sums paid by the Board. Before such an order is made, the magistrates' court must allow the legal or other representative a

---

[39] *ibid.* r. 28(4).
[40] *Holden v. C.P.S. (No. 2); sub nom. Steele Ford & Newton v. Crown Prosecution Service* [1993] 2 W.L.R. 934, H.L.
[41] Supreme Court Act 1981, s. 51 as amended by Courts and Legal Services Act 1990, s. 4.
[42] Supreme Court Act 1981, s. 51(8), (9) as inserted by Courts and Legal Services Act 1991, s. 4.
[43] Supreme Court Act 1981, s. 52(2A) as inserted by Courts and Legal Services Act 1990, s. 4(2).

reasonable opportunity to appear before it and show cause why it should not do so.[44]

19–13   Save in exceptional circumstances, no application for a wasted costs order should, in civil litigation, be sought against a party's legal representative until after the trial. The test to be applied on such an application has to be the same, whether the client was legally aided or not. No lawyer who acts in the public interest by accepting legally aided clients should stand any greater risk of being ordered to pay costs than if he was acting for a paying client.[45] When considering whether or not to make a wasted costs order it is important for a judge to bear in mind that it is a draconian order and to remember the daily demands of practice including difficulties with time estimates.[46]

A solicitor's failure to warn either the court or his opponent in sufficient time that because of his difficulties with the Board, he might have to seek at a late stage an adjournment of the hearing was an error of judgment on his part but did not warrant the making of a wasted costs order against him personally.[47] Before the court can make a wasted costs order against a firm of solicitors it need only find that their negligence, unvarnished by any pejorative adjective had resulted in their client unnecessarily incurring an order for costs.[48] A wasted costs order can only be made against counsel in respect of acts done after October 1, 1991 when the amendment to the Supreme Court Act 1981 came into force.[49]

Inherent jurisdiction in civil cases

19–14   Under its inherent jurisdiction, it was thought that the court would normally only deal with inexcusable conduct, not mere errors of judgment or negligence.[50] Where the legislature has stepped in with particular legislation in a particular area, then, within that particular area, the existing (inherent) jurisdiction is ousted or curtailed, at any rate, so far as the particular legislation is negative in character.[51]

The Master of the Rolls held in *Gupta v. Comer*[52] that *Myers v. Elman*[53] was authority for the proposition that, in the exercise of its inherent or common law jurisdiction over solicitors as officers of the Supreme Court,

---

[44] Magistrates' Courts Act 1980, s. 145A as inserted by Courts and Legal Services Act 1990, s. 112.
[45] *Filmlab Systems International Ltd v. Pennington, The Times,* July 9, 1993.
[46] *Re a Barrister* (Wasted Costs Order No. 4 of 1993) *The Times,* April 12, 1995 C.A.
[47] *Re A Solicitor (Wasted Costs Order),* 1993, 2 F.L.R. 959 C.A.
[48] *Philex plc v. Golban, The Times,* July 9, 1993.
[49] *Fozal v. Gofur, The Times,* July 9, 1993.
[50] *Re A Solicitor* (1978) 122 S. J. 264, C.A. *Thew R. & T. Ltd v. Reeves (No. 2)* [1982] 2 Q.B. 172; *Re A Solicitor (Taxation of Costs)* [1982] 1 W.L.R. 745; [1982] 2 All E.R. 683.
[51] *Shiloh Spinners Ltd v. Harding* [1973] A.C. 691; *Harrison v. Tew* [1987] 2 W.L.R. 1.
[52] *Gupta v. Comer* [1991] 1 Q.B. 629.
[53] *Myers v. Elman* [1940] A.C. 282.

the court should not make a costs order against a solicitor in his capacity as such, unless satisfied that the conduct which gave rise to those costs being incurred could properly be described as "a serious dereliction of duty as a solicitor either by himself or his clerks" or "gross negligence" or "a gross neglect". The *ratio* of *Sinclair-Jones v. Kay*[54] was that in civil proceedings governed by Ord. 62, r. 11 *Myers v. Elman* did not apply. The *ratio* of *Holden v. C.P.S.* was that Ord. 62, r. 11 did not apply in Crown Court proceedings where the court's jurisdiction was limited by *Myers v. Elman*. The powerful criticism of *Sinclair-Jones* in Lord Lane's judgment was accordingly *obiter*. In those circumstances, the Court of Appeal in *Gupta v. Comer* had to follow and apply *Sinclair-Jones*. In that case — which was on the subject of delay — L.J. May stated that the principles requiring gross misconduct laid down in older authorities were not applicable to an application under the modern Ord. 62, r. 11. That rule was to be given its ordinary English meaning and the court was to consider whether the particular conduct complained of was within its terms or not. Reasonably construed and applied it could work no injustice and could indeed be salutary.

Decided cases on the exercise of the penal jurisdiction

Lincoln J. held that there was a discretion to reduce the amount claimed if **19–15** there had been a long delay in submitting the bill even though the delay had not caused any prejudice. In that case, the delay was 19 months.[55] The power of the superior courts to order a solicitor personally to pay costs thrown away by his negligence exists whether or not the case is legally aided.[56]

> "But the jurisdiction to order a solicitor to pay the costs personally is to be exercised with great care and discretion and only in clear cases. It should not rest solely on inference without evidence. It is not for the solicitors or counsel to impose a screen through which a litigant has to pass before he can put his case before the Court".[57]

The judge must give the solicitors the opportunity of being heard as to whether or not such an order should be made.[58]

It is not sufficient merely to address counsel who has been briefed on behalf of the client and has no authority to answer for the solicitors.[59] Since counsel are not officers of the court, the court has no inherent powers in respect of counsel's fees. It will not exonerate a solicitor if he has blindly followed the view expressed by counsel (even experienced, leading

---

[54] *Sinclair-Jones v. Kay* [1989] 1 W.L.R. 114, C.A.
[55] *Re K (A Minor)* (1988) 138 New L.J. 262.
[56] Supreme Court Act 1981, s. 1(1)
[57] *Orchard v. South Eastern Electricity Board* [1987] Q.B. 565, *per* Donaldson M.R.
[58] *Myers v. Elman* [1940] A.C. 282.
[59] *R. v. Smith* [1975] Q.B. 531.

counsel) without exercising his own independent judgment.[60] But where a solicitor seeks counsel's advice as to the parties against whom proceedings should be brought and the form of the proceedings, and acts upon it without any notice of the inaccuracy of the advice, he will not be ordered personally to pay the costs thrown away.[61]

The Court of Appeal has indicated that, if counsel and solicitors fail to exercise the greatest possible diligence in complying with time-limits in the preparation of appeals in children's cases, the court will regard the matter as one of professional misconduct.[62] The Master of the Rolls wished it to be known, especially by those of the Bar who were peripatetic, that delays in such cases would not be tolerated. It was virtually impossible to dismiss an appeal in child cases without investigating the merits and the court's only alternative was, therefore, to regard the matter as professional misconduct.

19–16   The court has power under its inherent jurisdiction to order a solicitor to repay personally to the Fund, costs which have been incurred by a legally aided client as a result of a serious dereliction of duty on the part of the solicitor. The court will not exercise that power if the Board is dilatory in seeking an order that the solicitor pay the costs personally.[63]

Where it is obvious that the counsel who has been instructed is not competent to conduct the proceedings, the solicitors are always seriously at fault in not withdrawing instructions from him and ensuring that counsel competent to prosecute the proceedings is instructed. In those circumstances, it is no excuse for the solicitors to say that they were relying on counsel and that counsel has let them down.[64]

Where a case was set down on a defendant's application, the plaintiff having been an assisted person whose solicitor had exceeded the legal aid remit but continued to act, the court refused the plaintiff's application for an adjournment and dismissed the action against the defendant with costs to be paid by the plaintiff's solicitors.[65]

Wasted Costs

19–17   Section 51(6) of the Supreme Court Act 1981 empowers the Civil Division of the Court of Appeal, the High Court and the County Court to disallow or order the legal or other representative concerned to meet, the whole of any wasted costs or such part of them as may be determined in accordance with the rules of Court.

---

[60] *Davy-Chiesman v. Davy-Chiesman* [1984] Fam. 48.
[61] *R. v. Oxfordshire County Council, ex. p. Wallace* (1987) New L.J. 542.
[62] *Re M (A Minor)*, The Times, December 29, 1989.
[63] *Clark v. Clark (No. 2)* (1990) 140 New L.J. 140 at 206.
[64] *Re A (A Minor)* [1988] Fam. 339.
[65] *Castleton v. Anglian Windows*, The Times, December 13, 1989.

"Wasted costs" means any costs incurred by a party as a result of any improper, unreasonable or negligent act or omission on the part of any legal or other representative or any employee of such a representative; or which in the light of such act or omission occurring after they were incurred, the Court considers it unreasonable to expect that party to pay.[66]

The Court of Appeal has considered the wasted cost jurisdiction in a judgement covering six cases.[67] The Court considered the meaning of "improper, unreasonable or negligent". "Improper" covers but is not confined to conduct which would ordinarily be held to justify disbarment, striking off, suspension from practice or other serious professional penalty. "Unreasonable" aptly describes conduct which is vexatious, designed to harass the other side rather than advance the resolution of the case and it makes no difference that the conduct is a product excessive zeal and not improper motive. Conduct cannot be described as unreasonable simply because it leads to an unsuccessful result or because other more cautious legal representatives would have acted differently. The acid test is whether the conduct permitted of a reasonable explanation. "Negligence" should be understood in an untechnical way to denote failure to act with the competence reasonably expected of ordinary members of the profession. In adopting that approach the Court firmly discountenanced any suggestion that an applicant for a wasted cost order needed to prove, under the negligence head, anything less that he would have to prove in an action for negligence.[68]

The Court of Appeal also dealt with the question of pursuing a hopeless case. A legal representative cannot lend his assistance to proceedings which are an abuse of the process and is not entitled to use litigious procedures for purposes for which they were not intended, as by issuing or pursuing proceedings unconnected with success in the litigation or pursuing a case known to be dishonest; nor is he entitled to evade rules intended to safeguarded the interests of justice as by knowingly failing to make full disclosure on an ex parte application or knowingly conniving at incomplete disclosure of documents.

In relation to legal aid the Court held that the effect of section 31(1) of the Legal Aid Act 1988, was that the existence of Legal Aid should not affect the client/legal representative relationship nor the right of other parties to the proceedings or the principles on which discretion is exercised. It is incumbent on the courts to which the wasted cost applications are made to bear prominently in mind the peculiar vulnerability of legal

---

[66] Supreme Court Act 1981, s. 51 (7) and see para 19–10 above.

[67] *Ridehalgh v. Horsefield; Allen v. Unigate Dairies Ltd; Roberts v. Coverite (Ashphalters) Ltd; Philex Plc v. Golban; Watson v. Watson; Antonelli v. Wade Gery Farr (a Firm)*, [1994] 3 W.L.R. 462, C.A..

[68] See *Saif Ali v. Sidney Mitchell & Co.* [1980] A.C. 198 at 218.

representatives acting for assisted persons.[69] It would subvert the benevolent purposes of the legal aid legislation if such representatives were subject to any unusual personal risk. The Court should also bear prominently in mind that the advice and conduct of legal representatives is not to be tempered by the knowledge that their client is not their paymaster and so not, in all probability, liable for the costs of the other side.

The Court went on to deal with the question of immunity (of advocates) and privilege, then turned to causation. Demonstration of the causal link between the improper, unreasonable or negligent conduct and the waste of costs is essential. Where conduct is proved but no waste of costs shown to have resulted, the case might be referred to the appropriate disciplinary body or the legal aid authorities, it is not a matter for the exercise of the wasted cost jurisdiction.

The procedure to be followed in determining wasted cost orders is to be laid down by the Courts so as to meet the requirements of the individual cases before them. The overriding requirements are that any procedure has to be fair and as simple and summary as fairness permits. The respondent lawyer should be very clearly told what he is said to have done wrong and what is claimed. The requirements of simplicity and summariness mean that elaborate pleadings, should in general, be avoided. No formal process of discovery is appropriate. The Court could not imagine any circumstances in which the applicant should be permitted to interrogate the respondent lawyer or vice versa. Hearings should be measured in hours not days or weeks. Judges should not reject the weapon that Parliament intended to be used for the protection of those injured by the unjustifiable conduct of the other sides lawyers, they must be astute to control what threatens to become a new and costly form of satellite litigation.

The jurisdiction to make a wasted costs order also depends at two stages of the Court's discretion:

1 At the stage of initial application when the Court is invited to give the represensative an opportunity to show cause. This is not something to be done automatically. The costs of the enquiries compared with the costs claimed are always a relevant consideration. The discretion, like any other, is to be exercised judicially. However, Judges might not infrequently decide that further proceedings are not likely to be justified.

2 At the final stage, because even if the Court is satisfied that legal representatives have acted, improperly, unreasonable or negligently so as to waste costs, it is not bound to make an order but will have to give sustainable reasons for the exercise of its discretion in that way.

The Court of Appeal reiterated the undesirability of there being a

---

[69] *Symphony Group Plc v. Hodgson* [1993] 3 W.L.R. 830 at 842.

divergence in the practice of the Civil and Criminal Courts.[70] Parliament, it was said, had acted substantially to assimilate the practice in the two. The Court fully appreciated that the conduct of criminal cases would often raise different questions and depend on different circumstances, but expressed the hope that its judgement might give guidance that would be of value to both Civil and Criminal Courts.

Under the Civil Legal Aid (General) Regulations 1989

Without prejudice to the powers of the court, under the Supreme Court Act **19–18** 1981, s. 51(6), R.S.C., Ord. 62, rr. 10 and 11 or C.C.R., Ord. 38, r.1(3), on any taxation of an assisted person's costs in connection with proceedings (which are not authorised summary proceedings), any wasted costs must be disallowed or reduced; where the solicitor has, without a good reason, delayed putting in his bill for taxation, the whole of the costs may be disallowed or reduced.[71]

"Wasted costs" means any costs incurred by a party as a result of any improper, unreasonable or negligent act or omission on the part of a legal representative or an employee of such a representative, or which, in the light of such act or omission occurring after they were incurred, the taxing officer considers it unreasonable to expect that party to pay.[72]

No such reduction may be made until notice has been served by the taxing officer on the solicitor whose name appears on the certificate or, if the reduction relates to counsel's fees, on the assisted person's counsel, requiring the solicitor or counsel to show cause orally or in writing why those costs should not be disallowed or reduced.[73]

The solicitor is under a duty to inform the counsel in writing within seven days of taxation where the fees claimed on his behalf have been disallowed or reduced. The solicitor is also required to endorse the bill of costs with the date on which the notice was given or alternatively that no notice was necessary. The result of this is that where the bill of costs was endorsed that no notice was necessary, the certificate or allocatur may be issued immediately, but where such a notice has been given, no certificate or allocatur will be issued until 14 days have elapsed from the date of the endorsement.[74]

---

[70] See *Holden v. CPS*, [1992] Q.B. 261 and *Gupta v. Gomer* [1991], 1 Q.B. 269 C.A.
[71] Civil Legal Aid (General) Regulations 1989, reg. 109(1).
[72] *ibid.* reg. 109(3).
[73] *ibid.* reg. 109(2).
[74] *ibid.* reg. 112(1), (2).

WHAT COSTS ARE PAYABLE?

Remuneration

19–19   The amounts allowable to solicitors on assessment or taxation under regulation 107(A) of the Civil Legal Aid (General) Regulations 1989 will be in accordance with the Schedule to the Remuneration Regulations.[75]

Where the amount of a solicitor's remuneration in respect of non-contentious business is regulated (in the absence of agreement to the contrary) by the Solicitor's (Non Contentious Business) Remuneration Order 1994 or any similar Order, the amount of the costs to be allowed on taxation in respect of the like contentious business will be the same, notwithstanding anything contained in R.S.C., Ord. 62, App. 2.[76]

Where no provision is made in the Schedule to the Remuneration Regulations for the kind of work to which the costs relate, R.S.C., Ord. 62, App. 2, Pt. 1, para. 1(1) or C.C.R., Ord. 38, rule 3(3A) or (3B) will apply.[77]

In dealing with preparation work, the relevant authority must allow the higher specified rate where the office of the solicitor of the assisted person where the work was done is situated within legal aid area 1 (London).[78]

Disbursements, including counsel's fees, must be determined in accordance with R.S.C., Ord. 62 and C.C.R., Ord. 38.[79]

Subject to the Remuneration Regulations, the sums to be allowed to legal representatives in connection with the representation of an assisted person in proceedings to which the Remuneration Regulations apply, will be determined in accordance with Civil Legal Aid (General) Regulations 1989, Pt. XII, R.S.C., Ord. 62 and C.C.R., Ord. 38.[80]

Enhancement

19–20   On assessment or taxation, the relevant authority may allow fees of more than the prescribed rate where taking into account all the relevant circumstances — it appears that the work was done with exceptional competence, skill or expertise, with exceptional despatch, or the case invoved exceptional circumstances or complexity.[81]

---

[75] Legal Aid in Civil Proceedings (Remuneration) Regulations 1994, reg. 4(1)(a); similarly see Legal Aid in Family Proceedings (Remuneration) Regulations 1991, reg. 3(1)(a).
[76] R.S.C., Ord. 62, r. 17(2) and Legal Aid in Civil Proceedings (Remuneration) Regulations 1994, reg. 4(1)(B).
[77] *ibid.* reg. 4(1)(c).
[78] *ibid.* reg. 4(2).
[79] *ibid.* reg. 4(3).
[80] *ibid.* reg. 4(4).
[81] *ibid.* reg. 5(1). As to enhancement in Family proceedings see Re: Children Act 1989 (Taxation of Costs) 1994 2 FLR 934. Cazalet. J.

Enhancement may be applied to any item or class of work and takes the form of a percentage of the prescribed rate.[82] Fees may not be enhanced by more than 100 per cent,[83] except that in proceedings in the High Court the relevant authority may allow an enhancement exceeding 100 per cent when it considers that in comparison with work in other High Court proceedings which would merit a 100 per cent enhancement, the item or class of work relates to exceptionally complex matters which have been handled with exceptional competence or despatch. In those circumstances, the enhancement may exceed 100 per cent, but must not exceed 200 per cent.[84]

In determining what is exceptional within the meaning of the Regulations, the relevant authority may have regard for the generality of proceedings to which the Regulations apply.[85]

In determining the percentage by which fees should be enhanced above the prescribed rate, the relevant authority must have regard to:

(a) the degree of responsibility accepted by the solicitor;
(b) the care, speed and economy with which the case was prepared; and
(c) the novelty, weight and complexity of the case.[86]

Where a figure higher than the prescribed rate is sought for particular items of work, those items requiring an exercise of discretion by the taxing officer must be be identified.[87]

The work for which costs may be claimed

An assisted person's solicitor and counsel are entitled to be paid a **19–21** reasonable amount in respect of all costs reasonably incurred[88–89] — subject to the Regulations — within the scope of their client's certificate whether or not all that work comes within "the costs of the action" which would be payable *inter partes*. Legal aid covers representation to bring legal proceedings to an end whether by a contested hearing or by a compromise reached between parties. Implementation of the terms of a consent order necessarily involves the preparation of documentation; any other necessary work required to give effect to the order would fall within the scope of a legal aid order.[90–91] Before taking certain steps in an action, or doing certain acts on behalf of an assisted person, a solicitor may, and in some cases

---

[82] *ibid.* reg. 5(2).
[83] *ibid.* reg. 4(4).
[84] *ibid.* reg. 5(5), (6).
[85] *ibid.* reg. 5(7).
[86] *ibid.* reg. 5(3).
[87] *Re H(a Minor: Taxation of Counsel's costs) The Independent* August 14, 1995 Cazalet. J.
[88–89] R.S.C., Ord. 62, r. 12(1) and Civil Legal Aid (Remuneration) Regulations 1994; Legal Aid in Family Proceedings (Remuneration) Regulations 1991 as amended.
[90–91] *S. v. S. (Legal Aid Taxation)* [1991] Fam. Law, 271.

must, apply for authority from the Area Director, if this has not been given in the certificate. The effect of failing to obtain the authority in different cases has already been dealt with and must be kept in mind when considering the extent to which costs may be claimed from the Fund.

Where claims are made by a solicitor for payment of costs out of the Fund in respect of two or more cases — in which the work done, time spent or disbursements incurred are, in part or wholly, referrable to more than one case, the claims in respect of those cases should be so allocated as to avoid any duplication that would result in the total amount paid exceeding the total value of those items. The solicitor must ensure that the assessing authority is provided with sufficient information to enable it to perform its duty to ensure that no such duplication occurs.[92]

Legal aid granted after costs incurred

19–22 Where legal aid is granted to a party after proceedings have been instituted, the provisions of the 1988 Act apply only to so much of the costs of the proceedings as are incurred while the certificate is in force.[93]

Work done by a solicitor immediately prior to the issue of an emergency certificate, and at a time when no application for an emergency certificate could be made because the appropriate area office was closed, will be deemed to be work done while the certificate is in force if the solicitor applies for an emergency certificate at the first available opportunity and the application is granted.[94–95]

Where a solicitor has acted on behalf of an assisted person before the date of the legal aid certificate and where the solicitor has a lien on any documents necessary for the proceedings and has delivered them up subject to the lien, that solicitor may give notice of the fact to the appropriate area committee. If moneys are recovered for the assisted person, the Board will pay, to the solicitor giving notice, the amount to which that solicitor would have been entitled following a solicitor and own client taxation. If the amount recovered on behalf of the assisted person is insufficient to pay the solicitor's costs in full and also to meet the sums payable out of the Fund on the assisted person's account, the amount recovered in the proceedings will be divided between the Fund and the solicitor in the same proportions as the solicitor's costs and the cost to the Fund bear to the aggregate of the two. The statutory charge on property recovered or preserved in the proceedings will take effect accordingly. In such a case, where the amount of the costs payable to a solicitor or the *inter partes* costs incurred during the period in which the certificate was in

---

[92] *Re Rubie* (1975) L.S. Gaz, June 591, Solicitors Disciplinary Committee.
[93] Civil Legal Aid (General) Regulations 1989, reg. 103(1).
[94–95] *ibid.* reg. 103(6).

force have not been ascertained on taxation, they will be assessed by the appropriate area committee. In these circumstances, when the committee makes an assessment, it will do so with a view to allowing to the solicitor such costs as would have been allowed on a solicitor and own client taxation and, in respect of the *inter partes* costs, such costs as would have been allowed on a taxation under regulation 107A(2) of the Civil Legal Aid (General) Regulations 1989.[96]

Assessment by Area Director

In certain circumstances a legal aid taxation would cause undue expense, **19–23** would be inappropriate or would be contrary to the interests of the assisted person and assessment may then be the appropriate procedure.

Under the Civil Legal Aid (General) Regulations 1989, reg. 105

Under this head, "assessment" means an assessment of costs with a view **19–24** to ensuring that the amount of costs to be allowed are those which would be allowable on a taxation under regulation 107A(2) of the Civil Legal Aid (General) Regulations 1989.[97]

Where an assisted person has a financial interest in any assessment, review or appeal under regulation 105 of the Civil Legal Aid (General) Regulations 1989, he has a right to make written representations to the Area Director, appropriate area committee or committee appointed by the Board within 21 days of being notified of the right to make the representations.[98]

On an assessment, it is the duty of the assisted person's solicitor to: supply him with a copy of his bill, inform him of the extent of his financial interest and his right to make written representations, and endorse on the bill that the assisted person has a financial interest in the assessment and that he has complied with the above requirements.[99]

Where a legal representative wishes to apply for a review of the decision **19–25** of the Area Director or appeal against the decision of the area committee under regulation 105 of the Civil Legal Aid (General) Regulations 1989 and the assisted person has made representations prior to the assessment, the legal representative must notify the assisted person of the decision to be reviewed or appealed, the grounds of appeal and his right to make further representations.[1]

Subject to the provisions relating to assessment and taxation where

---

[96] Civil Legal Aid (General) Regulations 1989, reg. 103(2), (3), (4), (5).
[97] *ibid.* reg. 105(1).
[98] *Ibid.* reg. 105A (1).
[99] *Ibid.* reg. 105A(2).
[1] *ibid.* reg. 105A(3).

agreed costs have been paid[2] in any case where the retainer of the solicitor is determined before proceedings are actually begun and there has been no subsequent change of solicitor or counsel under the certificate, the amount of the costs and any fees payable to counsel must be assessed by the Area Director.[3]

Where proceedings have begun and the solicitor is of the opinion that the total amount which he and counsel would receive after taxation would not be more than £500, application must be made to the Area Director for an assessment in respect of the work done.[4]

19–26 Subject to the preceding paragraph, and to the provisions relating to assessment and taxation where agreed costs have been paid,[5] the assisted person's solicitor may, if he wishes, apply to the Area Director to have his costs, and any fees payable to counsel, assessed in any case where proceedings have been begun and:

(a) the solicitor is of the opinion that the total amount which he and any counsel who has been instructed would receive after a taxation would not be more than one thousand pounds; or

(b) there are special circumstances where a taxation would be against the interest of the assisted person or would increase the amount payable from the Fund; or

(c) after a direction or order that the assisted person's costs be taxed, the solicitor incurs costs for the purpose of recovering sums payable to the Fund.[6]

The provision for assessment of costs where taxation would be against the assisted person's interests is intended to serve as an escape clause in cases of difficulty, but it should not be construed so as to transfer the responsibility for ascertaining the costs from the taxing office to the Area Director merely because this would save expense. There must be special circumstances.

Assessment and taxation where agreed costs have been paid

19–27 Where proceedings to which an assisted person has been a party, as regards an assisted person,[7] settled without any direction of the courts as to costs on terms including a provision for the payment of agreed costs in favour of

---

[2] *ibid.* reg. 106A.
[3] *ibid.* reg. 105 (2).
[4] *ibid.* reg. 105 (2A) as amended by Civil Legal Aid (General) (Amendment) Regulations 1994, with effect from July 1, 1991.
[5] *ibid.* reg. 106A.
[6] Civil Legal Aid (General) Regulations 1989, reg. 105(3) as amended by Civil Legal Aid (General) (Amendment) Regulations 1994 (S.I. 1994 No. 229).
[7] Other than a person referred to in R.S.C., Ord. 62, r. 16, *i.e.* a minor or patient.

the assisted person, taxation or assesment must be dealt with as set out below.

Where proceedings to which an assisted person has been a party are brought to an end by a judgment, decree or final order and there has been agreement as to the cost to be paid in favour of the assisted person's solicitor or counsel is determined before proceedings are actually begun and there has been no subsequent change of solicitor or counsel under the certificate and there is an agreement for the payment of agreed costs in favour of the assisted person, the taxation or assessment must proceed as set out below.[8] For these provisions to apply, the agreed costs must, in each case, have been paid.[9]

In the above circumstances, the assisted person's solicitor may apply to the Area Director for an assessment limited to legal aid only costs, if the solicitor is of the opinion that the amount of those costs when determined, including counsel's fees, would not be more than £1,000.[10]

"Legal aid only costs" means those costs which would not be allowed as *inter partes* costs but which are payable from the Fund subject to determination under regulation 107A(2) of the General Regulations 1989.[11]

The assisted person's solicitor may apply for a taxation under regulation 107A(2) of the Civil Legal Aid (General) Regulations 1989 limited to legal aid only costs, if the solicitor is of the opinion that the amount of those costs when determined including counsel's fees would be more than £500.[12] Before any assessment or taxation takes place, the assisted person's solicitor must confirm in writing to the relevant authority that the agreed costs have been paid.[13] "The relevant authority" means the Area Director in the case of an assessment, and the taxing officer in the case of a taxation.[14] The relevant authority may require the production of any information which it considers relevant for the purpose of discharging its functions.[15]

The provisions of the Regulations[16] relating to review and appeal apply to assessments by the Area Director under these provisions.[17]

Where the Area Director has disallowed or reduced counsel's fees, counsel must be notified accordingly by the Area Director. If counsel is dissatisfied and wishes to make representations so that his fees can be reconsidered by the area committee, he must make them in writing. They

---

[8] Civil Legal Aid (General) Regulations 1989, reg. 106A(2).
[9] *ibid.* reg. 106A(2).
[10] *ibid.* reg. 106A(3).
[11] *ibid.* reg. 3.
[12] *ibid.* reg. 106A(4).
[13] *ibid.* reg. 106A(5).
[14] *ibid.* reg. 3.
[15] *ibid.* reg. 106A(6).
[16] *ibid.* reg. 105(4)(2)(8).
[17] *ibid.* reg. 106A(7).

are made directly to the area committee and not through instructing solicitors.

Where counsel has been instructed but not assigned, the instructing solicitor will be given an opportunity to comment on counsel's representations.

Notes for Guidance

19–28 The Board has approved guidance to be applied by area committees when dealing with claims for costs.

(a) Since there will no longer be a general right of appeal against area committee decisions to the Board, it is essential that area committees are seen to be carrying out an independent review in respect of each and every area office assessment against which representations are made. Area offices should therefore only place before the area committee a copy of the report on the case, a breakdown of the officer's assessment and the solicitor's and/or counsel's representations in support of their costs and fees claimed. Comments by the area office on the assessment made should be kept to a minimum, and where made should be restricted to issues of fact only. The Deputy Area Director (Finance) will be able to advise the committee on any matters of costs assessment practice affecting a particular case.

(b) Area committees should give reasons for their decisions in all cases. Where standard reasons would not be appropriate, the area committee should, of course, give a particular reason for its decision and, if necessary, refer to the relevant regulations and principles governing assessment of costs. The costs appeals committee has found that this cuts down considerably on the amount of correspondence received against decisions in particular cases since the profession is more satisfied that the issues involved have been considered properly.

(c) Where the area committee is satisfied that a point of principle of general importance arises, a certificate should be approved. The matters covered by the standard reasons for decisions are, generally speaking, issues of fact and would not, in the normal case, justify the certification of a point of principle of general importance. The Board considers that it is the area committee which should act as the final arbiter on all issues of fact such as attendance and preparation time.

Whilst the area committee must consider each case on its own merits, the types of case where points of principle are most likely to arise, are in respect of interpretations of the Regulations affecting assessment of costs and the principles governing their application on assessment. As the Regulations are new and their operation uncertain, area committees are asked at least for a 12-month period to give the benefit of the doubt to the appellant in those cases where it is uncertain whether a point of principle of general importance has been disclosed and to sanction an appeal to the Board.

The Board accepts that the area official should give reasons for his or her decision when disallowing costs. The officials should indicate the part of the bill considered unreasonable or not properly chargeable. This will enable the solicitor and/or counsel to formulate the representations which they wish the area committee to consider.

Proceedings in the magistrates' courts and the Crown Court

19–29 The remuneration of solicitors and counsel for work done in civil proceedings in magistrates' courts and the Crown Court (under Part IV of the 1988 Act) is assessed by the Area Director, and the costs are not taxed.[18-19] In the case of family proceedings, any assessment review or taxation is made in accordance with the Legal Aid in Family Proceedings (Remuneration) Regulations 1991.

Where an assessment or review is carried out in respect of such work (not family proceedings), it is done in accordance with the provisions of regulation 6 of, and Schedule 1, Part 1, paragraph 1(1)(a), to the Legal Aid in Criminal and Care Proceedings (Costs) Regulations 1989 as if the work done was work to which those provisions apply save that paragraphs 2 and 3 (relating to reduction and enhancement of the prescribed rates) do not apply.[20]

The provisions of the Civl Legal Aid (General) Regulations 1989 relating to assessment of costs, agreement in respect of costs, taxation of costs, failure to apply for taxation, the disallowance or reduction of costs and the solicitor's duty to safeguard the interests of the Fund do not apply to costs in relation to civil proceedings in the magistrates' court.[21]

Wilson J. sitting in the Family Division stated that there was an urgent need for reform of procedures in relation to the quantification of orders for costs in civil proceedings in the magistrates' court whether or not the successful party was legally aided. Pending reform, it was suggested that where the successful party was legaly aided and where the costs were large, the court should at least consider whether to adjourn pending the director's assessment or, where section 64(2) of the Magistrates' Courts Act 1980 did not apply (requiring any sum ordered to be paid to be specified in the order), to make an order in the amount of the future assessment rather than to proceed and to specify the amount in advance of the assessment. Justices

---

[18-19] *ibid.*, reg. 104(1).

[20] Civil Legal Aid (General) Regulations 1989, reg. 104(2), as amended by Civil Legal Aid (General) (Amendment) Regulations 1991.

[21] *Ibid.* reg. 104(4), (5), and see regs. 105–110.

are entitled to order a local authority to pay the costs of a successful appeal against its refusal to register an applicant as a child minder. The amount payable under a costs order made pursuant to rule 22 of the Family Proceedings Courts (Children Act 1989) Rules has to be ascertainable, but it does not have to be specified in the order.[22]

Counsel's fees

19–30 In legally aided cases, counsel's fees are not agreed by his instructing solicitor but are left to be fixed by the legal aid taxation or by assessment. No fees are marked on any set of papers delivered to counsel. Any instructions delivered to counsel must include a copy of the certificate (and any amendment to it) and any authority to incur costs obtained under Part VIII of the Civil Legal Aid (General) Regulation 1989. The instructions must be endorsed with the legal aid reference number and, in the case of authorised summary proceedings, show the authority for counsel to be instructed.[23]

The greatest cause of failure to recover counsel's fees is the failure by solicitors to comply with the above requirements. If those requirements are complied with, and counsel undertakes work which is not covered by a legal aid certificate, the solicitors have some protection. If, on the other hand, counsel is not given that information and undertakes work on the solicitors' instructions, the solicitors may find themselves the subject of a complaint to the Solicitors' Complaints Bureau, if counsel's fees are disallowed on taxation. It is not open to solicitors to pay counsel's fees personally because of the operation of regulation 64 of the Civil Legal Aid General Regulations 1989 which prevents an assisted person's solicitor or counsel from receiving or being party to the making of any payment for work done in the proceedings during the currency of the certificate (whether within the scope of the certificate or otherwise) except such payments as can be made out of the Fund.[24]

19–31 The Master of the Rolls has issued a number of Practice Statements concerning the taking of judgments and the submission of skeleton arguments by counsel. Counsel's brief fee includes his remuneration for taking a note of the judgment of the court, having the note transcribed accurately, submitting the note to the judge for approval where appropriate, revising it if so required by the judge and providing any copies required by the Court of Appeal, his instructing solicitors and his lay client. Accordingly, save in exceptional circumstances, there can be no justification for charging any additional fee for such work.[25]

---

[22] *Sutton London Borough Council v. Davis (No. 2)*, *The Times*, June 15 1994, *per* Wilson J.
[23] *ibid.* reg. 59(2).
[24] *ibid.* reg. 64.
[25] Practice Note, Master of the Rolls, May 9, 1989; [1989] 2 All E.R. 288.

With regard to skeleton arguments, a Practice Direction was issued by the Court of Appeal which applies to all appeals to the Civil Division which have a hearing date commencing on or after June 6, 1989.[26] The Direction makes skeleton arguments compulsory and lays down a timetable for their production and service. To ensure that counsel are entitled to appropriate remuneration for any extra work involved, the court has directed taxing masters to tax costs of preparing skeleton arguments separately from brief fees. If, for some reason, counsel is unable to comply with the Practice Direction, he should write to the Registrar of Civil Appeals explaining why that was so. Failure to lodge a skeleton argument within the appropriate time can result in the appeal being dismissed.[27]

The Practice Direction was subsequently extended and explained, and **19–32** counsel were asked to provide four, rather than three, copies of skeleton arguments so that one could be given to the court associate for availability to the press.[28] The request for a fourth copy was not intended to indicate that skeleton arguments would be made available in cases involving children or other cases in which special reporting restrictions applied.[29] The Court of Appeal subsequently confirmed that skeleton arguments were to be lodged four weeks before the date fixed for the hearing of the appeal and, where that time limit could not be complied with, counsel were to seek an extension from the Registrar of Civil Appeals.[30]

As soon as the work carried out by counsel has been completed, he should submit a note of his fees to his instructing solicitor in the normal way so that the solicitor can include these when submitting a bill of costs for taxation or assessment. It is open to counsel to supply the solicitor with the memorandum for the use of the taxing officer or the Area Director dealing with any factors which affect the amount of the fee for which he has asked.

Where counsel entrusts the conduct of the case to another member of the Bar, the latter is entitled to the fee unless he does part only of the work which is the subject of instructions, in which case division of the fee is a matter for arrangement between them.

OBTAINING PAYMENT OF COSTS

Recovery of Costs

Where an agreement or order provides for costs to be paid by any other **19–33** party in favour of the assisted person, the assisted person's solicitor may

---

[26] [1989] 1 W.L.R. 281.
[27] *Mardas v. Official Receiver* (1989) 139 New L.J. 1597, *The Times*, November 10, 1989.
[28] *Lombard North Central v. Pratt, The Times*, November 27, 1989.
[29] *Lombard North Central v. Pratt, The Times*, December 8, 1989.
[30] Practice Note Skeleton Arguments. *The Times*, January 19, 1990.

recover a sum in respect of costs from the paying party subject to certain conditions.[31]

The assisted person's solicitor may take proceedings for the recovery of costs.[32] Where the Board has paid costs but those costs have not been reimbursed by payment by the paying party, the solicitor must obtain the consent of the area director before taking proceeedings for recovery.[33]

The costs which the assisted person's solicitor may recover must not exceed the total of the sums of the amount of *inter partes* costs received by the Board in excess of the costs determined under regulation 107A(2) of the General Regulations 1989 and the balance of interest received by the Board after deduction of interest on the costs determined under regulation 107A(2).[34]

The assisted person's legal representatives will not be prevented from recovering from the paying party, sums in respect of costs due, by any rule of law which limits the costs recoverable by a party to proceedings to the amount which he is liable to pay his legal representatives, or by regulation 64 of the Civil Legal Aid (General) Regulations 1989 (restriction on payment otherwise and from the Fund.[35]

Subject to reimbursement of the Board in respect of costs determined under regulation 107A(2) and any interest thereon, any costs recovered from the paying party belong to the solicitor.[36]

The payment on account scheme

19–34 There are a number of cases in which a solicitor acting for an assisted person may apply for payment on account of costs. First, where he wishes to receive a sum on account of disbursements incurred or about to be incurred in connection with the proceedings.[37] This is useful in respect of disbursements which are likely to be heavy and also where considerable expenditure has to be incurred on a particular item. Even where individual expenditure is relatively low, the combined total of money paid out by a legal aid practice can be extremely high.

Secondly, where the proceedings to which the certificate relates have continued for more than 12 months, it appears unlikely that an order for taxation will be made within the next 12 months, and delay in the taxation of those costs or fees will cause hardship to the solicitor or counsel, application may be made to the appropriate area committee for the

---

[31] Civil Legal Aid (General) Regulations 1989, reg. 91(2B).
[32] *ibid.* reg. 91(2A).
[33] *ibid.* reg. 91(2B).
[34] *ibid.* regs. 92(1)(c),(d), 107B(2).
[35] *ibid.* reg. 107B(3).
[36] *ibid.* reg. 107B(4).
[37] Civil Legal Aid (General) Regulations 1989, reg. 101(1)(a).

payment of a sum on account.[38] No indication is given in the Regulations or Notes for Guidance as to what might constitute hardship — each case must be argued on its own merits.

In the case of counsel, where the proceedings have concluded or the solicitor is otherwise entitled to have his costs taxed and counsel has not received payment in respect of his fees for at least six months since the event which gave rise to the right to taxation, counsel may apply to the appropriate area committee for payment of 75 per cent of the amount claimed on account of fees for work done in connection with the proceedings.[39] This provision is totally separate from the payment on accounts scheme and it is not necessary to wait until the proceedings have continued for 12 months or to prove "hardship". Counsel's clerk simply has to wait for six months from the date of the right to taxation before having an absolute right to apply for payment of 75 per cent of the fee notes submitted. Usually the "right to taxation" will arise when an order for legal aid taxation is made by the court.[40]

Where a solicitor's retainer has been determined and another solicitor **19–35** (who is not a member of the same firm) is acting on behalf of the assisted person, the appropriate area committee may authorise payment of a sum on account of the original solicitor's costs where it appears unlikely that those costs will be taxed within six months of the date on which the retainer was determined.[41-42] A solicitor or counsel acting for, or instructed on behalf of, an assisted person under a certificate may, in certain circumstances, submit a claim to the financial controller of the Board on a form approved by the Board for the payment of sums on account of profit costs or of fees in respect of work done in connection with the proceedings.[43]

Claims for payments on account must be made at prescribed rates where the rates are prescribed for solicitors or counsel in the Legal Aid in Criminal Proceedings (Remuneration) Regulations 1994 or the Legal Aid in Family Proceedings (Remuneration) Regulations 1991.[44]

A payment on account may only be made when, in the case of a claim by a solicitor, a period of 12 months has elapsed since the date on which the certificate was issued or a further period of 12 or 24 months has elapsed since that date.[45] A claim must be made within two months before to four months after any period specified above.[46] The maximum payment for each claim in any one financial year is:

---

[38] *ibid.* reg. 101(1)(b).
[39] *ibid.* reg. 101(2).
[40] *ibid.* reg. 107(1).
[41-42] *ibid.* reg. 100(6).
[43] Civil Legal Aid (General) Regulations 1989, reg. 100(1), (2).
[44] Civil Legal Aid (General) Regulations. 1989, reg. 100(9).
[45] ibid. reg. 100(3).
[46] *ibid.* reg. 100(4).

(a) for the financial year 1994–95 ....70 per cent
(b) for the financial year 1995–96
    and thereafter..75 per cent
The fact that a payment on account has been made does not release a solicitor from any obligation to submit his costs and counsel's fees for taxation or assessment at the conclusion of the case. If, once taxation or assessment has taken place, the payments on account are found to exceed the final costs of the case, the solicitor or counsel must repay the balance due to the Fund on demand. Where the final costs exceed the payment on account, the balance will be paid from the Fund to the solicitor or counsel.[47]

Deferment of solicitor's profit costs

19–36 If an assisted person's solicitor fails to comply with any provisions of the Civil Legal Aid (General) Regulations 1989 and, as a result of his default or omission, the Fund incurs a loss, the appropriate area committee may defer payment of all or part of the solicitor's profit costs in connection with the proceedings to which the certificate relates until he has complied with those provisions. If the Board refers the conduct of the solicitor to the Solicitors' Disciplinary Tribunal, and the solicitor is disciplined, the Board is entitled to retain any sum, payment of which has been deferred in accordance with the findings of the Tribunal.[48]

19–37 The only profit costs, payment of which may be deferred, are those arising under the legal aid certificate in connection with which the solicitor's default or omission occurred. Payment of a solicitor's profit costs will normally only be deferred if he has failed to comply with any of the provisions of Part XI of the Civil Legal Aid (General) Regulations 1989. As regulation 102 is compensatory and not punitive, deferment will not be of an amount in excess of the loss to the Fund. The loss to the Fund may comprise:

(a) the net liability of the Fund as defined in section 16(9) of the 1988 Act;
(b) any additional costs incurred by the Fund, *e.g.* under regulation 91(1);
(c) the amount of any costs sought by section 16(5) of the Legal Aid Act 1988.

As the application of regulation 102 is discretionary, there is room for the evaluation of individual cases although the object of the 1989 Regulations suggests that in general the sanction should be applied.

---

[47] *Ibid.* reg. 100(7), (8).
[48] *Ibid.* reg. 102(a), (b).

The most common default or omission giving rise to the application of **19–38** regulation 102 is failure to comply with regulation 90 (requiring solicitors to pay moneys recovered to the Board). When considering regulation 90 it should be borne in mind that:

(a) Property (which includes money and costs) is recovered or preserved at the moment an action is disposed of either by compromise or judgment. It is at that moment that the statutory charge attaches. It continues to attach unless and until the judgment is reversed on appeal.

(b) Regulation 90(1)(a) requires an assisted person's solicitor to inform the Area Director of any property (including moneys and costs) recovered or preserved forthwith. This obligation to report arises immediately there is a compromise or judgment which gives rise to recovery or preservation.

How payment is obtained

Where costs have been taxed

The 1988 Act provides that a person who provides advice, assistance or **19–39** representation under the 1988 Act may not take any payment for so doing except such payment as is made by or authorised by the Board or by Regulations under the 1988 Act.[49–50] Neither the 1988 Act nor the Regulations contain any machinery for the method of payment, but in practice the Board authorises payment after the costs have been taxed or assessed on submission of the following documents:

(a) taxing officer's certificate;
(b) a completed copy of the taxed bill;
(c) counsel's fee note;
(d) a report on the case and any supporting documents.

These papers will be sent to the appropriate area commitee who will authorise payment. Payments are made to solicitors monthly, one cheque covering all payments authorised for a solicitor or his firm during the month. Counsel are paid in the same way.

Where costs are assessed by the Area Director

Where costs due to a solicitor or counsel are to be assessed under the Civil **19–40** Legal Aid (General) Regulations 1989, a solicitor must forward to the area committee a report on the case, a gross sum bill — which includes the fees claimed by counsel with counsel's fee note attached — and, if required, by the Area Director, a detailed bill of costs.

[49–50] Legal Aid Act 1988, s. 31(3); Civil Legal Aid (General) Regulations 1989, reg. 64.

Where *inter partes* costs are agreed and paid, but a further claim is made against the Fund, where the residual amount is less than £500, the additional claim must be assessed by the Board; where it does not exceed £1,000 it may be so assessed. Any claims for higher amounts must be taxed by a taxing officer. The prescribed forms should be used for such assessments and may, if appropriate, be used for taxation of such items. Both the Board and the taxing officer may call for such further information as is thought reasonable.[51-52]

Where costs are to be assessed for work done in a magistrates' court or in the Crown Court, the solicitor must lodge with the Area Director such papers and information as will be needed to assess the remuneration payable to the solicitor and to any counsel who acted in the case. These must include a report on the case setting out the claim for costs in respect of the work done, in accordance with regulation 6 of Schedule 1, Part 1, paragraph 1(a), to the Legal Aid in Criminal and Care Proceedings (Costs) Regulations 1989. There should be included any claim for disbursements, travelling and any other out-of-pocket expenses, actually and reasonably incurred.[53] The area committee will authorise payment by the Chief Accountant of the Board and payment will be made in the same way as where costs have been taxed.

In such a case, the costs payable are the aggregate amount allowed on taxation or on assessment, but these may be divided between the principal and the agent by agreement assuming that the agent is another English legal representative. A foreign lawyer's costs are treated as a disbursement. When drawing the bill of costs, the principal should include in it the items of his agent's charges as though they were his own and should not show them as a disbursement. This does not apply if the agent is outside the jurisdiction when the charges should be shown as a disbursement. In *McCullie v. Butler*,[54] Scottish solicitors were held not to be "solicitors" within the 1988 Act which applied only to the ordinary agency between solicitors in this country. "Solicitor" is defined as a solicitor of the Supreme Court.[55] The court said that, in such a case, there should be a detailed statement for the information of the taxing officer of the circumstances which required the services of a foreign lawyer.

Where a certificate is discharged or revoked

Generally

19–41 The retainer of any solicitor or counsel selected by or acting on behalf of an assisted person determines forthwith upon his receiving notice of

---

[51-52] Form CLA32; see Practice Direction No. 3 of 1994.
[53] See below, Chapter 20.
[54] [1962] 2 Q.B. 309.
[55] Legal Aid Act 1988, s. 43.

revocation or discharge of the certificate. If the assisted person appeals to the appropriate area committee against the revocation or discharge and that appeal is dismissed, the retainer forthwith determines after receipt by the solicitor or counsel of notice of dismissal.[56] If the revocation or discharge takes place after proceedings have commenced, the solicitor's retainer will not determine until he has sent a copy of the notice to the appropriate court office or registry and has served any notice of revocation or discharge required by the Regulations.[57] In such circumstances, the costs which have been incurred by or on behalf of the assisted person must, as soon as is practicable, be submitted for taxation or assessment by the Area Director. The Fund will remain liable for payment of those costs, notwithstanding the discharge or revocation of the certificate.[58]

Discharge

Where a certificate is discharged, the person whose certificate is discharged **19–42** ceases to be an assisted person from the date of discharge in the proceedings to which the certificate related. The solicitor and counsel are entitled to their taxed or assessed costs out of the Fund, the assisted person's liability being limited to his maximum contribution, or the amount paid out of the Fund, whichever is less.[59] Where the assisted person continues to take, defend or be a party to the proceedings to which the certificate related, that person's liability, under an order for costs made against him in those proceedings, will not exceed the amount (if any) which is a reasonable one for him to pay having regard to all the circumstances including the financial resources of all the parties and their conduct in connection with the dispute, in so far as the costs were incurred while that person was assisted.[60]

Revocation

Where a certificate is revoked, the person whose certificate is revoked is **19–43** deemed never to have been an assisted person in relation to those proceedings (save in relation to the costs of successful unassisted parties).[61]

Where a certificate has been revoked, the Board has the right to recover, from the person to whom the certificate was issued, the costs paid or payable to the solicitor or counsel, less any amount received by way of contribution. The solicitor who has acted under the certificate has the right

---

[56] Civil Legal Aid (General) Regulations 1989, reg. 83(1).
[57] *ibid.* reg. 83(2).
[58] *ibid.* reg. 84.
[59] *ibid.* regs. 74(2), 86(2).
[60] Legal Aid Act 1988, s. 17(1); Civil Legal Aid (General) Regulations 1989, reg. 86(2).
[61] Legal Aid Act 1988, s. 18; Civil Legal Aid (General) Regulations 1989, reg.74(2).

to recover from that person the difference between the amount paid or payable out of the Fund and the full amount of his solicitor and own client costs.[62] In this connection, the client's maximum contribution is irrelevant and the solicitor has the right to recover all costs incurred with the client's approval even though they are disallowed on legal aid taxation or assessment.

Where a person is legally aided for part only of the proceedings

19–44 Where a solicitor has been instructed to do work either before the issue of a certificate or after its discharge or revocation, or to act for an assisted person in matters falling outside the scope of the certificate, he is entitled to look to his client for costs on a solicitor and own client basis in the normal way, and the client has the usual right to have these taxed in accordance with the Solicitor's Act 1974. It is in the interests of a potential litigant to obtain legal aid, if available, as early as possible in any dispute, and for the certificate to extend to the whole of the case from the beginning and to remain in force until the proceedings are concluded. Otherwise that person will have to pay the extra costs to his solicitor as well as his maximum contribution and will not gain the protection of the provisions of the 1988 Act, which provide that the liability of a legally assisted person under an order for costs made against him with respect to any proceedings, must not exceed the amount, if any, which is a reasonable one for him to pay having regard to all the circumstances, including the financial resources of the parties and their conduct in connection with the dispute.[63]

Any solicitor who has acted on behalf of an assisted person whose certificate was issued after proceedings have been instituted or who has by law a lien on any documents needed in connection with the proceedings and has delivered them up subject to the lien, may give notice of the fact to the appropriate area committee.[64] Then if any damages, costs or any other sums are recovered for the assisted person, the Board must pay the solicitor, out of the moneys so recovered, his costs on the solicitor and own client basis, in respect of the period before the certificate was issued. If the sums recovered are insufficient to meet both those costs and the amounts paid are payable out of the Fund on the assisted person's account, they must be divided between the solicitor and the Fund. The division is to be in the same proportion as the pre-certificate costs and the cost to the Fund bear to the aggregate of the two.[65] If either of these sets of costs have not been ascertained by taxation, they are to be assessed by the appropriate

---

[62] Civil Legal Aid (General) Regulations 1989, reg. 6(1).
[63] Legal Aid Act 1988, s. 17(1).
[64] Civil Legal Aid (General) Regulations 1989, reg. 103(1), (2).
[65] *ibid.* reg. 103(4).

area committee for the purpose of the apportionment.[66] The solicitor is then entitled to look to his client for the balance of the pre-certificate costs which are due to him.

The Board has indicated that it considers that no lien arises in respect **19–45** of costs and disbursements payable under a legal aid certificate and that it is misleading to use the word "lien" in relation to such costs and disbursements. Accordingly where, under a legal aid certificate, a change of solicitors is authorised by the Area Director subject to:

(a) there being no lien in respect of pre-certificate costs and disbursements; and

(b) an undertaking being given by the new solicitor as to the eventual taxation or assessment of costs,

there is no reason why the papers should not be expeditiously transferred to the new solicitor.

Where a person is legally aided for part only of the proceedings, subject to the provisions relating to recovery of costs in excess of prescribed legal aid rates from the paying party on an *inter partes* basis,[67] once a legal aid certificate has been issued in connection with any proceedings, the assisted person's solicitor or counsel may not receive or be a party to the making of any payment for work done in those proceedings during the currency of that certificate (whether within the scope of the certificate or otherwise) except such payments as may be made out of the Fund.[68] This is an absolute rule that prevents the client being charged for work done even if it is outside the scope of the certificate. However, there is a distinction to be drawn. The Court of Appeal has held[69] that on its true construction, the word "proceedings" in regulation 65 of the Legal Aid (General) Regulations 1980 (which was identical to regulation 64 of the Civil Legal Aid (General) Regulations 1989) has a narrow meaning which reflects the fact that legal aid may be, and often is, granted to deal with one issue arising out of an action as a whole, and therefore refers only to the specific proceedings for which legal aid was granted even though those proceedings might only be incidental to the whole action. Accordingly, where a legal aid certificate has been granted to a defendant to purge his contempt of court in civil proceedings brought against him, the solicitor who represents him in the contempt proceedings will not be precluded from receiving payment from the defendant for representing him in the main civil proceedings brought against him by the plaintiff, nor will the solicitor be precluded from claiming a lien on the papers appertaining to those civil proceedings. However, apart from that exposition of the law, it is not

---

[66] *ibid.* reg. 103(5).
[67] Civil Legal Aid (General) Regulations 1989, reg. 107B(3).
[68] *ibid.* reg. 64.
[69] *Littaur v. Steggles Palmer* [1986] 1 W.L.R. 287.

possible to require a client to top up fees recovered under a legal aid certificate.

Joint parties

19–46 Where joint parties are not all assisted, the costs incurred on behalf of each must be apportioned on taxation. There will be allowed against the Fund not only those items of cost which are solely attributable to the assisted person, but also an equal proportion of those which are common.

Interest

19–47 The decision in *Hunt v. R.M. Douglas (Roofing) Ltd*[70] by the House of Lords, has clarified the situation with regard to interest on costs, *i.e.* interest is applied at the current rate[71] from the date of judgment not from the date of the taxation master's certificate or allocatur. As to Interest on damages see C16–06A. It is clear that the legal representative of an assisted person cannot recover from the Fund more than costs on the prescribed rates as laid down in the Legal Aid in Civil Proceedings (Remuneration) Regulations 1994 and the Legal Aid in Family Proceedings (Remuneration) Regulations 1991. However, it is possible to recover costs against an opposing party on either the standard or the indemnity basis. Subject to reimbursement of the Board in respect of costs and any interest thereon, any costs recovered from the paying party belong to the solicitor.[72]

Where a plaintiff accepts a payment into court in satisfaction of his claim, his entitlement to the costs of the action arises out of the Rules of the Supreme Court and not from any specific judgment or order to which the Judgments Act 1838 applies. Accordingly, such a plaintiff was unable to recover interest on costs so obtained unless he became entitled to apply for a judgment on costs under R.S.C., Ord. 45, r. 15.[73] Now, however, R.S.C., Ord. 62, r. 5(1) has been amended to provide that such acceptance is a deemed entry of a judgment and accordingly interest is recoverable.

19–48 Where interest is payable because of the postponement of enforcement of charges over money or land or by reason or substitution of charged property, interest continues to accure on the sum which the Board would have retained under the statutory charge until paid and the Board may not seek to recover interest until that payment is made.[74]

Where judgment is given with damages to be assessed, interest runs from

---

[70] [1988] 3 W.L.R.
[71] Eight per cent Judgment Debts (Rate of Interest) Order 1993.
[72] *ibid.* reg. 107B(4).
[73] Legal Aid Board v. Russell [1991] 2 A.C. 317, H.L.
[74] Civil Legal Aid (General) Regulations 1989, reg. 99(1).

the judgment recording or assessing the damages payable to the plaintiff. The word "judgment" in section 17 of the Judgments Act 1838 clearly contemplates a single final judgment for a quantified sum rather than an interlocutory judgment or order which merely establishes the defendant's liability.[75]

---

[75] *Thomas v. Bunn, Wilson v. Graham, Lea v. British Aerospace* plc [1991] 2 W.L.R. 27.

Chapter 20

TAXATION OF COSTS (PRACTICE)

Introduction

20–01 The nature of a legal aid taxation was summarised by Lord Denning M.R. in *Storer v. Wright.*[1]

> "A legal aid taxation is different from all others: in that there is no one to oppose it. It is not adversarial but inquisitorial. The taxing master is the inquisitor. The Legal Aid Act 1974 says . . . that 'a solicitor who has acted for a person receiving legal aid shall be paid for so acting out of the Legal Aid Fund . . .' but who is to challenge his bill? There is no one to contest the amount at all. If the client has lost the case — and has a nil contribution — he is not concerned in the least with the amount the solicitor charges. If he has won the case — and (been) awarded damages — he may be much concerned — because the solicitor gets a charge — for his costs — on the amount of damages recovered. The higher the solicitor's bill the less his damages but the client is never represented in the taxation or even told about it . . .
>
> Seeing that there is no one to oppose it seems to me that on a legal aid taxation, it is the duty of the taxing officer to bear in mind the public interest. He should himself disallow any item which is unreasonable in amount or which is unreasonably incurred. In short, whenever it is too high he must tax it down. Otherwise the legal aid system could be much abused by solicitors and Counsel."

The costs of legally aided proceedings are subject to taxation *inter partes* in the same way as ordinary cases. Whether the costs are assessed by the Area Director or by a taxing officer or are taxed, the costs of the assisted person's solicitor and counsel are ascertained subject to the Civil Legal Aid (Remuneration) Regulations 1994 and the Family Proceedings (Remuneration) Regulations 1991 in accordance with the standard basis

---

[1] [1981] 1 Q.B. 336.

under R.S.C., Ord. 62, that is: "a reasonable amount in respect of all costs reasonably incurred."[2]

The Civil Legal Aid (General) Regulations 1989 give both the assisted **20–02** person and his legal advisers the right to make representations and for review in respect of costs which have been assessed and to carry in objections to a taxation, to go to review and to appeal against any review by a judge of a taxation. A review or appeal may affect the adviser's position only, and the client may have no interest in the outcome. In other cases, he may have an interest which is adverse to theirs.

In order to meet this difficulty and so that the public interest may be represented, the Lord Chancellor is given the right to appoint a solicitor to intervene in the review of certain taxations and, in an appeal from any such review, the intervening solicitor may himself appeal.

This chapter deals only with the procedure and the principles to be followed on legal aid taxation and related ones *inter partes*; the rights and liabilities of assisted persons in respect of costs and the entitlement of solicitors and counsel to remuneration for legally aided work have already been dealth with. The procedure in the Supreme Court is dealt with first, followed by that in other courts where it differs from this.

A number of matters which may be relevant on a legal aid taxation have been dealt with earlier. For convenience, they are included in the summary of practical points at the end of this chapter.

BILL OF COSTS

Form of Bill

Where an assisted person's costs are wholly payable out of the Fund and **20–03** only a legal aid taxation is involved, a three-column bill is all that is needed. Where another party has been ordered to pay the costs there will have to be a taxation, both on the legal aid basis and *inter partes*. Bills should be drawn in the six-column format. The *inter partes* column should include the sums claimed on a normal R.S.C., Ord. 62 or C.C.R., Ord. 38 *inter partes* taxation at appropriate expense rates. The "Legal Aid Only" column will include only those items not claimed *inter partes* charged at the prescribed rates in accordance with the regulations. Each chargeable item in the bill must be consecutively numbered. The bill will need to be divided into parts dealing with pre-certificate and post-certificate costs and reflecting any changes in VAT rates. At the discretion of the solicitor, the bill may be prepared in parts for other purposes, but there is no need for

---

2–3 R.S.C., Ord. 62, r. 12(1).

the main bill to be divided into parts relating to changes in the prescribed rates.

20–04   In addition, the solicitor must prepare a schedule to be lodged with the main bill for taxation setting out the amount claimed for *inter partes* costs calculated at the prescribed rates. The schedule may be a plain paper schedule, but it should be divided vertically to provide the following information:

    (a) item number;
    (b) narrative;
    (c) VAT on disbursements;
    (d) disbursements;
    (e) profit costs.

The schedule should not include any item for which no *inter partes* claim is made in the main bill.[4]

The item numbers in the schedule must correspond with those in the main bill. The main narrative should be inserted in the main bill. The schedule will require a very brief narrative, simply to show how the sum claimed is calculated in accordance with the Regulations. Claims for increased percentages for care and conduct in respect of *inter partes* costs at appropriate expense rates should be made in the main bill; claims for enhancement of the prescribed legal aid rates should be set out in the schedule, either as a preamble to the schedule, or a part of the narrative for the particular item.[5]

Joint parties

20–05   Where joint parties to proceedings are not all legally aided, the bill should be drawn in a way which clearly distinguishes between them as there will be allowed against the Fund only those items which are solely attributable to the assisted person and an equal proportion of all those items which are common. In some cases, this will involve separate columns, in others, separate parts or the charging of only a proportion of the common items will be needed. If any doubt arises, it should be borne in mind that on the standard basis that doubt must be resolved in favour of the paying party.[6]

Documents to be lodged

20–06   The party beginning proceedings for taxation must lodge at the appropriate office the "requisite documents" giving authority to tax,[7] together with a

---

[4] *Practice Direction No. 3 of 1994*, para. 9 see appendix.
[5] *ibid.* paras. 13 and 14.
[6] R.S.C., Ord. 62, r. 12(1).
[7] *ibid.* App. 1.

statement of parties and the bill of costs duly signed. In addition, the papers and vouchers specified below must be lodged in this order:

- (a) a bundle comprising all civil legal aid certificates and amendments thereto, notices of discharge or revocation thereof and specific legal aid authorities;
- (b) unless the relevant information is included in the judgment or order or the parties have agreed the times of the hearing, a certificate of times or a copy of the associate's certificate;
- (c) a bundle comprising fee notes of counsel and accounts for other disbursements;
- (d) one complete set of pleadings arranged in chronological order with any interlocutory summonses and lists of documents next to it;
- (e) cases to counsel to advise, and his advice and opinions, and instructions to counsel to settle documents and briefs to counsel with enclosures arranged in chronological order;
- (f) reports and opinions of medical and other experts, arranged in chronological order;
- (g) the solicitor's correspondence and attendance notes; and
- (h) any other relevant papers duly bundled and labelled.[8]

If any written authorities have been issued by the Area Director, these must also be lodged. Delay in lodging a bill for taxation may prejudice the assisted person's position and can lead to the disallowance of costs or to disciplinary proceedings against the solicitor before a panel (complaints) tribunal.

ASSESSMENT AND AGREEMENT

In the magistrates' courts and Crown Courts

The procedure to be adopted is an set out in chap. 19, para. 19–29. Except **20–07** for family proceedings, both assessment and review are made in accordance with the provisions of regulation 6 of, and Schedule 1, Part I, paragraph 1(1)(a) to, the Legal Aid in Criminal and Care Proceedings (Costs) Regulations 1989, as if the work done was work to which those provisions apply, save that paragraphs 2 and 3 (relating to reduction and enhancement of the prescribed rates) do not apply.[9] In the case of family proceedings, any assessment review or taxation will be made in accordance with the Legal Aid in Family Proceedings (Remuneration) Regulations 1991.[10]

---

[8] *ibid.* r. 29(7).
[9] Civil Legal Aid (General) Regulations 1989, reg. 104(3).
[10] *ibid.* reg. 104(2).

411

With regard to review, the Civil Legal Aid (General) Regulations set out below apply where costs are assessed by an Area Director in the same way as indicated below, save that it is the above-mentioned Legal Aid in Criminal and Care Proceedings (costs) Regulations which apply.[11]

Procedure where *inter partes* costs are agreed and paid but a further claim is made against the Fund

20–08 It is permissible to agree the *inter partes* element and have the remaining legal aid only element assessed or taxed in accordance with the Civil Legal Aid (General) Regulations 1989.[12] Where the residual amount is less than £500 any additional claim must be assessed by the Area Director and, where it does not exceed £1,000, it may be so assessed. Any claims for higher amounts must be taxed by a taxing officer. In any event, the agreed costs must have been paid and the assisted person's solicitor must confirm in writing to the relevant authority that the agreed costs have been paid.[13] There will normally be two types of costs to be considered, namely: items in respect of which there is no *inter partes* order (*e.g.* costs of a summons where the assisted persons are not allowed costs), and items which are covered by an *inter partes* order but for which the paying party will not accept (full) responsibility (*e.g.* allegedly excess of attendance on a client).[14]

The solicitor will be required to identify the items, the times and details of the work done and the amount claimed. The solicitor will also need to state the amount claimed from the paying party in respect of each item concerned, the amount agreed and paid, and the equivalent cost of the shortfall recalculated at the prescribed rates. The solicitor must satisfy the appropriate authority that the paying party refused to accept the particular item, wholly or in part, and justify the reasonablenesss of the claim against the Fund. The prescribed form[15] should be used for assessments and may, if appropriate, be used for taxation. Both the Board and the taxing officer may call for such further information as is thought reasonable. In addition, the taxing officer may give directions for a full taxation of the relevant costs and for the filing of a bill and schedule if the circumstances require it. If the solicitor is dissatisfied with the provisional taxation, a full bill may be lodged or, unless the taxing officer otherwise directs, a formal taxation may take place on the original form CLA32.[16]

---

[11] *ibid.* reg. 104(4).
[12] Civil Legal Aid (General) Regulations 1989, reg. 106A.
[13] *ibid.* reg. 106A(2), (5).
[14] *Practice Direction No. 3 of 1994* para. 24.
[15] CLA32.
[16] *Practice Direction No. 3 of 1994* para. 26.

Review

If any solicitor or counsel is dissatisfied with any decision on an assessment **20–09** specified above, he may — within 21 days of that decision — make written representations to the appropriate area committee and that committee will review the assessment of the Area Director and either confirm it, increase it or decrease it.[17]

Appeal

A solicitor or counsel who is dissatisfied with the decision of the area **20–10** committee on review may — within 21 days of the decision — apply to the committee to certify a point of principle of general importance. Where the committee certifies such a point, the solicitor or counsel may — within 21 days of the certification — appeal in writing to a committee appointed by the Board.[18] On the appeal, the committee appointed by the Board may reverse, affirm or amend the decision of the area committee.[19]

Counsel

It is the duty of the assisted person's solicitor — within seven days after **20–11** an assessment or review — to notify counsel in writing where the fees claimed on his behalf have been reduced or disallowed on assessment or review.[20]

THE TAXATION

Procedure

The procedure on taxation of costs, either *inter partes* or under the Legal **20–12** Aid Act 1986, is, in general, the same as in unassisted proceedings. Representation on the taxation *inter partes* will be covered by the assisted person's certificate and he will be entitled to be represented by his solicitor. Where there has been both an order for costs *inter partes* in the proceedings and a direction for a legal aid taxation, the two sets of costs will be taxed at the same time as will be the case where more than one party is legally aided.

---

[17] Civil Legal Aid (General) Regulations 1989, regs. 105(4)–(8), 106A(7).
[18] *ibid.* regs. 105(5), (6), 106A(7).
[19] *ibid.* regs. 105(7), 106A(7).
[20] *ibid.* regs. 105(8), 106A(7).

On a taxation which is both legal aid and *inter partes*, if the solicitor is responsible for serving the bill on the paying party he should exclude the schedule which is of no relevance *inter partes*. Schedules should, however, be attached to the main bill lodged for taxation and to the main bill when this needs to be served on the assisted person.[21]

The existing procedures for provisional taxation will continue to apply.[22]

On the *inter partes* taxation, the taxing officer will first tax the main bill. He will consider objections to the bill and, where appropriate, disallow costs *inter partes*.

Whenever costs *inter partes* are disallowed or reduced, an appropriate deduction will be made to the amount claimed for the same item in the schedule. The taxing officer will consider whether it is appropriate to allow any enhancement claimed and will take this into account fixing the amount to be allowed.[23]

Where an item is disallowed *inter partes*, the taxing officer will then need to consider whether any part of the amount taxed off *inter partes* should be allowed against the Fund. Any sum so allowed will be added to the legal aid only column of the main bill.[24]

A taxing officer may give directions as to the parties who are entitled to attend the taxation of those costs, and may disallow the costs of attendance of any party not entitled to attend by virtue of the directions and whose attendance he considers unnecessary. Where the court has directed that a bill of costs be taxed under the 1988 Act, the taxing officer may direct the party whose bill it is, to send to any person having an interest in the Fund, a copy of the bill or any part of it, free of charge, together with a letter explaining that the bill has been referred to a taxing officer for taxation, giving the name and address of the taxing officer and the office at which the taxation is proceeding, giving notice of the time appointed for the continuation of the taxation and such other information as the taxing officer may direct.[25]

The costs of proceedings to which an assisted person is a party will be taxed *inter partes* in accordance with any direction or order given or made in the proceedings irrespective of the interest, if any, of the assisted person in the taxation.[26] The effect of this provision is to cover cases where, *e.g.* because the assisted person has a nil contribution, he has no interest in the outcome of the taxation of costs awarded in his favour. The Fund might suffer if his nominal interest were not argued and the CLA(G) 1989 Regulations provide that it is the duty of an assisted person's solicitor to

---

[21] In accordance with Civil Legal Aid (General) Regulations 1989, reg. 119; *Practice Direction No. 3 of 1994*, para. 18.

[22] *Practice Direction No. 3 of 1994*, para. 18.

[23] *ibid.* para. 19.

[24] *ibid.* para. 20.

[25] R.S.C., Ord. 62, r. 26.

[26] Civil Legal Aid (General) Regulations 1989, reg. 107(1).

safeguard the interests of the Fund on any *inter partes* taxation which takes place pursuant to an order for costs in favour of an assisted person where he himself may have no interest in the result of the taxation.[27]

Where the assisted person has a financial interest in the taxation, it is the duty of an assisted person's solicitor to: supply him with a copy of the bill; inform him of the extent of his financial interest and the steps which can be taken to safeguard that interest and — if the assisted person so requests — to give notice in accordance with the rules of court to the taxing officer that the assisted person has such an interest; and endorse on the bill that the assisted person has a financial interest in the taxation and that he has complied with the above requirements.[28] The assisted person may not be required to make any contribution to the Fund on account of the costs of taxation proceedings; the statutory charge does not apply in relation to any resulting increase in the net liability of the Fund arising from the costs of the taxation proceedings.[29]

Compromise

The costs of giving effect to a compromised action which may include work **20–13** (*e.g.* conveyancing) not normally covered by a certificate, is now generally considered to be covered under the terms of a legal aid certificate.[30]

Subsequent procedure

Where a party has begun proceedings for taxation, the taxing officer will **20–14** give to that party and to any other party entitled to be heard on the taxation not less than 14 days' notice of the day, time and place appointed for the taxation. The party whose costs are to be taxed must, within seven days after beginning the proceedings for taxation, send a copy of the bill of costs to every other party entitled to be heard on the taxation, and notify the proper officer that he has done so. If in beginning, or purporting to begin, any taxation proceedings, or at any stage in the course of or in connection with the proceedings, there is a failure to comply with the requirements of R.S.C., Ord. 62, whether in respect of time or any other respect, the failure is treated as an irregularity which does not nullify the taxation procedure or any steps taken in the proceedings. However, the taxing officer may, on the grounds that there has been a failure, on such terms as he thinks just, set aside, either wholly or in part, the taxation proceedings, or exercise his

---

[27] *ibid.* reg. 110.
[28] *ibid.* reg. 119(1).
[29] *ibid.* 1989, reg. 119.
[30] *Re Clarendon Villas (No. 26), Hove Trusts; Copeland v. Houlton* [1955] 3 All E.R. 178 at 180.

powers under R.S.C., Ord. 62 to make such order, dealing with the taxation proceedings generally, as he thinks fit. The requirement, under R.S.C., Ord. 3, r. 6, that notice must be given, where a year or more has elapsed since the last proceedings in a cause or matter, does not apply to the taxation proceedings.[31]

Provisional taxation

20–15   If the party lodging the bill so requests, and the taxing officer considers it appropriate, or so decides, the taxing officer may, instead of proceeding to appoint the taxation in the normal way, proceed with a provisional taxation. In such a case, the officer must send to each party entitled to be heard on the taxation, except the party whose bill it is, a notice requiring that party to inform the proper officer within 14 days after the receipt of the notice if he wishes to be heard on the taxation. If any party indicates a wish to be heard on taxation, the proper officer then fixes an appointment for taxation and gives not less than 14 days' notice of the appointment to every party entitled to be heard. If no party to whom notices have been given indicates a wish to be heard, the provisionally taxed bill will be sent to the party lodging the bill with a notice specifying the amount which the taxing officer proposes to allow in respect of it, requiring that party to inform the proper officer within 14 days after receipt of the notice, if he wishes to be heard on taxation. If that party does wish to be heard on taxation, an appointment will be fixed for taxation giving not less than 14 days' notice of the appointment.[32]

Legal aid only — provisional taxation

20–16   Where only the party who commenced the proceedings is entitled to be heard on the taxation, the proper officer must, unless the taxing officer otherwise directs, send to that party a notice specifying the amount which it is proposed to allow in respect of the bill and requiring that party to inform the proper officer within 14 days after the receipt of the notice if he wishes to be heard on the taxation. If that party indicates a wish to be heard, the proper officer will fix a date and time for the taxation and give not less than 14 days' notice of it to that party. In other words, a provisional taxation may take place in respect of a legal aid bill if only the party who commences the proceedings is entitled to be heard. The procedure applies unless the taxing officer otherwise directs. If more parties than one are

---

[31] R.S.C., Ord. 62, r. 30.
[32] *ibid.* rr. 31(3), (4), (5), (6), (7).

entitled to be heard, the procedure will only apply if the taxing officer at his discretion so directs.[33]

Party having a financial interest

Where costs are to be paid out of the Fund, the taxing officer may give **20–17** directions as to the parties who are entitled to attend on the taxation of the costs and may disallow the costs of attendance of any party not entitled to attend by virtue of the directions and whose attendance he considers unnecessary. Where the court has directed that a bill of costs be taxed for the purpose of being paid out of the Fund, the taxing officer may direct the party whose bill it is, to send to any person having any interest in the Fund, a copy of the bill or any part of it free of charge together with a letter containing the following information:

    (a) that the bill of costs, a copy of which is sent with the letter, has been referred to a taxing officer for taxation;

    (b) the name of the taxing officer and the address of the office at which the taxation is proceeding;

    (c) the time appointed by the taxing officer at which the taxation will be continued; and

    (d) such other information, if any, as the taxing officer may direct.[34]

For the purposes of R.S.C., Ord. 62, a legally assisted person is a "party entitled to be heard" if:

    (a) he has given notice to the party taxing and the proper officer that he has a financial interest in the outcome of the taxation; or

    (b) the taxing officer has exercised his powers by directing that a bill be sent to the legally assisted person.

In the Supreme Court Taxing Office, it is the practice of the taxing officers in all legal aid taxation to consider whether the assisted person may have an eventual liability to pay any part of the charges or fees of his solicitor or counsel, and, if so, whether it is desirable in the assisted person's interest (*e.g.* he was not consulted before some unusual expense was incurred), whether or not the assisted person has given notice that he has a financial interest in the outcome of the taxation, for the taxing officer to proceed to direct that the copy of the bill be sent to the assisted person. If, after the taxation has begun, it comes to the notice of the taxing officer that the assisted person ought to be given the opportunity to be heard, then the taxing officer will proceed to direct that a copy of the bill is served on the assisted person in accordance with his powers.[35]

---

[33] R.S.C., Ord. 62, r. 31(1), (2).
[34] *ibid.* r. 26(1), (2).
[35] *ibid.* rr. 26, 29(8) (c).

The basis of taxation

The standard basis

20–18 Subject to the Civil Legal Aid (Remuneration) Regulations 1994 and the Family Proceedings (Remuneration) Regulations 1991, every taxation, both *inter partes* and legally aided, is on the standard basis, that is "a reasonable amount in respect of all costs reasonably incurred". Where the court makes an order for costs without indicating the basis of taxation or an order that costs be taxed on any basis other than the standard basis or the indemnity basis, the costs must be taxed on the standard basis.[36]

The correct viewpoint for a taxing officer to adopt when deciding whether or not an item in a bill has been properly incurred is that of a sensible solicitor considering what, in the light of his then knowledge, is reasonable in the interest of his client. This test was laid down by Sachs J. in *Francis v. Francis and Dickerson*[37] where he said that it was:

> "wrong for a Taxing Officer to adopt an attitude akin to a revenue official called upon to apply rigorously one of those Income Tax Act rules as to expenses which have been judicially described as 'jealously restricted' and 'notoriously rigid and narrow in their operation'."

20–19 The correct viewpoint to be adopted is:

> "That of a sensible solicitor sitting in his chair and considering what in the light of his then knowledge is reasonable in the interests of his lay client ... the lay client ... should be deemed a man of means adequate to bear the expense of the litigation out of his own pocket and by 'adequate'. I mean neither 'barely adequate' nor 'super-abundant'."

The only difference between costs to be taxed on the standard basis and those to be taxed on the indemnity basis, is that any doubts which the taxing officer may have as to whether the costs were reasonably incurred or were reasonable in amount will be resolved in favour of the paying party on the standard basis and in favour of the receiving party where the taxation is on the indemnity basis.[38]

Distinction between standard basis and solicitor and own client costs

20–20 It is important to keep in mind the difference between standard basis costs and solicitor and own client costs (which are taxed on the indemnity basis). It is proper under the latter for the taxing officer to allow costs, although he

---

[36] *ibid.* r. 12.
[37] [1956] P. 87.
[38] R.S.C., Ord. 62, r. 12(1), (2).

considers that they have been incurred unreasonably, provided he is satisfied that the client either expressly or impliedly consented to their being incurred.[39] This does not apply to a standard basis taxation and a solicitor acting for an assisted person may have to exercise a degree of control over the client, should the client act in such a way as to incur costs unreasonably. Provided that the taxing officer is satisfied that the solicitor has taken any necessary steps to avoid unnecessary costs, he should be slow to disallow the costs in question on a legal aid taxation.

Counsel's fees

In general, the same principles apply to the taxation of counsel's fees under the 1988 Act as apply to the taxation of solicitor's costs, *i.e.* on the standard basis, a reasonable amount in respect of costs reasonably incurred.[40] For the purposes of a legal aid taxation, counsel's fees are taxed as if they have been paid by the solicitor. This means that the assisted person's solicitor must include counsel's fees in his bill despite the fact that, unlike other expenses incurred in the proceedings, the fees are paid direct from the Fund. Counsel's fees may also be allowed *inter partes* but, being payable out of the Fund, do not have to be vouched on taxation.

20–21

The instruction of distant counsel may be regarded as an act which by its nature involves unusually large expenditure and in respect of which authority may be obtained from the Area Director.[41] Unusual expenditure can include special fees for counsel which are unusual, extraordinary or generous fees.[42] On the other hand, a party is entitled to be allowed on taxation *inter partes* a brief fee to counsel which is a normal and reasonable fee for such a case heard out of London, even if it is heard in a town where there are a few local members of the bar who are prepared to do the work for less[43] and whether counsel has another brief in the same court on the same day.[44–45]

An assisted person's solicitor must do his best to secure the allowance of a proper fee for counsel on taxation and if the solicitor does not feel able to support the amount of the fees claimed by counsel, counsel should be informed before the taxation so that an appropriate memorandum may be supplied for the taxing master or district judge. In cases in which the appropriate authority has not been obtained for the instruction of two counsel or of Queen's Counsel alone, it is for the taxing officer to decide on any *inter partes* taxation whether the employment of any such counsel

---

[39] *ibid.* r. 15.
[40] *ibid.* r. 12(1).
[41] Civil Legal Aid (General) Regulations 1989, reg. 61(2) (d).
[42] *Cavendish v. Strut* [1904] 1 Ch. 524.
[43] *Self v. Self* [1954] P. 480; *Young v. Kohler* [1955] 1 W.L.R. 395.
[44–45] *Isaac v. Isaac* [1955] P. 333.

was justified. Unless the cost is allowed *inter partes* on the taxation in favour of the assisted person, it cannot be allowed on the legal aid taxation.[46]

The assisted person's solicitor must, within seven days after the taxation (or provisional taxation), notify counsel in writing where the fees claimed have been reduced or disallowed on taxation and must endorse the bill of costs with the date on which such notice was given or that no notice was necessary. Where the bill is endorsed that no notice was necessary, the taxing officer's certificate or allocatur may issue forthwith. Otherwise, 14 days must elapse from the date of notice being given before the certificate or allocatur may issue.[47]

Reserved costs and costs in any event

20–22 Where the costs of interlocutory proceedings are reserved, the party in whose favour an order for costs is made at the conclusion of the cause or matter, will be entitled to the costs of the proceedings in respect of which the order was made unless the court otherwise orders. The onus is on the paying party to apply to the court for a specific order if it is desired to avoid liability to pay the reserved costs.[48] That provision applies except in proceedings in the Family Division where, if reserved costs are not picked up in the final order, nothing will be recoverable *inter partes*. However, if a direction is made on a legal aid taxation, that direction will relate to all the costs of the action.[49]

An interlocutory order, under which costs are to be paid by the assisted party, *e.g.* "in any event", does not affect the remuneration payable to the assisted person's solicitor under the legal aid taxation. Should the final order be for payment by the opposing party of the assisted person's costs, those costs will not include, *inter partes*, the costs payable in any event although they will be recoverable out of the Fund.

Joint assisted parties

20–23 Where two or more joint parties are legally aided, it is not normally necessary to distinguish between the costs incurred on behalf of each, and only one allocatur or certificate is issued, the total being divided equally between them. Where, however:

     (a) some specific item or items of costs were incurred on behalf of one of the parties; and

---

[46] Civil Legal Aid (General) Regulations 1989, reg. 63(3).
[47] *ibid.* reg. 112(1), (2).
[48] R.S.C., Ord. 62, r. 3(6).
[49] *Paice v. Paice* [1957] 1 W.L.R. 1011.

(b) any of the parties are likely to be called on to meet part or all of
    the costs, either by contribution or under the statutory charge,
the taxing officer will certify on behalf of each party individually.

Two common examples are where one joint plaintiff settles and the other
continues with the action; and where in claims for damages by joint
plaintiffs on a running down case, one of them incurs more medical experts'
fees than the other. The bills should be drawn so that such items are readily
distinguishable.

In a case where there are large numbers of legally aided plaintiffs (*e.g.*
drug litigation) it has been held that whenever particular plaintiffs incurred
costs in pursuing lead actions, either personally or through the Fund, every
other plaintiff should contribute rateably on a *per capita* basis. Parties may
be given leave to apply to vary the order if there is a change of
circumstances.[50]

The problem of the procedures to be adopted in group litigation under
the English system of civil litigation is in need of investigation, and it would
be desirable that an outline procedure should be prescribed since section
51(1) of the Supreme Court Act 1981 provides that the costs of and
incidental to all proceedings in the High Court should be in the discretion
of the court. There is nothing in the rules of court or the guidance given by
the appellate courts which preclude a costs sharing order. In one case,
the plaintiff had sought an order that one judge be appointed to hear all
applications in the trial of the proposed actions between diverse plaintiffs
and defendants and that any costs incurred or ordered to be paid by any
plaintiff should be paid equally by all plaintiffs. The order was made
accordingly.[51]

Costs incurred in travelling

In general, the law relating to allowance on taxation of travelling expenses **20–24**
is the same in legally aided as in other cases. One difficulty which may
arise is where the assisted person's solicitor practices some way away from
the client's home town. Additional costs in travelling to see witnesses, to
view the *locus in quo* or to attend the court or the hearing may be incurred.
These will not be allowed *inter partes* on the standard basis unless they can
be shown to be reasonable. Since the test on a legal aid taxation is the
same, it is unlikely that such unusual expenses would be recoverable unless
specific authority to incur those expenses has been obtained.[52] Any expense
incurred by the assisted person travelling to the solicitor's office will not be
allowed since it does not amount to an item of costs.

---

[50] *Davies (Joseph Owen) v. Eli Lilly & Co.* [1987] 1 W.L.R. 1136, C.A.
[51] *Chrzanowska v. Glaxo Laboratories Ltd, The Times,* March 16, 1990.
[52] Civil Legal Aid (General) Regulations 1989, reg. 61(2)(d).

Costs wasted by delay or incompetence

R.S.C., Ord. 62, rr.28, 30

20–25 In the High Court the exercise of the penal powers under R.S.C., Ord. 62, r. 28 is restricted to a taxing master or district judge. If it appears to the taxing officer that anything has been done or any omission has been made unreasonably or improperly by or on behalf of any party in the taxation proceedings or in the proceedings which gave rise to the taxation proceedings, he may order that the costs of that party in respect of the act or omission shall not be allowed and that any costs occasioned by it to any other party should be paid by him to that other party.[53]

Where it appears to the taxing officer that costs have been wasted in the taxation proceedings or in proceedings which gave rise to the taxation proceedings, he may exercise the powers conferred on the court by section 51(6) of the Supreme Court Act 1981, *i.e.* make a wasted costs order.[54]

Where a party entitled to costs fails, without good reason, to commence or conduct proceedings for the taxation of those costs in accordance with R.S.C., Ord. 62 or any direction, or delays lodging a bill for taxation, the taxing officer may:

(a) disallow all or part of the costs of taxation that he would otherwise have awarded that party; and

(b) after taking into account all the circumstances (including any prejudice suffered by any other party as a result of such failure or delay, as the case may be, and any additional interest payable under section 17 of the Judgments Act 1838 because of failure or delay), allow the party so entitled less than the amount he would otherwise have allowed on a taxation bill or wholly disallow the costs.[55]

Thus, the taxing officer is entitled to reduce the bill in the case where there has been a long delay, even though there has been no prejudice to the paying party. It has been judicially suggested that taxing officers should use their punitive powers to reduce delay and speed up the administration of justice.[56]

Where, in beginning or purporting to begin taxation proceedings, or at any stage in the course of or in connection with those proceedings, there has been a failure to comply with the requirements of R.S.C., Ord. 62, whether in respect of time or in any other respect, the failure is treated as an irregularity which does not nullify the taxation proceedings or any step taken in the proceedings, but the taxing officer may, on the ground that

---

[53] R.S.C., Ord. 62, r. 28(1).
[54] *ibid.* r. 28(2).
[55] *ibid.* r. 28(4).
[56] *Re K (A Minor)* (1988) 138 New L.J. 262.

there has been such a failure, and on such terms as are thought fit, set aside wholly or in part the taxation proceedings or exercise his powers under R.S.C., Ord. 62 to make such order (if any) dealing with the taxation proceedings generally as he thinks fit.[57-58]

Civil Legal Aid (General) Regulations 1989, regs. 109, 108

Without prejudice to the Supreme Court Act 1981, s. 51(6), R.S.C., Ord. **20–26** 62, rr. 10, 11 (the penal powers of the Court vested in taxing masters and district judges under R.S.C., Ord. 62, r. 28) or to C.C.R., Ord. 38, r. 1(3), on any taxation of an assisted person's costs in connection with proceedings (except authorised summary proceedings), any wasted costs will be disallowed or reduced, and where the solicitor has, without good reason, delayed putting in his bill for taxation, the whole of the bill of costs may be disallowed or reduced.

"Wasted costs" means any costs incurred by a party as a result of any improper, unreasonable or negligent act or omission on the part of a legal representative or any employee of such a representative; or which in the light of any such act or omission occurring after they were incurred, the taxing officer considers it unreasonable to expect that party to pay. No costs will be disallowed or reduced under that provision until notice has been served by the taxing officer, on the solicitor whose name appears on the assisted person's certificate and, in a case where those costs relate to counsel's fees, on the assisted person's counsel, requiring the solicitor or counsel to show cause orally or in writing why those costs should not be disallowed or reduced.[59]

Where an order or agreement is made for the payment to an assisted party of costs and he has failed to ask for the costs to be taxed or for his certificate to be discharged before taxation, the Board may authorise the making of the application for taxation on his behalf and the costs of the application and the taxation are deemed to be costs in the proceedings to which the certificate related.[60-61]

Inherent jurisdiction

All the foregoing provisions are supplementary to the inherent jurisdiction **20–27** of the court.

Costs of taxation

The costs incurred on behalf of an assisted person as a result of his being a **20–28** party to a taxation *inter partes* are treated in the same way as other costs

---

57-58 R.S.C., Ord. 62, r. 30(4), (5).
59 Civil Legal Aid (General) Regulations 1989, reg. 109(1), (2), (3).
60-61 *ibid.* reg. 108.

incurred on his behalf and whether or not they are payable by the other party, they will be paid out of the Fund.[62] The assisted person is under the normal liability to recoup the Fund these costs up to the limit of his maximum contribution. As a general rule, the party whose bill is being taxed is entitled to his costs of the taxation proceedings, but where it appears to the taxing officer that in the circumstances of the case some other order should be made as to the whole or any part of the costs, the taxing officer has, in relation to the costs of taxation proceedings, the same powers as the court has in relation to the costs of the proceedings themselves.[63]

Calderbank procedure

20–29 The provisions of R.S.C., Ord. 62 dealing with *Calderbank* offers to pay a specific sum in satisfaction of costs "without prejudice save as to costs of taxation" do not apply where the person entitled to recover costs is an assisted person.[64]

Allocaturs and certificates

20–30 On completion of the taxation, the solicitor should make up the bill and the schedule in the usual way and certify the costings. The solicitor should then complete the legal aid taxation certificate and certify its accuracy. This form will replace the legal aid summary on the bill and when sealed by the court acts as a certificate authorising payment of the legal aid costs to the solicitor by the Board.[65] Additionally, the Board will require from the court an order or certificate showing total costs recoverable *inter partes* at appropriate expense rates.[66]

The certificate belongs to the successful party and where, because each is assisted it contains the costs of both parties, the Supreme Court Taxing Office will normally issue the certificate in two parts to enable each party to lodge the relevant part with the appropriate area committee. Alternatively, an office copy must be obtained. Where any party to a taxation is an assisted person, the certificate or allocatur may not, except by consent, be signed within 21 days of the taxing officer's decision.[67] Where, however, a bill is lodged within this period, whether legal aid only or *inter partes* and legal aid, the Supreme Court Taxing Office will infer that the

---

[62] Legal Aid Act 1988, s. 15(6), (7).
[63] R.S.C., Ord. 62, r. 27(1), (2).
[64] *ibid.* r. 27(5).
[65] *Practice Direction 3 of 1994*, para. 27.
[66] *ibid.* para. 4.
[67] Civil Legal Aid (General) Regulations 1989, reg. 121(1).

solicitors' consent to the issue of the certificate forthwith but their consent should be endorsed on the bill.

Where an assisted person's solicitor applies for authority to carry in objections or to have a taxation reviewed, that application must be made before the expiration of the time allowed under rules of court for applying to the taxing officer for a review of the taxation and the time so allowed will, for this purpose, be extended by two months, or such longer period as the taxing officer may allow. Notice of any application for authority to carry any objections or to have a taxation reviewed must be given to the taxing officer and to any opposing party.[68]

In the High Court, application for review of a taxing officer's decision must be made within 21 days after that decision and that time will be extended by one month as provided above.[69]

Failure to obtain a legal aid authority before lodging objections renders the review proceedings a nullity, but if the authority is subsequently obtained, the taxing officer has the power to extend the time for objection under R.S.C., Ord. 62, r.21 or r.33(2) to enable a further application for review to be made.[70]

A legally aided plaintiff does not have sufficient interest in the remuneration of his or her legal representatives and therefore lacks the *locus standi* necessary to apply for judicial review of the Board's refusal of authority to apply to a judge for a review.[71]

REVIEW OF TAXATION

General

An assisted person, his solicitor or counsel may be dissatisfied with the **20–31** taxation, the assisted person with that of the bill *inter partes* and the practitioner, either with that or with the legal aid taxation. The CLA(G) Regulations 1989 give all three the right, with the authority of the area commitee or the Board, to challenge a taxation by carrying in objections, by going to a review before a judge and by appealing from his decision. Any such proceedings are deemed to be proceedings to which the assisted person's certificate relates, whether or not it has been discharged or revoked, and the costs of those proceedings will be paid out of the Fund.[72] Where the assisted person has no interest in a taxation, or would but for

---

[68] *ibid.* reg. 121(1), (2); see regs. 113, 114, 116.
[69] R.S.C., Ord. 62, r. 33(2).
[70] *Morris v. Murphy (J) Cable* contractors & Civil Engineers, *The Times*, October 23, 1987.
[71] *R. v. Legal Aid Board, ex p. Bateman* [1992] W.L.R. 711, D.C.
[72] Civil Legal Aid (General) Regulations 1989, reg. 120.

the Regulations have an interest adverse to that of the solicitor, the assisted person will not be required to make any contribution to the Fund on account of the costs of the proceedings arising out of taxation or in consequence of any order made in those proceedings.[73] As the Fund may have an interest in the matter, the Lord Chancellor has power to appoint a solicitor to intervene and appear on the review by a judge of certain taxations and on an appeal from such a review.[74]

Carrying in objections

The assisted person

20–32 Where an assisted person is dissatisfied with any decision of a taxing officer as to the amount which he is entitled to recover by virtue of an order or agreement for costs made in his favour or for which he is liable by virtue of an order for costs made against him, the solicitor must apply to the area committee for authority to carry in objections to the taxation. If the area committee gives authority (but not otherwise), the solicitor may carry in objections in accordance with rules of court.[75]

The solicitor

20–33 Where the assisted person's solicitor is dissatisfied with any decision of the taxing officer on an *inter partes* taxation pursuant to an order for costs made in favour of the assisted person or on a legal aid taxation under regulation 107A(2) of the 1989 Regulations, the solicitor must apply to the area committee for authority to carry in the objections to the taxation and if the area committee gives authority (but not otherwise) the solicitor may carry in objections in accordance with rules of court.[76]

Counsel

20–34 It is the duty of the assisted person's solicitor within seven days after taxation or provisional taxation to notify counsel in writing where the fees claimed on his behalf have been reduced or disallowed and the solicitor must endorse the bill of costs with the date on which the notice was given or that no notice was necessary. Where the bill is endorsed that no notice was necessary, the taxing officer may issue the certificate or allocatur but where notice has been given, that certificate or allocatur will not issue until 14 days have elapsed from the date of the endorsement.[77]

---

[73] *ibid.* reg. 118(b).
[74] *ibid.* reg. 122.
[75] *ibid.* reg. 113(1), (2) (a); R.S.C., Ord. 62, rr. 33, 34.
[76] *ibid.* reg. 113(1), (2) (b); R.S.C., Ord. 62, rr. 33, 34.
[77] *ibid.* reg. 112(1), (2).

Where a counsel acting for an assisted person is dissatisfied with any decision on a legal aid taxation under regulation 107A(2) of the 1989 Regulations, it is the duty of the solicitor to report the matter to the appropriate area committee (or to the Board in the case of a review by a judge or an appeal from such a review) and if the committee (or the Board), gives authority to do so, to carry in objections to the taxation, to apply to a judge to review the taxation or to appeal from the decision of the judge as the case may be. The Civil Legal Aid (General) Regulations 1989 relating to applications for authority to carry in objections or to bring in a review, apply as if the solicitor were the person dissatisfied, and the costs of such proceedings are deemed to be proceedings to which the assisted person's certificate relates whether or not it has been discharged or revoked and the costs of those proceedings will be paid out of the Fund.[78]

Similarly, where there has been a provisional taxation and counsel is dissatisfied with the decision on that provisional taxation, it is the duty of the assisted person's solicitor to inform the taxing officer that he wishes to be heard on the taxation and to attend on the taxation.[79]

Although counsel has the right to appear in person on a review of his own fees in a legal aid taxation, it is usually preferable for him to be represented by a solicitor and the expense of that representation will be met out of the Fund. Similar principles apply to a review before a judge of a taxation and to an appeal from the judge's decision on a review.

By another party

If in proceedings to which an assisted person is a party any other party **20–35** carries in objections to the *inter partes* taxation or applies to a judge to review the taxation, the assisted person's solicitor may be heard on the objections or review notwithstanding that the assisted person himself may have no interest in the taxation.[80] The solicitor also has the right to appear by counsel and be heard on an appeal by the other party despite the fact that the client may have no interest in the appeal, or would but for the Regulations have an interest adverse to that of the solicitor.[81] In any such case it is unnecessary for the authority of the area committee or the Board to be obtained.

Procedure

Where a solicitor wishes to apply to the area committee for authority to **20–36** carry in objections either on his own behalf or on behalf of counsel or an assisted person, the application must be made within the time allowed by

---

[78] *ibid.* regs. 116(1), 113, 114, 115, 120.
[79] *ibid.* reg. 116(2).
[80] *ibid.* reg. 117.
[81] *ibid.* reg. 118.

rules of court for applying to the taxing officer to review his decision, *i.e.* 21 days.[82] The solicitor must give notice of the application to the taxing officer and to any opposite party and the time for carrying in objections is then extended by one month or such longer period as the taxing officer may allow.[83]

The position where the assisted person has no interest in taxation

20–37   Where the assisted person has no interest in the taxation or would but for the provisions of the CLA(G) Regulations 1989 have an interest adverse to that of the solicitor:

(a) it is the duty of the solicitor carrying in the objections under regulation 113 or applying for review under regulation 114 to ensure that all matters which are proper to be taken into account in consideration of the objections or on the review are placed before the taxing officer or the judge, as the case may be;

(b) the assisted person will not be required to make any contribution to the Fund on account of the costs of any proceedings arising under regulations 113 to 117 or in consequence of any order made in such proceedings; and

(c) the charge created by section 16(6) of the 1988 Act will not apply in relation to any resulting increase in the net liability of the Fund arising out of the costs of any proceedings under regulations 113 to 117 or in consequence of any order made in such proceedings.[84]

The position where the assisted person has a financial interest in taxation

20–38   Regardless of the provisions set out in the previous paragraph, where the assisted person has a financial interest in the taxation:

(a) It is the duty of his solicitor to explain to him the extent of his interest in the taxation and the steps which can be taken to safeguard that interest and, if the assisted person so requests, to give notice in accordance with the rules of court to the taxing officer, that the assisted person has such an interest;

(b) the assisted person will not be required to make any contribution to the Fund on account of the costs of the taxation proceedings;

(c) the charge created by section 16(6) of the 1988 Act will not apply

---

[82] R.S.C., Ord. 62, r. 33(2).
[83] Civil Legal Aid (General) Regulations 1989, reg. 121.
[84] *ibid.* reg. 118.

to any resulting increase in the net liability of the Fund arising out of the costs of the taxation proceedings.[85]

Application for review of taxation

The assisted person or solicitor

Where the assisted person, or the solicitor, is dissatisfied with the decision **20–39** of the taxing officer on any matter to which objection has been taken, the solicitor must apply to the Board for authority to have the taxation reviewed. If the Board gives authority but not otherwise, the solicitor may apply (or instruct counsel to apply) to a judge to review the taxation in accordance with the rules of court.[86]

The Court of Appeal has held that, in the absence of an appropriate authority, the court has no power to entertain a review under its inherent jurisdiction or its general powers under R.S.C., Ord. 62.[87]

In the rare cases where no relief is available under the Rules of the Supreme Court, it is possible for the High Court under its own inherent jurisdiction to examine the decisions of a taxing master, notwithstanding that judicial review does not extend to such decisions.[88]

The Court of Appeal has also held that the failure to obtain legal aid authority before lodging objections renders review proceedings a nullity, but, where authority is subsequently obtained, the taxing officer has power to extend time for objections under R.S.C., Ord. 62, r. 21 or r. 33(2) to enable a further application for a review to be made.[89]

It is open to a solicitor properly to apply for authority to carry any objections or to apply for a review in a situation where an expert witness had limited his claim for remuneration to the amount allowed on taxation. The expert has no right to be heard on taxation in person or by legal representation and the decision whether to admit evidence falls within the taxing master's discretion, although the court thought in one particular case that expert evidence should be permitted in respect of notes for the services performed. The court also considered it doubtful whether a taxing master could be ordered to give further particulars of his reasons.[90]

---

[85] *ibid.* reg. 119.
[86] *ibid.* reg. 114; R.S.C., Ord. 62, r. 35.
[87] *Storer v. Wright* [1981] Q.B. 336.
[88] *R. v. Taxing Officer, ex p. Bee Line Roadways (International) Ltd*, The Times, February 11, 1982.
[89] *Morris v. Murphy J. Cable Contractors & Civil Engineers*, The Times, October 23, 1987.
[90] *Cementation Construction Ltd. v. Keaveney* (1988) 138 New L.J. 242; *The Times*, July 21, 1988.

Counsel

20–40 Where counsel acting for an assisted person is dissatisfied with any decision on the legal aid taxation, it is the duty of the assisted person's solicitor to report the matter to the Board and, if the Board gives authority, to apply to a judge to review the taxation.[91]

Other party

20–41 If, in proceedings to which an assisted person is a party, any other party applies to a judge to review the taxation, the assisted person's solicitor may be heard on the review notwithstanding that the assisted person himself may have no interest in the taxation.[92]

Procedure

20–42 Where a solicitor wishes to apply to the Board for authority to have a taxation reviewed, either on his own behalf or on that of counsel or an assisted person, the same provisions apply as to the time in which this must be done and the notices which must be given as relate to an application to the area committee's authority to carry any objections.[93]

Where the assisted person has no interest in the taxation or has an interest which would, but for the Civil Legal Aid (General) Regulations 1989, be adverse to that of the solicitor, it is the duty of the solicitor applying for the review to ensure that all matters which are proper to be taken into account in consideration of the review are placed before the judge.[94]

Applicants for reviews of taxation are required to lodge with the Chief Clerk of the Supreme Court Taxing Office three bundles of documents for the use of the judge and assessors.

Upon receipt of the summons from the Queen's Bench or Chancery Divisions, the Chief Clerk will send notice to the applicants requesting that the bundles be lodged. The bundles should consist of copies of the following documents:

(a) the summons to review;
(b) the order, judgment or other instrument providing for the taxation;
(c) the bill of costs;
(d) the objections;
(e) the respondent's answers (if any);
(f) the master's and district judge's answers and certificate;
(g) any affidavits filed during the course of the taxation;
(h) the legal aid certificate — any relevant amendments thereto; and

---

[91] Civil Legal Aid (General) Regulations 1989, reg. 116.
[92] *ibid.* reg. 117.
[93] *ibid.* reg. 116.
[94] *ibid.* reg. 118(a).

(i) the authority to apply for review;

(j) any correspondence or other documents to which reference is intended to be made at the hearing of the review.

The bundles must be clearly paginated with an index at the front of the bundle listing all the documents and giving a page reference for each one. The bundles must be bound together, loose documents will not be accepted. The bundles must be lodged within 21 days from the receipt of the notice from the Chief Clerk or within such other time as the Chief Clerk may direct.[95]

Appeal from review of taxation

An assisted person's solicitor may, with the authority of the Board, appeal, **20–43** either on behalf of the assisted person or on his own behalf or on behalf of counsel, from the decision of a judge on a review of taxation and is entitled to appear by counsel for the purpose.[96] No right of appeal is conferred in proceedings to which an assisted person is not a party where no such right exists;[97] as an order by a judge on a review of taxation is an interlocutory order, leave is necessary.[98] Application to the Board for authority must be made before the expiry of the time allowed by rules of court to appeal from the judge's decision (presently four weeks).[99] When this is done, the time for appealing is extended by two months.[1]

The exercise by the Board of its power to grant or withhold authority under the Civil Legal Aid (General) Regulations 1989, reg. 114 is susceptible to judicial review proceedings on the grounds of public interest in the administration of justice by applicants with sufficient interest, which need not be financial. Feelings of gratitude or sympathy for the solicitors do not afford sufficient justification for bringing proceedings for judicial review.[2]

Appointment of solicitor to intervene

In the past, the courts sometimes experienced difficulty when hearing a **20–44** summons for the review of a legal aid taxation because the Regulations contained no provision for those responsible for the protection of the Fund to be represented at the hearing. The situation has been met since 1960 by

---

[95] *Practice Direction (Application to Review)* (No. 5 of 1986) Supreme Court Taxing Office [1986] 1 W.L.R. 1053.

[96] Civil Legal Aid (General) Regulation 1989, regs. 114, 115, 116.

[97] *ibid.* reg. 115(2).

[98] R.S.C., Ord. 59, r. 1A (6) (dd).

[99] *ibid.* r. 4(1).

[1] Civil Legal Aid (General) Regulations 1989, reg. 115(3).

[2] *R. v. Legal Aid Board, ex p. Bateman* [1992] 1. W.L.R. 711, D.C.

the Civil Legal Aid (General) Regulations 1989 which give the Lord Chancellor power to appoint a solicitor to intervene in any review by a judge of a taxation of the costs of proceedings to which an assisted person is a party. Such an appointment may be made in respect of the particular review or may extend to any review of taxation during the period for which the solicitor is appointed.[3]

Whenever the Board gives authority to an assisted person's solicitor to apply to a judge for a review of a taxation it must notify the Lord Chancellor and inform him of the name and address of the assisted person's solicitor.[4]

If in proceedings to which an assisted person is a party, any other party applies to a judge to review any *inter partes* or legal aid taxation the assisted person's solicitor must inform the Board and the Board must notify the Lord Chancellor and inform him of the name and address of the assisted person's solicitor and where the subject of the review is an *inter partes* taxation, the name and address of the solicitor acting for the other party.[5]

If a solicitor is appointed to intervene in this way, he is entitled to production of all relevant documents and to receive copies of them and to appear by counsel and to be heard on the review with a view to ensuring that all considerations, which are proper to be taken into account, are placed before the court, whether they relate to the interests of the Fund or of the assisted person or to the remuneration of the solicitors and counsel acting for assisted persons.[6] It is clear from this that the intervening solicitor is expected to take broader considerations into account than just the financial interests of the Fund and is more in the position of an *amicus curiae*.

The judge hearing the review may make an order for costs in favour of, or against, the intervening solicitor. Any sum which the solicitor receives in consequence of such an order must be paid by him to the Board and any costs which he is ordered to pay will be met by the Fund. The solicitor's own costs for intervening in the review will also be paid out of the Fund.[7] The same provisions apply in the case of an appeal against a judge's decision on a review and the intervening solicitor may himself appeal.[8]

The costs of objection and review

20–45   Any of the proceedings already referred to in connection with challenging a taxation (*i.e.* carrying any objections and review to a judge) are deemed to be ones to which the assisted person's certificate relates, whether or not

---

[3] Civil Legal Aid (General) Regulations 1989, reg. 122(1).
[4] *ibid.* reg. 122(2).
[5] *ibid.* reg. 122(3).
[6] *ibid.* reg. 122(4).
[7] *ibid.* reg. 122(5).
[8] *ibid.* reg. 122(6).

it has been discharged or revoked and the costs of such proceedings will be paid out of the Fund, provided the appropriate authority has been obtained.[9]

THE TAXATION OF COSTS IN INDIVIDUAL COURTS

The House of Lords

Taxation is carried out in the House of Lords by the taxing officer appointed **20–46** by the Clerk of the Parliaments under the standing order regulating judicial business.[10] Where an *inter partes* taxation and a legal aid taxation are to be carried out together, a four-column bill must be lodged in the same way as in the Supreme Court. Where a legal aid taxation only is involved, a two-column bill is required. Standard basis (and the indemnity basis) of taxation applies in the House of Lords.[11]

Any party to a taxation who is dissatisfied with the allowance or disallowance of any item by the taxing officer may apply to the Clerk of the Parliaments to review the decision of the taxing officer in respect of that item. Application is only permitted on a question of principle and not in respect of the quantum allowed on taxation. Application must be made within 14 days after the decision of the taxing officer or such longer period as may be fixed by him. No application is permitted after the signing of the taxing officer's certificate dealing finally with that item.

Any party who is dissatisfied with the Clerk of the Parliaments' decision on review, may, within 14 days of the date on which it is delivered to the parties, present an incidental petition to the House of Lords in accordance with direction 41 of *The Directions as to Procedure (Civil)*. Such a petition will be referred to an appeal committee who will consider whether it should be referred for an oral hearing. Such steps would, of course, require the authority of the area committee or the Board as the case may be.[12]

County court

In general, the position as to legal aid costs in civil proceedings is the same **20–47** in the county court as in the High Court.[13]

The County Court Rules 1981 contain provisions for objections to be

---

[9] *ibid.* reg. 120.
[10] Standing Order XIII.
[11] *Procedure Direction (House of Lords: Bills of Costs)* [1986] 1 W.L.R. 1133, H.L.
[12] Civil Legal Aid (General) Regulations 1989, regs. 113-120.
[13] See below, chap. 7 as to divorce proceedings in the county court.

made to a taxation and for the taxation to be reviewed by a judge.[14] There is a right to appeal to the Court of Appeal against a decision by a judge when reviewing a taxation.[15]

The Land's Tribunal

20–48   The provisions of the Civil Legal Aid (General) Regulations 1989 relating to assessment of costs and taxation of costs[16] do not apply in relation to proceedings in the Land's Tribunal to which an assisted person is a party. Where the Tribunal gives a final decision in writing, it must in addition to any direction as to costs, contain a direction that the costs of any assisted person be taxed on the standard basis and those costs will be taxed by the registrar of the Tribunal. Where the proceedings are brought to an end without such a direction having been given, the costs must be taxed by the registrar on the standard basis, and in taxing the costs of any assisted person, the registrar has power to determine as the appropriate scale for taxation one of the scales of costs for the time being prescribed by the County Court Rules 1981.[17] The regulations relating to objections and review apply in the same manner as they apply to the conduct of proceedings in any court.[18]

Employment Appeal Tribunal

20–49   Costs of an assisted person in respect of proceedings in the Employment Appeal Tribunal must be assessed by the Area Director, in accordance with the Civil Aid (General) Regulations 1989, reg. 105, or taxed on the standard basis by a taxing master of the Supreme Court. The provisions of R.S.C., Ord. 62 are specifically applied with necessary modifications to the taxation of those costs as if the proceedings were a cause or matter in the Supreme Court.[19] The Civil Legal Aid (General) Regulations 1989 apply to the conduct of all proceedings in the Appeal Tribunal in the same way as they apply to the conduct of proceedings in any court.[20]

   Where public money had been wasted in the preparation of 100 pages of an industrial tribunal chairman's notes of evidence when only 10 lines referred to on appeal were strictly relevant, the Appeal Tribunal had been minded to order the applicant's trade union to pay the costs thrown away by the requirement of the notes, but there was no power to do so under

---

[14] C.C.R., Ord. 38. r. 9 (as to the allowance of increased sums on taxation).
[15] County Courts Act 1984, s. 77; C.C.R., Ord. 38, r. 24.
[16] Civil Aid (General) Regulations 1989, regs. 105-107.
[17] *ibid.* reg. 148 (4) (a)–(c).
[18] *ibid.* reg. 148 (2).
[19] *ibid.* reg. 149 (7).
[20] *ibid.* reg. 148 (2).

rule 27 of the Employment Appeal Rules 1980,[21] since that rule referred to costs incurred "by that other party" that meant a party to the appeal.[22]

The Commons Commissioners

The costs of an assisted person in respect of proceedings before the Commissioners must be taxed or assessed as if they were costs of proceedings in the county court.[23] The Civil Legal Aid (General) Regulations 1989 apply to the conduct of all proceedings before the Commissioners in the same way as they apply to conduct of proceedings in any court.[24]

20–50

The Restrictive Practices Court

The costs of an assisted person in respect of proceedings in the Restrictive Practices Court must be assessed in accordance with the Civil Legal Aid (General) Regulations 1989, reg. 105, or taxed on the standard basis by a taxing master of the Supreme Court. The provisions of R.S.C., Ord. 62 apply with necessary modification to the taxation of those costs as if the proceedings in the court were a cause or matter in the Supreme Court.[25]

20–51

Save where otherwise provided, the Civil Legal Aid (General) Regulations 1989 apply to proceedings in the Restrictive Practices Court under Part 3 of the Fair Trading Act 1973 and to any proceedings in the court in consequence of an order made or an undertaking given to the court under that Act and for conduct of all such proceedings in the same way as they apply to the conduct of proceedings in any court.[26]

Where any power to do any act or exercise any jurisdiction or discretion is conferred by the Civil Legal Aid (General) Regulations 1989 on a court it must, in relation to proceedings in the Restrictive Practices Court, be exercised by that court and may, unless it is exercisable only during the hearing of any proceedings by a judge or by the court, be exercisable by the proper officer of the court.[27]

---

[21] S.I. 1980 No. 2035.
[22] *Wilson v. Knowsley Borough Council, The Times,* November 11, 1989.
[23] Civil Legal Aid (General) Regulations 1989, reg. 150(4).
[24] *ibid.* reg. 150(2).
[25] *ibid.* reg. 151(7).
[26] *ibid.* reg. 151(2).
[27] *ibid.* reg. 151(3).

Chapter 21

THE RIGHT OF AN UNASSISTED PARTY TO COSTS OUT OF THE FUND

INTRODUCTION

21–01 In any proceedings to which a legally assisted person is a party and which are finally decided in favour of an unassisted party, the court which decides the proceedings may, subject to certain conditions, make an order for the payment by the Board to the unassisted party of the whole or any part of the costs incurred by him in the proceedings.[1]

The 1988 Act states that "costs means costs as between party and party".[2] Since the old party and party basis of taxation was done away with in April 1986, the section must be interpreted as meaning costs *inter partes* and such costs will be taxed on the standard basis.[3] The costs include the costs of applying for an order in respect of a successful unassisted party. The principles governing when costs will be awarded against the Board and to an unassisted party are the same in children cases as in other areas of Law even though this could result in the unassisted party suffering severe financial hardship.[4]

CONDITIONS FOR THE MAKING OF AN ORDER

The proceedings must have been finally decided in favour of the unassisted party

21–02 Before the court can make an order, the proceedings must be finally

---

[1] Legal Aid Act 1988, s. 18(1), (2); and see also advice by way of representation (ABWOR), chap. 4.
[2] *ibid.* s. 18(6).
[3] R.S.C., Ord. 62, r. 12(3).
[4] *K. v. K. (Legal Aid: Costs) The Times*, October 28, 1994, C.A.

decided in favour of the unassisted party.[5] Proceedings are to be treated as finally decided in this way if:

(a) no appeal lies against the decision in the unassisted party's favour;

(b) an appeal lies against the decision with leave and the time-limit for applications for leave expires without leave being granted; or

(c) leave to appeal against a decision is granted or is not required and no appeal is brought within the time limited for appeal.[6]

The word "proceedings" includes an interlocutory appeal and where that interlocutory appeal has been "finally decided" in favour of unassisted defendants the court has jurisdiction to order that the defendants' costs be paid out of the Fund.[7]

Where an appeal against a decision is brought out of time, the court by which the appeal (or any further appeal in those proceedings) is determined, may make an order for the repayment by the unassisted party to the Board of the whole or any part of any sum previously paid to him in respect of those proceedings.[8]

For proceedings to be finally decided in favour of the unassisted party within the meaning of the 1988 Act, it is not necessary for those proceedings to be decided wholly in favour of the unassisted party, merely that they be substantially so decided.[9]

Where an unassisted defendant makes a payment into court, the proceedings are finally decided in favour of the unassisted party whenever that payment exceeds the sum eventually recovered by the legally aided plaintiff.[10]

The court must consider what order for costs should be made against the assisted party

Before making an order for costs in respect of the successful unassisted party, the court must consider what order for costs should be made against the assisted party and for determining his liability in respect of those costs.[11] This is something which the court will consider in any event whether the unassisted party makes an application or not.   **21–03**

---

[5] Legal Aid Act 1988, s. 18(1).

[6] *ibid.* s. 18(7).

[7] *Megarity v. The Law Society; Gayway Linings Ltd. v. The Law Society* [1982] A.C. 81; [1981] 2 W.L.R. 335.

[8] Legal Aid Act 1988, s. 18(7).

[9] *Kelly v. London Transport Executive* [1982] 1 W.L.R. 1055; [1982] 2 All E.R. 842; *General Accident Fire and Life Assurance Corporation Ltd v. Foster* [1972] 3 All E.R. 880.

[10] *Kelly v. London Transport Executive* [1982] 1 W.L.R. 1055.

[11] Legal Aid Act 1988, s. 18(3).

An order for costs would be made in the proceedings apart from the 1988 Act

21–04   An order in respect of the costs of a successful unassisted party may only be made if an order for costs would be made in the proceedings apart from the 1988 Act.[12] Thus, if apart from the 1988 Act, no order would have been made, the unassisted party would not be entitled to payment out of the Fund.

When a judge comes to consider whether, apart from the 1988 Act, he would have made an order for costs against the unsuccessful assisted party, he should be careful not to be influenced by the consideration that that conclusion (that he would have made such an order) is one step towards the making of an order in favour of the unassisted litigant against the Fund. He must come first to his independent conclusion that he would have made an order.[13]

Proceedings in a court of first instance must have been started by the assisted party

21–05   As regards the costs incurred in a court of first instance, those proceedings must have been instituted by the assisted party.[14] Provided this condition is fulfilled, an unassisted party may apply for an order if successful at first instance or on appeal.

An unassisted plaintiff may successfully apply for an order for costs out of the Fund where an assisted defendant makes a counterclaim;[15] it has, however, been held that the costs of the counterclaim should be only those exclusively referrable to the counterclaim, that is, the increased costs occasioned by the existence of the counterclaim.[16] This view is open to argument so as to enable the costs to be divided between the costs of the counterclaim and the costs of the claim.[17]

Although there is no reference to "appellate court" in section 18 of the 1988 Act, that section has precisely the same effect as its predecessor, section 13 of the Legal Aid Act 1974, although it is more clearly and simply expressed. The Divisional Court could never in any circumstances be called a court of first instance, since it is inevitably faced with a challenge to a decision or order of a lower court or inferior tribunal or a person or body exercising a public law function.[18]

---

[12] ibid. s.18(4)(a).
[13] Nowotnik v. Nowotnik [1967] P.83, and Hanning v. Maitland (No.2) [1970] 1 Q.B. 580, C.A.
[14] Legal Aid Act 1988, s. 18(4)(b).
[15] Millican v. Tucker [1980] 1 W.L.R. 640, C.A.
[16] ibid.
[17] R. & T. Thew Ltd v. Reeves [1982] Q.B. 172, C.A.
[18] R. v. Leeds County Court, ex p. Morris [1989] 2 W.L.R. 175; [1990] 1 All E.R. 550.

A district judge, who first hears and determines a case and makes an order which is effective and operative unless reversed on appeal, is "a court of first instance". Where a party appeals from that decision to a judge in chambers the judge sits as an appellate court.[19]

The unassisted party will otherwise suffer severe financial hardship

An order for the costs of a successful unassisted party, incurred in a court **21–06** of first instance, may only be made if the court is satisfied that the unassisted party will suffer severe financial hardship unless the order is made[20]:

> ". . . the words (severe financial hardship) should be constructed so as to exclude insurance companies; and commercial companies who are in a considerable way of business; and wealthy folk who can meet the costs without feeling it. But it should not be construed so as to exclude people of modest income or modest capital who would find it hard to bear their own costs."[21]

Where an individual was in receipt of an income which was quite substantial but was already committed to maintaining his lifestyle it was held that that person was likely to suffer severe financial hardship if he did not recover his costs from public funds.[22] The Court of Appeal has accepted that a limited company can suffer hardship, especially if it is a small company which is little more than the alter ego of its shareholder directors[23] but that the London Transport Executive would not suffer severe financial hardship merely because its already vast deficit would be increased.[24] There is thus a difference between making a company pay its own costs where the effect would be to force it into liquidation on the one hand and on the other hand where the effect is simply to increase the size of the company's overdraft and thus reduce its profitability to some extent.[25]

There is no reason in principle why a local authority or any other large body should not be able to establish that the amount expended on costs in legal proceedings placed an exceptional burden on its resources and that it would suffer severe financial hardship unless the Board paid the costs.[26]

It has been held that it is not right to aggregate the income and capital resources of the unassisted party and his spouse for the purpose of

---

[19] *Megarity v. The Law Society; Gayway Linings v. The Law Society* [1982] A.C. 81; [1981] 2 W.L.R. 335.
[20] Legal Aid Act 1988, s. 18(4)(b).
[21] *Per* Denning M.R. in *Hanning v. Maitland (No. 2)* [1970] Q.B. at 588.
[22] *Stewart v. Stewart* [1984] 1 W.L.R. 877, S.C.
[23] *R. & T. Thew Ltd v. Reeves* [1982] Q.B. 172, C.A.
[24] *Kelly v. London Transport Executive* [1982] 1 W.L.R. 1055.
[25] *ibid.* at 1067, *per* Akner L.J.
[26] *R. v. Greenwich London Borough Council, ex p. Lovelace* [1991] 3 W.L.R. 1015, C.A.

considering the existence of financial hardship. However, it was held that the resources of the spouse could and should be taken into account to the extent that the spouse was able to support herself and so relieve the defendant of the burden of providing her with financial support; following from this it was held that a finding of severe financial hardship did not mean that the unassisted party would automatically have all his costs paid by the Fund. Thus, the defendant should receive "only so much of his costs as would occasion him severe financial hardship if he himself had to pay them".[27] Where an unassisted party is concerned in proceedings only in a representative, fiduciary or official capacity, the court will not take into account his personal resources, but must have regard to the value of the property, estate or fund out of which the unassisted party is entitled to be indemnified and may, in its discretion, also have regard to the resources of the persons, if any, including the unassisted party where appropriate, who are beneficially interested in that property, estate or fund.[28]

It must be just and equitable for an order to be made

21–07 Before an order is made, the court must be satisfied that it is just and equitable in all the circumstances of the case, that provision for the costs should be made out of public funds.[29]

The current view of the Court of Appeal in respect of what is "just and equitable" appears to be a follows:
- (a) the words "just and equitable" are not a term of art nor are they capable of precise definition;
- (b) in considering whether they apply the court has a wide discretion and may consider the conduct of the parties;
- (c) if the applicant has brought the litigation on himself or could have avoided it or could have taken steps to have his opponent's certificate withdrawn, he may disentitle himself from obtaining an order;
- (d) it is unnecessary to inquire into the circumstances in which the assisted party received legal aid; so far as the applicant is concerned, this is *res inter alios acta*;
- (e) something more is needed than merely showing that the case is one where it is proper to apply the normal rule that the successful party is entitled to his costs;
- (f) the fact that the unassisted party may, as the result of an order, be put in a better position than a legally aided party would be in, in similar circumstances, is irrelevant.[30]

---

[27] *Adams & Adams v. Riley* [1988] Q.B. 372.
[28] Civil Legal Aid (General) Regulations 1989, reg. 135.
[29] Legal Aid Act 1988, s. 18(4) (c).
[30] *Hanning v. Maitland (No. 2)* [1971] Q.B. 580, C.A. and *Kelly v. London Transport Executive* [1982] 1 W.L.R. 1055.

Where a building society was sued by an assisted person claiming that an **21–08** alleged assignment of her property to a third party was void and the building society lost at first instance but was successful on appeal, an order was made that the building society should be at liberty to add its costs of the action and those occasioned by appeal to its security comprised in the mortgage. The House of Lords considered two questions:

    (a) whether the order of the Court of Appeal enabling the building society as the mortgagee to add its costs to its security should be set aside on the grounds that it conflicted with the Legal Aid Act 1949 s. 2(2)(e); and

    (b) whether it was just and equitable in all the circumstances that an order should be made under the Legal Aid Act 1964 s. 1(2) for payment out of the Fund to the building society of the whole or any part of its costs in the Court of Appeal and the House of Lords in so far as they were not covered by the security.

The House of Lords held that:

    (a) the order of the Court of Appeal did not conflict with the provisions of the Legal Aid Act 1949, it should not be set aside, and it did not impose any personal liability on the assisted person since it did no more than enable the building society as the mortgagee to operate an existing right against the legally assisted person's property;

    (b) for the same reasons the building society as the mortgagee was also entitled to add to its security its costs incurred in resisting the plaintiff's appeal to the House of Lords;

    (c) it would not be just and equitable in all the circumstances for an order to be made for the payment to the building society out of the Fund of the costs not covered by the security which it chose to incur by appealing to the Court of Appeal against a decision at first instance in favour of the legally aided party; and

    (d) it was just and equitable in all the circumstances that an order should be made for the payment to the building society out of the Fund of its costs in the House of Lords in so far as they were not covered by the security, since the appeal was by the legally aided party and leave was given for it because it involved important general questions of law.[31]

Who May Apply for an Order?

Any unassisted litigant is entitled to apply for an order. There is no **21–09** restriction as there is on eligibility for legal aid and a corporation or a partnership has the same right to apply as an individual litigant.

---

[31] *Saunders v. Anglia Building Society (No. 2)* [1971] A.C. 1039.

A successful respondent to an appeal is entitled to an order for costs against the Fund where the court is satisfied that the circumstances are so unsatisfactory that the appellant should not have been granted legal aid to pursue the matter.[32]

THE PROCEDURE WHEN A PARTY APPLIES FOR AN ORDER

21–10   An application for an order may be made at any time and in any manner in which an application for an order for costs might be made in respect of the same proceedings if none of the parties were receiving any legal aid. Any proceedings in respect of which a separate certificate could properly be issued must be treated as separate proceedings for the purposes of section 18 of the 1988 Act.[33]

Where a court decides any proceedings in favour of the unassisted party and an appeal lies (with or without leave) against that decision, the court may, if it thinks fit, make or refuse to make an order under section 18 of the 1988 Act forthwith. But, if an order is made forthwith, it will not take effect:

(a) where leave to appeal is required unless the time limited for applications for leave expires without leave being granted;

(b) where leave to appeal is granted or is not required unless the time limited for appeal expires without an appeal being brought.[34]

The unassisted party and the Area Director may appear at any hearing or inquiry in connection with an order for costs against an assisted person, or an order for costs of an unassisted party out of the Fund.[35] The usual practice is for an order to be made unless, within a specified time (usually 10 weeks), the Board makes representations to the contrary.[36]

The Area Director may, instead of appearing, submit written representations concerning the applications, and the representations must be supported by an affidavit sworn by the Area Director and sent to the proper officer of the court, with a copy to the unassisted party, not less than seven days before the hearing or the inquiry to which they relate.[37]

The magistrates' court

21–11   Where an application for an order for the costs of an unassisted party out

---

[32] *Aire Property Trust v. Treeweek* (1989) 07 E.G. 74.
[33] Civil Legal Aid (General) Regulations 1989, reg. 134(1), (2).
[34] Legal Aid Act 1988, s. 18(8).
[35] Civil Legal Aid (General) Regulations 1989, reg. 136(1).
[36] *Maynard v. Osmond* [1979] 1 W.L.R. 31 and *Scarth v. Jacobs-Paton, The Times,* November 2, 1978.
[37] Civil Legal Aid (General) Regulations 1989, reg. 136(2).

of the Fund is made in respect of authorised summary proceedings, the magistrates' court may, in its discretion, instead of making an order forthwith, either adjourn the hearing of the application or dismiss the application. If the application is adjourned, the unassisted party must swear an affidavit of costs and resources, containing the matters specified in Schedule 2 to the Civil Legal Aid (General) Regulations 1989. That affidavit must be produced at the adjourned hearing, and not less than 21 days before the unassisted party must serve notice of the date and time of the hearing on the Area Director with a copy of his affidavit of costs and resources together with any exhibits and supporting documents.[38]

The matters to be included in an affidavit of costs and resources are:
- (a) an estimate of the unassisted party's *inter partes* costs of the proceedings in respect of which his application is made supported by:
  - (i) particulars of the estimated costs in the form of a summary bill of costs;
  - (ii) all necessary documentary evidence to substantiate each item in the bill;
- (b) a statement, supported by evidence, of the unassisted party's financial resources of every kind during the period beginning three years before his application is made, and of his estimated future financial resources and expectation;
- (c) a declaration that, to the best of his knowledge and belief, the unassisted party has not, and at any relevant time has not had and will not have, any financial resources or expectations not specified in the statement described above;
- (d) a declaration that the unassisted party has not at any time deliberately foregone or deprived himself of any financial resources or expectations with a view to furthering his application;
- (e) a statement supported by evidence of the unassisted party's reasonable financial commitments during the period covered by his statement described at (b) above, including, if desired, his estimated solicitor and own client costs of the proceedings in respect of which his application is made:
  - (i) if the unassisted party has, or at any relevant time has had, a spouse, his statements and declarations described above must also take account of and (to the best of his knowledge and belief) specify that spouse's financial resources, expectations and commitments, unless he or she had a contrary interest to the unassisted party in the proceedings in respect of which his application is made, or the unassisted party and his spouse are, or at the relevant time were, living separately and apart,

---

[38] *ibid.* reg. 137(1), (2).

or for some other reason it would be inequitable or impracticable for the unassisted party to comply with the requirements
of this paragraph;

    (ii) paragraph (i) applies to a man and woman who are living with
each other in the same household, as husband and wife, as it
applies to the parties to a marriage;

  (g) full particulars of any application for legal aid made by the unassisted party in connection with the proceedings in respect of which
the application is made including the date and reference number
of his application and the Area Director to whom it was made.[39]

County Court Proceedings

21-12   Where an application for an order for an unassisted party's costs out of the
Fund is made in respect of proceedings in, or on appeal from, a county
court, the court must not make an order forthwith, but may, at its discretion,
refer the application to the district judge for hearing and determination or
adjourn or dismiss the application. The district judge means the district
judge of the county court in which the proceedings were tried or
determined or from which the appeal was brought.[40]

Reference to registrar for determination

21-13   Where an application is referred to the district judge for hearing and
determination:

  (a) within 21 days of the adjournment, the unassisted party must file
an affidavit of costs and resources (with any exhibits and
supporting documents) together with a copy;

  (b) not less than 21 days before the hearing, the court must serve on
the Area Director notice of the date fixed together with a copy of
the affidavit of costs and resources filed.[41]

An unassisted party seeking an order for costs against the Board is
required to comply in all significant respects with the requirements of
Schedule 2 to the Civil Legal Aid (General) Regulations 1989 by providing
a full affidavit of costs and resources which includes the matters specified
in that schedule.[42]

The unassisted party or the Area Director may appeal to the judge on a

---

[39] *ibid.* 1989, Sched. 2.
[40] *ibid.* reg. 138.
[41] *ibid.* regs. 139 (a), 142 (a), (b).
[42] *Jones v. Zahedi, The Times,* July 12, 1992.

point of law from the district judge's determination within 14 days of the date on which it was given.[43-44]

The procedure on reference to district judge for inquiry and report

Where a court adjourns the hearing of an application, it may make an order **21–14** referring it to the district judge for inquiry and report. If such an order is made:

(a) the court must serve a copy of its order on the unassisted party;

(b) within 21 days of the court making its order (or such longer time as the court may allow), the unassisted party must file an affidavit of costs and resources (with any exhibits and supporting documents) together with a copy;

(c) the court must serve a copy of its order and of the unassisted party's affidavit of costs and resources on the Area Director.[45]

As soon as the copy of the order of the court and the affidavit of costs and resources have been served on the Area Director, the district judge must give the unassisted party and the Area Director at least 21 days' notice of the date and time when it is proposed to conduct the inquiry. The district judge is given the same powers as the taxing officer in the exercise of his functions under the County Court Rules 1981. Once the inquiry is complete, the district judge must report to the court in writing and must, at the same time, send a copy of the report to the unassisted party and the Area Director. Once the report is received by the court, it must give the unassisted party and the Area Director 21 days' notice of the day appointed for the hearing and determination of the application in chambers.[46]

Procedure where application adjourned

Where the court simply adjourns an application without referring it to the **21–15** district judge for inquiry and report, the unassisted party must, within 21 days of the adjournment, file an affidavit of costs and resources (with any exhibits and supporting documents) together with a copy; and not less than 21 days before the adjourned hearing, the court must serve on the Area Director notice of the date fixed together with a copy of the affidavit of the costs and resources so filed.[47] The court has no jurisdiction to grant an

[43-44] Civil Legal Aid (General) Regulations 1989, reg. 139 (b).
[45] Civil Legal Aid (General) Regulations 1989.
[46] *ibid.* reg. 141(1), (2), (3), (4).
[47] *ibid.* reg. 142.

extension of time for the filing of an affidavit of costs by a successful unassisted party.[48]

APPLICATIONS IN RESPECT OF PROCEEDINGS IN THE SUPREME COURT AND THE HOUSE OF LORDS

21-16 Where an application for costs of an unassisted party out of the Fund is made in respect of proceedings in the Supreme Court (except proceedings on appeal from a county court) or in the House of Lords, the court must not make an order forthwith but may, in its discretion:

    (a) refer the application to a master or a registrar or district judge for hearing and determinations; or

    (b) adjourn the hearing of the application; or

    (c) dismiss the application.

In relation to proceedings in the Court of Appeal "registrar", means the registrar of civil appeals and in respect of appeals from the Employment Appeal Tribunal or from the Restrictive Practices Court, the registrar of that tribunal or court as the case may be.[49]

In proceedings under the Child Abduction and Custody Act 1985, where the defendant was successful throughout and had been legally aided for only part of the proceedings, the House of Lords ordered pursuant to section 18 of the 1988 Act that the defendant's costs prior to the issue of the legal aid certificate be paid out of the Fund. The order was suspended pursuant to regulations 143 and 147 of the Civil Legal Aid (General) Regulations 1989 to give the Board the opportunity to object. The House held that section 18(1) and (2) of the 1988 Act authorised an order in such terms and that the House had jurisdiction to make it. The prohibition in regulation 143[50] of the Civil Legal Aid (General) Regulations 1989 applied only to an order which was to take immediate effect and not to a suspended order.

Procedure on referral to a registrar or district judge for hearing and determination

21-17 Where the application is referred to a registrar or district judge, the unassisted party must, within 21 days, file an affidavit of costs and resources (with any exhibits and supporting documents) together with a copy; and not less than 21 days before the hearing date, the court must serve on the

---

[48] *Middleton v. Middleton* [1994] 3 All E.R. 236, C.A.
[49] *ibid.* reg. 143(1).
[50] *Re H (Minors) (Abduction Custody Rights) (No. 2)* [1992] W.L.R. 198, H.L.

Area Director notice of the date fixed together with a copy of the affidavit of costs and resources so filed.[51]

Procedure where application referred to a master for hearing and determination

Where the court refers an application to a master for hearing and **21–18** determination, the unassisted party must, within 21 days, file an affidavit of costs and resources together with original exhibits and any other documents necessary to support the affidavit and not less than 21 days before the adjourned hearing, the unassisted party must serve notice on the Area Director of the date and time of the adjourned hearing, together with a copy of the affidavit of costs and resources (and of any exhibits and supporting documents).[52]

The master is given the same powers as the taxing officer in the exercise of his functions under R.S.C., Ord. 62. The unassisted party or the Area Director may appeal to a judge in chambers on a point of law within 14 days from the determination of the master.[53]

Reference to master for inquiry and report

Where the court adjourns an application it may make an order referring it **21–19** to the master for inquiry and report. If such an order is made, then within the 21 days allowed, the unassisted party must:

(a) file an affidavit of costs and resources;

(b) lodge a copy of the order of the court and of his affidavit of costs and resources together with the original exhibits and any other documents necessary to support the affidavit with the master; and at the same time,

(c) serve a copy of the order of the court and of his affidavit of costs and resources (and of any exhibits and supporting documents) on the Area Director.[54]

Once the unassisted party has complied with the requirements as to the affidavit of costs and resources, the master must give the unassisted party and the Area Director not less than 21 days' notice of the date and time when he proposes to conduct his inquiry. The master is given the same powers as a taxing officer in the exercise of his functions under R.S.C., Ord. 62. On the completion of the inquiry, the master must report to the court in writing and must, at the same time, send a copy of the report to the

---

[51] Civil Legal Aid (General) Regulations 1989, regs. 139, 142, 143(2).
[52] *ibid.* regs. 144(a), 147.
[53] *ibid.* reg. 144(b), (c).
[54] *ibid.* reg. 145.

unassisted party and to the Area Director. When the court has received the report of the master, it is for the unassisted party to seek appointment for the hearing and determination of the application in chambers and to give the Area Director not less than 21 days' notice of the date and time so fixed.[55]

Procedure where application is adjourned

21–20 If the court adjourns the application without referring it for inquiry and report, the assisted party must within 21 days of the adjournment file an affidavit of costs and resources together with original exhibits and any other documents necessary to support the affidavit; and not less than 21 days before the adjourned hearing serve notice on the Area Director of the date and time of the adjourned hearing together with a copy of his affidavit of costs and resources (and of any exhibits and supporting documents).[56]

WHERE A PARTY IS LEGALLY AIDED FOR PART ONLY OF THE PROCEEDINGS

21–21 Where a party begins to receive representation after the proceedings have been instituted, or ceases to receive representation before they are finally decided or otherwise receives representation for part only of the proceedings, the court must, if it decides to make an order, make an apportionment covering the costs incurred by the unassisted party in the proceedings which are attributable to the part during which the other party was legally aided.[57]

APPEALS AGAINST ORDERS

21–22 Without prejudice to any other provision restricting appeals from any court, no appeal lies against an order in respect of the costs of successful unassisted parties or against a refusal to make such an order, except on a point of law.[58]

---

[55] *ibid.* reg. 146(1)–(4).
[56] *ibid.* reg. 147.
[57] Legal Aid Act 1988, s. 18(6).
[58] *ibid.* s. 18(5).

Chapter 22

CARE PROCEEDINGS AND PROCEEDINGS UNDER THE CHILDREN ACT 1989[1]

AVAILABILITY OF CIVIL LEGAL AID

On the implementation of the Children Act in 1989, legal aid for care **22–01** proceedings was moved across from what was effectively criminal legal aid dealt with by the magistrates' courts to civil legal aid administered by the Board. Although the 1989 Regulations dealing with criminal legal aid retain the word "care" in their titles they no longer have any relevance to care proceedings. Also, with effect from October 1989, the concept of summary jurisdiction civil legal aid (with its own application form and no possibility of an emergency certificate but rather a certificate granted on the basis of an undertaking) was abolished.

Civil legal aid is available for any proceedings under the Children Act **22–02** 1989. For the magistrates' courts, Children Act proceedings have been specifically added to the list of proceedings for which civil legal aid is available.[2] This means that a single civil legal aid certificate can cover proceedings under the Children Act in any court because for the higher courts civil legal aid is available on the basis of the forum itself.[3] No fresh certificate is therefore required if a matter is transferred out of the family proceedings court.

Note, however, that civil legal aid is specifically unavailable to local authorities, any other body which falls within a prescribed description (that is acting in a representative, fiduciary or official capacity, *e.g.* the NSPCC) and to guardians *ad litem* for the purposes of proceedings under the

---

[1] Sources: Legal Aid Act 1988, s. 15 and Pt. 1, Sched. 2; Civil Legal Aid (General) Regulations 1989, reg. 12A and Pt. XII; Legal Aid in Family Proceedings (Remuneration) Regulations 1991 and *Legal Aid Handbook 1995*, Notes for Guidance, paras. 7–01 to 7–24. See Chapter 4 and para. 22–26 regarding the availability of ABWOR.
[2] Legal Aid Act 1988, Para. 2(g) Pt. 1, Sched. 2 and Civil Legal Aid (General) (Amendment) (No. 2) Regulations 1991.
[3] Legal Aid Act 1988, Pt. 1, Sched. 2, para. 1.

Children Act 1989. A guardian *ad litem* who needs separate legal representation must look to the appropriate GALRO Panel — this cannot be funded by a legal aid certificate held by the guardian *ad litem* or the relevant child.

SPECIAL ARRANGEMENTS

22–03 Special provisions make civil legal aid available to certain parties in specified public law proceedings on a non-means, non-merits tested ("free") or means tested only basis. The relevant provisions are contained in section 15 of the 1988 Act. They make non-means, non-merits tested legal aid available to:
  (a) parents (including unmarried fathers);
  (b) children;
  (c) those with parental responsibility;
in proceedings relating to an application for:
  (a) a care or supervision order under section 31;
  (b) a child assessment order under section 43;
  (c) an emergency protection order under section 44; or
  (d) the extension or discharge of an emergency protection order under section 45.

22–04 For the same proceedings:
  (a) parties to the proceedings (that is those required to be parties by the Family Proceedings Court (Children Act 1989) Rules 1991 and the Family Proceedings Rules 1991); and
  (b) those applying to be joined;
have to satisfy only the means test but no merits test.[4] The position is untested where an assisted person ceases to qualify as their status changes *i.e.*, they no longer have parental responsibility (*e.g.* on an interim care order being made), although the proceedings are continuing. It is however, unlikely that the Board would, in normal circumstances, withdraw the certificate and require a fresh application to be made on the means tested basis.

22–05 In addition, non-means, non-merits tested civil legal aid must be granted to the child (only) where he or she is brought before a court under section 25 of the Children Act 1989 (use of secure accommodation) and is not but wishes to be legally represented.[5] This will not be necessary where the child is already represented in criminal proceedings to which the section

---

[4] Legal Aid Act 1988 and Civil Legal (General) Regulations 1989, reg 3A, Legal Aid Act 1988, s. 15(3C), (3E).
[5] Legal Aid Act 1988, s. 15(3B).

25 application relates; the criminal legal aid order will cover the section 25 proceedings.[6]

These special arrangements do not extend to other Children Act **22–06** proceedings. This means that education supervision order applications, applications to discharge care orders and other public law proceedings between individuals and the state, as well as private law proceedings between individuals are outside the special arrangements. Means and merits tested civil legal aid is available in the usual way. In those circumstances an emergency certificate could be applied for.

ADDITIONAL COVER AND AMENDMENTS

Where non-means, non-merits tested civil legal aid has been granted **22–07** representation must also be granted to cover an appeal against a care or supervision order made under section 31, regardless of means, but this cover is subject to the usual civil legal aid merits test.[7] The area office is unlikely to grant cover for an appeal against an interim order, given the limited benefit to be obtained.

Note that an existing certificate can only be amended to cover an appeal from a family proceedings court in the case of special Children Act proceedings, that is proceedings for which non-means, non-merits tested civil legal aid is available.[8] The Board will not amend a means tested only certificate to cover an appeal from the family proceedings court.

Legal aid certificates issued on a non-means, non-merits tested or means **22–08** tested only basis can also cover proceedings *relating to* an application for an order under sections 31, 43, 44 or 45 from the issue of the certificate or following a subsequent amendment (that is on application by the solicitor).[9] The concept of "relating to" an application for one of the specified orders is not defined and whether any particular case falls within the special provisions will be decided by the Board.

The Board in its Notes for Guidance has indicated that a related matter is one where an order is to be sought at the same time as, and as an alternative to, the order under sections 31, 43, 44 or 45. Applying for a section 8 order in care or supervision proceedings will be sufficiently closely related to the care or supervision proceedings for cover to be available under a non-means, non-merits tested or means tested only certificate.[10] Note, however, that specific cover (either in the certificate or

---

[6] *ibid* s. 19(2).
[7] *ibid* s. 15(3D).
[8] Civil Legal Aid (General) Regulations 1989, reg. 46(2).
[9] Legal Aid Act 1988, s. 15(3C).
[10] *Legal Aid Handbook 1995* Note for Guidance 7–04.

an amendment) would be needed to make (but not to oppose) such an application.

Ancillary matters between individuals (including applications for periodical payments in respect of the child who is the subject of care or supervision proceedings) and applications for injunctions under the Domestic Violence and Matrimonial Proceedings Act 1976 would require a separate means and merits tested application.

22–09   If the related proceedings are not considered by the Board to be sufficiently closely related to the proceedings which triggered the special provisions, then this will constitute the partial refusal of the legal aid application in question or of a request for an amendment. In either case this gives rise to a right of appeal to the area committee and the solicitor will have to decide whether to advise the client to exercise that right or to submit a fresh means and merits tested application. A certificate should be issued immediately for the section 31, 43 or 45 proceedings.

22–10   If proceedings covered by a non-means, non-merits tested or means tested only certificate are followed by subsequent private law proceedings, then the earlier certificate will not be amended (even if it has not been discharged) and a separate means and merits tested application will be required. Although a certificate may relate to more than one action, cause or matter in the case of family proceedings[11] the Board will not issue an amendment because both the means and merits tests will be applied to the fresh proceedings. The aim of the Board is to keep the different legal aid regimes (free, means tested only, and means and merits tested) separate. This also avoids potential difficulties as to the appropriate rate of payment and in relation to the possible operation of the statutory charge. A table on page 456 lists the circumstances in which the Board will/will not amend an existing certificate. The practitioner should remember that the overall aim of the Board is not to mix the different legal aid regimes in one certificate with the exception that a free certificate can be amended to cover an appeal which will be merits tested.

22–11   Where a solicitor wishes to seek additional cover within a non-means, non-merits tested or means tested only certificate, he should take care to make this entirely clear in his application form, giving sufficient detail to enable the area office to make a decision. He must also remember that he cannot rely on cover necessarily being granted for the "related proceedings". This will mean that in order to be sure of receiving payment under the certificate he will need to await confirmation of the position from the Board before undertaking work in that regard. The deeming provision which applies to non-means, non-merits tested certificates can extend to the related proceedings but the solicitor cannot be sure of the position until he has heard from the Board.

---

[11] Civil Legal Aid (General) Regulations 1989, reg. 46(3)(a).

Where proceedings under one of the specified sections are followed by **22–12** proceedings under another (*e.g.* emergency protection order proceedings are followed by an application for a care order) the Board is of the view that an amendment to an existing non-means, non-merits tested or means tested only certificate should be sought (if necessary over the telephone).[12] It could be argued that a fresh certificate should be obtained (thus avoiding the need for an urgent amendment) but, in means tested cases, this could involve the client in a further means assessment.

FORUM

The proceedings which attract non-means, non-merits tested or means **22–13** tested only legal aid are governed by the Children (Allocation of Proceedings) Order 1991. Civil legal aid certificates will not, therefore, specify the court covered. They permit representation in all the courts in accordance with the Order, including representation on an application for transfer to a county court following the refusal of the family proceedings court to order a transfer. This contrasts with the position in relation to proceedings which are not covered by the Order where the certificate will often include a condition as to jurisdiction: see below, para. 22–24.

EXTENT OF COVER

A non-means, non-merits tested or means tested only certificate will cover **22–14** the normal steps involved in the conduct of the proceedings. The Board has indicated that, in its view, this extends to representation as to:
- (a) an interim order;
- (b) applying for directions and their variation;
- (c) contact and the refusal of contact on the making of an emergency protection or care order;
- (d) an application for a search warrant under section 48 in emergency protection order cases;
- (e) the extension or discharge of an emergency protection order in emergency protection order cases.[13]

The Board also accepts that a certificate covers proceedings which are concluded with a different type of order (*e.g.* where care proceedings are concluded with a section 8 residence order applied for by another party or

---

[12] *Legal Aid Handbook 1995*, Note for Guidance 7–05.
[13] *ibid.*

made on the court's own motion) but it considers that specifically stated cover in the certificate or an amendment is needed;

    (a) to make (but not to oppose) an application for a section 8 order in care or supervision proceedings; or

    (b) to appeal against the making of a care or supervision order.[14]

FORMS

22–15 Currently application forms CLA5, CLA5A or CLA2 may be used for Children Act proceedings. Each form contains information as to its use. These forms are to be amended and re-numbered on the implementation of the Board's new Corporate Information System scheduled for late 1996.

Form CLA5A is a self-certification form which is used for non-means, non-merits tested cases only. It will be submitted alone without supporting documents or means forms. It is a very simple form but the experience of the Board's area offices is that it is not necessarily correctly completed. Particular care should be taken when completing this form because if it is incorrectly completed then the deeming provision may not apply[15].

Form CLA5 is to be used for free-standing Children Act proceedings (including those which are means tested only), as well as for wardship and adoption proceedings. Free-standing Children Act proceedings are those which are not in the context of matrimonial or other specific family proceedings.

Form CLA2, the matrimonial application form, is to be used where a Children Act order is sought in proceedings other than under the Children Act (*e.g.* in matrimonial proceedings or in proceedings under the Domestic Violence and Matrimonial Proceedings Act 1976). The appropriate means form must be submitted with Forms CLA2 and CLA5 and the emergency application form, CLA3, may also need to submitted with Forms CLA2 and CLA5.

22–16 Only one application form needs to be submitted for an individual client applicant where a number of children are involved. If the solicitor is applying for legal aid for a number of children an application must be submitted on behalf of each child. This is because the child is the assisted person and each child will hold a separate certificate.

The Board has indicated that form filling for multiple applications can be reduced by the information which is common to all the solicitors' clients being inserted in a single Form CLA5 which should be marked "ORIGINAL APPLICATION" in the top right-hand corner of the first page. The form

---

[14] *ibid.*
[15] See below, para. 22–18.

should then be photocopied the required number of times (without being signed) and the information particular to each child should then be inserted in a separate copy of the form. Each form should then be signed and the applications forwarded together to the area office. The photocopied applications must be firmly attached *behind* the original. Only one set of supporting enclosures is needed.

A solicitor can sign and make a civil legal aid application for a child/ **22–17** minor client but only where the child/minor is entitled to begin, prosecute or defend proceedings without a next friend or guardian *ad litem (i.e.* in accordance with the Family Proceedings Rules 1991, r. 9.2A). The nominated solicitor must sign the application personally. He will be treated as the child/minor's agent, including for the receipt of notices.[16] The solicitor should remember that documents will automatically be sent by the area office to the applicant's address (*i.e.* the child's address) as inserted in the application form. The solicitor should, therefore, insert his own address as the correspondence address for the application. He can then ensure that information is passed to the child applicant as appropriate.

A special means form, Form CLA4F, has been introduced for child applicants under 16 who have no significant assets. The solicitor must sign the form where he is applying for legal aid for a child who is entitled to begin, prosecute or defend proceedings without a next friend or guardian *ad litem.*[17] Note that there is no longer any requirement for an offer of legal aid to be made before a certificate is issued to a minor, although where a certificate is issued to a minor it is required to be in his name, stating the name of the person who applied for it on his behalf.[18]

DEEMING PROVISION

In non-means, non-merits tested cases costs will usually be covered **22–18** immediately as there is a deeming provision.[19] For the deeming provision to operate, a correctly certified Form CLA5A must be received by the appropriate area office within *three working days* of the solicitor receiving instructions to act. Where the deeming provision applies costs from the time of receipt of instructions to act will be deemed to be within the certificate. The solicitor will not need to telephone the area office. He will have immediate legal aid cover from instruction. Although previou Green Form costs (*i.e.* incurred for advice before the commencement of proceedings) can be claimed (under the Green Form itself), a solicitor

---

[16] Civil Legal Aid (General) Regulations 1989, reg. 16(1) and (4).
[17] *ibid.* reg. 16(1)(c).
[18] *ibid.* reg. 16(3).
[19] *ibid.* reg. 12A(3).

receiving immediate instructions to act in a non-means, non-merits tested ("free") legal aid case where proceedings have been commenced will not need to use the Green Form.

Difficulties have been experienced where solicitors have completed the self-certification form incorrectly or in cases to which the special provisions for free legal aid do not apply. This will either mean that there is a delay in issuing the free certificate (and the deeming provision will not apply) or, where the case is not a free legal aid case, a fresh application (and emergency application) would need to be submitted. There would then be no retrospective legal aid cover. Area offices will notify solicitors where Form CLA5A has been used incorrectly but the solicitor should not rely on the area office giving this priority in its workload and care should be taken in completing the form.

22–19   Where the deeming provision does apply, this will be shown on the face of the certificate issued. If the matter proceeds to taxation, rather than assessment by the area office, the appearance of the deeming provision in the certificate itself will confirm to the taxing officer that it applies.

For the deeming provision to operate, the requirement is that the form must be lodged with the area office at the first available opportunity and "in any event within three working days of receiving instructions to act".[20] The self-certification Form CLA5A asks for the date of instruction. The solicitor should take care to ensure that the correct date of instruction is inserted — time will run immediately from that date.[21] Any day when the appropriate area office is open for business is a working day and if the self-certificate form is received out of time costs will only be covered from the date of issue of the certificate.

The Board has accepted that time can be extended[22] but this will only be done where the area office thinks fit, *i.e.* for good reason. Oversight by the solicitor will not suffice. Self-certification application forms will be date-stamped upon receipt in the area office, but the solicitor should keep a copy on his file with a note of the date and method of dispatch to the area office.

If the deeming provision is to apply, the self-certification form must be received as follows:

Instructions to act received on:		Form CLA5A must be reveived at the area office on:
Monday	—	Thursday
Tuesday	—	Friday
Wednesday	—	Monday

---

[20] *ibid.* reg. 12A(1).
[21] *ibid.* reg. 7(1).
[22] *ibid.* reg. 7(2).

Instructions to act received on:		Form CLA5A must be reveived at the area office on:
Thursday	—	Tuesday
Friday	—	Wednesday
Saturday	—	Wednesday
Sunday	—	Wednesday

In cases outside the special non-means, non-merits tested provisions the **22–20** deeming provision contained in regulation 103(6) of the Civil Legal Aid (General) Regulations 1989 applies. This is only applicable where the area office is closed and the solicitor makes a telephone emergency application at the first available opportunity. He must then submit the written application to the area office within the time stipulated by the area office. If these conditions are satisfied, then work done immediately prior to the issue of the emergency certificate is deemed to be done while it is in force.

Outside the special non-means, non-merits tested provisions (where the **22–21** solicitor will have no need to telephone the area office), means tested only applications should be accepted by the Board's area offices as urgent enough to be dealt with over the telephone. The written application including an emergency application will need to submitted following the telephone call.

In means and merits tested cases involving children the solicitor should consider whether to submit an emergency application.

Discharge of Certificates

Where a certificate is not merits tested (*i.e.* is free or means tested only) the **22–22** Board has accepted that it can only effectively seek to apply the merits test to an amendment to cover an appeal or for a change of solicitor. In the latter case, the circumstances may be such that the show cause procedure is triggered on the basis that the assisted person is requiring the proceedings to be conducted unreasonably so as to incur an unjustifiable expense to the Fund.[23]

The Board has indicated that it does not envisage discharging a non-merits tested certificate on the basis of lack of reasonable grounds or that it is unreasonable for legal aid to continue in the particular circumstances. This may mean that the solicitor finds himself in the situation of representing a client who will not accept reasonable advice. The professional conduct aspects of this are not directly a matter for the

---

[23] *ibid.* reg. 77(1)(b).

Board, but it is conceivable that, if the solicitor withdrew, a change of solicitor amendment could be refused and the show cause procedure triggered.

A means tested only certificate could be discharged (or, if applicable, revoked) on any of the grounds relating to the means test, arrears of contribution, abuse of legal aid or failure to provide information.[24]

A means tested only or free certificate could also be discharged with consent, on the assisted person's death, on the making of a bankruptcy order against the assisted person, on the disposal of the proceedings or on the completion of the work authorised.

MEANS AND MERITS TESTED APPLICATIONS AND FORUM

22–23   If an application for Children Act proceedings is merits tested, then the usual legal merits and reasonableness tests will be applied. The Board has, however, indicated that relevant factors will include the likelihood of an order being made at all, having regard to the non-intervention principle, the likelihood of success in the light of the checklist at section 1(3) of the Children Act, the benefit to be obtained and the need for representation having regard to all the circumstances of the case (including the contested issues between the parties).[25]

22–24   Where cover is sought in respect of proceedings which are not required to be commenced in accordance with the Children (Allocation of Proceedings) Order 1991 the area office will expect the solicitor to commence proceedings in the family proceedings court where it has jurisdiction, unless there is a particular reason not to do so.

If the application does not indicate why the proceedings should be commenced in a higher court, then any certificate issued will bear a condition to the effect that the proceedings must be *commenced* in the family proceedings court. If that is the case, they may be transferred in accordance with the Children (Allocation of Proceedings) Order 1991 (either horizontally or vertically) without any amendment being required to the certificate. Applying for a transfer is considered to be within the scope of the certificate without the need for an amendment.

Certificates may also be issued with a condition that the proceedings be commenced in the county court. Such a condition permits transfer in accordance with the Children (Allocation of Proceedings) Order 1991 without a specific amendment being required.

Alternatively, the certificate may be issued with no condition at all and it is then a matter for the solicitor to commence proceedings in whichever

---

[24] *ibid.* reg. 76, 78, 79 and 80(b).
[25] *Legal Aid Handbook 1995*, Note for Guidance 7–21.

court he considers appropriate, subject to justification on assessment/ taxation.

The insertion of a condition may be appealed to the area committee, **22-25** although where a means assessment is available a certificate or offer will be issued immediately. This will mean that the solicitor can seek a transfer from the court or can pursue an appeal to the area committee. If the question of jurisdiction was not addressed in the original application or if further information is available which makes it likely that the solicitor's view as to jurisdiction will be accepted, then the solicitor should write in to the area office giving notice of appeal and providing the fresh information. This will trigger a review of the case and the matter need not necessarily proceed to a hearing before the area committee.

The Board has given a non-exhaustive list of examples of cases where it would be appropriate to commence proceedings other than in the family proceedings court[26] but solicitors will also need to be aware of any relevant case law indicating, e.g. that cases of a particular type should be dealt with in the High Court.

AVAILABILITY OF ABWOR

The Board accepts that, because of the provisions of the Interpretation Act **22-26** 1978, ABWOR is available to cover those proceedings under the Children Act for which ABWOR was previously available for proceedings under repealed statutes (e.g. the Guardianship of Minors Acts 1971 and 1973).

In cases of any doubt or where the proceedings are to be commenced in (or are likely to be transferred to) a court other than the family proceedings court, then civil legal aid should be applied for. ABWOR cannot cover proceedings other than in the family proceedings court and cannot be amended to cover an appeal.

Both ABWOR and civil legal aid will also be available where a Children Act order is to be sought in other family proceedings for which both ABWOR and civil legal aid are available, e.g. proceedings under the Domestic Proceedings and Magistrates' Courts Act 1978.

Where both civil legal aid and ABWOR are available the Board's area offices will not seek to refuse applications for ABWOR on the basis that civil legal aid should be applied for. Although there is a specific power to refuse civil legal aid if it appears to the Board more appropriate that ABWOR should be given,[27] there is no corresponding provision for the refusal of ABWOR.

---

[26] *ibid.* Note for Guidance 7-22.
[27] Legal Aid Act 1988, s. 15(3)(b).

AUTHORITIES

22–27 There are no special provisions relating to authorities for Children Act cases. The usual civil legal aid or ABWOR position applies so that the authority of the area office is required to instruct counsel in the family proceedings court.[28] Under an ABWOR approval authority is also mandatory to obtain an expert report/opinion or to tender expert evidence or to perform an act which is either unusual in its nature or involves unusually large expenditure.

The solicitor should also, when acting under a civil legal aid certificate, consider whether he wishes to obtain prior authority for an expert report. This is not mandatory (compare the position under an ABWOR approval) but if authority is to be sought and leave of the court is required for the child to be examined or assessed, then authority will not be given until that leave has been obtained. In short, the need to obtain the leave of the court will constitute an approval of the disbursement in principle and the solicitor will probably only wish to seek the Board's authority where the amount involved is such that he wishes to have the protection of the prior authority on assessment/taxation.

22–28 Although form CLA31, the mandatory application for civil legal aid prior authorities, currently asks whether alternative quotes have been obtained, an application for authority will not necessarily be refused in the absence of alternative quotes. However, if the solicitor is seeking to instruct a particularly expensive, or distant, expert then the reasons for this should be made clear in the application. It should also be remembered that for civil legal aid the maximum amount of the authority must be specified.[29] Although not a requirement, a maximum amount will also usually be specified in ABWOR authorities. For that purpose the Board's area office will need to know the amount sought (excluding VAT and travelling expenses) and the hourly rates upon which that amount is based.

STATUTORY CHARGE

22–29 The statutory charge applies in Children Act cases but Schedule 1 to the Children Act 1989 has been inserted:
    (a) in paragraph (vii) of regulation 94 of the Civil Legal Aid (General) Regulations 1989 so that the £2,500 exemption applies (this also

---

[28] Civil Legal Aid (General) Regulations 1989, reg. 59(1)(a); Legal Advice and Assistance Regulations 1989, reg. 22(7)(a).
[29] Civil Legal Aid (General) Regulations 1989, reg. 61(3).

applies to the solicitor's Green Form charge due to the provisions of the Interpretation Act 1978); and

(b) in regulation 96(1)(d) of the Civil Legal Aid (General) Regulations 1989 so that the enforcement of the charge may be postponed where the conditions in regulation 96 or 97 are satisfied.[30]

It is the view of the Board that only one £2,500 exemption is available in respect of any one order even if there is more than one beneficiary from the order.

Although a certificate may now cover more than one action, cause or matter in the case of family proceedings[31] this does not mean that a single certificate will always be issued.[32] The Board will try as far as possible to keep the different regimes of legal aid separate so that the difficulties of applying the different regimes to a single certificate are, so far as possible, avoided. The statutory charge can apply to public law cases in the usual way in that there is no specific exclusion or exemption from its operation. The operation of the statutory charge should not, however, arise in a public law case as the financial aspects between the parties are unlikely to be dealt with in the same proceedings or under the same certificate as the public law aspects. In particular, the Board does not consider that the financial aspects between the parties are related to the public law sections which trigger free or only means tested legal aid. This means that separate certificates will be issued for those separate proceedings and the operation of the statutory charge will not arise. **22–30**

REMUNERATION

Children Act cases dealt with under a civil legal aid certificate are remunerated in accordance with the Legal Aid in Family Proceedings (Remuneration) Regulations 1991, Part XII of the Civil Legal Aid (General) Regulations 1989 and the Family Proceedings (Costs) Rules 1991 (which to a great extent incorporate the Matrimonial Causes (Costs) Rules 1988). These are a part of the civil legal aid, rather than the criminal legal aid, regime and the usual civil legal aid provisions including those regarding payments on account, deferment, disallowance and reduction of costs, reviews and appeals, disclosure of the bill to an assisted person with a financial interest and objections, reviews and appeals against taxation apply.[33] **22–31**

There are two Schedules in the Legal Aid in Family Proceedings

---

[30] See Chapter 18.
[31] Civil Legal Aid (General) Regulations 1989, reg. 46(3)(a).
[32] See para. 22–10.
[33] See Chapters 19 and 20.

(Remuneration) Regulations 1991, the first cover care proceedings which are defined as "proceedings for an order under Parts IV or V of the Children Act 1989" and the second applies to "prescribed family proceedings" which covers proceedings under the Children Act 1989, excluding care proceedings, as well as proceedings to which rules made under section 50 of the Matrimonial Causes Act 1973 applied or would have applied (had they remained in force after October 14, 1991).[34] Family proceedings which are not within the definitions of care proceedings or prescribed family proceedings are (with only limited exceptions) remunerated in accordance with the Legal Aid in Civil Proceedings (Remuneration) Regulations 1994 (*i.e.* at prescribed hourly rates) or, for certificates issued before February 25, 1994, in accordance with R.S.C., Ord. 62 or C.C.R., Ord. 38. The most common examples are proceedings under Domestic Violence Act 1976 and adoption proceedings.

22–32   Where a certificate covers proceedings to which different rates would otherwise be applicable the aim of the Regulations is to ensure that only one rate is applied. Within a single certificate (including one covering different types of proceedings) it may be necessary to apportion the costs in accordance with the level of court in which the proceedings took place and in accordance with the rate applicable at the time the work was done, but it should not be necessary to apportion the work done to different rates applicable to the type of work.

The Legal Aid in Family Proceedings (Remuneration) Regulations 1991[35] provide that where a certificate covering family proceedings which are not care proceedings or prescribed family proceedings is extended to cover care proceedings or prescribed family proceedings, then the costs must be determined in accordance with Schedule 1 (care proceedings) or 2 (prescribed family proceedings) as the case may be. If a certificate is extended to cover both care proceedings and prescribed family proceedings, then the prescribed family proceedings rates in Schedule 2 prevail.

The current provisions do not necessarily reflect the reality of the position (which is that certificates may be be issued which from the start cover mixed proceedings, *i.e.* care proceedings and prescribed family proceedings). The provisions are under review and the Board's Costs Appeals Committee has made no relevant decisions. In the circumstances practitioners can seek to justify apportioning the costs between the Schedule 1 and Schedule 2 rates, although claiming all the costs on the basis of the higher Schedule (*i.e.* Schedule 1 for proceedings in the family proceedings court and Schedule 2(a) for proceedings in the High Court or county court) is not specifically excluded.

---

[34] Legal Aid in Family Proceedings (Remuneration) Regulations 1991, reg. 2(1).
[35] *ibid.* reg. 3(3).

Practitioners should note that there is no care and conduct element included in Schedule 1 which covers care proceedings, although there is a care and conduct element for prescribed family proceedings in the High Court and county court in accordance with Schedule 2(a) of the Legal Aid in Family Proceedings (Remuneration) Regulations 1991 (but not for Schedule 2(b) family proceedings court matters). Both Schedules have a higher preparation rate but for prescribed family proceedings in the High Court and county court this is triggered by the proceedings being conducted in the divorce registry or in another court on the South Eastern Circuit (as opposed to by the fee earner's office being situated within the No. 1 legal aid area).[36]

Enhanced (or reduced) rates are payable for preparation, conferences **22–33** with counsel, attendances and taxation/review of taxation in respect of care proceedings and prescribed family proceedings in the High Court and county court. No enhanced (or reduced) rates are payable in respect of prescribed family proceedings in the family proceedings court (where the rates are the same as in criminal proceedings).

Reduced rates may be allowed where it is considered "reasonable to do so having regard to any failure on the part of the solicitor to provide timely preparation or advice, or for any similar reasons".[37] Enhanced rates may be allowed where it appears reasonable to do so having regard to:

(a) the exceptional competence with which the work was done; or
(b) the exceptional expedition with which the work was done; or
(c) any other exceptional circumstances of the case including in the case of care proceedings, membership of the Law Society's "Children Act" panel.[38]

Membership of the Law Society's specialisation panel which is in fact called the Children Panel but which is accepted to be the panel referred to in the Legal Aid in Family Proceedings (Remuneration) Regulations 1991 has been a source of difficulty. The Board has taken the view that panel membership alone is not an exceptional enough circumstance to trigger the payment of an enhanced rate although it may be a factor contributing to the decision to pay an enhanced rate. The Board's Costs Appeals Committee's decision reference CLA8 which will be applied by all the Board's area offices and area committees states:

"Membership of the Law Society's Children Panel is not in itself an exceptional circumstances justifying payment of an enhanced rate under Regulation 3(4)(c)(iii) Legal Aid in Family Proceedings (Remuneration) Regulations 1991, but membership of the panel may be a factor which contributes to a decision that enhanced rates are

---

[36] *ibid.*
[37] *ibid.*
[38] *ibid.*

justified under Regulation 3(4)(c)(iii) Legal Aid in Family Proceedings (Remuneration) Regulations 1991."

22–34 The Costs Appeals Committee's decision CLA9 gives some guidance as to when the "exceptional circumstances" requirement may be satisfied and makes it clear that the requirement refers to the circumstances of the case rather than the manner in which the work was done. Decision CLA9 reads:

Care proceedings: Enhanced rates: Possible "exceptional circumstances"

When considering a claim for enhanced rates on the basis of regulation 3(4)(c)(iii) Legal Aid in Family Proceedings (Remuneration) Regulations 1991 consideration should, when deciding if there are "any other exceptional circumstances" of the case, be given to whether any of the following existed:

(i) the case fulfilled the complexity criteria requiring the transfer of the case to a Care Centre;

(ii) innate difficulties of communication with the client (*e.g.* mental health problems, deaf, speech impaired or autistic clients);

(iii) a *conflict* of expert evidence as opposed to merely contested expert evidence and/or a proliferation of expert witnesses;

(iv) serious *contested* allegations of abuse;

(v) long hearings (*i.e.* in excess of two days) undertaken by solicitors in person without reliance on counsel;

(vi) the involvement of a number of children with different needs.

The factors set out above are a non-exhaustive list. They relate to the circumstances of the case itself and not to claims for enhanced rates based on regulation 3(4)(c)(i) and (ii) Legal Aid in Family Proceedings (Remuneration) Regulations 1991 which have regard to the manner in which the work was done.

The presence of one or more of the above factors *may* justify payment of an enhanced rate. (Legal Aid Board reference CLA9.)

22–35 Furthermore, the Costs Appeals Committee has considered the calculation of enhanced rates in its decision CLA9 which makes it clear that claims will be assessed on the basis of broad average direct cost and a percentage uplift. Decision CLA11 reads:

Enhanced rates in family proceedings

Where the criteria for paying enhanced rates set out in regulation 3(4)(c) Legal Aid in Family Proceedings (Remuneration) Regulations 1991 are met, the relevant authority may exercise their discretion in determining the amount of costs to be allowed in accordance with regulation 3(7) Legal Aid in Family Proceedings (Remuneration) Regulations 1991.

Following the decision of *Freeman* v. *Freeman*, January 21, 1992 (reported in Butterworths Costs Service) such claims will be assessed on the basis of the broad average direct cost of the work (the "*A*" figure) to which is added a percentage uplift (the "*B*" figure) to take into account all the relevant circumstances of the case. (Legal Aid Board reference CLA11.)

All civil legal aid costs in respect of authorised summary proceedings including proceedings under the Children Act are required to be assessed by the Board's area offices.[39] The courts have no jurisdication even if the case is transferred up from a family proceedings court. This means that *all* family proceedings (magistrates') court costs must be assessed (rather than taxed), regardless of the amount claimed and any transfer of the proceedings. The Board accepts that claims for assessment may be submitted before the proceedings are finally concluded, that is to say the family proceedings (magistrates') court element may be claimed from the area office without awaiting the final outcome of the case. **22–36**

In a single particular case there may therefore be an assessed element for costs incurred in the family proceedings court followed by a further taxed or assessed element, depending on the amount of costs involved.[40] This may then possibly be followed by another assessed element in the event of the transfer of the proceedings back to the family proceedings court. The Lord Chancellor's Department has no plans to alter the position and it is likely that the Board's area offices will continue to have sole jurisdiction in respect of costs in the family proceedings/magistrates' court. Note that those costs are not taken into account by the Board's area offices in deciding whether or not the higher court costs fall within the £500/£1,000 assessment limit.

The Board is reviewing its claim forms and will be introducing a new form for care proceedings. In the meantime, existing Forms CLA16 and 17 must be used. These forms are unsuitable and practitioners will need to remember that no care and conduct element can be claimed in respect of care proceedings assessed in accordance with Schedule 1. Where the solicitor claims both the family proceedings court element and the higher court taxed/assessed element at the same time then he must submit a separate Form CLA16 for *each* element and a single Form CLA17, showing the date of transfer of the proceedings, for any assessed element. This may mean that, where the solicitor has delayed claiming the family proceedings court element, then on the conclusion of the case he may need to submit

---

[39] Civil Legal Aid (General) Regulations 1989, reg. 104(1).
[40] *ibid.* reg. 105(2A), (3).

two Forms CLA16 (one for the assessed element and one for the taxed element) and one Form CLA17 (for the assessed element only).

22-37 Where the assisted person has a financial interest, then he has a right to make written representations to the area office, area committee or Costs Appeals Committee of the Board.[41] The solicitor and counsel have the same rights of appeal on a family proceedings assessment as on any other assessment case.[42]

22-38 On considering a claim for assessment, the Board's area office will in particular check for:

    (a) the inclusion in the certificate of cover under the Civil Legal Aid (General) Regulations 1989, reg. 12A(3) deeming provision;

    (b) the date of instruction where the deeming provision applies — as costs before instruction cannot be claimed under the certificate (although they may be claimable under a Green Form);

    (c) commencement of the proceedings in accordance with any condition included in the certificate;

    (d) any necessary amendment to apply for a section 8 order in care or supervision proceedings or to appeal against the making of a care or supervision order; and

    (e) the payment of any court fees which should not have been paid in the light of the exemption from court fees for legally assisted persons contained in the Family Proceedings Fees Order 1991 (since amended) and the Magistrates' Courts' Fees (Amendment) Order 1992.

USE OF COUNSEL

22-39 The authority of the area office either contained in the certificate or issued subsequently is required to instruct counsel in authorised summary proceedings in the magistrates' court. This includes proceedings under the Children Act 1989.[43]

Any instructions delivered to counsel should show the authority for counsel to be instructed in the case of authorised summary proceedings (that is conducted under a civil legal aid certificate),[44] as well as a copy of the certificate (and any amendments) and be endorsed with the legal aid reference number.

If, however, counsel is instructed without authority the Board accepts

---

[41] *ibid.* reg. 104(4), 105A.
[42] *ibid.* reg. 104(4).
[43] *ibid.* reg. 59(1)(a).
[44] *ibid.* reg. 59(2).

that this may still be justified on assessment.[45] It is preferable for the solicitor to obtain prior authority. Authority will not be granted nor the instruction of counsel considered to be justified, if the reason for the application is merely that the other side has instructed counsel or that the solicitor is unable to attend at a particular hearing.

If counsel is instructed without authority and on assessment this is not considered justified for the proper conduct of the proceedings, costs will be assessed by estimating what would have been allowed to the solicitor had he undertaken the case without counsel. Counsel and the solicitor will then be allowed such reasonable costs as do not together exceed that sum. This is known as the "maximum fee principle" and is not directly provided for by the Legal Aid in Family Proceedings (Remuneration) Regulations 1991 although it can be justified on the basis that allowing a standard fee as specified by the Regulations would be unreasonable.[46] This approach allows a solicitor to employ junior counsel rather than a solicitor agent, although solicitors who are members of the Law Society's Children Panel do undertake to deal with cases themselves and prefer to instruct a solicitor agent.

Note that if an amendment is sought to cover an appeal against the making of a care or supervision order the Board's area office may wish counsel's opinion to be obtained on the merits, although this may be avoided if the solicitor makes out his own case as to the prospects of success of the proposed appeal.

---

[45] *ibid.* reg. 63(4).
[46] Legal Aid in Family Proceedings (Remuneration) Regulations 1991, reg. 3(5).

Part D

CRIMINAL LEGAL AID

Chapter 23

THE AVAILABILITY OF LEGAL AID (REPRESENTATION)

In which Proceedings?

Representation is available for criminal proceedings in specified courts.[1]

"Criminal proceedings" include proceedings for dealing with an offender **23–01** for an offence, or in respect of a sentence, or as a fugitive offender and also include proceedings under section 115 of the Magistrates' Courts Act 1980 (binding over), *e.g.* an actual or apprehended breach of the peace or other misbehaviour, and proceedings for dealing with a person for failure to comply with a condition of a recognisance to keep the peace or to be of good behaviour and also include proceedings under section 15 of the Children and Young Persons Act 1969 (variation and discharge of supervision orders) and under section 16(8) (appeals in such proceedings).[2]

"Proceedings for dealing with an offender as a fugitive offender" means proceedings before a metropolitan stipendiary magistrate under section 9 of the Extradition Act 1870 (as if the prisoner were charged with an indictable offence committed in England); section 7 of the Fugitive Offenders Act 1967 (proceedings for committal against a person arrested in pursuance of a warrant of arrest issued under section 6 of that Act); or section 6 of the Criminal Justice Act 1988; (under which a fugitive criminal may be dealt with as if charged with an indictable offence committed in England).

Representation under Part V of the 1988 Act extends to any proceedings **23–02** preliminary or incidental to the proceedings, including bail proceedings before any court.[3] Legal aid is not available to oppose an application either for continued detention of money intended for use in drug trafficking or

---

[1] Legal Aid Act 1988, s. 19(1). An application for the removal of disqualification from driving is within the meaning of "criminal proceedings". *R. v. Recorder of Liverpool, ex. p. McCann, The Times,* May 4, 1994, D.C.
[2] *ibid.* s. 19(5), as amended by the Children Act 1989, s. 99(3).
[3] Legal Aid Act 1988, s.19(2).

for forfeiture of that money, since neither application constitutes "criminal proceedings" for the purposes of section 19 of the 1988 Act.[4]

Representation also extends, in the case of the magistrates' court, to any proceedings before a juvenile court or other magistrates' court to which the case is remitted (*i.e.* under section 56(1) of the Children and Young Persons Act 1933 where a child or young person is found guilty of any offence (other than homicide).[5]

In respect of bail proceedings, representation does not extend to proceedings before a judge of the High Court exercising the jurisdiction of that court.[6-7] Civil legal aid is available for applications for bail to the judge in chambers in the High Court. There are certain proceedings for which criminal legal aid must be granted, provided that the applicant is financially eligible.

The Official Solicitor procedure should be used whenever it is appropriate to do so as the grant of legal aid for an application to a judge in chambers in the High Court is a very much more expensive procedure. In cases where legal aid is applied for, the application should deal with the following points:

   (a) whether the defendant is in the custody of the magistrates' court (although legal aid is not restricted to such cases, defendants in the custody of the Crown Court can apply to that court for bail under the Criminal Legal Aid Order) and a civil legal aid application would be likely to be refused either on the basis that no application had been made to the Crown Court or on the lack of prospect of success, if such an application were to be made;
   (b) the length of time the defendant may have to remain in custody pending trial;
   (c) whether the defendant can reapply for bail to the magistrates' court and why such an application would be likely to fail;
   (d) whether the defendant has been represented on previous applications for bail;
   (e) whether it is suggested that the reasons given by the court for refusing bail were unreasonable or the grounds for refusing bail have altered;
   (f) any special social or other reasons for making an application for bail.

A civil legal aid certificate is only likely to be granted where the Official Solicitor procedure is inappropriate, all possible bail applications to the

---

[4] *R. v. Crawley Justices, ex. p. Ohakwe, The Times,* May 26, 1994. Turner J. but see *R. v. Redbridge Justices, ex. p. Guppy, The Times,* February 23, 1995, D.C.
[5] *ibid.* s. 19(3).
[6-7] *ibid.* s. 19(4).

magistrates' court and Crown Court have been made and the application to the judge in chambers has a reasonable prospect of success.

TO WHOM AVAILABLE?

Representation, for the purposes of any criminal proceedings, is available **23–03** to the accused or convicted person but is not available to the prosecution except, in the case of an appeal to the Crown Court against conviction or sentence, for the purpose of enabling an individual who is not acting in an official capacity to resist the appeal.[8] Representation will not be granted to any person unless it appears to the competent authority that his financial resources are such as to make him eligible under the 1988 Act.[9]

IN WHICH COURTS?

Representation in criminal proceedings is available to any person, subject **23–04** to and in accordance with the 1988 Act and Regulations made under that Act, in a magistrates' court, the Crown Court, the Criminal Division of the Court of Appeal or the Courts Martial Appeal Court and the House of Lords in the exercise of its jurisdiction in relation to appeals from either of those courts.[10]

BY WHICH AUTHORITY?

Generally

The 1988 Act sets out the authorities competent to grant representation. **23–05** The court before which any proceedings take place or are to take place is always competent as respects those proceedings.[11]

Representation granted by a competent authority may be amended or withdrawn by either that or any other competent authority.[12]

Subject to the criteria for the grant of representation and to the various financial regulations, nothing in the Legal Aid in Criminal and Care Proceedings (General) Regulations 1989 affects the power of a court, a

---

[8] Legal Aid Act 1988 s. 21(1).
[9] *ibid.* s. (21)(5).
[10] *ibid.* s. 19(1).
[11] *ibid.* s. 20(2).
[12] *ibid.* s. 21(9).

judge or the registrar to make a legal aid order, whether an application has been made for legal aid or not, or the right of an applicant whose application has been refused or whose legal aid order has been revoked (under section 24(2)) to apply to the court at the trial or in other proceedings.[13] An accused whose grant of legal aid has been revoked for non payment of contributions cannot reapply for legal aid under regulation 11(1) of the General Regulations 1989 but must apply under regulation 10 to the court of trial.[14] But if there are other proceedings *i.e.*, pre-trial matters before the magistrates' court, the application may be made to that court.[15]

Where an application for a grant of representation for the purpose of an appeal to the Court of Appeal or the Courts Martial Appeal Court is made before the giving of notice of appeal or the making of an application for leave to appeal, the competent authority may, in the first instance, make a grant consisting of advice on the question whether there appears to be reasonable grounds of appeal and assistance in the preparation of an application for leave to appeal or in the giving of a notice of appeal.[16]

The Board

23–06 The Lord Chancellor has made an order under section 3(4) of the 1988 Act conferring on the Board the functions required to enable area committees to determine applications.[17] The Board is only empowered to deal with:
  (a) an application for review of a refusal by a magistrates' court to grant representation;
  (b) a renewed application for amendment or withdrawal of a grant of representation or for representation by counsel; and
  (c) an application for prior authority to incur expenditure.[18]

The magistrates' court

23–07 A magistrates' court is, in addition, competent to grant representation in respect of proceedings before the Crown Court where it:
  (a) commits a person for trial or sentence or to be dealt with in respect of a sentence;
  (b) has been given a notice of transfer in respect of a serious fraud case under section 4 of the Criminal Justice Act 1987; and

---

[13] Legal Aid in Criminal and Care Proceedings (General) Regulations 1989, reg. 10.
[14] *R. v. Liverpool Deputy Stipendiary Magistrate, ex p. Shacklady, The Times,* December 28, 1992, D.C.
[15] *R. v. Liverpool Magistrates' Court, ex. p. Pender, The Times,* July 22, 1993, D.C.
[16] Legal Aid Act 1988, s. 21(8).
[17] The Legal Aid (Functions) Order 1989 (S.I. 1989 No. 551).
[18] *ibid.* art. 2.

(c) is being appealed from the magistrates' court to the Crown Court against conviction or sentence.[19]

Where the magistrates' court sits as examining justices it is also competent to grant representation before it decides whether or not to commit the person for trial as respects any proceedings before the Crown Court on his trial (the "through" legal aid order).[20] If a through legal aid order has not been made, legal aid for the Crown Court proceedings is generally applied for on committal. Where a person has been arrested for an offence but has not appeared or been brought before a court, any magistrates' court is competent to make a grant of representation in respect of the proceedings in relation to the offence.[21]

The Crown Court

In addition to proceedings which take place or are to take place before it, **23–08**
the Crown Court is competent to grant representation in respect of applications for leave to appeal and proceedings on any appeal to the Court of Appeal under section 9(11) of the Criminal Justice Act 1987 (*i.e.* appeal against orders or rulings of a judge at preparatory hearings regarding any question of admissibility of evidence or any other question of law relating to the case).[22]

The Court of Appeal and the House of Lords

In addition to proceedings which take place or are to take place before it, **23–09**
a Court of Appeal (Criminal Division) and the Courts Martial Appeal Court is competent to grant representation in proceedings which may take place, if notice of appeal is given or an application for leave to appeal is made.[23]

Similarly, such a court is also competent as regards proceedings on appeal from their decisions to the House of Lords.[24]

Where a re-trial is ordered by the Court of Appeal or the House of Lords on fresh evidence (under section 7 of the Criminal Appeal Act 1968) the court ordering the retrial is also competent as regards the proceedings before the Crown Court.[25]

Section 2(4) of the 1988 Act provides that "representation" includes advice and assistance as to any appeal. This means that a defendant who was legally aided in the Crown Court can receive advice as to whether

---

[19] Legal Aid Act 1988, s. 20(4).
[20] *ibid.* s. 20(5).
[21] *ibid.* s. 20(8).
[22] *ibid.* s. 20(6).
[23] *ibid.* s. 20(2).
[24] *ibid.* s. 20(3).
[25] *ibid.* s. 20(7).

there are reasonable grounds for appeal to the Court of Appeal and, if so, be given assistance in preparing an application for leave to appeal or in the giving of notice of appeal. The Court of Appeal can, however, grant further legal aid, *i.e.* if work of an exceptional nature is contemplated or the expense will be great.

If counsel other than counsel who represented the defendant at the trial is instructed to advise on appeal under the original legal aid order, this will not be covered unless it can be justified as necessary and reasonable.

CRITERIA FOR GRANT OF REPRESENTATION

23–10 Representation may be granted where it appears to the competent authority to be desirable to do so in the interests of justice.[26]

Magistrates' court and Crown Court

23–11 In proceedings by way of trial by or before a magistrates' court or the Crown Court or on an appeal to the Crown Court against a person's conviction, the factors to be taken into account in determining whether it is in the interests of justice that representation be granted include the following:

(a) the offence is such that if proved it is likely that the court would impose a sentence which would deprive the accused of his liberty or lead to loss of his livelihood or serious damage to his reputation;

(b) the determination of the case may involve consideration of a substantial question of law;

(c) the accused may be unable to understand the proceedings or to state his own case because of his inadequate knowledge of English, mental illness or other mental or physical disabilities;

(d) the nature of the defence is such as to involve the tracing and interviewing of witnesses or expert cross-examination of a witness for the prosecution;

(e) it is in the interests of someone other than the accused that the accused be represented.[27]

These are the so-called "Widgery Criteria" originally introduced by the Widgery Committee, on the granting of legal aid, in its report in 1966. The list is not exhaustive and the Lord Chancellor is empowered to vary the factors listed by amending factors in the list or by adding new factors to it.[28]

---

[26] *ibid.* s. 21(2).
[27] *ibid.* s. 22(1),(2).
[28] *ibid.* s. 22(3).

Where doubt arises whether representation should be granted to any person, the doubt is to be resolved in that person's favour.[29]

The Lord Chancellor's Department, the Justices Clerks Society and the Board have jointly issued guidance to all magistrates' courts for use by those considering applications for criminal legal aid.[30]

The Court of Appeal and the House of Lords

In the Court of Appeal and the House of Lords there are no specific factors **23–12** mentioned in the LACCP(G)R1989 Regulations to be taken into account. Legal aid may, therefore, be granted where it appears desirable in the interests of justice.[31] This is subject to the applicant's financial resources being within the prescribed limits.[32] If any doubt arises whether representation should be granted, that doubt must be resolved in the applicant's favour.[33]

WHEN GRANTED?

Generally

Provided that a person is financially eligible, representation *must* be **23–13** granted:

(a) where a person is committed for trial on a charge of murder, for his trial;

(b) where the prosecutor appeals or applies for leave to appeal to the House of Lords for the proceedings on the appeal;

(c) where a person charged with an offence before a magistrates' court:

(i) is brought before the court in pursuance of a remand in custody when he may again be remanded or committed in custody; and

(ii) is not but wishes to be, legally represented before that court (not having been legally represented when he was so remanded), for so much of the proceedings as relate to the grant of bail; and

---

[29] *ibid.* s. 21(7).
[30] Guidance on the Interests of Justice Test for the Grant of Criminal Legal Aid, Lord Chancellor's Department, Justices Clerks Society, Legal Aid Board May 1994.
[31] Legal Aid Act 1988, s. 21(2).
[32] *ibid.* s. 21(5).
[33] *ibid.* s. 21(7).

    (d) where a person:
        (i) is to be sentenced or otherwise dealt with for an offence by a magistrates' court or the Crown Court; and
        (ii) is to be kept in custody to enable inquiries or a report to be made to assist the court,
for the proceedings on sentencing or otherwise dealing with him.[34]

There is no clear statutory answer to the question of whether the court has the power to backdate a legal aid order.[35]

Determination in private

23–14   Determination of any matters determinable otherwise than by a court may be carried out in private and in the absence of the applicant, the appropriate contributor of the person concerned or the legally assisted person as the case may be.[36]

Legal aid records

23–15   The proper officer is required to keep records of all cases in which a legal aid order was made by the court, or an application for legal aid was made to it. The records are to be kept in accordance with directions of the Lord Chancellor and the proper officer is required to send to the Lord Chancellor such information from those records as the Lord Chancellor may request.[37]

Persons under 18

23–16   The provisions with regard to the grant of representation have effect, in respect of a person who has not attained the age of 18, as if the references to "remand in custody" and to being "remanded" or "kept in custody", include references to being committed under section 23 of the Children and Young Persons Act 1969 to the care of a local authority or a remand centre.[38]

Murder

23–17   Where a person is committed for trial on a charge of murder it is for the magistrates' court which commits the person for trial and not for the Crown Court to make the grant of representation for his trial.[39]

---

[34] *ibid.* s. 21(3).
[35] *R. v. North Staffordshire Justices, ex. p. O'Hara*, 1994, C.O.D. 248 May J.
[36] Legal Aid in Criminal and Care Proceedings (General) Regulations 1989, reg. 7.
[37] *ibid.* reg. 8.
[38] Legal Aid Act 1988, s. 21(11).
[39] *ibid.* s. 21(4).

The interests of justice

The principle throughout is that representation may be granted where it **23–18** appears to the competent authority to be desirable in the interests of justice.[40]

The guidance issued by the Lord Chancellor's Department, Justices Clerk Society and Board is as follows.

LEGAL AID APPLICATIONS—GENERAL CONSIDERATIONS

(a) Every application for legal aid must be considered on its merits **23–19** and must be determined in accordance with the provisions of Part V of the 1988 Act.

(b) The specific criterion or other interests of justice consideration which is relied upon must be identified clearly in the application form.

(c) The decision must always be based on the information contained in the form of application for legal aid, together with any other oral or written information provided by or on behalf of the applicant, particulars of the offence(s) alleged as set out in the information(s) before the court, and any other relevant particulars which may be properly taken into account as a result of statements made in open court during the course of the proceedings against the applicant. If the decision to grant or refuse legal aid is influenced by information provided orally, then *the relevant information provided should be clearly recorded on the application.*

(d) In respect of offences triable either-way, the approach to the grant of legal aid should be the same whether the offence is to be tried in the Crown Court or the magistrates' court; accordingly, *e.g.* an accused charged with an offence triable either-way, who does not merit legal aid for summary trial, should not automatically be granted legal aid simply because he elects to be tried at the Crown Court.

(e) It is suggested that the need for a Newton hearing (*i.e.* a dispute on the facts following a plea of guilty) may justify a grant of legal aid if, *e.g.* witnesses need to be traced by a legal representative or expert cross-examination is necessary. This may also apply for other disputes of fact and/or law arising after a guilty plea.

---

[40] *Ibid.* s. 21(2) and see s. 22(2). In the Legal Aid in Criminal and Care Proceedings (General) Regulations 1989 the "Interests of Justice Criteria" means factors which the competent authority is required to take into account by s. 22(2) of the 1988 Act: Legal Aid in Criminal and Care Proceedings (General) Regulations 1989 Reg. 3(1).

THE INTERESTS OF JUSTICE CRITERIA—DETAILED CONSIDERATIONS

23–20   (a) The factors set out in section 22 of the 1988 Act apply to proceedings by way of a trial by or before a magistrates' court or the Crown Court or on an appeal to the Crown Court against conviction.

(b) Section 22(2) of the 1988 Act specifies five factors which must be taken into account when a competent authority is determining whether it is in the interests of justice that representation be granted.

(c) In some cases, the interaction of two or more of the factors may dictate that legal aid should be granted when neither by itself would have sufficed. For example, whereas a minor question of law could normally be dealt with under the Green Form Scheme, or a person's knowledge of English may be adequate rather than good, those two factors in combination could merit a grant of legal aid. Where such interaction is used this should clearly be noted on the application form.

(d) The five factors (considered below) are not exhaustive. Section 22(2) of the 1988 Act states: "The factors to be taken into account . . . shall include the following . . .". In *R. v. Liverpool City Magistrates, ex p. McGhee* it was stated that ". . . these magistrates were plainly wrong in regarding the factors statutorily identified [in section 22(2)(a)–(e)] as being exhaustive and there may be, according to the circumstances of a particular case, other than the identified factors which have to be taken into consideration in deciding whether or not the justice of the case requires that legal aid should be granted."

(e) While some applications may rely on all or several of the factors, an application which relies on only one must be given equal consideration. It also follows from *McGhee* that reliance on none of the statutory factors is not necessarily fatal. When a non-statutory factor is held to have founded or supported the grant of legal aid this should be clearly specified on the application form.

(f) For example, where the behaviour of a defendant is so disputive as to distract the court from the exercise of its judicial function, that alone could justify a grant of legal aid if the presence of a lawyer would mitigate the distraction—if only as a last resort, enabling the court to continue the hearing in the absence of the defendant but in the presence of his legal representative. It is further suggested that behaviour which affects the court's administrative performance is outside the scope of section 22 of the 1988 Act and cannot, therefore, be the basis for a grant of legal aid.

Section 22(2)(a) of the 1988 Act

The offence is such that if proved it is likely that the court would impose a sentence which would deprive the accused of his liberty or lead to loss of his livelihood or serious damage to his reputation

Likelihood of deprivation of liberty

(a) The person considering the application must be provided with **23–21** sufficient information to enable him to be satisfied that, in the event of a conviction, the accused's liberty would be at risk. Accordingly, information about the seriousness and circumstances of the offence alleged should be taken into account, including details of any aggravating circumstances which, in the event of the accused being convicted, might expose him to a more severe sentence than would normally be the case. Details relating to previous convictions should also be applied for the purposes of determining seriousness. Regard should also be had to the gravity of the offence. Where any aggravating factors influence the decision on the grant of legal aid, these should be clearly recorded.

(b) It is recommended that reference in appropriate cases be made to *The Magistrates' Association Sentencing Guidelines* issued on 20 September, 1993, which provide examples of "seriousness indicators" (aggravating factors and mitigating factors) for various types of offence.

(c) The onus is on the applicant to state why such a sentence is likely.

(d) Legal aid should normally be granted where there is a real and practical (as opposed to theoretical) risk of imprisonment or other form of deprivation of liberty. For example, an offender of previous good character, charged with possessing a small quantity of cannabis, would have difficulty in establishing that he was likely to lose his liberty because, although the offence is punishable with three months' imprisonment on summary conviction, it would be most unusual for any court to pass a custodial sentence for such an offence.

(e) For the purpose of determining whether the accused is likely to lose his liberty, etc., regard should be had to the sentencing approaches of courts generally and, in particular, to the sentencing approach of the court before which the accused is appearing.

(f) The likelihood of conviction should not be taken into account; the grant of legal aid should not be based on the merits of the defence and conviction should always be assumed.

(g) "Deprivation of liberty" includes any sentence of imprisonment (whether immediate or suspended), detention in a young offender

481

institution, custody for life, detention under section 53(2) of the Children and Young Persons Act 1933; hospital and guardianship orders.

(h) As noted above, section 22(2)(a) refers specifically to the likelihood of deprivation of liberty and it has been a matter of some debate whether community sentences are capable of falling within that category. This debate has now been settled by the judgment in *R. v. Liverpool City Magistrates, ex p. McGhee*. In giving judgment, Rose L.J. said that ". . . I am not persuaded . . . that the risk of a community service order amount[s] to a risk of deprivation of liberty within the meaning of that section" [section 22(2)(a)]. In concurring, Waller J. said ". . . I am also clear that the words in section 22(2)(a) 'The offence is such that if proved it is likely that the court would impose a sentence which would deprive the accused of his liberty', do not include a community service order." The judgment went on to state that the possibility of a community service order being made might be a factor to be considered when considering whether or not to grant legal aid, and Rose L.J. made plain that this should not be taken to imply that legal aid should be granted if community service was likely. It was, however, a factor other than the listed factors which could be taken into account in particular cases.

(i) Legal aid should normally be granted:
  (i) upon a committal to the Crown Court for sentence (*R. v. Serghiou*[41]);
  (ii) where the court is considering making a recommendation for deportation (*R. v. Edgehill*[42]);
  (iii) where the court is considering making a hospital order (*R. v. King's Lynn Justices, ex p. Fysh*[43]).

(j) A grant of legal aid for mitigation only might be appropriate, *e.g.* when the court's assessment of the gravity of the case is substantially altered by factors which come to light after conviction. Courts should also bear in mind the statutory restrictions on imposing certain sentences as referred to at (d) above.

Loss of livelihood

23–22

(a) It follows from the provisions of the 1988 Act that the granting authority should consider how likely it is that loss of livelihood will result from a sentence imposed by the court on conviction. It

---

[41] [1966] 3 All E.R. 637.
[42] [1963] 1 All E.R. 181.
[43] [1964] Crim. L.R. 143.

is suggested that legal aid should only be granted where there is a real risk of loss of livelihood.

(b) The applicant must explain why he believes that it is likely that he will lose his livelihood. In some cases this will be obvious, *e.g.* a bank clerk accused of an offence of dishonesty; in others it may be obscure, *e.g.* a teacher convicted of indecency with a child is likely to lose his livelihood, but a coach-driver convicted of a similar offence might not appear so vulnerable until he explains to the court that he drives school buses. The likely loss of livelihood should be a direct consequence of the conviction or the sentence.

(c) It is suggested that loss of livelihood would normally refer to current livelihood. Therefore, someone who is not currently employed, would be less likely to meet this criterion, although other criteria under section 22 may be met, such as "serious damage to reputation" (*e.g.* see paragraph 23–23e below).

(d) Assertions that disqualification from driving will result in a loss of livelihood should be examined critically. There can seldom be justification to grant legal aid to resist a mandatory driving disqualification alone arising from a drink/driving charge unless a cogent argument as to special reasons can be put forward. Though a grant could be justified in exceptional circumstances (*e.g.* if the applicant could show that the disqualification would result in a real risk of dismissal), legal aid would not usually be justified where the accused sought to avoid a "totting-up" disqualification, having acquired 12 or more penalty points.

Serious damage to reputation

(a) In many cases, conviction will damage the accused's reputation. **23–23** However, section 22 refers to *serious* damage. It is considered that this would relate to those cases in which the offence, or the offender's circumstances, are such that the disgrace of conviction, or consequent damage to the applicant's standing, would greatly exceed the direct effect of the penalty which might be imposed. "Reputation" for these purposes is a question of good character, including honesty and trustworthiness. Social class and position should not be taken into account. The loss of reputation consequent on a conviction for dishonesty is absolute and not relevant to the amount.

(b) As a general rule, offences of varying degrees of seriousness attract different levels of damage to reputation. The 1988 Act refers to *serious* damage as justifying the grant of legal aid.

(c) An effective plea in mitigation for any charge may lessen the severity of the sentence and thereby lessen the seriousness of the damage to reputation. An applicant who either has a previous conviction for a *like* offence or a conviction for a more serious offence can be assumed to have lost reputation and the criterion will not apply. However, the fact that a person has previous convictions should not preclude consideration of legal aid under this head. For example, it may be that someone with a previous conviction for a minor assault might still suffer serious damage to reputation if convicted of an offence of dishonesty or a sexual offence

(d) In deciding upon the seriousness of the damage to reputation, it is suggested that special factors about the accused (*e.g.* religious background) might aggravate the damage to reputation caused by a conviction which may not have the same effect on another person. This could also apply, *e.g.* to someone engaged in voluntary work such as drug-use prevention, where a conviction for possession of a drug could particularly undermine their integrity.

(e) Consideration should be given to whether an accused who is undertaking vocational or professional training might suffer damage to reputation so serious that there is a risk that future livelihood might be lost.

Section 22(2)(b) of the 1988 Act

The determination of the case may involve consideration of a substantial question of law

23–24

(a) Legal aid should only be granted under this criterion if a question of law is raised which the applicant cannot be expected to deal with unaided and is a substantial question and is relevant to the applicant's case. It should be noted that this criterion may also apply when legal aid is being considered for an appeal against conviction.

If the applicant intends to plead guilty, the likelihood of substantial questions of law arising must generally be remote, although there may be exceptions, such as some "special reasons" (such as laced drinks) in drink/driving cases. There may also be some instances in which sentencing considerations could give rise to a substantial question of law.

(b) The defence solicitor should specify the point of law on the application form. Quite often issues coming before the courts involve mixed questions of fact and law but again, in such circumstances, to justify the grant of legal aid the question of law must be a *substantial* one.

(c) Except in circumstances where the applicant faces serious or complex charges, legal aid should not generally be granted solely for the purpose of obtaining advice as to the appropriate plea since this can rarely be described as a substantial question of law. Preliminary advice as to plea can usually be provided satisfactorily by advice from the duty solicitor or from any solicitor under the Green Form Scheme.

SECTION 22(2)(C) OF THE 1988 ACT

The accused may be unable to understand the proceedings or to state his own case because of his inadequate knowledge of English, mental illness or other mental or physical disability

Inadequate knowledge of English

(a) Legal aid should not be granted unless the applicant's knowledge   **23–25**
is sufficiently poor to prevent him from following the proceedings or conducting his case. It is suggested that the fact that the services of an interpreter are available is not a sufficient ground for refusing legal aid under this criterion.

(b) The accused's difficulties of comprehension may differ with the complexity of the case; he may be able to manage in a very straightforward case but may be unable to do so in a more complex one. Courts should, therefore, consider carefully whether the stated impediment to understanding is likely to be operative in the particular case.

(c) Generally, it is the ability to understand spoken English which is important. It should be borne in mind that, while the language of the courts is often technical, it is the responsibility of those working in the courts to use plain English. A lack of fluent literacy will not, in most cases, impair the accused's ability to prepare and present his case. Relevant factors could include the degree of literacy, the complexity of the case and the extent of reading required.

Mental or physical disability

(a) Legal aid should be granted if the applicant is unable to follow the   **23–26**
proceedings or properly conduct his case by reason of substantial physical disability, e.g. deafness or blindness, or by reason of mental disorder, mental impairment or subnormality.

(b) Courts may think it appropriate to request a medical report or certificate, especially in cases where it is claimed that the applicant is suffering from a form of mental illness that is likely to worsen

485

significantly due to a court hearing and, as a consequence, is unlikely to be able to represent himself properly.

Section 22(2)(d) of the 1988 Act

The nature of the defence is such as to involve the tracing and interviewing of witnesses or expert cross-examination of a witness for the prosecution

Trace and interview witnesses

23–27   (a) Details of the witnesses, and why there is a necessity for representation to trace and/or interview them, should be included in the application. If details of witnesses are not included, consideration of the legal aid application should be deferred until the applicant has provided the court with sufficient information to make a determination.

Expert cross-examination of a prosecution witness

23–28   (a) In cases where the applicant requires legal aid for the benefit of expert cross-examination of prosecution witnesses, he should be expected to explain why this is necessary.

(b) It should be noted that section 22(2)(d) refers to expert cross-examination of a witness and *not* only to cross-examination of an expert witness. Giving judgement in *R. v. Liverpool City Magistrates, ex p. McGhee*, Rose L.J. said: "These justices . . . were clearly under the misapprehension . . . that because expert witnesses were not to be called, the factor identified in part of section 22(2)(d) was not satisfied. That, in itself, as it seems to me, is sufficient to flaw the approach of these justices."

Thus, legal aid should be granted under this heading when there is a need for professional cross-examination of a witness. This may very likely be the case when the evidence is provided by an expert, since an accused person would rarely be capable, *e.g.* of cross-examining a medical or handwriting expert. It may also apply in other cases, such as those where shades of emphasis in the evidence can make an action appear more sinister than it was in fact. But in considering applications under this heading, the emphasis should be clearly on the nature of the evidence, rather than on the status of the person providing the evidence.

SECTION 22(2)(E) OF THE 1988 ACT

It is in the interests of someone other than the accused that the accused be represented

(a) It should be borne in mind when considering legal aid under this heading that section 34A of the Criminal Justice Act 1988 provides that a defendant charged with certain offences specified in section 32(2) of that Act shall not cross-examine in person any child witness who is an alleged victim or alleged witnesss to the commission of the offence.   **23–29**

(b) It is suggested that legal aid should also be considered when, *e.g.* the accused is charged with a sexual offence where it is desirable that the complainant should be spared the great strain of being cross-examined by a person whom they believe has committed a sexual offence against them.

(c) This principle may also apply where the alleged victim or witness of, *e.g.* an offence against the person or a burglary, is very young or elderly, when cross-examination by the accused might put them under undue strain.

Chapter 24

HOW TO APPLY FOR LEGAL AID

THE MAGISTRATES' COURT

The application

24–01 In the magistrates' court the application for legal aid is made on the prescribed form with such variations as the circumstances of the particular case require.[1] A single form of application for a legal aid order is prescribed, the use of which is mandatory.[2] The magistrates' court must provide the relevant forms free of charge to persons (whether solicitors, prospective applicants or appropriate contributors) intending to use them to make application to that court or to notify the proper officer of a change in financial circumstances.[3]

The application is made to the justice's clerk on the prescribed form or orally to the court and the justice's clerk may grant or refuse the application.[4] Where the application is made orally the court may refer it to the justice's clerk for determination. Save where the applicant is not required to furnish a statement of means, no legal aid order will be made until the court or the justice's clerk has considered the applicant's statement of means.[5]

A justice's clerk is entitled to refuse to make a legal aid order until provided with a statement in writing of the defendant's financial circumstances.[6] The work carried out in connection with proceedings in a magistrates' court is not work done under a legal aid order if it is done before the order is made, unless and to the extent that the deeming provision is applied under regulation 44(7) of the Legal Aid in Criminal and

---

[1] Legal Aid in Criminal and Care Proceedings (General) Regulations 1989, reg. 4(1).
[2] *ibid.* reg. 4(1), Sched. 2, Form 1.
[3] *ibid.* reg. 4(2), Sched. 2, Forms 1 and 5.
[4] *ibid.* reg. 11(1), Sched. 2, Form 1.
[5] *ibid.* reg. 11(2), (3).
[6] Legal Aid Act 1988, s. 21(6) and Legal Aid in Criminal and Care Proceedings (General) Regulations 1989, reg. 23(2).

Care Proceedings (General) Regulations 1989.[7] A Justices' Clerk has no power to backdate a legal aid order and the practice of making an order on condition that supporting documentary evidence is supplied is unsatisfactory since the regulations require simultaneous consideration of statements of means and supporting evidence.[8]

A statement of means is required in every case, unless it appears to the court or the justice's clerk that by reason of the physical or mental condition of the applicant, he is for the time being incapable of furnishing such a statement; or the applicant has already submitted a statement in connection with a previous application in respect of the same case and his financial circumstances have not changed.[9]

An applicant whose application for legal aid is refused may renew the application either orally to the court or to the justice's clerk; this is without prejudice to any right there may be to have the decision reviewed by an appropriate area committee.[10].

Justices erred in hearing a case against a defendant, having heard an application for legal aid which included information as to the defendant's previous findings of guilt and an application by the local authority for a secure accommodation order. This was particularly so given the statutory form of words on the application form which provides that if the defendant pleads not guilty, the information given on the form will not be made known to the justices who try the case.[11]

Notification of refusal

Where an application for legal aid is refused, the court or the justice's clerk **24–02** must notify the applicant on the prescribed form[12] that the application has been refused on one or both of the following grounds:

  (a) it does not appear to the court or to the justice's clerk desirable to make an order in the interests of justice; or

  (b) it appears to the court or the justice's clerk that the applicant's disposable income and disposable capital are such that he is ineligible for legal aid.

The applicant must be informed of the circumstances in which he may renew his application or apply to an area committee for review.[13]

---

[7] *R. v. Newham Justices, ex p. Mumtaz* [1990] Crim. L.R. 589.
[8] *R. v. Highbury Corner Magistrates' Court, ex. p. Sonn & Co., The Times*, May 23, 1995, D.C. and see *R. v. North Staffordshire J.Js. ex. p. O'Hara*, 1994, C.O.D. 248 May, J.
[9] Legal Aid in Criminal and Care Proceedings (General) Regulations 1989, reg. 23(4).
[10] *ibid.* reg. 14(1).
[11] *R. v. Blyth Valley Juvenile Court, ex p. S. The Times*, April 11, 1987.
[12] Legal Aid in Criminal and Care Proceedings (General) Regulations 1989, Sched. 2, Form 2.
[13] *ibid.* reg. 12(1), (2).

Determination of contribution where legal aid is refused

24–03 Notwithstanding that an application for legal aid has been refused, the court or the justice's clerk is required to determine the applicant's disposable income and disposable capital and the amount of any contribution which would have been payable, and the manner in which it would have been payable had a legal aid order been made, and the applicant must be notified of the amounts so determined.[14] The purpose of this is to enable an applicant to decide whether to seek to renew or review the refusal and to enable a contribution order to be made if an area committee decides to make a legal aid order on review.

Renewal of application

24–04 Where an application for legal aid has been refused, the applicant may renew the application either orally to the court or to the justice's clerk. The notice of refusal must be returned,[15–16] and if the application is being renewed after a refusal upon review to an area committee, the notice of the committee's decision must also be returned.[17]

Where an application is renewed to the justice's clerk, he may either grant the application, or refer it to the court or to a justice of the peace. The justice's clerk is not entitled to refuse the renewed application of his own volition.[18] Where the application is renewed to the court, the court may grant or refuse the application or refer it to the justice's clerk who may grant the application, or refer it back to the court or to a justice of the peace. Again, the justice's clerk may not refuse the application.[19] The court or justice of the peace to whom an application is referred by the justice's clerk may grant or refuse the application.[20]

No legal aid order will be made until the court, a justice of the peace or the justice's clerk has considered the applicant's statement of means, unless the applicant is not required to furnish such a statement (where it appears that by reason of his physical or mental condition the applicant is for the time being incapable of furnishing such a statement; or the applicant has already submitted such a statement in connection with a previous application in respect of the same case and his financial circumstances have not changed).[21] A statement of means may be required if an incapable

---

[14] *ibid.* reg. 13.
[15–16] *ibid.* reg. 14(2), Sched. 2, Form 2.
[17] Legal Aid in Criminal and Care Proceedings (General) Regulations 1989, reg. 14(2), Sched. 2, Form 4.
[18] *ibid.* reg. 14(3).
[19] *ibid.* reg. 14(4), (6).
[20] *ibid.* reg. 14(5).
[21] *ibid.* regs. 14(7), 23(4).

patient becomes capable.[22] There are no time-limits for reviewing nor is there any limit on the number of times an application may be renewed. Clearly, a renewed application is unlikely to be granted in the absence of fresh information or a change of circumstances. There is nothing to stop a fresh application rather than a renewed application being made, and the court of trial can be asked to grant legal aid on the day of trial in any event.

Refusal of renewed application

Where a renewed application is refused by a magistrates' court or a justice **24–05** of the peace the applicant will be notified on the prescribed form[23] that the application has been refused on one or both of the following grounds:
  (a) it does not appear to the court desirable to make a order in the interests of justice; or
  (b) it appears to the court that the applicant's disposable income and disposable capital are such that he is ineligible for legal aid
and he will be informed of the circumstances in which he may renew his application or apply to an area committee for the decision to be reviewed.[24] In this connection "a justice of the peace" means a justice of the peace who is entitled to sit as a member of the magistrates' court.[25]

Application for review to an area committee

The 1988 Act makes provision for Regulations to be made for an appeal to **24–06** lie to a specified court or body against any refusal by a magistrates' court to grant representation, and for that other court or body to make any grant of representation that could have been made by the magistrates' court.[26] The Legal Aid in Criminal and Case Proceedings (General) Regulations 1989 provide the review procedure. Where an application for representation has been refused and where an application for review may be made, the court or the justice's clerk will send to the applicant notification of the refusal to grant legal aid and determination of contribution on the prescribed form as well as a copy of the original application for legal aid.[27]

Application for review may only be made where an application for a legal aid order has been refused after having been considered for the first time by a magistrates' court or a justice's clerk.

---

[22] *ibid.* reg. 23(5).
[23] *ibid.* reg. 14(8), Sched. 2, Form 2.
[24] *ibid.* reg. 12(1), (2).
[25] *ibid.* reg. 14(8), (9).
[26] Legal Aid Act 1988, s. 21(10).
[27] Legal Aid in Criminal and Care Proceedings (General) Regulations 1989, Sched. 2, Forms 1, 2.

Review lies to the appropriate area committee, which is the committee for the area in which the court to which the original application was made, is situated.[28]

An application for review only lies to an area committee where:
- (a) the applicant is charged with an indictable offence, or an offence which is triable either way, or appears or is brought before a magistrates' court to be dealt with in respect of a sentence imposed or an order made in connection with such an offence; and
- (b) the application for a legal aid order has been refused on the ground that it does not appear to the court or the justice's clerk desirable to make an order in the interests of justice; and
- (c) the application for a legal aid order was made no later than 21 days before the date fixed for the trial of an information or the inquiry into the offence as examining justices where that date had been fixed at the time that the application was made.[29]

A defendant's first appearance in the magistrates' court may be "the date fixed for trial" since the court alone has the power to fix the date of trial or inquiry into an offence. In the unlikely event of justices being in a position to deal with a case on the first appearance it is the justices' decision to proceed which makes it "the date fixed for the trial . . . or the inquiry" and not the fact that the date has been fixed for a first appearance by the Crown Prosecution Service.[30]

The Board accepts jurisdiction in criminal damage matters regardless of the amount involved but has no jurisdiction in respect of common assault. If a review application refers to summary offences as well as a qualifying offence or offences within regulation 15(2)(a) of the Legal Aid in Criminal and Care Proceedings (General) Regulations 1989 then the Board considers the area committee still has jurisdiction and legal aid may be granted for the summary offences.

The right of review does not arise where legal aid is refused on the basis of means, that is to say the refusal must be based on the "interests of justice" alone for a review application to be made.

Procedure on application for review

24–07 Application for review is made on the prescribed form (Form 3) to the appropriate area committee within 14 days of the date of notification of the refusal. The applicant must send a copy of the form to the justice's clerk at

---

[28] *ibid.* regs. 15(1), 3.
[29] *ibid.* 1989, reg. 15(2).
[30] *R. v. Bury Justices, ex p. N.* [1987] Q.B. 284.

the magistrates' court to which the first application for legal aid was made.[31] The applicant must also send to the appropriate Board area office a copy of the completed application for legal aid, which should have been returned by the court with the notification of refusal as well as a copy of the notice of refusal.[32] It may be possible for the application to be dealt with without the copy of the original legal aid application provided sufficient other information is submitted but the application cannot proceed without the notice of refusal as this confirms the basis of refusal and shows the contribution, if any.

The area committee will only have the information provided to it, and a review application will only succeed, if the information submitted indicates that it is in the interests of justice for legal aid to be granted. A lack of information will not be used to justify a grant based on the requirement contained in section 21(7) of the 1988 Act that doubt should be resolved in the applicant's favour. It is, therefore, in the applicant's interests that a review application be supported where possible by not only the original legal aid application but also a statement, any advance disclosure, and full details of the applicant's criminal record, if any. No information provided to the area committee will be made known to the court.

The area committee will accept review applications signed by a solicitor on behalf of the applicant for review.

The area committee may require further particulars, information and documents which the justice's clerk and the applicant must supply. The area committee may, for good reason, waive or extend the time-limit within which the application for review is to be made.[33] Good reason will usually mean matters outside the control of the applicant and solicitor, *e.g.* postal delays.

Determination of review

The area committee on a review may either refuse the application or make **24–08** a legal aid order. If area office staff are not prepared to grant legal aid then the review application will be referred to the committee for consideration and this will inevitably mean a delay as committees do not meet daily.

Where a legal aid order is made, the area committee will also make a contribution order in accordance with any determination made by the magistrates' court when the original application was refused.[34]

Where the contribution order which the area committee makes is in respect of a contribution from disposable capital, the area committee will

---

[31] Legal Aid in Criminal and Care Proceedings (General) Regulations 1989, reg. 16(1), Sched. 2, Form 3.
[32] *ibid.* reg. 16(2), Sched. 2, Forms 1, 2.
[33] *ibid.* reg. 16(4), (3).
[34] *ibid.* regs. 13, 17(1), (2).

send the legal aid order to the appropriate justice's clerk, and it will not take effect until the contribution is paid.[35] The area committee will give notice of its decision and the reasons for it on the prescribed form to the applicant and his solicitor, if any, and the justice's clerk of the magistrates' court to which the original application was made.[36] In cases where the interests of justice criteria apply (under section 22 of the 1988 Act) the statement of reasons must include specific reference to such of those criteria as appear to be relevant to the decision.[37]

THE CROWN COURT

The application

24–09 An application for legal aid in respect of proceedings in the Crown Court, may be made either to the appropriate officer of the Crown Court on the prescribed form[38] or:

    (a) orally to the Crown Court or to a magistrates' court at the conclusion of any proceedings in that magistrates' court; or

    (b) where a magistrates' court has been given a notice of transfer in a serious fraud case (under section 4 of the Criminal Justice Act 1987) to the justice's clerk of that magistrates' court on the prescribed form[39]; or

    (c) in the case of an appeal to the Crown Court from a magistrates' court to the justice's clerk of that magistrates' court on the prescribed form[40]; or

    (d) where the applicant was granted legal aid for proceedings in the magistrates' court and was committed for trial in the Crown Court, to the justice's clerk of the magistrates' court ordering the committal in such form as may be required; or

    (e) in the case of a re-trial ordered under section 7 of the Criminal Appeal Act 1968 orally to the court ordering the re-trial.

The appropriate officer, the court or the justice's clerk may grant or refuse the application or, where the application is made orally to the court, the court may refer it to the proper officer for determination. No legal aid order will be made until the appropriate officer, the court or the justice's clerk has considered the applicant's statement of means unless the applicant is not required to furnish a statement of means (because it appears that by

---

[35] *ibid.* reg. 17(3).
[36] *ibid.* reg. 17(4), Sched. 2, Form 4.
[37] *ibid.* reg. 17(5).
[38] *ibid.* reg. 18, Sched. 2, Form 1.
[39] *ibid.* Sched. 2, Form 1.
[40] *ibid.*

reason of his physical or mental condition the applicant is for the time being incapable of furnishing such a statement or he has already submitted such a statement in connection with a previous application in respect of the same case and his financial circumstances have not changed).[41]

Notification of refusal

Where an application for legal aid in the Crown Court is refused, the **24–10** applicant must be notified on the prescribed form of the refusal and that it is on one or both of the following grounds:
  (a) it does not appear to the officer, the court or the justice's clerk desirable to make an order in the interests of justice; or
  (b) it appears to the officer, the court or the justice's clerk that the applicant's disposable income and disposable capital are such that, in accordance with the LACCP(G) Regulations 1989 he is ineligible for legal aid.
The notice must inform the applicant of the circumstances in which he may renew his application.[42] A copy of the form will be sent to the applicant and his solicitor, if any.

Determination of contribution where legal aid refused

Where an application for a legal aid order has been refused, the appropriate **24–11** officer of the Crown Court, the court or the justice's clerk is required to determine the applicant's disposable income and capital and the amount of any contribution which would have been payable, and the manner in which it would have been payable by the applicant or the appropriate contributor had a legal aid order been made. This is to notify the applicant of the amount of any contribution and to facilitate the making of a contribution order in the event of an application being granted on renewal. The applicant is to be notified of the amounts determined.[43]

Renewal of application

Where an application for a legal aid order in respect of proceedings in the **24–12** Crown Court has been refused, the applicant may renew the application either orally to the court or to the appropriate officer of the Crown Court. The applicant must return the notice of refusal which should have been

---

[41] *ibid.* regs. 18(1), (2), (3), 23(4).
[42] *ibid.* reg. 19(1), (2), Sched. 2, Form 2.
[43] *ibid.* reg. 20.

returned to him by the court indicating the grounds upon which the application had been refused.[44]

The appropriate officer, (*i.e.* the chief clerk of the Crown Court or an officer designated by him to act on his behalf) may either grant the application, or refer it to a judge of the court; he may not refuse it. The court or a judge of the court may grant or refuse the application, and, if the application is made initially to the court, it may refer it to the appropriate officer who may grant it or refer it to a judge of the court. Again the application may not be refused by the appropriate officer.[45]

No legal aid order will be made in respect of a renewed application until the court or the appropriate officer has considered the applicant's statement of means (unless the applicant is not required to furnish such a statement because it appears to the court or the proper officer that by reason of his physical or mental condition he is, for the time being, incapable of furnishing such a statement or he has already submitted a statement in connection with a previous application in respect of the same case and his financial circumstances have not changed).[46]

Refusal of renewed application

24–13 If the renewed application is refused, the appropriate officer or the court will notify the applicant on the prescribed form that the application has been refused on one or both of the following grounds, namely:
   (a) it does not appear to the officer or the court desirable to make an order in the interests of justice; or
   (b) it appears to the officer or the court that the applicant's disposable income and disposable capital are such that he is ineligible for legal aid.

The applicant must be informed of the circumstances in which he may renew his application and a copy of the prescribed form must be sent to the applicant and his solicitor, if any.[47]

THE COURT OF APPEAL AND THE HOUSE OF LORDS

The application

24–14 An application for a legal aid order in respect of proceedings in the Court of Appeal or the House of Lords may be made orally to the Court of Appeal,

---

[44] *ibid.* reg. 21(1), (2).
[45] *ibid.* reg. 21(3), (4), (5), (6).
[46] *ibid.* regs. 21(7), 23(4).
[47] *ibid.* regs. 19, 21(8), Sched. 2, Form 2.

to a judge of the Court or the Registrar of Criminal Appeals (or the Registrar of the Courts Martial Appeal Court, including any person duly authorised to act on his behalf) or by giving written notice of the application to the Registrar in such form as he may direct.[48]

Subject to the limitations imposed by the LACCP(G) Regulations 1989, the powers of the Court of Appeal to determine an application for a legal aid order may be exercised by a judge of the Court or by the Registrar.[49]

Where an application is made orally to the Court of Appeal, the Court may refer it to a judge of the court or to the Registrar for determination. Similarly, if an application is made orally to a judge of the court, he may refer it to the Registrar. Where a judge of the court refuses to make a legal aid order the applicant may renew his application to the Court of Appeal.[50]

In considering an application for a legal aid order the Registrar must make an order or refer the application to the Court of Appeal or to a judge of the court; in other words, the Registrar has no power to refuse the application.[51] No legal aid order may be made until the notice of appeal or application for leave to appeal to the Court of Appeal or the House of Lords has been given, and the Court of Appeal or the judge of the court or the Registrar has considered the applicant's statement of means (unless the applicant is not required to furnish a statement of means because it appears to the court or the proper officer that by reason of his physical or mental condition he is, for the time being, incapable of furnishing such a statement or he has already submitted such a statement in connection with a previous application in respect of the same case and his financial circumstances have not changed.[52]

It is open to the Court of Appeal, the court, a judge of the court or the Registrar to specify the stage of the proceedings at which legal aid shall commence.[53]

This means that in a proper case an order for legal aid may be made retrospectively for work already done.[54] Whether the court chooses to backdate an order will depend on the whole of the circumstances including the need for the work to have been done.[55]

---

[48] *ibid.* reg. 22(1).
[49] *ibid.* reg. 22(7).
[50] *ibid.* reg. 22(2), (3).
[51] *ibid.* reg. 22(4).
[52] *ibid.* regs. 22(5), 23(4).
[53] *ibid.* reg. 22(6).
[54] *R.v. Kearney* [1983] 1 W.L.R. 1046, C.A.
[55] *R.v. Gibson* [1983] 1 W.L.R. 1038, C.A.

FINANCIAL CIRCUMSTANCES

Generally

24–15 Representation may not be granted to any person unless it appears to the competent authority that his financial resources are such as under the LACCP(G) Regulations 1989 make him eligible for representation.[56]

Before making any decision as to the eligibility of any person, the competent authority must, except in certain prescribed cases, require a statement of the financial resources to be furnished in the prescribed form.[57]

Where a doubt arises whether representation should be granted to any person the doubt is to be resolved in that person's favour.[58]

The statement of means

The statement of means must be in the appropriate form,[59] it may be submitted by the applicant or an appropriate contributor. The "applicant" is the person making the application or in relation to an application made on behalf of a person who has not attained the age of 17 years, his parent or guardian. An "appropriate contributor" in relation to a person who has not attained the age of 16 means his parent or guardian.[60] The form of statement of means is prescribed by the LACCP(G) Regulations 1989[61] Where a person applies for legal aid without submitting a statement of means, the proper officer, or the court to which he is making the application, must require him to do so.[62]

If the applicant is under 16 the proper officer may require either the applicant or an appropriate contributor or both to submit a statement of means.[63] Therefore, an applicant under 16 will be assessed on the basis of his and any contributor's circumstances, and an applicant over 16 will be assessed on his own circumstances, although up to the age of 17 the application will be by his parent or guardian.

Exceptions

24–16 A statement of means will be required unless it appears, to the court or the proper officer, that by reason of his physical or mental condition, the

---

[56] Legal Aid Act 1988, s. 21(5).
[57] *ibid.* s. 21(6).
[58] *ibid.* s. 21(7).
[59] Legal Aid in Criminal and Care Proceedings (General) Regulations 1989, reg. 23(1), Form 5.
[60] *ibid.* reg. 3.
[61] *ibid.* reg. 23(1), Form 5.
[62] *ibid.* reg. 23(2).
[63] *ibid.* reg. 23(3).

applicant is for the time being incapable of furnishing such a statement; the applicant has already submitted a statement in connection with a previous application in respect of the same case and his financial circumstances have not changed; or it appears to the court or the proper officer that certain benefits are being paid.[64]

Where an applicant has avoided furnishing a statement of means by reason of his physical or mental condition there is nothing to prevent the court or the proper officer from requiring the applicant to furnish a statement of means after a legal aid order has been made when it appears that he is no longer incapable of so doing.[65]

Provision of information

The court or the proper officer may at any time after the submission of the **24–17** statement of means require the applicant, the legally assisted person or the appropriate contributor to provide evidence of any information given in a statement of means, or of any change in his financial circumstances, together with such additional information as they may require.[66] Where an applicant submits a statement of means, but neither provides supporting documentary evidence, nor supplies an explanation in writing of why it was not reasonably practicable to do so, the proper officer, or the court to which the application is being made must require him to provide such evidence or supply a written explanation.[67]

Where representation is granted to an applicant who provided a reasonable explanation of why, at the time of submission of the statement of means, it was not reasonably practicable to supply supporting documentary evidence, the court or proper officer may subsequently require the assisted person to provide documentary evidence where it appears that it has become reasonably practicable to do so.[68]

Where documentary evidence is provided, the determination or redetermination of any contribution payable or the amount of any contribution order will be in accordance with the LACCP(G) Regulations 1989.[69]

Determination of contribution

When making a legal aid order the court or the proper officer is required **24–18** to determine the amount of any contribution payable in accordance with

---

[64] *i.e.* in accordance with *ibid* reg. 26(3), *ibid.* reg. 23(4)(a), (b), (c).
[65] *ibid.* reg. 23(5).
[66] *ibid.* reg. 24(1).
[67] *ibid.* reg. 23(2).
[68] *ibid.* reg. 24(2) as amended by the Legal Aid in Criminal and Care Proceedings (General) (Amendment) Regulations 1994.
[69] *i.e. ibid.* regs. 24(3), 32, 33.

LACCP(G) Regulation 26, 1989.[70-71] Where the applicant or the legally assisted person has paid or is liable to pay a contribution in respect of advice and assistance given in relation to the same proceedings (under section 9(6) of the 1988 Act), any contribution which he or an appropriate contributor is liable to make in respect of the cost of representation will be reduced by the total amount of any contribution paid or payable in respect of the advice or assistance[72] that is to say, any assessed Green Form contribution will be set off against the criminal legal aid contribution. The Means Form, Form 5, inquires as to this, in the section headed "4. Allowances and Deductions".

Assessment of resources

24–19 No grant of representation will be made for any purpose unless it appears that a person's financial resources are such that he requires assistance in meeting the costs which he may incur.

The court or the proper officer must consider the statement of means submitted by the applicant or the appropriate contributor and any other relevant information: and determine the disposable income and disposable capital in accordance with Schedule 3 to the Legal Aid in Criminal and Care Proceedings (General) Regulations 1989 and the applicant or appropriate contributor will then be required to pay a contribution in accordance with Schedule 4 if it appears that the applicant's financial resources "are such that he requires assistance in meeting the costs which he may incur."[73] Schedule 4 provides for weekly contribution from disposable income (as assessed under Schedule 3) and for the contribution from capital of the excess disposable capital (also as assessed under Schedule 3). A contribution from income and capital may be payable as there is no specified upper limit on either income or capital as eligibility depends on the need for assistance in meeting costs provided for by regulation 26(1).

No determination will be made where the applicant, the appropriate contributor or the spouse of either of them is in receipt of income support or family credit and this applies equally to a man and a woman who are living with each other in the same household as husband and wife.[74] This is because criminal legal aid will be available without a contribution on the basis of the receipt of benefit.

[70-71] *ibid.* regs. 25(1), 26.
[72] Legal Aid in Criminal and Care Proceedings (General) Regulations 1989, reg. 25(2).
[73] *ibid.* reg. 26(1), (2), (4).
[74] *ibid.* reg. 26(3).

Contribution orders

Once the financial resources have been assessed, the court or the proper **24–20** officer will make a contribution order and will endorse the legal aid order accordingly. A copy of the contribution order is sent to the person ordered to make the contribution, to the legally assisted person's solicitor or counsel and to the collecting court.[75]

Legal Aid Records

The Proper Officer[76] of each court is required to keep a record of every **24–21** application to that court for a Legal Aid Order. The record must state whether the application was granted; was refused on the ground that it did not appear that it was desirable to make an order in the interests of justice; or was refused on the ground that it did not appear that the applicant's disposable income and disposable capital were such that he was eligible for Legal Aid. Where the application is granted or refused on interests of justice grounds, the record must state the factors relied on by the applicant and the reasons for the decision.[77]

Where a Legal Aid order is granted or refused by an Area Committee following an application for review the proper officer must keep a record of the decision and the reasons of the Area Committee.[78] In the case of proceedings by way of trial before a Magistrates Court or the Crown Court or on Appeal to the Crown Court against conviction, the statement of reasons must include specific reference to such of the interest of justice criteria as appear to be relevant to the decision.[79]

---

[75] *ibid.* reg. 27(1) and (2) and Sched. 2, Form 6.
[76] *i.e.* in the House of Lords, the Clerk of the Parliaments; in the Court of Appeal, the Registrar; in the Crown Court, the Chief Clerk or an officer designated to act by him and in the Magistrates Court, the Justices Clerk: Legal Aid in Criminal and Care Proceeding (General) Regulations 1989 regulation 3(1).
[77] *ibid.* reg. 8(1), (2).
[78] *ibid.* reg. 8(3).
[79] *ibid.* reg. 8(4).

Chapter 25

THE LEGAL AID ORDER

GENERALLY

The Order

25–01 Where a legal aid order is granted, copies of the order in the prescribed form will be sent to the legally assisted person and to the solicitor assigned or to counsel; where the order is made for the purposes of proceedings before a magistrates' court a further copy (endorsed "Board copy") will also be sent.[1]

A clerk to a magistrates' court has power to issue a duplicate legal aid order to a solicitor and may make enquiries of the solicitor about the original before exercising his discretion. The exercise of the discretion is not susceptible to challenge unless irrational, perverse, or coming within another recognised *Wednesbury* ground.[2]

Contributions from disposable capital

25–02 Where a contribution out of disposable capital is to be paid immediately, the legal aid order does not take effect until the payment is made; the court or the proper officer of the court must give notice of this fact, in the prescribed form, to the applicant and the appropriate contributor and the solicitor assigned or counsel.[3] On a successful review application to the area committee in such a case, the area committee will send the legal aid order to the appropriate justice's clerk pending payment.[4] In any event, where a legal aid order is made by an area committee for the purposes of proceedings in a magistrates' court, one copy is sent to the proper officer of the court to which the application for legal aid was made.[5]

---

[1] Legal Aid in Criminal and Care Proceedings (General) Regulations 1989, reg. 40(1), (2), Sched. 2, Forms 11, 11A, 12, 13.
[2] *R. v. Liverpool Justices ex p. R. M. Broudie & Co., The Times,* April 6 1994; *Associated Provincial Picture Houses Ltd v. Wednesbury Corporation* [1948] 1 K.B. 223.
[3] *ibid.* reg. 29(3), Sched. 2, Form 7.
[4] *ibid.* reg. 17(3), Sched. 2, Form 7.
[5] *ibid.* reg. 40(3).

Counsel

Where the solicitor assigned instructs counsel, instructions delivered to   **25–03**
counsel must include a copy of the legal aid order and the solicitor must
inform counsel of any amendments made to the order.[6]

If legal aid is granted for counsel only in the Court of Appeal, an
application from counsel may be made in writing showing that there is
work to be done which only solicitors can undertake.

Notes of evidence and depositions

Where a legal aid order is made in respect of an appeal to the Crown Court,   **25–04**
the justice's clerk must supply, on the application of the solicitor assigned,
copies of any notes of evidence or depositions taken in the proceedings in
the magistrates' court.[7]

Transfer of documents

Where a person is committed by a lower court to a higher court or appeals   **25–05**
or applies for leave to appeal from a lower court to a higher court, the
proper officer of the lower court must send to the higher court:
- (a) a copy of any legal aid order previously made in respect of the
same proceedings;
- (b) a copy of any contribution order made;
- (c) a copy of any legal aid application which has been refused;
- (d) any statement of means already submitted.[8-9]

WITHDRAWAL, REVOCATION AND AMENDMENT

Revocation

Where a legally assisted person fails to pay a relevant contribution when it   **25–06**
is due, the court in which the proceedings for the purposes of which he
has been granted representation are being heard may, subject to certain
safeguards, revoke the grant.[10]

In the event of the legal aid order being revoked for refusal to pay a

---

[6] *ibid.* reg. 40(5).
[7] *ibid.* reg. 42.
[8-9] *ibid.* reg. 43.
[10] Legal Aid Act 1988, s. 24(2), (3).

contribution, similar provisions apply with any necessary modifications as if the order had been withdrawn.[11]

In the Court of Appeal where the legally assisted person applies for the order to be revoked, the power to revoke may be exercised by a judge of the court or by the registrar.[12]

A legal aid order made by a magistrates' court may only be revoked on the grounds set out in the 1988 Act or in the LACP(G)R 1989 so that a purported revocation of a legal aid order, made by the magistrates' court pursuant to a properly submitted application, was of no effect and the defendant remained legally aided throughout.[13]

Withdrawal

25–07 Where two legal aid orders are made in respect of the same proceedings, the second order is deemed to be of no effect and will be withdrawn.[14]

A legal aid order may be withdrawn where the legally assisted person declines to accept the terms on which the grant may be made at the request of the legally assisted person or in accordance with the LACP(G)R 1989 if the legal representative for the time being assigned under the order withdraws from the case and it appears to the court that because of the legally assisted person's conduct it is not desirable to amend the order.[15]

The order withdrawing legal aid will be on the prescribed from and a copy must be sent to the legally assisted person or the solicitor assigned or to counsel, and where the legal aid order is withdrawn by the area committee, to the proper officer of the court to which the application for withdrawal was made.[16]

Where a legal aid order is withdrawn, the counsel assigned must send all papers and other items in his possession relating to the proceedings to the solicitor assigned or (where no solicitor was assigned) to the legally assisted person. The solicitor assigned must send all papers and other items in his possession relating to the proceedings to the legally assisted person.[17]

It may be a material irregularity for a judge to refuse to revoke a legal aid order where a defendant seeks new legal representation but if the judge has before him information which would inevitably justify him in revoking the legal aid order under section 31(2)(a) of the Legal Aid Act 1974 (now Legal Aid in Criminal and Care Proceedings (General) Regulations 1989,

---

[11] Legal Aid in Criminal and Care Proceedings (General) Regulations 1989, reg. 41(5).
[12] ibid. reg. 22(8).
[13] R. v. Huntingdon Magistrates' Court, ex. p. Yapp [1986] Crim. L.R. 689.
[14] Legal Aid in Criminal and Care Proceedings (General) Regulations 1989, reg. 41(2).
[15] ibid. regs. 41(1), 50(2).
[16] ibid. reg. 41(3), Sched. 2, Form 14.
[17] ibid. reg. 41(4).

reg. 41) it is not material that formalities in accordance with the Act were not followed.[18]

The Divisional Court does not have jurisdiction to entertain a judicial review of the decision of a Crown Court Judge to reinstate a legal aid order which had previously been discharged.[19]

Amendment of legal aid orders

A court, having power to make a legal aid order, may, on application, **25–08** amend the order by substituting the legal representative or representatives previously assigned. The new representatives must be such as could have been assigned if the court had then been making the legal aid order.

The court may withdraw the legal aid order if the only legal representative, or all the legal representatives for the time being assigned under the order, withdraw from the case, and it appears to the court that because of the legally assisted person's conduct it is not desirable to amend the order.[20]

Where a defendant complained about the conduct of his solicitors, who were the third firm to have represented him, the solicitors and counsel were allowed to withdraw on the second day of the trial. However, the judge refused the defendant's application to instruct a fourth firm of solicitors. He was subsequently convicted of common assault having conducted his own case and on appeal it was held that the defendant was entitled to representation (by virtue of section 31(1) of the Legal Aid Act 1974 which is similar in form to regulation 50(2) of the Legal Aid in Criminal and Care Proceedings (General) Regulations 1989) until the judge revoked the order; as the judge had not done so, there had been a material irregularity and the appeal was allowed.[21]

Where an order is amended, the order must be in the prescribed form **25–09** and a copy of it will be sent to the legally assisted person, the solicitor assigned or counsel, and to any solicitor and counsel assigned by the amended legal aid order; and where the legal aid order is amended by an area committee to the proper officer of the court to which the application for amendment was made.[22]

The local Criminal Legal Aid Committee is entitled to amend a legal aid order if it is in the interests of justice to do so. The mere fact that the defendant wishes to instruct different solicitors is not of such importance that it can be said that the Committee wrongly exercised its discretion in

---

[18] *R. v. Dimech* [1991] Crim. L.R. 846, C.A.
[19] *R. v. Isleworth Crown Court, ex p. Willington, The Times,* October 6, 1992.
[20] Legal Aid in Criminal and Care Proceedings (General) Regulations 1989, reg. 50(1), (2).
[21] *R. v. Chambers* [1989] Crim. L. R. 367, C.A.
[22] Legal Aid in Criminal and Care Proceedings (General) Regulations 1989, reg. 50(3), Sched. 2, Form 15.

refusing to amend the order. It is incumbent on the applicant to put forward grounds or reasons to justify the desire to change solicitors.[23]

Where a new solicitor or counsel is assigned on amendment, the solicitor or counsel originally assigned must send all papers and other items in their possession relating to the proceedings to the new solicitor or counsel.[24]

A magistrates' court, inquiring into an offence as examining justices, may amend a legal aid order so that it applies both to proceedings before the court, and in the event of the defendant being committed for trial, to his trial before the Crown Court, *i.e.* a through legal aid order. The prescribed form must be used and copies of the order must be sent to the legally assisted person, to the solicitor assigned or to counsel and to any solicitor and counsel assigned by the amended legal aid order.[25]

---

[23] *R. v. Law Society Criminal Legal Aid Committee, ex p. Magerou and Braithwaite* [1989] C.O.D. 535, D.C.
[24] Legal Aid in Criminal and Care Proceedings (General) Regulations 1989, reg. 50(4).
[25] *ibid.* reg. 40(1), Sched. 2, Form 11.

Chapter 26

CONTRIBUTION ORDERS

Introduction

The 1988 Act provides that where representation is granted to any person **26–01** whose financial resources are such as make him liable to make a contribution the competent authority must order that person to pay the contribution in respect of the costs of his being represented under the Act.[1]

Where the legally assisted person has not attained the age of 16 years the competent authority may, either instead of or in addition to ordering him to make a contribution, order an appropriate contributor to make a contribution in accordance with that person's financial resources.[2]

The way in which the contribution is to be determined is prescribed by the Legal Aid in Criminal and Care Proceedings (General) Regulations 1989, Part III.

Availability of judicial review

A legal aid contribution order, like any other order with regard to costs, **26–02** which the Crown Court might make at the conclusion of a trial on indictment is an integral part of the trial process and belongs to the court's "jurisdiction relating to trial on indictment" and is not subject to judicial review. However, the House of Lords took the view in 1987 (under the previous legislation) that there was no reason why a legal aid contribution order should not be subject to review on appropriate grounds, for example that the order was made in the face of unchallenged evidence that the defendant's disposable income and capital did not exceed the prescribed limits.

Such an order could not affect the conduct of the trial and certainly could not be regarded as an integral part of the trial process.

---

[1] Legal Aid Act 1988, s. 23(1).
[2] *ibid.* s. 23(2).

On the other hand, the decision of the Crown Court at the conclusion of the trial, whether or not to exercise its discretion to remit or order repayment of any sums due from or paid by a defendant under a legal aid contribution order, was an integral part of the trial process and on that ground excluded from judicial review.[3]

Provision of Information

26–03 The court or the proper officer may at any time after the submission of the statement of means require the applicant, the legally assisted person or the appropriate contributor to provide evidence of any information given in a statement of means, or of any change in his financial circumstances, together with such additional information as they may require.[4] Where the person so required fails to provide the evidence or information, his disposable income and capital will be deemed to exceed the limits below which no contribution is payable and the contribution payable by him will be such amount as the court or the proper officer of the court may decide.[5]

Interpretation

26–04 "Applicant" means the person making the application for legal aid or, in relation to an application on behalf of a person who has not attained the age of 17 years by his parent or guardian, that person.[6] Where an applicant attains the age of 16 years after the date on which the application is made but before the legal aid order is made the applicant is treated as not having attained the age of 16.[7]

An "appropriate contributor" in relation to a person who has not attained the age of 16 years means: that person's father (or any person who has been adjudged to be the father) or mother; or that person's guardian.[8]

"Contribution" means the contribution payable in respect of the costs of representation.[9]

"Person concerned" means the person whose disposable income and disposable capital are to be determined or the person whose resources are to be treated as the resources of any other person under the regulations.[10]

---

[3] *Re Sampson* [1987] 1 W.L.R. 194, H.L.
[4] Legal Aid in Criminal and Care Proceedings (General) Regulations 1989, reg. 24(1).
[5] *ibid.* reg. 24(4) and Sched. 4.
[6] *ibid.* reg. 3(1).
[7] *ibid.* reg. 5.
[8] Legal Aid Act 1988, s. 23(10), 34(2)(c); Legal Aid in Criminal and Care Proceedings (General) Regulations 1989, reg. 3(1).
[9] Legal Aid in Criminal and Care Proceedings (General) Regulations 1989, reg. 3(1).
[10] *ibid.* reg. 3(1).

"Disability living allowance" means an allowance under the Social Security Contributions and Benefits Act 1992.[11]

"Disability working allowance" means an allowance under the Social Security Contributions and Benefits Act 1992.[12]

"Period of computation" means the period of three months next ensuing from the date of the application for a legal aid order.[13]

"Person concerned" means the person whose disposable income and disposable capital are to be determined or the person whose resources are to be treated as the resources of any other person under the Regulations.[14]

DETERMINATION OF CONTRIBUTION

Generally

When making a legal aid order the court or the proper officer is required **26–05** to determine the amount of any contribution payable.[15] Where the applicant or the legally assisted person has paid or is liable to pay a contribution in respect of advice and assistance given in relation to the same proceedings (under section 9(6) of the Legal Aid Act 1988 any contribution which he or an appropriate contributor is liable to make in respect of the cost of representation will be reduced by the total amount of any contribution paid or payable in respect of the advice or assistance.[16]

Determination of disposable income and disposable capital

In computing the disposable income and the disposable capital of the **26–06** person concerned, the financial resources of any spouse are treated as that person's resources. Those provisions apply to a man and a woman living with each other in the same household as husband and wife. Such resources are not taken into account where:

    (a) the person concerned and his spouse are living separate and apart; or

    (b) the spouse has a contrary interest in the proceedings in respect of which an application for legal aid has been made; or

---

[11] Legal Aid in Criminal and Care Proceedings (General) (Amendment) Regulations 1992, reg. 3.
[12] *ibid.* reg. 3.
[13] *ibid.* 1993, reg. 4.
[14] Legal Aid in Criminal and Care Proceedings (General) Regulations 1989, reg. 3(1).
[15] *ibid.* reg. s. 25(1), and 26.
[16] *ibid.* reg. 25(2).

(c) in all the circumstances of the case it would be inequitable to do so.

Where a spouse fails to provide information as to financial resources in response to the request of the proper officer, it is open to the proper officer to make an estimate of the likely resources of the spouse on the basis of any information which is available.

Where it appears to the proper officer that the person concerned has, with intent to reduce the amount of his disposable income or disposable capital, whether for the purpose of reducing his liability to pay a contribution towards legal aid or otherwise directly or indirectly deprived himself of any resources; or converted any part of his resources so that they might be disregarded or left out of account in determining his resources, those resources will be treated as part of his resources for the purpose of the determination.[17]

Disposable income

26–07 The income which the person concerned receives during the period of three months from the date of the application for a legal aid order (the period of computation) is taken to be his income for the purposes of determination. The income received during the period of computation may be estimated on the basis of the income received by the person concerned during the three months prior to the commencement of the period of computation.[18] Where a person concerned is in receipt of profits from any trade, business or gainful occupation, other than employment at a wage or salary, the profit which accrues during the period of computation is taken to be his income for the purpose of determination.[19]

Income disregarded

26–08 In computing disposable income the following payments made under the Social Security Contributions and Benefits Act will be disregarded:
　　(a) disability living allowance;
　　(b) attendance allowance;
　　(c) constant attendance allowance paid under section 104 as an increase to a disablement pension;
　　(d) housing benefit;
　　(e) any payments made out of the social fund.[20]

---

[17] *ibid.* Sched. 3, paras, 1,2 and 3 as amended by Legal Aid in Criminal and Care Proceedings (General) (Amendment) Regulations 1990, reg. 3(1)(a).
[18] Legal Aid in Criminal and Care proceedings (General) Regulations 1989, Sched. 3, para.4.
[19] *ibid.* Sched. 3, para. 5.
[20] *ibid.* Sched. 3, para. 6.

Income deducted in computing disposable income

The following will be deducted when computing disposable income: **26–09**
  (a) the total amount of any tax payable on that income;
  (b) the total amount of any contributions payable under the Social Security Contributions and Benefits Act 1992;
  (c) reasonable expenses of travelling to and from the place of employment;
  (d) the amount of any contribution paid, whether under a legal obligation or not to an occupational pension scheme within the meaning of the Social Security Pensions Act 1975 or to a personal pension scheme within the meaning of the Social Security Act 1986; and
  (e) reasonable expenses in respect of making a reasonable provision for the care of any dependent child living with the person concerned because of that person's absence from home by reason of employment.[21]

In computing the income of the person concerned there will be deducted any sums payable (net of council tax benefit) by the person concerned in respect of the council tax to which he is liable.[22]

Housing expenses

In computing disposable income, deduction may be made in respect of, the   **26–10**
main or only dwelling in the case of a householder, or the amount of the net rent payable or such part of it as is reasonable in the circumstances.[23]

"Rent" includes the annual rent payable and the sum in respect of yearly outgoings including in particular any domestic rates and water and sewerage charges, a reasonable allowance towards any necessary expenditure on repairs and insurance and any annual instalment (whether of interest or of capital) payable in respect of a mortgage debt or heritable security charged on the house in which the householder resides or has an interest. In calculating the amount of rent payable any housing benefit paid under the Social Security Contributions and Benefits Act 1992 is deducted from the amount of rent payable.

"Net rent" means the rent less any proceeds of sub-letting any part of the premises in respect of which the rent is paid or the outgoings are incurred. Where any person is accommodated otherwise than as a sub-tenant the rent may be deemed to be reduced by an amount reasonably attributable to that other person, *i.e.* there will be a reduction of a notional

---

[21] *ibid.* Sched. 3, para. 7.
[22] *ibid.* Sched. 3, para. 7A
[23] *ibid.* Sched. 3, para. 8(1).

rent. Where the person whose income is being determined is not a householder, a deduction will be made in respect of the cost of his living accommodation of such an amount as is reasonable in the circumstances.[24]

Maintenance, fines and other deductions

26–11 The proper officer will make a deduction, when computing disposable income, in respect of the maintenance of the spouse of the person concerned, where they are living together, and in respect of the maintenance of any dependent child, and of any dependent relative of the person concerned, where such persons are members of the household. Specific rates of reduction are prescribed:

1. In the case of a spouse at the rate equivalent to the difference between the income support allowance for a couple where both members are aged not less than 18 (which is specified in column 2 of paragraph 1 (3) (c) of Schedule 2 Part I of the Income Support (General) Regulations 1987), and the allowance for a single person aged not less than 25 (which is specified in column 2, paragraph 1 (1) (e) of Schedule 2, Part I, of those Regulations);

2. In the case of a dependent child or a dependent relative at a rate equivalent to the amount specified for the time being in paragraph 2, Part I of Schedule 2 to the Income Support (General) Regulations 1987 appropriate to the age of the child or relative.

The proper officer is empowered to reduce those rates by taking into account the income and other resources of the dependent child or other dependent, to such extent as appears to be just and equitable. In ascertaining whether a child is a dependent child or whether a person is a dependent relative, regard is to be had to their income and other resources.[25]

Where the person whose income is being determined is making, and "throughout such period as the proper officer may consider to be adequate" has regularly made, bona fide payments for the maintenance of a spouse who is living apart; a former spouse; a child; or a relative; who is not a member of the household, there will be a deduction at the rate of those payments or at such rate as is in all the circumstances reasonable but not exceeding those payments.[26]

A deduction may be made in respect of any sum or sums payable by the person concerned, under an order made by or arising from any conviction before the High Court, the Crown Court, a county court or a magistrates court in any proceedings, other than those in respect of which the legal aid order was made.[27]

---

[24] *ibid.* Sched. 3, paras. 8(2) 8(3) and 9 as amended by Legal Aid in Criminal and Care proceedings (General) (A) R 1990, reg. 3(1)(c) and (d).
[25] *ibid.* Sched. 3, para. 10.
[26] *ibid.* Sched. 3, para. 11
[27] *ibid.* Sched. 3, para. 12

The proper officer may make an allowance, of such amount as he considers reasonable in the circumstances, where the person concerned is required to or might reasonably, provide for any other matter.

In computing income from any source the proper officer may disregard such amount as is considered reasonable having regard to the nature of the income or to any other circumstances of the case.[28]

Disposable capital

The capital of the person concerned includes the amount or value of every **26–12** resource of a capital nature belonging to him on the date of the assessment. In so far as capital does not consist of money its amount or value is taken to be its open market value, or if there is only a restricted market, the amount which it would realise after deduction of any expenses incurred in sale, or if such an amount cannot be ascertained an amount which appears to the proper officer to be reasonable.[29]

Capital to be disregarded

In computing disposable capital the following are disregarded: **26–13**
- (a) any savings of mobility allowance paid under the Social Security Act 1975 or disability living allowance which the person concerned intends to use in connection with mobility or his disability;
- (b) for a period not exceeding twelve months from the date of receipt, any arrears of-
  - (i) attendance or mobility allowance paid under the Social Security Acts 1975–1988 or disability living allowance;
  - (ii) income support, family credit or disability working allowance; and
- (c) any payments paid out of the social fund under section 32 of the Social Security Contributions and Benefits Act 1992.[30]

Other funds left out of account

No sum will be included in the amount of disposable capital in respect of **26–14** the value of the assets of any business, owned in whole or in part by the person concerned, unless it is reasonable in the circumstances to do so.

No sum will be included in the amount of capital in respect of:

---

[28] *ibid.* Sched. 3, paras. 13, 14.
[29] *ibid.* Sched. 3, para. 15.
[30] *ibid.* Sched. 3, para. 16.

(a) household furniture and effects of the main or only residence occupied by the person concerned;

(b) articles of personal clothing; and

(c) tools and equipment of his trade;

except in exceptional circumstances.[31]

Main or only residence

26–15 The value of any interest in the main or only residence in which the person concerned resides is wholly disregarded in computing disposable capital. There may also be disregarded such amount of capital that as the proper officer decides to disregard, taking into account the nature of the capital or any other circumstances of the case.[32]

Contribution Orders

26–16 Once the court or the proper officer has made a determination of the financial circumstances the applicant or the appropriate contributor will be required to pay a contribution in accordance with the scale set out in the Regulations.[33] The court or the proper officer will make a contribution order and will endorse the legal aid order accordingly. A copy of the contribution order is sent to the person ordered to make the contribution, to the legally assisted person's solicitor or counsel and to the collecting court.[34]

PAYMENT OF CONTRIBUTIONS

Generally

26–17 Payments out of income will be paid weekly, fortnightly or monthly at the discretion of the court or the proper officer of the court for the period during which a legal aid order is in force (*i.e.* the period from the grant of the legal aid order to (a) the conclusion of the proceedings, or (b) the date of withdrawal or revocation of the order.[35] The first instalment will fall due seven days from the making of the legal aid order or the contribution order whichever is the later.[36]

---

[31] *ibid.* Sched. 3, paras. 17, 18.
[32] *ibid.* Sched. 3, paras. 19, 20.
[33] *ibid.* reg. 26(4) and Sched. 4.
[34] *ibid.* reg. 27(1) and (2) and Sched. 2, Form 6.
[35] Legal Aid in Criminal and Care Proceedings (General) (Amendment) Regulations 1993 reg. 6.
[36] Legal Aid in Criminal and Care Proceedings (General) Regulations 1989, reg. 29(1).

Contributions out of capital must be paid immediately if the sum is readily available, or at such time as the court of the proper officer of the court considers reasonable in all the circumstances. Where a contribution out of capital is to be paid immediately, the legal aid order will not take effect until payment has been made and the court or the proper officer must give notice of this fact in the prescribed form to the applicant and the appropriate contributor and the solicitor assigned or counsel.[37]

It is open to the competent authority granting representation when making a contribution order to direct that the grant shall not take effect until the contribution is paid.[38]

Method of payment of contributions

Where a legal aid order is not to take effect until a contribution out of **26–18** capital has been paid, that payment must be made to the court making the legal aid order, unless that court directs otherwise. In all other cases payment of contributions is made to the proper officer of the "collecting court."[39]

"Collecting court", in relation to a contribution order is the magistrates' court specified in the order and the court so specified must be:

(a) in a case where the court making the order is itself a magistrates' court that court;

(b) in a case where the order is made on an appeal from a magistrates' court or in respect of a person who was committed (whether for trial or otherwise by a magistrates' court) to the Crown Court the court from which the appeal is brought or as the case may be which committed him; and

(c) in any other case a magistrates' court nominated by the court making the order.[40]

Change in financial circumstances

If there is any change in the financial circumstances of the legally assisted **26–19** person or the appropriate contributor which has occurred since the submission of the statement of means the proper officer or the court should be informed if there is reason to believe that the change might make the person liable to pay a contribution where such a contribution is not already

---

[37] *ibid.* reg. 29(2) and (3) and Sched. 29(2) 2, Form 7.
[38] Legal Aid Act 1988, s. 24(1).
[39] Legal Aid in Criminal and Care Proceedings (General) Regulations 1989, reg. 30(1) and (2).
[40] Legal Aid Act 1988, Sched. 3, para. 1.

payable; or might affect the terms of any contribution order made in connection with the legal aid order.[41]

Determination where no contribution previously payable

26–20 Where further information has become available as to the amount of disposable income and disposable capital available *at the time when the legal aid order was made*; or the circumstances upon which the disposable income or disposable capital were determined at the time the legal aid order was made have altered during the period in which the legal aid order was in force; the court or the proper officer must determine the amount of the contribution payable by a legally assisted person or appropriate contributor who is not already liable to make a contribution; provided that it appears likely that if such a determination were to be made a contribution would be payable.[42]

Redetermination of contributions

26–21 Similarly a contribution must be redetermined in the above circumstances where the disposable income of the person concerned may have increased by an amount greater than £750 a year or decreased by an amount greater than £300 a year; or his disposable capital may have increased by an amount greater than £750 a year. If it appears unlikely that any significant change in liability would result there is no need for the proper officer to carry out a redetermination, otherwise he is empowered to vary or revoke the contribution order accordingly.[43]

The effect of error or mistake

26–22 Where there has been some error or mistake in the determination of the disposable income, the disposable capital or contribution and it appears to the court or the proper officer that it would be just or equitable to correct the error or mistake the contribution order may be varied accordingly, revoked, or a contribution order may be made.[44]

---

[41] Legal Aid in Criminal and Care Proceedings (General) Regulations 1989, reg. 31.
[42] *ibid.* reg. 32.
[43] *ibid.* reg. 33.
[44] *ibid.* reg. 34.

VARIATION AND REVOCATION OF CONTRIBUTION ORDERS

Generally

In certain circumstances the court may vary or revoke a contribution order. **26–23**
The order varying or revoking the contribution order must be in the
prescribed form and a copy of it must be sent to the person ordered to make
the contribution; to the legally assisted person's solicitor or counsel; and to
the proper officer of the collecting court.[45]
Where a contribution order is revoked or varied to an amount which is
less than that which has already been paid, the court or the proper officer
will order the repayment of any sum overpaid.[46]

Proceedings concluded

At the conclusion of the proceedings, the court in which those proceedings **26–24**
are "concluded" may if it thinks fit:
(a) remit any sum due under a contribution order which falls to be
paid after the conclusion of the proceedings; or
(b) remit or order the repayment of any sum due or paid under a
contribution order where the legally assisted person has been
acquitted.[47]
Where the legal aid order in connection with which a contribution order
was made is revoked the proceedings are treated as having been
concluded.[48]

Appeals

Where a legally assisted person successfully appeals against his conviction; **26–25**
or is respondent to an appeal which is unsuccessful, the court hearing the
appeal may remit or order the repayment of any sum due or paid under a
contribution order.[49]

Extension of period of computation

Where a contribution order is varied to an amount greater than that which **26–26**
was previously payable; or a contribution order is made after a

---

[45] *ibid.* reg. 35(6) and Sched. 2, Form 8.
[46] *ibid.* reg. 35(4).
[47] *ibid.* reg. 35(1).
[48] *ibid.* reg. 35(2).
[49] *ibid.* reg. 35(3).

determination where no contribution was previously payable, payment is made in the normal way, save that where payment is to be made out of disposable income, the court or the proper officer may extend the period within which the payment is to be made, beyond the conclusion of the proceedings.[50]

Failure to pay contribution

26–27 Where a legally assisted person fails to pay any relevant contribution when it is due, the court in which the proceedings are being heard, may revoke the grant. The court may not exercise the power of revocation unless after affording the legally assisted person an opportunity of making representation it is satisfied:

(a) that he was able to pay the relevant contribution when it was due: and

(b) that he is able to pay the whole or part of it but has failed or refused to do so.

In this connection "the relevant contribution" means any sum which the legally assisted person is required to pay under a contribution order which falls due after the making of the order and before the conclusion of the proceedings.[51]

Where a legally assisted person fails to pay a relevant contribution, the court or the proper officer may serve notice on the legally assisted person requiring him to comply with the contribution order and pay any sums due within seven days of receipt of the notice; and if he does not do so, serve notice on him inviting him to make representations as to why he cannot comply with the contribution order. Notices and the prescribed forms must be sent to the legally assisted person and to his solicitor or counsel.[52]

The court must consider any representations made by the legally assisted person and if satisfied that he was able to pay the relevant contribution when it was due; and is able to pay the whole or part of it but has failed or refused to do so, may revoke the grant of representation.[53] Where a legal aid order, in connection with which a contribution order was made, is revoked the court may if it thinks fit remit any sum due after the date of revocation or remit or order the repayment of, any sum due or paid under a contribution order where the legally assisted person is acquitted.[54] The revocation of a legal aid order does not necessarily mean that the

---

[50] *ibid.* reg. 35(5).
[51] Legal Aid Act 1988, s. 24(2), (3) and (4).
[52] Legal Aid in Criminal and Care Proceedings (General) Regulations 1989, reg. 36(1) and (2) and Sched. 2, Forms 9 and 10.
[53] *ibid.* reg. 36(3).
[54] *ibid.* reg. 35(2).

contribution is remitted. Revocation of the legal aid order and the contribution order are two separate matters.

The revocation of the grant of representation does not affect the right of any legal representative previously assigned to the legally assisted person to remuneration for work done before the date of the revocation.[55]

Termination of period of computation

If the legally assisted person, the appropriate contributor or the spouse of either of them (including a man and a woman living with each other in the same household as husband and wife) begins to receive income-related benefits the liability to pay any further contributions ends on the date the receipt of benefits commenced. The legally assisted person or appropriate contributor are under a duty to inform the collecting court of the date on which receipt of benefits commenced.[56] **26–28**

Where the court remits any sum due under a contribution order which falls to be paid after the conclusion of the relevant proceedings; or the legally assisted person is sentenced to an immediate term of imprisonment or a sentence of detention in a young offender institution,the liability to pay any further contributions ends on the date of that remission or sentence. The court in such a case must inform the collecting court that the liability to make further contributions ended on the date of the remission or sentence.[57]

Disposal of sums received from legally assisted persons after conviction

Where a legally assisted person who is ordered to pay any sum adjudged to be paid on conviction or an appropriate contributor who is ordered to pay a fine, compensation or costs under the provisions of section 55 of the Children and Young Persons Act 1933 or section 3 of the Children and Young Persons Act 1969 has been ordered to make a contribution,any amounts falling due after the conclusion of the proceedings and any extension of the period which has been given under regulation 35(5), will be applied first in accordance with the provisions of section 139 of the Magistrates' Courts Act 1980 (which deals with the disposal of sums adjudged to be paid on conviction). Any sum paid in addition to a sum adjudged to be paid on conviction will be paid to the Lord Chancellor.[58] **26–29**

---

[55] *ibid.* reg. 36(4).
[56] *ibid.* reg. 37(1)(a) (3) and (4).
[57] *ibid.* reg. 37(1)(b) and (c) and (2).
[58] *ibid.* reg. 38(1) and (2); Legal Aid Act 1988, Sched. 3, para. 4(2).

REPAYMENT OF CONTRIBUTIONS AND RECOVERY

Contributions

26–30   Where a contribution has been made in respect of the costs of representation and an order for costs is made in favour of that person and where sums due under the order for costs are paid to the Legal Aid Board or Lord Chancellor:

   (a) if the costs of the representation do not exceed the sums paid the contribution will be repaid;

   (b) if the costs of the representation do exceed the sums so paid the provisions set out below will apply as if the costs of the representation were equal to the excess.[59]

Once the costs payable to solicitors and counsel have been determined, the appropriate authority must notify the collecting court of the amount determined in each case in which a contribution order has been made.[60]

If the total contribution made in respect of the costs exceeds the costs of representation the excess will be repaid:

   (a) where the contribution was made by one person, only to him;

   (b) where the contribution was made by two or more persons, to them in proportion to the amount contributed by them.[61]

On receiving notification of the amount of the costs of representation as amended determined under the Legal Aid in Criminal and Care Proceedings (Costs) Regulations 1989 the collecting court must repay to the legally assisted person or the appropriate contributor the amount if any by which any contribution paid exceeds the costs.[62]

COSTS IN FAVOUR OF THE ASSISTED PERSON

26–31   When a contribution order has been made, then where sums due under the order for costs are paid to the Legal Aid Board or to the Lord Chancellor in accordance with directions given by him, if the costs of the representation do not exceed the sums so paid, the contribution will be repaid. If the costs of representation do exceed the sums so paid the balance of the costs of representation are taken into account when considering whether all or part of the contribution should be repaid.[63]

If the legal representative acting for the assisted person is the same one

---

[59] Legal Aid Act 1988, s. 23(8).
[60] Legal Aid in Criminal and Care Proceedings (General) Regulations 1989, reg. 11.
[61] Legal Aid Act 1988, s. 23(7).
[62] Legal Aid in Criminal and Care Proceedings (General) Regulations 1989, reg. 39.
[63] Legal Aid Act 1988, s. 23(7) and (8).

who gave advice or assistance, any charge or fee in respect of the advice or assistance is treated as if it were part of the costs of the representation.[64]

Where one party to any proceedings is a legally assisted person then for the purposes of sections 16 and 17 of the Prosecution of Offences Act 1985 (defendants' costs orders and orders in respect of prosecution costs) the assisted person's costs are taken not to include either the expense incurred on his behalf by the Legal Aid Board or the Lord Chancellor or, if he is liable to make a contribution, any sum paid or payable by way of contribution.

For the purpose of sections 18 and 19 of the Prosecution of Offences Act 1985 (awards of costs against the accused and costs wasted as a result of an unnecessary or improper act or omission) the assisted person's costs are taken to include the expenses incurred on his behalf by the Legal Aid Board or the Lord Chancellor (without any deduction on account of any contribution paid or payable) but if he is liable to make such a contribution his costs are taken not to include any sum paid or payable by way of contribution.[65]

The effect of these provisions is such that legal aid costs are only recovered under orders made under sections 18 and 19 and not under orders made under sections 16 and 17. The most common order for costs against someone other than the accused will be a defendants' costs order under section 16 but in making any order the court will take into account the existence of the legal aid order. Even if a defendants' costs order under section 16 is made it will cover only the defendant's expenses and a claim for costs out of the Legal Aid Fund will be made to the area office in the usual way.

ENFORCEMENT OF CONTRIBUTION ORDERS

Any sum required to be paid by a contribution order is recoverable as if it **26–32** had been adjudged to be paid by an order of the collecting court subject to the provisions described later.[66] Without prejudice to that right a contribution order is also enforceable by the High Court or a county court as if the sum were due to the clerk of the collecting court in pursuance of a judgement or order of one of those courts.[67] The clerk of the collecting court may not take proceedings in the High Court or county court unless authorised to do so by the court.[68]

"Collecting court", in relation to enforcement of contribution orders is

---

[64] *ibid.* s. 23(9) and 26(2).
[65] Prosecution of Offences Act 1985, s. 21(4A)(b).
[66] Legal Aid Act 1988, Sched. 3, para. 2.
[67] *ibid.* Sched. 3, para. 3.
[68] *ibid.* Sched. 3, para. 3(2).

the magistrates' court specified in the order and the court so specified must be:

    (a) in a case where the court making the order is itself a magistrates' court, that court:

    (b) in a case where the order is made on an appeal from a magistrates' court or in respect of a person who was committed (whether for trial or otherwise by a magistrates' court) to the Crown Court, the court from which the appeal is brought or as the case may be which committed him; and

    (c) in any other case a magistrates' court nominated by the court making the order.[69]

The Act does not authorise the enforcement of a sum due under a contribution order by issue of a writ of *fieri facias* or other process against goods or by imprisonment or attachment of earnings; or the enforcement by a county court of payment of any sum exceeding the amount which for the time being is the county court *limit* (for the purposes of section 15 of the County Courts Act 1984).[70]

Any costs awarded under section 64 of the Magistrates' Courts Act 1980 (which deals with the power to award costs and the enforcement of costs), on the hearing of a complaint for the enforcement of a contribution order are enforceable as a sum required to be paid by that order[71] (*i.e.* as a civil debt).

The collecting court may exercise in relation to a contribution order the power to dispense with immediate payment conferred by section 75 of the Magistrates' Courts Act 1980. Any provisions made by the authority which made the contribution order as to time for payment or payment by instalments is treated as having been made by the collecting court[72].

Sections 17 (not more than one committal for same arrears) and section 18 (power to review committal) of the Maintenance Orders Act 1958 apply as if a contribution order were a maintenance order[73].

The following provisions of the Magistrates Courts Act 1980 apply as if the contribution order were enforceable as an affiliation order:

    (a) section 80 application of money found on defaulter to satisfy sum adjudged;

    (b) section 93 complaint for arrears;

    (c) section 94 effect of committal on arrears (*i.e.,* no arrears while in custody); and

    (d) section 95 power to remit arrears.[74]

---

[69] *ibid.* Sched. 3, para. 1.
[70] *ibid.* Sched. 3, para. 3(3).
[71] *ibid.* Sched. 3, para. 2(5).
[72] *ibid.* Sched. 3, para. 3(3).
[73] *ibid.* Sched. 3 para. 3(2): Maintenance Orders Act 1958, ss.17, 18.
[74] *ibid.* Sched. 3 para. 2(4).

Transfer of enforcement proceedings to different court

Where the person who is the subject of a contribution order is residing in **26–33** an area other than that for which the collecting court acts the court may make a "transfer order" with respect to the contribution order specifying the other petty sessions area.

Where such an order is made payment becomes enforceable in the area specified in the transfer order and as from the date of the transfer order a magistrates' court[75].

Limitations on enforcement by proceedings

No sum due under a contribution order is recoverable nor is any payment **26–34** enforceable until the conclusion of the proceedings for the purpose of which the grant of representation was made; or if earlier the revocation or withdrawal of the grant[76].

Where the person liable to make payment under a contribution order is a member of Her Majesty's Armed Forces and the Secretary of State notifies the collecting court that any sum payable will be recovered by deduction from that person's pay, the collecting court may not enforce payment unless and until the Secretary of State notifies it that the person is no longer a member of the forces and that the sum has not been fully recovered[77].

Power to defer enforcement proceedings

The collecting court may defer recovering any sum due under a **26–35** contribution order if any appeal is pending in respect of the proceedings, for the purpose of which the grant of representation was made, or the person granted representation has been ordered to be retried[78].

---

[75] Legal Aid Act 1988, Sched. 3 para. 5
[76] *ibid.* Sched. 3, para. 6, 10.
[77] *ibid.* Sched. 3, para. 7, 11.
[78] *ibid.* Sched. 3, para. 8.

Chapter 27

THE CONDUCT OF THE ASSISTED PERSON'S CASE

THE NATURE OF REPRESENTATION

Introduction

27–01   The fact that a person receives advice, assistance or representation, is not to affect the rights or liabilities of other parties to the proceedings, or the principles on which the discretion of any court or tribunal is normally exercised.[1]

Where an order is made under sections 18 or 19 of the Prosecution of Offences Act 1985 (award of costs against the accused, or orders in respect of costs thrown away), the assisted person's costs are taken to include the expenses incurred on his behalf by the Board or the Lord Chancellor (without any deduction on account of any contribution paid or payable), but if he is liable to make a contribution, his costs are taken not to include any sum paid or payable by way of contribution.[2]

The fact that the services of a legal representative are given under the 1988 Act, is not to affect the relationship between or the rights of a *legal representative* and client, or any privilege arising out of that relationship,[3] but notwithstanding the relationship between or rights of a legal representative and a client or any privilege arising out of such a relationship, the legal representative is not precluded from disclosing to any person authorised by the Board any information relating to the cases of clients or former clients who are or were legally aided.[4] A person providing advice, assistance or representation under the 1988 Act may not take any payment, except such payment as is made by the Board or authorised by the 1988 Act or any Regulations.[5–6] The LACCP(G)R89 provide that, save in certain circumstances, where a legal aid order has been made, a legal

---

[1] Legal Aid Act 1988, s. 31(1) (b).
[2] Prosecution of Offences Act 1985, s. 21(4A).
[3] Legal Aid Act, 1988, s. 31(1) (a).
[4] Legal Aid (Disclosure of Information) Regulations 1991, reg. 2.
[5–6] Legal Aid Act, 1988. s. 31(3).

representative must not receive or be a party to the making of any payment for work done in connection with the proceedings in respect of which the legal aid order was made.[7]

The revocation of a grant of advice, assistance, or representation does not affect the right of any legal representative of the legally assisted person to remuneration for work done before the date of the revocation.[8]

As a general rule, a grant of representation provides for the services of both a solicitor and counsel.[9]

The following special rules apply:

Magistrates' court

A legal aid order granting representation in respect of proceedings before a **27-02** magistrates' court does not include representation by counsel except:
  (a) in the case of an indictable offence where the court is of the opinion that, because of circumstances which make the case unusually grave or difficult, representation by both solicitor and counsel would be desirable;
  (b) legal aid order in the magistrates' court may not include representation by counsel for the purpose of that part of any proceedings relating to the giving of bail.[10]

Administrative committals

The Home Office has issued guidance (Circular No. 71/1986) to **27-03** magistrates' courts and prosecuting agencies suggesting steps whereby defence solicitors could be enabled to take fuller advantage of the opportunity given by section 6(2) of the Magistrates' Courts Act 1980 (as amended by section 61 of the Criminal Justice Act 1982) not to attend committal proceedings involving only written statements.

The Home Office circular points out that, where an accused person has a solicitor acting for him, examining justices may commit him for trial on written statements alone. The solicitor does not need to be present in court unless he or she disputes the sufficiency of the evidence disclosed in the written statements or there are other circumstances in which the defendant may need to be represented. The use of the dispensation in appropriate cases can reduce calls on defence solicitors' time and result in savings in payment from the Fund to solicitors for attending committal proceedings.

The circular emphasises that to allow the procedure to work it is essential

---

[7] Legal Aid in Criminal and Care Proceedings (General) Regulations 1989, reg. 55.
[8] Legal Aid Act 1988, s. 31(4).
[9] Legal Aid in Criminal and Care Proceedings (General) Regulations 1989, reg. 44(1).
[10] *ibid.* reg. 44(2).

for the prosecution to provide written statements in good time before the date of hearing to enable the solicitor to take instructions from the accused person on the written statements and to decide whether or not an attendance is necessary.

27–04   The Board is of the opinion that, subject to the correct procedure being followed, solicitors should be expected to exercise the option not to attend court in appropriate cases. Accordingly the Board has decided that payment will not be made out of the Fund for attendances at committal proceedings by either solicitors or counsel except in any of the following circumstances:

(a) where a submission is to be made of no case to answer or there is a need to take oral evidence from witnesses;

(b) where there is to be an application for bail or for variation of the condition of bail;

(c) where there is to be an application to lift reporting restrictions:

(d) where there is to be an application in relation to the venue of the trial;

(e) where the written statements on which the committal will be based have been served less than 14 days before the date fixed for the committal proceedings;

(f) where the solicitor has to attend to make an oral legal aid application to the magistrates' court or to make representation about the grant of legal aid for the Crown Court proceedings; or

(g) where there is any other matter requiring the solicitor's or counsel's attendance at the hearing which may be reasonable in the particular circumstances of the case.

Solicitors will be expected, when submitting bills for payment, to state precisely why attendance was necessary on each occasion.

27–05   Attached to the Home Office circular is a copy of a form of notice of non-attendance for use by defence solicitors wishing to inform the court that they will not be present at committal proceedings based on written statements alone. This form was prepared by the Home Office in consultation with the Law Society and issued to courts with the request that in cases where the defence solicitor has applied for legal aid, the clerk to the justices should enclose a copy of the form with the court's response to the legal aid application.

The Costs Appeals Committee of the Board has decided[11] that attendance at formal remand hearings should not be necessary unless the solicitor is aware that he has an application to make or oppose, or the court appearance presents a convenient and economical opportunity for the solicitor to obtain further instructions from a client who is in custody. It has been held that justices, to whom applications for the assignment of counsel used to be made, should recognise that any competent solicitor could

---

[11] See decision CRIMLA 7.

realise at an early stage of many grave or difficult cases, that no useful purpose was likely to be served by opposing a simple committal. Mere multiplicity of charges could not make representation by counsel desirable. But in a single charge, complex facts might make it desirable for counsel at least to advise whether good grounds existed for opposing a simple committal. If there were affirmative reasons, in case of some weight, for supposing that counsel might discover a basis for sensible submission of no case to answer, or a sound forensic technical reason why certain of the written statements of witnesses should not be admitted, and the witnesses should not give sworn evidence and perhaps be cross-examined, the justices might be persuaded to assign counsel at the committal stage. An unusually grave or difficult case will almost always make representation by counsel desirable at trial, but in many such cases, undesirable at committal stage.[12]

Where the magistrates' court makes a grant of representation in respect of an appeal to the Crown Court, or in respect of proceedings in which a person is committed to the Crown Court for trial or sentence, the court may, if the proceedings are those in which solicitors have a right of audience, order that representation must be by a solicitor only.[13]

Crown Court

Where the Crown Court makes a grant of representation, in respect of an appeal to that court or proceedings in which a person is committed to, or appears before it for trial or sentence, or appears or is brought before it to be dealt with, the court may in cases of urgency where it appears that there is no time to instruct a solicitor, order that representation shall be by counsel only.[14] **27–06**

Where the Crown Court grants representation for the purpose of those proceedings, it may, if the proceedings are proceedings in which solicitors have a right of audience, order that representation should be by solicitor only.[15]

Where a trial judge allowed a trial to proceed against an unrepresented defendant who wished to be represented and was in possession of a legal aid certificate for that purpose which had not been revoked, that constituted a material irregularity in the trial. It was the view of the Court of Appeal (under section 30(3) of the Legal Aid Act 1974) that, while the Crown Court had power to grant legal aid for counsel only, that was only applicable to cases of urgency where there was no time to instruct a solicitor and it was

---

[12] *R. v. Guildford Justices, ex p. Scott* [1975] Crim.L.R.286.
[13] Legal Aid in Criminal and Care Proceedings (General) Regulations 1989, reg. 44(6).
[14] *ibid.* reg. 44(5).
[15] *ibid.* reg. 44(6).

doubted if that direction would have been given if regard had been paid to the terms of the Act (the Act was in terms similar to but not identical with the Civil Legal Aid (General) Regulations 1989).[16]

Court of Appeal

27–07 Where representation is granted for the purposes of appeal to the Court of Appeal, the court may order that representation should be by counsel only.[17]

Attendance at court with counsel

27–08 Where counsel has been instructed, the instructing solicitor is under a duty to attend, or arrange for the attendance of a responsible representative, throughout the proceedings; save that attendance may be dispensed with in the magistrates' court or in certain categories of Crown Court proceedings, where the solicitor is satisfied that it is reasonable in the particular circumstances of the case that counsel be unattended and that the interests of the client and the interests of justice will not be prejudiced.[18] It should be noted that if counsel is instructed in the magistrates' court on a non-assigned basis (*i.e.* where the legal aid order does not include the assignment of counsel) costs will be assessed on the so called maximum fee basis. That is to say the solicitor's costs are estimated as if he had undertaken the case without counsel and then counsel and the solicitor are allowed reasonable costs which together do not exceed that sum.[19]

The Law Society has expressed the view that attendance on counsel should only be dispensed with in the Crown Court in the following categories of case:

(a) committals for sentence;

(b) appeals against sentence; and

(c) guilty pleas where the solicitor was so instructed at the time he prepared the brief to counsel.

27–09 It is expected that a solicitor would normally attend counsel in the Crown Court where:

(a) the client is a person at risk (such as juveniles, persons with inadequate knowledge of English, persons subject to mental illness or mental handicap or with sight, speech or hearing impediments), whether someone is a person at risk is a matter as to which the solicitor must exercise his judgment; or

---

[16] *R. v. McAllister* [1988] Crim.L.R.380.
[17] Legal Aid in Criminal and Care Proceedings (General) Regulations 1989, reg. 44(4).
[18] *The Guide to The Professional Conduct of Solicitors*, Principle 18.03.
[19] Legal Aid in Criminal and Care Proceedings (Costs) Regulations 1989, reg. 7(3).

(b) the client is of such a difficult character that it is desirable that counsel be attended; or

(c) there is a probability that the client will receive a substantial sentence of imprisonment or will receive an immediate sentence of imprisonment for the first time; or

(d) witnesses to fact or opinion (*i.e.* not character witnesses) are required to be present whether or not they are actually called; or

(e) counsel actually appearing in the case is not counsel instructed, unless the solicitor is satisfied that the change of counsel is unlikely to be prejudicial to the interests of the client; or

(f) there are any other circumstances in which the solicitor considers the attendance on counsel is reasonable.

In the above circumstances, the solicitor will be remunerated for attending court with counsel. However, where a solicitor attends on counsel in an apparently straightforward case such as a guilty plea, the attendance may be disallowed, and solicitors must therefore be in a position to justify their attendance.

In any case where a solicitor proposes that counsel should appear unattended, counsel must be so informed and a full and detailed brief must be delivered sufficiently early before the hearing to enable counsel to consider the papers and to decide whether it would be appropriate for him to attend alone. The client must be informed that counsel will be unattended and the client must also be told the name of counsel instructed. The solicitor must still attend upon counsel where counsel originally instructed or subsequently substituted, informs the solicitor that he does not believe it is appropriate for him to be unattended.

Guidelines (issued by the Criminal Law Committee of the Law Society)

Where counsel is to be unattended, briefs to counsel should, whenever possible, be delivered not less than seven days in advance of the case in order to alert counsel and the clerk. The brief should be clearly marked where solicitors propose that counsel should be unattended. The brief will need to contain more than it would if the solicitor or his representative were in attendance, as counsel will have to undertake those duties normally carried out by the solicitor or his representative when attending court. Solicitors' should insert clear instructions in the brief so that counsel is aware of precisely what duties he will have to fulfil in the absence of the solicitor or his representative. Thus, the instructions should, where appropriate: **27–10**

(a) deal with counsel's early arrival at court in order to see the client;

(b) include sufficient details about the defendant and any witnesses to enable counsel to contact them if they do not appear;

(c) require the judge's comments on sentence to be fully recorded;

(d) require notice to be provided of the headings of counsel's speech in mitigation;

(e) require a telephone report to the solicitors after the case; *and*

(f) require counsel to deal with witness expenses;

(g) require counsel to deal with the client and any relatives who may be present after the case has been concluded;

(h) require counsel to find out where the client has been taken, if in custody and pass the information to the solicitor; and

(i) require counsel to endorse on the brief within two days what oral advice on appeal has been given to the client.

Both solicitors and counsel will receive an additional standard fee where counsel is unattended in the Crown Court. In non-standard fee cases, the assessment of what additional preparation should reasonably be allowed will be subjected to *ex post facto* determination in the normal way.

Appearance by Queen's Counsel alone in legal aid cases in the Crown Court

27–11 The Code of Conduct of the Bar makes it clear that a Queen's Counsel may accept instructions to appear as an advocate without a junior.

A Queen's Counsel is entitled to assume, unless the contrary is stated, when instructions in any matter are first delivered, that a junior will also be instructed.

A Queen's Counsel may decline to appear as an advocate without a junior if he would not be able to conduct the case or other cases properly, or to fulfill his professional or semi-professional commitments unless a junior were also instructed in the case in question. Whilst the final question as to whether or not a Queen's Counsel considers it appropriate to appear alone in a case lies with him, it is recognised that the instructing solicitor has a contribution to make in reaching the decision.

The Bar Council and the Law Society in a joint statement identified examples of cases where it was considered appropriate for a Queen's Counsel only to be briefed, namely:

(a) pleas of guilty in cases worthy of Queen's Counsel representation where the plea is certain in advance of the hearing;

(b) appeals to the Court of Appeal (Criminal Division), in cases worthy of Queen's Counsel representation which can properly be undertaken by Queen's Counsel alone; and

(c) cases of basic simplicity which have some sensitive overlay whether political, local or other.

The joint statement of the Bar Council and the Law Society acknowledges that the problem involved in encouraging the briefing of Queen's Counsel alone, is that in most cases, junior counsel will already have been instructed in the case at an early stage and may have met the lay client and gained his confidence and inspired his loyalty. Early identification of the "silk only" cases and the early grant of the appropriate legal aid order is essential.

REPRESENTATION OR ADVICE GIVEN BEFORE LEGAL AID ORDER MADE

Where representation or advice is given to a person in the magistrates' court **27–12** and a grant of representation is subsequently made, the representation or advice is deemed to be given under the order if:

(a) the interests of justice required that the representation or advice be provided as a matter of urgency;

(b) there was no undue delay in making an application for legal aid; and

(c) the representation or advice was given by the solicitor who was subsequently assigned under the legal aid order.[20]

The work carried out in connection with proceedings in a magistrates' court is not work done under a legal aid order if it is done before the order is made, unless and to the extent that the deeming provision is applied under regulation 44(7) of the Legal Aid in Criminal and Care Proceedings (General) Regulations 1989.[21]

Where a solicitor submits a claim for costs, and claims to be entitled to be paid for representation or advice given before the grant of representation was made, he must give full particulars in support of his claim.[22] The appropriate authority is required to consider the claim and to allow such work as appears to it to have been reasonably done including any representation or advice which is deemed to be work done under the legal aid order.[23]

---

[20] Legal Aid in Criminal and Care Proceedings (General) Regulations 1989, reg. 44(7).
[21] *R. v. Newham Justices, ex p. Mumtaz* [1990] Crim.L.R. 589.
[22] Legal Aid in Criminal and Care Proceedings (Costs) Regulations 1989, reg. 5(4)(a).
[23] *ibid.* reg. 6(2)(a).

ASSIGNMENT AND SELECTION OF LEGAL REPRESENTATIVES

Generally

27–13 A person entitled to receive advice, or assistance, or representation may select a legal representative to advise or assist him from among those willing to provide advice or assistance.[24] A person who is granted representation entitling him to the services of a legal representative may select any legal representative who is willing to act, and that representative will be assigned to him. Where a legal aid order provides the services for solicitor and counsel, the solicitor may instruct any counsel who is willing to act.[25] A legal representative may also select as his agent any other representative who is not for the time being excluded from selection.[26]

Where a solicitor is selected to act for a legally assisted person, that solicitor should, before accepting instructions, consider whether any disbursements likely to be incurred will be abnormally large by reason of the distance of the court or the assisted person's residence, or both, from the solicitor's office — since reimbursement of the expenses so incurred may be limited to what would otherwise, having regard to all the circumstances, be a reasonable amount (*i.e.* as if a more local solicitor had been instructed[27]).

When considering assignment under a legal aid order the proper officer should, where considered appropriate, bring to the attention of a solicitor whose practice is some distance from the legally assisted person and/or the court that the full costs may not be recoverable. However, if the solicitor is still prepared to act for the legally assisted person he should be so assigned.[28]

Counsel

27–14 Where a legal aid order granting representation for the purposes of proceedings in the Crown Court is made or amended so as to provide for counsel only, counsel will be assigned by the court, or its proper officer.[29]

Assignment of one solicitor or counsel to more than one legally assisted person

27–15 A solicitor or counsel may be assigned to two or more legally assisted persons whose cases are to be heard together, unless the interests of justice

---

[24] Legal Aid Act 1988. s. 32(1).
[25] Legal Aid Criminal and Care Proceedings (General) Regulations 1989, reg. 45(1), (2).
[26] Legal Aid Act 1988, s. 32(10).
[27] Legal Aid in Criminal and Care Proceedings (Costs) Regulations 1989, reg. 7(1)(a).
[28] Lord Chancellor's Department Circular: JC(93)1, March 29, 1993.
[29] Legal Aid in Criminal and Care Proceedings (General) Regulations 1989, reg. 47(1).

require that the persons should be separately represented.[30] In multi-handed cases, consideration should be given to the possibility of assigning a solicitor to more than one defendant. Unless the proper officer is already satisfied that joint representation would not be appropriate he should seek comments from the solicitors concerned before taking any decision.[31] In the absence of a conflict of interests, the court will assign the same solicitor to all co-defendants.

It has been held that the court has power to assign a solicitor but, save as indicated, does not also have the power to assign the counsel to be instructed by that solicitor to appear in the Crown Court. It cannot by its order fetter the right of the solicitor to select counsel. It has been held that it was wrong to construe regulation 14 of the Legal Aid in Contempt Proceedings (General) Regulations 1968 (which was in the same form as regulation 49 of the Legal Aid in Criminal and Care Proceedings (General) Regulations 1989, as giving a power to assign counsel when that power was not to be found in some other Regulation; still less should it be construed as giving the court the power to make a legal aid order which required two assisted persons to be represented by the same counsel when the authority making the order has not even got the power to assign counsel at all. It follows that any court which construes regulation 49 of the LACCP(G)R 1989 as giving it the power, when making an order for representation of an assisted person in the Crown Court by solicitor and counsel, to direct that the same counsel should appear for that person as for another, is mistaken in law and any such order is *ultra vires*.[32]

The Court of Appeal and the House of Lords

In the case of proceedings in the Court of Appeal or the House of Lords, **27–16** counsel may be assigned by the court, a judge of the court or the proper officer making or amending the legal aid order.

In assigning counsel, regard is to be had, as far as is reasonably practicable, to the wishes of the legally assisted person; the identity of the solicitor or counsel, if any, who represented him in any earlier proceedings; and the nature of the appeal.[33]

Where, in the Court of Appeal, or the Courts-Martial Appeal Court, the legal aid order is granted or amended, so as to provide for representation by counsel only, counsel will be assigned by the court, a judge of the court, or the proper officer.[34]

---

[30] *ibid.* reg. 49.
[31] Lord Chancellor's Department Circular: JC (93) 1, March 29, 1993.
[32] *R. v. O'Brien and Olliffe* [1985] W.L.R. 464, *per* Hobhouse J.
[33] Legal Aid in Criminal and Care Proceedings (General) Regulations 1989, reg. 46(1), (2).
[34] *ibid.* reg. 47(2).

Contempt

27–17 Where a person is granted representation in respect of proceedings for contempt, there is no right of selection of a legal representative, and the court may assign to the legally assisted person any representative who is within the precincts of the court at the time.[35]

Acceptance of instructions

27–18 The fact that a legal representative has been selected or assigned does not prejudice the law or practice relating to the conduct of proceedings by such a representative, or the circumstances in which he may refuse or give up a case, or entrust it to another.[36] No legal representative who is for the time being excluded from legal aid work may be selected or assigned.[37]

WHEN TWO COUNSEL MAY BE ASSIGNED

27–19 Where a legal aid order provides for the services of counsel, only one counsel may be instructed. More than one counsel may be instructed in certain circumstances with leave.[38]

The magistrates' court may only make an order providing for a Queen's Counsel with a junior counsel on a charge of murder, and then only in relation to the trial in the Crown Court. There is no provision for the magistrates' court to allow any other combination of counsel[39] That is to say, there is no power to assign Queen's Counsel for the magistrates' court proceedings although it should be noted that if both solicitor and counsel are assigned (due to the unusual gravity or difficulty of the case as provided for by regulation 44(3) of the Legal Aid in Criminal and Care Proceedings (General) Regulations 1989) then an application can be made to the appropriate area committee for prior authority under regulation 54(1)(d) of those Regulations to instruct Queen's Counsel alone without junior counsel. Some magistrates' courts have purported to grant legal aid orders assigning Queen's Counsel and junior counsel for the magistrates' court proceedings in murder cases. Such an order is void as to the assignment of Queen's Counsel and the Board, which is responsible for the determination of costs

---

[35] Legal Aid Act 1988, s. 32(4), (5).
[36] *ibid.* s. 32(6).
[37] *ibid.* s. 32(9); Solicitors Act 1974, s. 47(2) (Powers of Solicitors' Disciplinary Tribunal); Administration of Justice Act 1985, s. 42 (Exclusion of Barristers from Legal Aid Work).
[38] Legal Aid in Criminal and Care Proceedings (General) Regulations 1989 reg. 48(1).
[39] *ibid.* reg. 48(4).

in such cases, would disallow any costs and disbursements relating only to the instruction of Queen's Counsel.

In the Crown Court, Court of Appeal, or the House of Lords, it is possible **27–20** to obtain an order permitting the instruction of more than one counsel in the following circumstances:

(a) on a charge of murder; or

(b) where it appears to the Court, or the person making the legal aid order that the case is one of exceptional difficulty, gravity or complexity, and that the interests of justice require that the legally assisted person should have the services of two counsel.[40]

A legal aid order, which provides for the services of one counsel may be amended to provide for the services of two counsel, or if it provides for the services of two counsel it may be amended to provide for the services of the same number of counsel, but in a different combination, *e.g.* leader and junior or two juniors.[41]

A High Court judge, or circuit judge in the Crown Court, a judge of the Court of Appeal, or the Registrar of Criminal Appeals, may make a legal aid order to provide for the services of two counsel in the following terms:

(a) a Queen's Counsel with a junior counsel;

(b) a Queen's Counsel with a noting junior counsel;

(c) two junior counsel; or

(d) a junior counsel with a noting junior counsel.

Regard may be had to the choice by the legally assisted person of any one particular counsel.[42] The judge or the registrar must consider before making the order whether the services of the Queen's Counsel alone should be provided and, if so, is required to make an order accordingly.[43]

Where it appears to a legally assisted person's solicitor necessary for the proper conduct of proceedings in a magistrates' court or in the Crown Court, and where the legal aid order provides for the services of solicitor and counsel, the solicitor may apply to the appropriate area committee for prior authority to instruct a Queen's Counsel alone without junior counsel.[44] Where such prior authority has been obtained, no question as to the propriety of instructing Queen's Counsel alone may be raised on any determination of counsel's fees, unless the solicitor knew, or ought reasonably to have known, that the purpose for which the authority was given had failed or become irrelevant or unnecessary before the fees were incurred.[45]

---

[40] *ibid.* reg. 48(2).
[41] *ibid.* reg. 48(6).
[42] *ibid.* reg. 48(3).
[43] *ibid.* reg. 48(5).
[44] *ibid.* reg. 54(1)(d).
[45] Legal Aid in Criminal and Care Proceedings (Costs) Regulations 1989, reg. 9(7).

AMENDMENT OF LEGAL AID ORDERS

Amendment or withdrawal

27–21   A court which has the power to make a legal aid order may, on application, amend such an order by substituting for any of the legal representatives assigned, any other legal representatives whom the court could have assigned at the date of amendment. The court may withdraw a legal aid order if the legal representative, or all the legal representatives assigned, withdraw from the case and the court is of the opinion that, because of the legally assisted person's conduct, it is not desirable to assign other legal representatives.[46] Where an accused's legal representatives withdraw from the case and it appears to the court to be undesirable to amend the legal aid order by the assignment of fresh legal representatives, the court should withdraw the legal aid order.[47] Where an application is made to amend the legal aid order by substituting a different solicitor, the application must clearly state the reasons why it is felt necessary to amend the order. The existing solicitors should comment and inform the court of the extent of the preparation already undertaken. If granting the application is likely to lead to a delay in bringing the case on for trial the resident judge should be consulted.[48] Where a legal aid order is amended, an order in the prescribed form[49] must be sent to the legally assisted person, the solicitor or counsel originally assigned, and to any solicitor and counsel assigned under the amendment, and, where the order is amended by an area committee, to the proper officer of the court to which the application for amendment was made.[50] Where a legal aid order is amended and new legal representatives assigned, the solicitor or counsel originally assigned must send all papers and other items in their possession relating to the proceedings to the new solicitor or counsel.[51]

TO WHOM APPLICATION FOR AMENDMENT OR WITHDRAWAL IS MADE

27–22   An application for amendment or withdrawal, or for representation by counsel in the magistrates' court, must be made to the proper officer of the

---

[46] Legal Aid in Criminal and Care Proceedings (General) Regulations 1989, reg. 50(1), (2).
[47] *R. v. Dimech* [1991] Crim.L.R. 846, CA; and see *R. v. Kirk* (1983) 76 Cr.App.R. 194.
[48] Lord Chancellor's Department Circular: JC (93) 1, March 29, 1993.
[49] Legal Aid in Criminal and Care Proceedings (General) Regulations 1989, Pt. 2, Sched. 2, Form 15.
[50] *ibid.* reg. 50(3).
[51] *ibid.* reg. 50(4).

court stating the grounds on which the application is made. There is no application form for this so the application should be made by letter setting out the grounds in full. Courts may purport to deal with such applications made orally to the court, but the court has no power on an initial application, although application may be renewed to it (see para. 27–23 below).

That officer may grant or refuse the application.[52]

RENEWAL OF APPLICATION TO THE COURT

Where an application for representation by counsel, amendment or withdrawal is refused, the applicant may renew the application both to the court, and in certain circumstances, to an area committee. The proper officer must notify the applicant of the circumstances in which an application may be renewed. Where an application is renewed to the court, the court may grant or refuse the application or refer it to the proper officer. The proper officer may grant it or refer it back (in the magistrates' court) to the court or to the justice of the peace, or refer it to a judge of the court. On renewal, the proper officer may grant or refer the application, but has no power to refuse it. The court, a judge of the court, or a justice of the peace, to whom an application is referred, may grant or refuse it.[53]

27–23

RENEWAL OF APPLICATION TO THE AREA COMMITTEE

An application may be renewed to an area committee, unless an application for the assignment of counsel or the amendment or withdrawal of the order in the same proceedings has previously been refused by an area committee or by the court. In the magistrates' court, no application may be made less than 14 days before the date fixed for the trial of an information, or the inquiry into an offence as examining justices, where the date had been fixed at the time the application was made. Since the court alone has the power to fix the date for trial or inquiry into an offence, a defendant's first appearance at court could be "the date fixed for trial". In the unlikely event of justices being in a position to deal with the case on a first appearance, it is the justices' decision to proceed which makes it "the

27–24

---

[52] *ibid.* reg. 51(1). For amendment or withdrawal, see reg. 50(1), (2). For representation by counsel in the magistrates' court, see reg. 44(3). For a definition of "proper officer" see reg. 3.
[53] *ibid.* reg. 51(2)–(5).

date fixed for trial ... or the inquiry" and not the fact that the date has been fixed for a first appearance by police or the Crown Prosecution Service.[54]

In the Crown Court, no application for renewal may be made to an area committee more than 14 days after the committal for trial or sentence, or the date of giving notice of appeal.[55] No application may be made in respect of proceedings in the Court of Appeal, the Courts-Martial Appeal Court, or the House of Lords.[56]

When an application is renewed to the area committee, the legally assisted person must send to the Area Director a copy of the legal aid order, a copy of the notice of refusal, any papers presented in support of the original applications, and any other relevant documents or information. The area committee may require the proper officer, the legally assisted person or his solicitor to supply such further particulars, information and documents as it thinks fit.[57]

The area committee will grant or refuse the application and, where necessary, amend or revoke the legal aid order. The area committee must notify the proper officer of the court, the legally assisted person and his solicitor of its decision, although there is no prescribed form for this.[58]

APPEALS

27–25 Where an advice on appeal is given in the Crown Court, and legal aid is granted or renewed by the Court of Appeal, if notice of appeal is given, or application for leave to appeal is made, determination of the costs is carried out by the registrar whether or not the appeal is later abandoned. If no notice of appeal is given or application for leave to appeal made, the costs relating to the advice on appeal are determined by a determining officer in the Crown Court.[59]

In the case of costs relating to advice or assistance as to an appeal from the magistrates' court to the Crown Court, the appropriate authority is the Board, no matter whether the appeal proceeds or not.[60]

---

[54] *R. v. Bury Justices, ex p. N* [1987] Q.B. 284; Legal Aid in Criminal and Care Proceedings (General) Regulations, reg. 51(6)(a), (b)(ii).
[55] Legal Aid in Criminal and Care Proceedings (General) Regulations 1989, reg. 56(1)b)(i).
[56] *ibid.* reg. 51(6)(c).
[57] *ibid.* reg. 52(1), (2).
[58] *ibid.* reg. 53(1), (2).
[59] Legal Aid in Criminal and Care Proceedings (Costs) Regulations 1989, reg. 3(3)(a), (b); *R. v. Gibson* [1984] 1 W.L.R. 1038.
[60] *ibid.* reg. 3(4).

Where a legal aid order is made in respect of proceedings in the Court of Appeal, the order may specify the stage of the proceedings at which legal aid is to commence. In a proper case, therefore, an order for legal aid may be made retrospectively for work already done.[61]

---

[61] Legal Aid in Criminal and Care Proceedings (General) Regulations 1989, reg. 22(6); *R. v. Kearney* [1983] 1 W.L.R. 1046.

Chapter 28

ACTS FOR WHICH AUTHORITY MUST OR MAY BE OBTAINED

Topping up where a legal aid order has been made

28–01 The legally assisted person's solicitor or counsel may not receive, or be a party to the making of, any payment for work done in connection with the proceedings save out of the Fund or by the Lord Chancellor except in certain limited circumstances.

If the solicitors have previously made an application to the appropriate area committee for authority to incur certain expenses or fees and that authority has been refused by the area commitee, the solicitor may look direct to the client for reimbursement of the expenses. The expenses or fees are limited to those incurred in:

    (a) preparing, obtaining or considering any report, opinion, or further evidence whether provided by an expert witness or otherwise; or

    (b) bespeaking transcripts of shorthand notes or tape recordings of any proceedings including police questioning of suspects.[1]

There are no circumstances in which it is permissible for counsels' fees to be topped up in criminal proceedings.

Counsel

28–02 A Magistrates' Court which is competent to do so,[2] may make a Legal Aid Order providing for the services of a Queen's Counsel with one junior Counsel, where

    (a) the proceedings are a trial for murder and the order is made upon committal or transfer for trial or

    (b) the prosecution is brought by the Serious Fraud Office and the

---

[1] Legal Aid in Criminal and Care Proceedings (General) Regulations 1989, reg. 55.
[2] *i.e.* by the virtue of s. 20(4) or (5) of the Legal Aid Act 1988.

Order is made upon receiving a notice of transfer under section 4 of the Criminal Justice Act 1987. Apart from this the Magistrates' Court has no other power to make an order in relation to Counsel.[3] The Legal Aid in Criminal and Care Proceedings (General) Regulations 1989 provide for the authority granting a legal aid order to extend Legal Aid to provide for the services of a Queen's Counsel or more than one counsel in respect the whole or any specified part of any proceedings in certain specified cases, but not otherwise.[4] On a trial in the Crown Court, or in proceedings in the Court of Appeal or the House of Lords, on a charge of murder, or where it appears to the Court making the order that the case is one of exceptional difficulty, gravity or complexity and that a legal aid order for the provision of the services of Queen's Counsel or more than one counsel is required in the interests of justice, a decision to make or amend the legal aid order may only be made by a Circuit Judge or a High Court Judge where the proceedings are in the Crown Court, or by a Judge of the Court of Appeal or the Registrar when the proceedings are in the Court of Appeal.[5] Where the prosecution is being brought by the Serious Fraud Office a decision may only be made by the Judge expected to try the case or a High Court Judge where the proceedings are in the Crown Court, or by a High Court Judge or a Judge of the Court of Appeal where the proceedings are in the Court of Appeal.[6]

The Regulations enable the Court to amend existing legal aid orders to provide representation by Counsel appropriately.[7]

Where a legal aid order is made or amended so as to provide for the services of the Queen's Counsel or more than one counsel it may be in any of the following terms:

(a) a Queen's Counsel alone;
(b) where two counsel are required —
    (i) Queen's Counsel with a Junior Counsel, or
    (ii) Queen's Counsel with a noting Junior Counsel, or
    (iii) two Junior Counsel, or
    (iv) a Junior Counsel with a noting Junior Counsel[8]

In the case of a Serious Fraud Office prosecution the Court may, if it considers three Counsel are required, provide for the services of three Counsel in any of the terms provided for above plus an extra Junior Counsel or noting Junior Counsel.[9]

---

[3] Legal Aid in Criminal and Care Proceedings (General) Regulations 1989, reg. 48(9).
[4] Legal Aid in Criminal and Care Proceedings (General) Regulations 1989, reg. 48(1).
[5] Legal Aid in Criminal and Care Proceedings (General) Regulations 1989, reg. 48(2)(a), (b) and (14)(a) see Practice Direction (Crown Court: Counsel) 16th January 1995, [1995] 1 W.L.R. 261
[6] ibid. reg. 48(2)(c), (14)(b) see Practice Direction (Crown Court: Counsel) January 16, 1995, [1995] 1 W.L.R. 261.
[7] ibid. reg. 48(10), (11).
[8] ibid. reg. 48(3).
[9] ibid. reg. 48(4).

The fact that a Queen's Counsel is assigned under the legal aid order it is not of itself a reason for making an order for two or three Counsel.[10] Where Queen's Counsel is assigned the Court may not make an order for two or three Counsel where it appears, at the time of making the order, that there is a reasonable certainty that indictment will be disposed of by a guilty plea and there are no special circumstances requiring the provision of services of more than one Counsel, or the case relates to an appeal to the Court of Appeal or to the House of Lords and the case representation can properly be undertaken by a Queen's Counsel alone.[11] The application for a Queen's Counsel or more than one Counsel must be in writing unless the Court otherwise directs and must specify the terms of the order sought and the grounds of the application and if the application is for two or three Counsel, the reason why two or three Counsel are required.[12] Before making an order for Queen's Counsel or more than one Counsel the Court may require written advice from any Counsel already assigned to the applicant on the question of what representation is needed in the proceedings.[13]

Where Queen's Counsel or more than one Counsel is assigned under a legal aid order it is the duty of each legal representative to keep under review the need for more than one Counsel to be present and in Court or otherwise providing services and to consider whether the legal aid order should be amended. Queen's Counsel is under a duty to keep under review the question whether he or she could act alone.[14] If a legal representative is of the opinion that the legal aid order should be amended the representative is under a duty to notify that opinion in writing to the other legal representatives, to the assisted person and to the Court. The Court must, after considering the opinion and any representations made by any other legal representative to the assisted person, determine whether and in what manner the Legal Aid should be amended.[15]

Acts for which authorities may be sought

28–03   In proceedings in the magistrates' court or the Crown Court, where it appears to the legally assisted person's solicitor necessary for the proper conduct of the proceedings for costs to be incurred in taking certain steps, application may be made to the appropriate area committee for prior authority. The particular steps are:

---

[10] *ibid.* reg. 48(5).
[11] Reg. 48(6).
[12] *ibid.* reg. 48(7).
[13] *ibid.* reg. 48(8).
[14] *ibid.* reg. 48(12).
[15] *ibid.* reg. 48(13).

(a) obtaining a written report or opinion of one or more experts;

(b) employing a person to provide a written report or opinion (otherwise than as an expert);

(c) bespeaking transcripts of shorthand notes or of tape recordings of any proceedings including police questioning of suspects;

(d) where a legal aid order provides for the services of solicitor and counsel, instructing a Queen's counsel alone without junior counsel; or

(e) performing an act which is either unusual in its nature or which involves unusually large expenditure.[16]

All members of the legal profession are under a duty not to involve the Fund in unnecessary expenditure.[17]

Position where authority applied for

Where the area committee authorises the taking of any specific step (save **28–04** the instruction of Queen's Counsel alone) it must also authorise the maximum fee to be paid.[18]

When the solicitor's costs come to be determined, no question as to the propriety of any step taken with prior authority may be raised on the determination unless the solicitor knew or ought reasonably to have known that the purpose for which the authority was given had failed or had become irrelevant or unnecessary before the costs were incurred.[19]

Similarly, where costs are incurred in accordance with and subject to the limit imposed by prior authority, no question may be raised as to the amount of the payment to be allowed.[20]

If a particular step is taken without authority or costs are incurred in excess of a limit authorised by the area committee, payment may nevertheless be allowed on determination of costs in a proper case.[21]

Expert witnesses

The 1988 Act provides that the costs of an assisted person do not include **28–05** any allowance to witnesses attending to give evidence in the proceedings in any case where the allowance is payable under any other enactment.

---

[16] Legal Aid and Criminal and Care Proceedings (General) Regulations 1989, reg. 54(1).

[17] *R. v. Silcott, Braithewaite and Raghip, The Times,* December 9, 1991.

[18] *ibid.* reg. 54(2).

[19] Legal Aid in Criminal and Care Proceedings (Costs) Regulations 1989, reg. 7(4).

[20] *ibid.* reg. 7(5).

[21] *ibid.* reg. 7(6).

Regulations provide that where a witness attends to give evidence the expenses properly incurred are to be allowed out of central funds unless the court directs otherwise.[22] The effect of this is that all witness expenses should be paid by the Crown Court out of central funds and should not be included in a solicitor's bill. However, in the Legal Aid in Criminal and Care Proceedings (Costs) Regulations 1989 "disbursement" means travelling and *witness expenses* and other out of pocket expenses incurred by a fee-earner in giving legal aid.[23] Previous Regulations made provision for prior authority in respect of expert witnesses attending court and tendering evidence; that provision has now been omitted. Not all Crown Courts adopt the same stand-point, some paying witness expenses out of central funds, others allowing them as a disbursement in the solicitor's bill. The Lord Chancellor's Department is aware of this discrepancy and acknowledges that there is a difficulty. It would seem that if the Crown Court insists upon paying all witnesses' expenses out of central funds they are technically correct; however, there is no review procedure in respect of those expenses and this could leave a solicitor in a difficult position and perhaps contractually liable to the expert for fees that the Crown Court is not prepared to meet. In practice, it is better from the solicitor's (and the experts') point of view if the Crown Court can be persuaded to accept it, to include the claim for expert witnesses' fees in the solicitor's bill of costs — this would then enable the normal process of re-determination and review to take place.

In any event, it is in the solicitor's best interests to inform an expert who is being instructed that the case is legally aided. If the position is not made clear to the expert the solicitor could well be contractually liable for the expert's fees.

How to apply for authority

28–06   The application for authority to the area committee is made by the solicitor, who must set out the necessity for incurring the expense and give a detailed estimate of the fees or costs involved, including the likely cost of a court attendance if authority is sought for an expert's report (this is to avoid an expert being authorised who is subsequently discovered to have a high court attendance rate which is unlikely to be met from central funds). The solicitor should also submit any other relevant information or documents (*e.g.* a statement, related prosecution reports, form CR0609 as to the assisted person's record). It is sensible either to obtain an estimate or proposed rate of charge for the proposed work, and in any event, it is important to inform the person supplying the particular service of any limit imposed upon the cost. Failure to do this could leave the solicitor

---

[22] Legal Aid Act 1988, s. 25(3); Costs in Criminal Cases (General) Regulations 1986, reg. 16(1).
[23] Legal Aid and Criminal and Care Proceedings (Costs) Regulations 1989, reg. 2(1).

contractually liable to pay the amount not covered by the legal aid authority. The application must be accompanied by the copy of the legal aid order, endorsed "Board Copy" and the authority or refusal will be endorsed on the order which will then be returned to the solicitors. The Board accepts the solicitor's copy of the order in Crown Court cases where a through order was made.

Authority may be applied for over the telephone in very urgent cases but if the solicitor has delayed in applying, his telephone application is likely to be refused. Any telephone grant will be subject to submission of a written application including the legal aid order. In any event, a solicitor wishing to apply for authority should do so at the earliest opportunity although an application at the pre-committal stage for work which should be undertaken after committal will be refused.

The regulations do not preclude more than one application for prior authority being made in respect of the same matter but any subsequent application will be refused unless it is based on a change of circumstances or additional information.

The following points will be of assistance when considering whether to apply for prior authority:

Medical reports generally

In connection with applications for prior authority in respect of medical **28–07** reports, the area committee will consider the purpose of the report, and whether it is from a professional or expert witness and whether it has been ordered by the court.

Medical reports as to intention

Applications may be made for *expert* medical reports as to the defendant's **28–08** ability to form the intent required for some specific offences, *e.g.* shoplifting. If making such an application the report may be referred to as being as to "fitness, plea and disposal" so that it can cover not only the question of intention but also assist as to sentencing in the event of a conviction.

Medical reports ordered by the court

Reports as to possible probation/hospital order or otherwise to assist as to **28–09** sentencing can be ordered by the courts pursuant to section 32(2) of the Criminal Justice Act 1967 and regulation 25 of the Costs in Criminal Cases (General) Regulations 1986. The costs of such reports are payable out of central funds and will not be authorised.

Medical reports before conviction/consideration by the court

If an application for prior authority is made in respect of a referral for **28–10** assessment/reports before conviction or before cases have been considered

545

by the sentencing court and is for the purposes of disposal/sentencing, *only* then if the defendant is pleading not guilty such application will be refused on the basis that reports are premature prior to guilt being established and the court's consideration of the possibility of a report being ordered to assist in sentencing. If the defendant is pleading guilty, the area committee will consider whether the defendant's history is such that the application should be granted bearing in mind possible alternative funding and despite the fact that the sentencing court could order a report if it considers one is necessary even though this would involve the costs of an adjournment.

Medical reports after conviction/consideration by the court

28–11 Here the area committee will want to know the view of the court as to the preparation of the report (*e.g.* did the court endorse the need for a report but decline to order it), and also to establish the position as to alternative funding of the referral/report. Reports provided by private rehabilitation centres will usually be provided with a view to the possibility of a probation order with the condition of medical treatment. Such reports go to mitigation/sentencing and not to intention. A referral/assessment might be being considered by the defendant's general practitioner, by a Social Services Department if it is involved in the case, or, the most likely, by the probation service. The probation service may apply to the Home Office for funding of a report/assessment.

Murder cases (medical and post-mortem reports)

28–12 In murder cases, although a psychiatric report will be obtained by the prosecution, the defendant's solicitor is likely to be authorised to obtain a psychiatric report in any event if fitness to plead or diminished responsibility are in issue. Prior authority for a second post-mortem report on a murder victim may also be applied for.

Accountant's fees

28–13 The area committee will wish to know whether the accountant to be used is chartered or certified and the level of fee-earner as well as the hourly rate(s) involved. If a large amount is sought, the committee will consider the possibility of a preliminary report being authorised to establish whether, and to what extent, a more detailed report is necessary.

Transcripts

28–14 Regulation 54(1)(c) of the LACCP(G)R89 refers to bespeaking transcripts of shorthand notes or of tape recordings of any proceedings, including police questioning of suspects. If the transcription is undertaken in-house such work will be an overhead of the solicitor's practice and not recoverable from the Fund. Note that regulation 54(1)(c) refers to "bespeaking transcripts" which implies the use of an outside agency. The Costs Appeals Committee has made the following *Point of Principle* decision on this topic:

Where a solicitor applies for prior authority to transcribe a tape using an outside agency and satisfies the area committee that such a transcript is necessary, then authority should normally be granted. Where a solicitor chooses to transcribe a tape in-house, the work of transcription would not normally be regarded as fee-earner's work and will not therefore be remunerated under the legal aid order.[24]

If prior authority is sought in respect of a transcription outside the solicitor's office, the area committee will need to be satisfied:

(a) that the defence solicitor has listened to the tape;

(b) that the tape contains evidence which is relevant to the defence;

(c) that there is a dispute about the content or admissibility of such evidence and that such dispute has not been resolved by discussions with the prosecution, or that there are good reasons for not entering into such discussions, or for believing that such discussions would not lead to resolution;

(d) that the evidence on the tape cannot be adduced by means other than the provision of a transcript, or that the provision of a transcript will be the most efficient means of adducing such evidence;

(e) that the defence solicitor has ascertained from the prosecution whether they will be preparing a transcript;

(f) that the transcription will be confined where practicable to the material relevant to the dispute.

Listening to tapes of police interviews

It is the Board's view (although this has not been tested in the courts), that **28–15** requests under regulation 54(1)(e) for prior authority in respect of a solicitor's time spent listening to a taped interview do not fall within the Regulations and that a fee for listening to a taped interview would need to be justified to the determining officer on assessment.

Queen's Counsel alone

Pursuant to regulation 54(1)(d), prior authority may be sought to instruct a **28–16** Queen's Counsel alone without junior counsel where a legal aid order *provides* for the services of solicitor and counsel. The order *must* so provide. The area committee will consider all the circumstances of the case and in particular its legal complexity.

---

[24] See decision CRIMLA 10.

Unusual in its nature/unusually large expenditure

28–17 Regulation 54(1)(e) refers to acts which are either unusual in their nature *or* involve unusually large expenditure. The same wording is used in regulation 61 of the Civil Legal Aid (General) Regulaions 1989 in relation to civil authorities and can refer to acts on the part of the solicitor and his own disbursements (*e.g.* travelling expenses) although "unusually large expenditure" is narrowly interpreted. The solicitor must always justify his profit costs on assessment but an authority could be granted to perform a specific act unusual in its nature. Regulation 52(2) requires a maximum fee to be authorised for the act but the area committee will only indicate the act authorised and not specify a maximum fee where the authority relates to profit costs (as opposed to disbursements). When applying under regulation 54(1)(e), the solicitor should ensure that it is made clear why it is his view that the area committee has jurisdiction.

Photocopying

28–18 Prior authority can be sought for photocopying where it involves unusually large expenditure within regulation 54(1)(e). In-house copying is an office overhead and will not be authorised. If copying is to be undertaken by an outside agency the case for this must be made out, and authority is likely to be refused for copying a second set of committal statements (a) to take instructions; and (b) to provide a set to a second counsel where two counsel are authorised in the legal aid order (unless the prosecution has been requested and declined to provide a second set).

Interpreters' fees

28–19 Authority may be requested in respect of interpreters' fees under regulation 54(1)(e). If this is because a *witness*, rather than the *defendant*, cannot understand English then the application may be dealt with but if the application is based upon the defendant's lack of English the situation depends upon whether authority is for a court hearing or to enable the solicitor to take instructions away from the court. The former fees are payable from central funds under the Prosecution of Offences Act 1985 (solicitors will be told to approach the court/prosecution to arrange for an interpreter's attendance at court).

Solicitor's travelling time/expenses

28–20 A solicitor's travelling *expenses* may fall within regulation 54(1)(e) if "unusually large expenditure" is involved but this will be strictly interpreted and any travelling *time* must in any event be justified on assessment rather than authorised.

Inquiry agents

Inquiry agent's fees may fall within regulation 5(1)(b) or 54(1)(e) (as **28–21**
unusually large expenditure) depending on the work which is to be
undertaken although the service of a witness summons will not be within
either subsection and fees incurred for taking proofs of evidence will not
be authorised.

Chapter 29

THE RIGHT OF AN ASSISTED PERSON TO COSTS

UNDER THE PROSECUTION OF OFFENCES ACT 1985

Defendant's costs order out of central funds (section 16 of the Prosecution of Offences Act 1985)

29–01   Where a defendant's costs order is made it is for the payment out of central funds to the person in whose favour the order is made, of such amount as the court considers sufficient reasonably to compensate him for any expenses properly incurred by him in the proceedings.[1] Costs out of central funds are determined under the Regulations in the normal way.[2]

There is no basis in statute, regulation or order for the payment of interest on costs awarded from central funds in a criminal cause or matter. Sections 17 and 18 of the Judgments Act 1838 do not apply to criminal proceedings.[3]

Where a defendant's cost order is made in favour of a legally assisted person, his costs are taken not to include, either the expenses incurred on his behalf by the Board or the Lord Chancellor, or if he is liable to make a contribution, any sum paid or payable by way of contribution.[4] Therefore a legally aided defendant will only be able to recover his own expenses out of central funds pursuant to a section 16 defendant's costs order.

The making of such an order is of no assistance to the Fund in that legal aid costs are claimed in the usual way and are not recoverable under the costs order.

Where there is nothing extraordinary about a case and there is no criticism of the police in the conduct of the case, justices are not justified in making an order for costs of an acquitted, legally aided defendant to be paid by the prosecution on a private client basis on the assumption that the

---

[1] Prosecution of Offences Act 1985, s. 16(6).
[2] Costs in Criminal Cases (General) Regulations 1986, regs. 4–14.
[3] *Westminster City Council v. Wingrove (Lord Chancellor Intervening)* [1991] 4 All E.R. 692, D.C.
[4] Prosecution of Offences Act 1985, s. 21(4A)(a).

legal aid scale is insufficient to cover the actual costs incurred. The appropriate order would be no order as to costs, resulting in the costs being borne by the Fund.[5]

Where an innocent legally aided party successfully intervenes in restraint proceedings under the Drug Trafficking Offences Act 1986 properly brought by the Crown Prosecution Service, his costs should be paid out of central funds.[6]

Order for prosecution costs (section 17 of the Prosecution of Offences Act 1985)

Legal aid is only available to a private prosecutor in the case of an appeal **29–02** to the Crown Court against conviction or sentence by a defendant, and the legal aid order is for the purpose of enabling a prosecutor who is not acting in an official capacity to resist the appeal.[7]

In an appropriate case, the court may make an order for the payment out of central funds of such amount as the court considers sufficient reasonably to compensate the prosecutor for any expenses properly incurred by him in the proceedings.[8] Where such an order is made the legally aided prosecutor's costs will be taken not to include either the expenses incurred on his behalf by the Lord Chancellor or if he is liable to make a contribution, any sum paid or payable by way of contribution.[9]

Inter partes (sections 18 and 19 of the Prosecution of Offences Act 1985)

Where a legal aid order has been made in respect of a private prosecutor **29–03** for the purpose of enabling that person to resist an appeal to the Crown Court against conviction or sentence, the Crown Court may, in an appropriate case, make such order as to the costs to be paid by the accused to the prosecutor as it considers just and reasonable. The Court of Appeal may make such order, as to the costs to be paid by the accused to such persons as may be named in the order, as it considers just and reasonable.[10]

Where such an order is made, the legally aided prosecutor's costs will be

---

[5] *R. v. Oxford City Justices, ex p. Chief Constable Thames Valley Police, The Times,* April 24, 1987.
[6] *Re Mason, The Times,* November 26, 1992.
[7] Legal Aid Act 1988, s. 21(1).
[8] Prosecution of Offences Act 1985, s. 17(1).
[9] *ibid.* s. 21(4A)(a).
[10] *ibid.* s. 18(1), (2).

taken to include the expenses incurred on his behalf by the Lord Chancellor (without any deduction on account of any contribution paid or payable), but if he is liable to make a contribution, his costs will be taken not to include any sum paid or payable by way of contribution.[11]

Where costs are wasted or thrown away as a result of an unnecessary or improper act or omission by one party to criminal proceedings, the court may, in an appropriate case, make an order as to the payment of those costs to another party to the proceedings.[12] The court must specify the amount to be paid in accordance with the Regulations.[13]

Such an order can be made in respect of a legally assisted defendant or in respect of a private prosecutor who has been granted representation to resist an appeal. Where such an order is made, the costs of the legally assisted person will be taken to include the expenses incurred on his behalf by the Board or by the Lord Chancellor (without any deduction on account of any contribution paid or payable) but if he is liable to make a contribution, his costs will be taken not to include any sum paid or payable by way of contribution.[14]

THE EFFECT UPON CONTRIBUTION ORDERS

29–04 Where an order for costs is made in favour of a legally assisted person who has been ordered to pay a contribution in respect of those proceedings, then where the sums due under the order for costs are paid, if the costs of the representation do not exceed the sums so paid, the contribution will be re-paid to the legally assisted person; if the costs of the representation do exceed the sums paid in respect of costs, any surplus of the total of contribution and costs recovered, over the costs of representation will be re-paid to the legally assisted person.[15–16]

Topping up

29–05 Where a legal aid order has been made, the legally assisted person's solicitor or counsel may not receive or be a party to, the making of any payment for work done in connection with the proceedings in respect of which the legal aid order was made, save in certain limited circumstances.

---

[11] *ibid.* s. 21(4A)(b).
[12] *ibid.* s. 19(1).
[13] Costs in Criminal Cases (General) Regulations 1986, reg. 3.
[14] Prosecution of Offences Act 1985, s. 21(4A)(b).
[15–16] Legal Aid Act 1988, s. 23 (8), (9).

However, the fact remains that a considerable amount of costs may be incurred by a legally assisted person outside the scope of the legal aid order. If an order for costs out of central funds or *inter partes* is made, such costs will be recoverable in full if they have been reasonably incurred.[17]

---

[17] Legal Aid in Criminal and Care Proceedings (General) Regulations 1989, reg. 55.

Chapter 30

THE LIABILITY OF AN ASSISTED PERSON FOR HIS OPPONENT'S COSTS

INTRODUCTION

30–01 There are three circumstances in which an order for costs can be made against a legally aided person in criminal proceedings, namely:

(a) the award of costs against an accused under section 18 of the Prosecution of Offences Act 1985;

(b) an order for costs made where the court is satisfied that one party to criminal proceedings has incurred costs as a result of an unnecessary or an improper act or omission by or on behalf of another party to the proceedings under section 19 of the Prosecution of Offences Act 1985; and

(c) a wasted costs order made under section 19A of the Prosecution of Offences Act 1985.

AWARD OF COSTS AGAINST OFFENDERS AND APPELLANTS

Section 18 of the Prosecution of Offences Act 1985

30–02 In an appropriate case, the court may make such order, payable to the prosecutor, as it considers just and reasonable. The amount to be paid by the offender or appellant must be specified in the order.[1] An order will normally be made where the court is satisfied that the offender or appellant has the means and the ability to pay.[2] Where the costs of the prosecution are awarded against the defendant, those costs should be confined to the

---

[1] Prosecution of Offences Act 1985, s. 18(1), (3).
[2] *Practice Direction (Criminal Law: Costs)*, Pt. VI [1989] 1 W.L.R. 625; [1989] 2 All E.R. 604.

prosecution itself and not include the costs of investigations leading to prosecution.[3]

Where one party to criminal proceedings is a legally assisted person and an order is made under section 18 of the Prosecution of Offences Act 1985 his costs are taken to include the expenses incurred on his behalf under the 1988 Act (without any deduction on account of any contribution payable); but if he is liable to make such a contribution, his costs are taken not to include any sum paid or payable by way of contribution.[4]

Introduction to the award of costs

The fact that a person is receiving advice, assistance or representation under the 1988 Act does not affect the rights or liabilities of other parties to the proceedings or the principles on which the discretion of the court is normally exercised.[5] This means that the court will approach the making of an order for costs on the principles which apply generally in all cases regardless of whether or not a party is legally aided.

30–03

Before an order for payment of prosecution costs is made against a party, the court should have evidence of ability to pay.[6] The order must not be in the nature of a penalty, nor one which will only be satisfied on the offender's release from prison after a considerable term. The court has the power to make an offender criminally bankrupt in an appropriate case.[7]

In the case of multiple defendants, the order may be joint or several but the costs should relate to those in or about the prosecution of the individual accused.[8] The court is first concerned to consider generally what were the costs of bringing the particular accused to justice (e.g. different accused may be charged with different counts or appeal against different counts, or there may be a trial within a trial with respect to one accused but not to others), and then to exercise a more general discretion.

Where the amount of costs awarded amounted to more than twice the amount of a fine, the costs were subsequently reduced on appeal to a sum equal to four-fifths of the amount of the fine.[9] The order for costs should not be in the nature of a penalty.[10]

The amount payable must be specified in the order by the court. In exercising its discretion, the court is entitled to take into account all the circumstances, including the strength of the case against the offender and

---

[3] *R. v. Maher* [1983] Q.B. 784, C.A.; *R. v. Seymour* (1988) 9 Cr.App.R. (S.) 395, C.A.
[4] Prosecution of Offences Act 1985, s. 21(4A) (b).
[5] Legal Aid Act 1988, s. 31(1)(b).
[6] *R. v. Judd* [1971] 1 W.L.R. 89; *R. v. Pottage* (1922) 17 Cr. reg. 33.
[7] *R. v. Gaston* [1971] 1 W.L.R. 85.
[8] *R. v. Symmonds* [1969] 1 Q.B. 685, C.A.
[9] *R. v. Davis* [1962] 1 All E.R. 490.
[10] *R. v. Highgate Justices, ex p. Petrou* [1954] 1 W.L.R. 485; *R. v. St. Albans Crown Court, ex p. Cinnamond* [1981] Q.B. 480; *R. v. Tottenham Justices, ex p. Joshi* [1982] 1 W.L.R. 631.

his knowledge of its strength at the time he pleaded not guilty.[11] In fixing the sum, the court must have regard to the person's means and the amount payable should not be out of step with any fine which that person is called upon to pay.[12]

Magistrates' court

30–04   A magistrates' court may make an award of costs against an accused when any person is convicted of an offence before it,[13] but where any person is convicted of an offence before a magistrates' court and the court orders payment by way of fine, penalty, forfeiture or compensation of a sum not exceeding £5, the court will not order the accused to pay any costs, unless in the particular circumstances of the case it considers it right to do so.[14] The Prosecution of Offences Act 1985 gives no indication as to what particular circumstances might warrant the award of costs but the *Practice Direction* of May 3, 1991, which applies to the Crown Court, indicates that an order should be made where the court is satisfied that the offender or appellant has the means and the ability to pay.[15] Where a person under the age of 17 is convicted of an offence before a magistrates' court, the amount of any costs ordered to be paid by the accused must not exceed the amount of any fine imposed upon him.[16]

Section 18 of the Prosecution of Offences Act 1985 applies to proceedings in the magistrates' court where certain orders are made or sentences passed, as if the offender had been tried in those proceedings for the offence for which the order was made or the sentence passed. These include: probation orders and orders for conditional discharge, community service orders, orders in respect of suspended or partially suspended sentences or for breach of suspended supervision orders and orders in respect of breach of attendance centre order.[17]

It is wrong in principle for justices to order a convicted defendant to pay prosecution costs in such a sum that, through lack of means, the defendant is unable to pay within a reasonable time such as one year. Orders for costs and fines should be kept in step and an order for costs should be within the means of the person to pay.[18]

---

[11] *R. v. Yoxall* (1972) 57 Cr.App.R. 263, C.A.
[12] *R. v. Whalley* (1972) 56 Cr.App.R. 304, C.A.
[13] Prosecution of Offences Act 1985, s. 18(1)(a).
[14] *ibid.* s. 18(4).
[15] *Practice* Direction (*Criminal Law: Costs*) [1989] 1 W.L.R. 625; [1989] 2 All E.R. 604.
[16] Prosecution of Offences Act. 1985, s. 18(5).
[17] Costs in Criminal Cases (General) Regulations 1986, reg. 14(3).
[18] *R. v. Nottingham Justices, ex p. Fohmann* (1987) 84 Cr.App.R. 316.

Crown Court

The Crown Court may make an award of costs against the accused, where **30–05**
it dismisses an appeal against conviction for an offence before the
magistrates' court, against sentence imposed on the conviction, or where
any person is convicted of an offence before a Crown Court.[19]
    Where a person is committed by a magistrates' court to the Crown Court:
    (a) with a view to his being sentenced for an indictable offence in
        accordance with the powers of Criminal Court's Act 1973, s. 42;
        or
    (b) with a view to his being sentenced by the Crown Court under
        section 6(6) or 9(3) of the Bail Act 1976; or
    (c) with a view to the making of a hospital order with an order
        restricting his discharge under the Mental Health Act 1983, Part III;
section 18 of the Prosecution of Offences Act 1985 applies in the same
way as where the person is convicted in proceedings before the Crown
Court.[20]
    Section 18 also applies in proceedings in the Crown Court in respect of
a person committed by a magistrates' court as an incorrigible rogue under
section 5 of the Vagrancy Act 1824 as if he had been committed for trial
before the Crown Court and as if the committing court were examining
justices. Similarly, section 18 applies in respect of an appeal under section
14 of the Vagrancy Act 1824, as if the hearing of the appeal were a trial on
indictment and as if the magistrates' court from which the appeal was
brought were examining justices.[21]
    Section 18 of the Prosecution of Offences Act 1985 applies to
proceedings both in the magistrates' court and in the Crown Court:
    (a) for dealing with an offender under the Powers of Criminal Courts
        Act 1973, ss. 6, 8, or 10 (probation orders and orders for con-
        ditional discharge);
    (b) under the Powers of Criminal Courts Act 1973, ss. 16 or 17
        (community service orders);
    (c) under the Powers of Criminal Courts Act 1973, ss. 23(1), 27 or the
        Criminal Law Act 1977, s. 47 (for dealing with an offender in
        respect of a suspended or partially suspended sentence or for
        breach of a suspended sentence supervision order); or
    (d) under the Criminal Justice Act 1982, s. 19(5) (for dealing with an
        offender in respect of a breach of attendance centre orders);

---

[19] Prosecution of Offences Act 1985, s. 18(1)(b), (c).
[20] Costs in Criminal Cases (General) Regulations 1986, reg. 14(1).
[21] *ibid.* reg. 14(2).

as if the offender had been tried in those proceedings for the offence for which the order was made or the sentence passed.[22]

The Court of Appeal

30–06 The Court of Appeal may order an unsuccessful appellant to pay costs to such person as may be named in the order. Those costs may include the costs of transcripts obtained for proceedings in the Court of Appeal.[23]

AWARD OF COSTS INCURRED AS A RESULT OF UNNECESSARY OR IMPROPER ACT OR OMISSION

Section 19 of the Prosecution of Offences Act 1985

30–07 A magistrates' court, the Crown Court or the Court of Appeal, if satisfied that costs have been incurred in respect of the proceedings, by one of the parties, as the result of an improper or unnecessary act or omission by or on behalf of another party to the proceedings, may, after hearing the parties, order that all or part of the costs incurred by that party should be paid to him by the other party.[24]

Where one party to the criminal proceedings is a legally assisted person then for the purposes of section 19 of the Prosecution of Offences Act 1985 his costs are taken to include the expenses incurred on his behalf under the Legal Aid Act 1988 (without any deduction on account of any contribution payable); but if he is liable to make such a contribution, his costs are taken not to include any sum paid or payable by way of contribution.[25]

The court must hear the parties before making any order and must take into account any other order as to costs (including any legal aid order) which has been made in the proceedings and the order which is made must specify the amount of costs to be paid. The court is entitled to take such an order into account when making any other orders as to costs in respect of the proceedings.[26]

In the magistrates' court no order may be made which requires a person under the age of 17 who has been convicted of an offence, to pay an amount by way of costs which exceeds the amount of any fine imposed upon him.[27]

---

[22] *ibid.* reg. 14(3).
[23] Prosecution of Offences Act 1985, s. 18(2), (6).
[24] Costs in Criminal Cases (General) Regulations 1986, reg. 3(1).
[25] Prosecution of Offences Act 1985, s. 21(4A)(b).
[26] Costs in Criminal Cases (General) Regulations 1986, reg. 3(2)–(4).
[27] *ibid.* reg. 3(5).

WASTED COSTS ORDERS

Section 19A of the Prosecution of Offences Act 1985

An order in respect of costs incurred as a result of an unnecessary or **30–08** improper act or omission is appropriate only where the failure is that of the defendant or the prosecutor. Where the failure is that of the legal representatives, a wasted costs order may be made under section 19A of the Prosecution of Offences Act 1985 or the inherent jurisdiction of the court may be exercised.[28]

This is dealt with at Chapter 31.

---

[28] *Practice Direction (Crime: Costs in Criminal Proceedings)* [1991] 1 W.L.R. 498.

Chapter 31

THE REMUNERATION OF COUNSEL AND SOLICITORS

The Right to Costs

The statutory right

31–01 The 1988 Act provides that where representation in criminal proceedings has been granted to any person, the costs are to be paid by the Lord Chancellor or by the Board, as the Lord Chancellor directs.[1]

The scheme of legal aid criminal costs is described in chapter 32, namely standard fees for solicitors and *ex post facto* determination of solicitors' costs and the same for counsel.

Costs in respect of work done under a legal aid order are determined by the appropriate authority designated by the Regulations. In determining costs, the appropriate authority is required to take into account all the relevant circumstances of the case including the nature, importance, complexity or difficulty of the work and the time involved and allow a reasonable amount in respect of all work actually and reasonably done.[2]

It is for the appropriate authority to determine the costs, and the trial judge has no power to tax the fees payable to counsel or solicitors or to order what should or should not be allowed on taxation, although it is open to the judge to make observations for the benefit of the determining officer.[3] In the magistrates' court the bench may make observations to the Board's area office after giving the legal representative an opportunity to comment.

In all matters to do with the determination of costs, the test to be applied is one of reasonableness.

> "The correct view point to be adopted . . . is that of a sensible solicitor sitting in his chair and considering what in the light of his then knowledge is reasonable in the interests of his lay client . . . the lay

---

[1] Legal Aid Act 1988, s. 25.
[2] Legal Aid in Criminal and Care Proceedings (Costs) Regulations 1989, regs. 3, 4.
[3] *R. v. McFadden and Cunningham* (1976) 62 Cr.App.R. 187, C.A.; see *Practice Direction* May 3 1991, Part X, [1991] 1 W.L.R. 498.

client ... should be deemed a man of means adequate to bear the expense of the litigation out of his own pocket and by 'adequate' I mean neither 'barely adequate' nor 'super abundant'' '.[4]

Having regard to this principle, it follows that a taxing officer should not use hindsight in considering whether or not a particular item of work is reasonable.

Interim payments in cases awaiting determination

Where a solicitor has a total claim for costs of £4,000 or more (exclusive of VAT) or a barrister claims a basic fee of £4,000 or more (exclusive of VAT) or where there is a claim for costs for less than those amounts but the claim is related to a claim for costs or basic fee of £4,000 or more, the appropriate authority is required to make an interim payment subject to the Regulations.[5]   **31–02**

The following claims for costs are related to each other:

(a) the claims of a solicitor and counsel acting in the same proceedings for a defendant;

(b) the claims of any solicitor or counsel acting in any proceedings where different proceedings involving the same defendant are prepared or heard or dealt with together; and

(c) the claims of all solicitors or counsel acting for the defendants where proceedings involving more than one defendant arose out of the same incident so that the defendants are charged or tried or disposed of together.[6]

Entitlement to interim payment does not arise until three months has elapsed from the date on which the bill is ready to tax, or if earlier, the date three months after the conclusion of the last of any related proceedings. A bill is regarded as being ready to tax on the date on which it is received by the appropriate authority for determination, except that where there are related claims for costs all the bills relating thereto are regarded as ready to tax on the date the last bill is received.[7]   **31–03**

Proceedings are taken to be related to each other where:

(a) different proceedings involving the same defendant are prepared or heard or dealt with together;

(b) proceedings involving more than one defendant arose out of the same incident so that the defendants are charged or tried or disposed of together.[8]

A solicitor or barrister may submit a claim for interim payment if no

---

[4] See para. 20–19. *Francis v. Francis and Dickerson* (1956) Pt. 87, *per* Sachs J.
[5] Legal Aid and Criminal Care Proceedings (Cost) Regulations 1989, reg. 4C(1), (2).
[6] *ibid.* reg. 4(C)(6)–(8).
[7] *ibid.* reg. 4(C)(3), (4).
[8] *ibid.* reg. 4C(7).

payment has been made and six months have elapsed from the conclusion of the proceedings against the defendant represented under the legal aid order. No payment may be made unless (subject to extensions of time) a solicitor or barrister has submitted his claim for costs in accordance with the provisions of the Regulations.[9]

Where the entitlement to an interim payment arises the amount payable will be 40 per cent of the total claim for costs less any sum already paid. The provisions in the Regulations relating to redetermination and review do not apply to interim payment.[10]

Where representation is provided under a franchising contract in the Magistrates' Court, the franchisee may apply to the Board when the legal aid order is granted for an interim payment in respect of a claim for costs in accordance with the franchising contract.[11]

Recovery of overpayments

31–04 Where a solicitor or barrister is entitled to be paid a certain sum under the 1989 Regulations and for whatever reason he is paid a greater amount, the appropriate authority may require immediate repayment of the amount in excess of the amount due and a solicitor or barrister must repay the excess amount on demand or deduct the excess amount from any other sum which is or becomes payable to the solicitor or barrister by virtue of the Regulations.[12]

The appropriate authority may deduct the excess amount without first requiring repayment from the solicitor or barrister. These provisions apply notwithstanding that the solicitor or barrister to whom the excess amount was paid is exercising or may exercise a right to redetermination or appeal under the Regulations.[13]

Restriction on payment of costs

Topping up—restriction on payment

31–05 Where a legal aid order has been made, the legally assisted person's solicitor or counsel may not receive, or be a party to the making of, any payment for work done in connection with the proceedings except such payments as may be made:

    (a) out of the Fund or by the Lord Chancellor; or

    (b) in respect of any expenses or fees incurred in:

        (i) preparing, obtaining or considering any report, opinion further

---

[9] *ibid.* reg. 4C(5), (9).
[10] *ibid.* reg. 4D(1), (2).
[11] *ibid.* reg. 4E.
[12] *ibid.* reg. 10A(1), (2).
[13] *ibid.* reg. 10A(3).

       evidence, whether provided by an expert witness or otherwise; or

(ii) bespeaking transcripts of shorthand notes or tape-recordings of any proceedings including police questioning of suspects; where an application for authority to incur expenses or fees has been refused by the appropriate area committee.

There is no provision for the topping up of counsel's fees in respect of criminal proceedings.[14]

The court's inherent jurisdiction

In addition to the power of the judge to make observations where it appears **31–06** that work may have been unreasonably done, the Supreme Court (which includes the Crown Court) may, in the exercise of its inherent jurisdiction over officers of the court, order a solicitor personally to pay costs thrown away by reason of some improper act or omission on his part or on that of his staff. Such an order may not be made unless reasonable notice has been given to the solicitor of the matter alleged against him, and he is given a reasonable opportunity of being heard in reply. If the court considers it necessary to hold the hearing in chambers, a shorthand note ought to be kept. There is no power to award costs to be paid personally by counsel, but where counsel acts under legal aid, the court may make observations to the determining authority.

The whole question of the court's inherent jurisdiction has recently been considered by the Court of Appeal[15] (before the introduction of the powers in relation to wasted costs).

The court considered:

(a) the nature and degree of fault on the part of the solicitor sufficient to justify the exercise of the jurisdiction;

(b) the purpose of the jurisdiction;

(c) the extent to which common law rules have, if at all, been modified by more recent rules and directions;

(d) whether the jurisdiction in criminal trials differs from that in civil trials; and

(e) who, if anyone, should be respondent to any appeal.

The conduct which may give rise to the jurisdiction Having considered **31–07** and approved the decision in *Myers v. Elman*[16] the Court of Appeal defined the conduct which gives rise to the jurisdiction as:

"Any conduct of a solicitor which involves a serious dereliction on the part of the solicitor of his duty to the court."

---

[14] Legal Aid in Criminal and Care Proceedings (General) Regulations 1989, reg. 55.
[15] *ibid.*
[16] *Holden & Co. v. Crown Prosecution Service* [1990] 2 Q.B. 261, C.A.

That formulation takes account of the dictum of Lord Denning M.R. in *R. & T. Thew Ltd v. Reeves (No. 2)*[17] as follows:

"The cases show that it (the jurisdiction) is not available in cases of mistake, error of judgment or mere negligence. It is only available where the conduct of the solicitor is inexcusable and such as to merit a reproof."

31–08 What is the object of the jurisdiction? The Court decided that the object of the order is primarily to reimburse the litigant for costs which he has incurred because of the solicitor's default. The Court referred to *Weston v Central Criminal Courts' Administrator*[18] where Stevenson L.J. had held that the costs, which a solicitor would have to pay from his own pocket, would be those and only those which his default had caused. Nothing was to be added to that figure to mark the disapproval of the court or by way of deterrence. The Court of Appeal found that there was also a punitive element, following May L.J. in *Curry v. Law Society*[19] since the solicitor was having to pay a bill which would otherwise have to be paid by one of the parties to the litigation. There was also necessarily an element of deterrence in that solicitors would wish to avoid the expense and adverse publicity that the exercise of the court's jurisdiction entails.

31–09 Has the common law rule been altered or modified by more recent Rules of the Supreme Court and Practice Directions? Under this head, the Court went on to consider the decision in *Sinclair Jones v. Kay*[20] in which May L.J. held that the principles requiring gross misconduct laid down under older authorities were not applicable where there was an application to the court under R.S.C., Ord. 62, r. 11 (which applies to civil proceedings and to the Divisional Court in criminal matters). The Court of Appeal decided that it was clearly anomalous if, in civil proceedings, different criteria obtained as to the duties of the solicitor towards the court from those in criminal proceedings. The duty should be the same whatever the nature of the proceedings. The Court therefore concluded that, at least so far as criminal cases were concerned, neither R.S.C., Ord. 62, r. 11 nor the 1989 *Practice Direction* (relating to criminal costs[21]) altered the common law rules as to the jurisdiction of the court.

31–10 Does the jurisdiction of the court differ according to whether the trial is civil or criminal? The Court of Appeal reasserted that there seemed to be no logical reason why a lesser duty should be imposed on solicitors in criminal proceedings than is imposed upon them in civil proceedings and

---

[17] [1940] A.C. 282.
[18] [1982] 1 Q.B. 1283 at 1286.
[19] [1977] Q.B. 32 at 45.
[20] [1977] 1 Q.B. at 997.
[21] [1989] 1 W.L.R. 114.

that in any event there was an overlap so far as the Divisional Court was concerned. The Court went on to find that the reasoning of the court in *Sinclair Jones v. Kay* was inconsistent with the authority of the House of Lords in *Myers v. Elman* and that R.S.C., Ord. 62, r. 11 did nothing but restate the inherent jurisdiction of the court and provide the machinery for its implementation.

The Court of Appeal held that:

(a) there is no distinction between civil and criminal trials; and

(b) the recent changes in the Rules of the Supreme Court and the recent Practice Directions have not altered in any way the previous law.

Who, if anyone, should be respondent to an appeal?   In all but one of the **31–11** appeals before the Court of Appeal, the Crown Prosecution Service (C.P.S.) had been named as respondents. However, the Court was told that in many cases it was a matter of indifference to the C.P.S. whether an order was made or not, and that it was not the policy of the C.P.S. to make applications that costs thrown away should be paid by the defendant's solicitors personally. The Court of Appeal, whilst acknowledging that it was not its place to determine the policy of the C.P.S., suggested that the matter should be reconsidered. If costs had been thrown away as a result of a serious dereliction of the defence solicitor's duty, it meant that public funds had been wasted. It could see no reason in principle why the C.P.S. should not be under a duty to protect public funds by making an application that the solicitor pay costs personally if it appeared to the C.P.S. that it was an appropriate case for such an order. In civil cases it is usually the opposing party who initiates an application under R.S.C., Ord. 62, r.11, but the court could not see why there should be any policy precluding an application being made in an appropriate case by the C.P.S. Where an order is made as a result of an application by the C.P.S., then it would seem that on appeal to the Court of Appeal, the C.P.S. would be the proper respondent. Where the initiative is taken by the judge himself, the Court felt that it was not appropriate that the C.P.S. should be the respondent. It was equally inappropriate that the Crown Court should be named as respondent. In the view of the Court of Appeal, the solution is for the appeal to be entitled: *Re the Crown Court at, appeal by ABC (a firm)*.

The Court took the view that in most cases it would request the Treasury Solicitor to instruct counsel to assist the court. If the C.P.S. wished to appear by counsel, there was no reason why they should not do so. It was not necessary for any respondent to be named.

Wasted costs orders

The Courts and Legal Services Act 1990 amends the Prosecution of **31–12** Offences Act 1985 by inserting a new section 19A which provides for costs orders against legal representatives in criminal proceedings in respect of wasted costs.

In any criminal proceedings, the Court of Appeal, the Crown Court or a magistrates' court, may disallow or order the legal or other representative to meet the whole or part of any wasted costs. A "legal or other representative" means a person exercising a right of audience, or a right to conduct litigation, on behalf of any party to the proceedings.

"Wasted costs" are any costs incurred by a party:

(a) as a result of any improper, unreasonable or negligent act or omission on the part of any representative or any employee of a representative; or

(b) which in the light of any such act or omission occurring after they were incurred, the court considers it unreasonable to expect that party to pay.[22]

When making a wasted costs order the court must specify the amount to be paid, but before the order is made, the legal or other representatives and any party to the proceedings must be allowed to make representations. It is open to the court when making a wasted costs order to take into account any other order as to costs in respect of the proceedings and the court may take the wasted costs into account when making any other order. Where a wasted costs order has been made, the court will notify any interested party of the order and the amount disallowed or ordered to be paid. An "interested party" means the party benefitting from the wasted costs order and, where he is legally aided, includes the authority responsible for determining costs payable in respect of the work done under the legal aid order.[23]

Determination

31–13　Where the court has disallowed the whole or any part of any wasted costs the appropriate authority, in determining costs in respect of work done by the legal representative against whom the wasted costs order was made, must deduct the amount of the order from the amount otherwise payable. Where the determining officer is minded to disallow any amount of a claim for work done to which the wasted costs order relates, the officer must disallow that amount or the amount of the wasted costs order whichever is the greater.[24]

Appeals

31–14　A legal or other representative against whom a wasted costs order is made may appeal, in the case of an order made by a magistrates' court to the

---

[22] Courts and Legal Services Act 1990, s. 111.

[23] Prosecution of Offences Act 1985, s. 19A.

[24] Costs in Criminal Cases (General) Regulations 1986, regs. 3A and 3B (inserted by the Costs in Criminal Cases (General) (Amendment) Regulations 1991).

Crown Court, and in the case of an order made at first instance by the Crown Court, to the Court of Appeal. There is no provision in the 1986 Regulations for an appeal from an order made by the Court of Appeal. The appeal must be instituted within 21 days of the wasted costs order being made by the appellant giving notice in writing to the court which made the order stating the grounds of the appeal.[25]

The appellant must serve a copy of the notice of appeal and grounds including any application for an extension of time in which to appeal upon any interested party. The time limit within which an appeal may be instituted may, for good reason, be extended before or after it expires; in the case of an appeal to the Crown Court by a judge of the Crown Court, and in the case of an appeal to the Court of Appeal by a judge of the High Court or the Court of Appeal. In each case the court will give notice of the extension to the appellant, the court which made the wasted costs order and to any interested party.[26]

The court to which appeal is made will give notice of the hearing date to the appellant, the court which made the wasted costs order and any interested party and must allow the interested party to make representations which may be made orally or in writing. The court may affirm, vary or revoke the order as it thinks fit and must notify its decision to the appellant, any interested party and the court which made the original order.[27] The court has no power to order that the costs of solicitors' successful appeals against wasted costs orders should be paid from central funds.

The Court of Appeal Civil Division has considered in detail the wasted **31–15** costs jurisdiction introduced by the Courts and Legal Service Act 1990.[28] The Court held that, while litigants should not be financially prejudiced by the unjustifiable conduct of litigation by their or by their opponents' lawyers, the courts — in the exercise of the wasted costs jurisdiction — should be astute to control the threat of a new and costly form of satellite litigation. When a wasted costs order was contemplated a three-stage test should be applied:

(a) had the legal representative of whom complaint was made acted improperly, unreasonably or negligently?

(b) if so, did such conduct cause the applicant to incur unnecessary costs?

(c) if so, was it in all the circumstances just to order the legal representative to compensate the applicant for the whole or part of the relevant costs?

---

[25] Legal Aid in Criminal and Care Proceedings (Costs) Regulations 1989, reg. 9A (1) and (2) inserted by the Legal Aid in Criminal and Care Proceedings (Costs) (Amendment) (No. 2) Regulations 1991.

[26] Costs in Criminal Cases (General) Regulations 1986, reg. 3C (1), (2).

[27] *ibid.* 3C (4), (5) (6).

[28] *Holden & Co. v. Crown Prosecution Service (No. 2) sub. nom Steele Ford & Newton v. Crown Prosecution Service* [1993] 2 W.L.R. 934, H.L.

Demonstration of the causal link between the improper, unreasonable or negligent conduct and the waste of costs was essential. Where conduct was proved, but no waste of costs shown to have resulted, the case might be referred to the appropriate disciplinary body or the legal aid authorities. It was not a matter for the exercise of the wasted costs judrisdiction. The jurisdiction to make a wasted costs order depended at two stages on the court's discretion:

    (a) At the stage of initial application when the court was invited to give the representative an opportunity to show cause; this was not something to be done automatically. The costs of the inquiries compared with the costs claimed would always be a relevant consideration. The discretion, like any other, was to be exercised judicially, the judges might not infrequently decide that further proceedings were not likely to be justified.

    (b) At the final stage; even if the court were satisfied that legal representatives had acted improperly, unreasonably, or negligently, so as to waste costs, it was not bound to make an order, but would have to give sustainable reason for the exercise of its discretion in that way.

The Court of Appeal expressed the view that the approach to wasted costs should be the same in both civil and criminal cases.

It is unreasonable for a barrister in sole practice to rely wholly on instructing solicitors to notify him of the dates and times of his cases. It is his responsibility to adopt a system which enables him to keep abreast of the listing arrangements for his cases.[29]

Recovery of sums due under a wasted costs order

31–16   Where a person has been required to make a payment in respect of sums due under a wasted costs order and has failed to do so, payment may be recovered summarily as a sum adjudged to be paid as a civil debt by order of a magistrates' court by the party benefitting from the order, and where that party was legally aided the power to recover is exercisable by the Lord Chancellor.[30]

COSTS AND PAYMENT

Generally

31–17   The 1988 Act provides that the costs of representing a legally assisted person are to be paid by the Lord Chancellor or by the Board in accordance

---

[29] *Ridehalgh v. Horsefield; Allen v. Unigate Dairies Ltd; Roberts v. Coverite (Asphalters) Ltd; Philex Plc v. Golban; Watson v. Watson; Antonelli v. Wade Gery Farr (a firm)*, [1994] 3 W.L.R. 462 C.A.

[30] *Re a Barrister (Wasted Costs Order) (No. 4 of 1992), The Times*, March 15, 1994, C.A.

with the Lord Chancellor's directions and those costs are to include sums on account of the fees payable to the assisted person's legal representative and disbursements reasonable incurred by the representative for or in connection with the representation.[31] The relevant regulations are the Legal Aid in Criminal and Care Proceedings (Costs) Regulations 1989 which are dealt with briefly in outline below.

The expenses of witnesses attending to give evidence in the relevant proceedings are expressly excluded from the costs where such allowances or expenses are payable under any other enactment.[32] Where a witness attends at the insistence of the accused, a private prosecutor or the court, in any proceedings in a criminal cause or matter, in a magistrates' court, the Crown Court, a Divisional Court of the Queen's Bench Division, the Court of Appeal or the House of Lords, the expenses properly incurred by the witness will be allowed out of the central funds, in accordance with the 1986 Regulations unless the court directs that the expenses are not to be allowed out of central funds.[33] The effect of this is that unless the court gives a specific direction, that witness expenses are not to be allowed out of central funds they will be so allowed and no witness expenses will be paid out of the Fund. The Costs Appeals Committee of the Board has confirmed this in relation to magistrates' court cases and the stance of the Board is that witness expenses will be disallowed from costs claims unless the solicitor confirms that the court made a direction in which case expenses reasonably incurred will be allowed out of the Fund.[34] Expenses are defined by regulation 16(1) of the 1986 Regulations as "including compensation for trouble or loss of time and out of pocket expenses".

Payment for advice or assistance where representation subsequently granted

If a legal representative acting for a legally assisted person under a grant of representation is the same one who gave to that person advice or assistance on any matter which is, or becomes, the subject of criminal proceedings against him, any charge or fee in respect of the advice or assistance will be paid as part of the costs of representation rather than under a separate claim for advice and assistance.[35] The Board is at present accepting separate Green Form costs claims.   **31–18**

If a contribution order is made in respect of the grant of representation, any sum which the assisted person is required to pay in respect of the advice or assistance (whether or not it is already paid) will be credited against the contribution to be made by him under the contribution order,

---

[31] Costs in Criminal Cases (General) Regulations 1986, reg. 3D.
[32] Legal Aid Act 1988, s. 25(1), (2).
[33] *ibid.* s. 25(3).
[34] Costs in Criminal Cases (General) Regulations 1986, reg. 16(1).
[35] See decision CRIMLA 15.

and in so far as the charges and fees payable are concerned, any sum paid in respect of advice or assistance is treated as if it were part of the contribution made under the contribution order.[36]

The Legal Aid in Criminal and Care Proceedings (Costs) Regulations 1989

31–19 The Legal Aid in Criminal and Care Proceedings (Costs) Regulations 1989 (the Costs Regulations 1989) which are dealt with in detail hereafter encapsulate and consolidate the Costs Regulations made since 1982. The Costs Regulations 1989 now provide for standard fees for solicitors in both the magistrates' court and the Crown Court; *ex post facto* determination of solicitors costs: standard fees for counsel in the Crown Court and *ex post facto* determination of counsel's fees.

Standard fees for solicitors in the magistrates' court

31–20 In relation to proceedings in the magistrates' court standard fees are payable in respect of certain work regardless of the grade of fee-earner carrying out the work. The proceedings (which include any proceedings preliminary or incidental thereto whether before that or another court including bail applications made in the magistrates' court or the Crown Court) are the proceedings specified below.[37]

TABLE: CATEGORIES AND TYPES OF PROCEEDINGS

Column 1	Column 2	Column 3
Category 1	**Category 2**	**Category 3**
1.1 guilty pleas 1.2 uncontested proceedings arising out of a breach of an order of a magistrates' court (including proceedings in a magistrates' court relating to a breach of a Crown Court probation order, community service order or suspended sentence) 1.3 proceedings (other than committal proceedings) which are discontinued or withdrawn 1.4 proceedings (other than committal proceedings) relating to summary or either	2.1 contested trials 2.2 proceedings which were listed and fully prepared for trial in a magistrates' court but disposed of by a guilty plea on the day of trial before the opening of the prosecution case 2.3 proceedings which were listed and fully prepared for trial in a magistates' court but are discontinued or withdrawn or where the prosecution offers no evidence or which result in a bind over on the day of trial before the	3.1 committal proceedings under section 6(2) of the Magistrates' Courts Act 1980 including those which are discontinued or withdrawn 3.2 committal proceedings which are discontinued or withdrawn before the court has fixed the date for a section 6(1) committal hearing 3.3 proceedings transferred under section 4 of the Criminal Justice Act 1987 or section 53 of the Criminal Justice Act 1991

---

[36] Legal Aid Act 1988, s. 26(1), (2).
[37] *ibid.* s. 26(3).

Column 1	Column 2	Column 3
Category 1	**Category 2**	**Category 3**
way offences which result in a bind over 1.5 proceedings arising out of a deferment of sentence (including any subsequent sentencing hearing) under section 1 of the Powers of Criminal Courts Act 1973	opening of the prosecution case 2.4 contested proceedings relating to a breach of an order of a magistrates' court (including proceedings relating to a breach of a Crown Court probation order, community service order or suspended sentence) 2.5 proceedings where mixed pleas are entered	

Proceedings are treated as forming part of one case where they relate to one or more charges or informations which are preferred or laid at the same time or which are founded on the same facts or which form part or are part of a series of offences. Where a case includes proceedings referred to in the table above at 3.1 and 3.2 it is treated as if all the proceedings were category 3 proceedings.

Subject to that, where proceedings forming one case fall into more than one category, the proceedings are treated as forming part of the higher or highest in value of the categories concerned.[38]

Save where proceedings are treated as category 3 proceedings, where there is a change of solicitor assigned under a legal aid order in proceedings to which standard fees apply, the proceedings are treated as category 1 proceedings for the purposes of the claim for costs in respect of work done under the legal aid order by the solicitors formerly assigned. Where proceedings have not been concluded but a warrant of arrest has been issued the proceedings are treated as category 1 proceedings.[39]

Standard fees in the magistrates' courts do not apply to proceedings which counsel has been assigned under a legal aid order; or in which costs are allowed at an enhanced rate in accordance with paragraph 3 of Schedule 1, part 1.[40]

Standard fees for solicitors in the Crown Court

In relation to proceedings in the Crown Court, standard fees are payable in **31–21** respect of certain work, regardless of the grade of fee-earner carrying out the work. The proceedings to which standard fees apply are:

---

[38] Legal Aid in Criminal and Care Proceedings (Costs) Regulations 1989, Sched. 1, Pt. 3 inserted by Legal Aid in Criminal and Care Proceedings (Costs) (Amendment) Regulations 1993 from June 1, 1993.

[39] Legal Aid in Criminal and Care Proceedings (Costs) Regulations 1989, Sched. 1, Pt. 3, para. 2(3)–(5).

[40] *ibid.* Sched. 1, Pt. 3, para. 2(6), (7).

(a) committals for trial in which the indictment consists of counts in respects of an offence of Class 3 or 4; and
  (i) where the trial (including any case prepared for trial in which no jury was sworn) lasted two days or less and at the time of listing was reasonably expected to last two days or less;
  (ii) where the case was listed and disposed of as a guilty plea;
(b) appeals against conviction;
(c) appeals against sentence; and
(d) committals for sentence (including proceedings which arose out of a breach of an order of the Crown Court, proceedings in which sentence was deferred and other similar matters).

Under paragraph 1(5) of Schedule 1, Part II of the Costs Regulations 1989 a solicitor may elect to claim standard fees for Crown Court work.

Procedures are laid down for redetermination and appeal against the allowance of standard fees.[41]

Ex post facto determination of solicitors' fees

31–22 All other claims for costs and disbursements by solicitors are determined *ex post facto*. Fees may be claimed in respect of various classes of work and in respect of various grades of fee earner. The classes of work are:
  (a) preparation, including taking instructions, interviewing witnesses, ascertaining the prosecution case, advising on plea and mode of trial, preparing and perusing documents, dealing with letters and telephone calls which are not routine, preparing for advocacy, instructing counsel and expert witnesses, conferences, consultations, views and work done in connection with advice on appeal or case stated;
  (b) advocacy, including applications for bail and other applications to the court;
  (c) attendance at court where counsel is assigned, including conferences with counsel at court;
  (d) travelling and waiting;
  (e) dealing with routine letters written and routine telephone calls.

The categories of fee-earner applied to proceedings in the Crown Court and Court of Appeal are:
  (a) senior solicitor;
  (b) solicitor legal executive or fee-earner of equivalent experience;
  (c) articled clerk or fee-earner of equivalent experience.[42]

The rates are prescribed by the Costs Regulations 1989 although there is a safety measure for solicitors in that regulation 6(3) allows determining officers to allow such fees as appear to be reasonable having regard to the

---

[41] *ibid.* Sched. 1, Pt. III, para. 3.
[42] *ibid.* Sched. 1, Pt. II.

specified rates for work done after June 30. This is to allow for the possibility that the prescribed rates are not, as has become usual, updated in April and when the prescribed rates are reviewed the fail-safe date is also moved on by a year.

Ex post facto determination applies in all courts not merely the Crown Court. The appropriate authority is required to consider the claim and to allow such work as appears to it to have been reasonably done under the legal aid order (including any representation or advice deemed to be work done under the order) by a fee earner, and to allow such time in respect of each class of work as it considers reasonable.[43]

The appropriate authority is empowered to allow fees of more than the rate prescribed in the Costs Regulations 1989, where it appears that taking into account all the relevant circumstances of the case that the work was done with exceptional competence, skill or expertise; with exceptional dispatch or the case involved exceptional circumstances or complexity. Where the appropriate authority considers that any item or class of work should be allowed at more than the prescribed rate an enhancement may be applied.[44]

The appropriate authority must have regard to:

(a) the degree of responsibility accepted by the solicitor and his staff;
(b) the care, speed and economy with which the case was prepared;
(c) the novelty, weight and complexity of the case.[45]

The maximum permitted enhancement is 100 per cent save in the case of serious or complex fraud when the maximum is 200 per cent.[46] In determining what is exceptional regard may be had to the generality of proceedings to which the 1989 Costs Regulations apply.[47]

The Costs Regulations 1989 provide procedures for review and appeals in respect of determinations by the Board and redetermination, appeal to a taxing master and appeals to the High Court, in respect of other determinations.[48]

Standard fees for counsel

Standard fees are prescribed for junior counsel in the Crown Court and **31–23** must be allowed, unless the appropriate authority is satisfied that it would be inappropriate, taking into account the relevant circumstances of the case: in which case an *ex post facto* determination may take place.[49] The appropriate authority may not allow a standard fee in respect of:

---

[43] *ibid.* reg. 6(4).
[44] *ibid.* reg. 6(2).
[45] *Ibid.* Sched. 1, Pt. 1, para. 3(1).
[46] *ibid.* Sched. 1, Pt. 1, para. 3(2).
[47] *ibid.* Sched. 1, Pt. 1, para. 3(3).
[48] *ibid.* Sched. 1, Pt. 1, para. 3(4), (5).
[49] *ibid.* Sched. 1, Pt. 1, para. 3(6).

> (a) committals for trial in which the indictment includes counts in respect of an offence of Class 1 or 2;
> (b) proceedings in any other case:
>   (i) which lasted more than three days or which, at the time of listing, were reasonably expected to last more than three days;
>   (ii) in which the indictment is disposed of by a plea of guilty but which, if contested, would reasonably have been expected to last more than three days, unless counsel requests that a standard fee should be allowed.[50]

Ex post facto determination of counsel's fees

31–24 In all other cases, counsel's fees are determined on an *ex post facto* basis by the authority appropriate to the particular court. The appropriate authority is required to consider the claim and to allow such work as appears to it to have been reasonably done.[51]

In proceedings in the Crown Court or the magistrates' court the appropriate authority must allow such fees, in respect of the work, as it considers reasonable in accordance with the Costs Regulations 1989. Where it appears to the appropriate authority, taking into account all the relevant circumstances of the case, that owing to the exceptional circumstances of the case, the amount payable in accordance with the Costs Regulations 1989 would not provide reasonable remuneration for some or all of the work it has allowed, it may allow such amount as appears to it to be reasonable remuneration for the relevant work.[52]

In the case of proceedings in the Court of Appeal, the appropriate authority must allow such fees in respect of such work as it considers reasonable in such amounts as appear to it to be reasonable remuneration for such work.[53]

Review and appeals

31–25 The Costs Regulations 1989 provide for review of determinations by the Board and appeals to a committee appointed by the Board in respect of such determinations; and also for redetermination, appeal to a taxing master and appeal to the High Court in respect of all other cases.[54]

---

[50] *ibid.* reg. 9(2).
[51] *ibid.* reg. 9(3), Sched. 2, Pt. 1.
[52] *ibid.* reg. 9(1).
[53] *ibid.* reg. 9(5)(b).
[54] *ibid.* reg. 9(6).

The claim for costs

Solicitors

Subject to the provisions relating to the extension of time-limits,[55] a **31–26** solicitor's claim for costs must be submitted within three months of the conclusion of the proceedings to which the legal aid order relates. Where proceedings in a magistrates' court have not been concluded but a warrant of arrest has been issued, a claim by a solicitor for costs in respect of work done under a legal aid order must be made not earlier than six weeks and not later than 19 weeks from the date of issue of the warrant and the provisions relating to standard fees in the magistrates' court will apply.

The claim must be made in such form and manner as may be directed by the appropriate authority and must be accompanied by the legal aid order and any receipts or other documents in support of disbursements claimed.[56]

When a claim is submitted, it must summarise the items of work done by a fee-earner in respect of the classes of work specified by the Costs Regulations 1989. A "fee-earner" is a solicitor, a legal executive or any clerk who regularly does work for which it is appropriate to make a direct charge to a client. A "legal executive" is a fellow of the Institute of Legal Executives.[57]

The claim for costs must state, where appropriate, the dates on which the items of work were done, the time taken, the sums claimed and whether the work was done for more than one assisted person. In relation to proceedings in the Crown Court or Court of Appeal, the claim must specify the fee-earner who undertook each item of work claimed. The claim must give particulars of any work done in relation to more than one indictment or a re-trial and must specify any disbursements claimed, the circumstances in which they were incurred and the amounts claimed in respect of them.[58]

Where counsel has been instructed in the magistrates' court, although not assigned under the legal aid order, the solicitor must state the amount agreed in respect of counsel's fees, the time spent by counsel in preparation, advocacy, travelling and waiting and the amounts agreed for counsel's travelling and time and travelling costs.[59]

Where a solicitor claims: **31–27**

    (a) that representation or advice given before the legal aid order was made should be deemed to have been given under the order; or

    (b) that, taking into account all the relevant circumstances of the

---

[55] *ibid.* regs. 12–16.
[56] Legal Aid in Criminal and Care Proceeding (Costs) Regulations 1989, reg. 5(1A).
[57] *ibid.* Regs. 2(1), 5(3).
[58] *ibid.* reg. 5(1), (2). The appropriate forms are: magistrates' court, Crown Court, Court of Appeal.
[59] *ibid.* regs. 2(1), 5(3).

case, the amount of fees payable at the rate specified in the Costs Regulations 1989 would not reasonably reflect the exceptional competence and despatch with which the work was done or the exceptional circumstances of the case, the solicitor must give full particulars in support of the claim.[60]

The classes of work allowable on an *ex-post facto* determination are:

(a) preparation, including taking instructions, interviewing witnesses, ascertaining the prosecution case, advising on plea and mode of trial, preparing and perusing documents, dealing with letters and telephone calls which are not routine, preparing for advocacy, instructing counsel and expert witnesses, conferences, consultations, views and work done in connection with advice on appeal or case stated;

(b) advocacy including applications for bail and other applications to the court;

(c) attendance at court where counsel is assigned, including conferences with counsel at court;

(d) travelling and waiting;

(e) dealing with routine letters written and telephone calls.[61]

The classes of work allowable in respect of standard fees are:

(a) Preparation within the meaning of regulation 6 (1)(a) of the Costs Regulations 1989 but including routine letters and routine telephone calls;

(b) advocacy in respect of applications for bail;

(c) attendance at court, (including waiting) where counsel is assigned;

(d) travelling except:

(i) to undertake work for which standard fees are not payable; or

(ii) in respect of advocacy, in respect of applications for ball.

"Travelling" is deemed to include waiting in connection with preparation work.[62]

Where there are any special circumstances to be drawn to the attention of the appropriate authority, it is up to the solicitor to specify them in the claim for costs or in a letter or note annexed to it. The solicitor must supply such further particulars, information and documents as the appropriate authority may require.[63]

Counsel

31–28 Subject to the provisions relating to the extension of time-limits, a claim for fees for work done by counsel must be submitted within three months of

---

[60] *ibid.* reg. 5(4), Sched. 1, Pt. I, para. 3; Legal Aid in Criminal and Care Proceedings (General) Regulations 1989, reg. 44(7).

[61] Legal Aid in Criminal and Care Proceedings (Costs) Regulations 1989, reg. 6(1).

[62] *ibid.* Sched. 1, Pt. II, para. 4(2).

[63] *ibid.* reg. 5(5), (6).

the conclusion of the proceedings to which the legal aid order relates. The claim for fees must be in the form and manner directed by the appropriate authority.[64]

Counsel's claim must summarise the items of work in respect of which fees are claimed according to classes specified in the Costs Regulations 1989, state the dates on which the items of work were done, the time taken (where appropriate), the sums claimed and whether the work was done for more than one assisted person, and give particulars of any work done in relation to any indictment or re-trial.[65] The classes of work in respect of which counsel may claim fees are (save where standard fees apply):

(a) a basic fee for preparation including preparation for pre-trial review and, where appropriate, the first day's hearing including, where it took place on that day, short-conferences, consultations, applications and appearances (including bail applications), views and any other preparation;

(b) a refresher fee for any day or part of the day during which a hearing continued, including, where it took place on that day, short conferences, consultations, applications and appearances (including bail applications), views and any other preparation;

(c) a subsidiary fee for:
   (i) attendance at conferences, consultations and views not covered above;
   (ii) written advice on evidence, plea, appeal, case stated or other written work;
   (iii) attendance at pre-trial reviews, applications and attendances (including bail applications and adjournments for sentence) not covered above.[66]

Where counsel claims that it would be inappropriate to allow standard fees or that, owing to the exceptional circumstances of the case, the amount payable by way of fees prescribed by the Costs Regulations 1989 would not provide reasonable remuneration, counsel must give full particulars in support of the claim either on the claim itself or more usually in a letter or note accompanying the claim.[67] Counsel must also draw to the attention of the appropriate authority any special circumstances and must also supply such further particulars, information and documents as the appropriate authority may require.[68]

---

[64] *ibid.* reg. 8(1), (2). The appropriate forms are Magistrates Court, Crown Court, Court of Appeal.
[65] *ibid.* reg. 8(3).
[66] *ibid.* reg. 9(4).
[67] *ibid.* reg. 8(4).
[68] *ibid.* reg. 8(5), (6).

Determination of costs by the appropriate authority

Solicitors, determination

31–29 In the magistrates' court, the fees prescribed do not differentiate between the grade of fee-earner doing the work. However, in the Crown Court and the Court of Appeal, different rates are applicable to senior solicitors (Grade A fee-earners); solicitors, legal executives or fee-earners of equivalent experience (Grade B fee-earners); or articled clerks or fee-earners of equivalent experience (Grade C fee-earners). Fees will be allowed to whichever grade of fee-earner it was reasonable to employ to undertake the work.

Updating of rates

31–30 The prescribed rates are normally updated in April every year but the Costs Regulations 1989 provide that where any work allowed was done after June 30 in a particular year, the appropriate authority is given discretion to allow such fees as appear reasonable for the work done, having regard to the existing rates.[69]

Determination

31–31 In certain instances, preparation work is allowed at a higher rate for fee-earners whose office is situated within legal aid area 1, that is the London area. It is open to the appropriate authority to allow fees at less than the prescribed rate where it appears reasonable to do so having regard to the competence and despatch with which the work was done. This will normally only occur where the trial judge has made an adverse comment.[70]

It is also open to the appropriate authority to allow fees at more than the prescribed rate where it appears that taking into account all the relevant circumstances of the case the amount of fees payable at the specified rate would not reasonably reflect:

    (a) the exceptional competence and despatch with which the work was done; or

    (b) the exceptional circumstances of the case.[71]

Where a solicitor seeks enhanced rates full particulars must be given in support of the claim.[72]

When will enhanced rates be paid?

31–32 In *Fay v. Fay*[73] "exceptional" was described as "something out of the ordinary". The fact that the charge is one of murder will not of itself give

---

[69] *ibid.* reg. 6(3).
[70] *ibid.* Sched. 1, para. 2. As to wasted costs orders.
[71] *ibid.* Sched. 1, Pt. I, para. 3.
[72] *ibid.* reg. 5(4) (b).
[73] [1982] A.C. 835.

rise to an entitlement to enhanced rates. To qualify, a case does not have to be exceptional when compared with other cases of the same type, and the fact that a case is of a particular type will not automatically justify the payment of enhanced rates. Each case must be judged on its merits.

It is inappropriate to fetter or guide a taxing officer as to the choice of circumstances which he could regard as exceptional in determining an uplift to a solicitor's costs in excess of the standard rate and the Board was wrong to attempt to do so. It was also wrong when considering all the relevant circumstances in considering when a case was exceptional, to compare the case in question with others of the same type. The words "all the relevant circumstances" in the Costs Regulations 1989 are unrestricted.[74] It follows from this decision that it is appropriate to compare cases with the generality of criminal cases or the usual or ordinary criminal trial in order to decide whether or not the case is exceptional. A Legal Aid Committee is not obliged to give a solicitor notice of or an opportunity to make representations on its decision not to allow enhanced rates.[75]

Wasted costs

Where the court has disallowed the whole or any part of any wasted costs, **31–33** the appropriate authority, in determining costs in respect of work done by the legal representative against whom the wasted costs order was made, must deduct the amount of the order from the amount otherwise payable. Where the determining officer is minded to disallow any amount of a claim for work done to which the wasted costs order relates, the officer must disallow that amount or the amount of the wasted costs order whichever is the greater.[76]

Solicitors' disbursements

The appropriate authority must allow the disbursements claimed by a **31–34** solicitor providing that they have been reasonably incurred but regardless of whether standard fees are payable.[77]

Interim payment of disbursements in Crown Court proceedings

A solicitor may submit a claim to the appropriate authority for payment of **31–35** a disbursement for which he has incurred a liability in criminal proceedings in the Crown Court where:

---

[74] *R. v. Legal Aid Board, ex. p. R. M. Broudie & Co., The Times,* April 11, 1994, D.C.
[75] *R. v. Legal Aid Board, ex. p. R. M. Broudie & Co., The Times,* November 24, 1994, Macpherson, J.
[76] Legal Aid in Criminal and Care Proceedings (Costs) Regulations 1989, reg. 9A (1), (2) inserted by the Legal Aid in Criminal and Care Proceedings (Costs) (Amendment) (No. 2) Regulations 1991.
[77] Legal Aid in Criminal and Care Proceedings (Costs) Regulations reg. 7(1).

(a) a prior authority has been obtained to incur expenditure of £100 or more under regulation 54(1)(a), (b), (c) or (e) of the Legal Aid in Criminal and Care Proceedings (General) Regulations 1989; and

(b) a liability has been incurred for the disbursement under that authority of £100 or more.[78]

The claim for interim payment may be made at any time before the solicitor submits a claim for costs under regulation 5(2) of the Costs Regulations 1989 in the normal way.

Without prejudice to the power of the appropriate authority to allow fees in excess of any authority under regulation 7(6) of the Costs Regulations 1989 a claim for interim payment of disbursements must not exceed the maximum fee authorised under the prior authority.[79]

Procedure

31–36 A claim for interim payment of disbursements must be submitted to the appropriate authority in such form and manner as it may direct and must be accompanied by the authority to incur expenditure and any invoices or other documents in support of the claim. The appropriate authority must allow the disbursement subject to the limit imposed by the prior authority if it appears to have been reasonably incurred in accordance with the authority.

Where the disbursement is allowed, the appropriate authority must notify the solicitor and, where the disbursement includes the fees or charges of any person, that person, of the amount payable and must authorise payment to the solicitor accordingly.

There is no provision for redetermination or appeal in respect of interim payments of disbursements.[80]

The effect upon final determination

31–37 On a final determination of costs, the solicitor is still required to submit to the appropriate authority a completed claim in respect of all disbursements and must specify any disbursements claimed, the circumstances in which they were incurred and the amount claimed in respect of them. The determining officer must approach the determination of the disbursements in accordance with regulation 7 of the Costs Regulations 1989.

Where the amount found due under regulation 7 of the Costs Regulations 1989 in respect of a disbursement is less than the amount paid as an interim disbursement, the appropriate authority must deduct the difference from the sum otherwise payable to the solicitor on the determination and where the

---

[78] *ibid.* reg. 4A(1), (2).
[79] *ibid.* reg. 4A(3), (4).
[80] *ibid.* reg. 4A(5)–(8).

amount due exceeds the interim disbursement the appropriate authority will add the difference to the amount otherwise payable to the solicitor.[81]

Counsel's standard fees

Standard fees for counsel apply to work done by junior counsel in the **31–38** Crown Court. Standard fees are payable unless such a fee would be "inappropriate" taking into account all the relevant circumstances of the case.[82] It has been held that if the standard fee would not provide reasonable remuneration for work actually and reasonably done then it was inappropriate for the purposes of the Costs Regulations 1989.

Any case falling within the categories to which standard fees are required to be applied, must be a usual case of its kind, viewed as to weight, gravity or complexity. This applies equally to all cases falling within the categories without regard to the intrinsic weight, gravity or complexity which may be found in one class of case as a distinct from another.

What this decision actually appears to mean, is that in order to take, *e.g.* a simple theft out of the range of standard fees there would have to be significant factors involved. Whereas in the case of a more serious offence such as causing death by dangerous driving such factors could be of a relatively minor nature.[83]

Standard fees may not be paid in respect of:
  (a) committals for trial in which the indictment includes offences of Class 1 or 2;
  (b) Proceedings in any other case
    (i) which lasted more than three days or which at the time of listing were reasonably expected to last more than three days;
    (ii) in which the indictment is disposed of by a plea of guilty but which if contested would reasonably have been expected to last more than three days.
Counsel may request the allowance of a standard fee in any event.[84]

Counsel's fees ex post facto determination

Ex post facto determination of counsel's fees takes place where standard **31–39** fees are not appropriate, for work done by junior counsel in the Crown Court and in respect of all other work. The appropriate authority must consider the claim and any further particulars, information or documents

---

[81] *ibid.* reg. 4B(1), (2).
[82] *R. v. Hugget* [1988] T.C. 12.
[83] Legal Aid in Criminal and Care Proceedings (Costs) Regulations 1989, reg. 9(2).
[84] *ibid.* reg. 9(3).

submitted by counsel and any other relevant information and must allow such work as appears to it to have been reasonably done.[85]

Payment of costs

31–40 Once costs have been determined by the appropriate authority, the solicitor or counsel will be notified of the amount payable and payment will be authorised. On occasions, legal representatives have to wait considerable periods for notification and payment. The Costs Regulations 1989 lay down no times within which the authority must act.[86] Where the amount of costs payable is varied as a result of a redetermination or review, the appropriate authority will either authorise payment of the increase or solicitor or counsel must repay the amount of any decrease. Similarly, where the costs of any appeal are awarded, the appropriate authority must authorise the payment of such costs; again no time limit is imposed.[87] Where counsel who is not assigned appears in the magistrates' court any fee due to counsel will be paid direct.[88]

---

[85] *ibid.* reg. 9(4).
[86] *ibid.* reg. 10(1).
[87] *ibid.* reg. 10(2).
[88] *ibid.* reg. 10(2).

Chapter 32

TAXATION OF COSTS

APPROPRIATE AUTHORITY AND FORM OF BILL

Magistrates' court

The Board is the appropriate authority in respect of criminal proceedings **32–01** in the magistrates' court and in respect of advice or assistance as to appeal from a magistrates' court to the Crown Court.[1]

Crown Court

In the case of criminal proceedings in the Crown Court, the appropriate **32–02** authority is an officer appointed by the Lord Chancellor.[2] Each appropriate authority may appoint or authorise the appointment of determining officers to act on its behalf, under the Costs Regulations 1989 in accordance with directions given by it or on its behalf.[3]

In respect of advice or assistance as to appeal from the Crown Court to the Court of Appeal, the appropriate officer is the officer appointed by the Lord Chancellor in respect of criminal proceedings in the Crown Court unless, on the advice of counsel or the solicitor assigned, notice of appeal is given, or application for leave to appeal is made (whether or not the appeal is later abandoned), when the Registrar of Criminal Appeals is the appropriate authority.[4]

Determination is carried out in the Crown Court in the case of an appeal under section 9 (11) of the Criminal Justice Act 1987 regarding any question of admissibility of evidence or any other question of law relating to the case, which can only be pursued with leave.[5]

---

[1] Legal Aid in Criminal and Care Proceedings (Costs) Regulations 1989, reg. 3(1) (c), (d), (4).
[2] The appointed officer is currently the Permanent Secretary of the Lord Chancellor's Department; see Directions for Determining Officers in the Crown Court issued by the Lord Chancellor's Department.
[3] *ibid.* reg. 3(1) (b), (2).
[4] Legal Aid in Criminal and Care Proceedings (Costs) Regulations 1989 reg. 3(3) (a), (b).
[5] *ibid.* reg. 3(3).

Divisional Court

32–03 Appeals to the Divisional Court by way of case stated are dealt with under civil certificates.

Court of Appeal

32–04 In the case of proceedings in the Court of Appeal, the Registrar of Criminal Appeals is the appropriate authority or the Registrar of the Courts-Martial Appeal Court as the case may be.[6]

In the case of advice or assistance relating to an appeal from the Crown Court to the Court of Appeal, the Registrar is also the appropriate authority where, on the advice of counsel or the solicitor assigned, notice of appeal is given or application for leave to appeal is made whether or not the appeal is later abandoned.[7]

Determination is carried out in the Crown Court in the case of an appeal under section 9(11) of the Criminal Justice Act 1987 regarding any question of admissibility of evidence or any other question of law relating to the case which can only be pursued with leave.[8]

House of Lords

32–05 Costs payable to a solicitor or counsel in the case of proceedings in the House of Lords will be determined by an officer prescribed by an order of the House of Lords. That provision apart, the Costs Regulations 1989 do not apply to proceedings in the House of Lords.[9]

Time-limits

32–06 No claim by a solicitor for costs will be entertained unless it is submitted within three months of the conclusion of the proceedings to which the legal aid order relates, unless the time has been extended by the appropriate authority. Every claim for costs must be submitted in such form and manner as the appropriate authority may direct and must be accompanied by the legal aid order and any receipts or other documents in support of any disbursements claimed.[10]

Where proceedings in a magistrates' court have not been concluded but a warrant of arrest has been issued, a claim by a solicitor for costs in respect

---

[6] *ibid.* reg. 3(1) (a).
[7] *ibid.* reg. 3(3) (a).
[8] *ibid. reg.* 3(3).
[9] Legal Aid in Criminal and Care Proceedings (Costs) Regulations 1989, reg. 18(1), (2).
[10] *ibid.* reg. 5(1), (2).

of work done under a legal aid order must be made not earlier than six weeks and not later than 19 weeks from the date of issue of the warrant and the provisions relating to standard fees in the magistrates' court will apply.[11]

In the case of counsel, the same time-limit applies and the claim must be submitted in the form and manner directed by the appropriate authority.[12]

The Costs Regulations 1989 specify various time-limits in relation to applications for costs, redetermination and appeals. Those limits may, for good reason, be extended by the appropriate authority or in relation to an appeal to a taxing master, by the taxing master, or in relation to appeals to the High Court, by the High Court.[13]

Where a solicitor or counsel has, without good reason, failed to comply with a time-limit, the time may, in exceptional circumstances, be extended by the appropriate authority, a taxing master or the High Court as the case may be; but the person extending the time-limit must consider whether it is reasonable in the circumstances to reduce the costs. Costs may not be reduced unless the solicitor or counsel has been allowed a reasonable opportunity to show cause orally or in writing, that the costs should not be reduced. Such an application for time may be made after the time-limit has expired.[14]

As regards magistrates' court claims, the Board is continuing to apply **32–07** guidelines previously agreed by the Legal Aid Committee which can be summarised as follows:

To avoid difficulties on assessment, the solicitor should apply for an extension to the time-limit before submission of his cost claim. However, an assessing officer may still extend the time-limit, on receipt of a costs claim, where no prior extension was obtained, provided that he considers there to have been "good reason" for the solicitor's failure to observe the time-limits. The following are examples of what constitutes "good reason":

(a) the claim for costs is a particularly difficult one to prepare. This is unlikely to apply to the majority of magistrates' court claims. However, there may be a small number of magistrates' courts cases where this could constitute "good reason" (*e.g.* a large murder or drugs case or a large-scale VAT fraud involving complex evidential issues);

(b) a co-defendant's case is still awaiting disposal;

(c) there is a genuine misunderstanding about the submission of a claim (*e.g.* under the Advice at Police Stations Scheme an inexperienced solicitor's clerk does not realise that a separate

---

[11] *ibid.* reg. 5(1A).
[12] *ibid.* reg. 8(1), (2).
[13] *ibid.* reg. 17(1).
[14] *ibid.* reg. 17(2).

claim for work done must be submitted in addition to the claim for standby payments);

(d) where, following the committal of the defendant for trial or an appeal against conviction or sentence being lodged, the trial or appeal comes on so quickly that the solicitor cannot release his papers to the area office for assessment of his costs incurred in the magistrates' court;

(e) the defendant is involved in a multiplicity of cases (*e.g.* a juvenile charged with theft is also the subject of related care proceedings and the solicitor feels that he cannot release the papers until all the proceedings are concluded);

(f) the solicitor has been waiting for another party to render his account, *e.g.* counsel or a local solicitor agent;

(g) although, the court has granted legal aid, there has been a delay in issuing the legal aid order without which the solicitor cannot submit his claim.

These examples are, of course, by no means exhaustive. Each case must be judged on its merits and there may be other situations where the solicitor will be able to show "good reason" for submitting his bill out of time. Where the determining officer decides that the solicitor has shown "good reason", his claim for costs must be assessed in full. There is no jurisdiction to impose a penalty for late submission.

32–08 Where the solicitor has failed to show "good reason", the determining officer must then go on to consider whether there are "exceptional circumstances" which would justify extending the time-limit. The following are examples of "exceptional circumstances":

(a) the size of the claim is such that disallowance of all of the solicitor's costs would represent too harsh a penalty. This provision should be construed liberally so as to include any claim for costs in excess of £100;

(b) the solicitor's practice is a small one and, due to the illness of a senior member of staff, the work of the office has become so disrupted that it has become impossible to render bills on time;

(c) the solicitor concludes wrongly that the three-month time-limit runs from the date the Crown Court proceedings were concluded rather than from the date the proceedings in the magistrates' court were concluded;

(d) there has been a major upheaval in the solicitor's practice (*e.g.* amalgamation with another solicitor's practice or destruction of the solicitor's premises);

(e) the solicitor goes on holiday and hands his practice over to a locum who fails to submit bills on time.

These examples are not exhaustive and each case must be judged on its merits. There will be certain cases where what constitutes "exceptional circumstances" may also constitute "good reason".

Where the determining officer decides that there were "exceptional **32–09** circumstances", they must then go on to consider whether to impose a penalty for late submission. Where the only "exceptional circumstances" are that the bill exceeds £100 the following tariff scale of deduction is likely to be imposed:

(a) A maximum of 5 per cent for bills submitted up to three months out of time.

(b) A maximum of 10 per cent for bills submitted up to six months out of time.

(c) A maximum of 15 per cent for bills submitted up to nine months out of time.

(d) A maximum of 20 per cent for bills submitted up to twelve months out of time.

Deductions of more than 20 per cent should not be imposed normally. However, there may be cases where claims for costs are submitted so late that higher deductions would be warranted. Any such higher deduction should not exceed 50 per cent of the claim for costs as assessed.

Where a solicitor has failed to show either good reason or "exceptional circumstances" his claim for costs is likely to be disallowed in full.

Appeals in relation to time-limits

A solicitor or counsel may appeal to a taxing master against a decision as **32–10** to the enforcement of a time-limit by an appropriate authority, save in respect of proceedings before a magistrates' court. The appeal must be instituted within 21 days of the decision being given, by notice in writing to the Chief Taxing Master specifying the ground of appeal.[15]

THE INFORMATION TO BE PROVIDED

Solicitors

A solicitor's claim for costs must: **32–11**

(a) summarise the items or work done by a fee-earner according to the classes specified;

(b) state, where appropriate, the dates on which the items of work were done, the time taken, the sums claimed and whether the work was done for more than one assisted person;

(c) in the case of proceedings in the Crown Court or the Court of

---

[15] *ibid.* reg. 17(3).

Appeal, specify, where appropriate, the fee-earner who undertook
each of the items of work claimed;

(d) give particulars of any work done in relation to more than one
indictment or re-trial;

(e) specify any disbursements claimed, the circumstances in which
they were incurred and the amounts claimed in respect of them.

(f) state the amount agreed in respect of counsel's fee (including the
time spent in preparation, advocacy and waiting) in proceedings
where counsel has been instructed by the solicitor although not
assigned under the legal aid order.[16]

Where the solicitor claims that representation or advice, given before a
legal aid order was made, should be deemed to be given under the legal
aid order, or that enhanced rates should be paid owing to the exceptional
competence or despatch with which the work was done, or the exceptional
circumstances of the case, full particulars must be given in support of the
claim.[17] The solicitor is under an obligation to draw the attention of the
appropriate authority to any special circumstances and must supply such
further particulars, information and documents as the authority may
require.[18]

Counsel

32–12 A claim for fees by counsel must:

(a) summarise the items of work in respect of which fees are claimed
according to the classes specified in the LACCP(C)R89.

(b) state the dates on which the items of work were done, the time
taken where appropriate, the sums claimed and whether the work
was done for more than one assisted person;

(c) give particulars of any work done in relation to more than one
indictment or a re-trial.[19]

Where counsel claims that a standard fee would be inappropriate or that
owing to the exceptional circumstances of the case higher fees should be
paid, full particulars should be given in support of the claim.[20] Counsel is
under an obligation to draw any special circumstances to the attention of
the appropriate authority and must supply such further particulars,
information and documents as the authority may require.[21]

---

[16] *ibid.* reg. 5(3).
[17] *ibid.* reg. 5(4).
[18] *ibid.* reg. 5(5), (6).
[19] *ibid.* reg. 8(3).
[20] *ibid.* reg. 8(4).
[21] *ibid.* reg. 8(5), (6).

DETERMINATION BY THE APPROPRIATE AUTHORITY

Solicitors' ex post facto determination

In the magistrates' court, the fees prescribed do not differentiate between **32–13** the grade of fee-earner doing the work. However, in the Crown Court and the Court of Appeal, different rates are applicable to senior solicitors (Grade A fee-earners); solicitors, legal executives or fee-earners of equivalent experience (Grade B fee-earners); or articled clerks or fee-earners of equivalent experience (Grade C fee-earners). Fees will be allowed to whichever grade of fee-earner it was reasonable to employ to undertake the work.[22] Normally, the figures in respect of solicitors' costs are revised annually in April. However if the figures are not revised where work was done after June 30 in any year the appropriate authority may allow such fees in such amounts as appear to it to be reasonable remuneration having regard to the amount specified in the schedule. In those circumstances, it would seem reasonable to expect an increase in the fees in line with inflation.[23]

If a Grade A fee-earner undertakes work more properly conducted by a Grade C fee-earner, only the Grade C rate will be paid. If a Grade C fee-earner undertakes Grade B work or above, it is not correct to claim at a higher rate but a claim for enhanced rates should be made.[24]

There is no formal definition in the LACCP(C)R89 of "a senior solicitor". The precise point at which a solicitor becomes a senior solicitor must ultimately be decided by the determining authority. There is no rule that a senior solicitor is one of more than 10 years' standing, although it is probable that such a solicitor would be considered to be a senior solicitor. A solicitor with less than 10 years' post-admission experience may be deemed to be a senior solicitor if the greater part of his experience has been dealing with heavy or complex criminal matters which required the expertise which would normally be expected of a senior solicitor.[25]

Fee-earners of "equivalent experience" must be identified on the facts **32–14** relating to each particular fee-earner and each particular case. An unadmitted clerk may have experience equivalent to that of the solicitor or legal executive in one particular field but not possess such experience in another field (e.g. fraud) and might therefore be assessed at different rates in different cases. It is for the solicitor when submitting the claim for costs to justify the particular rates claimed and to set out the relevant factors

---

[22] *ibid.* Shed. 1, Pt. I.
[23] *ibid.* reg. 6(3).
[24] *ibid.* reg. 6(4).
[25] *R. v. Halcrow* [1984] T.C. S.14.

relied upon.[26] It should be noticed that only a senior solicitor can qualify for the "A" rate. It can, of course, be argued that because of the exceptional competence and dispatch with which the case was dealt, or the exceptional circumstances of the case, the legal executive should be allowed an enhanced rate.

An enquiry agent who, on behalf of a solicitor, has performed the function of a solicitor's clerk, or even of the solicitor himself was held to be a "clerk" (within the meaning of section 43(1) of the Solicitor's Act 1974) and that did not necessarily imply that a master and servant relationship had to exist between the agent and the solicitor.[27]

32–15 The reference to "legal executive" in the Costs Regulations 1989 means a fellow of the Institute of Legal Executives and a "fee-earner" is a solicitor, legal executive or any clerk who regularly does work for which it is appropriate to make a direct charge to the client.[28]

Solicitors may claim for work done in the following classes:

    (a) preparation, including taking instructions, interviewing witnesses, ascertaining the prosecution case, advising on plea and mode of trial, preparing and perusing documents, dealing with letters and telephone calls which are not routine, preparing for advocacy, instructing counsel and expert witnesses, conferences, consultations, views and work done in connection with advice on appeal on a case stated;

    (b) advocacy, including applications for bail and other applications to the court;

    (c) attendance at court where counsel is assigned, including conferences with counsel at court;

    (d) travelling and waiting;

    (e) dealing with routine letters written and routine telephone calls.[29]

The appropriate authority must consider the claim and any further particulars, information or documents submitted by the solicitor at the request of the authority and any other relevant information (including any observation by the trial judge) and allow such work as appears to it to have been reasonably done under the legal aid order by a fee-earner. The work to be allowed includes any work done prior to the granting of the legal aid order which is deemed to be work done under the order. The work must have been carried out by a fee-earner (for this purpose, a non fee-earner can temporarily be deemed a fee-earner when undertaking fee-earner's work).

32–16 In dealing with the question of fee-earners and non fee-earners, the Chief Taxing Master stated in *R. v. Pullum*.[30]

---

[26] *R. v. Ali* TC S.12; *R. v. Zavala* TC S.11; *R. v. Green* [1984] TC S.13; *R. v. Neale* [1984] TC S.17.
[27] *Re B (A Solicitor's Clerk), The Times,* April 19, 1988, C.A.
[28] Legal Aid in Criminal and Care Proceedings (Costs) Regulations 1989, reg. 2(2).
[29] *ibid.* reg. 6(1).
[30] (1983) 133 New L.J. 1017, D.C.

"I will put the general principle in this way: a solicitor as an officer of the court has a duty to ensure that, in all cases where counsel is instructed and appears at a trial, a solicitor or a responsible member of his staff must attend. In my view the Regulations clearly provide that if that duty is performed, then, providing the person attending regularly does that class of work, the determining officer must treat him as a fee-earner. A determining officer in the Crown Court or Court of Appeal who has to consider a claim for costs made pursuant to the Regulations should apply regulation 6 to each item or class or items of work for which payment is claimed, by satisfying himself upon the following matters:

(a) Was the person who did the work a fee earner as defined by regulation 2;

(b) Did the work fall within the classes set out in regulation 6(1);

(c) Was the work actually and reasonably done or was the time spent on it reasonable?

Having satisfied himself on these matters, he must then decide which of the grades of fee-earner set out in regulation 6(4) he considers reasonably applied when assessing the fee."

It will be seen that it is necessary to look at the nature of the work which is being carried out in order to ascertain whether or not the person doing the work is in fact a fee-earner. The items of work claimed must, of course, come within the specified classes.

The work allowed by the appropriate authority will be divided up into the classes listed above, as the authority considers appropriate. In addition to allowing items of work, the appropriate authority must allow such time in respect of that work as it considers reasonable. Routine letters written and routine telephone calls are paid at a unit price regardless of time. Where it is sought to claim a letter or telephone call on a timed basis, these will fall into the non-routine category and should be claimed under (a) above rather than under (e).[31]

As to the specific classes of work allowable, Mustill J. in his judgment in **32–17** R. v. Sandhu[32] said:

"Certainly regulation 6(1) (of the 1982 Regulations which were in similar terms) creates an exclusive code for the ascertainment of the type of work which may properly be allowed. This does not mean however that nothing except what is explicitly described in the various sub-paragraphs can be claimed. The definitions of the type of work are contained (so far as concerns sub-paragraphs (a), (b), (c)) in the words which precede the first comma. What follows thereafter is added by

---

[31] Legal Aid in Criminal and Care Proceedings (Costs) Regulations 1989, reg. 6(2).
[32] November 11, 1984; TC SJ 1.

way of illustration. Thus the fact that supervisory work of the type performed by the senior solicitor in this case cannot be fitted within any of the activities described in the latter part of sub-paragraph (a), does not mean that no fee can be allowed in respect of it.

What matters is whether it constitutes 'preparation'. If it does, then the determining officer can and must allow . . . such fees in respect of it as he shall consider reasonable."

Letters and telephone calls

32–18 In *R. v. Hudson*[33] Evans J. was asked to deal with the question of certain routine correspondence and telephone calls. The particular types of item were specified as correspondence with and telephone calls to and from:

    (a) counsel's chambers dealing with matters such as the availability of counsel, arrangement of conferences and listing difficulties;

    (b) the Crown Court in connection with listing and other administrative matters;

    (c) witnesses to arrange appointments.

Evans J. stated:

"Correspondence and telephone calls of the kind as described in paragraphs (a) (b) and (c) of the question which are 'routine letters written and routine telephone calls actually and reasonably dealt with by a fee-earner' should not be disallowed on the ground either that they form part of the solicitor's overheads or that they should be assumed to be covered by a care and conduct element deemed to be included in the rates prescribed by the Regulations."

It now appears settled beyond doubt that routine letters written should be allowed at the unit rate, unless it is unreasonable for the letter to have been written or the letter was not fee-earners' work; in relation to telephone calls, all calls should be allowed, save abortive calls and those which are unreasonable or not fee-earners' work. A person who is not otherwise a fee-earner may be treated as a fee-earner when doing fee-earners' work.[34]

SOLICITORS' STANDARD FEES IN THE MAGISTRATES' COURT

32–19 The classes of work covered by standard fees in the magistrates' court are:

    (a) any preparation within the meaning of regulation 6(1)(a) including

---

[33] July 11, 1985, TC SJ 2.

[34] *R. v. Pullum* (1983) 133 New L.J. 1017; see now *Re B (A Solicitor's Clerk), The Times*, April 19, 1988, C.A.

listening to, or viewing, any tape or video recording of interviews or evidence;

(b) routine letters written and routine telephone calls within the meaning of regulation 6(1)(e);

(c) advocacy, including bail and other applications made in either a magistrates' court or the Crown Court;

(d) work done by a fee-earner acting as agent for the solicitor assigned under the legal aid order;

(e) unassigned counsel's preparation, and advocacy.[35]

Where the solicitor acts for more than one defendant in the proceedings the claim for payment of a standard fee covers all the legally aided defendants whom he represents.

Where a legal aid order is granted to a defendant in respect of more than one charge or information, the claim for payment of the standard fee covers all the charges or informations which form part of one case.[36]

Certain costs are payable in addition to the standard fee and are determined in accordance with regulations 6 and 7 and 7A of the Costs Regulations 1989. Those costs are:

(a) travelling and waiting time of fee-earners and unassigned counsel which is payable at the rate provided in paragraph 1(1)(a) of Schedule 1, Part 1 of the Costs Regulations 1989; and

(b) disbursements.[37]

Procedure

Allowance of standard fees

The Board must allow a lower standard fee where the core costs (*i.e* the **32–20** costs relating to the classes of work specified in paragraph 4(2)) would not, if they had been determined, have exceeded the lower limit.

Where the core costs claimed by the solicitor exceed the lower limit, the Board must determine the core costs in accordance with regulation 6(2) of the Costs Regulations 1989 and if the core costs so determined:

(a) do not exceed the lower limit, allow the lower standard fee;

(b) exceed the lower limit but do not exceed the higher limit, allow the higher standard fee;

(c) exceed the higher limit, allow the core cost as determined.

The rates specified in paragraph 1(1)(a) of Schedule 1, Part 1 of the Costs Regulations 1989 apply to the costs claimed subject to the fact that the Board may allow fees at less than the basic rate specified where it appears

---

[35] Legal Aid in Criminal and Care Proceedings (Costs) Regulations 1989, Sched. 1, Pt. III, para. 4.

[36] *ibid.* Sched. 1, Pt. III, para. 5.

[37] *ibid.* Sched. 1, Pt. III, para. 6.

reasonable to do so having regard to the competence and dispatch with which the work was done.[38]

Fees payable

32–21 The standard fees payable in the magistrates' court are set out in Schedule 1, Part III, to the Costs Regulations 1989.[39]

A solicitor is entitled to the relevant standard fee at the London rate where his office is situated within legal aid area 1.[40]

The costs payable in respect of standard fees in the magistrates' court are (subject to any deductions or reductions made pursuant to any wasted costs order or penalty imposed on an application for redetermination or review out of time):

> (a) the relevant standard fee together with the costs in respect of travelling and waiting time for fee earners and disbursements determined in accordance with the provisions of paragraph 6; or
>
> (b) where the core costs allowed exceed the higher limit of the relevant standard fee, the costs as determined in accordance with regulations 6 and 7 of the Costs Regulations 1989.[41]

Where proceedings have not been concluded but a warrant of arrest has been issued and a solicitor has been paid prior to the final disposal of the proceedings, any costs which would have been payable upon the final disposal of the proceedings will be reduced to the extent that they formed part of the costs previously, claimed.[42]

SOLICITORS' STANDARD FEES IN THE CROWN COURT

32–22 Standard fees are payable only in respect of certain classes of work, if other work is properly carried out which is not covered by standard fees, the claim must be made for *ex post facto* determination in respect of those items of work in the normal way.

The classes of work covered by standard fees are:

> (a) preparation, including taking instructions, interviewing witnesses, ascertaining the prosecution case, advising on plea and mode of trial, preparing and perusing documents, dealing with letters and telephone calls *both routine and non routine*, preparing for advocacy, instructing counsel and expert witnesses, conferences,

---

[38] *ibid.* Sched. 1, Pt. III, para. 7, Sched. 1, Pt. I, para. 2.
[39] *ibid.* Sched. 1, Pt. III, para. 8(1).
[40] *ibid.* Sched. 1, Pt. III, para. 8(2), Sched. 1, Pt. I, para. 1(2).
[41] *ibid.* Sched. 1, Pt. III, para. 8(2), Sched. 1, Pt. I, para. 8(3).
[42] *ibid.* Sched. 1 Pt. III, para. 8(2), Sched. 1, Pt. I, para. 8(4).

consultations, views and work done in connection with advice on appeal or case stated;

(b) advocacy (including waiting) in respect of applications for bail;

(c) attendance at court (including waiting) where counsel is assigned;

(d) travelling except:

    (i) to undertake work for which standard fees are not payable, or

    (ii) in respect of advocacy appertaining to bail applications.

In this context, "travelling" includes waiting time in connection with preparation work.[43]

Where a fee-earner travels to appear as an advocate in respect of a bail application, the rate payable will be the prescribed rate for travelling and waiting applicable to that grade of fee-earner on an *ex post facto* determination.[44]

Waiting

The allowance for attendance at court includes waiting, and is calculated   **32–23** from 30 minutes before the case was listed, and ends, where the client was present at court, 15 minutes after the hearing ended on that day, or, if the client was not present, at the time when the hearing ended on that day. Nothing is payable during the luncheon adjournment save in exceptional circumstances.[45]

If the fee-earner is attending court in respect of more than one case, a duplicate claim may not be made, thus a full attendance claim is made in respect of one case, and in respect of the second or subsequent cases only the time spent in attendance in addition may be claimed.[46]

Increases to standard fees

The standard fees payable are set out in the Table to the Costs Regulations   **32–24** 1989, Sched. 1, Pt. II. That Table sets out the "lower fee limit" and the "upper fee limit" and prescribes a "lower standard fee" and a "principal (higher) standard fee" in respect of the various classes of work. "London rate" is prescribed for solicitor with offices situated within legal aid area 1.[47] In certain circumstances, the standard fee can be increased either by a percentage or by a prescribed sum. Where such an increase is made, the upper and lower fee limits are increased by the same amount by which the

---

[43] *ibid.* Sched. 1, Pt. II, para. 4.

[44] *ibid.* Sched. 1, Pt. II, para. 4(7), Sched. 1, Pt. I, para. 1(1)(c).

[45] *R. v. Wanklyn* [1985] TC S.28; Legal Aid in Criminal and Care Proceedings (Costs) Regulations 1989, Sched. 1, Pt. I, para. 4(5).

[46] Legal Aid in Criminal and Care proceedings (Costs) Regulations 1989, Sched. 1, Pt. II, para. 4(6).

[47] *ibid.* Sched. 1, Pt. II, para. 4(3), (4).

standard fee has been increased.[48] Where a solicitor acts for more than one defendant or in respect of more than one indictment, appeal against conviction, appeal against sentence or committal for sentence, the standard fee will be increased by 20 per cent for each additional defendant and for each additional indictment, appeal, etc. Advocacy in respect of bail applications will also be increased by 20 per cent for each additional defendant represented. No increase is made for a solicitor's attendance at court where counsel is assigned or for travelling.[49]

Counsel

32–25 Where a solicitor prepares a case with a view to counsel appearing at the substantive hearing alone, the standard fee will be increased by a prescribed amount.[50]

Tape recordings

32–26 Where a fee-earner listens to a tape recording of an interview conducted under the Police and Criminal Evidence Act 1984, the standard preparation fee will be further increased by a prescribed amount for every 10 minutes or part thereof spent listening to tapes. The Costs Regulations 1989 refer to "the total running time of all tapes or parts of tapes listened to".[51]

Supplementary provisions relating to standard fees

32–27 Where in proceedings which would otherwise attract standard fees, the trial judge is dissatisfied with the solicitor's conduct of the case, or considers that, for exceptional reasons (*e.g.* because of the exceptional competence displayed), standard fees should not apply, the judge may direct *ex post facto* determination. This would enable the appropriate authority to allow either more or less than the standard fees prescribed depending upon the tenor of the judge's direction.[52]

It is open to a solicitor to claim standard fees for work done nothwithstanding that the proceedings would not otherwise attract standard fees. The Costs Regulations 1989 and Schedule apply with the necessary

---

[48] *ibid.* Sched. 1, Pt. II, para. 4(12).
[49] *ibid.* Sched. 1, Pt. II, para. 4(8), (9).
[50] *ibid.* Sched. 1, Pt. II, para. 4(10); at present £30 (£31 in London).
[51] Legal Aid in Criminal and Care Proceedings (Costs) Regulations 1989, Sched. 1 Pt. II, para, 4(11) as amended by Legal Aid in Criminal and Care Proceedings (Costs) (Amendment) Regulations 1990, reg. 3(6). The current increase is £10.45.
[52] Legal Aid in Criminal and Care Proceedings (Costs) Regulations 1989, Sched. 1, Pt. II, para. 1(3).

modifications, except that where the solicitor claims the principal standard fee in respect of a trial which lasted more than two days that fee together with any other appropriate standard fees *must* be paid.[53]

Where the principal or higher standard fee for preparation is claimed the appropriate authority may allow the lower standard fee if it considers that the fee claimed is excessive.[54] The Costs Regulations 1989 do not enlarge upon the circumstances in which such a fee might be considered to be excessive and in the absence of observations by the trial judge it is difficult to envisage any circumstances in which this provision could properly be applied.

Procedure

Where a principal standard fee is claimed and a lower standard fee is allowed

A solicitor who has claimed the principal standard fee but been allowed **32–28** the lower standard fee, may accept that lower fee, request the appropriate authority in writing to review its decision, or provide the appropriate authority with a detailed claim form requesting in writing that the fees for preparation be determined *ex post facto*.[55]

Where the appropriate authority is requested to review its decision, it must either allow the principal standard fee, or request the solicitor to provide a detailed claim form. It is *not* open to the appropriate authority to affirm the allowance of the lower standard fee.[56]

The time-limit

If the solicitor does not request a review or supply a detailed claim within **32–29** six weeks of the decision or the request to supply a detailed claim form, whichever is the later, the decision to allow the lower standard fee is deemed to be confirmed.[57]

Procedure where a detailed claim is submitted

Where a solicitor submits a claim for *ex post facto* determination in **32–30** proceedings which attract standard fees, or disputes the allowance of the lower standard fee and provides a detailed claim form as described above, the appropriate authority must first determine the preparation work in accordance with the standard fee provisions. If the fees so determined are

---

[53] *ibid.* Sched. 1, Pt. II, para. 1(4).
[54] *ibid.* Sched. 1, Pt. II, para. 2(1).
[55] *ibid.* Sched. 1, Pt. II, para. 2(2).
[56] *ibid.* Sched. 1, Pt. II, para. 2(3).
[57] *ibid.* Sched. 1, Pt. II, para. 3(4).

less than the lower fee-limit, the lower standard fee is payable: if between the lower and the upper limit, the principal standard fee is payable and; if more than the upper fee-limit, standard fees are not payable and a full *ex post facto* determination must be carried out. If a standard fee is found to be payable, standard fees for all other classes of work specified are also payable.[58]

Solicitors' disbursements

32–31 The appropriate authority must allow the disbursements claimed by a solicitor providing that they have been reasonably incurred, regardless of whether standard fees are payable.[59] Where prior authority has been obtained, no question may be raised as to the propriety of any step or act authorised, unless the solicitor knew or ought to have known that the purpose for which the authority was given had failed or become irrelevant or unnecessary before the disbursement was incurred. Amounts in excess of any authority may be justified and allowed.

If the disbursements are abnormally large by reason of the distance of the court or the assisted person's residence or both from the solicitor's office, reimbursement may be limited to what would otherwise be reasonable, *i.e.* if a local solicitor had been instructed. For this reason, if a legally assisted person chooses a solicitor who is not local, that solicitor must, before accepting instructions, consider whether the distance involved is such that the disbursements are likely to be reduced.

In the Court of Appeal where a transcript is obtained of the proceedings in the court below, nothing will be recoverable unless the transcript was obtained through the registrar or it was reasonable in all circumstances for the transcript to be obtained.[60]

COSTS IN PROCEEDINGS INVOLVING COUNSEL NOT ASSIGNED UNDER THE LEGAL AID ORDER

32–32 In proceedings in a magistrates' court, a solicitor may instruct counsel even though counsel is not assigned under the legal aid order and, subject to the Costs Regulations 1989 the Board will pay counsel the fees agreed between him and the solicitor.[61] Counsel's agreed fees will also include any fees agreed in respect of travelling and waiting time and travelling costs.[62]

---

[58] *ibid.* Sched. 1, Pt. II, para. 3(1), (2).
[59] *ibid.* reg. 7(1).
[60] *ibid.* reg. 7(1) (a), (b).
[61] *ibid.* reg. 7A(1).
[62] *ibid.* reg. 7A(1A).

The solicitor must claim the costs (including the time spent by counsel in preparation, and advocacy) at the rates applicable to solicitors' fees in magistrates' courts proceedings. The Board will determine the costs which would have been payable to the solicitor if he had undertaken the case without counsel.[63]

The costs payable in respect of counsel's agreed fee will be reduced only where, and to the extent that, they would exceed:

(a) the costs determined as above; or
(b) in a standard fee case the total payable under those provisions and the travelling costs allowed in respect of counsel.

The Board will pay the fee to counsel direct and pay the balance to the solicitor.[64]

Counsel's brief must include a copy of the legal aid order to enable counsel to be satisfied as to the legal aid position.[65]

The position where leading counsel is instructed alone without junior counsel has been dealt with earlier.[66]

EXPERTS' FEES AND WITNESSES

The situation with regard to the instruction of experts and payment of **32–33** witnesses fees generally has been dealt with earlier.

COUNSEL'S STANDARD FEES

Standard fees for counsel apply to work done by junior counsel in the **32–34** Crown Court. Standard fees are payable unless such a fee would be "inappropriate" taking into account all the relevant circumstances of the case. It has been held that if the standard fee would not provide reasonable remuneration for work actually and reasonably done then it was inappropriate for the purposes of the Costs Regulations 1989.

Any case falling within the categories to which standard fees are required to be applied, must be a usual case of its kind viewed as to weight, gravity or complexity. This applies equally to all cases falling within the categories without regard to the intrinsic, weight, gravity or complexity which may be found in one class of case as a distinct from another.[67]

What this decision actually appears to mean is that in order to take, *e.g.*

---

[63] *ibid.* reg. 7A(2),(3).
[64] *ibid.* reg. 7A(4),(5).
[65] *ibid.* reg. 40(5).
[66] *ibid.* reg. 7(4) (6).
[67] *R. v. Hugget* [1988] TC C12.

a simple theft, out of the range of standard fees, there would have to be significant factors involved. Whereas in the case of a more serious offence such as causing death by dangerous driving, such factors could be of a relatively minor nature.[68]

Standard fees may not be paid in respect of:
    (a) committals for trial in which the indictment includes offences of Class 1 or 2;
    (b) proceedings in any other case:
        (i) which lasted more than three days or which at the time of listing were reasonably expected to last more than three days;
        (ii) in which the indictment is disposed of by a plea of guilty but which, if contested, would, reasonably have been expected to last more than three days.

Counsel may request the allowance of a standard fee in any event.[69]

TYPES OF STANDARD FEE

32–35 The types of standard fee allowable are:
    (a) a standard basic fee;
    (b) a standard refresher fee;
    (c) a standard written work fee;
    (d) a standard appearance fee.

The Table of standard fees is set out at the end of Schedule 2, Part I to the Costs Regulations 1989.

Standard basic fee

32–36 This covers preparation, and the first day's hearing including, where they took place on that day, short conferences, applications and appearances (including bail applications), views and any other preparation.[70]

Where junior counsel appears in respect of proceedings arising out a breach of an order of the Crown Court or similar matters, the standard basic fee specified for "committals for sentence" is allowed.[71]

Where a case listed for jury trial does not proceed on the day for which it is listed, counsel is entitled to a sum equal to half the standard basic fee for a jury trial.[72]

---

[68] Legal Aid in Criminal and Care Proceedings (Costs) Regulations 1989, reg. 9(2).
[69] *ibid.* reg. 9(3).
[70] *ibid.* Sched. 2, Pt. I, para. (a)
[71] *ibid.* Sched. 2, Pt. I, para. 3.
[72] *ibid.* Sched. 2, Pt. I, para. 4.

Standard refresher fee

This covers any day during which the hearing continued, including where **32–37**
they took place on that day, short conferences, applications and
appearances (including bail applications), views and any other
preparation.[73]
Refresher fees are calculated as follows:
(a) A half-day refresher is allowed where:
(i) the hearing begins and ends before the luncheon
adjournment; or
(ii) a hearing begins after the luncheon adjournment and ends
before 5.30 pm.
(b) A full-day refresher is allowed where:
(i) a hearing begins before and ends after the luncheon
adjournment but before 5.30 pm; or
(ii) a hearing begins after the luncheon adjournment and ends
after 5.30 pm.
(c) A more than full-day refresher is allowed where a hearing beings
before the luncheon adjournment and ends after 5.30 pm.[74]

Standard written-work fee

This covers written advice on evidence, plea, appeal, case stated and other **32–38**
written work.[75]

Standard appearance fee

This covers attendance, applications and appearances (including bail **32–39**
applications and adjournments for sentence) together with, where they took
place on that day, short conferences where attendance is not covered by
the basic fee or refresher fee. The standard appearance fee does not cover
attendance at a pre-trial review.[76]
Where a case is listed for plea and adjourned for trial, or a case is listed
for hearing but not opened due to the failure of the defendant or a witness
to attend or the non-availability of a social inquiry report, or some other
good reason, counsel will be paid the standard appearance fee.[77]

---

[73] *ibid.* Sched. 2, Pt. I, para. 1 (b); *R. v. Gadhim, R. v. Gerhards* [1984] TC C2.
[74] *ibid.* Sched. 2, Pt. I, para. 2.
[75] *ibid.* Sched. 2, Pt. I, para. 1(c).
[76] *ibid.* Sched. 2, Pt. I, para. 1(d).
[77] *ibid.* Sched. 2, Pt. I, para. 5 as amended by Legal Aid in Criminal and Care Proceedings
(Costs) (Amendment) Regulations 1990, reg. 3(7).

PLEAS

32–40 Where a case is listed for plea, and a guilty plea is taken and the case is then adjourned part-heard, counsel is entitled to a standard basic fee for the first hearing and the standard appearance fee for the hearing at which the case is disposed of.[78]

ADDITIONAL DEFENDANTS AND ADDITIONAL INDICTMENTS, ETC.

32–41 Where counsel represents more than one defendant, the standard basic fee is increased by 20 per cent for each additional defendant who is substantively dealt with at the hearing in respect of which the basic fee is paid. There is no provision for percentage increases in respect of refresher fees or any other standard fees.[79]

The basic fee is similarly increased by 20 per cent where counsel appears on behalf of a defendant on the same day in respect of more than one indictment, appeal against conviction, appeal against sentence, or committal for sentence. A combination of additional defendants and additional indictments, etc., entitles counsel to an increase in respect of each defendant and/or indictment.[80]

COUNSEL APPEARING ALONE

32–42 Counsel who appears at the substantive hearing of a case without his instructing solicitor attending court, is entitled to an increase in the standard basic fee, irrespective of any percentage increase to which counsel may be entitled because of multiple defendants or indictments.[81]

TAPE RECORDINGS

32–43 A further increase is payable on the standard basic fee where counsel listens to a tape recording of an interview conducted under the Police and

---

[78] Legal Aid in Criminal and Care Proceedings (Costs) Regulations 1989, Sched. 2, Pt. I, para. 6 as amended by Legal Aid in Criminal and Care Proceedings (Costs) (Amendment) Regulations 1990, reg. 3(8).
[79] *ibid.* 1989, Sched. 2, Pt. I, para. 7(a) and (b).
[80] *ibid.* Sched. 2, Pt. I, para. 8.
[81] *ibid.* Sched. 2, Pt. I, para. 9. Current increase £18.50.

Criminal Evidence Act 1984. The increase is payable for every 10 minutes or part thereof spent listening to the tapes. The Regulations refer to "the total running time of all tapes or parts of tapes listened to".[82]

TRAVELLING AND HOTEL EXPENSES

Where counsel is instructed to appear at a distant court (*i.e.* not within 25 miles of his chambers) the appropriate authority may allow an amount to cover any travelling and hotel expenses reasonably incurred and necessarily and exclusively attributable to counsel's attendance at court provided that the amount allowed is not greater than the amount which would be payable to counsel practising from the nearest local bar, unless counsel is able to justify his attendance having regard to all the relevant circumstances of the case.[83] This provision encapsulates the decision in *R. v. Crittenden*[84] a decision of the Chief Taxing Master under earlier Regulations. It is a question of fact in each case whether or not counsel can justify his attendance instead of counsel from the local bar, but the local bar must be of sufficient strength to give the legally assisted person and instructing solicitor a reasonable choice of counsel of sufficient weight and experience. Circuit leading counsel are not regarded as being "local" to any particular court and are entitled to their reasonable travelling and hotel expenses anywhere on circuit not merely at distant courts.[85]

32–44

Where leading counsel claimed to be entitled to expenses for attending a court which was distant from his home, it was held that the basic principle was that travelling expenses were calculated from counsel's chambers unless the journey undertaken commenced from home or from some other location which was nearer to the destination than chambers, in which case the actual mileage was reimbursed. Since counsel's chambers were, in this case, in Leeds, and the hearing was in Leeds, he was not therefore entitled to travelling expenses to court. The Master also held that hotel or accommodation expenses could not be divorced from travelling expenses. Hotel expenses were paid instead of travelling expenses where counsel chose, or by reason of distance was obliged, to stay near to the distant court rather than to travel daily. It followed that if travelling expenses were not payable, then neither were hotel or accommodation expenses.[86]

---

[82] *ibid.* Sched. 2, Pt. I, para. 10 as amended by Legal Aid in Criminal and Care Proceedings (Costs) (Amendment) Regulations 1990, reg. 3(10). Current increase £10.45.
[83] Legal Aid in Criminal and Care Proceedings (Costs) Regulations 1989, Sched. 2, Pt. I, para. 11.
[84] 1985 T.M.D. 2 68.
[85] *R. v. Hutton* 1985 TC C5.
[86] *R. v. Khan* 1989 TC C.

COUNSEL EX POST FACTO DETERMINATION

32–45 *Ex post facto* determination of counsel's fees takes place where standard fees are not appropriate, for work done by junior counsel in the Crown Court and in respect of all other work. The appropriate authority must consider the claim and any further particulars, information or documents submitted by counsel and any other relevant information and must allow such work as appears to it to have been reasonably done.[87]

When determining fees, the appropriate authority may allow a figure, not exceeding the maximum amounts specified, in respect of each item of work as appears to it to provide reasonable remuneration.[88] Normally, the figures in respect of counsel's fees are revised annually in April. However, if the fees are not revised, where work was done after June 30 in a particular year, the appropriate authority may allow such fees in such amounts as appear to it to be reasonable remuneration having regard to the amount specified in the schedule. In those circumstances, it would seem reasonable to expect an increase in the fees in line with inflation.[89]

Where an hourly rate is specified in the Table to the Schedule, a minimum amount is also prescribed. The appropriate authority will determine the work at the hourly rate but may not allow less than the minimum amount specified.[90]

The types of fees payable are:

    (a) a basic fee;

    (b) a refresher fee; and

    (c) subsidiary fees covering conferences and views, written advice and attendances at pre-trial reviews and other applications.[91]

Basic fee

32–46 This covers preparation including preparation for pre-trial review and, where appropriate, the first day's hearing including, where they took place on that day, short conferences, consultations, applications and appearances (including bail applications), views and any other preparation.[92]

Preparatory work undertaken during the course of the trial is allowed as part of the daily refresher, not as part of the brief fee.[93]

---

[87] Legal Aid in Criminal and Care Proceedings (Costs) Regulations 1989, reg. 9(4).
[88] *ibid.* Sched. 2, Pt. II, para. 1.
[89] *ibid.* reg. 9(5)(a).
[90] *ibid.* Sched. 2, Pt. II, para. 2.
[91] *ibid.* reg. 9(4).
[92] *ibid.* reg. 9(4)(a).
[93] *R. v. Ghadim and Gerhards* [1984] TC C2.

In the Crown Court where junior counsel appears in proceedings arising out of a breach of an order of the Crown Court or other similiar matters, the fee allowed will not exceed the maximum amount specified for committals for sentence.[94]

Refresher fees

Refresher fees cover any day or part of a day during which a hearing continued including, where they took place on that day, short conferences, consultations, applications and appearance (including bail applications), views and any other preparation.[95]   **32–47**

Since the Costs Regulations 1989 refer to "any other preparation" in relation to refresher fees, it is necessary for counsel to keep a note, or to be in a position to satisfy the determining officer, of the actual preparation work done on a particular day. Thus, if several hours' preparation is done at night, there may well be a claim for an enhanced refresher in respect of that day. Where preparation is carried out on a day on which the court does not sit, clearly no refresher is payable and the additional preparation must be claimed as part of the basic fee.[96]

The Costs Regulations 1989 specify a maximum amount in respect of refresher fees, thus, where a refresher is claimed in respect of less than a full day, there will be allowed whatever appears reasonable having regard to the fee which would be allowable for a full day.[97]

Subsidiary fees

These include: **32–48**
  (a) attendance at conference, consultations and views not otherwise covered;
  (b) written advice on evidence, plea, appeal, case stated or other written work;
  (c) attendance at pre-trial reviews, applications and appearances (including bail applications and adjournments for sentence) not otherwise covered.[98]

---

[94] Legal Aid in Criminal and Care Proceedings (Costs) Regulations 1989, Sched. 2, Pt. II, para. 4.
[95] *ibid.*, reg. 9(4) (b).
[96] *R. v. Ghadim and Gerhards* [1984].
[97] Legal Aid in Criminal and Court Proceeding (Costs) Regulations 1989, Sched 2, Pt. II, para. 3.
[98] *ibid.* reg. 9(4)(c).

Enhanced fees

Magistrates' court and Crown Court

32–49   In the magistrates' court and the Crown Court the appropriate authority will allow fees in respect of such work as is considered reasonable and at amounts determined in accordance with the Schedule 2 to the Costs Regulations 1989. Where it appears to the appropriate authority, taking into account all the relevant circumstances of the case, that owing to the exceptional circumstances of the case, the amount payable by way of fees in accordance with the Schedule 2 to the Costs Regulations 1989 would not provide reasonable remuneration for some or all of the work it has allowed, it may allow such amount as appears to it to be reasonable remuneration for the relevant work.[99] Counsel seeking the application of this provision must give full particulars in support of his claim for fees. Normally, this is done in the form of a case assessment by counsel and may also be supplemented by observations of the trial judge.[1]

There is nothing in the Costs Regulations 1989 which makes it mandatory for counsel to make an express reference to regulation 9(5)(b) of the 1989 Regulations when making a claim for costs. But counsel must make it perfectly clear that dispensation contained in the regulation is being sought.[2]

Court of Appeal

32–50   In the Court of Appeal, the appropriate authority may allow fees, in respect of work considered to have been reasonably undertaken, in such amounts as appear to it to be reasonable remuneration for the work. In other words, the prescribed fees do not apply to proceedings in the Court of Appeal although, determining officers in the Court of Appeal have regard to the level of prescribed fees in the Crown Court and magistrates' court when considering what fees to allow in respect of work undertaken in the Court of Appeal.[3]

Queen's Counsel appearing alone

32–51   Where authority has been obtained for the instruction of Queen's Counsel alone, no question as to the propriety of that act will be raised on any determination of counsel's fees unless the solicitor knew, or ought reasonably to have known, that the purpose for which the authority was

---

[99] *ibid.* reg. 9(5)(b).
[1] *ibid.* reg. 8(4)(b).
[2] *R. v. Uchegbo* [1985] TC C6.
[3] *ibid.* reg. 9(6).

given had failed or become irrelevant, or unnecessary before the fees were incurred.[4]

Travel and hotel expenses

The provisions with regard to travelling and hotel expenses are identical **32–52** whether the fees are standard fees or *ex post facto*.[5]

Travelling to conferences

Where counsel actually and reasonably incurs expenses in travelling from **32–53** chambers to a prison or other place where a defendant is confined, for the purpose of holding a necessary conference, regulation 9(5)(b) of the Costs Regulations 1989 can be applied in exceptional circumstances, to enable the appropriate authority to increase subsidiary fees payable under regulation 9(4)(c)(i) of the 1989 Regulations to take account of travelling expenses. The expenses must be necessarily and exclusively attributable to the attendance in question. It has been held that if it is necessary for counsel to have a conference with his client who is detained in prison or elsewhere and the prison authorities will only produce the client at the place of detention, then counsel is under a duty to travel to attend the conference and that it is an exceptional circumstance for him to have to do so. The fact that in criminal proceedings this situation may often arise has no bearing on the question of whether it is an exceptional circumstance, nor is the size of the expenses relevant.[6]

REVIEW AND REDETERMINATION

By the Board

Where the Board is the appropriate authority, that is in the case of criminal **32–54** proceedings in a magistrates' court, a solicitor or counsel dissatisfied with a determination (including a decision concerning standard fees in the magistrates' courts) may, within 21 days of receipt of notification of the costs payable, apply to the appropriate area committee to review the decision. The area committee may confirm, increase or decrease the amount of the original determination, or in the case of standard fees,

---

[4] Legal Aid in Criminal and Care Proceedings (Costs) Regulations 1989, reg. 9(7).
[5] *ibid.* Sched. 2, Pt. II, para. 5.
[6] *R. v. Hindle* [1987] TC C11.

confirm or amend the decision,[7] and its decision can only be appealed further to a committee appointed by the Board (the Costs Appeals Committee) if the area committee subsequently certifies that a point of principle of general importance is involved. Although there is no right of audience as such, the area committee may be prepared to hear oral representations (on the review only).

The Board has issued guidance to area offices when dealing with claims for costs:

(a) Since there is no longer a general right of appeal against area committee decisions to the Board, it is essential that area committees are seen to be carrying out an independent review in respect of each and every area office assessment against which representations are made. Area offices should, therefore, only place before the area committee a copy of the report on the case, a breakdown of the officer's assessment and the solicitors' and or counsel's representative in support of their costs and fees as claimed. Comments by the area office on the assessment made should be kept to a minimum and, where made, should be restricted to issues of fact only. The finance manager will be able to advise the committee on any matters of costs assessment practice affecting a particular case.

(b) Area committees should, in all cases, give reasons for their decisions where standard reasons would not be appropriate. The area committee should, of course, give a particular reason for its decision and, if necessary, refer to the relevant regulations and principles governing assessment of the costs.

   The Costs Appeals Committee has decided[8] that, where the Board disallows a specific item for a specific reason, the item should be identified and the reason given but the Board is not precluded from reducing claims for classes of work without specifically identifying particular items of work. An area committee may determine a review of an assessment without considering the solicitor's file of papers provided that it otherwise has sufficient information to determine the appeal or the solicitor has failed to provide that information after having been given an opportunity to do so. Where, in determining costs, the Board has taken into account some specific factor or factors other than the nature, importance, complexity, or difficulty of the work and time involved it should indicate that factor or factors.

---

[7] Legal Aid in Criminal and Care Proceedings (General) Regulations 1989, reg. 12(1), (2); see also reg. 3(1) (c) and (d).

[8] See decision CRIMLA 12.

By an appropriate authority other than the Board

Solicitors' standard fees

A solicitor who has submitted a detailed claim for fees and is dissatisfied **32–55** with the decision to allow standard fees may apply for the costs to be redetermined. The provisions which apply to redetermination in respect of *ex post facto* determination apply to redetermination in these circumstances with the appropriate modifications.[9]

When redetermining, the appropriate authority must determine the fees for preparation work on the standard-fee basis and if the fees determined are less than the lower fee-limit, the lower standard fee is payable. If between the lower fee-limit and the upper fee-limit, the principal standard fee is payable and if more than the upper fee-limit a full *ex post facto* determination must be carried out. Where a standard fee is found to be payable standard fees for all other classes of work are also payable.[10]

Procedure where standard fees acceptable

Even where a solicitor is satisfied with the decision to allow standard fees **32–56** but contends that a standard fee which is not apt for the type of work has been allowed, or the fee has been wrongly calculated, he may make a written request setting out his reasons why the decision should be reviewed. This must be done within six weeks of receipt of notification of the decision. If the appropriate authority confirms its original decision written reasons *must* be given to the solicitor.[11]

Solicitors' ex post facto *determination, counsel's standard fees, counsel's* ex post facto *determination*

There is no provision for review other than by the area committee of the **32–57** area office assessment in respect of criminal proceedings in the magistrates' court. In all other proceedings if a solicitor or counsel is dissatisfied with the allowance of costs, application may be made to the appropriate authority to redetermine those costs or to review the decision (to allow counsel standard fees).[12]

Time-limit

Subject to the provisions as to extension of time-limits applications must be **32–58** made within 21 days of receipt of notification of the costs payable.

---

[9] Legal Aid in Criminal and Care Proceedings (Costs) Regulations 1989, reg. 14(2), (8), Sched. 1, Pt. II, para. 6(1).
[10] *ibid.* Sched. 1, Pt. II, para. 6(2).
[11] *ibid.* Sched. 1, Pt. II, paras. 4(4)–(12), 7.
[12] *ibid.* reg. 14(1).

Procedure

32–59 Application is by notice in writing to the appropriate authority setting out the matters in respect of which application is made and the grounds of objection. No specific form is prescribed and applications are by letter setting out the relevant points at issue.[13]

It is open to either solicitor or counsel to appear or to be represented on the redetermination, and if the applicant wishes to appear the appropriate authority *must* give an appointment. There have been frequent instances of determining officers refusing or declining oral representation but this is wholly wrong.[15] The appropriate authority may require the production of further particulars, information and documents, which it is the duty of the solicitor or counsel to provide.[16]

The appropriate authority may increase or decrease the amounts previously determined or leave them as originally determined; and may review the decision to allow counsel standard fees and confirm it, or allow fees to counsel on an *ex post facto* basis. The result of the redetermination must be notified to the applicant. Either counsel or solicitor may request written reasons for the decision and, if the request is made, the appropriate authority must comply with it.

Subject to the power to extend time, the application for reasons in writing must be made within 21 days of receiving notification of the decision.[17]

APPEALS

To committee appointed by the Board

32–60 In a case in which the Board is the appropriate authority, any solicitor or counsel, dissatisfied with the decision of an area committee on review may, within 21 days of receipt of notification of the decision, apply to that committee to certify a point of principle of general importance.

Where the area committee is satisfied that a point of principle of general importance arises, the certificate should be approved. The matters covered by the standard reasons for decisions are, generally, issues of fact and would not in the normal case justify the certification of a point of principle of general importance. The Board considers that it is the area committee

---

[13] *ibid.* reg. 14(2).
[14] *ibid.* reg. 14(3).
[15] *ibid.* reg. 14(4).
[16] *ibid.* reg. 14(5).
[17] *ibid.* reg. 14(6)–(8).

which should act as the final arbiter on all issues of fact, such as attendance and preparation time.

While the area committee must consider each case on its merits, the types of case where points of principle are most likely to arise are in respect of interpretation of Regulations affecting assessments of costs and the principles governing their application. A point must also be of general importance if it is to be certified. If such a point of principle is certified, the applicant may, within 21 days of receipt of the notification of certification, appeal in writing to the Costs Appeals Committee.

The committee appointed by the Board may reverse, affirm or amend the decision of the area committee, and there is no further appeal. There is no provision for oral representation[18] and if a point is certified it will be notified to the solicitor or counsel who then has to submit any representations and relevant documents to Legal Aid Head Office himself if he wishes the appeal to proceed automatically.

To a taxing master

Solicitors' standard fees in the Crown Court

A solicitor may appeal to a taxing master if dissatisfied with a decision on a redetermination where a detailed claim form has been submitted or a decision on a review as to the aptness, or calculation of standard fees.[19] **32–61**

Where detailed claim form is submitted On an appeal to a taxing master **32–62** where a detailed claim form has been submitted, the taxing master must determine the fees for preparation on the standard fee basis and if the fees so determined are less than the lower fee-limit, the lower standard fee is payable; between the lower and the upper fee-limit the principal standard fee is payable; if above the upper fee-limit, all the work must be determined by the taxing master on an *ex post facto* basis. Where it is found that a standard fee is payable, standard fees for all other classes of work are also payable.[20]

Where there is a dispute as to the standard fee Where the solicitor **32–63** accepts that a standard fee is payable, but contends that a fee which is not apt has been paid, or that the standard fee has been wrongly calculated, the taxing master may allow whatever standard fee he considers to be apt or recalculate the standard fee as he sees fit.[21]

Costs If the appeal is successful in whole or in part, the taxing master may **32–64**

---

[18] Legal Aid in Criminal and Care Proceedings (General) Regulations 1989, reg. 13(1)–(3).
[19] Legal Aid in Criminal and Care Proceedings (General) Regulations 1989, Sched. 1, Pt. II, para. 8(1).
[20] *ibid.* Sched. 1, Pt. II, para. 8(2).
[21] *ibid.* Sched. 1, Pt. II, para. 8(3).

allow the solicitor a sum in respect of part or all of any reasonable costs (including any fee payable in respect of the appeal) incurred by him in connection with the appeal.[22]

All other cases

32–65 Once reasons have been received from the appropriate authority, a solicitor or counsel who is still dissatisfied may, within 21 days of receipt of written reasons, appeal to a taxing master by giving notice in writing to the Chief Taxing Master. A copy of the notice must be sent to the appropriate authority. The notice must be in the form laid down by the Chief Taxing Master.[23]

The notice must also set out in separate numbered paragraphs, each fee or item of costs or disbursements in respect of which the appeal is brought showing the amount claimed for the item, the amount determined, and the grounds of the objection to the decision on the taxation or determination.[24]

The notice must be accompanied by the appropriate fee and state whether or not the appellant wishes to appear or to be represented; or whether he will accept a decision in his absence. The applicant must also forward, at the same time, a legible copy of the bill of costs (or counsel's fee claim) and any supporting submission or memorandum copy of the determination and redetermination, a copy of the original written representations in support of the application for redetermination, the appropriate authority's written reasons for its decision, a copy of the legal aid order and any authorities and the particulars, information and documents supplied to the appropriate authority in support of the redetermination.[25]

32–66 **The Lord Chancellor** Where a point of principle arises, the taxing master will send to the Lord Chancellor a copy of the notice of the appeal, together with such other documents as may be required, and, with a view to ensuring that the public interest is taken into account, the Lord Chancellor may arrange for written or oral representations to be made on his behalf. It is open to the Lord Chancellor to require the Chief Taxing Master to send details of every appeal.

If the Lord Chancellor proposes to make representations, he must inform the Chief Taxing Master and the appellant. Copies of any written representations will be sent to both the Chief Taxing Master and the appellant and, in the case of oral representations, they will be informed of the grounds on

---

[22] *ibid.* Sched. 1, Pt. II, para. 8(4); *R. v. Boswell* [1987] 1 W.L.R. 705.
[23] See *Practice Direction* No. 5 of 1994.
[24] *ibid.*
[25] Legal Aid in Criminal and Care Proceedings (Costs) Regulations 1989, reg. 15(1)–(5).

which the representations will be made. The appellant is granted a reasonable opportunity to make representations in reply.[26]

Appointment The taxing master will appoint the appeal and inform the appellant, and if relevant, the Lord Chancellor, and it is open to the taxing master to give directions as to the conduct of the appeal.[27] **32–67**

It is open to the taxing master to consult the trial judge, the appropriate authority or the determining officer; and the appellant may be required to provide any further information required for the purposes of the appeal. No further evidence may be received on the hearing of the appeal and no ground of objection will be valid, which was not raised on redetermination, unless the taxing master otherwise directs. Normally, unless there is good reason for the late introduction of evidence or grounds for objection, no such direction will be given.[28]

In hearing the appeal, the taxing master has the same powers as the appropriate authority and may accordingly increase or decrease the redetermined figure or leave it unaltered, confirm the decision to allow standard fees or allow fees to counsel on an *ex post facto* basis.

The taxing master's decision is given in writing with reasons and copies are sent to the appellant, the Lord Chancellor and the appropriate authority.[29]

Costs The taxing master may allow the appellant a sum in respect of part or all of any reasonable costs (including any fee payable in respect of the appeal) save where the decision on redetermination is confirmed or decreased.[30] **32–68**

To the High Court

Regulations 15 (appeals to a taxing master), 16 (appeals to the High Court), and 17 (time-limits) of the Costs Regulations 1989 relating to appeals by solicitors, apply with the necessary modifications to appeals in proceedings for which standard fees are payable, as they apply to appeals and proceedings for which standard fees are not payable.[31] **32–69**

Appeals by solicitors or counsel

An appellant, solicitor or counsel who is dissatisfied with the decision of a taxing master may, within 21 days of notification of the decision, apply to **32–70**

---

[26] Legal Aid in Criminal and Care Proceedings (Costs) Regulations 1989, reg. 15(6)–(9).
[27] *ibid.* reg. 15(10).
[28] *ibid.* reg. 15(10), (11).
[29] *ibid.* reg. 15(12), (13).
[30] *ibid.* reg. 15(14); *R. v. Boswell* [1987] 1 W.L.R. 705.
[31] Legal Aid in Criminal and Care Proceedings (Costs) Regulations 1989, Sched. 1, Pt. II, para. 8(6).

the master to certify a point of principle of general importance. If the taxing master certifies the point of principle of general importance, the solicitor or counsel may appeal to the High Court. The Lord Chancellor must be made a respondent to the appeal. The appeal must be instituted within 21 days of receipt of the taxing master's certificate. Time-limits relating to certification and appeal may be extended in accordance with the Costs Regulations 1989.[32] There is no appeal against the refusal of the Master to Certify but the decision may be susceptible to Judicial Review.[33]

Appeals by the Lord Chancellor

32–71   If the Lord Chancellor is dissatisfied with the decision of a taxing master, whether or not any representations have been made before the taxing master, he may appeal to the High Court against that decision. No certificate of a point of principle is required. The solicitor or counsel will be made a respondent to the appeal. It is not open to the Lord Chancellor to appeal if the solicitor or counsel have themselves appealed. Such an appeal must be instituted within 21 days of receipt of notification of the taxing master's decision. The time-limit may be extended in accordance with the Costs Regulations 1989.[34]

32–72   **Procedure**   The appeal is by way of originating summons in the Queen's Bench Division and is heard and determined by a single judge from whose decision there is no further appeal.[35]

32–73   **Powers of the judge**   The judge has the same powers as the appropriate authority and the taxing master, including the power to allow costs in an appropriate case. The judge may reverse, affirm or amend the decision appealed against or make such other order as he thinks fit.[36]

Extension of the time-limit

32–74   The time-limit within which any act is required or authorised to be done may for good reason be extended by the appropriate authority, or under regulation 15 (appeals to a taxing master) of the Costs Regulations 1989 by a taxing master or under regulation 16 (appeals to the High Court) of the Costs Regulations 1989 by the High Court.[37]

    Where a solicitor or counsel has failed to comply with a time-limit without good reason, the appropriate authority, a taxing master or the High

---

[32] *ibid.*, reg. 16(1)–(4).
[33] *R. v. Supreme Court Taxing Office ex p. John Singh & Co. The Times* May 3 1995. *Latham J.*
[34] *ibid.* reg. 16(5), (6).
[35] *ibid.* reg. 16(7).
[36] *ibid.* reg. 16(8) *R. v. Boswell;* [1987] 1 W.L.R. 705.
[37] *ibid.* reg.17(1) as amended by Legal Aid in Criminal and Care Proceedings (Costs) (Amendment) Regulations 1991.

Court may, in exceptional circumstances, extend the time-limit and must consider whether it is reasonable in the circumstances to reduce the costs. There may be no reduction of costs unless the solicitor or counsel has been allowed a reasonable opportunity to show cause orally or in writing why the costs should not be reduced.[38]

A solicitor or counsel may appeal to a taxing master against a decision under these provisions by an appropriate authority (save in respect of proceedings before a magistrates' court). The appeal is by notice in writing to the Chief Taxing Master within 21 days of the decision being given. The notice must specify the grounds of the appeal.[39]

General Principles of Determination under the Costs Regulations 1989

Rate of charge

Where it is sought to exceed the prescribed rates for solicitors' costs, solicitors must be able to show exceptional *competence and dispatch*. Both elements must be present at the same time. Alternatively it is necessary to show the exceptional circumstances of the case.[40]   **32–75**

The Taxing Officers' *Notes for Guidance*, para. 8, require the following factors to be taken into account:

(a) the importance of the case, including its importance to each defendant in terms of its consequences to his livelihood, standing or reputation, even where his liberty may not be at stake;

(b) the complexity of the matter;

(c) the skill, labour, specialised knowledge and responsibility involved;

(d) the number of documents prepared or perused with due regard to difficulty or length;

(e) the time expended;

(f) all other relevant circumstances, including travelling and hotel expenses where appropriate.

"The correct viewpoint to be adopted . . . is that of a sensible solicitor sitting in his chair and considering what in the light of his then knowledge is reasonable in the interests of his lay client . . . the lay client . . . should be deemed a man of means adequate to bear the

---

[38] *ibid.* reg. 17(2) as amended by Legal Aid in Criminal and Care Proceedings (Costs) (Amendment) Regulations 1991.

[39] *ibid.* reg. 17(3) as amended by Legal Aid in Criminal and Care Proceedings (Costs) (Amendment) Regulations 1991.

[40] Legal Aid in Criminal and Care Proceedings (Costs) Regulations 1989, Sched. 1, para. 3.

expense of the litigation out of his own pocket and by 'adequate' I mean neither 'barely adequate' nor 'super abundant'."[41]

When claiming enhanced rates the correct approach is to use a figure for the broad average direct cost of the work (the A figure, expense rate) and to add to that an allowance for care and conduct expressed as a percentage (the B figure).[42]

The backward limit — work undertaken before the making of the order

32–76 As a general premise, no costs are recoverable prior to the issue of a legal aid order and an order will not be backdated. But representation and advice given before the making of a legal aid order is deemed to be work done under that order provided that the appropriate authority is satisfied that:

(a) the interests of the justice required that the representation or advice be provided as a matter of urgency;

(b) there was no undue delay in making an application for legal aid;

(c) the representation and advice was given by the solicitor who was subsequently assigned under the legal aid order.[43]

Apart from that exception no costs are allowable prior to the issue of the legal aid order in the Crown Court or magistrates' court.[44] The Court of Appeal has power to make legal aid orders which are retrospectively effective.[45]

The broad average direct cost

32–77 In *R. v. Wilkinson*, Goff J. was asked to decide whether a taxing officer ought to accept, as sufficient evidence of the broad average direct costs of work done in the particular area by a principal solicitor in a particular year, the expense rates shown in tables prepared by a group of solicitors practising in that area's Crown Court on the basis of the methods suggested in the Law Society's booklet '*The Expense of Time*'. The judge held that although the booklet was laudable in many ways it did not, in its present form, provide a reliable basis for the taxation of costs. Nevertheless, taxing officers should not entirely disregard calculations of expenses submitted to them on the basis of the booklet, but should merely regard such calculations with reserve and treat them as no more than one matter to be taken into account.[46] The judge offered a great deal of practical criticism of the Law

---

[41] *Francis v. Francis and Dickerson* [1956] P. 87, *per* Sachs J.

[42] *R. v. Backhouse* [1986] TC S.30 following *Re Eastwood* [1975] Ch. 112; *Leopold Lazarus Ltd v. Secretary of State for Trade and Industry* (1976) S.J. 268.

[43] Legal Aid in Criminal and Care Proceeeings (General) Regulations 1989, reg. 44(7).

[44] *R. v. Rogers* [1979] 1 All E.R. 693.

[45] *R. v. Kearney* [1983] 1 W.L.R. 1046, C.A.; *R. v. Gibson* [1983] 1 W.L.R. 1038, C.A.

[46] *R. v. Wilkinson* [1980] 1 W.L.R. 396.

Society's booklet, which has since appeared in several revised editions. None of those editions has ever been tested before the court.

Supervision

The question of supervision was dealt with at some length by Mustill J. in **32–78** R. v. Sandhu[47]:

> "Certainly regulation 6(1) creates an exclusive code for the ascertainment of the type of work which may properly be allowed. This does not mean, however, that nothing except what is explicitly described in the various paragraphs can be claimed. The definitions of the type of work are contained (so far as concerns, sub-paragraphs (a), (b) and (c)) in the words which precede the first comma. What follows thereafter is added by way of illustration. Thus the fact that supervisory work of the type claimed by the senior solicitor in this case, cannot be fitted within any of the activities described in the latter part of sub-paragraph (a), does not mean that no fee can be allowed in respect of it. What matters is whether it constitutes "preparation". If it does then the determining officer can and must allow ... such fees in respect of it as he shall consider reasonable ... Many items of what may loosely be called supervision will not fall within the framework of the Regulations at all. Every senior solicitor will wish to keep an eye on what is going in his office to make sure that it is operating efficiently and that the standards set by the senior solicitor who bears the ultimate responsibility for the conduct of all work carried out by the practice is being scrupulously maintained."

Again, a senior solicitor, who has a proper regard for his broader **32–79** responsibilities, will find it necessary to discuss matters with his more junior staff as a method of practical instruction, with a view to making them better fitted to perform their allotted work. Very often in both of these spheres the solicitor may occupy some time on a particular case. It would not, however, by any means, necessarily follow that this time would be attributable to the preparation of that case so as to entitle the solicitor to remuneration (under paragraph 6(1)) of the Costs Regulations 1989.

It would simply be part of the overhead expense incurred by the solicitor in the proper conduct of his practice.

The determining officer could properly have regard to the nature of the case and the grade of fee-earner whose time is claimed for elsewhere in the bill when deciding whether it was reasonable for time to be spent by the senior solicitor on the supervisory work. There must be many cases where, once the case has been allocated to a fee-earner of the appropriate

---

[47] November 11, 1984 TC SJ. 1.

grade, he or she can be allowed to carry on the work unaided without any need for intervention by somebody more senior. On the other hand, there may equally be cases where even if the matter is in the hands of someone who could ordinarily be considered competent to deal with it there might be an unexpected turn of events where that senior solicitor's extra experience and weight would be an essential reinforcement.

The determining officer can reasonably expect the senior solicitor to provide an explanation of the reasons why the nature of the case made his participation necessary and of the occasions, duration and circumstances of such participation. Without such particulars, the determining officer might well consider that where an allowance has been claimed for a fee earner of a particular grade, there was no case made out for a further allowance in respect of someone more senior.

Counsel

32–80   When assessing a brief fee each case must be assessed separately and a lower brief fee should not be allowed because counsel appears in more than one case in the same Crown Court centre on the same day.[48] This is the general principle which is overridden by the scheme of standard fees for junior counsel in the Crown Court.[49] If counsel has only one case which lasts less than a day and is involved in waiting he is not entitled to a higher brief fee. Where the case is listed for a particular day but is not called for some time, so that the actual time occupied by the hearing is substantially less than five hours, the brief fee may be adjusted downwards. In such cases counsel should, if it be the case, certify by endorsement on his brief, that he was unable to do any other work because he was waiting in court. The determining officer must then take this into consideration when assessing the brief fee. Since the refresher will not normally be paid until counsel has spent five hours in court, a better course would seem to be to allow the full brief fee and adjust the subsequent refresher.

The Chief Taxing Master has considered in detail the principles to be applied where a trial goes short.[50] The brief fee should be determined having regard to the principle of reasonable remuneration in respect of all work reasonably done and taking into account all the circumstances of the individual case. The time spent in court is only one of a number of factors and should not be regarded as the sole or even major criterion. The weight of the case has to be judged according to all its elements and not simply as to its weight as a fight. On this basis, it is incorrect to determine the fee appropriate to a case by deciding what would have been allowed had there been a fight and then applying a discount to the figure in order to determine

---

[48] *Isaac v. Isaac* [1955] P. 333.
[49] Legal Aid in Criminal and Care Proceedings (Costs) Regulations 1989, Sched. 2, Pt. I.
[50] *R. v. Bellas* [1986] TC C. 9.

the brief fee. Each case must be taken on its own merits, the determination being carried out on the basis of all the circumstances of the individual case.

Retrials

It is sometimes necessary for there to be a change of counsel and if this is **32–81** reasonable and proper an entirely fresh brief fee is payable. If the change over is merely for the convenience of counsel, the brief fee allowed for the retrial will be the full fee but the fee for the first trial will be reduced so that the overall cost is no more than that which would have been allowed had the same counsel acted throughout.

Whenever counsel has conducted himself reasonably and properly but, through no fault of his own or of his clerk is unable to appear at the trial, he should not be penalised. Any fees for subsidiary work, including the settlement of the indictment, written advices or advices in conference, undertaken before the change in counsel should be assessed in accordance with paragraph 28.1 of the Bar's Code of Conduct (which provides that a barrister should be separately instructed and remunerated by a separate fee for each item of work that he undertakes) and should take into account the time reasonably spent on preparation for such item or work. The fees for second counsel should be assessed in accordance with the normal principles. If the change of counsel was unreasonable, the preparation will not be paid for twice, and the loss will fall upon the first counsel.[51]

Photocopying

Normally extra copies of depositions are obtainable from Crown Courts **32–82** free of charge. However, increasing difficulty appears to be experienced by solicitors in obtaining extra copies, thus, solicitors must either pay for photocopying to be carried out, or have it done within their own office. The Costs Regulations 1989 make no provision for photocopying save as a disbursement. Accordingly, the photocopies made in the solicitor's office cannot be a disbursement.[52] In *R. v. Sandhu*,[53] Mustill J. made it plain that the powers to make allowances for any kind of work are created and exclusively defined by the Costs Regulations 1989. In the absence of express provision, determining officers cannot and must not, remunerate the services claimed, even if they think such a course would be reasonable. If solicitors have copies made outside their office and make a payment for them, that is a disbursement; in such a case the determining officer would have to consider whether the course taken was reasonable on the facts of

---

[51] *R. v. Davies* TC C. 7; T.M.D. I. 78.
[52] *R. v. Zemb* [1986] TC S27.
[53] [1984] TC SJ.1.

the case, given that the making of copies is, in the ordinary way, part of the solicitor's work.[54]

Disbursements

32–83 Where a solicitor, *bona fide* acting in what he considers the best interest of his client, has incurred expenditure, which unless allowed on taxation will fall on him personally, it would be wrong for the court to be astute in seeking reasons to disallow the items and, in particular, care must be taken not be affected by hindsight.[55] All disbursements which have been reasonably incurred and are reasonable in amount should be allowed. Disallowance of a disbursement may result in the solicitor having to pay the sum out of his own pocket and this is a factor to be taken into account by taxing authorities. The fact that counsel has advised that a particular step should be taken will usually indicate that the disbursement is reasonable. However, failure to obtain counsel's advice is, of course, not fatal to the claim, and solicitors must still exercise their own independent judgment even when advised by counsel including experienced leading counsel.[56]

Where it ought to be obvious that counsel who has been instructed is not competent to conduct the proceedings, the solicitors will be seriously at fault in not withdrawing instructions from that counsel and ensuring that someone competent to prosecute the proceedings is instructed. It is no excuse for solicitors to say they were relying on counsel and counsel has let them down. It is the duty of solicitors to ensure that counsel instructed on their client's behalf is competent.[57]

Experts' fees

32–84 If solicitors choose to instruct an agency instead of instructing an expert direct they will generally not be able to recover more than the expert's reasonable fee (*i.e.* nothing will be paid in respect of any agency charges).[58] If prior authority is sought involving the use of an agency it is likely to be granted at a reduced amount to reflect the fact that it should be possible to contact an expert direct.

Attendance at court with counsel

32–85 Where counsel has been instructed, the instructing solicitor is under a duty to attend, or arrange for the attendance of a responsible representative, throughout the proceeding (save that attendance may be dispensed with in

---

[54] *R. v. Zemb* [1986] TC S27.
[55] *Francis v. Francis and Dickerson* [1956] P. 87, *per* Sachs J.
[56] *Davy-Chiesman v. Davy-Chiesman* [1984] Fam. 48; *R. v. Oxfordshire County Council, ex. p. Wallis* [1987] 2 F.L.R. 193.
[57] *Re A (A Minor), The Times*, February 25, 1988.
[58] *R. v. Powar* [1984] T.C. S22.

the magistrates' court or in certain categories of Crown Court proceedings, where the solicitor is satisfied that it is reasonable in the particular circumstances of the case that counsel be unattended and, in particular, that the interests of the client and the interests of justice will not be prejudiced).[59] In the magistrates' court unassigned counsel's fees will be dealt with on the maximum fee principle.

The Law Society has expressed the view that attendance on counsel should only be dispensed with in the Crown Court in the following categories of case:

(a) committals for sentence;
(b) appeals against sentence; and
(c) guilty pleas where the solicitor was so instructed at the time he prepared the brief to counsel.

It is expected that a solicitor would normally attend counsel in the Crown Court where:

(a) the client is a person at risk (such as juveniles, persons with inadequate knowledge of English, persons subject to mental illness or mental handicap or with sight, speech or hearing impediments), whether someone is a person at risk is a matter as to which the solicitor must exercise his judgment; or

(b) the client is of such a difficult character that it is desirable that counsel be attended; or

(c) there is a probability that the client will receive a substantial sentence of imprisonment or will receive an immediate sentence of imprisonment for the first time; or

(d) witnesses to fact or opinion (*i.e.* not character witnesses) are required to be present whether or not they are actually called; or

(e) counsel actually appearing in the case is not counsel instructed, unless the solicitor is satisfied that the change of counsel is unlikely to be prejudicial to the interests of the client; or

(f) there are any other circumstances in which the solicitor considers the attendance on counsel is reasonable.

In the above circumstances, the solicitor will be remunerated for attending **32–86** court with counsel. However, where a solicitor attends on counsel in an apparently straightforward case such as a guilty plea, the attendance may be disallowed, in those circumstances therefore solicitors must be in a position to justify their attendance.

In any case where a solicitor proposes that counsel should appear unattended, counsel must be so informed and a full and detailed brief must be delivered sufficiently early before the hearing to enable counsel to consider the papers and to decide whether it would be appropriate for him to attend alone. The client must be informed that counsel will be

---

[59] *The Professional Conduct of Solicitors*, Principle 12.03.

unattended and the client must also be told the name of counsel instructed. The solicitor must still attend upon counsel where counsel originally instructed or subsequently substituted, informs the solicitor that he does not believe it is appropriate for him to be unattended.

Guidelines issued by the Criminal Law Committee of the Law Society.

32–87 Where counsel is to be unattended, briefs to counsel should, whenever possible, be delivered not less than seven days in advance of the case in order to alert counsel and the clerk. The brief should be clearly marked where solicitors propose that counsel should be unattended. The brief will need to contain more than it would if the solicitor or his representative were in attendance, as counsel will have to undertake those duties normally carried out by the solicitor or his representative when attending court. Solicitors should insert clear instructions in the brief so that counsel is aware of precisely what duties he will have to fulfil in the absence of the solicitor or his representative. Thus, the instructions should where appropriate:

    (a) deal with counsel's early arrival at court in order to see the client;

    (b) include sufficient details about the defendant and any witnesses to enable counsel to contact them if they do not appear;

    (c) require the judge's comments on sentence to be fully recorded;

    (d) require notes to be provided of the headings of counsel's speech in mitigation;

    (e) require a telephone report to the solicitors after the case;

    (f) require counsel to deal with witness expenses;

    (g) require counsel to deal with the client and any relatives who may be present after the case has been concluded;

    (h) require counsel to find out where the client has been taken, if in custody, and pass the information to the solicitor; and

    (i) require counsel to endorse on the brief within two days what oral advice on appeal has been given to the client.

Both solicitors and counsel will receive an additional standard fee where counsel is unattended in the Crown Court. In non-standard fee cases the assessment of what additional preparation should reasonably be allowed will be subject to *ex post facto* determination in the normal way.

Appearance by Queen's Counsel alone in legal aid cases in the Crown Court

32–88 The Bar's Code of Conduct makes it clear that a Queen's Counsel may accept instructions to appear as an advocate without a junior. A Queen's Counsel is entitled to assume, unless the contrary is stated, when instructions in any matter are first delivered, that a junior will also be instructed.

A Queen's Counsel may decline to appear as an advocate without a junior if he would not be able properly to conduct the case or other cases, or to fulfil his professional or semi-professional commitments unless a junior were also instructed in the case in question. Whilst the final question as to whether or not a Queen's Counsel considers it appropriate to appear alone in a case lies with him, it is recognised that the instructing solicitor has a contribution to make in reaching the decision.

The Bar Council and the Law Society in a joint statement identified examples of cases where it was considered appropriate for a Queen's Counsel only to be briefed, namely:

(a) pleas of guilty in cases worthy of silk representation where the plea is certain in advance of the hearing;

(b) appeals to the Court of Appeal (Criminal Division), in cases worthy of Queen's Counsel representation which can properly be undertaken by Queen's Counsel alone; and

(c) cases of basic simplicity which have some sensitive overlay whether political, local or other.

The joint statement of the Bar Council and the Law Society acknowledges that the problem involved in encouraging the briefing of Queen's Counsel alone is that, in most cases, junior counsel will already have been instructed in the case at an early stage and may have met the lay client and gained his confidence and inspired his loyalty. Early identification of the "silk only" cases and the early grant of the appropriate legal aid order is essential.

Costs of appeal

Where a taxing master allows an appeal against a redetermination of costs, **32–89** he has the power under the Costs Regulations 1989, to allow counsel the costs of a professional fee for appearing on his own behalf or on behalf of another member of the Bar on appeal under the Regulations.[60]

---

[60] *R. v. Boswell* [1987] 1 W.L.R. 705.

PART E

SUPPLEMENTARY

Chapter 33

LEGAL REPRESENTATIVES (SOLICITORS AND BARRISTERS) RIGHTS AND OBLIGATIONS

INTRODUCTION

The rights and obligations of legal representatives towards their (lay) clients **33–01** who may be eligible for legal aid and when providing advice and assistance or representation under the 1988 Act are:

(a) found in the Solicitors' Practice Rules, "The Guide to the Professional Conduct of Solicitors", in the Code of Conduct of the Bar of England and Wales, and in the General Council of the Bar's Legal Aid Guidelines;

(b) expressed in legal aid legislation;

(c) expressed in or may be inferred from decided cases.

The Board also expresses its views in its Notes for Guidance in the *Legal* **33–02** *Aid Handbook* and imposes some requirements in the Duty Solicitor Arrangements 1994.

However, at the root of these rights and obligations is the fact that the Board is essentially responsible for paying the legal representative for the work which he does for a legally assisted person, so in providing legal services to assisted persons the legal representative is spending taxpayers' money. Section 31(3) of the 1988 Act provides:

"a person who provides advice, assistance or representation under this Act shall not take any payment in respect of the advice, assistance or representation except such payment as is made by the Board or authorised by, or by regulations under, this Act."

For advice and assistance (including ABWOR), section 9(5) of the 1988 Act **33–03** provides:

"except as provided by Sub-Section (6) or (7) below, the legally assisted person shall not be required to pay his legal representative any charge or fee."

Sub-section (6) concerns the legally assisted person's contribution.

Sub-section (7) concerns the charge on property recovered or preserved created by section 11(3) which provides:

> "in so far as the charge is created by sub-section (2) above in respect of any charges of fees to which this section applies is insufficient to meet them, the deficiency shall, subject to sub-section (5) below, be payable to the legal representative by the Board."

In respect of advice and assistance (including ABWOR) the Board must pay (legal representatives') charges or fees above the amount of
> (a) the legally assisted person's contribution plus
> (b) the value of the charge created by section 11(2).

The contribution provided by section 9(6) is payable to the legal representative and the charge created by section 11(2) is a first charge for the benefit of the legal representative.

33–04 For representation, section 15(6) of the 1988 Act provides:

> "Except in so far as he is required under section 16 to make a contribution, a legally assisted person shall not be required to make any payment in respect of representation under this Part and it shall be for the Board to pay his legal representative."

Section 16(1) of the 1988 Act provides for the legally assisted person to pay a contribution to the Board in respect of the costs of his being represented. Section 16(5) of the 1988 Act provides that:

> "Any sums recovered by virtue of an order or an agreement for costs made in favour of the legally assisted person with respect to the proceedings shall be paid to the Board."

Section 16(6) of the 1988 Act goes on to create a first charge for the benefit of the Board on any property recovered or preserved for the legally assisted person in the proceedings.

In respect of representation, the Board must pay all the legal representatives' costs. The Board may recoup its outlay from:
> (a) the amount of the legally assisted person's contribution plus
> (b) any sums recovered by virtue of the an order or agreement for costs made in favour of the legally assisted person plus
> (c) the value of the charge created by section 16(6).

THE SOLICITORS' PRACTICE RULES AND THE LAW SOCIETY GUIDE TO THE PROFESSIONAL CONDUCT OF SOLICITORS

33–05 The Practice Rules and the other requirements of solicitors' professional conduct apply equally whether the client is in receipt of legal aid or not. Some of the main specific obligations which solicitors have in respect of legal aid are set out below. References are to The Guide to the Professional Conduct of Solicitors 1993.

It is a principle of professional conduct (Principle 5.01) that:

"a solicitor is under a duty to consider and advise the client on the availability of legal aid where the client might be entitled to assistance under the Legal Aid Act 1988."

Commentary 2 to that principle states:
"a failure to advise clients promptly of their rights under the Legal Aid Act can amount to unbefitting conduct and may also lead to a claim in negligence against the solicitor for breach of duty owed to the client".

Commentary 6 to that principle states:
"Legally aided clients must be treated in the same way as privately funded clients and the same standards of care apply."

Commentary 5 to that principle states:
"Where a solicitor considers that legal aid is likely to be available to the client the availability of an emergency certificate should also be borne in mind. A solicitor who commences work without legal aid cover runs the risk of being unable to recover his pre-certificate costs."

Commentary 4 to that principle states:
"The duty to advise applies not only at the outset of the retainer but, as the matter proceeds. It is a duty of the solicitor to ensure that any material change of which he or she becomes aware in the client's means is at once taken into consideration in the context of eligibility for legal aid."

The Written Professional Standards in particular Standard (e) (Principle **33–06** 13.13) the information which solicitors should give legally aided clients:

"Where clients are legally aided they should be informed at the outset of a case and at appropriate stages thereafter:

(i) of the effect of the statutory charge on the case;
(ii) that if they lose the case they may still be ordered by the court to contribute to their opponent's costs even though their own costs are covered by the legal aid;
(iii) that even if they win, their opponent may not be ordered to pay the full amount of their costs and may not be capable of paying what they have been ordered to pay;
(iv) of their obligations to pay any contribution assessed and of the consequences of any failure to do so."

In respect of payment to witnesses, the Guide to Professional Conduct of **33–07** Solicitors states:

"In legal aid cases, whether civil or criminal, a solicitor should draw

629

the attention of the witnesses to the fact of legal aid and that the witnesses' fees and disbursements will have to be taxed or assessed and that only such amounts can be paid to the witness. A solicitor should expressly disclaim personal responsibility for payment of fees beyond those allowed on taxation or assessment."

In practice, witnesses may often not be prepared to contract with the solicitor on this basis i.e. that they will receive only what is allowed on taxation.[1,2]

33–08   Finally, as the solicitors' lien does not arise in legal aid cases, Commentary 5 to principle 12.18 states:

"Where the client is legally aided, The Law Society takes the view that a solicitor's costs are secured by a Legal Aid Order or certificate and it follows that it would be inappropriate to call for a professional undertaking from the successor solicitor to pay the costs except in respect of any outstanding pre-certificate costs. A solicitor should not part with the papers on a legally aided matter until the certificate is transferred to the successor solicitor, although the papers should be made available for inspection in the meantime or copies provided. In respect of legal aid costs it is permissable to ask for an undertaking requiring the successor solicitor to:
   (a) return the papers on completion; or
   (b) have the first solicitor's costs included in the successor solicitor's bill."

THE CODE OF CONDUCT OF THE BAR OF ENGLAND AND WALES

33–09   The Code of Conduct makes special reference to legal aid in Part II "Fundamental Principles" paragraphs 203 and 207, and in Part V "Briefs and Instructions to Practising Barristers" (paragraphs 502 and 504). Paragraph 209 provides:

"A barrister in independent practice must comply with the 'Cab-rank rule' and accordingly except only as otherwise provided in paragraphs 501, 502 and 503 he must in any field in which he professes to practise in relation to waste appropriate to his experience and seniority and irrespective of whether his client is paying privately or is legally aided or otherwise publicly funded:

   (a) accept any brief to appear before a court in which he professes to practise;

---

[1] For greater detail on the legal aid position see para. 33–15 (civil legal aid) and para. 33–52 (criminal legal aid).

[2] Dated March 31, 1990 and incorporating amendment No. 1 of October 22, 1990.

(b) accept any instructions;

(c) act for any person on whose behalf he is briefed or instructed;

and do so irrespective of (i) the party on whose behalf he is briefed or instructed (ii) the nature of the case and (iii) any belief or opinion which he may have formed as to the character reputation cause conduct guilt or innocence of that person."

Paragraph 203 provides:

"A practising barrister:

(a) must promote and protect fearlessly and by all proper and lawful means his lay client's best interests and do so without regard to his own interests or to any consequences to himself or to any other person (including his professional client or fellow members of the legal profession);

(b) subject only to compliance with the specific provisions of Legal Aid Regulations owes his primary duty:

(i) as between his lay client and his professional client; and

(ii) as between the Legal Aid Fund and his lay client; to his lay client and must not permit the Legal Aid Fund or his professional client to limit his discretion as to how the interests of his lay client can best be served;

(c) must act towards his lay client and his professional client at all times in good faith."

Paragraphs 502 provides:

"A barrister in independent practice is not obliged to accept a brief or instructions:

(a) requiring him to do anything other than during the course of his ordinary working year;

(b) other than at a fee which is proper having regard to the complexity length and difficulty of the case and to his ability experience and seniority and any brief or instructions in a legally aided matter shall for this purpose unless the Bar Council or the Bar in general meeting otherwise determines (either in a particular case or in any class or classes of case or generally) be deemed to be at a proper professional fee;

(c) if the expenses which will be incurred are likely to be unreasonably high in relation to the fee likely to be paid and are not to be paid additionally to such fee;

(d) save in the case of legal aid work:

(i) unless and until his fees are agreed;

(ii) if having required his fees to be paid before he accepts the brief or instructions to which the fees relate those fees are not paid."

Paragraphs 504 provides:

"A practising barrister must cease to act and if he is a barrister in independent practice must return any brief or instructions:

(c) if in any legally aided case (whether civil or criminal) it has become apparent to him that legal aid has been wrongly obtained by false or inaccurate information and action to remedy the situation is not immediately taken by his client;

(d) if the circumstances set out in Regulation 67 of the Civil Legal Aid (General) Regulations 1989 arise at a time when it is impracticable for the Area Committee to meet in time to prevent an abuse of the Legal Aid Fund."

LEGAL AID LEGISLATION

33–10   Section 2(6) of the 1988 Act provides:

"Advice, assistance and representation under this Act, except when made available under Part II, shall only be by legal representative(s), but in the case of Part II, may be by other persons."

Part II of the 1988 Act gives the Board power to provide advice and assistance and representation under Part II. It also gives the Board power to secure the provision of advice assistance and representation under Part II or under the other Parts of the 1988 Act by means of contracts with, or grants or loans to other persons or bodies. The Board has exercised its power to secure advice, assistance and representation by contact, through the franchising contract and in several multi party actions.

"Legal representative" is defined in section 43 of the 1988 Act:

"Legal representative" means an authorised advocate or authorised litigator as defined by Section 119(1) of the Courts and Legal Services Act 1990."

Section 119(1) of the Courts and Legal Services Act 1990 provides that an "authorised advocate" or "authorised litigator" is a person who has been approved as such by an "authorised body". Section 43 of the 1988 Act provides that "authorised body" has a meaning assigned by section 119(1) of the Courts and Legal Services Act 1990. At present, only the Law Society and the General Council of the Bar are "authorised bodies" and only solicitors and barristers are "legal representatives". However, in future other professionals may become "legal representatives" even if the scope of their authorised "advocate" or "authorised litigator" status is limited, *e.g.* patent agents.

Presently, only the 1988 Act uses the term "legal representative". The Regulations continue to refer to "solicitor" or "barrister".

The Legal Aid Act 1988

Section 32(1) of the 1988 Act provides: **33–11**

"Subject to the provisions of this Section, a person entitled to receive advice, assistance or representation may select the legal representative to advise, assist or act for him from among the legal representatives willing to provide advice, assistance or representation under this Act."

The exceptions provided by section 32 are:

(a) Where the Board exercises Part II contracting powers to secure representation under Part IV [section 4(6)] it may restrict choice of legal representative[3] (section 32(2)).

(b) In certain criminal cases legal representatives may be assigned (section 32(3) and (8)).

(c) There is no right of selection in relation to proceedings under section 29 for contempt where the court may assign any legal representative who is at the time within the precincts of the court (section 32(4) and (5)).

(d) Regulations may restrict the choice of legal representatives to those who are members of a panel. For example, Regulations could limit choice in certain Children Act proceedings to representatives who are members of the Law Society Child Care Panel. No such Regulations are presently in force (section 32(7)).

(e) Any legal representative who is excluded from legal aid work by his professional body may not be selected (section 32(9)).

It is clear from section 32(1) that the 1988 Act does not oblige legal   **33–12** representatives to act for legally assisted persons. The choice of legal representative is from among those "willing to provide" advice assistance or representation under the 1988 Act. Some solicitors or barristers, subject to their rules of professional conduct, are simply not willing to act for legally assisted persons. This is usually because they consider that the costs and fees payable under the 1988 Act are insufficient. This is particularly so in the case of large city firms of solicitors.

Section 32(6) also makes it clear that even when a solicitor or barrister is generally willing to provide advice assistance and representation under the 1988 Act, he is not obliged by legal aid legislation to agree to act for the person who wishes to select him.

Section 6(4)(a) of the Legal Aid Act 1949 provided:

"Where a person is entitled to receive legal aid, the solicitor to act for him and, if the case requires counsel, his counsel, shall be selected from the appropriate panel, and he shall be entitled to make the selection himself; provided that —

---

[3] The Board has done so in the smoking related diseases multi-party action.

(a) This sub-section shall not prejudice the rights of solicitor or counsel where he has good reason to refuse or give up a case or entrust it to another,"

Under this section a solicitor's and barrister's normal rights to refuse instructions could be exercised only for good reason, whereas the 1988 Act does not require the solicitor or barrister to provide justification.[4]

The Legal Aid Act 1949 created panels of solicitors and barristers who were willing to do legal aid work. In *Brown v. Brown*[5] Singleton L.J. expressed the view that if a solicitor on the panel was asked by a client to undertake a legal aid cases, prima facie he was bound to do so. "At least the Committee would expect them to show good reason if they declined".

As the panels no longer exist, solicitors and counsel cannot really be said to be holding themselves out to do legal aid work in the same way. Section 32(1) refers to legal representatives who are "willing to provide advice assistance or representation under the Act" but this not quite the same.

Section 32(6) provides:

"The selection by or assignment to a person of a legal representative shall not prejudice the law and practice relating to the conduct of proceedings by solicitor or counsel or the circumstances in which a solicitor or counsel may refuse or give up a case or entrust it to another"

and the circumstances in which he may choose to cease to act are not affected by his client's being a legally assisted person — though he will be required to give his reasons to the Area Director.[6]

Furthermore, the selection under the 1988 Act by a person of a legal representative does not oblige the legal representative to do any more of the work personally for the client than if he had been instructed privately. He may still instruct agents (subject to the agent's not having been excluded from selection). Section 32(10) provides:

"Notwithstanding sub-section (1) above, a legal representative who has been selected to act for a person under that sub-section may himself select to act for that person, as a legal representative's agent, any other legal representative who is not for the time being excluded from selection."[7]

33–12 Section 31 of the 1988 Act is entitled "Act not generally to effect the

---

[4] *Rondel v. Worsley* [1967] 3 All E.R. 995 at 1029. (Regulation 18 of the Legal Advice and Assistance Regulations 1989 does appear to require good cause for refusing to accept on application for advice and assistance.)

[5] [1952] All E.R. 1018, C.A. at 1019.

[6] Civil Legal Aid (General) Regulations 1989, reg. 69.

[7] In *R. v. Legal Aid Board, ex p. Bruce* [1992] 3 All E.R., however, the House of Lords accepted the Board's argument that solicitor agents could not be used under the green form scheme.

position of legal representatives or other parties" and encapsulates the principle that although the Board is responsible for paying a legally assisted person's legal representative, this does not affect:

(a) the relationship between the legally assisted person and his legal representative; or
(b) the rights of other parties to the proceedings; or
(c) the principles on which a court or tribunal normally exercises any discretion except where expressly provided by the Act or regulations.

Although section 15(6) provides that a legally assisted person's payment in respect of representation is limited to the amount of his assessed contribution and that it is for the Board to pay his legal representative, section 15(8) provides:

"Nothing in sub-section (6) above affects the duty of the legal representative to pay in the first instance expenses incurred in connection with the proceedings that would ordinarily be paid in the first instance by a person's legal representative."

In a similar vein section 16(8) provides:

"The charge created by sub-section (6) above [The Legal Aid Statutory Charge] on any damages or costs shall not prevent a court allowing them to be set off against other damages or costs in any case where a legal representatives lien for costs would not prevent it."

Section 34 deals with the Lord Chancellor's Regulation-making powers. **33–13** These are wide. Section 34(2)(f) provides that Regulations may make provision for recovery of sums due to the Board and for making effective the statutory charge. Section 34(8)(b) goes on to provide that such Regulations may include provision:

"For making a legal representatives' right to payment by the Board wholly or partly dependant on his performance of the duties imposed by him by regulations made for the purposes of that paragraph."

The relevant Regulations are the Civil Legal Aid (General) Regulations 1989 which impose a number of duties on legal representatives in this and other areas. Although there is no regulation, making the right to payment dependent on performance of duties, if the legal representative fails to comply with the Regulations and, as a result, there is a loss to the Fund, the area Comittee may, under regulation 102, defer payment of his profit costs.

Although the Civil Legal Aid (General) Regulations 1989 impose obligations on legal representatives, these all relate to the provision of representation and derive from the fact that the individual legally assisted person's case will be financed by the Board.

However, as well as providing that the Board has a general function of securing this advice, assistance and representation are available in accordance with the 1988 Act (section 3(2)) the 1988 Act also gives the Board general powers (section 4). It is clear from sections 3 and 4 that the Board is also expected to consider in what other ways advice assistance and representation could be provided and to make recommendations.[8]

33–14 As part of its research into franchising legal aid the Board required researchers to examine legal aid files in the possession of solicitors. While under the Civil Legal Aid (General) Regulations 1989, the Board can call for such files for the purpose of carrying out its functions under those Regulations (*e.g.* assessing the financial or legal merits of the case or assessing a claim for costs), it was less clear that it could call for such files for the purpose of carrying out its functions under the 1988 Act. To enable this, the Legal Aid (Disclosure of Information) Regulations 1991 were made. These provide that:

> "Notwithstanding the relationship between or rights of a legal representative and client or any privilege arising out of such relationship, the legal representative shall not be precluded from disclosing to any person authorised by the Board to request it, any information which relates to advice, assistance and representation provided to a client or former client of his where that client is or was a legally assisted person which is requested for the purpose of enabling the Board to discharge its functions under the Legal Aid Act 1988."

Civil Legal Aid (General) Regulations 1989

Counsel

33–15 Regulation 59(1) of the Civil Legal Aid (General) Regulations 1989 requires the authority of the Area Director to instruct a counsel only when instructing counsel in a magistrates' court or a Queen's Counsel or more than one counsel in other courts is proposed. In the case of *Re A solicitor (Taxation of Costs)*[9], the court said that because of the possible effect of the statutory charge, solicitors should also obtain their clients' consent before taking any unusually expensive steps. The fact that the Board is primarily liable to pay the solicitor's costs does not mean that the legally assisted person will not ultimately pay them (via the operation of the statutory charge) and solicitors should therefore consult a legally aided client in the same way that they would consult a private client before incurring such expense.

Regulation 59, which provides how instructions are to be delivered to counsel, also provides:

---

[8] See, especially, section 4(2)(e), (f), (8).
[9] [1982] 2 All E.R. 683.

"No fees shall be marked on any set of papers so delivered."

This is because counsel's fees, like solicitors' costs are a matter for taxation. If the Taxing Officer considers that counsel should not have been instructed, no counsel's fees and solicitors' costs of preparing instructions will be allowed on taxation.

Experts and other non-lawyers

Legal representatives have the right to be paid out of the Fund[10] but they must pay disbursements themselves in the usual way. Regulation 61 gives solicitors the discretion to apply to the Board for authority to incur certain disbursements. If an authority is granted it will specify the maximum amount authorised. The effect of obtaining an authority is that no question as to the propriety of the step or (up to the maximum amount authorised) the amount of the disbursement (unless the solicitor or the assisted person knew or ought reasonably to have known that the purpose for which the authority was given had failed or become irrelevant or unnecessary before the costs were incurred) can be raised on taxation.[11] Of course, the principle stated in Re A solicitor (Taxation of Costs), applies equally to disbursements.   **33–16**

If the solicitor obtains an authority he can confidently contract with his chosen expert to pay him the amount stated in the authority for his work. If he does not obtain an authority, he must contract either to pay such amount as may be allowed on taxation — which is maybe unattractive to the expert — or he must contract otherwise, in which case he himself bears the taxation risk.

Regulation 64 is entitled "Restriction on Payment Otherwise from the Fund" and the first part is in tune with sections 31(3), 15(6) and 15(8) of the 1988 Act.   **33–17**

However, regulation 64 goes further than this and provides:

"Where a certificate has been issued in connection with any proceedings, the assisted person's solicitor or counsel shall not receive or be a party to the making of any payment for work done in those proceedings during the currency of that certificate (whether within the scope of the certificate or otherwise) except such payments as may be made out of the Fund."

The regulation provides that solicitors and counsel shall not "be a party to the making of any payment for work done in those proceedings". This regulation does not prevent the solicitor from making such a payment himself e.g. when he has contracted to pay an expert £500 for a report and

---

[10] See Legal Aid Act 1988 s. 15(8).
[11] Civil Legal Aid (General) Regulations 1989, reg. 63.

only £300 is allowed on taxation, he may (and must under his contract) pay the expert the additional £200 from his own pocket but the solicitor may not recoup the £200 from his client or anyone else, as this would make him a party to the making of the payment. Effectively, the solicitor would have been the conduit for the payment from another source.

33–18   Regulation 101(a) of the Civil Legal Aid (General) Regulations 1989 gives the solicitor acting for a legally assisted person the discretion to apply for a payment on account of disbursements incurred or about to be incurred in connection with the proceedings to which the certificate relates. The Board's standard form asks whether the disbursements will be incurred within three months which indicates the Board's view of the phrase "about to be incurred".

Regulation 101(a) highlights another feature of this contract between the solicitor and his expert. How soon should the expert expect to be paid? The solicitor cannot assume that the expert will wait for a taxation. This is not an implied term of instruction. Therefore, unless the contract with the expert makes such provision, the solicitor will have to pay for his work within a reasonable time of receiving his account. He can fund such a payment from his office account or cover the payment by a payment on account by the Board.

Other persons

33–19   Section 32(10) of the 1988 Act provides that legal representatives may instruct other legal representatives as their agents. Regulation 65(1) makes similar provision which must be read in the light of section 32(10) so that it is not necessary for the legally assisted person to select the solicitor's agent. Regulation 65(1) provides:

> "No solicitor or counsel acting for an assisted person shall entrust the conduct of any part of the case to any other person except another solicitor or counsel so selected under section 32(1) of the Act."

Regulation 65(2) touches on the actual practice of conducting a case for a legally assisted person. It provides:

> "Nothing in paragraph (1) shall prevent a solicitor from entrusting the conduct of any part of the case to partner of his or to a competent and responsible representative of his employed in his office or otherwise under his immediate supervision."

33–20   As solicitors may be in partnership only with other solicitors or with registered foreign lawyers, the first part of this regulation is straight forward. The second part of the regulation concerns representatives employed "in his office" and "office" here presumably means "his office or where he has more than one office—one of his offices". The third part "or otherwise under his immediate supervision" arguably implies that a representative in the solicitor's office as well as one employed elsewhere, must be under his immediate supervision.

Having established that a solicitor may instruct counsel, agents and experts and may delegate work to representatives, specific duties under the Legal Aid (General) Regulations 1989 need to be examined.

First, regulation 73 provides:

"No solicitor at counsel shall be precluded, by reason of any privilege arising out of the relationship between counsel, solicitor and client, from disclosing to an Area Director or an area committee any information, or from giving any opinion, which he is required to disclose or give to the Area Director or that committee under the Act or these Regulations, or which may enable them to perform their functions under the Act or these Regulations.

(2) For the purpose of providing information under the Act or these Regulations or to enable an Area Director or an area committee to perform its functions under the Act or these Regulations, any party may disclose to an Area Director or an area committee communications in relation to the proceedings concerned sent to or by the assisted person's solicitor, whether or not they are expressed to be "without prejudice"."

What the Area Director will be concerned about are the financial and merits criteria. These are assessed on the application for legal aid but they must continue to be satisfied while the certificate is in force as the Regulations make provision for the certificate to be discharged if they cease to be satisfied and if certain appropriate information is not provided to the Area Director, the certificate may be revoked. Furthermore, a change in financial circumstances could lead to a reassessment of means and an increase (or decrease) in the financial contribution.

Before a solicitor can report to the Area Director any change in the legally **33–21** assisted person's financial position or in the merits of his case, he may first have to be able to obtain that information from the legally assisted person himself. Regulation 66 of the Legal Aid (General) Regulations 1989 provides:

"The assisted person shall forthwith inform his solicitor of any change in his circumstances or the circumstances of his case, which he has reason to believe might affect the terms or continuation of his certificate."

This obligation on the legally assisted person is in addition to those **33–22** provided by regulation 11 of the Civil Legal Aid (Assessment of Resources) Regulations 1989 which provides:

"The person concerned [which in most cases will be the legally assisted person] shall inform the Area Director of any change in

639

his financial circumstances which has occurred since the original assessment was made and which he has reason to believe might affect the terms on which the certificate was granted or its continuation."

33–23   When the solicitor receives any information from his client, what do the regulations require him to do? Regulation 67(2) provides:

"Where the solicitor or counsel is uncertain whether it would be reasonable for him to continue acting for the assisted person, he shall report the circumstances to the Area Director."

Regulation 67(1) also imposes further duties on the legally assisted person's solicitor and counsel. It provides:

"Where an assisted person's solicitor or counsel has reason to believe that the assisted person has —

(a) required his case to be conducted unreasonably so as to incur an unjustifiable expense to the fund or has required unreasonably that the case be continued; or

(b) intentionally failed to comply with any provision of regulations made under the Act concerning the information to be furnished by him or in furnishing such information has knowingly made a false statement or false representation,

the solicitor or counsel shall forthwith report the fact to the Area Director."

33–24   Given the provisions of regulation 73 and the nature of the relationship between the legally assisted person, the solicitor and counsel and the Board through its Area Director, deriving from the fact that public funds are supporting the litigation, solicitors and counsel if they have any doubt about whether to report to the Area Director under either regulation 67(1) or (2) should, resolve it in favour of reporting. Without prejudice to their rights generally to give up a legally assisted person's case, solicitors and counsel are specifically permitted by regulation 69(3) to give up the case in the circumstances specified in regulation 67 and, if they do so, must report to the Area Director.

33–25   Regulation 70(1)(a) provides:

". . . Without being required to do so, the assisted person's shall —

(a) make a report" (to the Area Director) "where the assisted person declines to accept a reasonable offer of settlement or a sum which is paid into court."

So, where an offer of settlement is made the assisted person's solicitor must decide whether it is reasonable. Where any sum is paid into court, the assisted person's solicitor must report to the Area Director. It would be sensible for the solicitor, at the same time as reporting a payment into

640

court, to comment on whether he considers the payment is reasonable or not.

The purpose behind regulation 70(1)(a) is to enable the Area Director to consider whether it is reasonable in the particular circumstances of the case for legal aid to continue. If he considers it is unreasonable, this is a ground for discharge of the certificate under regulation 77(c) (just as on an application for legal aid it is a ground for refusal under section 15(3)(a) of the 1988 Act).

Regulation 70(1)(b) provides: **33–26**

"... Without being required to do so, the assisted person's solicitor shall —
    (b) notify the Area Director where a legal aid certificate is issued to another party to the proceedings".

The assisted person's solicitor should know this soon after such a certificate is issued because of the provisions of regulation 50, which require the assisted person's solicitor to serve all other parties with notice of issue of the certificate.

The purpose of regulation 70(1)(b) is the same as regulation 70(1)(a). The **33–27** grant of a legal aid certificate to another party to proceedings is a material consideration because it means that that the prospects of recovering costs from that party will be restricted by his having the protection of the provisions of section 17 of the 1988 Act. If the first legally assisted person is, *e.g.* a plaintiff who is seeking damages, the fact that he may not be able to recover costs from a legally aided defendant will mean that at the end of the case, there is likely to be a deficit on his account with the Fund which will have to be satisfied by the application of the statutory charge on any damages be recovers. The grant of a legal aid certificate to the other party also indicates that he is a person of limited resources, which may be a relevant consideration.

Regulation 71 (which relates to the Area Director's discretion to **33–28** discharge a certificate under regulation 80) requires a solicitor who has acted or is acting, for an assisted person (so the obligation continues after the retainer is determined *e.g.* by death or by the cause of action vesting a trustee) on becoming aware that the assisted person has (a) died (b) had a bankruptcy order made against him, to report the fact to the Area Director.

Each of these factors is a ground for discharge of the legally assisted person's legal aid certificate under regulation 80(c)(i) and (ii) respectively. Neither the personal representative nor the trustee in bankruptcy of a (deceased) assisted person becomes entitled to the (deceased's) legal aid certificate.

Regulation 72(a) (which relates to the Area Director's discretion to **33–29** discharge a certificate under regulation 80) requires a solicitor to report forthwith to the Area Director "upon the completion of the case if he has completed the work authorised by the certificate".

Even if a case is "completed" on entry of final judgment, it would be rare for the certificate, before then, to cover subsequent (*e.g.* enforcement) proceedings. This could occur if the certificate had been amended for enforcement proceedings after entry of a first instance judgment and the certificate was later amended to cover opposing an appeal, which was opposed successfully.

Each of these facts, namely, the disposal of "the proceedings to which the certificate relates" and the completion of "the work authorised by the certificate" is a ground for discharge of the legally assisted person's legal aid certificate under regulation 80(c)(iii) and (iv) respectively.

Regulation 72(b) (which relates to the Area Director's discretion to discharge the certificate under regulation 80) requires the solicitor to report forthwith to the Area Director "if for any reason he is unable to complete the work". "The work" in this context must mean work authorised by the certificate. The most usual example will be where the solicitor is unable to obtain his client's instructions. This, and other reasons why the solicitor is unable to complete the work, are likely to raise the issue of whether it is reasonable in the particular circumstances of the case for legal aid to continue. If it is unreasonable, the Area Director may discharge the certificate under regulation 77(1)(c).

33–30   Regulation 70 also obliges the solicitor and counsel to respond to enquiries from the Area Director. Regulation 70(1) requires him to give such information regarding the progress of the proceedings to which the certificate relates as the Area Director may from time to time require for the purpose of performing his functions under the Regulations. (The solicitor is not prevented by reason of privilege from disclosing other information to the Area Director.[12])

Regulation 70(1) enables the Area Director to write for information to the legally assisted person's solicitor at any time for the purpose of performing his functions under the Regulations. The prime relevant function here is the function of discharging a certificate, particularly under regulation 77. Under this regulation, the Area Director must discharge a certificate if the conditions in the regulation are satisfied.[13]

Regulation 70(1) refers to "information which has come to his" (the Area Director's) "knowledge". Such information may come from, *e.g.* the court (under regulation 68) or from the legally assisted person's opponent in the proceedings, or from any other source. On receipt of such information, the Area Director will write to the solicitor under regulation 70(1).

Regulation 70(2) is expressed to be without prejudice to the generality of regulation 70(1). It was introduced to be a complement to the annual

---

[12] "See the Legal Aid (Disclosure of Information) Regulations 1991.
[13] Unreasonable grounds, unreasonable in the particular circumstances or the legally assisted person requiring proceedings to be conducted unreasonably so as to incur unjustifiable expense to the Fund.

payment on account scheme covered by regulation 100 so that solicitors would receive payments on account under the scheme only after being asked for reports on all or some eligible cases.

Regulation 70(2) requires the legally assisted person's solicitor "when **33–31** required to do so by the Board" to "make a report to the Area Director on a form approved by the Board, specifying the grounds on which he certifies that it is reasonable for the assisted person to receive legal aid in respect of the proceedings to which the certificate relates."

Where the legally assisted person's solicitor fails to make a report within 21 days, regulation 70(3) provides that the Area Director shall:

"(a) give notice to him and the assisted person that the legal aid certificate may be discharged; and

(b) invite the assisted person to show cause why the certificate should not be discharged."

The provisions of Part X of the Regulations, which relates to revocation and discharge of certificates, applies with any necessary modification if such notice is given.

Regulation 69 imposes a duty on solicitors and counsel to give the Area **33–32** Director "reasons for refusing to act or for giving up a case after being selected". Counsel must also give reasons if after being selected by an "assisted person" he refuses to accept instructions" or gives up the case and if, required to do so by the Area Director, shall "inform the Area Director of his reasons for entrusting" the case "to another" (if he has done so).

The regulation does not impose a duty on solicitors and counsel until they have been selected — in the case of counsel, by an assisted person. Such solicitors or counsel may be selected only if they are one of the class of "legal representatives willing to provide advice assistance or representation under the Act".[14] If, however, they are generally willing to provide advice assistance and representation under the Act but do not wish to act in this particular case, the position is not entirely clear.

If "selection" is a unilateral process performed by a legally assisted person as was apparently the position under the Legal Aid Act 1949, then regulation 69 imposes such duties even if the solicitor and counsel decline at the outset to act. It is hard to see how it can be other than a unilateral process. In which case, there seems to be a duty to report if a solicitor or counsel decline at the outset to act.

This would be difficult in practice as, if the client has not applied for legal aid, the Area Director will probably have no information about him and it rarely, if ever, occurs in practice.

Perhaps the best that can be said is that if the solicitor or counsel consider

---

[14] Legal Aid Act 1988, s. 32(1).

that they ought, because of special factors, e.g. they believe the client may be attempting wrongfully to manipulate the scheme to his advantage to report their refusal to act or accept instructions then they should do so — and if they do not know which legal aid area office to write to, they should write to the office in whose area their own office is situated. This is likely to happen only rarely. Where the client already has legal aid, the regulation is perhaps more pertinent and the solicitor and counsel should then know to which office to write to.

33–33 Regulation 69(4) provides:

> "Where any solicitor or counsel exercises his right to give up an assisted person's case in the circumstances specified in regulation 67,[15] the solicitor shall make a report to the Area Director of the circumstances in which that right was exercised."

Regulation 69(5) provides that if, following a report under regulation 69(4) of the circumstances in which counsel or the solicitor gives up a case the Area Director does not discharge or revoke the assisted person's certificate, he shall require the assisted person to select another solicitor to act for him. Thus, on a strict interpretation, even if it is counsel who has expressed his right to give up an assisted person's case, if the certificate is not discharged or revoked, the Area Director must require the assisted person to select another solicitor to act for him.[16]

33–34 Finally, in this part of the Regulations (and this regulation is not strictly concerned with obligations, rights yet discretions of legal representatives but with conduct of proceedings and falls in the same part of the Regulations as the other Regulations mentioned here) regulation 68 gives a court power in certain circumstances, on the application of the Board, or of its own motion, to make an order referring to the Area Director the question of whether the assisted person's certificates should continue. It provides:

> "(1) Subject to paragraph (2), at any time during the hearing of any procedings to which an assisted person is a party, the court may, on the application of the Board or of its own motion, make an order referring to the Area Director the question whether the assisted person's certificate should continue where the court considers that the assisted person has —
> (a) in relation to any application for a certificate, made an untrue statement as to his financial resources or had failed to disclose any material fact concerning them, whether the statement was made or the failure occurred before or after the issue of the certificate and notwithstanding that it was made or occurred

---

[15] Civil Legal Aid (General) Regulations 1989, reg. 67 is considered in detail at paras. 33–15.
[16] There must be some doubt as to whether this was the true intent of the draftsman.

in relation to an application to another area office in connection with the same procedings; or

(b) intentionally failed to comply with these Regulations by not furnishing to his solicitor or the Area Director any material information concerning anything other than his financial resources; or

(c) knowingly made an untrue statement in furnishing such information;

and the court shall notify the Area Director of the terms of any order so made.

(2) No order shall be made under paragraph (1) by reason of any such mis-statement or failure as is referred to in paragraph (1)(a) if the assisted person satisfies the court that he used due care or diligence to avoid such mis-statement or failure but the assisted person's solicitor shall nevertheless report the circumstances to the Area Director"

Regulation 50 is concerned with notifying the other parties to the proceedings of the issue of the legal aid certificate. It requires an assisted person's solicitor forthwith whenever the assisted person becomes a party to proceedings or whenever a party to proceedings becomes an assisted person, to serve notice of issue of legal aid on all other parties to the proceedings and if at any time thereafter a person becomes a party, to serve him with a similar notice. Regulation 54 requires a solicitor to serve and file similar notices where a (non financial) amendment has been made to the assisted person's certificate. These provisions are required because the issue of a legal aid certificate to a party may materially affect the actions of other parties to the proceedings. **33–35**

Regulation 50(4) also requires the assisted person's solicitor to send a copy of the legal aid certificate to the appropriate court, office or registry if proceedings have begun or when they begin. **33–36**

Regulation 50(3) provides that if a solicitor files at court a copy of the notice of issue which he must serve under regulation 50(1) then if proceedings are commenced in the county court or are certain matrimonial proceedings, a copy of the notice shall be annexed to the originating process of service. Regulation 50(2) provides that copies of the notice shall form part of the court papers. **33–37**

Regulation 82 requires the solicitor similarly to serve and file notice of discharge/revocation of his client's legal aid certificate forthwith upon receipt or, if an appeal under regulation 81(2) against discharge or revocation has been brought forthwith, upon receipt of a notice of dismissal of the appeal. Regulation 87 provides that if proceedings have been commenced, the solicitor's retainer does not determine until such appropriate notices have been filed and served — otherwise the retainer determines on his receipt of the notice of discharge/revocation — or his receipt of the notice of dismissal of the appeal against discharge/revocation. **33–38**

645

In first instance proceedings, there is no obligation to give notice of limitiations on legal aid certificates. But the position is different in appeal proceedings.

In *Scarth v. Jacobs-Paton*[17] the Court of Appeal stated *obiter* that when a certificate has been granted for an appeal and is expressed to be limited to filing notice of appeal and conditional upon counsel's opinion, the other party should be given notice of the limitation so that they do not carry out what may be unnecessary work in preparing for the appeal.

33–39   If the purpose of the notice of issue is to alert the parties so that they may consider their position, it follows that the notice should describe the scope of the legal aid granted. Otherwise, e.g. a third party to proceedings might not know whether the legally assisted person has legal aid to proceed against him or a defendant would not know whether the legally assisted plaintiff had legal aid to defend the defendant's counterclaim. These are material considerations not least because such proceedings are separate proceedings for the purposes of section 18 of the 1988 Act (costs against the Board).

33–40   Once a solicitor's retainer has determined, his obligation (under regulation 84) is to submit the costs of the proceedings to which the certificate relates for taxation or assessment as soon as is practicable.

Where the legally assisted person's certificate is revoked (which by regulation 74(2) means that he has never been an assisted person in relation to the proceedings to which the certificate related, except for the purpose of section 18 of the 1988 Act) regulation 86(b) gives the solicitor the right to recover from him the difference between the amount paid or payable out of the Fund and the full amount of his solicitor and own client costs.

33–41   The Civil Legal Aid (General) Regulations 1989 gives the assisted person's solicitor particular obligations so far as the recovery and receipt of property including costs and other monies is concerned. The first obligation created by regulation 87(1), is to be the recipient of all monies otherwise payable to the legally assisted person as a result of the proceedings.[18]

33–42   The Civil Legal Aid (General) Regulations impose an important duty on solicitors forthwith to inform the Board's Area Director of any property recovered or preserved for the assisted person and to send to him a copy of the order or agreement by virtue of which property was recovered or preserved. Property (which includes money[19] is clearly "preserved" when the order or agreement is made. It is almost certainly "recovered" for the purpose of section 16(6) at that time, too.

33–43   If the statutory charge does arise when the order or agreement is made, regulation 91 falls into place. It enables the Board to take proceedings in

---

[17] *The Times*, November 2, 1978.
[18] The detailed provisions are found in Civil Legal Aid (General) Regulations 1989 reg. 87(1).
[19] See *Law Society v. Rushman* [1955] 2 All E.R. 544.

its own name where an order or agreement is made providing for the recovery or preservation of money.

Only the solicitor (or the Board if the legally assisted person is no longer represented by a solicitor) is capable of giving a good discharge for monies so payable. Therefore, if they are wrongly paid to the legally assisted person or to some other person, the payer does not receive from the payee, a good receipt for the monies and the Board may sue for payment to it.

Regulation 87(2) imposes another duty on the solicitor. It provides:

"where the assisted person's solicitor has reason to believe that an attempt may be made to circumvent the provisions of paragraph (1), he shall inform the Board."

An assisted person may be successful (by obtaining an order for payment of monies covered by regulation 87(1)(b) against a company in liquidation or against the estate of a bankrupt or against a person who has made a deed of arrangement. If so, regulation 88 imposes a duty on his solicitor to send the liquidator, trustee or to an assignee of the deed of arrangement, notice that a legal aid certificate has been issued to the assisted person. This is to ensure that payment under the order is made to the assisted person's solicitor (which is one of the reasons for serving notice of issue of a legal aid certificate on an opponent (or his solicitor) in the proceedings.

Once the solicitor has received monies, his position is governed by regulation 90 which, broadly, requires him to pay all moneys received by him under the terms of an order or agreement made in the assisted person favour to the Board unless the Area Director directs otherwise. **33–44**

Regulation 110 imposes a duty on solicitors to safeguard the interests of the Fund on any *inter partes* taxation. It provides: **33–45**

"It shall be the duty of an assisted person's solicitor to safeguard the interests of the fund on any inter partes taxation pursuant to an order for costs made in favour of the assisted person where that person may himself have no interest in the result of the taxation, and for this purpose to take such steps as may appear to the solicitor to be necessary to obtain a review of taxation under regulation 113 or 114."

Regulation 105(8) (assessment of cost) and 112 impose duties on solicitors to notify counsel within seven days if his fees have been disallowed or reduced on assessment or taxation. By regulation 116, if counsel is dissatisfied with any decision, the solicitor must carry in objections, apply for a review or appeal. **33–46**

This part of the Regulations also makes provision for appeals against assessment/taxation. For assessments, there is a right of review by the Area Committee under regulation 105(4) and then if the area committee certifies a point of principle of general importance under regulation 105(5) a right of appeal to the Board's costs appeals committee. For taxations, there is a right to carry in objections under regulation 130(2)(b) and the right, with **33–47** authority, to apply to a judge for a review under regulation 114 and thereafter to appeal from the review under regulation 115. Regulation 118(a) imposes a duty on solicitors carrying in objections under regulation 113 or applying for a review under regulation 114 where the assisted person has no interest in the taxation or would, but for the provisions of regulation 118, have an adverse interest to that of his solicitor, to ensure that all matters which are proper to be taken into account are placed before the taxing officer or the judge, as the case may be. It follows that solicitors should point out matters to their disadvantage as well as points in their favour.

33–48   If any other party to the proceedings carries in objections or applies for a review the assisted person's solicitor may be heard even though the assisted person himself may have no interest in the taxation.[20]

33–49   Where the assisted person does have a financial interest in the taxation or assessment (an assisted person has such an interest if he has a contribution or the statutory charge will apply and such an interest should be assumed if there is a reassessment of means pending or the statutory charge may apply) the solicitor has a duty under regulation 119 to (a) supply him with a copy of the bill (b) inform him of the extent of his financial interest and of his right to make representations and (c) endorse on the bill that the assisted person has a financial interest and that (a) and (b) have been complied with.

Legal Advice and Assistance Regulations 1989

33–50   As Green Form advice, including advice by duty solicitors, is basically a simple advice scheme and as the proceedings covered by ABWOR are generally less expensive and less protracted than those covered by civil legal aid, the Legal Advice and Assistance Regulations 1989 include little relating to the rights and obligations of solicitors or barristers in providing advice and assistance or ABWOR.

Regulation 18 provides that a solicitor may for good cause, refuse to accept an application for advice and assistance. This requirement for there to be "good cause" is over and above the provision of section 32(6) of the 1988 Act which is that the selection of a legal representative does not prejudice the circumstances in which a solicitor or counsel may refuse a case. It also provides that, for good cause, a solicitor, having accepted an application, may decline to give, or to continue to give, advice and assistance. Whether he refuses an application or later refuses to continue, the solicitor may refuse to disclose his reasons except to the Area Director, if the Area Director requires information.

Regulation 19 provides that, if required by the Area Director, the solicitor

---

[20] Civil Legal Aid (General) Regulations 1989, reg. 117.

must give him information for the purposes of his functions under the Regulations and that professional privilege does not prevent this.

Regulations 24 and 25 include the requirement to give notice of approval and withdrawal of ABWOR

The Legal Aid (Disclosure of Information) Regulations 1991

The Legal Aid (Disclosure of Information) Regulations 1991 were made to **33–51** enable solicitors to show clients' files to the Board's franchise auditors. Other legal aid regulations include requirements to provide information to Area Directors for the purpose of their functions under the Regulations but whether information could be provided for the Board's purposes under the 1988 Act was less clear.

The Regulations provide that a legal representative is not prevented by reason of confidentiality or professional privilege from providing, to the Board's authorised representatives, information relating to advice, assistance or representation provided to a client or former client, which is requested for the purpose of enabling the Board to discharge its functions under the 1988 Act.

The Legal Aid in Criminal and Care Proceedings (General) Regulations 1989

Regulation 40(5) of these Regulations requires that if the assigned solicitor **33–52** instructs counsel, his instructions must include a copy of the legal aid order and that the solicitor must inform counsel of any amendments to the order.

Regulation 50(4) provides that if a legal aid order is amended to show a new assigned solicitor or (if counsel only was assigned) a new assigned counsel, the solicitor or counsel originally assigned shall send all papers and other items in his possession relating to the proceedings to the new solicitor or counsel.

Regulation 41(4) and (5) requires, if a legal aid order is withdrawn or revoked, assigned counsel to return all papers and other items relating to the proceedings to the assigned solicitor or, if there is none, to the assisted person and requires the assigned solicitor similarly to return such papers and items to the assisted person.

Regulation 55 provides a restriction on payment similar to (but not the same as) that provided by regulation 64 of the Civil Legal Aid (General) Regulations 1989. It provides that when a legal aid order has been made, the assisted person's solicitor or counsel shall not receive or be a party to the making of any payment for work done in connection with the proceedings in respect of which the legal aid order was made except such payments as may be made out of the Fund or by the Lord Chancellor.

In this respect, the regulation is similar to regulation 64 of the Civil Legal

Aid (General) Regulations 1989. However it goes on to make a further exception in respect of any expenses or fees incurred in (a) preparing, obtaining or considering any report, opinion or further evidence, whether provided by an expert witness or otherwise; or (b) bespeaking transcripts of shorthand notes or tape recordings of any proceedings, including police questioning of suspects, where an application under regulation 54 for authority to incur such expenses has been refused by the area committee.

Regulation 56 provides that, despite the rules of privilege or confidentiality, where a legal representative knows that his client, whether as an applicant or as a legally assisted person has failed to comply with any provision of Regulations under the 1988 Act concerning information to be furnished by him or, in furnishing such information, has knowingly made a false statement, the legal representative must forthwith report that fact to the proper officer. "Proper officer" is defined in regulation 3 and is, broadly, the relevant official in the court in which the proceedings will take place.

DECIDED CASES

33–53 Given the nature of the relationship between the solicitor and the Board and the requirements of the 1988 Act and the Regulations, the solicitor is bound to conduct proceedings reasonably. He should bear in mind that public moneys are being spent and he should not use legal aid as a weapon against his client's opponent. A leading case which illustrates how legally aided proceedings should be reasonably conducted is *Francis v. Francis & Dickerson*[21] in which Sachs J. Said:

> "the correct view point to be adopted by a Taxing Officer is that of a sensible solicitor in his chair and considering what in the light of his then knowledge is reasonable in the interests of his lay client [who] . . . .should be deemed a man of means adequate to bear the expense of the litigation out of his own pocket — and by "adequate" I mean neither "barely adequate" nor "super abundant"."

If proceedings are not so reasonably conducted, or if, on a legal aid taxation, the taxing officer has any doubts that they have been, those doubts must be resolved in favour of the paying party — *i.e.* the Board.

In the same case, it was also said that before advising an assisted person to take proceedings, the solicitor should make the same inquiries and investigations as would normally be carried out for a private client,

---

[21] [1955] 3 All E.R. 836 at 840.

provided these are within the scope of the certificate and are designed to achive the purposes which are contemplated by it.

The solicitor's duty to act reasonably is not ousted by taking a course advised by counsel. In *Davy-Chiesman v. Davy-Chiesman*[22] the court held that it would not exonerate a solicitor if he blindly followed the view expressed by counsel (even experienced leading counsel) without exercising his own independent judgment.

The case of *Re Trusts Affecting Clarendon Villas (No. 26)*[23] confirms that an assisted person has the same right as any other litigant to settle an action or to enter into a compromise to avoid proceedings or bring them to an end.

In *Orchard v. South Eastern Electricity Board*[24] the defendent sought an order for costs against the plaintiffs solicitors, presumably on the basis initially that the plaintiffs solicitors were guilty of serious misconduct in failing to inform the legal aid authorities of the circumstances and prospects of the plaintiffs claim (which had failed). Although the defendents application failed, the court did not dismiss the proposition that such a failure could give rise to such an order.

[22] [1984] 1 All E.R. 321.
[23] [1955] 3 All E.R. 178.
[24] [1987] 1 All E.R. 95.

Chapter 34

THE EFFECT OF LEGAL AID ON OTHER PARTIES AND ON THE COURT

INTRODUCTION

34–01 The fact that a party to litigation has certain rights arising from being legally aided is normally to be treated as irrelevant by the court when considering the position of the assisted person's opponent and the basis on which the court is to reach its decision. This is provided by section 31(1)(b) of the 1988 Act. This principle was contained in previous Legal Aid Acts although in some cases decisions have been made by the courts which could not easily be reconciled with the statutory provision. Generally decisions have been made under previous statutory provisions with the principles being established before the implementation of the 1988 Act. The position has, however, recently been confirmed by the Court of Appeal in *Ridehalgh v. Horsefield* [1994] 3 All E.R. 848.

The main effects which a grant of legal aid have on the assisted person's opponent and on the court are dealt with more fully in other chapters, but a short summary of them is set out below.

THE GENERAL PRINCIPLE

The effect of section 31(1)(b) of the 1988 Act

34–02 Commenting on the Legal Aid Act 1949 and the Regulations made under it, Scarman J. observed that they "should provide the sinews of war without ever obtruding into the forensic battle between the parties".[1] This is now provided for by section 31(1)(b) of the 1988 Act which directs that, save as is expressly provided by the Act itself or by the Regulations, "the rights

---

[1] *Carter v. Carter* [1964] 2 All E.R. 968 at 974.

conferred by this Act on a person receiving advice, assistance or representation under it shall not affect the rights or liabilities of other parties to the proceedings or the principles on which the discretion of any court or tribunal is normally exercised."

The test which should be applied is that laid down by Lord Denning M.R. in *Re Saxton, Johnson v. Saxton*[2] In that case the trial judge had granted an interlocutory application by legally aided plaintiffs for delivery of a disputed document to an expert for scientific tests. When doing so he took into account the fact that the defendants, in order to meet the case, would have to employ their own expert to make independent tests and as the plaintiffs were legally aided the chance of recovering the resulting expense would be small (because of the limitation on an assisted person's liability for costs under what is now section 17(1) of the 1988 Act). To avoid this prejudice to the defendants he imposed a condition that the plaintiffs should disclose their expert's report to the defendants. The Court of Appeal held that the condition was not one that would ever normally be imposed in an ordinary case and ordered it to be struck out.

The Court of Appeal has also held that the availability or otherwise of legal aid within alternative jurisdictions where a case might be tried was not a consideration to be taken into account in deciding which would be the most appropriate jurisdiction.[3]

It is only the assisted person's *rights* which are relevant and there is nothing **34–03** to prevent the court from taking into account his or her liabilities. It is proper to have regard, *e.g.* to the effect which the Board's statutory charge under section 16(6) of the 1988 Act will have on damages awarded to an assisted person in deciding how the court should exercise its discretion in making an order for costs against the assisted person's opponent.[4]

The courts have had to apply the provision to a variety of cases. The following are some examples of decisions made under section 1(7)(b) of the Legal Aid Act 1949 and now section 31(1)(b) of the 1988 Act.

The rights of other parties to the proceedings

In *Edwards v. Edwards*[5] Sachs J. held that the effect of section 1(7)(b) of the **34–04** Legal Aid Act 1949 was to leave untouched the court's power to protect a litigant by ordering his legally aided opponent's solicitor personally to pay costs which had been unnecessarily incurred. He also decided that a decision by the area committee not to revoke the assisted person's

---

[2] [1962] 2 All E.R. 92, C.A.
[3] *Connelly v. RTZ Corporation plc and another*; Court of Appeal, *The Times*, October 20, 1995.
[4] *Cook v. S.* [1967] 1 All E.R. 299, C.A.: but now see postponement of enforcement of the charge.
[5] [1958] 2 All E.R. 179.

certificate could not affect the other party's right to costs on the basis that the proceedings had been unreasonably continued. Wasted costs orders were recently considered by the Court of Appeal in *Ridehalgh v. Horsefield* [1994] 3 All E.R. 848.

It is consistent with the principle that the courts have made orders against assisted persons to give security for costs. In *Burton v. Holdsworth*[6] the defendant in an action for damages for negligence had applied to the High Court to transfer the action to a county court in default of the plaintiff's giving security for the defendant's costs. The plaintiffs objected that the court had no jurisdiction to make the order as one of them was legally aided. The Court of Appeal rejected this argument although in the earlier case of *Conway v. George Wimpey & Co. Ltd*[7] it had held that, generally speaking and in the absence of special circumstances, it would be inappropriate to make an order for security for costs against an assisted person. Section 1(7)(b) was not brought to its attention in that case but the position regarding security for costs is now specifically dealt with in regulation 123 of the Civil Legal Aid (General) Regulations 1989 which provides that "where in any proceedings an assisted person is required to give security for costs, the amount of such security shall not exceed the amount which could be ordered under section 17(1) of the Act". In other words the security is limited.

The liabilities of other parties to the proceedings

34–05   The liability of an unsuccessful party to pay costs, which is in the nature of an indemnity[8] was held in *Daley v. Diggers Ltd.*[9] to be unaffected by the fact that his opponent was legally aided and under no personal liability for costs against which he needed to be indemnified. Section 31(2) of the 1988 Act provides that, without prejudice to the generality of section 31(1)(b), for the purpose of determining the costs of a legally assisted person in pursuance of an order for costs or an agreement for costs in his favour (other than an order under Part II of the Prosecution of Offences Act 1985) the services of his solicitor and counsel shall be treated as having been provided otherwise than under the 1988 Act and his solicitor shall be treated as having paid counsel's fees.

34–06   The effect of the provision now contained in regulation 31(1)(b) of the 1988 Act on the court's discretion to order the opponent of an assisted person to give security for costs has caused some difficulty in the past and there have been conflicting decisions of the Court of Appeal. In *Wigley v. Wigley*[10] which was decided soon after the Legal Aid Act 1949 came into

---

[6] [1951] 2 All E.R. 381.
[7] [1951] 1 All E.R. 56, C.A.
[8] See *Gundry v. Sainsbury* [1910] 1 K.B. 645, C.A. at 649.
[9] [1951] 1 All E.R. 116.
[10] [1950] 2 All E.R. 1218.

force, counsel for the unassisted party argued that the effect of that Act was to change the whole basis on which security for costs should be ordered. The Court of Appeal held that the right of an assisted party to ask for security was not affected by the Act (although their decision on this point was, strictly, *obiter*). Three years later in the case of *Williams v. Williams*[11] it reiterated its view, without referring to *Wigley's* case, that the effect of section 1(7)(b) was to leave the position with regard to security for costs unaffected and it ordered the unassisted party to provide security. Later in *Carter v. Carter*[12] the facts were exceptional in that the unassisted husband had been ordered to provide security for his assisted wife's costs (the right of a spouse to apply for security for the costs of matrimonial proceedings has now been abolished) but the parties became reconciled and the proceedings were dismissed. The wife refused to apply for costs but Scarman J. accepted the argument of counsel for the Law Society that the court had jurisdiction to make an order nonetheless, and directed the husband to pay a sum not exceeding the amount lodged in court as security.

Finally, in *Norris v. Norris*,[13] the Court of Appeal rejected an application by a legally aided wife for an order against her husband for security for her costs of an appeal.

It is important to keep clear two separate issues; namely, whether the **34–07** unassisted party should be required to provide security, and whether he should be ordered, at the conclusion of the case, to pay costs.

(a) *Should security be ordered?* The fact that the party applying for security is legally aided should, by reason of section 31(1)(b) of the 1988 Act, be disregarded. The court should ask itself the question: "If the applicant did not possess the rights he does by reason of being legally aided, how would the discretion of the court normally be exercised in such a case as this?"

(b) *Should the unassisted party be ordered to pay costs?* The question is a general one which has to be dealt with whenever a legally aided litigant is successful in proceedings.[14] It has been accepted since *Daley v. Diggers*[15] that such a litigant has the same right to an order as any other successful party despite the principle that costs are award by way of indemnity.

The principles on which a court's discretion is normally exercised

Where section 31(1)(b) of the 1988 Act has been applied

The Court of Appeal has, in a number of cases, had to consider the effect **34–08** of the provision which is now contained in section 31(1)(b) on the way in

---

[11] [1953] 2 All E.R. 474.
[12] [1966] P. 1.
[13] [1969] 3 All E.R. 134.
[14] See Chapter 17.
[15] [1951] 1 All E.R. 116.

which its discretion should be exercised. In *Re G.*[16] it held that to take any account of the fact that the case was legally aided in deciding whether the wardship of a child should come to an end would be contrary to the express terms of section 1(7)(b) of the Legal Aid Act 1949. In *Howell v. Howell*[17] it decided that on the assumption that there was jurisdiction in exceptional circumstances to make an order for costs against a successful defendant, this should not, in view of section 1(7)(b), be exercised in such a way as to relieve the taxpayer.

Whether section 31(1)(b) of the 1988 Act applies before legal aid is granted

34–09 It is not easy to apply section 31(1)(b) to circumstances occurring before a certificate is granted. It is arguable that the words in the sub-section "the rights conferred by this Act on a person receiving advice, assistance or representation" apply only after a certificate has been granted and a person is in receipt of legal aid entitling him or her to those rights. On this basis of construction it is open to the court, *e.g.* to give leave to appeal out of time where the delay in appealing is attributable to obtaining legal aid. In practice, the courts may take into account any delay in obtaining legal aid notwithstanding the fact that to do so puts an applicant for legal aid in a stronger position than an assisted person, whose rights under his or her certificate must, by section 31(1)(b) be ignored by the court when exercising its discretion. It is submitted that the fundamental difference in this respect between an applicant for legal aid and an assisted person is that it is the requirement for legal aid which creates the very problem, namely delay, which the court is asked to take into account in favour of an applicant. It should, however, be noted that in *Jordan v. Jordan*[18] the Court of Appeal indicated that, where the liberty of the subject is involved and the solicitor considers that there are grounds for appeal he should lodge notice of appeal in accordance with the time-limits despite the absence of legal aid.

Leave to appeal to the House of Lords

34–10 An appeal to the House of Lords from the Court of Appeal can be brought only with leave of that court or of the House of Lords. In several cases the Court of Appeal, when exercising discretion on an application for leave to appeal, appears to have taken account of the rights possessed by the party applying by reason of his being legally aided. In *Chapman v. Honig*[19] Lord Denning M.R. said that the case was one in which in the ordinary way leave would certainly have been given on account of the issue of general importance,

---

[16] [1956] 2 All E.R. 876.
[17] [1953] 2 All E.R. 628.
[18] *The Times*, June 22, 1992.
[19] [1963] 2 All E.R. 513 at 526.

namely whether an action for damages for contempt was maintainable in law, but in view partly of the small amount involved and, of much more importance, in view of the then state of the law under which an unassisted person might incur heavy costs which would not be payable by the legally aided party, leave would not be granted. That case was decided prior to the introduction of the Legal Aid Act 1964 which gave, for the first time, a successful unassisted party an opportunity to claim costs out of the Fund. In *Shepherd v. Lomas*[20] the Court of Appeal reached a similar decision.

Neither of the above decisions is easy to reconcile with the requirements of section 1(7)(b) of the Legal Aid Act 1949 which was the relevant provision at the time. In both cases, however, the position would now be different as a result of the rights created by the Legal Aid Act 1964 whereby a successful unassisted party may claim costs out of the Fund.[21] As a general principle, it is submitted that where either party to an appeal before the Court of Appeal is legally aided, the effect of the provision now contained in regulation 31(1)(b) makes it necessary for the Court of Appeal to ignore his or her rights when considering an application by either party for leave to appeal to the House of Lords.

Other main effects of legal aid

On other parties

A litigant's position is affected in a variety of ways if his or her opponent is **34–11** legally aided. The main effects are as follows:

(a) He or she is entitled to give information to an area office with a view to dissuading the office or the area committee from granting a legal aid certificate to the applicant. There is no statutory right to do this but it is not precluded. There is, however, the practical difficulty of knowing an application has been made and to which area office. As much detail as possible about the applicant and application should be given but if the application cannot be identified (or the representations actually pre-date the application) they can be made after any grant of legal aid in any event.

(b) He or she may give the area office or area committee information after a certificate is granted, with the intention that it should be discharged or revoked. There is no set procedure for doing this but the relevant reference under taken from the certificate should be quoted and consent given for the disclosure of the representations to the assisted person. The representations should be focussed on the relevant aspects of the case (as against the statutory criteria for

---

[20] [1963] 1 W.L.R. 962 at 975.
[21] See Chap. 21.

the grant of legal aid), bearing in mind that it is not for the area office to usurp the function of the court in deciding the issues. Representations should be clearly marked "REPRESENTATIONS" at the top to assist the area office in identification/handling.

(c) He or she may challenge the validity of the certificate (*i.e.* as against the provisions of the 1988 Act as to availability of legal aid or as to the validity of an amendment including a back-dated "corrective" amendment).

(d) Communications sent to or by the assisted person's solicitor may in certain circumstances be disclosed to the area office or area committee, even if marked "without prejudice".

(e) His or her right to costs is severely limited by section 17(1) of the 1988 Act and his or her right to execution is also restricted.

(f) He or she may be required to file an affidavit in court giving evidence of his or her own costs and means for the purpose of section 17(1) of the 1988 Act (an "affidavit of costs and resources").

(g) He or she may be able to obtain an order for payment of costs out of the Fund under section 18 of the 1988 Act.

(h) With certain exceptions, he or she must pay all damages, costs and other sums due to the assisted person to the latter's solicitor or, if the assisted person is no longer represented, to the Board. No-one else, including the assisted person, has power to give the assisted person's opponent a good discharge.

On the court

34–12 The way in which the court exercises its discretion may be affected by the fact that one of the parties is legally aided. The following are the main effects which the issue of a certificate has on the court's powers and functions:

(a) it may have to pronounce on the validity of a certificate;

(b) it may refer abuse of legal aid by an assisted person to the appropriate Area Director, that is, in practice the area office;

(c) it must accept legal aid documents for filing;

(d) its discretion in respect of costs is much restricted in the case of the assisted person;

(e) it may make an order for payment of the unassisted party's costs out of the Fund under section 18 of the 1988 Act;

(f) its discretion in taxing the assisted person's costs is affected by the requirement that an assisted person with a financial interest must be notified of his/her rights.[22]

(g) It may disallow wasted costs.[23]

---

[22] For the position of assisted persons who have or do not have a financial interest in the taxation see Chap. 20.

[23] See Chap. 19.

Chapter 35

CONTROL OF DECISION-MAKING BY THE COURTS

INTRODUCTION

The Board, the Area Directors, the area committees and the assessment **35–01** Officers of the Legal Aid Assessments Office of the Benefits Agency (formerly Department of Social Security) who between them are responsible for administering civil legal aid are, in general, autonomous and the legislation provides no right of appeal to the courts from any of their decisions. Nevertheless, an unsuccessful applicant for legal aid or other person who may be dissatisfied with a decision by one of the authorities can in certain circumstances enlist the help of the courts. He or she may be able to do this by obtaining a decision in the course of legally aided proceedings, by an application for judicial review or by an application for a declaration.

AUTONOMY OF THE LEGAL AID AUTHORITIES

There is a right of appeal to the area committee from a decision by an Area **35–02** Director refusing to grant an application for legal aid for proceedings as well as against the refusal of an amendment or the revocation or, in certain circumstances, discharge of a certificate.[1] There is no appeal to an area committee from a refusal of an emergency certificate, from an assessment of means by the assessment officer[2] nor from any decision by an Area Director as to the amount or method of payment of a contribution.

There is, however, a right of appeal from a decision by an Area Director

---

[1] See Chaps. 7, 8 and 15.
[2] But see Chap. 6 as to the right to ask the Assessment Officer to reconsider the assessment and to ask for a breakdown of the assessment.

to require the applicant to obtain a contribution towards the cost of the proceedings from persons concerned jointly with or having the same interest as the applicant under regulation 32 of the Civil Legal Aid (General) Regulation.[3]

In addition, solicitors who are dissatisfied with an assessment of their costs by an Area Director may seek review of the assessment by an area committee and thereafter may only appeal on a point of principle of general importance to a committee of the Board.[4] These rights of appeal are the only ones conferred by the Regulations.

35–03 The effect is that decisions of the Board, the assessment officers at the Benefits Agency's Legal Aid Assessment Office and, subject to what is said above, Area Directors and area committees are final and, provided these bodies act in accordance with the 1988 Act and the Regulations, their decisions are not, judicial review apart, subject to any general review by the courts. The intention was and remains that the authorities administering legal aid should be autonomous:

> "It may no doubt be on occasion the court may think. ... that the Legal Aid Committee has erred in granting a certificate. But the High Court — and still less the Court of Appeal — is not vested with appellate powers over the transactions of the legal aid committees."[5]

The courts have made it clear on a number of occasions that they have no power to give directions to legal aid committees as to how they should carry out their duties, judges saying, *e.g.* "I have no authority to order the Legal Aid Committee to do anything."[6] "I have no power to sit in judgment on the decisions of the area committee"[7]; and "I have no power to give the area committee any direction whatsoever."[8]

Judicial review aside the most that the court will normally be prepared to do is to give general guidance to the legal aid authorities on the law[9] or the way in which they should carry out their duties[10] or to give an indication to a committee, which it may decide to ignore[11], that it would be desirable for a certificate to be issued in a particular case.[12]

Although decisions of area committees and determinations of means by

---

[3] As to Civil Legal Aid (General) Regulations 1989, reg. 32, generally, see Chaps. 7 and 8.
[4] See Chap. 20.
[5] *Per* Evershed, M.R. in *Page v. Page* [1953] 1 All E.R. 626, at 629.
[6] *Per* Sachs, J. *In the Estate of Wells, The Times*, 27 March, 1958. In that case the applicant had sought a declaration by the court inviting the committee to reconsider its decision to refuse him legal aid.
[7] *Per* Willmer, J. in *Moss v. Moss* [1956] 1 All E.R. 291 at 294.
[8] *Per* Sachs, J. in *Neill v. Glacier Metal Co. Ltd.* [1963] 3 All E.R. 477 at 485.
[9] *Littler v. Liverpool Corporation* [1968] 2 All E.R. 343 at 345.
[10] See *Page v. Page op. cit.*
[11] See *Berry v. British Transport Commission, The Times*, December 15, 1960; *The Times*, January 17, 1961 and February 23, 1961, C.A.
[12] See, *e.g. B. (B.P.M.) v B. (M.M.)* [1969] All ER 891 at 897.

the assessment officers are final[13], an applicant or an assisted person who is dissatisfied with a decision may in practice complain, lodge a fresh application, (subject only to the making of a prohibitory direction against him or her) or apply for leave in judicial review proceedings.[14] Although, in principle, the applicant or assisted person could apply to any area office an Area Director in another area is likely to transfer a fresh application to the area which dealt with the previous application.[15]

METHODS OF CONTROL BY THE COURTS

Although no formal right of appeal to the courts exists against the decisions   **35–04**
of the authorities administering legal aid there are certain circumstances in which the courts can exercise control. The examples given below are not exhaustive and do not deal with remedies which are little used in this field, such as control by injunction or an action for damages.[16]

By decisions in the course of proceedings

It sometimes happens that the validity of the certificate or the legality of   **35–05**
some act by a legal aid authority has to be considered by a court during the course of proceedings and in such a case the court has power to pronounce on it. It would seem that the court can do this at any stage, for example, during proceedings before a Master or District Judge. Also a taxing Officer should disallow on a legal aid taxation any costs incurred under a certificate which is invalid on the face of it. However, regulation 49 of the Civil Legal Aid (General) Regulations 1989 provides that any document purporting to be a certificate issued in accordance with the regulations shall, until the contrary is proved, be deemed to be a valid certificate issued to the person named in it and for the purposes set out.

In *Lacey v. W. Silk & Sons Ltd*[17] Slade J. held a certificate to be invalid, and ineffective to protect the holder from liability in respect of his opponent's costs[18] because the committee issuing it had purported to back-date it, which under the Regulations they had no power to do. The Limited circumstances when cover can be back-dated relate to corrective amendments, although cover can be "deemed" in respect of special Children Act proceedings and, if certain criteria apply, work undertaken

---

[13] See n. 2, above.
[14] Civil Legal Aid (General) Regulations 1989, reg. 41 and see Chap. 36.
[15] *ibid.* reg. 17.
[16] See Wade, *Administrative Law.*
[17] [1951] 2 All E.R. 128.
[18] Under what is now Legal Aid Act 1988, s. 17(1).

before the issue of an emergency certificate.[19] The position regarding corrective amendments has most recently been considered in the case of *Nicholson*.[20]

In another case, expense was incurred by an assisted person in obtaining a shorthand transcript for the purpose of an appeal.[21] On taxation of his costs under the provision then in force[22] the Taxing Master disallowed the cost of the transcript on the ground that the area commitee had not given authority for it (at the time it was mandatory to obtain such authority, but for the present position see Chapter 14). The plaintiff's solicitors then approached the area committee who stated that the original legal aid certificate had been intended to cover the cost of the transcript and issued an amended one to authorise the expense. On a summons to review the taxation, the court upheld the Taxing Master's decision and held that authority to incur the expense of a transcript had to be given before the expense was incurred and could not be given retrospectively. This authority is still good.

By application for judicial review

35–06 A person seeking to challenge an administrative act or omission may obtain from the Divisional Court of the Queen's Bench Division a judicial review including an injunction and damages, as may be appropriate. Judicial review proceedings taken in legal aid matters are, as with judicial review cases generally, increasingly common. They include applications made by opponents who are dissatisfied by the grant/continuation of legal aid in the light of representations made by them and by solicitors dissatisfied with decisions on points of principle of general importance by the Board's Costs Appeals Committee.

A letter before action should be written before commencing proceedings. This enables the decision made to be reviewed without unnecessary costs being incurred. The Board's Legal Department at Legal Aid Head Office will accept service of any proceedings.

35–07 Judicial review by way of what was formerly an order of certiorari applies to the proceedings of an inferior court or tribunal, its object being to correct any fundamental defect of judicial process, the commonest being excess of jurisdiction. A defective decision will be quashed. The quashing order will issue against an area committee, the Board or the Benefits Agency. It would also issue against an Area Director in circumstances where the decision of

---

[19] See Chap. 22.
[20] See Chap. 13.
[21] *Wallace v. Freeman Heating Co. Ltd.* [1955] 1 All E.R. 418.
[22] Legal Aid Act 1949, Sched. 3.

the Area Director is final, for example, on refusal to issue an emergency certificate.[23]

The starting point for deciding when judicial review on this basis will lie is the statement by Atkin L.J. in *R. v. Electricity Commissioners ex parte London Electricity Joint Committee Co.* (1920) Ltd.,[24] when he said that:

"... the operation of the writs (of certiorari and prohibition) has extended to control the proceedings of bodies which do not claim to be, and would not be regarded as, Courts of Justice. Wherever any body or persons having legal authority to determine questions affecting the rights of subjects, and having the duty to act judicially, act in excess of their legal authority they are subject to the controlling jurisdiction of the King's Bench Division exercised in these writs."

The first occasion when the courts considered the position of a legal aid committee in this context was in *R. v. Manchester Legal Aid Committee, exparte R.A. Brand & Co. Ltd.*[25] when the Divisional Court held that certiorari would issue to a local committee (the local committees, which dealt with all pre-certificate work other than applications for the purpose of appeals were abolished in 1980 and all committee decisions are now made by the area committees). Parker J. considered the definition in the Electricity Commissioners case and said:

"That the local committee was a body of persons having legal authority to determine questions affecting the rights of subjects was admitted and, indeed, is clear. The real contest in the present case is whether they also had the duty to act judicially."

He went on later to say:

"Though the local committees may be said to be administrative bodies in the sense that they are responsible for administering the Act, they are quite unconcerned with questions of policy. They cannot refuse legal aid because the fund is being depleted or because they think that certain forms of action should be discouraged. They have to decide the matter solely on the facts of the particular case, solely on the evidence before them and apart from any extraneous considerations. In other words, they must act judicially, not judiciously."[26]

In that case, the local committee issued a certificate to a trustee in bankruptcy to continue a bankrupt's claim against a company but exceeded their jurisdiction. This was because there had been no determination of the trustee's financial resources but only the means of the bankrupt (there was

---

[23] See Chap. 10.
[24] [1924] 1 K.B. 171, C.A. at 205.
[25] [1952] 1 All E.R. 480.
[26] *ibid.* at pp. 487 and 490.

at that time no provision that in such a case the trustee's resources should not be taken into account).[27] The Divisional Court granted an order of certiorari on the application of the company and directed that the certificate be quashed. This case is of course, also the first example of the other party in the proceedings seeking to challenge the grant (continuation of legal aid).[28]

In *Ex p. Rondel*[29] the Divisional Court gave the applicant leave to apply to the court for an order of certiorari to quash the decision of an area commitee who had refused him legal aid to prosecute an appeal to the House of Lords in an action against his former counsel. He applied for certiorari to quash the decision and mandamus to compel the area committee to decide his application according to law. Although the application was subsequently dismissed[30] on the ground that the committee had not exceeded their discretion, the fact that certiorari would lie was not disputed

In *R. v. Legal Aid Committee No. 9 (North Eastern) Legal Aid Area, ex parte Foxhill Flats (Leeds) Ltd*[31] the plaintiff to an action successfully applied to the Divisional Court for an order of certiorari to quash two legal aid certificates which had been granted to the defendants. Lord Parker C.J. who delivered the judgment of the court, said that the *Manchester Legal Aid Committee* case was "authority, which is not challenged in this court, that a party to proceedings such as in that applicants case *R.A. Brand & Co Ltd*, and in the present case the applicants, are aggrieved persons and that certiorari will lie to quash a legal aid certificate."[32]

The Legal Aid Board has since its inception accepted the court's jurisdiction in judicial review of decisions relating to the exercise of its statutory powers as a public body.

35–08 Where a committee's decision was challenged as being erroneous in law the error must have been shown to exist on the face of the record. However, in *Ex p Rondel*, the Divisional Court refused to look at a letter from the Area Secretary (now Area Director) to the applicant's solicitor indicating the points the committee were likely to bear in mind regarding the application for legal aid, or at the case note considered by the committee, although counsel for the committee raised no objection. The court did not consider such documents to be part of the record.

It is, however, now accepted by the Board that papers which are before

---

[27] Civil Legal Aid (General) Regulations 1989, reg. 33 and Civil Legal Aid (Assessment of Resources) Regulations 1989, reg. 6.
[28] See also London Docklands Development Corporation and Another v. Legal Aid Board, Court of Appeal, March 22, 1994, unreported.
[29] *The Times*, 8 February, 1967.
[30] See [1967] 2 All E.R. 419.
[31] [1970] 1 All E.R. 1176.
[32] *ibid.* at p. 1179.

the area committee when they consider any matter do form part of the record and are accordingly subject to discovery on judicial review.

There appears to be little restriction on the persons who may apply by way of judicial review. **35–09**

> "Anybody can apply for it — a member of the public who has been inconvenienced, or a particular party or a person who has a particular grievance of his own. If the application is made by what for convenience one may call a stranger, the remedy is purely discretionary. Where, however, it is made by a person who has a particular grievance of his own, whether as a party or otherwise, then the remedy lies ex debito justitiae."[33]

In the Manchester *Legal Aid Committee* case[34] the court considered whether the applicants, who were the assisted person's opponents in the main action, were persons aggrieved as, if so, certiorari would be granted *ex debito justitiae*. *Parker J.* said that "the applicants seem to us to be persons aggrieved within this principle. They are persons who incur the risks inherent in having to fight a party who has legal aid." He pointed out also that the legislation contemplated that they were persons interested in that when a party to proceedings became an assisted person his solicitor had to serve all other parties with notice of the fact.[35] Whether persons are aggrieved persons for this purpose depends on whether they have a particular grievance of their own beyond some inconvenience suffered in common with the rest of the public.[36]

In *ex p. Rondel*[37] the person applying for an order was an unsuccessful applicant for legal aid and these are the people most likely to apply for an order although it is clear that an assisted person's opponents may apply.

In *R. v. Supplementary Benefits Commission, ex parte Singer*[38] the Divisional Court granted certiorari against the Commission to an applicant for legal aid whose disposable income have been determined at a figure above the then legal aid limit.[39] **35–10**

In *R. v. No. 14 (London West) Legal Aid Area Committee, ex parte*

---

[33] *Per* Lord Partier C.J. in *R. v. Thames Magistrates' Court ex parte Greenbaum* [1957] 55 L.G.R. 129, C.A.

[34] See para. 35–07, above.

[35] See Civil Legal Aid (General) Regulations 1989, reg. 54(2).

[36] See *R. v. Nicholson* [1899] 2 Q.B. 455, C.A. at 470 but see also *London Docklands Development Corporation and Another* (see n. 28 above), *R. v. No. 8 Area Committee of the Legal Aid Board, ex p. Megarry and others*, Q. B., July 1, 1994, unreported and *R. v. Legal Aid Board, ex p. Bateman* [1992] 3 All E.R. 390.

[37] See para. 35–07, above.

[38] [1973] 2 All E.R. 931.

[39] See Chap. 6 regarding eligibility. See also *R. v. Legal Aid Assessment Office, ex p. Cocker, The Independent*, July 23, 1993, 143 NLJ 1259 and *R. v. Legal Aid Assessment Office, ex p. Saunders, The Times*, December 22, 1989 for examples of other challenges to assessments.

Bunting[40] an unsuccessful applicant for legal aid applied without success for orders to quash the area committee's decisions and to direct the committee to determine his legal aid applications according to law. Lord Widgery C.J. in an unreported part of his judgement, discussed the application of certiorari to legal aid committees and said:

> "On what basis should we approach the problem? Of course, this is a committee which . . . has the widest possible discretion to deal with the issues which are required to be put before it. It is clearly not the function of this Court to act as a court of appeal reviewing the decisions of legal aid committees and substituting our views as to what those decisions should be for the views of the committee itself. All that we can do is to allow certiorari to go in appropriate cases to quash the decision below and leave the committee to proceed to reach their conclusion afresh. I think that in relation to legal aid committees the ordinary principles which govern the use of the prerogative orders should apply. In other words, I think that this Court should allow certiorari to go to quash a decision of a legal aid committee if it is made without jurisdiction, or if it is made in such a fashion as to show an error of law on the face of the record.
>
> Furthermore, of course, it is possible to show an error of law on the face of the record not only by indicating an incorrect statement of the law therein contained, but also by showing that the decision is so perverse that no reasonable committee properly applying its mind to the problem could possibly have reached that decision. The point is sometimes put an other way by saying that certiorari could go if the decision is so strange that one is driven to the view that the committee must have taken into account the irrelevant or ignored the relevant. Once that stage is reached, then an error of law is disclosed and an opportunity for this Court to intervene is created."

Numerous decisions have since been challenged mostly following the refusal of civil legal aid on the merits and the application of the merits test has been judicially considered in that context.[41]

35–11 To obtain what was formerly an order of mandamus (to secure the performance of the public duty) the applicant must be able to show that he or she has a sufficient interest in the performance of the duty and that performance of it has been demanded and has been refused.

---

[40] (1974) 118 S.J. 259, D.C.
[41] See by way of example *R. v. Legal Aid Board, ex p. Belcher and Another*, Q. B., July 15, unreported; *R. v. Legal Aid Board, ex p. Hughes*, C. A., 24 H.L.R. 698, July 23, 1992 (regarding the civil legal aid merits test where leave has been granted in judicial review proceedings); *R. v. Legal Aid Board Area Committee No. 10 (East Midlands Area), ex p. McKenna, The Times*, December 20, 1989 and *R. v. Legal Aid Area No. 8 (Northern) Appeal Committee, ex p. Angell and others, The Times*, March 1, 1990.

In *Lacey v. W. Silk & Son Ltd.*[42] the court left open the question of whether mandamus would lie against a legal aid committee to compel them to issue a legal aid certificate to an applicant on his compliance with the requirements of the Regulations.[43]

In *Ex p Rondel*,[44] however, the Divisional Court gave the applicant leave to apply for orders both of mandamus and certiorari against an area committee who had refused him legal aid.

It is unlikely that anyone but an applicant for legal aid would normally wish to apply for an order to compel an action against an area committee but in a proper case such a person's opponent would be entitled to apply. It should, however, be noted that since the inception of the Legal Aid Board applicants for judicial review have only been successful in having decisions quashed so that they can then be given appropriate consideration.

By declarations

The High Court has power to make binding declarations of right, whether **35–12** or not any consequential relief is or could be claimed.

In *Taylor v. National Assistance Board*[45] the applicant applied for a declaration that in an application by her for a legal aid certificate the Board (a predecessor of the Benefits Agency) had incorrectly determined her disposable income.[46] The Board took the preliminary point that the relevant regulations provided that its computation of an applicant's disposable income was to be final and that any challenge to this should be by way of certiorari. Merriman P. overruled the objection and his decision on this point was endorsed *obiter* by Denning L.J. in the Court of Appeal who said:

"The remedy by declaration is available at the present day so as to ensure a board or other authority set up by Parliament makes its determinations in accordance with the law; and this is so, no matter whether the determinations are judicial or disciplinary, or, as here, administrative determinations."[47]

A different viewpoint was expressed by the Court of Appeal, also *obiter*, in the case *Punton v. Ministry of Pensions and National Insurance (No.2)*[48] where a declaration was sought that the National Insurance Commissioner had come to a wrong decision in law as to certain claims to unemployment benefit. The court refused to grant the declaration and said that the question

---

[42] [1951] 2 All E.R. 128.
[43] See what is now regulation 45(2) of the General Regulations.
[44] See para. 35–07, above.
[45] [1956] 2 All E.R. 455.
[46] See also Chap. 6.
[47] [1957] 1 All E.R. 183, at 185.
[48] [1964] 1 All E.R. 448.

whether the Commissioner was right in law "would have been the precise issue if proceedings had been taken by way of certiorari." Certiorari, *i.e.* judicial review proceedings (unlike the action for a declaration) would not usurp the function of the tribunal but would have required it, having quashed its decision, to hear the case and determine it correctly.

Since these cases were dealt with a number of challenges including of means assessments have proceeded by way of judicial review rather than declaration.

It is, however, clear that where the decision of an area committee is a nullity, because of lack of jurisdiction, a declaratory order can be sought.[49] Where, however, a committee acts within its jurisdiction but it is desired to set the decision aside as being wrong in law the court may refuse to make a declaratory order on the ground that judicial review is the proper remedy. Decisions regarding the operation of the statutory charge have tended to be challenged by way of declaration rather than judicial review.[50]

Decisions that may be challenged

Area committees and the Board

35–13 A large number of decisions are taken each year by area committees, in connection with applications for legal aid (civil or criminal) or ABWOR, with litigation by assisted persons and with assessment of solicitors' costs and counsel's fees for work done on behalf of assisted persons. These decisions relate to appeals from decisions by Area Directors refusing applications for legal aid or refusing amendments to certificates, discharging or revoking certificates, and assessing costs claims. Decisions are also made in the area of criminal legal aid — on reviews against refusal of legal aid, renewed applications, authorities and costs assessments.

Decisions are also made by the Board (or its sub-committees); making prohibitory directions against vexatious applicants,[51] granting/refusing authority to solicitors to have taxations reviewed[52] and dealing with appeals from assessment by area committees of costs claims, where a point of principle of general importance is involved.[53]

Whether any particular decision can be successfully challenged will depend upon the circumstances and the nature of the decision.[54] Any right

---

[49] See, *e.g. Ridge v. Baldwin* [1964] A.C. 40.

[50] See Chap. 18 for examples of such cases.

[51] See para. 36–05.

[52] See Chap. 20.

[53] See Chap. 20 and e.g. *R. v. Legal Aid Board ex parte R.M. Broudie & Co* (Co-2564–93) March 1994 for a judicial review of a point of principle decision.

[54] See e.g. *R. v. Legal Aid Board, ex p. Gilchrist* (1993) 137 Sol Jo LB 146 — regarding Healthcall and advice and assistance at police stations. Also *R. v. Legal Aid Board ex parte Bruce* [1992] 1 W.L.R. 694, [1992] 3 All E.R. 321 — regarding green form disbursements.

of appeal should be pursued and exhausted and an appropriate letter before action written to enable the decision to be reviewed without unnecessary costs being incurred.

It should be noted that in a civil legal aid matter if a solicitor challenges the refusal of authority to review a taxation by the Board Costs Appeals Committee (a sub-committee of the Board), any judicial review will be seen as for the benefit of the solicitor rather than the assisted person. The judicial review proceedings should not be pursued under the cover of a civil legal aid certificate granted to the assisted person.[55] This decision is likely to apply to challenges of any decision connected with the assessment of costs, although an assisted person *may* arguably have a sufficient interest to benefit from the challenge of a refusal of prior authority for expenditure if it significantly affects the conduct of the assisted person's case.

Area Directors

Most decisions relating to applications for legal aid or legal aid certificates are made in the first instance on behalf of the Area Directors. Their main duties are to consider applications for legal aid certificates, or orders, extensions to the Green Form costs limit, ABWOR, requests for amendments to certificates, requests for authority for acts which are likely to be unusually expensive or which are unusual in their nature, the discharge or revocation of certificates and assessment of solicitors' and counsels' costs claims.   **35–14**

Area Directors may also perform on behalf of the area committee any function which that committee is required or entitled to perform, the only exception provided for in the regulations being that an Area Director may not determine an appeal under regulation 39 of the Civil Legal Aid (General) Regulations.[56] Under the Civil Legal Aid (General) Regulations 1989[57] the Area Director carries out an assessment of costs in civil legal aid matters and any solicitor or counsel who is dissatisfied with the assessment may apply to the area committee for the assessment to be reviewed. Area offices regard themselves as not being empowered to hear an application for a review and all such applications are considered by the appropriate area committee following an assessment by the area office (rather than a provisional assessment as was previously the case).

In cases where the Regulations provide that a decision is to be made by the Area Director, or where an Area Director is entitled to make a decision on behalf of the area committee, an aggrieved person may seek to challenge that decision.[58]

---

[55] *R. v. Legal Aid Board, ex parte Bateman* [1992] 3 All E.R. 490.
[56] See regulation 6 of the General Regulations.
[57] Civil Legal Aid (General) Regulations 1989, reg. 105.
[58] See *R. v. Boycott, ex parte Keasby* [1939] 2 All E.R. 626 and *R v. Kent Police Authority ex parte Godden, The Times*, 18 June 1971, C.A.

35–15   It is, however, a fundamental principle of judicial review that the applicant must first have exhausted his or her remedies. Where, therefore, an aggrieved person has a right of appeal from an Area Director's decision, that right of appeal must be exercised before any application for judicial review is made. If the appeal against the Area Director's decision is dismissed by the area committee it will be the area committee's decision which would be challenged on judicial review.

An Area Director's decision is, however, final:

    (a) when determining an application for an emergency certificate;[59] or

    (b) when deciding the payable amount and method of payment of an applicant's contribution.

It is not often that an applicant for legal aid would wish to contest an Area Director's decision in either of these cases. By the time an challenge regarding refusal to grant an emergency certificate had been mounted it is likely that the application for a full certificate would have been considered. Regarding payment of contribution, although an applicant might well consider that his or her financial resources had been incorrectly determined the applicant's dispute would be with the Benefits Agency (Legal Aid Assessment Office) and not with the Area Director. It would therefore be more appropriate to apply for judicial review of the assessment officer's decision.

It should also be noted that there is no stated right of appeal against the refusal of a prior authority application and no right of appeal against a refusal to grant an extension to the Green Form legal advice and sssistance costs limit. Such area office decisions are therefore susceptible to and indeed have been judicially reviewed.[60]

The Benefits Agency — Legal Aid Assessment Office

35–16   The functions of the Benefits Agency (Legal Aid Assessment Office) are limited to determining the financial resources of applicants for legal aid and redetermining the resources of assisted persons. In *Taylor v. National Assistance Board*[61] a determination of the Board (a predecessor of the Agency) was challenged in the courts. In that case a declaratory order was sought when the court did not have to decide the question whether prerogative proceedings would lie (counsel for the Board in fact conceded that there would).[62] Subsequently a number of judicial review applications have been successfully mounted against the Benefits Agency Legal Aid Assessment Office and its predecessors.[63]

---

[59] See Chap. 10.

[60] See *e.g. R. v. Legal Aid Board, ex p. Higgins, The Times,* November 19, 1993 regarding disbursements under Green Form Legal Advice and Assistance.

[61] See Chap. 10.

[62] [1956] 2 All E.R. 455 at 459.

[63] See *e.g. R. v. Legal Aid Board ex parte Clark* [1992] The Times, November 25, 1992 and n. 39 above.

In such cases where the decision to be challenged is a decision relating to the assessment of a person's financial eligibility for legal aid, those assets which are disputed as between the applicant and the Assessment Office would be disregarded (as subject-matter of the dispute) in an application for legal aid to cover the judicial review proceedings.

The conduct of the defence of applications for judicial review involving the Legal Aid Assessment Office is generally undertaken by the Benefits Agency (rather than Legal Aid Head Office on behalf of the Board).

Declaration with regard to the operation of the statutory charge

Where the appropriate area office takes the view that the statutory charge   **35–17** under section 16(6) of the 1988 Act applies to the circumstances of an assisted person's case, that decision may be challenged in the courts by an application for a declaration that the charge does not apply.

Area offices are not prepared to discuss with the legal advisers for assisted persons whether proposed terms of settlement will or will not result in the charge being applied. If an area office were willing to discuss the applicability of the charge with solicitors before any order or agreement was made, clearly the office would be put in an invidious position. The office would find itself acting in the capacity of an adviser. The area offices take the view, therefore, that it is for the solicitors and counsel acting for an assisted person, after considering the 1988 Act, the relevant Regulations and any decided cases relating to the charge, to advise their client as to whether the charge will apply in any particular circumstances.

Solicitors acting for assisted persons are entitled to endeavour to resolve their clients' claims in ways which will minimise the effect of the statutory charge. The courts have, however, drawn a distinction between actions which result in perfectly acceptable avoidance of the statutory charge and artificial devices which result in unacceptable evasion of the charge.[64]

Although an area office will not be prepared to discuss the applicability   **35–18** of the statutory charge with an assisted person's solicitor before the final order or agreement is made, the office will be prepared to explain to solicitors why they consider that the statutory charge applies in a given case.

If solicitors do not accept the area office's view the case should be referred to the Legal Department at Legal Aid Head Office by the solicitor or the area office. The Legal Department will look at the matter afresh and decide whether or not it agrees with the decision made by the area office. If the Legal Department agrees with the area office's decision the only further remedy open to an assisted person is an application to the High Court for a declaration (or for judicial review).

Civil legal aid is available for such an application but the legal aid

---

[64] See *Manley v. The Law Society* [1981] 1 W.L.R. 385 and para. 18–35 above.

application would be considered by another area office (see below) and itself be subject to the possible operation of the statutory charge.

Legal aid to challenge decisions

35–19 It is open to a person seeking an application for judicial review or a declaration to apply for a legal aid certificate for the purpose of those proceedings. Such an application should be made to an area office other than that which made the decision which is being challenged.

The area office dealing with the application for legal aid will not communicate any information furnished in connection with the applicant's case to either the original area office which dealt with the matter or to Legal Aid Head Office.

Applicants seeking legal aid to challenge decisions of other area offices may provide all material information to the area office dealing with the legal aid application, without fear that any of that information will be disclosed to his or her opponent. For the purpose of proceedings the opponent is the appropriate area committee but in practice the proceedings will be handled on behalf of the Board at Legal Aid Head Office. Service will be accepted by the Head Office Legal Department and the area office dealing with the legal aid application for the proposed proceedings will expect a letter before action to be written in the usual way so that the decision to be challenged can be reviewed and no unnecessary costs incurred.

It should, however, be noted that the Board considers that it should not be placed in a position different from any other opponent facing an assisted person in that it remains open to the Board to make representations against the grant/continuation of legal aid. This would not, however, be done without the knowledge of the assisted person's solicitor and often only after giving him/her an opportunity to report to the relevant area office him or herself.

Chapter 36

ABUSES — SANCTIONS AND CONFIDENTIALITY

SANCTIONS

Through legal aid, the state provides public monies to fund private **36–01** litigation. To ensure that such monies are spent only in appropriate cases, the 1988 Act provides that, for most proceedings, applicants and assisted persons must satisfy financial eligibility criteria[1] and that their cases must satisfy merits tests.[2]

To enable financial eligibility and the merits of cases to be assessed, the 1988 Act and the Regulations require applicants and assisted persons to provide information to their solicitors to the Board (including the Legal Aid Assessment Office) and, in the case of criminal proceedings, to the court. If this information is either intentionally not provided or is knowingly false, the applicant or assisted person is liable on summary conviction to a fine not exceeding level 4 on the standard scale or to imprisonment for a term not exceeding three months or to both.[3] Note that the offence can be committed not only by someone receiving advice, assistance or representation but also by someone seeking it.

In addition, the Board may bring civil proceedings in a county court (regardless of the amount of the claim) to recover any loss sustained by as a result of an assisted person's failure to comply with the Regulations as to the information to be provided by him.

There are also the sanctions contained in the Regulations regarding discharge/revocation for abuse[4] as well as the particular sanctions dealt with below.

---

[1] See Chap. 6.
[2] See Chap. 7.
[3] Legal Aid Act 1988, s. 39.
[4] See Chap. 15.

Time-Limits and Prosecutions

36–02 Although the 1988 Act[5] provides an absolute limitation on criminal prosecutions — proceedings cannot be commenced more than two years after the date on which the offence was committed — so long as a certificate remains in force an assisted person is at risk of time running. For example, if an assisted person made a false statement in support of his application for legal aid, he might repeat that false statement on, *e.g.* a further assessment of means.

Note also that if an offence under the 1988 Act itself could not be pursued due to the time-limit, a prosecution based on deception rather than a Legal Aid Act offence could still be mounted.

36–03 Cases for prosecution are referred to the police by the criminal courts (regarding criminal legal aid) and by the Legal Aid Assessment Office or the Board (regarding civil legal aid). The Board has an Investigations Section which is part of Legal Aid Head Office and which is primarily concerned with deception/fraud on the part of solicitors undertaking legal aid work including the provision of Green Form advice and police station advice.

Provisions in Regulations

Legal advice and assistance — recovery of losses

36–04 The Legal Advice and Assistance Regulations 1989 set out the procedure to be followed before the Board may take proceedings to recover losses sustained either as a result of a person's failure to provide information, or as a result of his providing false information, as required by those Regulations.[6] A criminal prosecution within section 39 of the 1988 Act is also possible in respect of advice and assistance including ABWOR.

Civil legal aid-prohibitory direction

36–05 An abuse of the system by repeated civil legal aid applications can be prevented by the making of a "prohibitory direction" against the particular applicant. Such a direction can only be made by the Board following a report from the Area Director to the area committee and from the area committee to the Legal Aid Board itself. The person involved must be given an opportunity to make written representations and, if the Board is satisfied

---

[5] *ibid.* s. 39(3).
[6] Legal and Advice and Assistance Regulations, 1989 reg. 36.

his conduct has not amounted to an "abuse of the facilities provided by the Act", it can direct that, for a period not exceeding five years, no consideration shall be given to any future (or pending) application regarding any particular matter or, in exceptional circumstances, any application at all.

The direction can extend to a receiver, next friend or guardian *ad litem* and can be varied or revoked in whole or in part at any time (although there is no right of appeal as such).[7] The Board is required to inform the Lord Chancellor of the making of a prohibitory direction and, if requested, its reasons for making it.

Civil legal aid — obligations to report

The Civil Legal Aid (General) Regulations 1989[8] require an assisted person **36–06** to inform his solicitor forthwith of any change in his circumstances or in the circumstances of his case which he has reason to believe might affect the terms or the continuation of his certificate.

An intentional failure to comply with the provision will be sufficient for section 39(1)(a) of the 1988 Act to apply. This means that, while a person is legally aided, an intentional failure to inform his solicitor of any change in his circumstances or in the circumstances of his case which he has reason to believe might affect the terms or the continuation of his certificate may lead to proceedings being taken against him under section 39.

The Civil Legal Aid (Assessment of Resources) Regulations 1989 contain a similar provision. They require the person concerned to inform the Area Director of any change in his financial circumstances which has occurred since the original assessment of means was made and which he has reason to believe might affect the terms on which his certificate was granted, or its continuation.[9]

It follows from this, that if an assisted person tells his solicitor of a change in his financial circumstances, the solicitor should have in mind the provisions of this regulation and advise his client to report to the Area Director, if appropriate.

Furthermore, a solicitor has an obligation, under regulation 67 of the Civil Legal Aid (General) Regulations 1989, to report suspected abuse of legal aid to the Area Director[10] and if he (or counsel) is uncertain whether it would be reasonable for him to continue acting for the assisted person, regulation 67(2) requires that he must report the circumstances to the Area Director.

---

[7] Civil Legal Aid (General) Regulations 1989, regs. 40 and 41.
[8] *ibid.* reg. 66.
[9] Civil Legal Aid (Assessment of Resources) Regulations 1989, reg. 11
[10] *S. v. S. (Abuse of Process of Appeal)* [1994] 2 F.C.R. 941, C.A.

These provisions are normally used to trigger the show cause procedure on the merits of the case but are not confined only to that.

It is an abuse of the appeal process to bring an appeal using legal aid funds, which is of academic interest only to lawyers and which no reasonable privately paying client would fund merely to benefit lawyers.

Civil legal aid — representations

36–07 The re-examination of an assisted person's means of case may be triggered by a report from him or his legal representative or by the increasing use of "other side's representations".

Anyone can make representations against the grant of an application for legal aid or the continuation of a legal aid certificate, but it is usually the opponent, their solicitors or another party in the proceedings who does so.

The Board cannot normally deal with representations until an application has been received and a reference number allocated to it.

Representations can be on either legal merit/reasonableness (merits) or financial grounds (means), or both; and can be against the granting or the continuation of a certificate.

Representations should be made in writing to the relevant area office, with the assisted person's name and reference number, if known, clearly stated at the top of the letter. The letter should be boldly marked "Representations".

36–08 Merits representations are dealt with by the area office which issued the certificate.

Frequently, representations raise issues which may only be properly decided by the court. If this is apparent from the outset then the area office may decline to take any action. Action can only be taken where the representations may have a material bearing on the continuation of the legal aid certificate.

It is possible that the area office will already hold information showing that the representations are unfounded but, if not, the assisted person and solicitor are given the opportunity to comment on the representations. The Board will seek the consent of the representor to disclose a copy of the representations, unless consent is expressly given or the representor has already sent a copy to the assisted person and/or their solicitor.

If consent is not given, then the matter cannot usually be taken any further, because a legal aid certificate cannot be discharged or revoked without giving the assisted person an opportunity to show cause why the certificate should not remain in force.

The assisted person and solicitor will be given sufficient time to respond to the representations and then the matter will be considered by the area office. Investigations do take some time because enquiries have to be followed, the area office may have to engage in correspondence and may require appropriate documents to be produced.

The result of the representations will normally be disclosed to the representor i.e. whether the certificate has been discharged or revoked, or allowed to continue. However, the Board's general duty of confidentiality and the confidentiality provisions in section 38 of the Legal Aid Act 1988 prevent the disclosure of any information supplied by or on behalf of the assisted person without their consent.

Means representations should be addressed to the relevant area office. **36–09** The representations are normally then referred for investigation to the Benefits Agency's Legal Aid Assessment Office in Preston.

The action taken by the Assessment Office may include issuing forms to the assisted person for them to provide their current financial circumstances or contacting the local benefit payment office for information where this is relevant.

The Assessment Office reports the outcome of its investigation to the area office which takes the appropriate action. Normal procedures will be followed to discharge or revoke the certificate, if appropriate. The representor will normally be notified whether the certificate has been discharged or revoked, or allowed to continue.

The court itself has the power to make an order referring the question of **36–10** whether an assisted person's certificate should continue to the Area Director. This can be done on the application of the Board or of the court's own motion and is based on what effectively amounts to a finding of abuse by the court.[11] There is a defence of due care or diligence but even if no order is made there is an obligation on the assisted person's solicitor to report the circumstances to the Area Director,[12] who can then consider the position in any event.

Criminal legal aid — obligations to disclose/report

In relation to criminal legal aid a statement of means is required to be **36–11** provided supported by documentary evidence (subject only to certain exceptions). Changes liable to affect an assisted person's contribution liability are required to be reported to the court or proper officer of the court.[13] The proper officer may require further evidence to be provided of any information or change in circumstances, together with such additional information as the court or the proper officer may require.

There is also a specific obligation placed on the legal representative to **36–12** report "forthwith" to the proper officer, notwithstanding any professional privilege, where he knows that the applicant or assisted person has intentionally failed to comply with a regulatory requirement concerning the

---

[11] Civil Legal Aid (General) Regulations 1989, reg. 68(1).
[12] *ibid.* reg. 68(2).
[13] Legal Aid in Criminal and Care Proceedings (General) Regulations 1989, Pt III.

information to be given or has made a false statement or false representation. This is a new provision specifically inserted to deal with those cases where the legal representative would otherwise consider information to be privileged.[14]

CONFIDENTIALITY

On the part of the Board

36-13   The general position is that no information furnished for the purposes of the Legal Aid Act 1988 to the Legal Aid Board, or to any court, or other person or body of persons upon whom functions are imposed or conferred by regulations, and so furnished in connection with the case of a person seeking or receiving advice, assistance or representation, may be disclosed. The exceptions to the rule are:

(a) to enable or assist the Lord Chancellor to perform his functions under or in relation to the 1988 Act;

(b) to enable the Board to discharge its functions under the Act;

(c) to facilitate the proper performance of any court, tribunal or other person or body of persons of functions under the Act;

(d) with a view to the institutution of, or otherwise for the purpose of, any criminal proceedings for an offence under the Act;

(e) in connection with any other proceedings under the Act;

(f) to facilitate the proper performance by any tribunal of disciplinary functions as regards legal representatives.[15]

The restriction on disclosure of information does not apply to information in the form of a summary or collection of information so framed as not to enable information relating to any particular person to be ascertained from it, nor does it prevent the disclosure of information for any purpose with the consent of the person in connection with whose case it was furnished and, where he did not furnish it himself, with that of the person or body of persons who did.

Contravention renders a person liable on summary conviction to a fine not exceeding level 4 on the standard scale, but no proceedings may be brought without the written consent of the Attorney General.[16]

The Act provides, for the avoidance of doubt, that information furnished to a legal representative as such by or on behalf of a person seeking or receiving advice, assistance or representation under the 1988 Act is not

---

[14] Legal Aid in Criminal and Care Proceedings (General) Regulations 1989, reg. 56.
[15] Legal Aid Act, s. 38.
[16] *ibid.* s.38(4) and (5).

information unfurnished to the Board or a person upon whom functions are imposed or conferred by regulations.[17]

Care will be taken not to breach the confidentiality provisions and although it is clear that they relate only to information provided "in connection with the case" (which has been treated by the Board as extending to means information) the Board has successfully opposed/set aside Court orders for production of documents/disclosure in the context of proceedings (civil and criminal). Furthermore, the Board is of the view that obligations of confidentiality are owed to applicants/assisted persons outside section 38, *i.e.* in accordance the general principles of confidentiality. The Board will not, therefore, in the absence of appropriate consent disclose information which might be called administrative (*e.g.* as to the status of an application/certificate) other than in accordance with any relevant Regulations (*e.g.* as to notice or as to information to a person who has made representations against the grant/continuation of legal aid). **36–14**

On the part of the legal representatives

Section 31 of the 1995 Act makes it clear that the fact that legal services are given under the Act does not affect the general position and section 38(6) confirms that information given to a legal representative is not furnished to the Board or court or other person/body of persons with regulatory functions. Furthermore the Legal Aid (Disclosure of Information) Regulations 1991 waive the rules of privilege and confidentiality to permit the Legal Aid Board representatives information relating to the cases of clients or former clients who were legally aided. **36–15**

There are also specific provisions requiring the solicitor to supply information as to declining to give or continue to give advice and assistance (backed by a power for the Area Director to require information, professional privilege being waived)[18] as well as the various civil legal aid obligations on the solicitor or counsel to report to the Area Director under Part IX Civil Legal Aid (General) Regulations 1989[19] which are again not subject to professional privilege and in addition which would otherwise be "without prejudice".[20] Note that any party may disclose "without prejudice" or other communications in relation to the proceedings sent to or by the assisted person's solicitor, provided that the disclosure is for the purpose of providing information under the Act or the General Regulations or to enable an Area Director or area committee to perform their functions. **36–16**

In relation to criminal legal aid there is an obligation on the legal **36–17**

---

[17] *ibid.* s.38(b).
[18] Legal Advice and Assistance Regulations 1989, regs. 18 and 19.
[19] See Chap. 15.
[20] Civil Legal Aid (General) Regulations 1989, reg. 73(1) and (2).

representative to report "forthwith" to the proper officer the fact that an applicant or legally assisted person has intentionally failed to furnish information required by regulations or has knowingly made a false statement or representation. The legal representative must "know" the position and professional privilege is waived.[21]

A contribution order may be varied or revoked and the legal aid order itself may be withdrawn.[22]

---

[21] Legal Aid in Criminal and Care Proceedings (General) Regulations 1989, reg. 56 (inserted by the Legal Aid in Criminal and Care Proceedings (General) (Amendment) (No. 2) Regulations 1993.

[22] *ibid.* regs. 35 and 41.

Chapter 37

REPRESENTATION IN CONTEMPT PROCEEDINGS

IN WHICH PROCEEDINGS AVAILABLE

A grant of representation may be made in respect of any proceedings where **37–01** a person is liable to be committed or fined:
   (a) by a magistrates' court under section 12 of the Contempt of Court Act 1981 (for wilfully insulting the court, a witness or any officer of the court, or wilfully interrupting proceedings or otherwise misbehaving in court);
   (b) by a county court under section 14, (for assaulting an officer of the court in the execution of his duty); section 92, (for rescuing goods seized in execution under process of a county court); or section 118 (for wilfully insulting the judge, any juror or witness or any officer of the court, or wilfully interrupting the proceedings or otherwise misbehaving in court) of the County Courts Act 1984;
   (c) for contempt in the face of that or any other court by the Court of Appeal, the High Court, the Crown Court, the Courts-Martial Appeal Court, the Restrictive Practices Court, the Employment Appeal Tribunal, or any other court exercising, in relation to its proceedings, powers equivalent to those of the High Court, and including the House of Lords in the exercise of its jurisdiction in relation to appeals from courts in England and Wales.[1]
This type of legal aid does not apply to breaches of civil court orders or applications for committal for which civil legal aid may be granted, subject to means and merits.

---

[1] Legal Aid Act 1988, s. 29.

CRITERIA FOR GRANT OF REPRESENTATION IN CONTEMPT PROCEEDINGS

37–02 The grant of representation is made by the court not by the Board, and a grant will be made if it appears to the court to be desirable to do so in the interests of justice.[2] The court may assign the representative from any legal representative[3] within the precinct of the court in accordance with section 32(5) of the 1988 Act but this does not preclude any legal representative from seeking a grant of representation.

There is no provision for a test for financial eligibility for representation in contempt proceedings. It follows that there are no contribution Regulations and no enforcement Regulations.

In cases where the Board is the authority for payment there is a single form CLA35 to confirm the grant of the order by the court and apply for payment. Such representation is rarely granted and the courts are not familiar with the statutory requirements. A legal representative who is nominated may find it helpful to refer the court to Note for Guidance 18 in the Legal Aid Handbook 1995 and to check that the grant is appropriate.

COSTS AND PAYMENT

37–03 A claim for remuneration by a legal representative must be submitted to the appropriate authority in such form and manner as it may direct and any such claim must be submitted within three months of the completion of the work in respect of which the claim is made.[4]

The legal representative is under an obligation to supply such further information and documents as the appropriate authority may and the time limit may be extended for good reason.[5]

37–04 The appropriate authority for determination of costs claims is the registrar of criminal appeals for the Court of Appeal, Criminal Division, an officer appointed by the Lord Chancellor for criminal proceedings in the Crown Court and the Board for any other case.[6] The Board's London area office deals with all claims where the Board is the appropriate authority.

37–05 A set standard fee (currently £71.75 plus VAT) is payable for all work done on each day (or part of a day) of appearance, although where the

---

[2] *ibid.* s. 29(2).
[3] Legal representative is defined as an authorised advocate or authorised litigator, as defined by section 119(1) of the Courts and Legal Services Act 1990 — section 43 of the Legal Aid Act 1988.
[4] Legal Aid in Contempt Proceedings (Remuneration) Regulations 1995, reg. 5(1).
[5] *ibid.* reg. 5(2), (3),
[6] *ibid.* reg. 4(1).

appropriate authority considers there are exceptional circumstances, it may allow an assessed reasonable fee having regard to the amount of the standard fee.[7]

Where the assisted person is represented by two legal representatives, the standard fee for each day of appearance is required to be divided (currently as to £45.75 for the advocate and £26.00 for the other legal representative—solicitor).[8] **37–06**

The solicitor or barrister should submit the grant/claim form direct to the Board's London area office — only that office processes claims for payment. The form includes full instructions as to its completion and will be rejected for resubmission if it is incorrectly completed.

If the representative seeks an assessed fee the form allows him/her to:

(a) indicate that he/she wishes to apply for a non-standard fee;

(b) give details of the exceptional circumstances of the case to justify the payment of a non-standard fee (*e.g.* work required to be undertaken by the court after the court hearing and before a further court hearing);

(c) give full details of the work done and time spent.

The standard fee will be authorised where it is not considered that there are exceptional circumstances.

The fee allowed to a legal representative (other than counsel) on a non-standard basis cannot exceed the assessed rates allowable for criminal work in the relevant court by the relevant level of fee earner, franchisee or non-franchisee. For this purpose the Crown Court rate applies to all courts other than Magistrates' Courts.[9] Where the representative is not assigned by the court (as a representative within the precincts of the court in accordance with section 32(5) of the 1988 Act) the fee allowed cannot exceed the criminal rate appropriate to the lowest grade of fee-earner which the appropriate assessing authority considers would have been competent to do the work.[10]

The maximum assessed fee payable to counsel cannot exceed the amounts set out in the Table in Part II of Schedule 2 to the Legal Aid in Criminal Care and Proceedings (Costs) Regulations 1989 for a single junior counsel instructed in an appeal to the Crown Court against conviction.[11]

The same rights of review/appeal are available as in relation to other area office costs assessments (see Note for Guidance 17 in The Legal Aid Handbook 1995) and there is a right of appeal against a refusal to extend the time for claiming and against the payment of a standard fee where a non standard fee is claimed. **37–07**

---

[7] *ibid.* reg. 7(3).
[8] *ibid.* reg. 6(2).
[9] *ibid.* reg. 7(4) and (5).
[10] *ibid.* reg. 7(6).
[11] *ibid.* reg. 7(7).

Chapter 38

LEGAL AID ABROAD AND THE FOREIGN ELEMENT

Introduction

38–01 Some of the material in this chapter will be found elsewhere in this book but it is gathered in this separate chapter for ease of reference. This chapter deals with the availability of legal advice and assistance and legal aid in England and Wales and abroad in matters involving a foreign or international element. It also deals with the procedures for applying.

Legal aid in Scotland and Northern Ireland are dealt with by the Scottish Legal Aid Board, based in Edinburgh, and the Incorporated Law Society of Northern Ireland, based in Belfast, respectively.

Legal Advice and Assistance under the Green Form

38–02 Green Form advice is not available in relation to matters of foreign law. This is due to the definition of "advice" contained in section 2(2) of the 1988 Act. This definition refers specifically to "the application of English law". The definition of "assistance" contained in section 2(3) of the 1988 Act uses the same term. European law (but not the European Convention on Human Rights) is part of English law and therefore Green Form advice is available. However, due to the subject areas where it is likely to have an impact (*e.g.* company, competition) the client may not be financially eligible. Furthermore, costs incurred researching the law would be unlikely to be allowed.

38–03 Section 2(8) of the 1988 Act permits the Lord Chancellor to direct by order that advice and assistance relating to the application of other laws than English law as specified in the order shall be advice or assistance for any of the purposes of the 1988 Act where it appears to him to be necessary to do so for the purpose of fulfilling international (*i.e.* treaty) obligations. No such orders have been made. However, section 2(9) extends the reference to advice or assistance relating to the application of laws other than English law to advice or assistance for the purposes of making and

684

transmitting applications for legal aid under such laws — that is to say it covers the Strasbourg Agreement (see Para. 38–04 below).

European or "Strasbourg" Agreement

The Board accepts that advice or assistance is available (subject to financial **38–04** eligibility) for the making and transmission of applications under the European Agreement on the Transmission of Applications for Legal Aid (the "Strasbourg Agreement"). The Green Form can be used to take instructions and prepare the legal aid application as well as to deal with queries arising on the application and the costs of any necessary translations. Applications for extensions and payment under the Green Form should be sent to the local area office of the Board in the usual way making it clear that the subject-matter is the transmission of a legal aid application. The Green Form will not cover foreign law (*e.g.* research) nor any work after the application has been decided by the foreign authority and that decision notified to the client. The cover is only for making and transmitting the application. This is not considered by the Board to be a separate matter from any initial work undertaken to consider the case and decide upon the appropriate jurisdiction. That is to say one Green Form should be used and extended if necessary.

The Strasbourg Agreement is a Council of Europe Agreement which has **38–05** been ratified by the United Kingdom and which came into operation for the United Kingdom on February 18, 1978. Its purpose is to facilitate the steps which need to be taken by any person of limited means to obtain legal aid in civil, commercial or administrative matters in a contracting state of the Council of Europe other than that of his residence. It does not cover criminal proceedings.

A person wishing to take proceedings in another ratifying state and who wishes to have legal aid can submit his application to the transmitting authority in his country of residence without being obliged to apply direct to the foreign authority. The transmitting authority will transmit his application for legal aid to the receiving authority for the foreign country. Under the Agreement, the Board (Legal Aid Head Office) is the transmitting *and* receiving authority for England and Wales.

This means that an application for legal aid in any of the ratifying states **38–06** may be sent to the Legal Aid Head Office using a standard combined application and means form (available from Legal Aid Head Office — Legal Department, 85 Gray's Inn Road, London WC1X 8AA) and the Board will transmit the application to the appropriate authority in the foreign country.

Similarly, as the receiving authority, the Legal Aid Head Office accepts applications transmitted to England and Wales under the Agreement and passes them to the appropriate legal aid area office (at present London legal aid area). In short, the Board will act as a postbox.

Because of the availability of Green Form advice abroad (*i.e.* the Green Form can be sent by post with prior authority from an area office) and because there are no nationality or residence rules governing availability of civil legal aid in England and Wales, applications for legal aid from abroad will generally be prepared by a solicitor in England and Wales and submitted direct to the London area office. That is to say they will not be dealt with as transmissions at all but simply as applications from those resident abroad.

How to Transmit an Application

38–07 Contact Legal Aid Head Office (Legal Department) to obtain the standard application form (which is briefer than the Board's usual forms) and check for any particular requirements of the relevant receiving authority. Most countries accept applications in English but it is preferable to use the relevant foreign language. France requires the application and supporting documents to be translated into French (including the statement of means). Austria requires applications to be accompanied by translations in German. Spain does accept applications in English but, for Spain only, the Board's appropriate means forms must also be completed (as a means assessment will be carried out by the Legal Aid Assessment Office).

Advice and assistance under the Green Form can be used to cover the cost of any necessary translations, although in some cases the client may have sufficient command of the relevant language to complete the forms in, and translate any supporting documents into, the relevant language. If that is so, English versions need not be provided.

38–08 Applications for transmission must be sent to Legal Aid Head Office, (and *not* to any of the Board's area offices). The Legal Aid Assessment Office carries out a means assessment for Spain but not for any other country. The receiving authority abroad (as well as the applicant/applying solicitor) is notified of the outcome of that means assessment, although it then will apply its own eligibility rules.

Countries which have ratified the Agreement are:

(a) Austria;	(h) Luxembourg;
(b) Belgium;	(i) Norway;
(c) Denmark;	(j) Portugal;
(d) Eire;	(k) Spain;
(e) France;	(l) Sweden;
(f) Greece;	(m) Turkey;
(g) Italy;	(n) Finland.[1]

---

[1] Up to date details of ratifications may be obtained from: The Council for Europe, Palace of Europe, BP 431 R6, 67006 Strasbourg — CEDEX, France, Telephone 010 33 88 41 2000.

PRACTICAL DIFFICULTIES

Applications which are transmitted abroad take a period of months rather **38–09** than weeks to process and, although the Board can, for Spain, ask the Legal Aid Assessment Office to expedite the means assessment and, for any country, inform the foreign legal aid authority of the urgency of a particular case, it is unlikely that legal aid would be obtained in time for any forthcoming hearing. There are no specific provisions for emergency cases.

It has to be borne in mind that the Transmission Agreement is only a **38–10** method of ensuring access to the legal aid systems of the countries which have ratified the Agreement. They will apply their own rules regarding eligibility and scope. It should also be remembered that the legal aid system in England and Wales is by comparison with many others both sophisticated and extensive.

Even if legal aid is obtained it may be strictly limited in scope and the **38–11** expectation will be that the client will communicate direct with the lawyer abroad who will generally be *assigned* (rather than selected by the client). The foreign system will not generally know the concept of agency and it will not be possible for the solicitor who submitted the legal aid application to remain involved. Apart from the fact that any cover granted may be limited in scope it will generally only allow for very limited translation/ interpreting. This can mean that clients who eventually obtain legal aid cover for proceedings abroad find that, unless the assigned lawyer speaks English or they themselves know the language involved, have access to someone who does or are able to meet the necessary translating/interpreting costs, they will not be able to communicate with the foreign lawyer to progress the case. Green Form legal advice and assistance is *not* available once the application has been dealt with by the foreign authority.

The Board accepts that the transmission of the application *includes* dealing with queries by the foreign authority on the application and any necessary translation to deal with those queries up to the decision of the foreign authority. This will mean that any necessary translation or interpreting work *after* the grant of legal aid by the foreign authority which is not covered by the foreign legal aid will have to be met on a private-client basis.

The transmission agreement does not cover criminal proceedings so a **38–12** direct approach would have to be made to the legal aid authority of the country involved. The position is the same regarding civil proceedings in countries which have not ratified the Strasbourg Agreement. Legal Aid Head Office has some limited information about foreign legal aid schemes but it is probably advisable to approach the national Bar Association or Law Society or the United Kingdom representative (*e.g.* embassy, High Commission) of the country concerned.[2]

---

[2] See also para. 24 of the Hague Convention.

CIVIL LEGAL AID IN ENGLAND AND WALES

38–13 Representation in civil or criminal proceedings abroad is not available, as Part I of Schedule 2 to the 1988 Act (in relation to Part IV — civil legal aid) and section 19 of the 1988 Act (in relation to criminal legal aid) list the courts and Tribunals for which legal aid is available and none are outside the jurisdiction (England and Wales).

The definitions contained in section 2 of the 1988 Act do not, however, exclude any foreign law element which is directly relevant to the proceedings covered by the certificate or order. It is therefore possible to obtain counsel's opinion (or that of an appropriate foreign lawyer) on particular points of foreign law in a case involving, *e.g.* conflict of laws. This is not, however, permissible under Green Form legal advice and assistance and it may therefore be necessary to apply for a limited legal aid certificate just to do this (*e.g.* to obtain advice as to the validity of a foreign marriage/divorce and hence its recognition).

38–14 Under regulation 51(b) (vi) of the Civil Legal Aid (General) Regulations 1989 a certificate may be extended to cover proceedings in the Court of Justice of the European Communities on a reference for a preliminary ruling and under regulation 51(b) (vii) for representation by an EEC [*sic*] lawyer. In these cases, any application for an amendment to the existing legal aid certificate must be made to the appropriate area office. It should be noted that this cover would also be available on a fresh application for a certificate, although in practical terms that would be unlikely to arise (as there would need to be existing proceedings to trigger the reference for a ruling).

38–15 It should be noted that E.C. law forms part of English law and is covered by a legal aid order or certificate provided that the steps involved fall within the scope of the order or certificate.[3] Note also that the Board's Costs Appeals Committee has made a relevant decision on a point of principle of general importance.[4]

Section 2(6) of the 1988 Act provides that advice, assistance and representation except under Part II (contracts) "shall only be by legal representative". Legal representative means an authorised advocate or litigator as defined by section 119(1) of the Courts and Legal Services Act 1990. Therefore it covers any person exercising a right of audience or right to conduct litigation (on behalf of a party to proceedings). This catches both

---

[3] *R.v. Marlborough Street Metropolitan Stipendiary Magistrate, ex p. Bouchereau* [1977] 3 All E.R. 365.
[4] See decision CLA16 reproduced at Note for Guidance 13–31 *Legal Aid Handbook 1995* which reads: "Where an application to the European Commission is an essential preliminary step in court proceedings in England and Wales, such an application would be within the scope of a certificate granted to cover such court proceedings."

solicitors and barristers as well as any other authorised person (*e.g.* patent agents).

COURT OF JUSTICE OF THE EUROPEAN COMMUNITIES— LUXEMBOURG

Legal aid is available on a reference by a domestic court to the Court of **38–16** Justice for a preliminary ruling.[5] Here, the European Communities Court is advising the domestic court on a preliminary point of Community law.

The European Communities Court can, however, provide legal aid to any party who is wholly or in part unable to meet the costs of proceedings before it. The application must be made by the party (or on his behalf) and be accompanied by evidence of the applicant's means. If the applicant does not indicate his choice of lawyer or the court finds the choice unacceptable, it will appoint a lawyer to act.

Legal aid may be granted by the Court not only to those involved in proceedings started in the Court but also referred on a preliminary ruling. It is unlikely that the Board would refuse civil legal aid (including amendment to an existing certificate) on the basis that the applicant should seek legal aid from the European Court.[6]

EUROPEAN COURT OF HUMAN RIGHTS AND EUROPEAN COMMISSION OF HUMAN RIGHTS

Proceedings in the Council of Europe's European Commission of Human **38–17** Rights and European Court of Human Rights in Strasbourg are outside the scope of civil and criminal legal aid. Legal advice and assistance under the Green Form is not available as the European Convention on Human Rights does not form part of English law.

However, legal aid may be granted by the Council of Europe for proceedings before the Commission and the European Court of Human Rights in Strasbourg. Should a means assessment be required by the Council from the Legal Aid Assessment Office the usual, applicable legal aid form of the applicant's financial circumstances should be sent to Legal Aid Head Office which will ask the Assessment Office to carry out an assessment and forward it direct to the solicitor for the applicant.

Legal aid will, in any event, only be granted once an application to the

---

[5] See Civil Legal Aid (General) Regulations 1989, reg. 51(b) (vi).
[6] Further details about legal aid available from the European Communities Court may be obtained from: The Court of Justice of the European Communities, BP L-2925, Luxembourg.

Commission has been made although the grant may be on a legal aid application or of the Commission's own volition.[7]

THE HAGUE CONVENTION

38–18 A Convention on International Access to Justice was concluded by members of The Hague Conference on Private International Law on October 25, 1980. The Convention provides that nationals and residents of any contracting state are to be entitled to legal advice and to legal aid in court proceedings in civil and commercial matters in each contracting state on the same basis as if they were nationals and residents in that state. The Convention also covers former nationals and residents if the cause of action arises out of their former residence in the state.

The Convention operates like the Strasbourg Agreement in that each state designates a receiving and transmitting authority, although applications must be made in a particular form.

The United Kingdom has not yet signed this Convention but direct applications for legal aid in countries which have not ratified the Strasbourg Agreement can be made direct to the foreign authority involved. Enquiries could be made to the United Kingdom representative, the national Bar Association or Law Society of the country concerned to obtain details of any local legal aid schemes.

CHILD ABDUCTION AND CUSTODY ACT 1985

38–19 Applications under the Child Abduction and Custody Act 1985 for enforcement abroad are dealt with by the relevant state authority which will, at no charge, give information and forward applications for enforcement to the appropriate foreign state authority which will take steps to enforce the domestic order.[8]

The Child Abduction Unit (part of the official solicitor's office) deals also with children abducted to England and Wales and can supply up-to-date details of contracting countries as well as information regarding procedure. They have a useful free leaflet entitled "Child Abduction".

38–20 The Child Abduction and Custody Act 1985 came into force on August 1, 1986 and enabled the United Kingdom to ratify the Hague Convention

---

[7] Further details may be obtained from: The Council of Europe, Palace of Europe, PO Box 431 R6, F.67006 Strasbourg — CEDEX, France. Telephone 010 33 88 41 2000.

[8] The relevant state authority for England and Wales is the official solicitor's office at: Child Abduction Unit, 81 Chancery Lane, London WC2A 1DD; telephone 0171 911 7127; fax 0171 911 7248.

of October 25, 1980 on the Civil Aspects of International Child Abduction and the European Convention of May 20, 1980 on Recognition and Enforcement of Decision concerning Custody of Children and on the Restoration of Custody of Children.

The purpose of the Conventions is to enable a person (whether an individual or an institution such as a local authority) who has rights of custody (residence) over a child who has been taken overseas in breach of those rights, to secure the return of the child (to the United Kingdom). The Conventions also enable a person in the United Kingdom to enforce rights of access (contact) to a child overseas.

Under the Hague Convention application can be made: **38–11**

(a) for the return of a child removed or retained in breach of rights of custody;

(b) for organising or securing rights of access to a child removed in breach of those rights;

by

(a) any person who claims that a child has been removed or retained in breach of rights of custody;

(b) any person who claims that child has been removed in breach of rights of access.

Under the European Convention application can be made:

(a) for the recognition and enforcement of a custody order (including enforcement by means of returning the child to the person in whose favour the custody order was made);

(b) for recognition and enforcement of an access order or for organising rights of access if no decision as to access has been made;

by

(a) any person who has a court order giving them rights of custody;

(b) any person who has a court order giving them rights of access.

Certain conditions must be fulfilled and the date of coming into force of the Conventions between the United Kingdom and the relevant country is crucial. The Child Abduction Unit can supply details of the conditions and dates.

The procedure for enforcement is that the Child Abduction Unit contacts   **38–21**
the central authority of the country to which the child has been taken and that authority should take immediate steps to:

(a) discover the whereabouts of the child;

(b) prevent further harm to the child;

(c) initiate or facilitate the institution of judicial or administrative proceedings in that country with a view to obtaining the return of the child to the United Kingdom, or the effective organising or securing of rights of access to the child;

(d) provide or facilitate the provision of legal aid and advice.

Once the application, which is based on a form of questionnaire issued for completion by the Child Abduction Unit, has been received by the foreign authority that authority has responsibility for it. There is no bar on applying direct to the foreign authority or applying direct to the foreign court but this is not advisable as the Child Abduction Unit, as a source of information and assistance, would be bypassed. Together with the questionnaire the applicant should submit a letter of authority (supplied by the Unit), a certified copy of any court order and evidence of service (if the order was made in the absence of the alleged abductor), as well as an affidavit as to the applicant's rights.

38–22   Payment for legal work in England and Wales can be under:

(a) the Green Form subject to all the usual rules;

(b) a civil legal aid certificate — if this is to obtain, *e.g.* a residence order or to defend proceedings then the usual means and merits tests apply but if this is under the Hague or European Conventions to the Child Abduction Unit for enforcement, then the usual means and merits tests are not applicable.

Legal aid applications for enforcement under the Conventions in England and Wales are dealt with by the Board's London legal aid area. Regulation 14(1) of the Civil Legal Aid (General) Regulations 989 provides that a person whose application has been submitted to the Lord Chancellor's Department (now the Child Abduction Unit which is part of the official solicitor's office) pursuant to section 3(2) or section 14(2) of the Child Abduction and Custody Act 1985 and on whose behalf a solicitor in England and Wales has been instructed in connection with the application:

(a) *shall* be eligible to receive legal aid whether or not he would be eligible under the usual Regulations as to eligibility;

(b) *shall not* be refused legal aid by virtue of the merits test contained in section 15(2) and (3) of the 1988 Act; and

(c) *shall not* be required to pay a contribution.

Therefore, there is no means or merits test applied or contribution payable for civil legal aid for *taking* proceedings under the Child Abduction and Custody Act 1985.

Note, however, that it is the view of the Board that the merits test may be applied in relation to any appeal, including an appeal to the House of Lords. Note also that non-means; non-merits tested legal aid does not extend to applying for a contact order where a means and merits tested legal aid application must be made.[9] The Child Abduction Unit will, however, assist the applicant in locating and instructing a suitable solicitor.

38–23   Initially, an approach can be made to the Lord Chancellor's Department which will arrange for the instruction of a solicitor who then applies for legal aid to the London area office. A defendant can apply to the usual area

---

[9] *Re T (Minors) (Convention on the Aspects of International Child Abduction: Access)* [1993] 1 W.L.R. 1461; [1993] All E.R. 127.

office for legal aid to defend proceedings in the normal way — the application does not need to be submitted to the London area office of the Board.

Payment of legal and other costs in the foreign country will depend on whether the application is under the Hague or European Conventions.

Under the Hague Convention:

(a) an applicant is not required to make any payment toward the costs and expenses of proceedings although some countries do require a contribution towards legal costs after the conclusion of the proceedings;

(b) an applicant is required to meet the cost of repatriating the child to the United Kingdom;

(c) it is possible for an application to be made to the overseas court for an order that the abducting parent meet any costs incurred.

Under the European Convention an applicant is not required to meet any costs incurred on his behalf, except those of repatriating the child.

REGISTRATION OF FOREIGN MAINTENANCE ORDERS AND JUDGMENTS

Regulation 15 of the Civil Legal Aid (General) Regulations 1989 applies the **38–24** same waiver of the means and merits tests and payment of any contribution[10] to:

(a) appeals to a magistrates' court against the registration of or the refusal to register a maintenance order made in a Hague Convention country pursuant to the Maintenance Orders (Reciprocal Enforcement) Act 1972; and

(b) to applications for the registration of a judgment under section 4 of the Civil Jurisdiction and Judgments Act 1982.

It should, however, be noted that in order to benefit from this provision the applicant must have had "complete or partial legal aid or exemption from costs or expenses in the country in which the maintenance order was made or the judgment was given".[11]

Both Part IV civil legal aid and ABWOR are available in respect of proceedings under Part I of the Maintenance Orders (Reciprocal Enforcement) Act 1972.[12] There are, however, no provisions corresponding to regulation 15 in the Legal Advice and Assistance Regulations 1989 governing ABWOR. Clearly it is advisable to apply for Part IV civil legal

---

[10] As is applied by reg. 14 to Child Abduction and Custody Act applications. See para. 38–22 above.

[11] Civil Legal Aid (General) Regulations 1989, reg. 15(3).

[12] Legal Aid Act 1988, para. 2(d), Pt I, Sched. 2 and Legal Advice and Assistance (Scope) Regulations 1989, para. 2(f), Sched.

aid as ABWOR would be subject to the usual means and merits test and could require the payment of a contribution. There is no power to refuse a Part IV civil legal aid application on the basis that ABWOR should be applied for as that ground for refusal is contained in section 15(3) of the 1988 Act which is excluded from regulation 15.

Chapter 39

FRANCHISING

INTRODUCTION

Legal Aid Franchising is based on the contracting provisions in Part II of the **39–01** Legal Aid Act 1988. In short, firms of solicitors which meet the Board's "specification" are, through the franchise contract, on an office by office basis, granted improved payments on account and have devolved to them some of the powers of area directors under the Regulations. These are known as "devolved powers". Franchised firms are also able to accept applications for advice and assistance made by telephone or by post.

Since April 24, 1995 franchised firms have been entitled to higher hourly rates for green form, ABWOR and Duty Solicitor work and higher standard fees for magistrates' court criminal work.[1]

Franchised firms are allowed to display the Board's franchise logo at each of their franchised offices and on their letter and publicity material. They must display at each franchised office the Board's certificate showing in which categories of work they are franchised.

A QUALITY SERVICE
Approved by The Legal Aid Board

---

[1] See Sched. 6 to the Legal Advice and Assistance Regulations 1989, para. 8 (1a) part III, Sched. 1 to the Legal Aid in Criminal and Care Proceedings (Costs) Regulations 1989, para. 3 to the Sched. to the Legal Advice and Assistance at Police Stations (Remuneration) Regulations 1989 and reg. 5(2) of the Legal Advice and Assistance (Duty Solicitor) (Remuneration) Regulations 1989.

STATUTORY PROVISIONS

39–02 The relevant regulations to establish franchising are set out below:
Regulation 2 of the Legal Advice and Assistance Regulations 1989 which defines terms:

> " 'contract' means a contract entered into by the Board with other persons or bodies pursuant to its powers under section 4 of the Act"
> " 'franchisee' means a person or body (other than the Board) acting under the terms of a franchising contract"

39–03 Regulation 3A of the Legal Advice and Assistance Regulations 1989 which provides:

> "Where and to the extent that a franchising contract so provides, any functions of an Area Director are conferred on a franchisee, the functions may be exercised by the franchisee on the Area Director's behalf"

It enables green form devolved powers to be granted by contract.

39–04 Regulation 9(3A) of the Legal Advice and Assistance Regulations 1989 provides:

> "Where a franchising contract so provides and subject to compliance with any provisions specified in the contract, an application for advice and assistance may be made by telephone or by post".

This enables the Board to grant by contract the power to accept applications for green form advice and assistance by telephone or post.

39–05 Regulation 30(4) of the Legal Advice and Assistance Regulations 1989 provides:

> "Where advice and assistance is provided under a franchising contract, regulations 29 and 30 shall apply except to the extent that the contract makes different express provision."

This enables payment criteria for green form work to be determined by contract.

39–06 Regulation 30A(1A) of the Legal Advice and Assistance Regulations 1989 provides:

> "Where ABWOR is provided under the franchising contract, the Franchisee may apply to the Area Director for the payment of a sum on account of his charges and fees."

This enables the contract, as it does, to allow payments on account to be made on the grant of ABWOR.

Regulation 30A(1B) of the Legal Advice and Assistance Regulations 1989 **39–07**
provides:

> "Where advice and assistance (other than ABWOR) is provided under
> a franchising contract, the Franchisee may apply to the Area Director
> for the payment of a sum on account of his costs."

This enables the contract to allow payments on account to be made in
green form work, *e.g.* as it does on the grant of green form extensions.

Regulation 2(2) of the Civil Legal Aid (General) Regulations 1989 provides: **39–08**

> "Where the Board has entered into a franchising contract, regulations
> relevant to the remuneration and payment of expenses of legal
> representatives and the manner in which any determination which may
> be required for those purposes may be made, reviewed or appealed
> shall apply except to the extent that the franchising contract makes
> different express provision."

This enables, with section 15(7) of the Act, the contract to determine
remuneration for civil legal aid.

Regulation 3 of the Civil Legal Aid (General) Regulations 1989 defines **39–09**
terms:

> " 'contract' means a contract entered into by the Board with other
> persons or bodies pursuant to its powers under section 4 of the Act"
> " 'franchisee' means a person or body (other than the Board) acting
> under the terms of a franchise contract"

Regulation 4(3) of the Civil Legal Aid (General) Regulations 1989
provides:

> "Where and to the extent that a franchising contract permits the
> Franchisee to exercise any of the functions of an Area Director, the
> functions may be exercised by the Franchisee on the Area Director's
> behalf."

This enables area directors' civil legal aid powers to be devolved by
contract.

Regulation 152(1) of the Civil Legal Aid (General) Regulations 1989 **39–10**
provides:

> "The classes of case in respect of which the Board may enter contracts
> for the provision of representation under Part IV of the Act shall be any
> proceedings for the time being specified in Part I, Schedule 2 to the
> Act except—
> (a) proceedings listed as 5. or 6. of Part I of that Schedule;

(b) proceedings for the time being specified in Part II of that Schedule."

This regulation, which has been drafted so wide as to include almost every (but not all) classes of case is necessary because section 4(5) of the Act provides:

"The power to secure the provision of representation under Part IV by means of contracts with other persons shall only be exercisable in the classes of case prescribed in regulations."

39–11 Regulation 2 of the Legal Aid in Criminal and Care Proceedings (Costs) Regulations, which defines terms provides:

" 'contract' means a contract entered into by the Board with other persons or bodies pursuant to its powers under section 4 of the Act."
" 'Franchisee' means a person or body (other than the Board) acting under the terms of a franchising contract."

39–12 Regulation 4E(1) of the Legal Aid in Criminal and Care Proceedings (Costs) Regulations 1989 provides:

"Where representation under Part IV of the Act is provided under a franchising contract for criminal proceedings in a magistrates' court, the Franchisee may apply to the Board when the legal aid order is granted for an interim payment in respect of a claim for costs in accordance with the contract."

This enables payments on account in criminal cases to be made by contract.

39–13 Regulation 2 of the Legal Advice and Assistance at Police Stations (Remuneration) Regulations 1989 which defines terms provides:
" 'contract' means a contract entered into by the Board with other persons or bodies pursuant to its powers under section 4 of the 1988 Act"
" 'franchisee' means a person or body (other than the Board) acting under the terms of a franchise contract."

39–14 Regulation 5(7) of the Legal Advice and Assistance at Police Stations (Remuneration) Regulations 1989 provides:

"Paragraph (5) shall not apply where a franchisee certifies that advice and assistance as required in the interest of justice to begin as a matter of urgency."

This regulation enables the contract to allow franchisees to exceed the £90 initial costs limit on duty solicitor police station work (section 10 of the Act and reg. 4(1)(a) Legal Advice and Assistance Regulations 1989) on certifying that advice and assistance had to be given as a matter of urgency.

Paragraph 2(2) of the Schedule to the Legal Advice and Assistance at Police **39–15** Stations (Remuneration) Regulations 1989 which provides:

> "Sub-paragraph (1) shall not apply where the duty solicitor is a franchisee providing advice and assistance under a franchising contract."

This provision enables the contract to allow franchisees to be paid in full for standby work on the police stations duty solicitor scheme *i.e.* without any reduction for advice and assistance actually provided.

Regulation 2 of the Legal Advice and Assistance (Duty Solicitor) **39–16** (Remunerations) Regulations 1989, which defines terms, provides:

> " 'Contract' means a contract entered into by the Board with other persons or bodies pursuant to its powers under section 4 of the 1988 Act."
> " 'Franchisee' means a person or body (other than the Board) acting under the terms of a franchising contract."

Regulation 5(2) of the Legal Advice and Assistance (Duty Solicitor) **39–17** (Remunerations) Regulations 1989 provides:

> "Subject to paragraph 3, the determining officer shall allow remuneration:
> (a) in respect of (1)(a) above at such rate as is the average of the two separate prescribed rates provided for advocacy and preparation paragraph 1(1)(a) (or paragraph 1A in the case of work done by a franchisee) of Part 1 of Schedule 1 to the 1989 Regulations; and
> (b) in respect of (1)(b) above at the same rate as the prescribed rate providers for travelling and waiting in paragraph 1(1)(a) (or paragraph 1A in the case of work by a franchisee) of Part 1 of Schedule 1 to the 1989 Regulations."

The 1989 Regulations means the Legal Aid in Criminal and Care (Costs) Regulations 1989 so these regulations permit the highest remuneration for franchisees provided by the 1989 regulation and apply to duty solicitor work.

APPLYING FOR A FRANCHISE

Categories of Work

At present, applications for franchises may be made in one or more of the **39–18** following categories of work:

Matrimonial/Family
Crime
Housing
Debt
Employment
Personal Injury
Welfare Benefits
Consumer/General Contract
Immigration/Nationality

To qualify an applicant should be capable of providing advice, assistance and representation at the magistrates' court, county court or tribunal, as appropriate to the category of work applied for. If organisations are unable or unwilling to provide representation, perhaps because full legal aid is not available for the case, clients should be told at the outset and, if possible, and at an appropriate stage, referred to an appropriate source of representation.

39–19   Organisations which apply for a crime franchise and which are involved in either of the duty solicitor schemes must meet the criteria for both criminal and duty solicitor work.

The Application Form and Self-Assessment Audit Check-List

39–20   Applicants for a franchise will be expected to complete an application form. The Board will supply applicants with a self-assessment audit check-list for use with the specification. The purpose of this is to assist applicants to assess their readiness for applying. The completed check-list will need to be submitted with each application, together with the documented procedures and arrangements for all the relevant mandatory requirements. These documents would normally form part of an office manual and it may be simpler for organisations to submit the whole manual. Copies of the documented procedures or the office manual are returned to the organisation at the preliminary audit.

Applications should be sent to the legal aid Area Office covering the geographic location of the office applying. Applications must not be made to more than one Area Office even where the office applying deals with other Area Offices.

Single Office and Multi-Office Organisations

39–21   Where the applicant is a single office, the office must comply with the specification in full and be audited against the requirements. If organisations have offices in more than one legal aid area, one Area Office will deal with all applications unless special arrangements are made to the contrary.

Therefore, the multi-office application should be submitted to one Area Office only. That Area Office then decides in consultation with other relevant Area Offices, which Area Office should deal with all the applications.

Where an organisation wishes to apply for a franchise in more than one office, a separate application form must be completed for each office, together with a separate form which will allow the organisation to set out clearly how the different offices for which applications are made relate to each other. All the relevant application forms should be submitted together. Different offices in the same organisation may apply at different times. It is not a requirement that all offices should apply together though many organisations will wish to take that course.

Legal Aid Account Numbers

Each office should have a single identifying legal aid account number. This **39–22** is to enable the Board to link statistical information to individual franchises and properly monitor the effect of franchising on access to legal services.

General

There is no closing date for applications and there is no limit to the number **39–23** of franchises that will be granted either by category of work or geographical area. Applications are processed in chronological order of receipt in the Area Office.

Upon receipt of a completed application form and the accompanying documents the Area Manager will appoint a Liaison Manager for the organisation. The appointed Liaison Manager reviews all the documentation for completeness. If the documentation is incomplete the Liaison Manager will not accept the application and will return the form to the applicant with guidance, requesting that the form be resubmitted. The Liaison Manager's guidance will describe where omissions were observed. To be accepted the application must be properly completed and accompanied by all the necessary supporting documentation.

Application, Audit and Monitoring Process

Applications proceed through the stages set out below. **39–24**
  (a) Acceptance of application for preliminary audit.
  (b) Preliminary audit based on self-assessment audit check-list.
  (c) Pre-contract monitoring.
  (d) Pre-contract audit.
  (e) Decision (to grant or refuse).
  (f) Appeal against decision (where relevant).

FRANCHISING DOCUMENTS

39–25 The franchise documents comprise:
1. A one-page contract for signature on behalf of the Board and the franchisee;
2. The contract Standard Terms;
3. The Franchising Specification (current edition being the second edition, March 1995);
4. Guidance on the Exercise of Devolved Powers (the Franchise Manual) current edition being the Interim Edition July 1994.

The contract is made pursuant to a direction of the Lord Chancellor under section 4(4) Legal Aid Act 1988. Although it is a contract under Part II of the Act, it provides for advice, assistance and representation to be provided under the "usual" other parts of the Act, *i.e.* advice and assistance continues to be provided under Part III, civil legal aid continues to be provided under Part IV and criminal legal aid continues to be provided under Part V. The consequence of this is that all the legal aid regulations apply to work done under the contract though, as is outlined above, some regulations provide for the contract to "rule".

No special regulations are required to provide for improved payments on account in civil legal aid because section 15(7) of the Act provides that where representation is provided under Part IV of the Act, pursuant to a contract, remuneration is governed by the contract.

The (one-page) Contract

39–26 This is merely the vehicle by which the Standard Terms are given effect. It is signed on behalf of the franchisee and the Board. The Standard Terms provide that, after signature, the contract comes into force on such date as the Board notifies to the franchisee.

Standard Terms

39–27 The Standard Terms, which the Board negotiated with The Law Society are, in essence, the framework for giving force to the obligations on franchisees which ar largely set out in the Franchising Specification. They specify the work covered by the contract, how each contract starts and when it will end.

Each franchise contract starts on 00.01 hours on the date notified to the franchisee by the Board as the date the franchisee shall begin to provide the franchise services and all franchise contracts will end at 24.00 hours on July 31, 1999. The Standard Terms, however, provide for a three-year extension on whatever standard terms are then in force, from 00.01 hours on August 1, 1999.

The Standard Terms also set out the franchisee's principal obligations and duties and the rights and obligations of the Board. The main obligation on the franchisee is to comply with the Specification and to demonstrate such compliance. The Standard Terms also make specific provision for how the franchisee must use the franchise certificate and the franchise logo and other promotional items.

The franchise certificate is the document showing the name of the franchise firm, the address of the relevant franchised office and the devolved powers which the franchisee has been granted.

Although franchise contracts are made with franchised firms, it is individual offices of each such firm which are actually "franchised". Even then, once an office is "franchised" only the work which is done in "franchised" categories of work is covered by the franchise contract.

The Standard Terms require the franchised firm to notify constitutional changes and impose obligations of confidentiality on both the franchise firm and the Board. This is clearly important—particularly for franchised firms—because the Board audits compliance with its specification and the Board's auditors may well discover information which a franchisee would wish to be kept confidential.

The Standard Terms set out the circumstances in which amendments may be made to the Specification and the Manual. There are significant restrictions on the Board's freedom to make changes—particularly to the Specification.

The Standard Terms also set out sanctions which the Board may apply when a firm fails to comply with the Specification or otherwise does not comply with the contract. Sanctions include suspension or termination of approval of devolved powers, of a category of franchise work or of a franchised office or termination of the contract.

The Franchising Specification provides for appeal mechanisms where the Board applies contract sanctions and the Standard Terms set out the circumstances in which matters which are still in dispute may be referred to arbitration.

THE SPECIFICATION

The introduction to the Franchising Specification sets out the essential **39–28** elements of the Franchising Scheme as:
(1) An improvement in the service offered by suppliers of legal services to their clients and a reduction of their administrative costs by:
    (i) delegating some powers which traditionally have been exercised by the Board;

      (ii) improving the working relationship between suppliers and the Board by the appointment of a nominated Liaison Manager for each applicant; and

      (iii) providing regular information about any perceived problems in the relationship between the Board and the supplier.

(2) The specification of quality assurance standards that the Board would expect suppliers to achieve in order to assure a good service to clients covering:

      (i) management, including case management, recruitment, training and supervision of staff, client care, accounting and forward planning;

      (ii) the handling of cases as assessed after the event by the auditing of case files on a confidential basis;

      (iii) work submitted to area offices;

      (iv) arrangements for audits by the Board to ensure that the standards are being achieved and maintained;

      (v) the control of case costs;

      (vi) an effective appeal procedure where the decision is to refuse, suspend, or terminate a franchise and additionally, a binding arbitration procedure where the decision is to suspend or terminate a franchise;

      (vii) the continuous monitoring of the scheme involving the profession and others to ensure that it is achieving its objective;

      (viii) obtaining the views of clients about franchised organisations.

The Specification includes information about how to apply for a franchise and the Board's objectives in establishing the Franchising Scheme. It also outlines appeal mechanisms which apply where an application has been refused, or where sanctions have been applied to a franchised firm. However, the main body of the Specification is concerned with the obligations on franchised firms.

39–29   Broadly, these are the obligations to have in place certain management systems, certain systems of supervision of staff and certain systems about the management of the legal aid case files. These requirements include the Law Society's Practice Management Standards, where appropriate, standards published by other bodies *e.g.* the National Association of Citizens Advice Bureaux (NACAB) membership scheme.

It is compliance with these requirements which the Board's auditors will check before a firm will be granted a franchise and, once a franchise has been granted, which will be checked by the Board's auditors periodically.

It is not essential to have computer systems in place in order to comply with the requirements of the Specification and firms without such systems have been granted franchises. However, particularly for firms which are not small, the possession of computer systems makes the task of compliance much simpler.

Essentially, franchising is a scheme to assess and to quality assure solicitors firms doing legal aid work. Any firm can apply to the Board to become a "franchisee". Before obtaining a franchise, the applicant firm must demonstrate that the work they do is properly supervised, that their employees are properly recruited and trained, that their files are properly run, that clients are fully and regularly advised about their cases and any costs clients may incur as a result of pursuing a case are clear to them in advance. They must also prove they have proper financial controls in place and that their businesses are properly managed and planned.

Following application, firms are audited twice and must be assessed as **39–30** sufficiently compliant with the Specification's requirements at each audit before they can be granted a franchise. The audits are designed to make sure that the firm's proper management systems are in place and operating effectively and to assess the work done by members of the firm's staff by auditing legal aid case files. Additionally, the applications and bills which the firm sends to the Board are monitored for about six months to make sure that the standard of such submissions is of a satisfactory quality. Once franchised, all firms are audited at least once a year.

Franchising covers nearly all areas of legal aid work—which fall into **39–31** nine broad categories. Firms' offices are audited in these nine categories, independently. Some firms may have a franchise in only one category, others may have been approved in any or all of the other categories covered, depending on their areas of expertise. The franchise certificate, which must be displayed at each franchise office, will state in which areas of work that office has been approved by the Board. The nine categories of work are:

Personal injury
Debt
Immigration
Matrimonial and Family
Housing
Welfare Benefits
Crime
Employment
Consumer/Contract

Within these categories, franchised firms may be granted the devolved powers referred to above and improved payment terms, on an office-by-office basis. Entitlement depends on (a) the firm having a franchise contract in force, (b) the franchised firms's office being approved by the Board as a "franchised office", and (c) the work being done in one of the above categories of work which the Board has approved as a "franchised category of work" at the franchised office. In order to exercise the devolved powers (as distinct from merely being able to claim the improved payment

705

terms) the Board must have granted devolved powers in the relevant category of work at the relevant office.

39–32   Under the Legal Advice and Assistance Regulations 1989, the devolved powers are the power to grant Green Form extensions and to exercise all the other powers of Area Directors under these regulations, except the power to grant authority not to enforce the charge arising under section 11 of the Legal Aid Act 1988 but including the power to grant or refuse ABWOR. They also include the power to receive applications for advice and assistance by telephone or by post.

Under the Civil Legal Aid (General) Regulations 1989, the power is the power to grant emergency legal aid.

When a franchised firm grants a Green Form extension or submits an extension application to the Board, it may apply to the Board for payment on account of the equivalent of two or three hours work.

When a franchised firm approves an ABWOR or submits an ABWOR application to the Board, it may apply to the Board for a payment on account of £150.

If a franchised firm grants emergency legal aid or submits an application to the Board then, it may apply to the Legal Aid Board for a payment on account of £250.

In civil legal aid cases, franchisees may claim 75 percent of profit costs incurred to date and still outstanding nine months after the issue of a civil legal aid certificate and every nine months thereafter.

Franchised firms may apply for payment of a category I lower standard fee on the grant of a criminal legal aid order to them. Crime franchisees who make claims for police station duty solicitor work will be paid in full for standby and for work done during the standby period, *i.e.* the "clawback" provision in paragraph 2 in the Schedule to the Legal Advice and Assistance at Police Stations (Remuneration) Regulations 1989 (as amended) will not apply.

Crime franchisees which make claims for police station advice and assistance do not have to justify to the Board exceeding the £90 limit where the interests of justice require advice and assistance to be given as a matter of urgency (regulation 5(6) Legal Advice and Assistance at Police Stations (Remuneration) Regulations 1989).

Devolved Powers and Financial Incentives

Green Form

39–33   The green form financial limit continues to apply but franchisees have power to exceed it without authority within the category or categories of work for which they are franchised. Franchisees will not be able to waive the solicitors' charge in green form cases; this decision should continue to be referred to the Area Office. However, all other decisions relating to applications for green form advice and assistance may be devolved.

When exercising a devolved power, franchisees must note on the case **39–34** file:

(a) the date the devolved powers were exercised;

(b) the decision made, including the financial limit imposed under regulation 21(3) of the Legal Advice and Assistance Regulations 1989;

(c) the reasons for exercise of the powers; and

(d) a note, *e.g.* a reference, of who exercised the powers.

After exercising a devolved power to grant a green form extension (or if the **39–35** franchisee decides not to exercise it but, instead, to apply for an extension to the Area Director) the franchisee may apply to the Board, on the appropriate form, for payment of the amount of the green form's initial cots limit *i.e.* the equivalent of either two or three hours' work.

When exercising the devolved powers franchisees must follow the Board's published guidelines and must impose a financial limit upon themselves in accordance with regulation 21(3) of the Legal Advice and Assistance Regulations 1989. When that limit is reached further extensions may be self authorised but no further payment on account will be made.

If the final green form bill is not submitted within 18 months the Board will recoup automatically the payment on account and the franchisee will be notified of that recoupment. If the franchisee will not be able to submit the final bill within 18 months of receiving the payment on account they may notify the Area Office so that the automatic recoupment of the payment of account can be prevented.

Once work under the green form is complete the final claim is submitted **39–36** to the Area Office for assessment in the usual way. If the claim is reduced or disallowed for any reason the franchisee has the usual right of appeal against the assessment to the Area Committee.

Where justifiable, franchisees may claim under the green form for **39–37** telephone advice without a personal attendance by or on behalf of a client to sign a green form and for the cost of outward travel (but not travelling time) to attend on the client away from the office before the signature of a green form. Where justifiable, franchisees may also accept postal applications from clients residing in England and Wales.

Payment may be claimed under the green form for telephone advice **39–38** given before the client has signed the green form, but the Board will meet claims for costs only where the client is financially eligible and has signed a green form. Costs must also have been reasonably incurred, for example taking account of the distances involved and must be justifiable on access grounds. The Specification suggests that claims might be justified where the client is elderly and infirm, disabled, a single parent without child care, in

707

prison, hospitalised or in a very isolated rural area. Finally, franchisees are entitled to higher hourly rates for green form work.

ABWOR

39–39 Franchisees can self-grant ABWOR without reference to the Area Office but, in doing so, must follow the guidelines published by the Board. Within seven days of exercising this devolved power the franchisee must send the Board the appropriate form, giving brief reasons for exercising the devolved power and, if required, a claim for a payment on account of £150.

If this is done, the ABWOR approval will be issued and dated the day of exercise of the devolved power and the payment on account will be made.

If the franchisee submits the appropriate form more than seven days after exercising the devolved power they must also submit a written explanation for the delay. The Area Office then has a discretion to allow the payment on account and the costs incurred in the light of the explanation. If costs are disallowed for late submission a costs appeal can be made to the Area Committee in the normal way.

If, in the view of the Area Office, the devolved power was exercised inappropriately the ABWOR approval will nevertheless be issued, dated the day of exercise of the devolved power, but with an amendment which may limit the ABWOR approval to all work done before the date of the Area Office decision. Notice of withdrawal of ABWOR may also be given. In these circumstances the client will have the usual right of appeal against the Area Office decision.

Any disbursements may be incurred by the franchisee, including the use of counsel, where it can be justified, without reference to the Area Office. At the end of the case, the usual costs claim is submitted to the Area Office for assessment. The Area Office will look particularly carefully at cases where counsel has been used. If the bill is reduced an appeal can be made in the usual way to the Area Committee. Finally, franchisees are entitled to high hourly rates for ABWOR work.

Emergency Legal Aid and Civil Aid Payments on Account

39–40 Franchisees can self-grant emergency legal aid without reference to the Area Office but, in doing so, must follow the guidelines published by the Board.

Within seven days of exercise of the devolved power the franchisee must send to the Area Office applications for emergency legal aid and for full legal aid and, if required, the appropriate form claiming £250 payment on account.

If this is done, an emergency certificate will be issued and dated the day of exercise of the devolved power and the payment on account will be made.

If the franchisee submits the applications for emergency and full legal aid more than seven days after exercising the devolved powers, they must also submit a written explanation for the delay. The Area Office then has a discretion to allow the payment on account and costs incurred in the light of the explanation. If costs are disallowed for late submission an appeal can be made to the Area Committee in the normal way.

Even if, in the view of the Area Office, the devolved powers have been exercised inappropriately an emergency certificate will still be issued and dated the day of exercise of the devolved power. This certificate may be amended from the date of the Area Office decision so as to limit the emergency legal aid to all work done before the date of the Area Office decision. There is no right of appeal against the Area Office decision but, if circumstances change so that legal aid is urgently required, an application for an amendment to the emergency legal aid certificate may be made.

Franchisees may claim 75 per cent of profit costs incurred and still **39–41** outstanding nine months after the issue of a civil legal aid certificate, and every nine months thereafter. The Board does not send reminders of when these payments fall due so franchisees should set up their own systems to ensure they claim at the appropriate time.

After the start date of the franchise contract franchisees can claim on certificates issued up to six months before that date. Thus, the first payments become due three months after the start date of the contract. Franchisees are not able to claim under the permanent payment on account scheme in franchised categories but remain eligible for hardship payments under regulation 101 of the Civil Legal Aid (General) Regulations 1989.

Franchisees may, when claiming a payment on account, apply enhanced rates if they believe such enhanced rates will be allowed on taxation or assessment. However, where an enhanced rate is not allowed on assessment or taxation, or is allowed at a lower rate than that claimed, the Board's Liaison Manager will discuss the matter with the franchisee with the objective of ensuring that enhanced rates for payments on account are applied for only where they can be justified.

Crime

Crime franchisees can apply, on the appropriate form, for payment of the **39–42** category I lower standard fee as soon as a criminal legal aid order is granted to them covering proceedings in a magistrates' court. Payment will normally be made within 28 days. If the final bill is not submitted within

18 months, this payment on account will be automatically recouped and the franchisee will be notified of that recoupment.

If a franchisee has a long running case which will not enable them to submit a final bill within 18 months of receiving a payment on account, they may notify the Area Office so that the automatic recoupment of the payment on account can be prevented.

Crime franchisees who make claims for police station duty solicitor work are paid in full for standby and for work done during the standby period, *i.e.* paragraph 2 in the schedule to the Legal Advice and Assistance at Police Stations (Remuneration) Regulations 1989 (as amended) does not apply.

39–43 Crime franchisees who make claims for police station advice and assistance do not have to justify to the Board exceeding the £90 costs limit where they determine that the interests of justice require advice and assistance to be given as a matter of urgency (regulation 5(6) Legal Advice and Assistance at Police Stations (Remuneration) Regulations 1989).

Finally, crime franchisees are entitled to higher hourly rates and standard fees.

Mandatory Requirements of the Specification

39–44 The franchising specification sets out mandatory requirements and detailed explanatory notes. The mandatory requirements, which set out the basic requirements are set out below. "PMS" means that there is an equivalent requirement in the Law Society's Practice Management Standards.

FRANCHISE REPRESENTATIVE AND LIAISON MANAGER

Organisations must appoint a named representative ("Franchise Representative"), who will act as a focal point for the Legal Aid Board Liaison Manager (Board Requirement).

The Franchise Representative must be available during any audits conducted by the Legal Aid Board (Board Requirement).

Organisations must notify the Liaison Manager where the Franchise Representative is changed or leaves (Board Requirement).

Welfare Benefits

39–45 Even where the organisation does not hold or apply for a franchise in welfare benefits, it must have at least one employee suitably qualified to recognise the need for welfare benefits advice. The organisation must ensure that all legal aid caseworkers/advisers in franchised categories are able to recognise the need for welfare benefits advice and refer clients to the appropriate source of advice (Board Requirement).

Status Inquiries

Organisations must give their authority to the Board to enable it during both **39–46** the pre-contract application period and the contract phase to submit status inquiries and to obtain information from the appropriate bodies (Board Requirement).

Organisations must provide a list of personnel, with their responsibilities, *i.e.* job titles, when requested by the Board for the purpose of conducting periodic status inquiries (Board Requirement).

Independent Advice

Organisations must comply with the requirements for independent advice **39–47** laid down by one of the following national organisations: The Law Society, Federation of Independent Advice Centres, Law Centres Federation or the National Association of Citizens Advice Bureaux (Board Requirement).

Equal Opportunities, Non-Discrimination and Professional Indemnity Insurance

Organisations must not discriminate on grounds of race, gender, sexual **39–48** orientation, religion or disability in deciding whether to accept instructions from clients, instructing counsel or in the provision of services (Board Requirement).

All job applicants and personnel in organisations must receive equal treatment in accordance with the relevant legislation and the guidance issued by the Law Society and other relevant national organisations, in respect of advice sector applicants (Board Requirement).

Organisations must maintain all necessary professional indemnity insurance cover either in accordance with Solicitors Act 1974 s.37 or as is provided by the relevant association (*e.g.* NACAB) or as reasonably required by the Board. Details of such cover, *e.g.* in the form of a current receipted notification of premium and renewal notice, must be provided to the Board (Board Requirement).

Forward Planning

Organisations must have a written outline strategy to provide a background **39–49** against which performance may be reviewed and decisions taken about the future (PMS B1(a)).

Services Plan

39–50   Organisations must have a written services plan which must include:
   (a) the services the organisation wishes to offer;
   (b) the client groups to be served;
   (c) how the services are to be provided; and
   (d) the organisation's approach to marketing (PMS B1 (b) and (c)).

Management Structure

39–51   Organisations must have a written description of their management structure (PMS A1).

   Organisations must designate the responsibilities of individuals within the management structure (PMS A1.2 (a) and E1).

Supervisors, Supervision and File Review

39–52   There must be a named supervisor or supervisors for each category of work for which an application for a franchise has been made or a franchise granted (PMS A1).

   The supervisor must either be a member of a relevant Law Society specialisation panel or possess experience of work within the category of law for which the franchise application is made, or the franchise is held, which must have been gained over a period of at least two years (Board Requirement).

   Organisations must ensure that arrangements are documented and are in place to supervise the conduct of case work. These arrangements must take into account the knowledge and experience of the caseworker/adviser being supervised (PMS F10).

   Organisations must have documented arrangements for periodic reviews of the management of files. The review must, except where there is only one caseworker/adviser in the organisation, be carried out by a caseworker/adviser who has not been involved in the day-to-day conduct of the matter (PMS F10).

   Where an individual supervisor's responsibilities extend to more than one office the arrangements for discharging those responsibilities must be documented (Board Requirement).

   Organisations must have documented arrangements to monitor the number and type of matters undertaken by each caseworker/adviser to ensure that they are within his or her capacity (PMS F1 (c)).

   The supervisory arrangements must ensure that the devolved powers are exercised in accordance with the Board's guidance. The arrangements for achieving this must be documented (Board Requirement).

File Management

Organisations must: **39–53**
  (a) have a system which enables them to identify all open and closed
      legal aid cases, including green form, from the time of making their
      application for a franchise (PMS F2);
  (b) have procedures to ensure that they are able to identify and trace
      all documents, correspondence and other information relating to
      a matter (PMS F6);
  (c) have arrangements designed to identify any conflict of interest
      (PMS F1(b));
  (d) maintain a back-up record of key dates in matters (PMS F1 (d));
  (e) ensure proper authorisation and monitoring of undertakings given
      on behalf of the practice (PMS F1 (e));
  (f) have a system which enables all relevant matters to be identified
      when acting for a client in a number of matters (PMS F2);
  (g) have arrangements to ensure that the status of a matter and action
      taken can be easily checked by someone other than the casework/
      adviser (PMS F9 (a));
  (h) have arrangements to ensure that documents are arranged in the
      file in an orderly way (PMS F9 (b));
  (i) ensure that key information is shown clearly on the file including,
      in particular, details of any undertakings given on behalf of the
      practice (PMS F9 (c)); and
  (j) record on case files the exercise of any devolved powers including
      the date of and reason for exercise, the decision made and a note,
      e.g. reference, of who exercised the devolved power (Board
      Requirement).

Individual Cases—At the outset of a case

Organisations must have documented procedures for taking instructions **39–54**
which ensure that caseworkers/advisers agree and record:
  (a) the requirements or instructions of the client (PMS F4 (a)(i));
  (b) the advice given (PMS F4 (a)(ii));
  (c) action to be taken by the organisation (PMS F4 (a)(iii));
  (d) the possible effect of the statutory charge (PMS F4 (a)(v));
  (e) advice to the client on the best information possible about likely
      total cost of the matter and any potential liability for costs (Written
      Professional Standard: Information on Costs for Clients (a)(i), (e)(ii)
      and (iii));
  (f) the client's potential obligation to pay any legal aid contributions
      assessed and of the consequences of any failure to do so (Written
      Professional Standard: Information on Costs for Clients (e)(iv));

(g) who will be responsible for the conduct of the case (PMS F4 (a)(vi)); and

(h) key dates in the matter, and record these in the file and in a back-up system (PMS F4(d)).

Organisations must confirm (a) to (g) above with the client, ordinarily in writing (PMS F4(b)).

Organisations must inform the client of any limits, if any, on their ability or willingness to act, for example in representing the client at court or before a tribunal (Board Requirement).

Individual Cases—Progress of the case

39–55 Organisations must have documented procedures which ensure that:

(a) in a complex case a case plan is prepared, agreed with the client and periodically reviewed and updated (PMS F5 (e));

(b) information on the progress of a case is given to the client at appropriate intervals (PMS F5 (a));

(c) information about changes in the action planned to be taken in the case, or its handling, is given to the client promptly (PMS F5 (b)); and

(d) information about changes in the client's potential cost liability, including the effect of the statutory charge, if any, is given to the client at least every six months (PMS F5(d)).

Individual Cases — at the end of a case

39–56 Organisations must have documented procedures to ensure that at the conclusion of the matter, the organisation:

(a) reports to the client on the outcome and explains any further action the client is required to take in the matter and what, if anything, the organisation will do (PMS F7 (a));

(b) accounts to the client for any outstanding money (PMS F7 (b));

(c) returns to the client original documents and other property belonging to the client if required (save for items which are by agreement to be stored by the organisation (PMS F7 (c));

(d) if appropriate, advises the client about arrangements for storage and retrieval of papers and other items retained (PMS F7 (d)); and

(e) advises the client whether the matter should be reviewed in future, and if so, when (PMS F7 (e)).

Services of Others

39–57 Organisations must have a documented procedure for using barristers, agents, and expert witnesses, etc., in providing legal services which must include provision for the following:

(a) use of clear selection criteria (PMS F8 (a));
(b) where appropriate, consultation with the client in relation to selection, and proper advice to the client on choice of advocate (PMS F8 (b));
(c) maintenance of records (centrally, by department or by office) of barristers, agents or experts used which must comply with the law relating to defamation, discrimination and data protection (PMS F8 (c));
(d) giving of instructions which clearly describe what is required (PMS F8 (d));
(e) checking of opinions and reports received to ensure they adequately provide the information sought (PMS F8 (e));
(f) payment of fees (PMS F8 (f)); and
(g) a record on the case file of why a barrister, agent or expert was selected who had not previously been used or approved for further use (Board Requirement).

Financial Management

Organisations must be able to demonstrate who exercises responsibility for **39–58** financial affairs (PMS C1).

Solicitors in private practice must be able to demonstrate that they have the management and financial information necessary for monitoring income, expenditure and cost, and for forward planning; and this must include the following:

(a) an annual budget including, where appropriate, any capital expenditure proposed;
(b) a quarterly variance analysis of income and expenditure against budget;
(c) an annual profit and loss account; and
(d) an annual balance sheet (PMS C2).

Law Centres and Advice Agencies must have an equivalent system of financial control which includes:

(a) an annual budget based on grant aid due, income projections and, where appropriate, any capital expenditure proposed;
(b) a quarterly variance analysis of income and expenditure against budget;
(c) an annual income and expenditure account;
(d) an annual balance sheet; and
(e) quarterly monitoring of these accounts by the management committee.

Organisations must have a system that ensures that time spent on casework can be properly recorded and attributed (PMS C3).

Organisations must keep a running record of costs incurred for each legal aid case (Board Requirement).

Managing People

39–59 Organisations must document the skills, knowledge and experience required of all staff including partners, caseworkers/advisers and support staff, directly or indirectly involved in work in the franchise category and the tasks that they are required to perform, usually in the form of a job description or person specification (PMS D1).

Organisations must have documented recruitment arrangements which evaluate the skill, knowledge and experience possessed by applicants for posts in the organisation, and their integrity and suitability (PMS D2).

Organisations must have documented arrangements to provide an induction process for new postholders (PMS D3).

Organisations must have procedures to:

(a) document the responsibilities and objectives of all personnel in the organisation;

(b) evaluate the performance of staff at least annually against those responsibilities and objectives; and

(c) record in writing the performance appraisal (PMS D4).

These procedures must be documented.

Organisations must have arrangements to ensure that:

(a) all personnel are trained to a level of competence appropriate to their work;

(b) training and development needs are assessed for each person against the objectives of the organisation and are reviewed at least annually;

(c) skills and knowledge required for the management and organisation of the organisation, as well as for the provision of legal services, are provided for in training and development; and

(d) appropriate written training records are maintained (PMS D5).

Client Care and Complaints

39–60 Organisations must comply with Solicitors' Practice Rule 15 or any equivalent complaints procedure specified by, *e.g.* NACAB (Law Society and Board Requirement).

Organisations must have documented arrangements for:

(a) reporting and recording centrally every formal complaint made by a client;

(b) responding appropriately to any complaint;

(c) identifying the cause of any problem of which a client has complained, offering any appropriate redress, and correcting any unsatisfactory procedure (PMS F11).

Franchise organisations must ensure that all legal aid clients and prospective clients have ready and early access to the information contained in the Board's leaflet, Legal Aid: A Quality Service (Board Requirement).

Office Manual

Organisations must maintain an office manual collating information on **39–61** organisational practice which must be available to all personnel in the organisation (PMS E2).

Legal Reference Materials

Applicant organisations must have the current Legal Aid Handbook at each **39–62** office for which application for a franchise is made, and the elements of the "Franchise Manual" at each of the franchised offices (Board Requirement).
Organisations must have arrangements to ensure that:

(a) caseworkers/advisers have ready access to up-to-date legal reference material for the categories of work for which application for a franchise is made or a franchise is held; and

(b) caseworkers/advisers receive timely information about changes to the law in the relevant category of work (PMS E3).

Franchise Forms

A franchisee must use the prescribed forms in connection with the **39–63** operation of its contract and in the way prescribed by the Board in the guidance that appears in the "Franchise Manual" or is otherwise published by the Board (Board Requirement).

THE GUIDANCE ON THE EXERCISE OF DEVOLVED POWERS (FRANCHISE MANUAL)

Having devolved powers to franchised firms, the Board must ensure that **39–64** such firms will exercise those powers as the Board would have done, had they not been devolved. The Franchise Manual includes guidance which franchised firms must follow when exercising their devolved powers.

The Franchise Manual makes frequent reference to the Board's notes for guidance found in the Legal Aid Handbook. The intention is that both franchised firms and the Board's own staff will be approaching decision-making in the same way so that the likelihood of consistent decision-making is enhanced.

SUSPENSION OR TERMINATION BY THE BOARD IN ACCORDANCE WITH THE SPECIFICATION

39–65 Clause 13.5 and 13.6 of the Standard Terms provide:

> "Subject to Clause 13.7, where the Board considers that the Franchisee has committed any breach or breaches of Clauses 6.3 to 6.8 which the Board reasonably considers constitute, either alone or together, a Major Non-Compliance the Board shall be entitled to terminate this Agreement or to terminate or suspend (indefinitely or for such period as it thinks fit) approval of any or all of the Franchised Offices and/or of any or all of the Franchised Categories of Work and/or of any or all of the Devolved Powers in accordance with the provisions of and procedures in the Specification. For the avoidance of doubt, the fact that the Franchisee, having failed to comply with, perform or observe the obligations in Clauses 6.3 to 6.8, thereafter operates so as to do so, shall not prevent the Board from terminating or suspending in accordance with the provisions of and procedures in the Specification.
>
> Without prejudice to Clause 13.5, where the Board considers that the Franchisee has committed any breach or breaches of Clauses 6.3 to 6.8 which the Board reasonably considers is alone or are together such as to justify the Board's terminating or suspending approval of any or all of the Devolved Powers to protect the legal aid fund or the Board's or Clients' interests, the Board shall be entitled forthwith to terminate or suspend (indefinitely or for such period as it thinks fit) approval of any or all of the Devolved Powers. For the avoidance of doubt, arbitration (Clause 19), does not apply to the provisions of this Clause 13.6."

Clause 6 sets out the requirement to comply with the Specification and to demonstrate such compliance.

Paragraph 5.8 of the Specification provides:

39–66 There are four types of major non-compliance: major (a); major (b); major (c); and major (d). Thee are defined as follows:

> A major (a) non-compliance is where there is no written plan, procedure or arrangement for one of the mandatory general and management requirements set out in section 3 above;
>
> A major (b) non-compliance is where a written plan, procedure or

arrangement exists but it does not meet the mandatory general and management requirements in section 3 above;

A major (c) non-compliance is where there is no or insufficient evidence that a plan, procedure or arrangement that is a mandatory general and management requirement in section 3 above is in effective operation;

A major (d) non-compliance is where the organisation is not able to comply with one of the following mandatory requirements of the specification:

(i) monitoring;
(ii) transaction criteria;
(iii) average cost criteria;
(iv) outcome measures.

Section 9 of the Specification sets out how the Board will approach suspension and termination. Paragraphs 9.5 to 9.10 provide:

The Board may consider that there is an urgent need to suspend or ter- **39–67** minate the franchise. Normally, this will happen only where the Board considers there is a risk to clients or to the Legal Aid Fund. The Board's general approach will be to follow a graded procedure which allows the franchisee time to address any problems. The procedure is set out in para 9.6.

If the monitoring information and/or audits reveal that the specification's mandatory requirements are not being met, or there is some other cause for concern, the Liaison Manager will notify the Franchise Representative of the concern and ask for remedial steps to be taken, normally within a period of 21 days.

If the area of concern is not dealt with to the satisfaction of the Liaison Manager within the required period (including any extensions of time which might be granted) the Liaison Manager will recommend suspension of franchises in particular offices or categories or the termination of the contract to the Area Manager and will invite the franchisee to make representations within 14 days or such other period as might be specified.

After representations have been received or after the period for making representations has expired, the Area Manager will consider the matter and the franchisee will be notified of the Area Manager's decision, the date the decision is to take effect, being at least 14 days after the date of notification, and of the right of appeal.

Appeals and Arbitration (Section 8)

If the franchisee appeals against the decision to suspend or terminate a **39–68** franchise and, if that appeal fails, wishes to proceed with arbitration, the franchise will continue, unless there are extreme circumstances where the Board needs to suspend or terminate the franchise to protect the Fund or clients' interests.

If the franchisee seeks to appeal against the decision to suspend the operation of devolved powers the suspension will continue until the appeal is determined. There is no recourse to arbitration for the suspension of devolved powers.

If a franchise in any category is suspended for any reason, the organisation may apply for a suspension to be lifted if it feels it has successfully addressed the issues which led to the suspension. It may do this by writing to the Liaison Manager who may either recommend lifting the suspension forthwith, or direct an audit to be carried out to verify that the issues that led to the suspension have been addressed. The decision to lift the suspension or not will be the Area Manager's. An appeal from the Area Manager's decision not to lift a suspension will be to the appeal body described in para 8.3.

39–69   The specification also sets out how appeals will be managed and the arbitration procedure. It will be noted that if the Board considers that the situation is urgent it may suspend a franchise without following the normal graded procedure, in which case the franchise will remain suspended notwithstanding an appeal or reference to arbitration, or until the appeal or arbitration is decided in the franchise's favour.

Chapter 40

MULTI-PARTY ACTION CONTRACTS

GENERAL

The Board has, following competitive tendering, entered into a number of **40–01** contracts with firms or groups of firms to do the generic work in multi-party actions. Such contracts are made under Part II of the Legal Aid Act 1988 for provision under Part IV of the Legal Aid Act of civil legal aid. By section 15(7) of the Act, payment for such work is governed by the contract and, pursuant to section 32(2) of the act, the Board could assign solicitors to individual clients. The Legal Aid Board Multi-Party Action Arrangements (1992) (as amended) set out how the Board's tender procedure works and include most of the contract terms.

The majority of multi-party action contracts have been for generic work so the assignment provisions have not been used. Assisted persons continue to instruct the solicitor of their choice but the work which such a solicitor can do is limited to work specific to that client's case. They cannot do the research and other generic work which such litigation requires.

However, the Board has awarded an all-work contract for the smoking related diseases litigation. This means that one or more solicitors in the group of firms which was successful in securing the contract will, if the Board directs, be the solicitors for all assisted persons.

The Legal Aid Board's area offices notify the Board's Head Office when, in any case, 10 legal aid certificates have been issued. It is the issue of 10 legal aid certificates which defines a potential multi-party action. If the nature of the action appears to be one where there will be common generic issues, or if there are other reasons why the Board considers the matter would best be dealt with by a contract, the Board issues application forms to all firms which have submitted applications for legal aid for the relevant proceedings by what is termed the "set closing date".

Any firm which has submitted an application for legal aid by such date may tender for the work in its own right. Firms which have not submitted applications by the set closing date may, nevertheless, join with any qualifying firm and a group of firms to tender for the work. Up until the tender closing date (the date by which tenders for the work must be submitted to the nominated area office), the Board continues to send out application forms to all firms of solicitors submitting applications for legal aid for the relevant proceedings as such firms will be affected by any decision to award a contract and are the firms most likely to wish to combine in a group with a qualifying firm.

40–02 Essentially, the Board's multi-party action contract and arrangements require firms to take more of a project management approach towards the litigation and require them to provide regular reports to clients and to the Board.

Although the Board's contract could control the price payable for the work, instead, the usual regulations apply and work done under a multi-party action contract is subject to taxation in the usual way. Price, therefore, is not a factor in the selection of tenders. Instead, the tender documentation asks for information about individual firms, about the strength of the team which would be put together to manage the litigation, about how the work would be co-ordinated and about how the firms would manage should unexpected circumstances arise. The forms also ask for firms' assessments of the litigation and how they would intend to progress it.

40–03 Examples of the tender inquiries currently made by the Board are set out below.

Instructions to Tenderers—example

Tender reports must comprise the following attached documents and the replies to them:
1. Officer
2. Overall resource strength, group information liaison information and client information
3. Team information
4. Firm information
5. Claims information
6. General and confidential information

Tenderers should carefully note and comply with the instructions on each of the documents. Additional sheets of paper may be used to reply where necessary—every additional sheet of paper used to reply should (1) bear the relevant firm's name, the name of the document and number of the request to which it relates; and (2) be attached to the document to which it relates.

Tenderers should note the timetable which will be strictly followed:
1. */**/**   Set Closing Date. (The date by which at least one bona fide written application for legal aid must have been submitted).
2. */**/**   Questions Closing Date. (The date (and time)

until which the Liaison Officer will accept questions on the tender procedure. No questions will be accepted after this date).

3. */**/**   Tender Closing Date. (The date (and time) by which tender reports must be received at the relevant Legal Aid Area Office by hand or by recorded delivery.

4. To be fixed   Multi Party Actions (Operational) Committee meeting to consider tender reports.

1. Offer—example

The firm or firms whose name(s) is/are written below and whose letter(s) is/are attached to this offer (each) hereby offers:

"To provide representation to legally assisted persons in accordance with the provisions of the Legal Aid Board Multi-Party Action Arrangements 1992 (as amended) and the Legal Aid Board Multi-Party Action Contract (Ref: MPA 95/*)".

The name(s) of the firm(s) whose letter(s) is/are attached to this offer is/are set out below:

1. ....
2. ....
3. ....
4. ....
5. ....

NB: Attached letters must be on the firm's headed note paper, be signed by a partner and be addressed to the Board's Liaison Officer. When a group of firms (*i.e.* more than one firm) is involved, such letters are required from every firm in the group. Letters must be in the following terms only:

"Management of the ** claims"

"We hereby offer to provide representation to legally assisted persons in accordance with the provisions of the Legal Aid Board Multi-Party Action Arrangements 1992 (as amended) and the Legal Aid Board Multi-Party Contract (Ref: MPA 95/*). We agree that this offer, with your written acceptance shall constitute a binding agreement on the contract terms."

NB: To be eligible to tender a firm (or, when a group of firms is concerned, at least one firm in the group) must have submitted in writing at least one bona fide application for legal aid in connection with the above claims by the set closing date. A partner in the firm which submitted that application for legal aid must provide an appropriate certification to confirm this on his or her

723

firm's headed paper. The certification must state the relevant legal aid reference number.

2. Overall resource strength, group information, liaison information and client information—example

Parts A, C and D should be replied to in all cases. Part B should also be replied to if the tender report is submitted by a group of (more than one) firms.

A. Overall Resource Strength

The Board is looking for an overview of the total resources of the tendering firm, or group of firms, and of the total resources which would (and could if required) be applied to progressing the claims. Firm and team information will be evaluated against the background of overall resource strength.

Please state in no more than 500 words on a separate sheet what human and other resources the firm or group of firms (a) possesses; (b) intends to apply to progressing the claims; and (c) could realistically apply should unforeseen circumstances arise.

B. Group Information

1. Number of firms in the group ....
2. Please explain why this number of firms is involved.

....
....
....
....

3. You have tendered for the work specified in the contract. Please describe on a separate sheet in no more than 500 words the intended division of such work between the firms.
4. The Board needs to be satisfied that there will be effective coordination of firms in the group. Please describe on a separate sheet in no more than 500 words how you intend to achieve this.

C. Liaison Information

1. Person and Firm responsible for liaison with the Board on this tender:
Name .... (position) ....
Firm's Name .... (phone no. ....)
2. Person and Firm responsible for liaison with the Board during contract:
Name .... (position) ....
Firm's Name .... (phone no. ....)

3. Person and Firm responsible for submitting reports to the Board:
Name .... (position) ....
Firm's Name .... (phone no. ....)
4. Person and Firm responsible for submitting reports to Claimants:
Name .... (position) ....
Firm's Name .... (phone no. ....)

D. Client Information

The Board would like to know how many clients (if any) have already instructed the firm or group of firms in connection with the claims. Please provide the following information:

	Name of Firm	Number of Private Clients	Number of Legal Aid Clients
1.	....	....	....
2.	....	....	....
3.	....	....	....
4.	....	....	....
5.	....	....	....
	Total:	Total:	

3. Team Information—example

The Board expects that the firm or group of firms will have one team of people who will be primarily devoted to pursuing the above claims. The Board is interested in the experience and abilities of such people and in how the team will be managed.

In respect of such team, the firm or group of firms must provide the following information:

1. The names of the people in the team. Each name to be followed by (1) age (2) qualifications and dates obtained (3) position in their firm (4) percentage time expected to be devoted to the above claims (5) the level of supervision and/or training (if any) they will need (6) their role in the team.

2. In respect of key team members C. V.s, including (as appropriate) general experience, experience of management, experience of information technology, experience of research, experience of multi-party actions. Information about any . relevant expertise which the team member considers s/he possesses.

3. A summary of the team's strengths and weaknesses and experience of multi-party actions.

4. A description (in under 500 words) of how the team will be managed.

725

5. A description of the team's ability to cope with unplanned circumstances which might arise in pursuing the claims including details of any mechanisms for reviewing whether sufficient resources (human, financial and other) and expertise exist, and what steps might be taken following such review.

4. Firm Information—example

Every firm, whether tendering alone or as one of a group, should reply (in a maximum of 500 words per reply) to each of the following requests using a separate sheet of paper for each numbered request. Each firm's sheets should be placed in order and fixed by a treasury tag at the top left-hand corner. As well as replying in respect of present procedures/management etc. firms may also set out the procedures/management etc. which they propose to operate if awarded the contract.

1. Please describe the structure, management and organisation of the firm.
2. If the firm has more than one office, please describe the structure, management and organisation of the office which will be primarily responsible for the claims.
3. Please set out your firm's complaints procedures.
4. Please set out your firm's training procedures and include details of any special training which you would introduce if awarded the contract.
5. Please set out details of your firm's support services;
   (a) secretarial;
   (b) administrative;
   (c) library;
   (d) information technology;
   (e) other.
6. Please describe how your firm approaches the issue of quality of service.
7. Please provide a summary of your firm's general litigation experience.
8. Please provide a summary of your firm's personal injury litigation experience.
9. Please state your firm's experience of multi-party actions.

5. Claims Information—example

The Board would like to know how the tendering firm, or group of firms now envisages progressing the claims. The tendering firm, or group of firms, should respond to the following requests in no more than 500 words per response, using (except in the case of question 9 a separate sheet of paper for each numbered request.

1. Please state your assessment of the present position including, so far as is practicable an estimate of the potential number of claimants.
2. Please outline what generic work (if any) has been carried out by your firm or group of firms. Please outline any other experience/ knowledge/expertise specifically relevant to this multi-party action.
3. Please state what you consider to be the significant features (including any significant difficulties) of the claims, the generic issues to be addressed and the major obstacles to be overcome.
4. Please outline any opportunities you see for securing improved value for money through economies of scale or otherwise.
5. So far as is practicable, please provide a report in accordance with paragraphs 29–31 of the Legal Aid Board Multi-Party Arrangements 1992 (as amended) including estimates of costs and damages. If this is impracticable please provide, so far as is practicable, plans for the next six months as required by paragraphs 30(vii) and 31(ii) of the Arrangements.
6. Please outline briefly how you propose to consult and liaise with claimants and any action groups.
7. Please outline briefly how you propose to deal with the media.
8. Please tick box ☐ to confirm that, if your tender is not accepted, there will be no delay in making available to any successful tenderer all information held by you (the tendering firm or any or all of the firms in the group) which may assist.

6. General and Confidential Information—example

Responses to the following requests must be provided by the tendering firm or group of firms.

1. Please state how you propose to arrange for private clients to contribute to the cost of progressing the claims.

....
....
....

2. Please state whether your firm is, or (where the tender report is submitted by a group of firms) whether all firm sin the group are, able to receive payments from the Board by BACS? YES/NO
If not, please provide details

....
....
....

3. Each firm whether tendering alone or as one of a group of firms must disclose:

727

(a) Any adjudication in respect of any partner or employee of the firm by the Solicitors Complaints Bureau within the last five years and any pending hearing.

(b) Any criminal convictions in respect of any partner or employee of the firm and any pending hearings.

This information should be supplied on the firm's headed notepaper marked "Tender Report—6. Confidential Information." and should be in a separate envelope also so marked and endorsed with the firm's name. Where a group of firms is concerned one envelope may be used, if convenient.

Obligation in the Arrangements

40–04 The main obligations on contracted firms in multi party actions are set out in the Legal Aid Board Multi Party Action Arrangements 1992 (as amended).

40–05 An extract from the Arrangements is set out below.

Part V—Standard Contracting Provisions

General

25. Contracting firms will carry out only such work as is authorised by the Board and will comply with such limitations on contract work as the Board may from time to time impose.

26. Subject to any directions given by the liaison officer:
    (i) contracting firms shall divide the contract work between them and may amend such division from time to time; but contracting firms shall notify the liaison officer of any major change of responsibilities within a group;
    (ii) each contracting firm shall individually record the contract work which it does;
    (iii) contracting firms may instruct counsel in respect of contract work but may not delegate or assign contract work to non-contracting firms.

27. A nominated contracting firm shall be primarily responsible for liaising with the Board.

28. In carrying out contract work, contracting firms will exercise reasonable skill and care.

Monitoring Multi-Party Actions

29. A nominated contracting firm shall submit a report to the liaison officer every six months (or such shorter period as the Board may prescribe). Such reports shall be divided into two sections:
    (i) legal and financial;

(ii) management and administration.

30. The legal and financial section of the report shall include:
  (i) an up-to-date appraisal of the current position, including:
    (a) an assessment of the present strength and financial viability of the action, setting out the information which is relevant to the assessment and taking into account any developments since the last report;
    (b) an estimate of costs to date;
    (c) anticipated future costs;
    (d) present estimates of quantum;
    (e) a costs benefit assessment;
  (ii) a description of the work carried out since the last report;
  (iii) statistics, including:
    (a) number of claimants;
    (b) number of private clients in the action;
    (c) number of inquiries from prospective clients;
    (d) best estimate of likely numbers of claimants or private clients who have yet to join the action;
  (iv) copies of all reports and circulars sent to claimants and local firms over the last six months;
  (v) details of unresolved complaints;
  (vi) details of any relevant time limits or deadlines in the action, the steps taken to comply with them and the extent to which such deadlines are being or will be complied with;
  (vii) a plan to progress the action over the next six months.

31. The management and administration section of the report shall include:
  (i) details of how the action has been managed and co-ordinated over the lat six months, including any changes in administration, personnel or IT since the last report;
  (ii) a plan for the management and administration of the action over the next six months.

32. If the nominated contracting firm fails to provide an adequate report the liaison officer may:
  (i) withhold any payments on account pending submission of the report;
  (ii) limit work to submitting the report only;
  (iii) recommend to the Committee termination of the contract.

33. The liaison officer may during any action make enquiries of claimants as to the standard of service they are receiving from contracting firms.

Keeping Claimants and Local Firms Informed

34. Contracting firms will keep claimants fully informed as to the preparation and prosecution of their claims.

729

35. Without prejudice to the obligation under paragraph 34, a nominated contracting firm shall make reports on at least a three-monthly basis to claimants on the preparation and progress of their claims. Such reports may be sent via local firms to claimants with an instruction that local firms should pass the reports on and deal with any queries from their clients. Reports sent to claimants must be in language readily understandable to the layman.

36. Contracting firms will keep local firms informed of the progress of the action and will give them sufficient guidance and information to enable them:

    (i) properly to advise and assist their clients;

    (ii) to make representations on behalf of their clients on the conduct of the litigation;

    (iii) to assess so far as possible the likely impact of the statutory charge on claims of their clients;

    (iv) to progress the individual claims of their clients in accordance with the latest orders or directions from the Court.

37. Nothing in these arrangements shall oblige contracting firms to comply with all requests for information from local firms or claimants or to disseminate information which in the opinion of contracting firms might prejudice the interests of claimants in the action generally.

Remuneration

38. Save where these arrangements expressly provide otherwise, contracting firms will be paid at the same rates and in the same manner as they would be paid under regulations, and their fees shall be subject to taxation on the standard basis or assessment in accordance with the provisions of the regulations. For the avoidance of doubt contracting firms may obtain authority to incur costs in accordance with the provisions of Part VIII of the regulations.

39. Contracting firms may apply for payments on account only as provided for by these arrangements. Contracting firms may apply to the liaison officer for the payment of a sum on account of:

    (i) disbursements incurred or about to be incurred in connection with contract work;

    (ii) profit costs or counsel's fees in respect of contract work as soon as such work has been undertaken, including contract work undertaken under a legal aid certificate prior to the date of the contract.

In relation to applications under sub-paragraph (ii) above the Board will pay 75 per cent of what it considers to be a reasonable amount for work reasonably done. Payments on account will be made as soon as practicable, provided that sufficient details are submitted to enable the Board to consider the reasonableness of the claim.

40. Where contract work is carried out for the benefit of private clients as well as claimants the Board will be responsible only for the legal aid proportion of the costs of the action and at the conclusion of the action the Board will immediately recoup any excess sums paid on account.

Subject to paragraph 41, payments on account will be reduced by a percentage to take into account the current proportion of private clients in the action as a whole. For this purpose only private clients who have commenced proceedings or are otherwise clearly identified to the satisfaction of the liaison officer will be taken into account, but contracting firms shall provide the liaison officer with such information as he requires to enable a fair estimate of numbers to be given.

41. In exceptional circumstances the Board may, if it thinks fit, agree to payments on account being made as if there were fewer private clients or no private clients in the action, but only if it is satisfied that:

(i) reducing payments on account to take account of private clients would cause delay or otherwise prejudice the interests of claimants; and

(ii) contracting firms have taken all reasonable steps to obtain appropriate levels of funding from private clients in the action generally; and

(iii) it would be reasonable to make payments on account at a higher rate having regard to the proportion of private clients in the action.

42. Contracting firms may apply to the liaison officer for payment of the travelling costs of claimants in connection with:

(i) claimants' meetings organised by contracting firms;

(ii) committees organised by contracting firms which include claimant representatives.

The liaison officer may approve such payment if the purpose of the meeting or committee is clear and will progress the conduct of the litigation, and the objectives of the meeting or committee cannot be achieved as effectively through other procedures. If such approval is given the Board will pay claimants' reasonable travelling costs within the United Kingdom (equivalent to Second Class return rail fare) to contracting firms for distribution to claimants, or reimburse contracting firms for any such reasonable sums as they have paid.

Contracting firms will explain to claimants the effect of the statutory charge should such expenses not be allowed on *inter partes* taxation.

43. Where contracting firms have failed to comply with any relevant provision of the regulations, arrangements or contract:

(i) payments on account may be deferred or suspended; and

(ii) where as a result of such default or omission the Board incurs loss, such loss may be deducted from payment of profit costs in respect of contract work until the loss is recovered.

Complaints

44. Contracting firms shall issue details of their complaints procedure to claimants and should ensure that, so far as possible, the following procedure is adopted in respect of obligations and procedures contained in these arrangements:

(i) claimants should in the first instance complain to their own solicitors;

(ii) complaints unresolved by a local firm should be referred to contracting firms;

(iii) complaints unresolved by contracting firms should be referred to the liaison officer.

45. The liaison officer will monitor and keep records of complaints. The liaison officer will refer complaints to the Committee where the complaints relate to the arrangements themselves or where the volume or severity of the complaints might lead the Committee to consider termination.

Publicity

46. The Board may, in consultation with contracting firms, take such steps as it considers appropriate to publicise a multi-party action.

Conflicting Instructions and Compromises

47. Nothing in these arrangements shall affect the normal professional duties of solicitors to their clients. Where as a result of instructions received contracting firms or local firms consider that they cannot reasonably be expected to act for any claimant they shall inform the liaison officer and certificates may be amended or discharged as appropriate/.

48. Where a contracting firm receives conflicting instructions (whether in relation to an offer of compromise or otherwise) and cannot resolve such conflict, it shall report the problem to the liaison officer. The normal procedures as to amendment or discharge of certificates shall apply in such circumstances but where it appears to the liaison officer that there may be grounds for terminating the contract or for dividing the claimants into groups and entering into one or more new contracts, he will inform the Committee and make appropriate recommendations.

Termination

49. The Board may terminate any contract, either in respect of a specific firm within a group or all firms, where in the opinion of the Board:

(i) any contracting firm in the group is in breach of its obligations under the contract or under these arrangements or has otherwise acted or is proposing to act in a way likely to cause substantial prejudice to claimants or to the Board;

(ii) information set out in a tender report is inaccurate or misleading; or

(iii) it is no longer appropriate to continue representation by means of a contract in the action.

By way of examples only, potential grounds for termination are set out in the Schedule hereto.

50. The Board may terminate immediately in case of urgency, but otherwise:

(i) the liaison officer will notify the contracting firm of the area of concern and ask for remedial steps to be taken within 21 days, or such other period as he may specify; and

(ii) failure to remedy the problem will result in the liaison officer referring the matter to the Committee to consider termination.

51. Where a termination has occurred the Committee will consider how best to proceed in the interests of claimants and the Board may enter into a new contract or contracts without applying the procedures set out in Part III of these arrangements.

52. Subject to paragraph 43, after termination a former contracting firm may apply for payment on account under paragraph 39 in respect of work done up to the date of termination. On termination contracting firms will deliver up documents relating to contract work as required by the Board.

Apportionment of Costs

53. In this and the remaining paragraphs of the arrangements, "costs" refers to all costs, counsel's fees and disbursements incurred in respect of contract work on behalf of claimants, and "generic costs" refers to such costs in respect of generic work. Costs will be apportioned between the accounts of claimants by the Board where required pursuant to sections 16(10) and 40(4) of the Act.

54. Contracting firms will keep such records and supply such information as is necessary to enable the Board to carry out apportionment of costs. When lodging for taxation any bill of costs in respect of contract work, contracting firms will serve a copy of the bill on the liaison officer.

55. When apportioning costs the Board will seek to give effect to any costs sharing order made by the Court. Subject to any such order, the following principles will operate as guidelines only in the apportionment of costs:

(i) subject to the following guidelines, generic costs will be divided equally between all claimants and all other costs will be placed on the account of the individual claimant concerned;

(ii) generic costs attributable to a particular group of claimants will be divided equally between the members of that group. This would apply where there are issues in the action which relate only to that

733

group, or where a group of claimants continue with the action after others have discontinued or accepted offers of settlement;

(iii) generic costs will be apportioned between claimants *ab initio,* regardless of when they joined the action;

(iv) claimants who leave an action before it is concluded, whether by discontinuing, death, accepting an offer of settlement or otherwise ("early leavers") will be liable for their share of generic costs only up to the time they left, or up to the end of the next accounting period chosen for this purpose by the Board;

(v) travelling costs to meetings paid under paragraph 42 will be placed on the account of the claimant concerned; travelling costs to committees under that paragraph will be treated as generic costs.

56. At the request of an early leaver the Board may if it thinks fit specify a figure pursuant to section 16(10) of the Act before the conclusion of the action. Any such determination shall then be binding on both the Board and the claimant, leaving the balance of the costs to be apportioned amongst the remaining claimants at the conclusion of the action.

Schedule

Examples of Potential Grounds for Termination

1. Serious or persistent failure to comply with relevant provisions of regulations, arrangements or contract after appropriate notice of default. Examples include:

(i) unauthorised delegation of generic work;

(ii) failure to co-operate with other contracting or local firms, including failure to provide information needed for monitoring reports;

(iii) failure to comply with monitoring requirements including material non-disclosure which could substantially prejudice claimants or the Board;

(iv) failure to comply with any complaints procedure;

(v) failure to provide proper information to claimants either as specifically required in the arrangements or in response to reasonable requests;

(vi) failure to maintain accurate records of costs incurred as apportioned between claimants.

2. Material alteration to partnership or team membership of any firm affecting ability to fulfil obligations to the Board or to claimants (*e.g.* in the case of a split or merger in a contracting firm, the Board may wish to terminate and enter new contracts if the team left its old firm and transferred to a new one which met the selection criteria. Alternatively as a result of

the move neither firm might meet the criteria and a completely new firm might be required).

3. Failure properly to control the conduct and progress of the action.

4. Failure/inability to maintain adequate support services for the conduct of the action, *i.e.* the breakdown of suitable secretarial, administrative and information technology facilities.

5. Poor quality of work and advice identified by the Board.

6. Continuing substantiated complaints or an adverse adjudication by the SCB whether regarding work in the multi-party action or otherwise, including an adjudication on delay, or persistent discrimination against staff or clients.

7. Continuing excessive claims for payment, including for payments on account.

8. Major loss of confidence by claimants.

9. The contracting firm being unable on ethical grounds to continue representing the claimants.

10. The firm's financial condition being such that to continue might at worst lead to the bankruptcy of its partners, at best lead to diminished quality of work and advice.

11. Dishonesty or criminal conviction of relevant personnel.

12. Bankruptcy of partner members of the team.

13. Termination requested by contracting firms and agreed to by the Board.

Appendix 1

QUEEN'S BENCH DIVISION

*Practice Direction (Crown Court: Counsel)

1. Regulation 48(14)(a) of the Legal Aid in Criminal and Care Proceedings (General) Regulations 1989, as amended by the Legal Aid in Criminal and Care Proceedings (General) (Amendment) (No. 2) Regulations 1994, empowers a High Court judge or a circuit judge to make, or subsequently amend, a legal aid order to provide for the services of two counsel ("a two counsel order") or a Queen's Counsel alone in proceedings in the Crown Court in the terms set out in that paragraph.

2. Regulation 48(14)(b) of the Legal Aid in Criminal and Care Proceedings (General) Regulations 1989, as amended, empowers a High Court judge or the anticipated trial judge to make, or subsequently amend, a legal aid order to provide, where the prosecution is being brought by the Serious Fraud Office, for the services of three counsel ("a three counsel order") in proceedings in the Crown Court in the terms set out in that paragraph.

3. An application for a two counsel order, Queen's Counsel alone or any subsequent amendment made to the Crown Court shall be placed before the resident or designated judge of that Crown Court (or, in his absence, a judge nominated by a presiding judge of the circuit) who shall determine the application, save that where the application relates to a case which is to be heard before a named High Court judge or a named circuit judge, he should refer the application to the named judge for determination.

4. Paragraph 3 above shall not apply where an application for a two counsel order is made either during a pre-trial review or during a trial when it shall be for the judge seized of the case to determine the application.

5. In the event of any doubt as to the proper application of this direction, reference shall be made by the judge concerned to a presiding judge of the circuit who shall give such directions as he thinks fit.

6. *Practice Direction (Crown Court: Two Counsel Order)* [1989] 1 W.L.R. 618 of May 26, 1989 is hereby withdrawn.

Lord Taylor of Gosforth C.J.

January 16, 1995

PRACTICE DIRECTION No. 3 OF 1994

The Civil Legal Aid (General) (Amendment) Regulations 1994, the Legal Aid in Civil Proceedings (Remuneration) Regulations 1994, and the Legal Aid in Family Proceedings (Remuneration) (Amendment) Regulations 1994 (Legal Aid taxations).

1. This Practice Direction applies only to taxations in which there is both a legal aid and an inter partes element. It applies only to taxations where the legal aid certificate was granted on or after 25 February 1994.

2. It sets out the practice to be followed in the Supreme Court Taxing Office, the Principal Registry of the Family Division, District Registries of the High Court and divorce county courts, and is made by the Chief Taxing Master and the Senior District Judge of the Family Division with the concurrence of the Lord Chancellor (under Rule 10.22 of the Family Proceedings Rules 1991).

3. The above Regulations came into force on 25 February 1994. The general effect of the regulations is

— to prescribe rates recoverable from the Legal Aid Fund for all bills in the High Court and County Court
— to permit inter partes costs to be taxed, and recovered by the assisted party's solicitors, at rates allowed under the normal principles of RSC Order 62 and CCR Order 38 ("appropriate expense rates") even though the Legal Aid Board's liability to remunerate such solicitors is limited to the prescribed rates
— to enable the solicitor in certain circumstances to take proceedings in default of payment to recover inter partes costs exceeding the costs taxed at the prescribed rates
— to enable the assisted person's solicitor to agree the inter partes costs with the paying party and where such costs are paid to have taxed or assessed only such further costs as may be reasonably recoverable under the terms of the legal aid certificate. If the inter partes costs are not paid it will be necessary to have the whole bill taxed
— to disapply the indemnity principle in inter partes taxations to the extent indicated above.

4. The Legal Aid Board will require from the court certificate(s) showing
— the inter partes costs payable by the Board calculated in accordance with the prescribed rates
— the "legal aid only costs", i.e. those which are not the subject of any inter partes order for costs or costs which have been disallowed inter partes but allowed in whole or part against the fund
— the costs of taxation allowed against the Legal Aid Fund.

737

The form of certificate appears at Annex A, (see also paragraph 27). Additionally, the Board will require from the Court an order or certificate showing the total costs recoverable inter partes at appropriate expense rates.

5. To enable such certificate(s) to be given the normal procedures on taxation will require modification where there is to be a taxation of inter partes costs at appropriate expense rates and also pursuant to the Regulations (a mixed taxation).

6. A separate procedure is also required to assess or tax the legal aid only costs where inter partes costs have been agreed without taxation and paid.

Procedure on a Mixed Taxation

7. Form of Bill:
Bills should be drawn in the normal six column format (preferably on A4) as at present. The inter partes column should include the sums claimed as on a normal RSC Ord 62 or CCR Ord 38 inter partes taxation at appropriate expense rates. The "legal aid only" column will include only those items not claimed inter partes charged at the prescribed rates.

8. Practice Direction No. 2 of 1992 applies to the preparation of this bill (the "main bill"). In addition it is essential that each chargeable item in the bill be consecutively numbered. The bill will need to be divided into parts dealing with pre certificate and post certificate costs and reflecting any changes in VAT rates. At the discretion of the solicitor the bill may be prepared in parts for other purposes but there is no need for the main bill to be divided into parts relating to changes in the prescribed rates.

9. In addition the solicitor must prepare a schedule to be lodged with the main bill for taxation setting out the amount claimed for inter partes costs calculated at the prescribed rates. The schedule may be a plain paper schedule but should be divided vertically to provide the following information—

> Item No.
> Narrative
> VAT on Disbursements
> Disbursements
> Profit Costs

The schedule should not include any item for which no inter partes claim is made in the main bill.

10. The item numbers must correspond with those in the main bill. However, where because of changes in the prescribed rates the single preparation item in the main bill needs to be split into two or more parts in the schedule the item number should accord with that of the main bill but be followed by the suffix "(pt)".

11. The main narrative will be found in the main bill. The schedule will

require a very brief narrative simply to show how the sum claimed is calculated in accordance with the Regulations. In the case, *e.g.* of an attendance at court this should appear as follows—

```
"35        Hearing 1 hour              65
           Travel and
           waiting 1 hour              28.75
           Travel expenses 1.75   10.00    "
```

In the case of the preparation item(s) a summary only is required as follows—

```
"64(pt)    Attendances                 5 hours
           Timed Telephone
           attendance                  1 hour
           Preparation                 8 hours
           Unit Telephone
           attendances                 17
           Letters Written             27    "
```

and the total sum claimed should be inserted in the Profit costs column.

Enhancement

12. For Legal Aid taxations the system of increasing costs in exceptional circumstances is governed by the Legal Aid in Family Proceedings (Remuneration) Regulations 1991 reg.3 and by the Legal Aid in Civil Proceedings (Remuneration) Regulations 1994 reg.5.

13. Claims for an increased percentage for care and conduct in respect of inter partes costs at appropriate expense rates should be made in the main bill in accordance with present practice.

14. Claims for enhancement of the prescribed rates in the legal aid inter partes claim in the schedule should be set out in the schedule either as a preamble to the schedule or as part of the narrative for the particular item. Solicitors are reminded that enhancement may well apply to certain items of work only and that different rates may apply.

Division of Schedule into Parts

15. It is expected that the prescribed rates will be reviewed from time to time. The schedule should be divided into separate parts for each change of rate. This will commonly involve dividing the preparation item to cover the work done in each part (see para. 10 above as to numbering the item in such cases). The schedule will also need to be divided to correspond with any such divisions in the main bill.

16. It may be desirable to divide the schedule (and possibly the main bill) into further parts
— to reflect differing elements of work done (*e.g.* in Family matters, injunction and ancillary relief)
— to reflect areas of work for which differing rates of enhancement are claimed.

Any such division is at the discretion of the solicitor.

Taxation Procedure

17. Taxation is commenced as at present. Where the solicitor is responsible for serving the bill on the paying party he should exclude the schedule which is of no relevance inter partes. The schedule should however be attached to the main bill lodged for taxation and to the main bill when this needs to be served on the assisted person in accordance with the Civil Legal Aid (General) Regulations 1989 Reg. 119.

18. The existing procedures for provisional taxation will continue to apply.

19. On taxation the taxing officer will first tax the main bill. He will consider objections to the bill and where appropriate disallowed costs inter partes. Whenever costs inter partes are disallowed or reduced an appropriate deduction will be made to the amount claimed for the same item in the Schedule. The Taxing Officer will consider whether it is appropriate to allow any enhancement claimed and will take this into account in fixing the amount to be allowed.

20. Where an item is disallowed inter partes the taxing officer will then need to consider whether any part of the amount taxed off inter partes should be allowed against the fund. Any sums so allowed will be added to the "legal aid only" column of the main bill.

"Taxing Off" the Schedule

21. To achieve simplicity no "taxing off" column is to be provided in the schedule. The Taxing Officer if reducing the amount claimed in the schedule will strike through that sum and insert the sum actually allowed on taxation.

Procedure where Inter Partes Costs are Agreed and Paid but Further Claim made Against the Fund

22. Solicitors are reminded that where the residual amount is less than £500 any additional claim must be assessed by the Board and where it does not

exceed £1000 it may be so assessed. Any claims for higher amounts must be taxed by a taxing officer.

23. It is expected that many such claims will be relatively straightforward and it is proposed that the Legal Aid Board and taxing officers will initially follow a similar procedure and use similar forms.

24. There will be two types of costs to be considered

(a) items in respect of which there is no inter partes order (e.g. costs of a summons where the assisted person was not allowed costs)

(b) items which are covered by an inter partes order but for which the paying party will not accept (full) responsibility (e.g. allegedly excessive attendance on a client). (See also paragraph 25 below).

25. In respect of (a) the Board/taxing officer will require the solicitor to identify

— the item(s)
— times and details of work done
— amount claimed.

In respect of (b) rather more information will be required. The solicitor will need to state:

(i) the amount claimed from the paying party in respect of each item concerned;

(ii) the amount agreed and paid; and

(iii) the equivalent cost of the shortfall recalculated at the prescribed rates.

The solicitor will also need to satisfy the Board/taxing officer by reference to correspondence or otherwise that the paying party refused to accept the particular item wholly or in part and justify the reasonableness of the claim against the Board.

26. Form CLA32 (Annex B) should be used for assessments and may (if appropriate) be used for taxation of such items. Both the Board and the taxing officer may call for such further information as is thought reasonable. In addition the taxing officer may if he thinks fit give directions for a full taxation of the relevant costs and for the filing of a bill and schedule as described above. If the solicitor is dissatisfied with the provisional taxation a full bill may be lodged or, unless the taxing officer otherwise directs, a formal taxation may take place on the form CLA32.

Completion of Taxation

27. On completion of taxation the solicitor should make up the bill and schedule in the usual way and certify the castings. The solicitor should then complete the legal aid taxation certificate (Annex A) and certify its accuracy. This form will replace the legal aid summary and when sealed

by the court will act as a certificate authorising payment of the legal aid costs to the solicitor by the Legal Aid Board.

28. The taxing fee (if any) will be calculated on the total amount allowed both legal aid only and inter partes. No further fee is playable on amounts allowed in the Schedule.

Dated the 28th day of April 1994

P. T. Hurst, Chief Taxing Master

Dated the 28th day of April 1994

G. Angel, Senior District Judge of the Family Division

Legal Aid Taxation Certificate

Plaintiff/Petitioner

Defendant/Respondent

In the	
County Court / District Registry	
Case No.	
Legal Aid Certificate No.	
Solicitors Ref.	

Seal

The costs in this matter have been taxed as set out in boxes A, B and C below and are claimed from the Legal Aid Fund. *(please tick)*

The costs are those of the ☐ Plaintiff ☐ Petitioner

☐ Defendant ☐ Respondent ☐ Other

They were taxed in the ☐ High Court ☐ County Court

Total pre-certificate costs, which are not being claimed, were £
(Include disbursements, profit costs and VAT)

Dated _____ Signed _____

(Solicitor)

A. Legal aid inter partes costs
(Do not include any pre-certificate costs, inter partes costs or the costs of taxation.)

Profit costs	
VAT	
Counsel's Fees	
VAT	
Disbursements	
VAT (where appropriate)	
Total	£

B. Legal aid only costs
(Do not include the costs of taxation.)

Profit costs	
VAT	
Counsel's Fees	
VAT	
Disbursements	
VAT (where appropriate)	
Total	£

C. Costs of taxation
(Allowed in respect of A and B above)

Part A Taxation costs	
VAT	
Taxing fee (where appropriate)	
Part B Taxation costs	
VAT	
Taxing fee (where appropriate)	
Total	£

D. Total Claimed
(Add totals A, B and C)

Total part A	
Total part B	
Total part C	
Total	£

Sealed by the court on _____

Ex80A Legal Aid Taxation Certificate

743

Civil Legal Aid

CLA 32
Legal Aid Board Legal Aid Act 1988

Claim for taxation or assessment of legal aid only costs where inter partes costs have been paid in full

➤ For all work covered by an inter partes order which was claimed but not accepted by the paying party, please identify (a) the amount claimed from the party, (b) the amount agreed and paid, and (c) the reason for non-payment of the balance claimed from the Fund.

➤ If necessary, you may continue on a second form or a separate piece of paper and attach it to this form.

Name of petitioner/plaintiff _____

Name of respondent/defendant _____

Name of assisted person _____

Name of court _____ Case No. _____

Legal Aid certificate No. ☐ ☐ ☐ ☐   Date of Legal Aid certificate ____ / ____ / ____

Summary of the case
Please set out here a brief summary of the case

Disbursements

	Claimed £ p	Allowed £ p
a) Not liable to vat		
b) Liable to vat		
Total a + b		
VAT on b		
TOTAL		

Fees payable to counsel
Please give details of work claimed

	Claimed £ p	Allowed £ p
Net total		
VAT		
TOTAL		

April 1994

744

Profit costs claimed
If you are seeking an enhanced rate of remuneration please identify the item of work, the reason for the enhancement and the enhanced rate claimed.

| Please tell us | the total profit costs (excluding VAT) **claimed** inter partes | £ _____ |
| | the total profit costs (excluding VAT) **recovered** inter partes | £ _____ |

Section 1	Work not covered by an inter partes order	Time or no. of items	Claimed £ p	Allowed £ p
Please give details of the work claimed				
		Total section 1		

Section 2	Work covered by inter partes order but not accepted by the paying party	Time or no. of items	Claimed £ p	Allowed £ p
Please give details of the work claimed				
		Total section 2		
		Net profit costs (total of sections 1 & 2)		
		VAT		
		TOTAL		

Declaration for assessment (delete if not appropriate)

I certify that a copy of this bill has been provided to the assisted person with an explanation of their rights under Regulation 105A Civil Legal Aid (General) Regulations 1989 and that 21 days have passed since the copy was so provided.

Declaration for taxation (delete if not appropriate)

I certify that a copy of this bill has been provided to the assisted person pursuant to the regulations, with an explanation of his/her interest in the taxation and the steps which can be taken to safeguard that interest. He/she has/has not requested that the Taxing Officer be informed of his/her interest and has/has not requested that notice of the taxation appointment be sent to him/her.

SIGNED (partner in the firm) _____ DATE _____

745

Practice Direction—Legal Aid Taxations

The Lord Chancellor in exercise of his powers under Order 50 Rule 1 of the County Court Rules 1981 makes the following Direction.

The Practice Direction Number 3 of 1994 made by the Chief Taxing Master and the Senior District Judge of the Family Division and dated 28 April 1994 shall be applied in the County Courts.

Dated 28 April 1994

Supreme Court Taxing Office
Practice Direction
No. 5 of 1994

Appeals to a taxing master pursuant to the Costs in Criminal Cases (General) Regulations 1986 and the Legal Aid in Criminal and Care Proceedings (Costs) Regulations 1989

1. Solicitors and Counsel dissatisfied with the determination of costs under the above Regulations may apply to the appropriate authority for a review of the determination. Appeal against a decision on such a review is made to a Taxing Master of the Supreme Court Taxing Office. Written notice of appeal must be given to the Chief Taxing Master within 21 days of receipt of the reasons given for the decision, or within such longer time as the Taxing Master may direct.

2. The Notice of Appeal must be in the Form 'A' annexed hereto setting out in separate numbered paragraphs each fee or item of costs or disbursement in respect of which the appeal is brought showing the amount claimed for the item, the amount determined and the grounds of the objection to the decision on the taxation or determination.

Counsel and solicitors must provide detailed grounds of objection in respect of each item in accordance with Regulation 10(2) of the Costs in Criminal Cases (General) Regulations 1986 and Regulation 15(5)(b) of the Legal Aid in Criminal and Care Proceedings (Costs) Regulations 1989. A reference to accompanying correspondence or documents is insufficient and will result in the appeal being dismissed.

3. The appeal must be accompanied by a cheque for the appropriate fee made payable to 'HM Paymaster General'. The Notice must state whether the appellant wishes to appear or to be represented or whether he will accept a decision given in his absence.

The following documents should be forwarded with the notice of appeal:
(a) a legible copy of the bill of costs (with any supporting submissions) showing the allowances made;

(b) Counsel's fee claim, fee note any memorandum by Counsel submitted to the determining authority;

(c) a copy of the original determination of costs and a copy of the redetermination;

(d) a copy of the appellant's representations made to the determining authority on seeking re-determination;

(e) the reasons of the Taxing Officer or Determining Officer;

(f) a copy of the Legal Aid Order and of any authorities given under Regulation 54 of the Legal Aid in Criminal and Care Proceedings (General) Regulations 1989.

Supporting Papers

4. Appellants who do not intend to appear at the hearing of their appeal should lodge all *relevant* supporting papers with the documents listed above.

Appellants who do wish to attend at the hearing of their appeal should not lodge their supporting papers until directed to do so by the Supreme Court Taxing Office.

5. Appellants are reminded that it is their responsibility to procure the lodgement of the relevant papers even if they are in the possession of the Crown Court or other persons. Appeals may be listed for dismissal if the relevant papers are not lodged when required.

6. Delays frequently arise in dealing with appeals by Counsel because the relevant papers have been returned by the Court to the Solicitor whose file may not be readily available or who may have destroyed the papers. These problems would be avoided if Counsel's clerk were, immediately on his lodging with the Court a request for redetermination, to ask his instructing solicitor to retain safely the relevant papers.

Time Limits

7. Appellants who are unable to lodge an appeal within the time limits should make an application to the Taxing Master for leave to appeal out of time setting out in full the circumstances relied upon.

Appeals should not be delayed because certain relevant documents are not available. An accompanying note setting out the missing documents and undertaking to lodge them within a specified time, not exceeding 28 days, should be sent with the appeal.

Appeals to the High Court

8. An appellant desiring to appeal to a Judge from the decision of the Taxing Master should, within 21 days of receipt of the Master's decision, request

him to certify that a point of principle of general importance (specifying the same) is involved. An appeal is instituted by originating summons in the Queen's Bench Division within 21 days of the receipt of the Master's certificate. The times may be extended by a Taxing Master or the High Court, as the case may be.

9. The originating Summons by which such appeal is to be instituted must contain full particulars of the item or items or the amount allowed in respect of which the appeal is brought. After the issue of the Summons the appellant must forthwith lodge with the Clerk of Appeals, Supreme Court Taxing Office, all the documents used on the appeal to the Taxing Master.

10. The summons is to be served within three days after issue returnable on a day to be appointed and must be indorsed with an estimate of the length of hearing. The Chief Clerk of the Supreme Court Taxing Office will obtain from the Judge a date for hearing and will notify the parties.

11. After the appeal has been heard and determined the Chief Clerk will obtain the documents, together with a sealed copy of any order of the Judge which may have been drawn up, and will notify the Court concerned of the result of the appeal.

12. The Practice Direction listed below is hereby withdrawn:

26 May 1989 — Chief Taxing Master
1989 1 WLR 637; 1989 2 All ER 645

13. This Practice Direction is issued with the concurrence of the Lord Chief Justice.

Dated 16 June 1994

P. T. Hurst, Chief Taxing Master

Appendix 2

Form of Notice of Appeal

APPEAL PURSUANT TO THE COSTS IN CRIMINAL CASES (GENERAL) REGULATIONS 1986 AND THE LEGAL AID IN CRIMINAL AND CARE PROCEEDINGS (COSTS) REGULATIONS 1989
_____ CROWN COURT/DIVISIONAL COURT/COURT OF APPEAL CRIMINAL DIVISION

Regina -v- _____

Appeal of _____

Case No. _____

To: The Chief Taxing Master and to the appropriate authority of the _____ Crown Court/Divisional Court/Court of Appeal Criminal Division.

The Appellant _____ appeals to a Taxing Master against the re-determination of the costs in the above matter.

The following are the items in respect of which the Applicant appeals:

ITEM	DESCRIPTION	AMOUNT CLAIMED	AMOUNT ALLOWED	TOTAL AMOUNT IN DISPUTE AFTER RE-DETERMINATION
1.				
2.				
3. etc				

Grounds of Objection (TO BE SET OUT IN FULL)

1. We confirm that a copy of this notice has been served upon the appropriate authority.

The Appellant should attach to this Notice of Appeal his/her Grounds of Objection and in so doing provide the Taxing Master with a detailed response to the written reasons provided by the Determining Officer.

Do you wish to attend the hearing of your Appeal? Yes/No.

Dated the   day of   1988

(Signed _____

Appellant

Address _____

_____

_____

Tel No. _____

Ref: _____

Fax No: _____

Dx No: _____

INDEX

(All references are to paragraph number)

750

Relator actions
eligibility, 07–15
Remuneration (assistance by way of representation)
amount, 04–39 – 04–40
application for, 04–35 – 04–38
assessed deficiency, 04–37
assessment procedure
appeal, 04–42 – 04–43
generally, 04–41
disbursements, 04–36
generally, 04–26
payments on account, 04–36
prior authority, 04–28
solicitors charge, 04–37 – 04–38
Remuneration (care proceedings)
enhancement, 22–34 – 22–38
exceptional circumstances, 22–34 – 22–35
generally, 22–31 – 22–32
rates, 22–33
Remuneration (civil legal aid)
agreed costs, 19–27
amount
enhancement, 19–20
generally, 19–19
pre-certificate work, 19–22
reasonably incurred, 19–21
assessment
agreed costs, 19–27
Crown Court proceedings, 19–29
family proceedings, 19–29
generally, 19–23
magistrates proceedings, 19–29
regulations, under, 19–24 – 19–26
basis
contribution, 19–05
generally, 19–04
paying party, excess from, 19–05, 19–33
revoked certificate, 19–06
claim
assessment, 19–40
deferment of profit costs, 19–36 – 19–38
discharge, 19–41 – 19–42
LAB guidance notes, 19–28
payment on account scheme, 19–34 – 19–35
pre-certificate costs, 19–44
revocation, 19–41 , 19–43
taxation, 19–39
compromise, effecting, 20–13

Remuneration (civil legal aid)—*cont.*
contempt proceedings, 37–04 – 37–06
counsels fees, 19–30 – 19–32
Crown Court proceedings, 19–29
discharge, 19–09
family proceedings, 19–29
generally, 19–01 – 19–02
interest, 19–47 – 19–48
magistrates court proceedings, 19–29
multi-party action contracts, 40–02
revocation, 19–09
statutory right, 19–03
taxation, *see* Taxation on remuneration (civil legal aid)
Remuneration (criminal legal aid)
appeal, 31–25
claim
counsels fees, 31–28
solicitors fees, 31–26 – 31–27
counsels fees
ex post facto, 31–24, 31–39
standard, 31–23, 31–38
determination
enhanced rates, 31–31 – 31–32
generally, 31–29
increase of rates, 31–30
wasted costs, 31–33
disbursements
generally, 31–34
interim payment, 31–35 – 31–37
interim payments
disbursements, 31–35 – 31–37
entitlement, 31–03
generally, 31–02
recovery of excess, 31–04
payment
ex post facto determination, 31–22
generally, 31–17, 31–19, 31–40
pre-order work, 31–18
standard fees
Crown Court, 31–21
magistrates court, 31–20
restrictions
court powers, 31–06
disallowance, 31–06 – 31–13
topping up, 31–05
review, 31–25
statutory right, 31–01
taxation, *see* Taxation on remuneration (criminal legal aid)
wasted costs order, 31–06 – 31–16, 31–33